Contents

Concise Dictionary of American Literary Biography

The Twenties,
1917-1929

Concise Dictionary of American Literary Biography

The Twenties, 1917-1929

A Bruccoli Clark Layman Book
Gale Research Inc. • Book Tower • Detroit, Michigan 48226

6 v. set 11-12-91

Advisory Board for
CONCISE DICTIONARY
OF AMERICAN LITERARY BIOGRAPHY

Matthew J. Bruccoli and Richard Layman, *Editorial Directors*
C. E. Frazer Clark, Jr., *Managing Editor*

Printed in the United States of America

Published simultaneously in the United Kingdom
by Gale Reseach International Limited
(An affiliated company of Gale Reseach Inc.)

**Library of Congress Cataloging in
Publication Data**

Concise dictionary of American literary biography.
   "A Bruccoli Clark Layman book."
   Includes bibliographies and index.
   Contents: [1] Colonization to the American Renaissance, 1640-1865– [2] Realism, naturalism, and local color, 1865-1917– [3] The Twenties, 1917-1929– [etc.]
   1. Authors, American–20th Century–Biography–Dictionaries. 2. American literature–20th century–Dictionaries. 3. American literature–20th century–Bio-bibliography.
PS129.C66   1987   810'.9'0054 [B]   86-33657

ISBN 0-8103-1824-5

Plan of the Work

The six-volume *Concise Dictionary of American Literary Biography* was developed in response to requests from high school and junior college teachers and librarians, and from small- to medium-sized public libraries, for a compilation of entries from the standard *Dictionary of Literary Biography* chosen to meet their needs and their budgets. The *DLB,* which comprises over ninety volumes as of the end of 1987, is moving steadily toward its goal of providing a history of literature in all languages developed through the biographies of writers. Basic as the *DLB* is, many librarians have expressed the need for a less comprehensive reference work which in other respects retains the merits of *DLB.* The *Concise DALB* provides this resource.

This series was planned by a seven-member advisory board, consisting primarily of secondary school educators, who developed a method of organization and presentation for selected *DLB* entries suitable for high school and beginning college students. Their preliminary plan was circulated to some five thousand school librarians and English teachers, who were asked to respond to the organization of the series and the table of contents. Those responses were incorporated into the plan described here.

Uses for the Concise DALB

Students are the primary audience for the *Concise DALB.* The stated purpose of the standard *DLB* is to make our literary heritage more accessible. *Concise DALB* has the same goal and seeks a wider audience. What the author wrote; what the facts of his life are; a description of his literary works; a discussion of the critical response to his works; and a bibliography of critical works to be consulted for further information: These are the elements of a *Concise DALB* entry.

The first step in the planning process for this series, after identifying the audience, was to contemplate its uses. The advisory board acknowledged that the integrity of *Concise DALB* as a reference book is crucial to its utility. The *Concise DALB* adheres to the scholarly standards established by the parent series. Thus, within the scope of major American literary figures, the *Concise DALB* is a ready reference source of established value, providing reliable biographical and bibliographical information.

It is anticipated that this series will not be confined to uses within the library. Just as *DLB* has been a tool for stimulating students' literary interests in the college classroom—for comparative studies of authors, for example, and, through its ample illustrations, as a means of invigorating literary study—the *Concise DALB* is a primary resource for high school and junior college educators. The series is organized to facilitate lesson planning, and the contextual diagrams (explained below) that introduce each entry are a source of topics for classroom discussion and writing assignments.

Organization

The advisory board further determined that entries from the standard *DLB* should be presented complete—without abridgment. Their feeling was that the utility of the *DLB* format has been proven, and that only minimal changes should be made.

The advisory board further decided that the organization of the *Concise DALB* should be chronological to emphasize the historical development of American literature. Each volume is devoted to a single historical period and includes the most significant literary figures from all genres who were active during that time. Thus, the volume that includes modern mainstream novelists Saul Bellow, Bernard Malamud, and John Cheever will also include poets who were active at the same time—such as Allen Ginsberg, Lawrence Ferlinghetti, and John Berryman—and dramatists who were their contemporaries—such as Tennessee Williams, Arthur Miller, and William Inge. It should be noted that the volume of the *Concise DALB* that includes these authors comprises thirty-six entries, while the volumes in the standard *DLB* covering the same period include some four hundred author biographies. The *Concise DALB* limits itself to major figures, but it provides the same coverage of those figures as the *DLB* does.

The six period volumes of the *Concise DALB* are *Colonization to the American Renaissance, 1640-1865; Realism, Naturalism, and Local Color, 1865-*

1917; The Twenties, 1917-1929; The Age of Maturity, 1929-1941; The New Consciousness, 1941-1968; Broadening Views, 1968-1987. The sixth volume will also contain a comprehensive index by subjects and proper names to the entire *Concise DALB*. (As in the standard *DLB* series, there is a cumulative index to author entries in each *Concise DALB* volume.)

Form of Entry

The form of entry in the *Concise DALB* is substantially the same as in the standard series, with the following alterations:

1) Each entry has been updated to include a discussion of works published since the standard entry appeared and to reflect recent criticism and research of interest to the high school audience.

2) The secondary bibliography for each entry has been selected to include those books and articles of particular interest and usefulness to high school and junior college students. In addi- tion, the secondary bibliography has been annotated to assist students in assessing whether a reference will meet their needs.

3) Each entry is preceded by a "contextual diagram"–a graphic presentation of the places, literary influences, personal relationships, literary movements, major themes, cultural and artistic influences, and social and economic forces associated with the author. This chart allows students– and teachers–to place the author in his literary and social context at a glance.

It bears repeating that the *Concise DALB* is restricted to major American literary figures. It is anticipated that users of this series will find it advantageous to consult the standard *DLB* for information about those writers omitted from the *Concise DALB* whose significance to contemporary readers may have faded but whose contribution to our cultural heritage remains meaningful.

Comments about the series and suggestions about how to improve it are earnestly invited.

A Note to Students

The purpose of the *Concise DALB* is to enrich the study of literature. In their various ways, writers react in their works to the circumstances of their lives, the events of their time, and the culture that envelops them (which are represented on the contextual diagrams that precede each *Concise DALB* entry). Writers provide a way to see and understand what they have observed and experienced. Besides being inherently interesting, biographies of writers provide a basic perspective on literature.

Concise DALB entries start with the most important facts about writers: What they wrote. We strongly recommend that you also start there. The chronological listing of an author's works is an outline for the examination of his or her career achievement. The biographies that follow set the stage for the presentation of the works. Each of the author's important works and the most respected critical evaluations of them are discussed in *Concise DALB*. If you require more information about the author or fuller critical studies of the author's works, the annotated references section at the end of the entry will guide you.

Illustrations are an integral element of *Concise DALB* entries. Photographs of the author are reminders that literature is the product of a writer's imagination; facsimiles of the author's working drafts are the best evidence available for understanding the act of composition—the author in the process of refining his work and acting as self-editor; dust jacket and advertisements demonstrate how literature comes to us through the marketplace, which sometimes serves to alter our perceptions of the works.

Literary study is a complex and immensely rewarding endeavor. Our goal is to provide you with the information you need to make that experience as rich as possible.

Acknowledgments

This book was produced by Bruccoli Clark Layman, Inc. Karen L. Rood is senior editor for the *Dictionary of Literary Biography* series. Laura Ingram was the in-house editor.

Production coordinator is Kimberly Casey. Art supervisor is Susan Todd. Penny L. Haughton is responsible for layout and graphics. Copyediting supervisor is Joan M. Prince. Typesetting supervisor is Kathleen M. Flanagan. William Adams and Michael D. Senecal are editorial associates. The production staff includes Brandy H. Barefoot, Rowena Betts, Charles D. Brower, Joseph M. Bruccoli, Amanda Caulley, Teresa Chaney, Patricia Coate, Mary Colborn, Sarah A. Estes, Cynthia Hallman, Judith K. Ingle, Kathy S. Merlette, Sheri Beckett Neal, and Virginia Smith. Jean W. Ross is permissions editor.

Walter W. Ross and Jennifer Toth did the library research with the assistance of the reference staff at the Thomas Cooper Library of the University of South Carolina: Daniel Boice, Cathy Eckman, Gary Geer, Cathie Gottlieb, David L. Haggard, Jens Holley, Dennis Isbell, Jackie Kinder, Marcia Martin, Jean Rhyne, Beverly Steele, Ellen Tillett, Carol Tobin, and Virginia Weathers.

Concise Dictionary of American Literary Biography

The Twenties, 1917-1929

Concise Dictionary of American Literary Biography
Sherwood Anderson

This entry was updated by Walter B. Rideout (University of Wisconsin-Madison) from his entry in DLB 9, American Novelists, 1910-1945, Part 1.

Places	Clyde, Ohio Chicago	New Orleans Southwestern Virginia	The Midwest
Influences and Relationships	George Borrow Walt Whitman Mark Twain	Theodore Dreiser Gertrude Stein D. H. Lawrence	Van Wyck Brooks Ernest Hemingway William Faulkner

Literary Movements and Forms	Journalism
	Modern American
	   Short Story
	"Lyric" Novel
		Opposition to "Poison
		   Plot" Fiction
		"Organic" Fiction
		Character Sketch
			Impressionistic
			   Nonfiction
			Rejection of European
			   Literary Standards

Major Themes	Industrialism as a
	   Dehumanizing Force
	Obsession with Mate-
	   rial Success vs. the
	   Inner Life
	The Promise of
	   America
		Small Town Life as
		   Repressive yet
		   Rewarding
		The Need for Sexual
		   Honesty and
		   Sensitivity
		Honesty in Literature
			Importance of the
			   Imagination
			The "Buried" Psychic
			   Life of the
			   Individual
			Loneliness and Long-
			   ing for Community

Cultural and Artistic Influences	Postimpressionist
	   Painting
		Collapse of Traditional
		   Values
			King James Bible

Social and Economic Influences	Growth of
	   Industrialism
	World War I
		The Great Depression
		Prohibition
		The New Deal
			The Proletarian
			   Movement

See also the Anderson entries in DLB 4, American Writers in Paris, 1920-1939 *and* DLB, Documentary Series 1.

BIRTH: Camden, Ohio, 13 September 1876, to Irwin M. and Emma Smith Anderson.

MARRIAGES: 16 May 1904 to Cornelia Lane (divorced); children: Robert, John, Marion. 31 July 1916 to Tennessee Mitchell (divorced). 5 April 1924 to Elizabeth Prall (divorced). 6 July 1933 to Eleanor Copenhaver.

AWARDS: The *Dial* Award, 1921; elected, National Institute of Arts and Letters, 1937.

DEATH: Colón, Panama, Canal Zone, 8 March 1941.

BOOKS: *Windy McPherson's Son* (New York: Lane, 1916; London: Lane/Bodley Head, 1916; revised edition, New York: Huebsch, 1922; London: Cape, 1923);

Marching Men (New York: Lane, 1917; London: Lane/Bodley Head, 1917);

Mid-American Chants (New York: Lane, 1918; London: Lane/Bodley Head, 1918);

Winesburg, Ohio: A Group of Tales of Ohio Small Town Life (New York: Huebsch, 1919; London: Cape, 1922);

Poor White (New York: Huebsch, 1920; London: Cape, 1921);

The Triumph of the Egg: A Book of Impressions from American Life in Tales and Poems (New York: Huebsch, 1921; London: Cape, 1922);

Horses and Men: Tales, long and short, from our American life (New York: Huebsch, 1923; London: Cape, 1924);

Many Marriages (New York: Huebsch, 1923);

A Story Teller's Story: The tale of an American writer's journey through his own imaginative world and through the world of facts, with many of his experiences and impressions among other writers—told in many notes—in four books—and an Epilogue (New York: Huebsch, 1924; London: Cape, 1925);

Dark Laughter (New York: Boni & Liveright, 1925; London: Jarrolds, 1926);

The Modern Writer (San Francisco: Lantern Press, 1925);

Sherwood Anderson's Notebook: Containing Articles Written During the Author's Life as a Story Teller and Notes of his Impressions from Life scat-

Sherwood Anderson (by permission of the Sherwood Anderson Papers, the Newberry Library)

tered through the Book (New York: Boni & Liveright, 1926);

Tar: A Midwest Childhood (New York: Boni & Liveright, 1926; London: Secker, 1927);

A New Testament (New York: Boni & Liveright, 1927);

Alice and The Lost Novel (London: Matthews & Marrot, 1929);

Hello Towns! (New York: Liveright, 1929);

Nearer the Grass Roots (San Francisco: Westgate Press, 1929);

The American County Fair (New York: Random House, 1930);

Perhaps Women (New York: Liveright, 1931);

Beyond Desire (New York: Liveright, 1932);

Death in the Woods and Other Stories (New York: Liveright, 1933);

No Swank (Philadelphia: Centaur Press, 1934);

Puzzled America (New York & London: Scribners, 1935);

Kit Brandon: A Portrait (New York & London: Scribners, 1936; London: Hutchinson, 1937);

Plays, Winesburg and Others (New York & London: Scribners, 1937);

A Writer's Conception of Realism (Olivet, Mich.: Olivet College, 1939);

Home Town (New York: Alliance Book Corporation, 1940);

Sherwood Anderson's Memoirs (New York: Harcourt, Brace, 1942);

The Sherwood Anderson Reader, edited by Paul Rosenfeld (Boston: Houghton Mifflin, 1947);

The Portable Sherwood Anderson, edited by Horace Gregory (New York: Viking, 1949; revised, 1972);

Return to Winesburg: Selections From Four Years of Writing for a Country Newspaper, edited by Ray Lewis White (Chapel Hill: University of North Carolina Press, 1967);

The Buck Fever Papers, edited by Welford Dunaway Taylor (Charlottesville: University Press of Virginia, 1971);

The "Writer's Book," edited by Martha Mulroy Curry (Metuchen, N.J.: Scarecrow Press, 1975);

France and Sherwood Anderson: Paris Notebook, 1921, edited by Michael Fanning (Baton Rouge: Louisiana State University Press, 1976);

Sherwood Anderson: The Writer at His Craft, edited by Jack Salzman, David D. Anderson, and Kichinosuke Ohashi (Mamaroneck, N.Y.: Appel, 1979);

The Complete Works of Sherwood Anderson, edited by Ohashi (Kyoto, Japan: Rinsen Book Company, 1982);

The Sherwood Anderson Diaries, 1936-1941, edited by Hilbert H. Campbell (Athens: University of Georgia Press, 1987).

Although Sherwood Anderson is not one of the major figures in twentieth-century American literature, he is for several reasons a writer of very considerable significance. At his best in short fiction, this "teller of tales" produced many remarkable individual stories—"I Want to Know Why," "The Egg," "I'm a Fool," "The Man Who Became a Woman," "Death in the Woods," and "Brother Death," to take only the most frequently anthologized pieces—as well as the book of related tales, *Winesburg, Ohio* (1919), which is generally considered his masterpiece. His effect on the development of the modern American short story as a genre was of great importance, for he rebelled against what he termed the "poison plot"—that is, fiction written according to standardized formulas, readily marketable but unrealistic as portrayals of actual human beings and human experience—in favor of stories which developed

their individual shapes "organically" out of the play of the imagination over observed reality. Never fully successful in handling the longer form of the novel, he nevertheless influenced later novelists as well as short-story writers through his example and sometimes through personal encouragement. In Malcolm Cowley's words, he became "the only story teller of his generation who left his mark on the style and vision of the generation that followed. Hemingway, Faulkner, Wolfe, Steinbeck, Caldwell, Saroyan, Henry Miller . . . each of these owes an unmistakable debt to Anderson, and their names might stand for dozens of others."

Anderson's career as storyteller, novelist, essayist, and even in a small way as dramatist, began relatively late in his life, for he published his first story in a literary magazine in 1914 and his first novel two years later, just before his fortieth birthday. Yet his earlier years as unskilled laborer, soldier, advertising copywriter, and businessman gave him the perspective of a representative American spokesman. He sensed and articulated the dreams, desires, frustrations, hopes, and longings that constitute much of each individual's imaginative life and explored that creative life buried beneath the surface of daily routines and the scramble for material success. In his deceptively simple prose he dealt, often lyrically, with this buried life, at his best showing acute insight into the psychological relationships of men and women and the lives of commonplace individuals. Characteristically he found beauty in failure rather than in success; he attacked the destructive aspects of the industrialism that swept over the United States during his lifetime; he affirmed the power of the imagination within both the artist and the ordinary person. Admitting—sometimes humbly, sometimes proudly—that he functioned through intuitive perception rather than reasoned analysis, he insisted that Americans were a lonely people longing for community. Though he could at times be simplistic and sentimental in his fictional and nonfictional writings, he could also perceive fundamental developments in American life.

The critic Maxwell Geismar called him the "last of the townsmen," an appropriate term for one who, rather like Mark Twain, located some of his values in the preindustrial small town of the American heartland. Born in Camden, Ohio, in 1876, he spent his formative years, from 1884 to 1896 or 1897, in Clyde, Ohio, where his father, Irwin M. Anderson, a harness maker and

Anderson and his sons John (standing) and Marion (seated) (by permission of the Sherwood Anderson Papers, the Newberry Library; and the Sherwood Anderson Literary Trust)

then a housepainter, was better known for his Civil War stories than for his industriousness. The third child in a family of five boys and a girl, Anderson never finished high school because he had to work to help support the family. He held so many jobs in succession that he was nicknamed "Jobby," but he was also known as a dreamer often lost in imagining a glorious future for himself. A year or two after the death of his beloved mother, Emma Smith Anderson, in 1895, he went to Chicago, worked there as an unskilled laborer, and then saw military service in Cuba after the end of the Spanish-American War. After a final year of precollege education in 1899-1900 at Wittenberg Academy in Springfield, Ohio, he became an advertising copywriter in Chicago, satisfying his growing interest in creative writing by contributing essays and sketches to his company's house periodical. After his marriage in 1904 to Cornelia Lane, daughter of a Toledo businessman, he established his own mail-order business in Elyria, Ohio, where in an attempt to cope with his growing financial and marital problems, he began writing novels around 1910. He suffered a nervous breakdown late in 1912, returned to his advertising job in Chicago early in 1913, and for the next ten years sup-

ported himself by that work while making writing his main preoccupation. The actual facts of his breakdown he would fictionalize as a deliberate conscious decision to walk out of business into art, and in the early 1920s this only partially true legend would make him a cultural hero for the postwar generation of American writers.

His first novel, *Windy McPherson's Son* (1916), was written in its original form while he was still a businessman in Elyria, and it contains many elements of disguised autobiography. During the first third of the book, the novel's best part, young Sam McPherson grows up in a small Iowa town. Partly out of shame at his boastful, incompetent father, "Windy," he becomes intensely committed to making money, an activity encouraged by several older townsmen who befriend Sam but fail to recognize, as he himself fails to, that the boy's longing for material success actually springs from the blindly dreaming aspect of his personality.

After the death of his mother, Sam goes to Chicago to seek his fortune and finds it there, as his creator did not. As in the popular novel of business success, Sam rises swiftly, through strong will, boldness, and imagination, to the presidency of the Rainey Arms Company. Meanwhile he has married the boss's daughter, Sue Rainey, but their marriage is threatened by her inability to bear children, and she leaves him when he betrays her father in a business deal. Thereafter Sam becomes increasingly corrupt in his financial operation until news of his father-in-law's suicide makes him abruptly walk out of his business office in order to "try to spend his life seeking truth."

For a year Sam wanders on foot among the people of the Midwest and the East, having a series of adventures, each of which strengthens his conviction that America is corrupt and disordered yet potentially vital. Disillusioned, he goes through a period of debauchery; then paying one of his women for her three unwanted children, he takes them with him and returns to Sue, who calmly accepts him and the children in what has usually been considered a happy ending.

Windy McPherson's Son thus displays early in Anderson's career several of his typical subjects and themes—the American small town with its atmosphere at once repressive and warmly human; the damage done to one's emotional and imaginative life by single-minded dedication to material success; the uncertainty of national purpose; the stresses which "the force of sex," in Anderson's (for 1916) forthright phrase, may produce in male-female relationships. An apprentice novel, it too often shows the influence of other writers, including those of popular romance; yet it also shows Anderson's ability to probe "beneath the surface of lives" and to communicate unexpected insights to the attentive reader. If one reads the return of Sam to Sue as the formulaic happy ending, for example, one misses the point that Sam, son of the failure Windy, has himself failed to find "truth" and may either surrender to a life of petty circumstance or, driven by his dreamer self, may in the future go forth rebelliously again. In actual life Anderson had separated from his wife soon after his breakdown; and in 1916, after Cornelia, against her own wishes, had generously obtained a divorce from him, he married Tennessee Mitchell, an independent and talented woman who taught music and dance in Chicago.

Anderson's first novel received generally favorable reviews and went into two printings. His second, *Marching Men* (1917), received, and deserved, less recognition. This novel likewise recounted a young man's growing up in a small town, success in Chicago, and eventual rejection of that success in favor of an idea. The first draft had been written in Elyria, but *Marching Men* went through repeated revisions which left the final version confused in focus and direction and chiefly notable as a first experiment by its author in the form of the "lyrical" or "poetic" novel.

The protagonist, "Beaut" McGregor, grows up as a huge, homely young man in an ugly Pennsylvania coal-mining town. Hating town and townspeople, he goes to Chicago where he eventually becomes a crusading lawyer. When he reluctantly returns to the town for his mother's funeral, however, he is deeply impressed by the orderly procession into which the miners unconsciously organize themselves as they march to the cemetery to honor his mother and is inspired to found a labor movement called the Marching Men. The silent, rhythmic marching of thousands of workers frightens many industrialists, but McGregor never explains how a political program or a social revolution can evolve out of mere marching. Indeed, the author appears not to have known how either; rather, the novel seems to have been rooted in Anderson's own psychological needs. As a soldier he had once been profoundly stirred by a sense of unified power when he saw a long line of his fellows marching. In his present life he felt a need for order to replace the social disorder he observed in industrialized Chicago, to-

gether with a need for internal order to resolve his painful conflict between the necessity to compose advertising copy–to him a perversion of language–and his urge to write fiction–to him the one sure honest use of language. Although an image of desired order dominates the book, the novel ends with the Marching Men Movement destined to fail and with an implied question: is not McGregor more artist than labor leader since the creation of "living beauty in our everyday affairs" comes not from success but from the deliberate acceptance, like McGregor's, of failure and defeat? *Marching Men* leaves that question unanswered, but under the disillusioning impact of World War I Anderson had concluded that social improvement in the United States would come, if at all, not through politics or a labor movement, but through the ameliorative cultural influence of the country's awakened artists.

Even while he was revising his first two novels and working on at least two others that would never be published, Anderson was discovering his authentic voice as a writer. In the fall of 1915 he had begun writing what he called "a series of intensive studies of people" in a town he named Winesburg, Ohio, though its physical presence was clearly that of his hometown of Clyde. By the following spring he had completed about a dozen of these studies, tales artfully simple in language and apparently casual in manner but making highly compressed revelations of the "buried lives" of individuals, many of whom perceive themselves as isolated within the community and who long to connect emotionally with other individuals. After his initial outpouring of these stories in the winter of 1915-1916, Anderson continued to write others from time to time over two more years; throughout this period he published a number of them in little magazines hospitable to new kinds of writing–the *Masses*, the *Little Review*, and the *Seven Arts*–while he was gradually collecting enough of them for book publication.

His third published volume, however, was a collection of free-verse poems which he wrote rapidly during the first half of 1917 under the stimulus of a visit to New York and acquaintance with the men associated with the *Seven Arts*, especially Van Wyck Brooks, Waldo Frank, and Paul Rosenfeld. These were college-trained men who saw in the relatively uneducated Anderson an artist already creating out of native materials the new literature their magazine was encouraging in opposition to the materialism and sexual repres-

Note written by Anderson while under treatment for amnesia in a Cleveland hospital, 1912 (by permission of the Sherwood Anderson Papers, the Newberry Library; and the Sherwood Anderson Literary Trust) siveness which, to them, characterized present-day "Puritanical" America. Anderson's poems, minor verse indebted to Walt Whitman and the King James Bible, constituted a bardic vision of American development from a golden age of small-town community into the physical ugliness and social disorder of the industrial age and beyond to a new golden age of order, community, and love. Published in April 1918 as *Mid-American Chants*, the poems received mostly unfavorable reviews. Few copies were sold, and John Lane, the publisher of Anderson's first three volumes, decided not to accept the book of Winesburg stories.

During the late summer and fall of 1918 Anderson lived in New York City, wrote much of what was to be his best novel, *Poor White* (1920), and found a publisher for *Winesburg, Ohio* in the small firm of B. W. Huebsch, who had already printed American editions of books by such experimental foreign writers as D. H. Lawrence and James Joyce. *Winesburg, Ohio* was published in May 1919; and though a few reviewers condemned the book as sex-obsessed, most acclaimed it as presenting a true picture of American life, as creating a new form resembling a novel but more fluid, and as providing in the individual tales a major break with the neatly constructed formula story. One of the most acute summaries of Anderson's technique was made by reviewer Burton Rascoe in the *Chicago Tribune* when he pointed out that the writer "frequently suggests rather than depicts; that he respects the imaginative faculty of his reader by refusing to be explicit where overtones of emotion are already invoked in the reader; that he is selective, indefinite, and provocative instead of inclusive, precise, and explanatory."

The introductory tale of *Winesburg, Ohio*, entitled "The Book of the Grotesque," describes an old writer who has a theory, expressed in parable form, that most human beings are "grotesques" because they cling rigidly to single-minded perceptions of themselves and life. The old writer escapes being a grotesque because of his ability to enter empathetically through his imagination into the lives of other men and women. Following this introduction are twenty-one tales about individual inhabitants of the town of Winesburg, many of whom are frustrated in their longing for community with others, turn in on themselves, and lead isolated lives as "grotesques," yet—and this is the characteristic Anderson note—have a hidden sweetness in them like the twisted fruit left by the apple-pickers on the trees in the orchards around Winesburg. A few of the inhabitants achieve some true understanding of self and community, especially young George Willard, son of a success-seeking father and a dreamer mother. A reporter of trivial surface events for the weekly newspaper, he wants to become a writer. Gradually, though not by conscious steady progression, he learns not to exploit others for his own satisfaction, a form of grotesqueness he exhibits toward the young woman who provides him with his first sexual experience. He learns to treat language honestly rather than "playing" with words and learns to "know what people are thinking about, not what they say." Shocked into maturity—that is, recognition and acceptance of the brevity of the individual life—by the death of his mother, he spends an evening with a girlfriend, Helen White, achieving with her a nonsexual closeness of intuitive understanding and a sense of overwhelming love for all the emotionally damaged yet humanly valuable inhabitants of Winesburg. He then leaves for the city and a probable, though not certain, future as a storyteller like the old writer of the introductory sketch or like Anderson himself.

Winesburg, Ohio brought its author more critical than financial success, and over the years since its publication became, as he himself would claim, "a kind of American classic." Yet despite his growing reputation as a leader in the literary revolution of the post-World War I United States, he was still forced to work at his advertising job, and he became increasingly desperate to leave Chicago for good. The first half of 1920 he spent in Alabama, first by himself in Mobile, then with Tennessee Anderson in the village of Fairhope on the east side of Mobile Bay. In the warmth and colorfulness of the southern spring he quickly finished the novel *Poor White* and enthusiastically took up painting with watercolors, typically rejecting academic training in favor of self-taught self-expression. When they returned to Chicago in the fall of 1920, Tennessee Anderson continued living in her apartment on the Near North Side, while Anderson settled for much of the next two years in a tiny house in the Chicago suburb of Palos Park.

B. W. Huebsch published *Poor White* in October 1920. This unusual, sometimes poetically written novel is partly a realistic description of the transformation of a Midwest town like Winesburg into an industrial city, partly a symbolic history of American development as a whole, partly a psychological exploration of the attempts by a man and a woman to break through the wall of alienation which, according to Anderson, surrounds each individual, and partly a lesson in attaining a warm human relationship. Hugh McVey, a "poor white" boy who resembles both Huck Finn and the young Abraham Lincoln, grows up a lazy dreamer in a Mississippi River town. He is goaded into constant aimless activity by a success-oriented New England woman and eventually wanders to Bidwell, Ohio, in the mid 1880s. Shy, inarticulate, introspective, Hugh finds an outlet for his suppressed dreaminess in inventing a series of labor-saving agricultural machines, which are put into production by the entrepreneur Steve Hunter. Factories, along with shoddy houses for incoming foreign-born workers, are built in Bidwell, and the village crafts are slowly destroyed by the influx of machine-made goods. The townspeople are warped out of their placid lives by greed for quick money destroying the sense of community that had once covered Bidwell "like an invisible roof."

During these years Clara Butterworth, daughter of a wealthy farmer and investor in the factories, has been growing to maturity. After attending the state university, where she has quietly rebelled against a routinized life, she returns to Bidwell, becomes interested in Hugh, and abruptly marries him when, for once overcoming his shyness and humility, he blurts out a proposal. The marriage is not consummated for several days, however, and even then the emotional wall between the couple continues for some years until two shocking events—a crazed old craftsman's murder of his craft-despising assistant and the old man's subsequent attack on Hugh—at last arouse in Clara deep emotion for her husband. Hugh has meanwhile become dissatisfied with his own alienated life and with the psychic injury he has unintentionally done to the people of Bidwell while attempting to save them from backbreaking labor. Rejecting the "mechanical . . . and . . . business age" and its success worship which he has unknowingly helped to establish, Hugh begins to accept "the life of the imagination." As the book ends, he and Clara are reaching out toward each other more successfully, and Hugh strives to be "not an inventor but a poet."

Poor White sold better than had *Winesburg,* but the reviews were mixed. Some critics argued that the book lacked structure, that the industrialization and the man-woman themes were not integrated. Others, however, praised it for its in-

sights into the way industrialism distorts individual human beings, accentuating alienation and destroying communal feeling, and for the book's combination of realism and symbolism. For some time Anderson had in fact been trying to push his style beyond realism. In the spring of 1919 he had begun a series of experimental prose sketches designed to be "the autobiography of the fanciful life of an individual." As he wrote these pieces over several years, they gradually became experiments in poetic prose that he would subsequently publish as *A New Testament* (1927). But even some of the prose tales he was writing around 1920 relied heavily for their organization on intricate patterns of motifs, symbols, repeated events. Sometimes, as in "Milk Bottles," the patterns seem too obvious and mechanical, but other times they are subtle and complex, providing both aesthetic structure and psychological insight. Among the best are "Brothers," concerning the family relation imagined by a half-crazed old man in Palos Park between himself and a murderer in a sensational case based on one actually being reported in the Chicago newspapers, and the long story "Out of Nowhere Into Nothing," concerning a young woman's rebellion against her sexually repressed parents in a small town and her decision to take a lover in the city.

Early in 1921 Paul Rosenfeld offered to pay Anderson's fare to Europe, and the two men, together with Tennessee Anderson, spent seven weeks of that summer in France, chiefly in Paris, and a month in London and Oxford. On this first trip abroad Anderson met Gertrude Stein and James Joyce, both of whom he admired. He delighted at being in the midst of older civilizations, and he was pleased to see that his work was beginning to receive international attention; yet the trip confirmed in him his desire to remain in and write about his native land. Shortly before the European trip he had met the young Ernest Hemingway and had encouraged him to write about his own Midwest experience, and on his return from Europe he urged Hemingway and his wife not to go to Italy as planned but to Paris, advice that would make an enormous difference in the development of that writer.

In October 1921 Huebsch published Anderson's *The Triumph of the Egg,* a collection of short stories loosely organized around the themes first of psychological constriction and then liberation, culminating in "Out of Nowhere Into Nothing." Many of these "Tales . . . from our American life" were in his new intricately patterned form, and the book was widely praised by reviewers both for its craftsmanship and its delicate probing into emotionally starved lives. Even more satisfying for him was his receipt in December of the first award by the *Dial* magazine, which had inaugurated an annual prize of two thousand dollars to honor one of the magazine's contributors for his or her literary career.

The prize money assured him of a period of freedom from the advertising agency and of time for creative work. Restive with his life in Chicago and with his marriage, Anderson spent the winter of 1921-1922 by himself in the French Quarter of New Orleans working intensively on *Many Marriages*, a short "lyrical" novel which in form grew out of his experiments in the "autobiography of the fanciful life of an individual." In this new writing venture he combined realism and fantasy to depict the inner life of a man in the process of being awakened to his emotional and imaginative self. John Webster, the repressed middle-aged owner of a small factory, falls in love with his stenographer and resolves to run away with her from a dull business life and a dull marriage. He begins a nightly ritual of walking around naked in his bedroom in front of a picture of the Virgin Mary. One evening his wife and their seventeen-year-old daughter, puzzled by the sound of his walking, enter his bedroom. Still naked, he begins to tell his daughter of how her mother and he had first met when they were, by chance, naked and how each through self-deceit entered into a sexually inhibited marriage. Unable to face Webster's "naked" revelations of their unsuccessful life together and his announcement that he is leaving her, the wife commits suicide, but the daughter, as her father had hoped, is brought to a new sense of self-respect and emotional freedom. Having thus liberated his daughter from repressed conventionality, Webster leaves town with his stenographer.

When *Many Marriages* was published early in 1923 it was condemned as a scandalous book and perhaps for that reason sold some nine thousand copies quickly before sales dropped off almost completely. Most reviewers strongly objected to what they considered merely a sordid tale of marital disharmony and the perversion of an innocent girl's mind; and in fact Anderson had bravely set out to attack the "Puritan" spirit which, in his view, had perverted his country through deflecting healthy sexual energy into an emotionally devastating obsession with material success. Between the critics' offended sensibilities

and Anderson's own tendency toward didacticism, his formal achievement, the interweaving of fantasy and reality into the complex patterns of the lyrical novel, was, and too often remains, largely unrecognized.

Anderson had lived alone in New Orleans, and during his brief return to Chicago in spring of 1922 tension between him and Tennessee Anderson rapidly increased. Late in June he started driving east in a newly purchased Ford, stopped in Ohio along the way, and by August was settled a few houses away from Theodore Dreiser in New York's Greenwich Village. Only rarely would he visit Chicago thereafter, and he would never see his second wife again. Instead he fell in love with Elizabeth Prall, manager of a bookstore. In February of 1923, after he had made final revisions of *Many Marriages* and seen it through Huebsch's press, he and Elizabeth Prall left New York for Reno, Nevada, where he hoped to obtain a quick divorce from Tennessee Anderson. She raised objections and proceedings dragged on for months. Anderson resigned himself to exploring the mountain areas, visiting Elizabeth Prall's university-bred family in Berkeley, California, and working on a volume of short stories and a book of fanciful autobiography. The former, published in October 1923 as *Horses and Men*, contained some of his weakest and strongest stories. Of the latter, two, " 'Unused' " and "An Ohio Pagan," are long excerpts from an unfinished novel, "Ohio Pagans," which drew on memories of his hometown, Clyde, and developed familiar themes. Both the young woman of the first story and the young man of the second are Andersonian "quester" protagonists, each attempting to achieve understanding of self and others. The first story ends with the pathetic death of a woman whose potentialities for affection are "unused," while the second reaches its astonishing climax in a young man's mythopoeic vision of the land around Sandusky Bay as a giant woman reclining in sexual invitation. Two other stories have a racetrack milieu as a background. "I'm a Fool" is a relatively simple tale told by a first-person narrator, a racehorse groom who "puts on airs," falls in love with a girl he meets in the grandstand at a racetrack, lies to her about his social standing, and recognizes too late that his foolish lie makes it impossible for a love letter from her ever to reach him.

"The Man Who Became a Woman," however, is a highly complex story in both form and meaning, one of the most remarkable tales Ander-

Anderson in 1939 (by permission of the Sherwood Anderson Papers, the Newberry Library; and the Sherwood Anderson Literary Trust)

son ever wrote. Again a first-person narrator, Herman Dudley, now middle-aged, recalls an emotionally traumatic event from his youth, telling the experience at last in order to discover why it should still trouble him. At age nineteen Herman leaves home and becomes a racehorse groom on the West Pennsylvania county fair circuit along with, first, another young white man who aspires to write with the strength and beauty of horses running a race, and then with a black groom named Burt. Burt helps Herman when the latter, feeling confused in his sexual identity, enters a period of working at his job very listlessly. One rainy night at a racetrack above an ugly mining town and bordered by a slaughterhouse around which the bones of killed animals are scattered, Herman becomes lonely. He goes to a sordid country bar and is startled to see in a mirror that his face is that of a young girl. After witnessing a half-crazed giant of a miner beat up a man, he returns to the track in the drenching rain to bed down naked near his horse. Two black grooms, either drunk or playing a prank, approach him as a woman, whereupon he escapes, runs terrified through the rainy night, pitches headlong into the skeleton of a slaughtered horse, and in overwhelming relief feels that he is cured of his notion that he might be a woman.

Among several meanings of this mysterious and powerful story one understands that Anderson, in his intuitive, nonprogrammatic way, is exploring the efforts of a man to come to terms with the feminine part of his psyche and is suggesting that such efforts will remain difficult even for self-aware males in so masculine-oriented a society as that of the United States.

Because of the still-lingering shock over *Many Marriages* and because of the unevenness in the quality of the stories, *Horses and Men* received a mixture of good and bad reviews and sold poorly. That Anderson was now at the height of his creative powers, however, is indicated by his completion late in 1923, while still in Reno, of *A Story Teller's Story*, a book so skillfully combining real and fanciful autobiography that for years afterward some of its self-created legends, such as the author's having had a lusty, one-eyed Italian grandmother and his pretending insanity so that he could abruptly leave business for art, were accepted as facts. Influenced in conception by the 1907 autobiography *The Education of Henry Adams*, though hardly its intellectual equal, *A Story Teller's Story* recounts in apparently rambling but actually controlled style and structure Anderson's development from small-town boy to itinerant laborer to success-worshipping businessman to writer and his becoming, in this process of finding himself and his art, an example for other artists struggling to express American life. The book received enthusiastic reviews after its publication in October 1924, but in the years following Anderson's death it was rejected on the charges of being factually inaccurate and structurally lax. More recently it has been recognized as one of his finest and most characteristic achievements, indeed as a turning point in his career as a writer.

After Anderson's divorce from Tennessee Anderson in early April of 1924, he married Elizabeth Prall. After a brief stay in Berkeley, where he began a never-finished impressionistic book on Abraham Lincoln, he and his new wife settled in the French Quarter of New Orleans. During a hot summer he began writing what he thought of as more a fantasy than a realistic novel about postwar America and the new sexual freedom of the 1920s. Troubled by the public's reception of *A Story Teller's Story*, which was to sell only about six thousand copies in the six months after its publication, he soon began seriously considering leaving Huebsch's small publishing firm for the larger, more aggressive one headed by the flamboyant Horace Liveright, who had for some time been trying to persuade Anderson that his company could sharply increase the sale of his books and hence his income from royalties. It was not until April 1925, however, that Anderson finally made the change, signing a contract with Liveright which guaranteed him a weekly income of one hundred dollars in exchange for delivering to the publisher one full-length book a year. Anderson felt guilty about deserting Huebsch, who had loyally helped build his reputation as a leading writer, but he was relieved to have an assured income.

That assurance was especially welcome since during the first two months of 1925 he had been away from New Orleans on a lecture tour to earn money and had found lecturing distinctly not to his taste. Returning to the city in March, he became friendly with a young Mississippian named William Faulkner, a poet who had begun to write fiction. Anderson urged this promising young man to write about the people of his own region, as he himself had written about in Ohio, and he generously helped persuade Liveright to publish Faulkner's first novel. Having completed the "fantasy" novel of postwar America, which he would eventually call *Dark Laughter*, he returned imaginatively to his origins and began a semi-autobiographical "Childhood" book. The serial rights were sold to the *Woman's Home Companion*, which promised him access for the first time to a large popular audience. Not wishing to face another summer of writing in the steamy heat of New Orleans, he was advised to board with a family named Greear who lived in the village of Troutdale in the cool mountainous area of western Virginia. Here, surrounded by a large family of boys who reminded him of his own family in Clyde days, Anderson found life so congenial that he wrote rapidly at the childhood book and even located a farm on nearby Ripshin Creek which some months later he would purchase as a site for a permanent home.

In September 1925 Liveright published *Dark Laughter*, Anderson's first book to appear under the new imprint. The action of this novel is simple enough when its events are put in chronological order. A Chicago newspaperman named John Stockton walks out of his job and loveless marriage, lives briefly and happily among blacks in New Orleans, and under the assumed named of Bruce Dudley returns to his hometown of Old Harbor, Indiana, on the Ohio River. Here Bruce works in a factory owned by Fred Grey, a successful businessman and unsuccessful human being,

whose wife Aline is passionate but as yet unawakened. Aline hires Bruce as her gardener, and they become lovers. When she becomes pregnant with his child, they go away together, leaving Fred listening to the knowing laughter of his black servants. What is not simple about the book is its mode of narration. Frequently Anderson introduces a self-conscious, choppily written commentary in his own voice on the sterility of industrialism and business life. At other times he enters the minds of his chief characters, creating for each a stream of consciousness that moves about in time with great flexibility. These explorations vary in tone from, for example, Bruce Dudley's lyric memory of a moment of wordless communication that he observed between his mother and an unknown young man when as a child he accompanied her on a trip on a riverboat, to bitter recollections of his wife's inability to write a story because her imagined situation was too artificial, her language too much an arty playing with words. The world of such artists, one understands, is as sterile as the conventional business world which they think themselves to be rebelling against. In contrast to both worlds are set representations of a more natural mode of life—the relation of Bruce and Aline, the "dark laughter" of the blacks, and one of Anderson's most successful creations, the figure of Sponge Martin, skilled craftsman and independent-minded worker who retains his sexuality and youthful zest into old age. *Dark Laughter* is a very uneven book, self-consciously primitivistic, heavy-handed in some of its satire, yet also lyrical, tender, filled with startling imaginative juxtapositions. It is the work of a writer bent on a bold experiment over which he does not have full control.

Horace Liveright fulfilled his prediction, however, for his skillful promotion of *Dark Laughter* made it, despite very mixed reviews, Anderson's one modest commercial success. In three and a half months the novel sold over twenty-one thousand copies and brought him just over eight thousand dollars; in its first nine months it went through eight printings. With this income, supplemented by lecturing fees and several thousand dollars in serial rights to the childhood book, Anderson felt affluent for the first time since he had become a writer. Finally he could afford to commission the building by local Virginia craftsmen of a fine stone house on the land he had bought along Ripshin Creek.

The summer of 1926 was an exciting and exhausting one for Anderson. In the late winter be-

Anderson with Eleanor Copenhaver, whom he married in 1933 (courtesy of the Newberry Library)

tween lecture engagements he had read final proofs on a second book for Liveright, *Sherwood Anderson's Notebook* (1926), a miscellaneous collections of articles, notes, and sketches, most of them previously published. Even before moving to Troutdale, he had thrown himself into a new novel, "Another Man's House," which, like many other projects, he would never complete. As the building of the house proceeded under his constant observation, he suddenly found the right form in which to cast one of his most famous stories, "Death in the Woods," which he had been trying to write off and on for five years, and he sent it to his literary agent in early June. By mid July he had finished and mailed to Liveright the manuscript of the childhood book, now titled *Tar: A Midwest Childhood* (1926), and had begun submitting to *Vanity Fair* a series of articles commissioned by that elegant magazine.

The strain of that frenetically busy summer was increased by the many antagonistic reviews of *Dark Laughter*; by the generally unenthusiastic

critical comment on *Sherwood Anderson's Notebook*; by the parody of his style in Hemingway's *The Torrents of Spring* (published in May 1926) and the ensuing praise by reviewers of that ungenerous attack from one he had befriended; and by his concern over the possible reception of *Tar*, which was to be published in November. The semi-autobiographical *Tar* is a pleasant, nostalgic recollection-invention of the author's small-town childhood, often effective in its presentation of a child's growing awareness of self, family, neighbors, townspeople, but marred by occasional passages of hasty, vague prose. Placed beside the first part of *A Story Teller's Story*, it seems both less skilled in its writing and repetitive in its use of childhood material. Anderson was beginning to fear that he had written himself out, and the weekly remittances from Liveright, welcome as they might be as a steady income, were also steady reminders that he must produce a book each year, a constricting situation for a writer who had been proud of his commitment to endless experimentation. In addition, he was becoming aware that Elizabeth Anderson and he were of widely different temperaments, were indeed incompatible.

All these deeply troubling concerns, together with a prolonged bout with flu, made his second visit to France, from December 1926 to March 1927, an emotional disaster. Returning to Ripshin, he was painfully despondent for months despite having Liveright stop weekly remittances. Then in the fall he learned that the two weekly newspapers of nearby Marion, the *Smyth County News* and the *Marion Democrat*, were for sale, and on 1 November he purchased them as an escape from his situation as a writer unable to write. For about a year and a half he edited the newspapers, finding pleasure in making them readable through his personal way of presenting local news events, through his weekly column of comment on literature or on state or national affairs, through his circumspect editorializing on the need for certain city improvements, through his invention, because he could not afford a real one, of an imaginary reporter named Buck Fever around whom he invented a whole cast of imaginary characters with farcical names. In April 1929 he collected excerpts from his first year of newspaper writings in the book *Hello Towns!* The book was too fragmentary in form and too local in its references to sell well, and Anderson's self-confidence was further shaken.

Late in 1928 he and Elizabeth Anderson separated–a divorce would follow in 1932–and he began increasingly to turn over the editorship of the newspapers to his oldest son, Robert. Left to himself, feeling that his talent was lost and his reputation as a writer declining, he drifted in and out of Marion. He worked unsuccessfully on a novel and went through periods of terrible depression, then took to making long automobile trips through the South, observing the mountain people at work in the textile mills or on desperate strikes in violently anti-union mill towns. From magazine articles that he wrote at this time he put together a small book entitled *Perhaps Women*, published in September 1931, which argued that while machines have a clean beauty of their own, they have become a dominating and dehumanizing force in modern life, robbing the men who tend them of, both figuratively and literally, their male potency. Women, on the other hand, because of their biological function as bearers of children, can resist the dehumanizing effects of the factory much more successfully and perhaps may bring machines under some sort of human control.

In 1931 and 1932 he was drawn briefly toward communism as a possible solution to the problems facing Depression America. In the late spring of 1932, for example, he joined Edmund Wilson, Waldo Frank, and other American writers and intellectuals in signing a manifesto supporting the Communist candidate in the presidential elections of that year. In August he made a quick trip to Amsterdam as part of the American delegation to a Communist-organized World's Congress Against War. Yet communism repelled him intellectually by its dogmatic theory and its authoritarianism as much as it attracted him emotionally for its appeal to the "invisible roof" of comradeship among workers in opposition to the money-valuing, self-centered owning class. This conflict is apparent in his novel *Beyond Desire*, written, too hastily, in this period and published in September 1932. Red Oliver, the novel's major figure, is a young Georgian caught in his allegiances between his upper-class father and working-class mother. Siding with the working class, he becomes involved in a strike in his hometown and eventually, though he is confused about whether to become a Communist or not, in a Communist-led strike in a North Carolina mill town. In a confrontation between strikers and National Guard troops under the command of a young officer who is equally confused about his role in a chaotic America, Red steps forward despite the officer's warning to the strikers not to move and is shot instantly dead.

The true focus of *Beyond Desire*, however, is not political, though Anderson sometimes ineptly obscures his larger subject: the effect of industrialism on the complex socioeconomic structure of the present-day South. Acutely perceptive of this structure because of his newspaper experience, his travels, and his intuitive understanding of human beings, Anderson portrays the collapse of traditional southern values before the amoral thrust of the machine age as that collapse is reflected at various class levels. By far the best section of the book is the one entitled "Mill Girls," the second of the four books into which the novel is divided as though into four interconnected short novels. Writing with the creative intensity and subtlety of *Winesburg, Ohio* or his finer short stories, he gets beneath the surface of the lives of four young women mill workers, presenting them with great technical dexterity and a moving sympathy. "Mill Girls" shows that his writer's gift was by no means gone, though he could not always count on it being with him.

For the unevenness of *Beyond Desire* Anderson himself must be faulted; for the fate of his next book, *Death in the Woods and Other Stories*, outside circumstance was to blame. Liveright's financial affairs went into disarray early in the Depression. This final collection of Anderson's stories was hardly distributed at all because its appearance in April 1933 coincided with Liveright's bankruptcy. This was a heavy blow, for Anderson had counted on this volume to restore his declining literary reputation. He had reason to hope that it would, for the collection opens with the simple but mythic "Death in the Woods," written in 1926, and ends with the equally strong "Brother Death," a tale he had condensed from an abortive novel depicting the tensions between life-giving independence and death-dealing subordination within a western Virginia farm family. Both tales represented a bold risk on the author's part that the reader's total understanding of each story's meaning would not be limited to the partial meaning explicitly stated at each story's conclusion. In both tales, and in several of those in between, Anderson displayed his final short story form–a plain, discursive, literal surface through which one looks into receding depths of meaning.

A much more important event in Anderson's life than his publisher's failure was about to occur, however. As early as 1928 he had met Eleanor Copenhaver, daughter of the Marion superintendent of schools, who for some years had been working in the Industrial Program of the National YWCA. Twenty years younger than Anderson, energetic, socially minded, she had encouraged him to visit the southern cotton mills and observe the strikes and had helped him move out of his long period of despairing self-doubt. In July 1933 she became his fourth wife in a marriage that would provide him relative stability during the last eight years of his life.

Although he would continue writing fiction during these remaining years, he turned more and more to doing articles, and his next two books after his marriage were nonfiction. In the first, *No Swank* (1934), he collected a number of impressionistic essays about individuals, primarily literary figures, both alive and dead, whom he admired–George Borrow, Dreiser, Stein, D. H. Lawrence. The second, *Puzzled America*, which appeared in March 1935, brought together the articles he wrote in 1934 for *Today* magazine recording his travels in the South and Midwest and his conversations with many kinds of people who were attempting to find out what had gone wrong with their lives and their country and how these might be set right. These articles show Anderson's gift for quick rapport with average people and his ability to understand and sympathize with their bewilderment in difficult times. *Puzzled America* reflects their lack of bitterness or revolutionary temper, their reliance on each other, their faith in President Roosevelt's New Deal, and their persistent hope for a more democratic, more united America to come. As a record of how ordinary people felt in the middle of the Depression, the unostentatious, human, and humane journalism of *Puzzled America* has few equals.

In the summer of 1935 he began writing his last novel, *Kit Brandon: A Portrait*, which was published in October 1936. Combining his skills as an interviewer and as an oral narrator, he worked out a double narrative technique in which part of the time he, the author, is purportedly obtaining information about or directly from the woman whose name provides the novel's title and part of the time the woman herself is recounting to him in her own words episodes of her life. (Shortly before beginning his novel, Anderson had in fact interviewed, over several weeks prior to her court trial, a woman who had become famous in southwestern Virginia for her

daring as one of a gang running moonshine in defiance of federal liquor laws.) Kit Brandon's life has been a special version of the American dream, embodying in its unusual way a desire for improvement both of her physical surroundings and of her self-knowledge. An intelligent but uneducated Appalachian mountain girl raised in a poor, slovenly home, Kit runs away at fourteen to a piedmont mill town and takes a job in a cotton mill, as other mountain people were doing in the 1920s. Here she begins to learn, through a radical fellow worker, about the class structure of the South in which she lives, and here she takes her first lover merely out of pity because he is dying of tuberculosis. Subsequently she meets and marries Gordon Halsey, the weak son of Tom Halsey, a wealthy bootlegger as daring and ruthless in getting what he wants as Kit is. Not satisfied with expensive clothes and high-powered cars, and despising her husband, Kit joins Tom's organization, which is running moonshine, and begins to build a reputation as a courageous and resourceful driver in Tom's car caravans. Tom is killed by his son when federal agents close in on the gang, but Kit escapes with the help of a young drunkard named Joel Hanaford. Perhaps too manipulatively, Anderson casts Hanaford as the son of a wealthy judge and legislator to show the hypocrisy and corruption that flourished in high places as well as low under Prohibition. Kit does not take Joel as one of her many lovers, but she realizes that through him she "had been carried out of herself . . . and into the life of another puzzled human," and she intends to find some other work "that did not so separate her from others."

Through Kit's varied and unusual career, Anderson was able to bring to focus the knowledge of the South which he, a curious and perceptive outsider, had picked up from years of close observation. Beyond that, he was able to condemn aspects of the larger American civilization that he had begun attacking twenty years earlier in his first novel–the repression of sexuality, the dedication to material success, the surrender of community and self-awareness to the social fragmentation and dehumanizing force of the machine. In Kit herself, moreover, he created one of his most attractive woman figures. An outlaw in the eyes of the conventional, as Anderson often felt himself and other honest artists to be, she moves essentially uncorrupted through a society corrupt in both its "legal" and "illegal" levels, gradually learning that the material aspect of the American dream is less admirable than its emotional, spiritual aspect, that aspect which values both individual integrity and the ability to live in human community. Like Anderson's seven other novels, *Kit Brandon* has its flaws, but perhaps more fully than any of the others except *Poor White* it succeeded in embodying his final beliefs about the failure and the promise of American life.

During his few remaining years Anderson and his wife traveled much about the United States, but their living arrangements tended to follow a pattern. They spent winter in New York for its cultural activities and Eleanor Anderson's job. In the spring, summer, and fall they lived at Ripshin or in Marion, where Anderson had come to feel a sense of personal roots and of community. He would celebrate this sense of home in a long essay, illustrated with many pictures of small towns, in the documentary volume *Home Town* (1940), the last of his books to appear during his lifetime. He worked desultorily on a variety of projects, the most important being assembling the reminiscences of his life that would appear, in still somewhat fragmented form, the year after his death under the title *Sherwood Anderson's Memoirs* (1942). Unlike *A Story Teller's Story*, the *Memoirs* was a fairly serious attempt to write "straight" autobiography, and it provided much information about its author; yet in his preface Anderson rightly warns the prospective reader that facts "elude" him. There are varying degrees in everything Anderson recounts in his pleasant, shrewd narrator's voice; but his memory is often selective—even when he is not, in the manner of all good storytellers, deliberately turning what did happen into what ought to have happened to give a reminiscence interest and aesthetic shape.

Late in February 1941 Anderson and his wife set out from New York for a trip to South America. At a cocktail party given in their honor the night before they sailed, he swallowed part of a toothpick. This fragment perforated his intestine. As the ship neared the Panama Canal, he became seriously ill, and he was taken to a hospital in Colón, where he died of peritonitis on the operating table.

In the preface to the *Memoirs* Anderson speaks of his life as having been "a most fortunate one" though he knows that in his literary career he has been "but a minor figure." He was being humble, perhaps too humble. Measured against the leading American fictionalists, he indeed is minor; but because of his best stories and

his fundamental influence on modern American fiction, he must be considered one of the most important minor figures of this century's literature.

Letters:

Letters of Sherwood Anderson, edited by Howard Mumford Jones in association with Walter B. Rideout (Boston: Little, Brown, 1953).
Contains 401 letters from the Newberry Library's Sherwood Anderson Collection emphasizing Anderson's concerns with writing and with public issues.

Sherwood Anderson/Gertrude Stein: Correspondence and Personal Essays, edited by Ray Lewis White (Chapel Hill: University of North Carolina Press, 1972).
Prints complete correspondence between these two friends along with their published writings about each other.

Sherwood Anderson: Selected Letters, edited by Charles E. Modlin (Knoxville: University of Tennessee Press, 1984).
Letters chosen from various collections to show Anderson's literary and personal interests from 1916 to 1941.

Letters to Bab: Sherwood Anderson to Marietta D. Finley, 1916-33, edited by William A. Sutton (Urbana: University of Illinois Press, 1985).
Over three hundred letters written by Anderson to a woman friend between 1916 and 1933 revealing many of his attitudes and feelings, particularly toward writing and events in his daily life.

Bibliographies:

Eugene P. Sheehy and Kenneth A. Lohf, *Sherwood Anderson: A Bibliography* (Los Gatos, Cal.: Talisman Press, 1960).
Only full-scale bibliography but needs updating.

Ray Lewis White, *The Merrill Checklist of Sherwood Anderson* (Columbus, Ohio: Merrill, 1969).
Designed for students; useful listing of Anderson's books and periodical publications and of selected books, articles, and reviews about him and his works.

Walter B. Rideout, "Sherwood Anderson," in *Sixteen Modern American Authors: A Survey of Research and Criticism,* edited by Jackson R.

Bryer (Durham, N.C.: Duke University Press, 1974), pp. 3-28.
Commentary on books and articles about Anderson and his work up through 1972 under five headings: Bibliography, Editions, Manuscripts and Letters, Biography, Criticism.

Douglas G. Rogers, *Sherwood Anderson: A Selective, Annotated Bibliography* (Metuchen, N.J.: Scarecrow Press, 1976).
Lists Anderson's books and periodical publications and books, articles, and reviews about him and his works; selective, but helpfully summarizes and evaluates the secondary items.

White, *Sherwood Anderson: A Reference Guide* (Boston: G. K. Hall, 1977).
Inclusive, accurate listing of 2,550 domestic and foreign books and shorter pieces about Anderson and his works, with items arranged by year from 1916 through 1975 and each item briefly summarized.

Biographies:

James Schevill, *Sherwood Anderson: His Life and Work* (Denver: University of Denver Press, 1951).
Solid, somewhat outdated life of Anderson in relation to his times with brief analyses of individual works.

Irving Howe, *Sherwood Anderson* (New York: Sloane, 1951; Stanford: Stanford University Press, 1966).
Somewhat sketchy on details of Anderson's life, but often highly perceptive in its discussions of certain of his best short and long works.

Elizabeth Anderson and Gerald R. Kelly, *Miss Elizabeth: A Memoir* (Boston: Little, Brown, 1969).
Often undependable on dates and details but valuable for its portrait of Anderson by his divorced third wife.

William A. Sutton, *The Road to Winesburg: A Mosaic of the Imaginative Life of Sherwood Anderson* (Metuchen, N.J.: Scarecrow Press, 1972).
Confusingly organized but full of indispensable information about Anderson's life and career up to 1919.

Kim Townsend, *Sherwood Anderson* (Boston: Houghton Mifflin, 1987).
By far the best biography despite some inaccuracies; a well-written, coherent presentation of Anderson and his work.

References:

David D. Anderson, *Sherwood Anderson: An Introduction and Interpretation* (New York: Holt, Rinehart & Winston, 1967).
Able chronological study of Anderson and his works, arguing that his central themes are the isolation of human beings and their attempts to achieve community with others.

Anderson, ed., *Critical Essays on Sherwood Anderson* (Boston: G. K. Hall, 1981).
Contains selected reviews of Anderson's books and articles on him and his work; three articles on women in his fiction.

Anderson, ed., *Sherwood Anderson: Dimensions of His Literary Art: A Collection of Critical Essays* (East Lansing: Michigan State University Press, 1976).
Essays on various aspects of Anderson's writings assembled in celebration of the centennial of his birth.

Rex Burbank, *Sherwood Anderson* (New York: Twayne, 1964).
Often acute survey of Anderson's life, work, attitudes, and ideas.

Hilbert H. Campbell and Charles E. Modlin, eds., *Sherwood Anderson: Centennial Studies* (Troy, N.Y.: Whitston, 1976).
Divided into two sections: "Source Materials"—a selection of letters by Anderson, an interview with Eleanor Copenhaver Anderson, articles on the Newberry Library's Sherwood Anderson Collection, a catalog of Anderson's library—and "Critical Essays."

Cleveland B. Chase, *Sherwood Anderson* (New York: McBride, 1927).
Unsympathetic survey of Anderson's work, concluding that only *Winesburg, Ohio*, despite limitations, and a few stories are artistically satisfactory.

Malcolm Cowley, "Introduction," *Winesburg, Ohio* (New York: Viking, 1960), pp. 1-15.

Excellent brief overview of Anderson as a writer to accompany Cowley's corrected edition of *Winesburg, Ohio*.

N. Bryllion Fagin, *The Phenomenon of Sherwood Anderson: A Study in American Life & Letters* (Baltimore: Rossi-Bryn, 1927).
Somewhat emotional discussion of Anderson as representative of American history and culture.

John H. Ferres, ed., *Sherwood Anderson, Winesburg, Ohio: Text and Criticism* (New York: Viking, 1966).
Reprints Cowley's edition and helpfully collects twenty articles and commentaries on the book.

Maxwell Geismar, *The Last of the Provincials: The American Novel, 1915-1925* (Boston: Houghton Mifflin, 1947), pp. 223-284.
Sympathetic discussion of Anderson as a significant writer and of his work as a perceptive record of American culture.

Forrest L. Ingram, *Representative Short Story Cycles of the Twentieth Century: Studies in a Literary Genre* (The Hague: Mouton, 1971), pp. 143-199.
Extensive, intelligent analysis of *Winesburg, Ohio* as a book of related short stories.

Newberry Library Bulletin, Sherwood Anderson Memorial Number, second series, no. 2 (December 1948); Special Sherwood Anderson Number, 6 (July 1971).
The first contains several memoirs of Anderson and "A Bibliography of Anderson's Contributions to Periodicals 1914 to 1946"; the second contains essays on Anderson and his work.

Burton Rascoe, "Winesburg, Ohio," *Chicago Tribune*, 7 June 1919, p. 13.
Review showing acute understanding of Anderson's method in *Winesburg, Ohio*.

Walter B. Rideout, ed., *Sherwood Anderson: A Collection of Critical Essays* (Englewood Cliffs, N.J.: Prentice-Hall, 1974).
Reprints essays and reviews on Anderson and his writings from a review of his first novel to a memoir and appreciation by William Faulkner.

Shenandoah, Sherwood Anderson Number, 13 (Spring 1962).
Includes a general article on Anderson, a recollection of him, and essays on "I Want to Know Why," *Winesburg, Ohio*, and *Kit Brandon*.

Story, Homage to Sherwood Anderson Issue, 19 (September-October 1941); reprinted in *Homage to Sherwood Anderson: 1876-1941*, edited by Paul P. Appel (Mamaroneck, N.Y.: Appel, 1970).
Prints the letters Anderson wrote to Van Wyck Brooks and two selections by Anderson, and provides memoirs of the writer by many who had known him.

Welford Dunaway Taylor, *Sherwood Anderson* (New York: Praeger, 1977).
An admirable brief introduction to the man and his work.

Twentieth Century Literature, Sherwood Anderson Issue, 23 (February 1977).
Contains a portfolio of photographs of Anderson and persons and places associated with him, six essays on various of his works, and two articles on his reception abroad, in France and Japan.

Brom Weber, *Sherwood Anderson* (Minneapolis: University of Minnesota Press, 1964).
Pamphlet; brief but perceptive examination of Anderson's writings, ideas, and literary achievement.

Ray Lewis White, ed., *The Achievement of Sherwood Anderson: Essays in Criticism* (Chapel Hill: University of North Carolina Press, 1966).
Twenty articles, reviews, book chapters covering many aspects of Anderson's literary career.

White, ed., *The Merrill Studies in Winesburg, Ohio* (Columbus, Ohio: Merrill, 1971).
Convenient gathering of materials on the book in four sections: Composition, Reviews, Aspects, Achievement.

The Winesburg Eagle, Official Publication of The Sherwood Anderson Society, 1975-
Originally edited by Welford D. Taylor; now edited by Hilbert H. Campbell and Charles E. Modlin, Department of English, Virginia

Polytechnic Institute and State University. Prints articles and notes on Anderson and his writings.

Papers:
The major collection of Anderson's papers is in The Newberry Library in Chicago.

Hart Crane

This entry was updated by J. M. Brook from the entry by Joseph Miller in DLB 48, American Poets, 1880-1945, Second Series.

Places	Cleveland Brooklyn	Paris	Mexico
Influences and Relationships	Charlie Chaplin Walt Whitman Harry & Caresse Crosby T. S. Eliot	Padraic and Mary Colum Plato Waldo Frank	Ralph Waldo Emerson Friedrich Nietzsche Sir James G. Frazer (*The Golden Bough*)
Literary Movements and Forms	Romanticism Symbolism	Postimpressionism Modernism	Greek and Latin Classics
Major Themes	Idealized Love The Inviolability of Art The Vulgarity and Materialism of Society	The Power of Imagination to Transform Reality Homoerotic Love	Nature as a Means of Renewal The Agony of the Creative Life
Cultural and Artistic Influences	Christian Science Mexican Architecture	Mexican Religious Rituals	The Bible The Silent Film
Social and Economic Influences	World War I	Rise of Industrialism	The Jazz Age

See also the Crane entry in DLB 4, American Writers in Paris, 1920-1939.

BIRTH: Garrettsville, Ohio, 21 July 1899, to Clarence A. and Grace Hart Crane.

AWARD: Guggenheim Fellowship, 1931.

DEATH: At sea, 27 April 1932.

BOOKS: *White Buildings* (New York: Boni & Liveright, 1926);
The Bridge (Paris: Black Sun Press, 1930; New York: Liveright, 1930);
The Collected Poems of Hart Crane, edited by Waldo Frank (New York: Liveright, 1933);
The Complete Poems and Selected Letters and Prose of Hart Crane, edited by Brom Weber (Garden City, N.Y.: Doubleday/Anchor, 1966; London: Oxford University Press, 1968);
Seven Lyrics (Cambridge, Mass.: Ibex Press, 1966);
Ten Unpublished Poems, edited by Kenneth Lohf (New York: Gotham Book Mart, 1972).

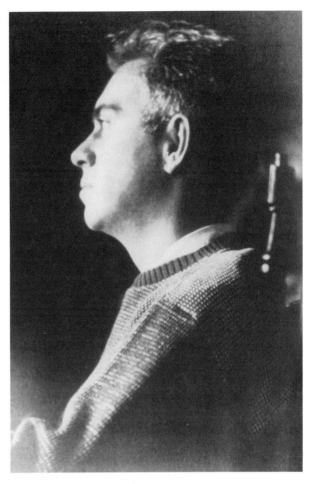

Hart Crane, 1931 (photograph by William Wright)

The years immediately preceding World War I saw the introduction of international modernism to America, and the years immediately following saw American artists in all the arts adopting and adapting the new ideas and grafting them onto a distinctly American consciousness. By 1923 Hart Crane was writing *The Bridge* (1930), in which he endeavored to unite the style of modernism—the heritage of the symbolists and postimpressionists—with the spirit of American romanticism—the heritage of Ralph Waldo Emerson and Walt Whitman. *The Bridge* is Crane's longest and most ambitious work, and he saw its problematic nature even as he wrote it. "At times the project seems hopeless, horribly so," he wrote to a friend, "and then suddenly something happens inside one, and the theme and the substance of the conception seem brilliantly real, more so than ever! At least, *at worst,* the poem will be a *huge* failure!" Apart from questions of its ultimate success or failure, *The Bridge* retains its character as a monumental experiment, and as such stands as a landmark in twentieth-century American poetry. In the truest sense the poem came from "inside" the poet, and indeed Hart Crane's entire life and career can be seen as a grand experiment: a projection of the ever-expanding, all-absorbing, all-consuming optimism of Emerson upon the cold cruel realities of modern life.

He was born Harold Hart Crane in Garrettsville, Ohio, on 21 July 1899, the only child of Clarence A. and Grace Hart Crane. Both the Cranes and the Harts were old mercantile families, and the poet's father, known as C. A., built up for himself a large fortune in the manufacture and sale of chocolate candy. The style and values of the Cranes' life were quintessentially bourgeois: they lived in comfort, and they maintained a certain superficial culture without any serious commitment to the arts. The marriage of C. A. and Grace Crane was a thoroughly unhappy one, and they made one another miserable from the day of their wedding in 1898 until long after their divorce in 1917. Grace Crane was famously beautiful and profoundly neurotic. She was terrified of sex, and spent her life alternately in suffering from psychosomatic illnesses and in undergoing Christian Science therapy. She smothered her son with affection, involved him in all her marital quarrels, turned him against his father, and established with him a bond of mutual dependence. Hart Crane found this bond stifling, but for all his life he could free himself from it only sporadically and with difficulty. C. A. Crane was an ambitious, unromantic man, generous and well meaning but unable by nature to cope with his unhappy wife or to understand his oversensitive, bookish, homosexual son. After the divorce C. A. Crane was married twice again, both times happily, first to a woman who died in 1928, and then to one who survived him. He died in 1931, after a reconciliation with his son, who was drowned at sea the following year. Grace Crane, who had been alienated from her son for some time as the result of a dispute over his inheritance from his grandmother, survived his death by fifteen years, during which time she devoted herself to his memory and to his reputation as a poet, assisting his editors and biographers. She lost her money and her beauty, and she, who had been raised in wealth and innocence, always sheltered and always something of a snob, was reduced in her last years to poverty, making her living as a charwoman. She met old age, loneliness, and poverty with a stoic dignity completely unknown in her earlier life, which had been characterized more by hysterical fits and sentimental blackmail.

Both the strengths and weaknesses of Hart Crane as a poet are evidenced in his character as a man, which is inexplicable apart from the atmosphere of emotional turmoil in which he lived his life. His was a volatile personality, excitable and exuberant, and not notably stable. He was given to passionate enthusiasms and to intense attachments to people, who, finding themselves overwhelmed by his attentions, invariably withdrew and disappointed him. Euphoric delight was followed by gloom and anger, followed by another passion. Although from an early age he was a dedicated and hardworking poet, he wrote with bursts of inspiration and suffered, when there was no inspiration, from fears that his gift had evaporated. He never achieved a calm detachment from his poetry any more than he did from his family.

When Crane was four years old the family moved to Warren, Ohio, where C. A. Crane founded a syrup factory, and in 1908, while Grace Crane was in a private sanatorium recovering from a nervous breakdown, Hart moved from Warren to Cleveland to live with his maternal grandmother, whose house served thereafter as the family home. It was a big three-story frame house with a pair of turrets on the front, one of which Hart maintained as his own private "ivory tower," complete with books, a Morris chair, a phonograph and records, and a Corona portable typewriter. Here as an adolescent he began his serious involvement in poetry. He took piano lessons from his Aunt Alice and remained all his life an avid, if undisciplined, amateur pianist, and it was Aunt Alice's collection of standard editions–Emerson, Whitman, Victor Hugo, Robert Browning–that inspired in him an admiration for great literature. She later remembered him at ten: "Once he stood there looking at all the books. 'This is a wonderful collection, Aunt Alice,' he said. He ran his fingers through his hair–he had a habit of doing that–and then he turned to me, very seriously: 'This is going to be my vocation,' he said. 'I'm going to be a poet.'" Hart Crane had a long apprenticeship ahead of him, but he seems never to have wavered in his decision to become a poet.

In 1914 Crane entered East High School, which was then one of the showplaces of the Cleveland educational system, with high academic standards and a record of successful graduates. Here he studied the "Classical" program, which emphasized English literature and composition, mathematics, and languages. He was a good student and learned easily, but his academic record was complicated by frequent and excessive absences from school, caused by upheavals in the family. There was a long and, as far as school was concerned, disastrous winter vacation in 1915 on the Isle of Pines (now the Isle of Youth), south of Cuba, where Mrs. Hart, the poet's grandmother, had a house, and twice Hart made long trips around the country with his mother. In 1916 they toured the West, including San Francisco, Yellowstone National Park, and the Canadian Rockies. Hart kept up with his schoolwork as best he could, but most of his real learning was done on his own. In the provincial metropolis of Cleveland he could indulge his passions for art and music and the theater, and in the "ivory tower" he pursued a course of private reading in literature that could only be called ambitious and precocious, including such writers as Plato, Plutarch, Honoré de Balzac, Voltaire, and Boccaccio. He read Nathaniel Hawthorne, Oscar Wilde, and Edgar Allan Poe, and in poetry Percy Bysshe Shelley and Algernon Swinburne. His earliest poems were long rhapsodies in the manner of Swinburne, full of gods and goddesses. He haunted

Richard Laukhuff's literary bookshop in downtown Cleveland, where he read all the newest avant-garde journals and little magazines. Hart Crane was by temperament and practice essentially an autodidact, and one is inclined to think that the style and content of his mind would not have been greatly different had he finished high school or attended a university. In 1916, following his parents' separation, Hart, a very green, very idealistic seventeen-year-old, was allowed to go to New York and make his mark on the world.

The plan was originally that Hart would study with a tutor toward passing the examination that would allow him to enter Columbia University without a high-school diploma, but this proved from the beginning to be little more than a pretense that permitted him to stay in New York. He was far too eager to become a successful poet immediately to be willing to spend four more years in school. While still in Cleveland he had made the acquaintance of Harriet Moody, widow of William Vaughn Moody, shown her his poems, and solicited her patronage. In September of 1916 he had actually published a poem in a New York journal called *Bruno's Weekly,* and, now that he was in New York, he lost no time in following up on every possible connection he could muster. He was never shy about pressing himself and his poems upon anyone who might prove useful, and because of his youth and guileless charm he seldom failed to make them his friends. Carl Schmitt, a painter he had known in Cleveland, became his first mentor in New York, introduced him to a wealth of modernist ideas about art and literature, and served as a critic and sounding board for his early poems. Schmitt introduced Crane to Padraic and Mary Colum. "Really," he wrote his mother, "as I expected, I am right in the swing. Tomorrow I call on the noted Irish poet & dramatist, Padraic Colum. Then I shall meet Frank Harris, editor of 'Pearsons,' and friend-biographer of Oscar Wilde. . . . Within a few weeks I expect to be printed in the columns of the 'New York Evening Sun.' Fine, isn't it." It was the Colums who gave him Arthur Symons's book on the symbolist movement and introduced him to the poetry of Charles Baudelaire, Arthur Rimbaud, and Paul Verlaine.

At this time, almost simultaneously, Crane came under the influence of two very different, but perhaps complementary, spheres of literary activity. One was that of the *Little Review,* which Margaret Anderson had brought from Chicago to New York in 1917. It was the champion of the English and French modernist circles. Ezra Pound was the "foreign editor" of the *Little Review,* and he filled its pages with the works of writers he admired, especially T. S. Eliot, W. B. Yeats, Wyndham Lewis, and James Joyce. Crane was excited about these writers; the offices of the *Little Review* became his second home in New York; and he worked there off and on, never with much success, selling advertisements. The other important sphere of influence centered upon the journal *Seven Arts,* founded in 1916 by Waldo Frank, Van Wyck Brooks, James Oppenheim, and Paul Rosenfeld. This group was the American school, whose guiding spirit was Walt Whitman. The editors of *Seven Arts* promoted writers such as Theodore Dreiser, Sherwood Anderson, and Robert Frost, and anyone whom they felt to be in the great tradition of Emerson, Thoreau, Melville, Whitman, and Emily Dickinson. Crane was a friend and enthusiastic admirer of Sherwood Anderson, and Waldo Frank became a kind of spiritual older brother to Crane and later edited his first *Collected Poems* (1933). Crane moved freely between these two circles and drew upon them both. Although his was essentially a magpie's attitude toward ideas and theories, the synthesis Crane effected between these two very dissimilar sources is an important part of his contribution to modern American literature.

Crane's life in New York was not easy. He was not interested in any kind of occupation apart from writing poetry, and so he was often short of money, especially when the strained communications between his parents caused his allowance to be delayed. Hart sided totally with his mother in the divorce disputes, but as a result her emotional demands on him were greater than ever. She went to Florida to socialize and forget, but she insisted nonetheless upon daily letters from her son and telegraphed him if they were late. She wrote him: "You, in my trouble, have been able to pay me for all the care & anxiety I have had for you since you came to me nearly eighteen years ago–I am expecting great things from you & when we see each other again we can talk over our plans which look very beautiful to me now. I am asking you to send me your love every day as I shall you." And in another letter: "So I am asking you to write me often Harold because your letters even though short are a stimulus to me, & surely you love me enough to do what you can to help me fight my way back to peace, happiness, & health. . . . Do not allow your-

Grace Hart Crane

Clarence A. Crane

self to become an egotist & unmindful of others–
But just remember that true happiness is largely
due to service & no matter how rich your day
may have been in opportunities, it is not entirely
complete unless you have done or thought of
someone else–Please write me often." Hart was
completely in his mother's thrall and had no defenses whatsoever against such manipulation
until years later, and then only by breaking with
her. After Grace Crane returned from Florida,
she brought her mother to New York, where
they lived with Hart in a one-bedroom apartment on Gramercy Park. From here Mrs. Crane
negotiated an abortive reconciliation with her husband and otherwise spent her time in bed with
fits of "nerves," nursed by her mother with Christian Science and by her son with sympathetic attention. It is a wonder that Hart could write anything under such conditions, but it is during this
time that he wrote some of his best early poems,
such as "Annunciation" and "Fear," and these
poems as well as several others were published
within the year in Joseph Kling's *Pagan,* a Greenwich Village journal. Crane's earliest poems are interesting now primarily as a prelude to what was
to follow. They were never reprinted during his

lifetime, but Frank included them in *The Collected
Poems of Hart Crane* (1933) as an appendix.

Crane found friendship and encouragement
among the New York literati, but the presence of
his mother only prolonged his childhood. She
moved restlessly back and forth between New
York and Cleveland, always on the brink of a nervous collapse or hoping to recover from one.
Crane depended upon his parents for money,
and early in 1918 C. A. Crane became increasingly difficult and threatened to withhold Hart's
allowance unless his son produced some evidence
of being employed or even of seriously seeking employment. The entrance of the United States into
World War I added further uncertainty to the
young man's life. He looked upon the army as a
possible escape from his family, but when he
tried to enlist he was turned away because he was
still a minor. Instead he worked for a time in a mu-
nitions plant in Cleveland as a contribution to the
war effort.

When the war had ended Crane took a job
as a reporter for the *Cleveland Plain Dealer.* He
left the *Plain Dealer* in February 1919 to return to
New York and become "advertising manager" of
the *Little Review* for four months. In August, on

the recommendation of his father, he got a job with Rheinthal and Newman in New York, the firm that supplied the Crane company with the Maxfield Parrish reproductions that they featured on their candy boxes. He began as a shipping clerk and finished as a shipping clerk three months later. He then returned to Ohio to work for his father, first in Akron, then in Cleveland, until father and son had a violent argument on 20 April 1921, whereupon Crane quit his job and broke decisively with his father. He worked briefly for an advertising firm in Cleveland, writing copy, and then went back to New York to work briefly for the J. Walter Thompson Company, an advertising agency. This job was followed by others in advertising and sales, always brief, and indeed he never held a job with any success. In 1925 and again in 1927 the financier and philanthropist Otto Kahn gave Crane money, which somewhat alleviated his poverty, but it was nonetheless a persistent discouragement to him to be unable to keep a job, especially in the prosperous and optimistic environment of the 1920s. This condition was in part a result of his restless nature and in part a result of his uncompromising dedication to poetry, which kept him from giving himself wholeheartedly to any other enterprise.

During these years Crane's love relationships were no more stable or long lasting than his jobs, characterized as they were by the peaks of elation and the depths of despair. He had a penchant for merchant sailors, the nature of whose work occasioned sad partings and jealous separations. He suffered attacks of "homesickness" for the security of his childhood family, but from a distance he felt too strongly the emotional greed of his mother ever to succumb to her again by returning to Cleveland. If he neglected his letters to her, she would write, "I wish you to realize that you treat me very badly indeed. . . . It isn't fair at all to me, Hart . . . dead silence for two weeks. . . . Now I won't *have* such neglect–and I won't love you at all any more if you ever repeat such indifference." Yet Crane was not morbid or melancholy by nature. On the contrary, he was full of vitality and eager for experience and for success, had an abundance of friends, and was widely regarded as very good company. But peace and fulfillment eluded him.

One might say that Crane sought to discover in poetry what he found lacking in life. As early as 1919, at the precocious age of twenty, he had already begun the poems of his early matur-

ity, which would be collected eventually and published in his first volume of verse, *White Buildings*, in 1926. With "My Grandmother's Love Letters" and "Garden Abstract" Crane establishes the connection between his poetry and his personal experience, in the one between his poetry and his family, in the other between his poetry and his sexuality. "My Grandmother's Love Letters" is a wistful poem in which the poet seeks in vain to reconstruct from old letters, "brown and soft,/And liable to melt as snow," the emotional life of his grandmother, Elizabeth Belden Hart, with whom he spent much of his childhood. There is pathos in this attempt to reassemble the shards of a broken family, but the poem ends on a note of self-protective irony: "And so I stumble. And the rain continues on the roof/With such a sound as gently pitying laughter"–as if to ward off any charges of sentimentality. "Garden Abstract" is a personal poem of a very different sort. In it the poet projects his own homosexual impulses upon the figure of a young girl who is experiencing an erotic surrender to the larger forces of nature: "The apple on its bough is her desire," and "She is prisoner of the tree and its green fingers." The sexual symbolism of this garden, that of male sexuality to be precise, was not lost on its first readers, at a time when Freud was fad and fashion, although there is no evidence that Crane ever read any of the works of Freud. The girl's ravishment by the forces of nature is, however, more than merely sexual. Crane called the poem a piece of "pure pantheistic aestheticism," and indeed in "Garden Abstract" the beginnings of Crane's visionary aspirations are apparent, as he seeks through the materials of his own life some archetype of unity, beauty, and escape from self-consciousness. At the end of the poem, "She has no memory, nor fear, nor hope/Beyond the grass and shadows at her feet."

In "Praises for an Urn," within the strict conventions of the English elegy, Crane transforms the grief and sense of loss experienced upon the death of a friend into a reflection upon the inviolability of art. His friend was Ernest Nelson, a Norwegian immigrant, a well-read and intelligent man and a would-be poet and painter, who lived in Cleveland and died in autumn 1921. Crane sees him as the type of the artist-victim who is pitted against the vulgarity and materialism of an uncaring society. "He was one of the many," he wrote to a friend, "broken against the stupidity of American life in such places as here." Together Ernest Nelson and the poet had specu-

Hart Crane, Allen Tate, and William Slater Brown in a Times Square photographer's gallery, February 1925

lated upon the immortality of the soul, and now one of them is dead and the other is left to confront the "insistent clock" which is "perched in the crematory lobby." The poet refuses to mourn, but scatters his verses instead, like ashes, like seeds perhaps, upon the world and succeeds thereby in robbing the sun of its triumph over the moon, that is, in robbing the world of facts of its triumph over the world of imagination. In "At Melville's Tomb," also an elegy of sorts, it is the sea—always an important symbol for Crane— that is the all-encompassing element which reconciles the tormented artist to the tribulations of life and death: "Then in the circuit calm of one vast coil,/Its lashings charmed and malice reconciled,/Frosted eyes there were that lifted altars;/And silent answers crept across the stars."

The religious image of the "lifted altars" is continued in "Lachrymae Christi," one of Crane's most overtly religious poems and one of his most difficult. There is no logic in this poem but for the logic of metaphor and the link and association of sounds and connotations, moving elusively around a central theme: again redemption and serenity achieved through suffering. The power of the imagination (the moon) transforms the cruel world of mills and machinery into a pastoral spring. In nature perhaps there is a hope of renewal for the poet who has lost his way, a kind of baptism that will "Anoint with innocence,– recall/To music and retrieve what perjuries/Had galvanized the eyes." His theme is now "Not penitence/But song, as these/Perpetual fountains, vines,–/Thy Nazarene and tinder eyes." The abundance and extravagance of images in this poem are reminiscent of the imagery of Richard Crashaw's "St. Mary Magdalene, or The Weeper," and in the parenthesis that directly follows the lines quoted above, the poet interjects a note upon his own experience of the cleansing power of tears and suffering–like benzine, a liquid both flammable and caustic, which in line two rises "from the moon." In the end of the poem the redemptive sacrifice of Christ is associated with the death and regeneration of nature, as personified in Dionysus, and with the renewal of poetry, symbolized by the "grail." "Lachrymae Christi" is an excellent example of Crane's stretching and straining language in order to suggest if not wholly to express some phenomenon that is utterly mysterious: the triumph of grace over the cruelties of nature. In the end the "Unmangled target smile" of Christ/Dionysus is held up as a goal, a target, in contrast to the "unyielding smile" of the "sure machinery," that is, of the mangle itself, the world of vulgar commercialism.

In "Lachrymae Christi" the suffering is the suffering of a poet, and the redemption is the renewal of his song. He is recalled "To music," "Not penitence/But song," and the "sphinxes from the ripe/Borages of death have cleared my tongue/Once and again." This theme of suffering as the source and occasion of poetry, and of poetry as the release from suffering, is a central one in Crane's verse, as it was in his life. The poem "Legend," for example, which he placed significantly at the opening of *White Buildings* (1926), is, as it were, the legend of these poems, the story of their origins, and a key to reading them. The poet is confronted by the chaotic flux of the world: "As silent as a mirror is believed/Realities plunge in silence by." But rather than lose himself in repentance and vain regrets and be destroyed like the moth in the flame, he approaches life as a lover. Order and meaning in the chaotic world can be grasped "only by the one who/Spends out himself again," and it is he who will see some "bright logic" in it, however unarticulated, "Unwhispering," experienced directly and immediately, "as a mirror/Is believed." This knowledge is not necessarily comforting: it is called "This cleaving and this burning," "the smoking souvenir,/Bleeding eidolon!" It is the price the poet pays for his art: "Then, drop by caustic drop, a perfect cry/Shall string some constant harmony,–/Relentless caper for all those who step/ The legend of their youth into the noon." There is a suggestion in the third and fourth stanzas of "Legend" that the reader must also share the poet's burden, become a lover, and spend himself again and again, if he is to arrive at the poet's bright logic.

The agony of the creative life and the poet's problematic acceptance of it are also the theme of "Passage." The poet seeks to escape his destiny, again in a pastoral setting: "In sapphire arenas of the hills/I was promised an improved infancy." (Little could have appealed to Crane more than an improved infancy.) But this flight involves leaving memory "in a ravine," and while the abandonment of memory means the loss of pain, it also means a loss of all the pleasures that memory and the imagination have to offer. The boon is not worth the sacrifice, he decides, and "So was I turned about and back, much as your smoke/Compiles a too well-known biography." He returns, retrieves his stolen book of memory, and proposes "To argue with the laurel," when he is immediately granted a vision of some esoteric Egyptian mystery, which baffles him. The poet does not achieve any certainty or lasting satisfaction, but here at least in the world of visions is an intensity of life that far surpasses the vegetable state of forgetfulness.

In "Black Tambourine" the poet compares his own plight in life to that of "The Black man, forlorn in the cellar," shut off from society by "the world's closed door." In this life he "Wanders in some mid-kingdom" between the heaven of art, "his tambourine," and death, "a carcass quick with flies."

The comic aspects of this position of the poet at odds with society did not escape Crane. Early on he saw himself as a bit of a clown, and the lines: "The everlasting eyes of Pierrot/And,

of Gargantua, the laughter," which in "Praise for an Urn" he employs to describe Ernest Nelson, he wrote originally to characterize himself. Crane wrote "Chaplinesque" in October 1921, shortly after seeing Charlie Chaplin's film The Kid, of which he wrote to Gorham Munson that "comedy . . . has never reached a higher level in this country before." He called Chaplin a "dramatic genius." The spirit of the age and the medium of the silent film were perfectly matched in Chaplin, whom the French adopted as their own, nicknaming him "Charlot," because they saw in him a reincarnation of Pierrot, that favorite of the French and Italian stage, who has his origins in the commedia dell'arte of the Renaissance. Crane saw in Chaplin the archetype of the poet in the modern world, a combination of clown, Everyman, and fool, rueful, witty, and self-deprecating, evading with a sidestep and a smirk the "inevitable thumb" of the police? of death? of a cruel world? "And yet these fine collapses are not lies," he says, if they permit the clown to preserve "the heart." By way of paraphrase Crane wrote to Gorham Munson: "I have made that 'infinitely gentle, infinitely suffering thing' of Eliot's into the symbol of the kitten. I feel that, from my standpoint, the pantomime of Charlie represents fairly well the futile gesture of the poet in U.S.A. today, perhaps elsewhere too. And yet, the heart lives on." In the last stanza of "Chaplinesque" the moon–again the poetic imagination–transforms "an empty ash can" into "a grail of laughter," which suggests that while the pursuit of poetry, especially amid the rejected debris of the world, is ludicrous and clownish, it is at the same time very serious, even sacred.

The idea of the poet as wry comedian is characteristic of the euphoric postwar period, the Jazz Age, the 1920s–an idea that found its fullest expression in Wallace Stevens's long quasi-autobiographical poem "The Comedian as the Letter C" (1923)–but it is from Jules Laforgue (1860-1887), particularly through the mediation of Ezra Pound and T. S. Eliot, his greatest disciples, that the hesitant, mocking, ironical manner of melancholy comedy came into the English poetry of this century, Eliot's "The Love Song of J. Alfred Prufrock" (1917) being the most notable example. In 1886 Laforgue published twenty-three "Pierrot poems" in his L'Imitation de Notre Dame La Lune, a volume that Crane ordered from Paris in the fall of 1920. The following summer Crane translated three of the "Locutions des Pierrots" into English, but in his translations of Laforgue he dilutes the ironic spirit considerably and substitutes a more robust, more typically American style of braggadocio, more characteristic of his own nature than the irony of Laforgue and closer to the broad humor of Whitman than to the urbane wit of Eliot.

It is instructive to note that after "Chaplinesque" Crane never again attempted a poem in the ironic manner of Laforgue, and in this respect "Chaplinesque" marks a decisive point in his career. He could still be ironical when he chose, as in the second section of "For the Marriage of Faustus and Helen," which he wrote early in 1922 and which appeared in the January 1923 issue of *Broom* as "The Springs of Guilty Song." Here there is a certain detachment and a jazzy smartness in the images and in the rhythms, but Crane soon found himself repelled by the mordant humor, the alienation, and the increasing pessimism of Eliot and his followers. He wrote to Allen Tate at this time: "The poetry of negation is beautiful–alas, too dangerously so for one of my mind. But I am trying to break away from it. Perhaps this is useless, perhaps it is silly–but one *does* have joys." He had no doubt already experienced too much misery in his life to wish to pursue it in his poetry, and he was by temperament an optimist. Crane found sympathy and encouragement in his optimism among his friends of the *Seven Arts* camp, who called themselves "Young America" and were intent upon humanizing and revitalizing American civilization through the arts, restoring the optimism of Emerson and Whitman, and defeating the cruel powers of materialism. Waldo Frank, for one, was an avowed idealist in the style of the New England transcendentalists and professed such things as: "The essence of all reality lies in the Ideal" and "America is a mystic Word. We go forth to seek America." It was in the spirit of Young America, in reaction to Eliot's *The Waste Land*, published in 1922, that Crane envisaged "For the Marriage of Faustus and Helen," which he finished the following year. "There is no one writing in English who can command so much respect, to my mind, as Eliot," he explained. "However, I take Eliot as a point of departure toward an almost complete reverse of direction. . . . I would apply as much of his erudition and technique as I can absorb and assemble toward a more positive, or . . . ecstatic goal. . . . I feel that Eliot ignores certain spiritual events and possibilities as real and powerful now as, say, in the time of Blake."

Crane at Harry and Caresse Crosby's country retreat in Ermenoville, France, spring 1929

"For the Marriage of Faustus and Helen" was Crane's longest and most ambitious poem to date. It is presented as a prothalamion–that most affirmative kind of poem–to celebrate the union of Faustus, "the poetic or imaginative man of all times," and Helen, "the symbol of this abstract 'sense of beauty.'" To underscore his affirmation of the existence of ideal love and ideal beauty in the modern world, Crane couches his myth aggressively in modern, urban, and technological images. In section one Faustus pursues his vision of Helen even while riding a streetcar: "Then I might find your eyes across an aisle,/Still flickering with those prefigurations." He ends the section by praying that Helen accept his adoring eye, "One inconspicuous, glowing orb of praise." Praise of an ideal as yet unattained, perhaps unattainable, is his theme. The second section is less strong than the other two, lapsing from mystic reverence to a tone almost of condescension, and it seems somewhat incongruous in the context. The scene is a jazz club on a roof garden, and the beautiful young woman–she is not called Helen by name–is less a goddess than a flapper. In section three Crane presents Helen as the ideal of beauty that survives the carnage and devastation of war. Of it he wrote to Waldo Frank, "This last part begins with *catharsis*, the acceptance of tragedy through destruction (The Fall of Troy, etc., also in it). It is Dionysian in its attitude, the creator and the eternal destroyer dance arm in arm, etc., all ending in a restatement of the imagination as in Part I." On the strength of this catharsis Faustus can say, "Let us unbind our throats of fear and pity." The combat pilot is called "religious gunman" and "eternal gunman" to suggest the liberating and religious function of material destruction when the ideal remains intact. The poem ends with a plea for praise rather than blame of "the years," the modern era, because of the triumphs it has witnessed of the imagination over despair. It is a blatant plea for optimism. Upon completing "For the Marriage of Faustus and Helen" Crane wrote to Gorham Munson that he felt himself "quite fit to become a suitable *Pindar* for the dawn of the machine age, so called. I have lost the last shreds of philosophical pessimism during the last few months. O yes, the 'background of life'—and all that is still there, but that is only three-dimensional. It is to the pulse of a greater dynamism that my work must revolve. Something terribly fierce and yet gentle." It was in this spirit of buoyancy and idealism that Crane conceived his first plans for *The Bridge,* a project that would occupy him intermittently for the next seven years.

The background of life was, indeed, still there, and Crane did not cease to write lyrics inspired by the tribulations of his private life just because he was also intent upon creating a larger, more impersonal myth of affirmation. Such poems as "Possessions" and "Recitative" call up the same tensions between aspirations and fulfillment as "For the Marriage of Faustus and Helen," and each ends with a similar call to optimism. Around Easter 1923, just weeks after finishing "For the Marriage of Faustus and Helen," Crane left Cleveland for good and settled in New York. There he caught up with old friends and made new ones, hoping to find "some kind of community of interest . . . something better than a mere clique," only to find, as the months passed, "factions, gossips, jealousies, recriminations, excoriations," a good many of which were instigated by Crane himself. He disliked his job at J. Walter Thompson, he was beset with problems from Cleveland, and a mutilated version of his "For the Marriage of Faustus and Helen" was published in the journal *Secession.* In October he

wrote to his mother, "My state of nerves and insomnia here due to the mad rush of things, and the noisy nights around the place I am obliged to live in, make it imperative that I get away before I have a real breakdown." He first intended to spend the winter on the Isle of Pines, but he decided instead to stay with his friends Edward Nagle and William Slater Brown, who had rented a house near Woodstock, New York. This stay in the country was one of the happiest times in Crane's life. To one friend he wrote: "I really am happy to hear the wind in the boughs, use the axe and saw, and even enjoy the bit of cooking which I share in doing. There is not much time for other things except on rainy days like the last, when I sat reading the Golden Bough. . . ." And to another he wrote: "To speak briefly, I have never felt so fine in my life before. So quiet it is here! No cats fighting, people quarrelling or subways beneath you to make the ground tremble." Two years later Crane enjoyed a similar winter pastoral as the guest of Allen and Caroline Gordon Tate in Patterson, New York, while he was doing the "research" and first drafts of *The Bridge.*

There is a hint of an "appalling tragedy"—presumably sexual—that took place the evening before he left New York for Woodstock, of which he wrote to a friend, "It keeps coming to me, though, in a kind of terrible rawness. . . . It does cry for words, however,—and I'm wondering if I am equal to such an occasion, such beauty and anguish, all in one." Such is the background of "Possessions" and "Recitative," which he brought back with him from Woodstock shortly after the new year. Both poems deal with the anguish of lust and the abiding hope for some kind of fulfillment in love. "Possessions" presents a "Record of rage and partial appetites," followed directly by the flat statement that "The pure possession, the inclusive cloud/Whose heart is fire shall come." "Recitative" presents a vivid and haunting picture of man as a creature divided against himself, "Janus-faced," "Twin shadowed halves," like someone looking in a mirror, "Borne cleft to you, and brother in the half." But when the sun rises, "The bridge swings over salvage," the morning bells are heard, "All hours clapped dense into a single stride," and the poet addresses his doppelgänger, his alienated self: "Forgive me for an echo of these things,/And let us walk through time with equal pride." It is significant that in neither "Possessions" nor "Recitative" is there any resolution or fulfillment beyond a tenacious determination to avoid despair. Even that determination is a kind of grace, an intimation of something positive. Of "Recitative" he wrote to Allen Tate: "Against this paradoxical DUALITY is posed the UNITY, or the conception of it (as you got it) in the last verse." And to his mother in the same month he wrote: "I have a revived confidence in humanity lately, and things are going to come very beautifully for me—and not after so very long, I think. The great thing is to Live and NOT Hate. (Christian Science, in part, I think; and a very important doctrine of belief. Perhaps the most important.)"

Perhaps the strongest statement of this doctrine of belief in the face of unsatisfactory personal experience, and Crane's profoundest expression of his striving for unity and perfection in love, is to be found in "Voyages," a suite of love poems that he wrote in the fall of 1924 and included in *White Buildings*. The summation and crowning achievement of the volume, these six poems doubtless contain some of Crane's finest lyric poetry, firmly rooted as they are in the facts of his own life and aimed at a visionary resolution strictly within the context of his own emotional and imaginative existence.

Shortly after returning to New York from Woodstock, Crane fell in love with a young man called Emil Opffer and in April 1924 moved with him into an apartment at 110 Columbia Heights in Brooklyn, "in the shadow of that bridge," as he wrote to Waldo Frank. The relationship seems to have been a passionate friendship, based on affection and mutual understanding and intensely heightened by eroticism. Opffer was a merchant marine sailing out of New York for periods of eight weeks at a time followed by the same amount of time or less with Crane in Brooklyn. For Crane this experience was "Heaven and Hell." Of the heaven he wrote to Frank: "I have seen the Word made Flesh. I mean nothing less, and I know now that there is such a thing as indestructibility. In the deepest sense, where flesh became transformed through intensity of response to counter-response, where sex was beaten out, where a purity of joy was reached that included tears." The hell of separation from Opffer involved Crane in states of "almost hysterical despair," fits of jealousy, fears of venereal disease, and binges of drinking and carousing. The relationship cooled into a casual friendship within the year, but while it lasted it offered Crane the material out of which he forged "Voyages."

Much of the success of "Voyages" is the result of Crane's happy use of the sea as a symbol of human love, its overwhelming grandeur, its beauty, its dangers, and its power to transport a person beyond what is familiar. Crane associated his own experience of love with the sea, as he wrote in the same letter to Frank: "I think the sea has thrown itself upon me and been answered, at least in part, and I believe I am a little changed—not essentially, but changed and transubstantiated as anyone is who has asked a question and been answered." "Voyages I," borrowing a theme from Melville, presents the sea (and love) as something dangerous: "there is a line/You must not cross nor ever trust beyond it," because "The bottom of the sea is cruel." It is something larger than man, beyond his control. In "Voyages II" the poet calls the sea "this great wink of eternity," a glimpse of the perfection of love in a timeless sphere, where "sleep, death, desire,/Close round one instant in one floating flower." In part 3 the poet continues "this tendered theme" of the sea, of the "Infinite consanguinity it bears," in a realm "through black swollen gates," where the lover surrenders himself totally, "and where death, if shed,/Resumes no carnage, but, this single change—/Upon the steep floor flung from dawn to dawn/The silken skilled transmemberment of song." In part 4 the lovers, having surrendered themselves totally to one another, are separated, but the sea is now the medium of a spiritual union between them, overcoming the limitations of space as it has those of time. And the communication between the parted lovers is one of song; "No stream of greater love advancing now/Than, singing, this mortality alone/Through clay aflow immortally to you." This vision of unity despite separation, "in mingling/Mutual blood, transpiring as foreknown," fills the poet with hope of a complete spiritual fulfillment in love, of a "pure possession": "In this expectant, still exclaim receive/The secret oar and petals of all love." Part 5 marks the death of the love that had once bridged the sea, and now "The cables of our sleep so swiftly filed,/Already hang, shred ends from remembered stars." The faithless lover takes the poet's gift of total love and sails away with it: "No,/In all the argosy of your bright hair I dreamed/Nothing so flagless as this piracy." Crane does not leave the poem with an image of love sundered and pirated. He was candid about his own failure to find satisfaction in love, but the vision of the possibility of perfect love was also a part of his experience, and ultimately the most important part. In "Voyages VI," beyond the stormy sea of mundane love, is a celestial sphere, of "rivers mingling toward the sky," in which "Creation's blithe and petalled word" is addressed to Venus, the goddess of love, "the lounged goddess when she rose/Conceding dialogue with eyes/That smile unsearchable repose–" intimating a possible fulfillment in Love. The goddess is then replaced by the image of an island, Belle Isle, which is called "Still fervid covenant," and "white echo of the oar," an echo, that is, of "The secret oar and petal of all love." In the last stanza this mystery is called "the Word": "The imaged Word, it is, that holds/Hushed willows anchored in its glow./It is the unbetrayable reply/Whose accent no farewell can know." "The imaged Word" is the poet's final name for his vision, "the Word made Flesh." Crane is borrowing, of course, St. John's expression for God's revelation of himself to mankind in the flesh of Jesus Christ, and suggesting at the same time the "imaged word" of poetry, the medium by which the poet's vision is made available to his readers. The vision is a vision of faith in the possibility of a sublime fulfillment in love–"a very important doctrine of belief "–and not a mystical experience of that fulfillment, and it is Crane's humility in not extending the poem beyond what he had himself seen and felt that accounts for the authenticity of "Voyages."

The final image in "Voyages," of the poet-voyager sailing to a Belle Isle of the imagination, firmly establishes Crane in the symbolist tradition, and it is not without justice that Carl Sandburg called him "the Cleveland Rimbaud." But there was too much of Cleveland in Crane–too much of modern industry and commerce and too much of the expansive optimism of the American heartland–to allow him to accept the isolation and alienation from society that comes with the role of *poète maudit*. Emerson, in his essay "Art," says that the artist of genius must "find beauty and holiness in new and necessary facts, in the field and road-side, in the shop and mill," and "raise to divine use the railroad, the insurance office, the joint stock-company." Crane, in his essay "Modern Poetry" (1930), says, "For unless poetry can absorb the machine, i.e., *acclimatize* it as naturally and casually as trees, cattle, galleons, castles and all other human associations of the past, then poetry has failed of its full contemporary function." It was Crane's ambition to build upon the spiritual illuminations of his private life and extend them into an optimistic vi-

Peggy Baird Cowley and Hart Crane, Mexico, 1932

sion of all America, acclimatizing the industrial world to all the human associations of its past, that informs his longest and most ambitious work, *The Bridge*. His model and mentor was not Rimbaud but Whitman.

As noted above, the initial idea for *The Bridge* came to Crane directly upon his finishing "For the Marriage of Faustus and Helen," while he was still living in Cleveland. In February 1923 he wrote to Gorham Munson: "I am ruminating on a new longish poem under the title of *The Bridge* which carries on further the tendencies manifest in 'F and H.' " He intended it originally to be "something of equal length" to "For the Marriage of Faustus and Helen," and he expected to finish it for inclusion in a first volume of his poems, but as he worked on *The Bridge* its scope and length expanded. The project was begun with great enthusiasm and announcements far and wide of his ambitious plans, but in fact very little of *The Bridge* had yet been written in the winter of 1926, when Crane had his *White Buildings* published by Boni and Liveright (without *The Bridge*) and returned to *The Bridge* after an interval of two years. Then came a brief period of prodigious creativity, between April and November

1926, when Crane retired to the Isle of Pines, thanks to the grant from Otto Kahn, and wrote ten of the fifteen sections of *The Bridge*. The following year he saw most of these sections published separately in various periodicals. It was not until 1929, however, stimulated by a promise from Harry and Caresse Crosby to publish it in Paris, that Crane actually finished his poem, and *The Bridge* was finally published by the Crosbys' Black Sun Press in February 1930, and by Horace Liveright in New York in April. The order of the separate parts of the poem as it was published bears no relation to the order of their composition, and at one point (in August 1926) Crane wrote, "I skip from one section to another now like a sky-gack or girder-jack." Despite the seven years of its gestation, the singleness of its inspiration and the simultaneous composition of many of its parts contributed greatly to a sense of organic unity in *The Bridge* as a whole.

Again T. S. Eliot's *The Waste Land* offers a useful focus of comparison and contrast to Crane's intention and achievement in *The Bridge*. Structurally and stylistically there are considerable similarities: both poets are thoroughly eclectic, drawing upon a wide range of cultural and historical material and assimilating it in a nonnarrative, thematic web of associations and allusions. Even the "gloss notes" were suggested by Eliot's notes for *The Waste Land*. After *The Bridge* was published Crane wrote to a sympathetic but confused reviewer (Herbert Weinstock) to suggest that "with more time and familiarity with *The Bridge* you will envisage it more as one poem with a clearer and more integrated unity and development than was at first evident.... It took me nearly five years, with innumerable readings to convince myself of the essential unity of [Eliot's *The Waste Land*]. And *The Bridge* is at least as complicated in its structure and inferences as *The Waste Land*—perhaps more so." But Crane's admiration of *The Waste Land* was more for its style than for its ideas. When it first appeared he was "rather disappointed" and found it "good, of course, but so damned dead." And later he wrote, "I tried to break loose from that particular strait-jacket [the fashionable pessimism of T. S. Eliot], without however committing myself to any oppositional form of didacticism.... [*The Bridge*], as a whole, is, I think, an affirmation of experience, and to that extent is 'positive' rather than 'negative' in the sense that *The Waste Land* is negative."

Both Eliot and Crane were mythologizing poets, and it is precisely in their use of myth that they are at the same time so similar and so different. Crane in all probability read T. S. Eliot's review of Joyce's *Ulysses* in the *Dial* (November 1923), where Eliot wrote: "In using the myth, in manipulating a continuous parallel between contemporaneity and antiquity, Mr. Joyce is pursuing a method which others must pursue after him.... It is simply a way of controlling, of ordering, of giving a shape and significance to the immense panorama of futility and anarchy which is contemporary history." In outlining his project for *The Bridge* to Otto Kahn in 1927, Crane wrote: "What I am after is an assimilation of this experience, a more organic panorama, showing the continuous and living evidence of the past in the inmost vital substance of the present." These words explain how Crane adopted the method propounded by Eliot and adapted it to idealistic purposes.

Unlike Eliot, Crane seems to have known very little about mythology or history, but he did have a strong intuitive sense of the mythic or symbolic qualities in persons, places, and things, be they contemporary, historical, or fictional. Brooklyn Bridge itself, the controlling symbol of the poem, with which it begins and ends, is at the same time a historical object, a work of art, a product of modern technology, and a perfect metaphor for the desire, the spiritual ambitions, and the unifying and reconciling aspirations of American idealism. In the "Ave Maria" section Crane introduces Christopher Columbus, a man whose courage and faith led him to discover a New World. It was Columbus who forged the union of European culture and religion with the native soil of Pocahontas, "Powhatan's Daughter." For Crane, Rip Van Winkle represented a man who carries the past around with him in his experience of modern life. The Land, the vast American continent drained by the Mississippi, is celebrated in "The River" section, the Sea in "Cutty Sark," and the Air in "Cape Hatteras," where the Wright brothers once again manifest that spiritual urge to transcend time and space, to fly. In "The Dance" the mythic material of America is invested with mystery and eroticism. At every turn in *The Bridge* it is the visionary trend in the American experience that inspires Crane to praise and poetry.

"The Dance" can be seen as the high point or turning point in this visionary celebration; and vision is indeed the very lock and key of *The*

Bridge, but Crane was too honest as an observer of modern life to claim that the visionary experience in America is, or ever has been, an easy one. The powers of darkness–materialism and vulgarity–are too great to ignore. In "National Winter Garden," for example, Love, the very basis of idealism, is cheapened and compromised by lust and commercialism, combined in the burlesque theater. In "Quaker Hill" the once sacred New England landscape–the Promised Land and New Jerusalem of the Puritan Fathers–is now nothing but real estate, golf courses, and antique auctions. And "The Tunnel"–the tunnel that goes under the East River where the Brooklyn Bridge flies over it–is a kind of modern Hades, a mockery of everything that has gone before. It is only in "Atlantis," the last section of the poem but the first to be written, that a balance is restored, but this balance is achieved only by the transformation of the bridge into a spiritual reality, a spiritualization and interiorization of the entire myth and history of America. The epigraph from Plato– "Music is then the knowledge of that which relates to love in harmony and system"–indicates that the fulfillment of this journey toward idealism is ultimately in the world of ideas, where music is not sound but knowledge. The bridge becomes "Love" and "Answerer of all," and the poet dedicates himself and his song to it: "So to thine Everpresence, beyond time,/Like spears ensanguined of one tolling star/That bleeds infinity– the orphic strings,/Sidereal phalanxes, leap and converge:/–One Song, one Bridge of Fire!" In the end it is Fire, that sanguine element, that transcends Earth, Air, and Water.

Crane was well aware of the contradiction existing in a vision that never gets beyond the mind of the visionary. In June 1926 he wrote to Waldo Frank: "The validity of a work of art is situated in contemporary reality to the extent that the artist must honestly anticipate the realization of his vision in 'action' (as an actively operating principle of communal works and faith), and I don't mean by this that his procedure requires any bona fide evidences directly and personally signalled, nor even any physical signs or portents. The darkness is part of his business. It has always been taken for granted, however, that his intuitions were salutary and that his vision either sowed or epitomized 'experience' (in the Blakeian sense)." Crane's confidence in "what has always been taken for granted" was entirely emotional and not at all intellectual. In the same letter he said, "Emotionally I should like to write *The Bridge;* in-

Crane in February 1932, two months before his death (collection of Richard Rychtarik)

tellectually judged the whole theme and project seems more and more absurd. . . . These 'materials' were valid to me to the extent that I presumed them to be (articulate or not) at least organic and active factors in the experience and perceptions of our common race, time and belief. The very idea of a bridge, of course, is a form peculiarly dependent on such spiritual convictions. It is an act of faith besides being a communication. The symbols of reality necessary to articulate the span–may not exist where you expect them, however. By which I mean that however great their subjective significance to me is concerned–these forms, materials, dynamics are simply non-existent in the world. I may amuse and delight and flatter myself as much as I please– but I am only evading a recognition and playing Don Quixote in an immorally conscious way."

Here Hart Crane is placing himself precisely at the center of the essential dilemma of romanticism. Not only did he feel that the values and vision he found in the past seem to have evaporated in the twentieth century, but even in the present the values and vision he felt within himself appear to have no necessary connection to the world outside the self. Crane seems never to have resolved this dilemma–indeed resolution is not possible without recourse to some transcendent absolute–but he did, within a few months following this letter, go on to write the greater part of *The Bridge*, presumably trusting that what has always been taken for granted can safely be taken for granted again. In this trust he had a considerable weight of authority from the nineteenth century behind him, in the romantic poets, and especially in Thomas Carlyle and Emerson. Carlyle advocated a blind leap of the will, a pronouncement of the "Everlasting Yea" to the validity of personal experience. Emerson, in his essay "The Poet," claimed that the products of the poetic imagination have "a certain power of emancipation and exhilaration for all men. . . . We are like persons who come out of a cave or cellar into the open air. This is the effect on us of tropes, fables, oracles and all poetic forms. Poets are thus liberating gods. Men have really got a new sense, and found within their world another world, or nest of worlds; for the metamorphosis once seen, we divine that it does not stop. . . . [The poet] unlocks our chains and admits us to a new sense." It is this blind faith in the creative, transforming, revivifying power of the individual imagination that is the spiritual heritage of Whitman. In the same letter to Waldo Frank quoted above, Crane wrote, "If only America were half as worthy today to be spoken of as Whitman spoke of it fifty years ago there might be something for me to say–not that Whitman received or required any tangible proof of his intimations, but that time has shown how increasingly lonely and ineffectual his confidence stands." How much more lonely and ineffectual did Crane's confidence seem to many of his first readers in the wasteland of the Depression era.

Unlike Crane, T. S. Eliot had no such confidence; he trusted the intellect more than the emotions, and he rejected the romantic theory of visionary imagination. In this he was the guiding spirit of an entire generation of literary critics who were essentially antipathetic to Crane's poetry. For many years the consensus of opinion on *The Bridge* was roughly that which Elizabeth Drew expressed in 1936, that "Structurally, on both spiritual and formal planes, the poem remains a muddle." In 1939 F. R. Leavis wrote that "Crane's symbolism amounts to nothing more than a turgidly rhetorical 'shall.' . . . The poem is wordy chaos, both locally and in sum . . . I cannot see that, apart from his conviction of genius and his confidence, he had any relevant gift." Two of the severest indictments of Crane came finally from two of his greatest admirers, Allen Tate and Yvor Winters. Both felt in the 1920s that Crane was a poet of genius, but with the fur-

ther development of their critical ideas, and in light of Crane's demise, they both came to think that his lack of a system of knowledge or of rational means for defining his experience was the cause of the failures in both his life and his art and offered proof of the self-destructiveness inherent in romanticism. Tate wrote (in the 1930s): "Far from 'refuting' Eliot, his whole career is a vindication of Eliot's major premise–that the integrity of the individual consciousness has broken down. . . . The poet did not face his first problem, which is to define the limits of his personality and to objectify its moral implications in an appropriate symbolism. Crane could only assert a quality of will against the world, and at each successive failure of the will he turned upon himself." Winters wrote (in 1947): "The Emersonian doctrine, which is merely the romantic doctrine with a New England emotional coloration, should naturally result in madness if one really lived it; it should result in literary confusion if one really wrote it. Crane accepted it; he lived it; he wrote it." For Tate and Winters, as for other proponents of the New Criticism, such as Kenneth Burke, John Crowe Ransom, and R. P. Blackmur, it was the entire romantic tradition that was on trial: Hart Crane was only their monitory example. Both Tate and Winters had lost their enthusiasm for *The Bridge* even before it was finished, and when it appeared Winters wrote an unfavorable review of it in *Poetry* (June 1930), which Crane interpreted as a personal attack and the bitterest betrayal.

The generally hostile, bewildered, or indifferent reactions to his great poem were only one of the many reversals that Crane met with in the last few years of his life. In 1928 there was the permanent break with his mother and the death of his grandmother, followed in 1930 by the death of his father, to whom he had been warmly reconciled. Largely to escape his mother's emotional demands, Crane took his small inheritance from his grandmother and sailed to Europe, where he spent the first six months of 1929. In Paris, which he called "the most interesting madhouse in the world," he met scores of prominent people in the arts, but the endless partying and drinking took its toll both on his health and on his spirits, and he got very little writing done. His European sojourn ended with a fracas with the police in a Paris café and a stint in jail. Harry Crosby, with whom Crane spent most of his time in France, shot his mistress and himself in New York in December 1929, and it was Crane who bore the bad news to Crosby's wife and mother. By far the most serious grief for Crane was what seemed like the failure of his powers as a poet. After 1927 he wrote next to nothing but for two brief periods (in the summer of 1929 and the winter of 1932), and what he did write, he realized, was far inferior to his best early work. Most of his time was spent in drunkenness and debauchery. In March 1931 he received a Guggenheim Fellowship for the purpose of studying "European culture, classical and romantic, with especial reference to contrasting elements implicit in the emergent features of a distinctive American poetic consciousness"; but, if indeed he ever had any serious intention of pursuing such a study, he promptly abandoned it and went instead to Mexico, where he gave himself up extensively to alcoholic and sexual intemperance.

Crane did, however, take an interest in Mexican culture–architecture and religious rituals in particular–and he had a love affair, his only heterosexual attachment, with Peggy Baird, an old friend from New York who was at the time married to Malcolm Cowley. He had periods of hopefulness about his writing, and in one of those periods, in the winter of 1932, he wrote his last and one of his finest poems, "The Broken Tower." "The Broken Tower" is a poignant recapitulation of his entire career as the "sexton slave" of the "antiphonal carillons" of poetry: "The bells, I say, the bells break down their tower." He "entered the broken world/To trace the visionary company of love." He poured out his words without knowing whether they were "cognate, scored/Of that tribunal monarch of the air" or "cleft to despair." He looked forward to building a new tower, "a tower that is not stone/(Not stone can jacket heaven)," a spiritual tower that will join earth and heaven, so that "the commodious, tall decorum of that sky/Unseals her earth, and lifts love in its shower." This is the same private vision of love and perfect union that we find at the end of "Voyages," and this vision is the most essential and authentic motive in all of Crane's life and work. He sought to reunite what had been sundered–his parent's marriage, or the broken world–through the power of love and poetry. His failure to connect this vision with the world outside himself does not invalidate the desire, but whenever he wearied and the force of his will could not hold out against the unhappy facts of reality, he was in despair. His was not generally thought to be a suicidal personality, but it was in such a period of despair, after a night of riotous behavior on board ship, around noon on 27 April 1932, that he leapt to his death from the deck of the *Orizaba,* on which he and Peggy Baird were sailing back to New York.

The report of his suicide fueled the legend of Hart Crane the tragic-romantic poet-hero driven to an early death, like Keats, by hostile critics, and that legend together with the antiromantic position of the New Critics served for many years to prevent any just evaluation of Crane's poetry. And yet, Harold Bloom has said that in the 1930s, "when I was eleven years old," it was the poetry of Hart Crane that "cathected me onto poetry, a conversion or investment fairly typical of many of my generation." Crane's world view is considered to have had a significant influence upon such later poets as Charles Olson and Robert Creeley, but it has been only since the 1960s, when the New Criticism began to give way to a more sympathetic, or at least more historical and objective, view of romanticism, that Hart Crane has come into his own. The difficulties and obscurities of his poems and the problems of pattern and structure in *The Bridge* have been solved by works of scholarly explication, most notably those by L. S. Dembo and R. W. B. Lewis. Any questions that could have been left by the earlier biographies by Philip Horton and Brom Weber have been more than answered in John Unterecker's encyclopedic biography *Voyager* (1969). There is now an abundance of learned studies of Crane's life and work, and the interest that he continues to inspire among poets and readers of poetry today is enough to justify Allen Tate's original opinion (1925), that "Hart Crane's poetry, even in its beginnings, is one of the finest achievements of this age."

Letters:

The Letters of Hart Crane, 1916-1932, edited by Brom Weber (New York: Hermitage House, 1952).
    Extensive collection of Crane's correspondence to friends, family members, and literary associates.

Letters of Hart Crane and His Family, edited by Thomas S. W. Lewis (New York & London: Columbia University Press, 1974).
    Collection of the Crane family's correspondence from 1910 to 1932, including the full text of many letters excerpted in Brom Weber's 1952 edition of Crane's letters.

Bibliographies:

Joseph Schwartz and Robert C. Schweik, *Hart Crane: A Descriptive Bibliography* (Pittsburgh: University of Pittsburgh Press, 1972).
Illustrated primary bibliography of Crane's writings.

Schwartz, *Hart Crane: A Reference Guide* (Boston: G. K. Hall, 1983).
Annotated listing of writings about Crane covering the years 1919 to 1980.

Biographies:

Philip Horton, *Hart Crane: The Life of an American Poet* (New York: Norton, 1937).
Sympathetic analysis of Crane's life and works, which, though partially supplanted by later, more detailed accounts, remains a valuable contemporary assessment.

Brom Weber, *Hart Crane: A Biographical and Critical Study* (New York: Bodley Press, 1948).
Primarily a critical study of Crane's work up through *The Bridge*, within the context of the poetry.

Susan Jenkins Brown, *Robber Rocks: Letters and Memories of Hart Crane, 1923-1932* (Middletown, Conn.: Wesleyan University Press, 1968).
Crane's letters to William Slater Brown and Susan Jenkins Brown interspersed with comments and reminiscences by the latter.

John Unterecker, *Voyager: A Life of Hart Crane* (New York: Farrar, Straus & Giroux, 1969).
Fully detailed life of the poet drawn from all available sources, perhaps overwhelming in its presentation of the facts, but thorough and complete.

References:

Edward Brunner, *Splendid Failure: Hart Crane and the Making of "The Bridge"* (Urbana & Chicago: University of Illinois Press, 1983).
Argues against the claim, as put forth by Waldo Frank and R. W. B. Lewis, that Crane is an obscure and mystical poet, and attempts to delineate a logical progression and structural unity in Crane's work.

R. W. Butterfield, *The Broken Arc: A Study of Hart Crane* (Edinburgh: Oliver & Boyd, 1969).

Examination of Crane's poetry in light of his personal and poetic "disintegration," with emphasis on the cultural significance of Crane's life and art.

David R. Clark, ed., *Critical Essays on Hart Crane* (Boston: G. K. Hall, 1982).
Includes contemporary reviews of Crane's work by Allen Tate, Malcolm Cowley, Yvor Winters, and Waldo Frank, early critical studies by R. W. B. Lewis and L. S. Dembo, and three previously unpublished essays by John T. Irwin, Allen Grossman, and Donald Pease.

Clark, ed., *The Merrill Studies in "The Bridge"* (Columbus, Ohio: Merrill, 1970).
Collection of critical essays on *The Bridge*.

L. S. Dembo, *Hart Crane's Sanskrit Charge: A Study of The Bridge* (Ithaca: Cornell University Press, 1960).
A defense of Crane's best-known poem which attempts to dispute the claim that it is a failed epic, flawed in its design and obscured by its imagery.

Margaret Dickie, "The Bridge," in her *On the Modernist Long Poem* (Iowa City: University of Iowa Press, 1986), pp. 47-76.
Structural analysis of *The Bridge* as a modernist poem in the tradition of T. S. Eliot's *The Waste Land*, William Carlos Williams's *Paterson*, and Ezra Pound's *Cantos*.

Lee Edelman, *Transmemberment of Song: Hart Crane's Anatomies of Rhetoric and Desire* (Stanford: Stanford University Press, 1987).
Examination of the rhetoric of Crane's three major works: "For the Marriage of Faustus and Helen," "Voyages," and *The Bridge*.

Paul Giles, *Hart Crane: The Contexts of "The Bridge"* (Cambridge, London & New York: Cambridge University Press, 1986).
Treats the theme of ambiguity in *The Bridge*, especially Crane's use of puns and paradoxes.

Alfred Hanley, *Hart Crane's Holy Vision: "White Buildings"* (Pittsburgh: Duquesne University Press, 1981).

Study of Crane's first book as it informs a major theme in his poetry, namely his search for an absolute and ideal truth.

Samuel Hazo, *Hart Crane: An Introduction and Interpretation* (New York: Barnes & Noble, 1963).
Attempts to place Crane and his work in the historical context of the 1920s.

Herbert A. Leibowitz, *Hart Crane: An Introduction to the Poetry* (New York: Columbia University Press, 1968).
A study of Crane's shorter poems that stresses his Americanism and places his poetry in a modernist context.

R. W. B. Lewis, *The Poetry of Hart Crane: A Critical Study* (Princeton: Princeton University Press, 1967).
Defines Crane as a visionary and religious poet in the tradition of English and American romanticism; one of the first full-length critical studies of Crane in which he is regarded as a major figure in American literature.

Helge Normann Nilsen, *Hart Crane's Divided Vision: An Analysis of The Bridge* (Oslo: Universitetsforlaget, 1980).
Examination of Crane's spirituality and pessimism as conflicting elements of *The Bridge*; also traces the influence of Walt Whitman and Waldo Frank on *The Bridge*.

Thomas Parkinson, *Hart Crane and Yvor Winters: Their Literary Correspondence* (Berkeley, Los Angeles & London: University of California Press, 1978).
Utilizes the letters between Crane and Winters in order to examine their friendship, both literary and personal, and its disintegration after Winters published an unfavorable review of *The Bridge*.

Sherman Paul, *Hart's Bridge* (Chicago: University of Illinois Press, 1972).

A study of Crane's life, his self-awareness as a poet, and the environmental forces that shaped his art; features a lengthy analysis of the poems collected in *White Buildings*, as well as a close reading of *The Bridge*.

Robert L. Perry, *The Shared Vision of Waldo Frank and Hart Crane* (Lincoln: University of Nebraska Press, 1966).
Treats Frank's ideological influence on Crane and the way in which Walt Whitman influenced Crane in part through Frank's writings.

Vincent G. Quinn, *Hart Crane* (New York: Twayne, 1963).
Brief overview of Crane's life and career, with discussions of the major works and a summary of critical opinion.

Alan Trachtenberg, ed., *Hart Crane: A Collection of Critical Essays* (Englewood Cliffs, N.J.: Prentice-Hall, 1982).
Includes Crane's essay "General Aims and Theories" and critical discussions by Tate, Winters, Cowley, and Frank, as well as essays by William Carlos Williams, Derek Savage, R. P. Blackmur, John Unterecker, R. W. B. Lewis, and Harold Bloom.

M. D. Uroff, *Hart Crane: The Patterns of His Poetry* (Urbana, Chicago & London: University of Illinois Press, 1974).
Stresses the continuity of Crane's poetry by identifying and tracing textual and thematic patterns.

Jack C. Wolf, *Hart Crane's Harp of Evil: A Study of Orphism in "The Bridge"* (Troy, N.Y.: Whitson, 1986).
Argues that *The Bridge* is a coherent poem unified by Crane's use of the myth of Orpheus.

Papers:
The major collection of Hart Crane's manuscripts is in the library of Columbia University.

Countee Cullen

This entry was updated by Shirley Lumpkin (Marshall University) from her entry in DLB 48, American Poets, 1880-1945, Second Series.

Places	New York City (Harlem)	France Harvard	Atlantic City
Influences and Relationships	James Weldon Johnson Charles S. Johnson (*Opportunity*) W. E. B. Du Bois	Alain Locke Owen Dodson Langston Hughes Arna Bontemps	Claude McKay John Keats Robert Hillyer
Literary Movements and Forms	Harlem Renaissance Lyric Poetry	Romanticism Children's Literature	The "Negritude" Movement
Major Themes	Christian Upbringing vs. Pagan Inclination The Pains and Joys of Love	The Spiritual Beauty of the Negro The Importance of Being a Poet	Celebration of Sensuous Experience Idealism vs. Reality
Cultural and Artistic Influences	Afro-Caribbean Culture *Crisis* and *Opportunity* Magazines	Afro-American Protestantism French Language and Culture	Jazz Theater Harlem Life
Social and Economic Influences	Racism The Execution of Sacco and Vanzetti	Harlem Riot Commission Education	The Scottsboro Case The Depression

See also the Cullen entries in DLB 4, American Writers in Paris, 1920-1939 *and* DLB 51, Afro-American Writers from the Harlem Renaissance to 1940.

BIRTH: Probably Louisville, Kentucky, 30 May 1903, to Elizabeth Lucas.

EDUCATION: B.A., New York University, 1925; M.A., Harvard University, 1926.

MARRIAGES: 9 April 1928 to Nina Yolande Du Bois (divorced); 27 September 1940 to Ida Mae Roberson.

AWARDS AND HONORS: Witter Bynner Poetry Contest Prizes: 1923, 1924, 1925; John Reed Memorial Prize (*Poetry* magazine), 1925; *Crisis* Magazine Spingarn Award, 1925; Harmon Foundation Literary Award, 1927; Guggenheim Fellowship, 1928.

DEATH: New York, New York, 9 January 1946.

BOOKS: *Color* (New York & London: Harper, 1925);
The Ballad of the Brown Girl: An Old Ballad Retold (New York & London: Harper, 1927);
Copper Sun (New York & London: Harper, 1927);
The Black Christ and Other Poems (New York & London: Harper, 1929);
One Way to Heaven (New York & London: Harper, 1932);
The Medea and Some Poems (New York & London: Harper, 1935);
The Lost Zoo (A Rhyme for the Young, But Not Too Young) (New York & London: Harper, 1940);
My Lives and How I Lost Them (New York & London: Harper, 1942);
On These I Stand: An Anthology of the Best Poems of Countee Cullen (New York: Harper, 1947).

PLAY PRODUCTION: *St. Louis Woman,* by Cullen and Arna Bontemps, New York, Martin Beck Theatre, 31 March 1946.

OTHER: *Caroling Dusk: An Anthology of Verse by Negro Poets,* edited, with contributions, by Cullen (New York & London: Harper, 1927);
St. Louis Woman, by Cullen and Arna Bontemps, in *Black Theatre,* edited by Lindsay Patterson (New York: Dodd, Mead, 1971).

Countee Cullen

PERIODICAL PUBLICATIONS: "Poet on Poet– *The Weary Blues," Opportunity,* 4 (February 1926): 73;
"The Dark Tower," *Opportunity,* 4 (December 1926): 388; 5 (February 1927): 53-54; 5 (March 1927): 86-87; 5 (April 1927): 118-119; 5 (May 1927): 149-150; 5 (June 1927): 180-181; 5 (July 1927): 210-211; 5 (August 1927): 240-241; 5 (November 1927): 336-337; 5 (December 1927): 373-374; 6 (January 1928): 20-21; 6 (February 1928): 52-53; 6 (March 1928): 90; 6 (April 1928): 120; 6 (July 1928): 210; 6 (September 1928): 271-273.

Countee Cullen became a central figure in the Harlem or New Negro Renaissance and in American poetry in general with the publication of his first book, *Color* (1925), which black and white critics hailed as both beautiful and promising. While his reputation for writing beautiful lyrical poetry remained high throughout his poetic career, which was cut short by his untimely death in 1946, critics began to question how well he fulfilled his poetic promise. Many came to believe that his education was something of a handicap, leading him to exclude from his poetry a wide range of feelings and ideas, and any hint of vernacular or folk-based musical styles, in favor of traditional American and English versification and such standard romantic subjects as love and death. Nonetheless, Cullen was a bright star of the New Negro Renaissance. As one of the primary figures in the development of Negro literature, he was well acquainted with all the major writers in the New Negro Movement and Negro literature in general, from the older James Weldon Johnson, Charles S. Johnson (editor of *Opportunity*), W. E. B. Du Bois (editor of *Crisis*), and Alain Locke, to his contemporaries, including Langston Hughes and Arna Bontemps.

Despite the waning of his reputation and perhaps of his muse, Cullen continued to be known for poems characterized by beauty and nobility, filled with his favorite image for the goodness and promise of life, spring. While he insisted that he should be considered a poet rather than a Negro poet, black and white critics commented rather acidly that, whatever Cullen thought, his best poetry was informed by racial experience. His ambivalence about what he was to call the Christian and pagan values struggling for dominance in his art and in his life led to suggestions that he could not create a sustained worldview or that he romanticized and failed to understand the African experience. Yet his carefully crafted poems, especially those in *Color,* had tremendous influence. Langston Hughes called "Heritage" the most beautiful poem he knew. Other readers responded to Cullen's brief ironic epitaphs, his tension-laden sonnets (such as "Yet Do I Marvel" and "From the Dark Tower"), or his lyrical celebrations of the sensuous and painful love of brown boys and girls. His work came to be identified with the best of the academic or traditional versification of the New Negro Renaissance, and it has been praised for expressing some of the most painful and ironic archetypal experiences of black people. In his time, Cullen was as much a sensation on the American poetry scene as Edna St. Vincent Millay. Yet later generations of white Americans have been less familiar with his work than black Americans. Perhaps his race, more than his failure to sustain his early promise and his tendency to use conservative versification and poetic

clichés, is partly responsible for this partial eclipse. Until recently his poems were anthologized primarily in black poetry anthologies rather than in more general collections of American poetry.

Popular and appreciated for his gentleness and selfless concern for others, Countee Porter Cullen was shy and not particularly open about his life, even with his closest friends. He once remarked in a letter to Claude McKay that he did not see why a poet's life should be an open book for the public, and Cullen's certainly is not. His exact birth date was questionable for a number of years, although 30 May 1903 is now firmly established. There is still some uncertainty about the place of his birth. His second wife, Ida Mae Roberson Cullen, said he was born in Baltimore; Langston Hughes and his longtime best friend Harold Jackman said Louisville, Kentucky; and Cullen himself is reported to have said New York. Such confusion about the details of Cullen's life is related to the deliberate silence Cullen maintained about the painful experiences in his life. In his reticence about the date and place of his birth, for example, Cullen seemed to be obscuring his lack of contact with his mother, Mrs. Elizabeth Lucas of Louisville, Kentucky, who neither raised nor once got in touch with her son from the time of his birth until he became well known in the 1920s. Cullen helped his mother financially after she contacted him, and, when she died in Louisville on 28 October 1940, he attended her funeral–actions suggesting a complex set of feelings he never wished to share with the general public or even his close friends. Cullen was raised by another woman, possibly his grandmother, a Mrs. Porter, who had brought him to New York City when he was about nine years old. They settled in an apartment near Salem Methodist Episcopal Church; and when Mrs. Porter died in 1918, the Reverend and Mrs. Frederick Cullen of this same church adopted Cullen as their son. While the adoption was informal, Cullen considered this couple his mother and father and was devoted to them. The conflicting emotional currents in his feelings about his childhood were not subjects Cullen desired to explore in conversation or in poetry, and he never did so.

Countee Cullen began writing poetry during his distinguished career at DeWitt Clinton High School, publishing "I Have a Rendezvous with Life (with apologies to Alan Seeger)"–which became a popular and prizewinning poem–in the January 1921 issue of the school's well-known liter-

Cullen in his youth (courtesy of the Schomburg Center for Research in Black Culture, the New York Public Library, Astor, Lenox and Tilden Foundations)

ary magazine the *Magpie.* Cullen was one of the few Negroes at the school, but one of several prominent Afro-American graduates. In his later years he was to be interviewed for the *Magpie* by another DeWitt Clinton student, James Baldwin.

After graduating from DeWitt Clinton in January 1922, Cullen entered New York University the same year and continued to write poetry which appeared in *Opportunity, Crisis,* the *Bookman, Poetry, Harper's,* and the *American Mercury.* During his undergraduate years Cullen spent his summers working as a waiter in Atlantic City to help defray the costs of his education. He began entering poetry contests and winning prizes in them, gradually becoming known within the black and white literary communities. In 1923 he won second prize in the Witter Bynner undergraduate poetry contest with his "The Ballad of the Brown Girl," which was published in 1927. In

1924 he again won second prize in the Witter Bynner contest, and in 1925 he won first prize. *Poetry* magazine's John Reed Memorial Prize was awarded him in 1925 for "Threnody for a Brown Girl." Significantly, that same year he was second in the *Opportunity*-sponsored poetry contest with the poem "To One Who Said Me Nay" (first prize went to Langston Hughes for "The Weary Blues," a poem in a vernacular, jazz, blues-based poetic language which was the polar antithesis of the style and the subject matter of Cullen's work). The two poles of New Negro poetry, the literary, individualistic lyricism of Cullen and the folk-derived people's voice of Langston Hughes, were thus established.

In 1925, the year Cullen was elected to Phi Beta Kappa and earned a B.A. from New York University, Harper and Brothers published *Color,* which won the Harmon Foundation Literary

Requiescam

I am for sleeping and forgetting
All that has gone before;
I am for lying still and letting
Who will beat at my door;
I would my life's gold sun were
              setting
To rise for me no more,

                    Countee Cullen

Fair copy of Cullen's poem "Requiescam" (by permission of the Estate of Countee Cullen; courtesy of the Clifton Waller Barrett Collection, University of Virginia Library; copyright © 1925 by Harper & Brother; copyright renewed 1953 by Ida M. Cullen)

Award in 1927 and received praise from black and white critics alike. Although Mark Van Doren suggested that, because some of the poems in *Color* seemed too long for their content, the young poet should not hurry his next book and William Stanley Braithwaite, almost alone among black or white critics, deplored what he called the racial content or flavor, Walter White and Alain Locke, leaders of the New Negro Movement, were enthusiastic about both the racial flavor and the style of writing.

The poems in *Color,* written during his undergraduate years, are Cullen's enduring work, and the grouping of the poems was one Cullen was to follow in later books. *Color* is divided into three sections: one group titled "Color," on the beauty of brown boys and girls and the bitter ironies and cruelties inflicted on brown people by the color line; one group on love, "For Love's Sake"; and one group on death, "Varia." All the poems are carefully constructed, employing a wide range of traditional versification forms, including sonnets, quatrains, and epitaphs. Neither his themes, nor his admiration for the great romantic poets such as John Keats, nor his being, in his words, "a rank conservative, loving the measured line and the skillful rhyme" were to change throughout his poetic career. The amount of poetry he wrote and the number of poems he wrote on the theme of color–both on its beauty and on the horrifying effects of racism–were to diminish, but his theme did not significantly change. As Cullen wrote for *Twentieth Century Authors* (1942): "Most things I write I do for the sheer love of the music in them. Somehow I find my poetry of itself treating of the Negro, of his joys and sorrows–mostly of the latter–and of the heights and depths of emotion I feel as a Negro."

Always motivated by a powerful love of poetry and the ideal of being a poet, Cullen attended Harvard and studied literature and poetry writing with Robert Hillyer, among others, earning an M.A. in 1926. Known as an omnivorous reader with a taste for the classics and the romantics, Cullen was not unacquainted with the oral tradition of song, dance, speech, and religion in the Afro-American community. Since he loved to dance, he loved jazz and other Afro-American and Afro-Caribbean dance music. He certainly heard, responded to, and possibly participated in the shouting church services and the chanted sermon of the black Protestant Christian church. He was also aware of the imagists and of

Cullen as a junior high school teacher in the late 1930s

the New Poetry movement; for during his many lectures and readings in his tuned and musical voice, Cullen made many contemporary contacts and by 1925 and 1926 had met Harriet Monroe, Edwin Arlington Robinson, and Robert Frost, and had had many poems published in Monroe's *Poetry* magazine, as well as in black magazines such as *Crisis* and *Opportunity.* He had a wide range of acquaintances among black writers, such as Hughes, who were deliberately using free verse, the vernacular, jazz rhythms and phrasing, blues, and the concentrated concrete images of black life in their work. He never lost his taste, however, for Tennyson, Millay, Keats, and other traditional versifiers; nor did he, while he freely and modestly admitted that other poets were more innovative and experimental in style, ever become convinced that the oral folk tradition of black (or any other) people should be the basis for or should appear in poetry unrefined by conventional versification. Thus in his February 1926 *Opportunity* review of Langston Hughes's *Weary Blues,* Cullen wrote that he considered the jazz poems interlopers among the "truly beautiful poems" because such poems "move me along with the frenzy and electric heat of a Methodist or Baptist revival meeting" and such "chills and fevers of emotion" are not really spiritual, nor do they seem to belong "to the dignified company, that select and austere circle of high literary expression which we call poetry."

In addition to his selective love of refined poetic versification, Cullen believed that poetic themes should be "austere" and chose the dignified styles of the sonnet, metered couplets, or brief ironic epitaphs because he sought controlled emotion to express his conception of beauty in his poetry. When he wrote about himself and selected poems from his own works for inclusion in his 1927 anthology of poetry by black poets, *Caroling Dusk*, Cullen explained more fully why he chose control in poetry, explaining that "his chief problem has been that of reconciling a Christian upbringing with a pagan inclination" and that "his life so far has not convinced him that the problem is insoluble." This issue, rather than whether to write about color, was the one he thought was central in his poetry; and to reconcile the Christian and the pagan he needed effective formal control.

The issue of color was continually raised, however, sometimes by Cullen himself, as he did in his anthology when he reiterated, with what he admitted might be "sickening" frequency, that he wished "no racial consideration" to bolster the reputation of his poetry. Acting upon his idea that "poet" was a more important category than "Negro," he called his anthology, one of several anthologies of black poetry to appear in the 1920s, *Caroling Dusk: An Anthology of Verse by Negro Poets* rather than "An Anthology of Negro Poetry" because, he stated in the foreword, he believed that Negro poetry "must emanate from some country other than this in some language other than our own." Since he argued Negro poets like himself used the heritage of the English language and were more individuals than men of the same color (what he called "the individual diversifying ego" transcending "the synthesizing hue"), he felt that Negro poets' work did not represent any "serious aberration from the poetic tendencies of their times." Selecting his own and other Negro poets' poems on that basis, he rejected the plantation-dialect of Dunbar and others, because of what he called "certain sociological considerations and the natural limitations of dialect for poetic expression" and because of the times' condemnation of artificiality. Although he praised the folk vernacular and musically based

styles of James Weldon Johnson and Langston Hughes, he never looked to the oral tradition or to free verse for his own poetry about colored folk and tended to exclude Hughes's and other black poets' most vernacular, jazz, blues, and free-verse work from his anthology. For example, he chose Fenton Johnson's earlier work written in traditional versification over his more powerful, free-verse poems of urban despair, such as "Tired," for his *Caroling Dusk* anthology.

This emphasis on conservative versification and exclusion of disrupting emotions or new styles marked his 1927 books, *The Ballad of the Brown Girl* and *Copper Sun*. Although *The Ballad of the Brown Girl* may have had its origin in a ballad that Cullen said he heard in Kentucky in 1915, the poem is essentially Cullen's rewriting of the black folk ballad in the form of an English literary ballad in quatrains. His changes make the motivations of the black girl, who is queenly and wishes to avenge the insult hurled at her blackness by a white woman, different enough to change the flavor of the story. *Copper Sun* has the same divisions that he had used in *Color,* but the "color" section is much shorter, including only "From the Dark Tower," "Threnody for a Brown Girl," and a small number of other poems on the beauty and pain of color. The longest sections are "The Deep in Love," poems about the pains and joys (more pains than joys) of love, and "Varia," poems about death and memorials to fallen poets, especially romantic ones. Two other short sections, "At Cambridge," containing the poems Cullen wrote as exercises in different verse forms for Robert Hillyer's class, and the poems "Juvenalia," are lighter in tone and consciously less serious poems, although love and its loss figure prominently in them. While critics such as Lyman Kittredge were enthusiastic about *The Ballad of the Brown Girl*, reactions to *Copper Sun* were mixed. E. Merrill Root in *Opportunity* and *New York Times* book reviewer Herbert S. Gorman applauded *Copper Sun*, but others such as Emanuel Eisenberg in the *Bookman* were negative. The critics generally enjoyed *Copper Sun* but agreed that the book was slighter and less intense than *Color*. Perhaps critical reaction would have been less mixed if *Copper Sun* had been the first, rather than the second, of Cullen's books. As it was, critics such as Harry Alan Potamkin, in the *New Republic,* were beginning to remark on Cullen's lack of growth.

Cullen's personal life during the period 1926-1928 had the same combination of ups and

Cullen in 1941 (photograph by Carl Van Vechten; by permission of Joseph Solomon, the Estate of Carl Van Vechten)

downs, successes and shadowy hints of failure or at least a loss of vigor, as his literary career. A successful assistant editor and columnist in his "From the Dark Tower" column for *Opportunity*, which was edited by Charles S. Johnson in 1926-1928, Cullen was able to review books and write on subjects of interest to blacks, gather material for his anthology, and write. As a result of his literary achievements he won a Guggenheim grant in 1928 to study in France for a year. Before he departed for France he married W. E. B. Du Bois's daughter, Yolande Du Bois, whom he had known since the summer of 1923, on 9 April 1928. Their wedding was a glittering social affair, drawing Afro-Americans from all circles. Cullen's relationship with Yolande is shrouded in the same kind of mystery as the circumstances of his birth and intimate family relationships. He and Yolande traveled together after the wedding, but she did not accompany Cullen when he left for

France on 30 June 1928 with his father, Rev. Frederick Cullen, and his intimate personal friend Harold Jackman. Yolande joined him in France for July 1928 but returned to the United States and to her job. The marriage was apparently over. While many of the poems Cullen wrote during this period and published in *The Black Christ and Other Poems* (1929) explore the bitterness and pain caused by disappointment over the character of a beautiful beloved and by the agony of lost love, the exact reasons for his break with Yolande remain obscure. Certainly her father, W. E. B. Du Bois, harbored no bitterness toward Cullen; Cullen's family and friends never mentioned his situation.

After his fellowship was extended, Cullen remained in France a year longer than he had originally planned, writing poems he published in *The Black Christ and Other Poems* and a series of articles for the *Crisis*. Upon his return to the United States in 1930, he and Yolande were divorced.

Cullen loved France, and he returned there, especially to Paris, for vacations until 1939. He savored his study at the Sorbonne, speaking French, dancing madly in the music halls, partying with sculptors, poets, and writers. He savored the freedom to write. Feeling released in France from the self-consciousness, the restraints, and the cruel horrors of Jim Crow racism, Cullen was also at home among the artifacts of French civilization.

What was invigorating for Cullen did not seem to have such a happy effect upon his poetry. *The Black Christ and Other Poems* was one of his least successful books with critics. Composed of a long "Varia" section and a short "color" section, with an "interlude," a group of poems that were primarily ironic and bitter in tone, the book had as its centerpiece the "color" poem "The Black Christ," which was considered one of Cullen's weakest works. Written in couplets, the poem attempts to fuse the dramatic story of two southern black brothers—one of whom is lynched—with an allegorical representation of Christ's crucifixion and resurrection and the romantic image of the tragic death of spring. This attempted merger was ambivalently received by a critical community clearly divided over the success of such a combination. More than half the critics considered the poem's style inappropriate, its content ambiguous, confused, and unrealistic, and the work as a whole lacking in the ability to confront or re-create the horrifying and concrete truth of lynching. Ironically, the "color" section also contains Cullen's response to critics who wanted him to write more poems on racial subjects and in a particular style. An angry and ironic work, "To Certain Critics" opens with the well-known lines: "Then call me traitor if you must,/Shout treason and default!" Cullen replied to the stinging accusation of treason to his race by saying, "I'll bear your censure as your praise,/For never shall the clan/Confine my singing to its ways/Beyond the ways of man." Cullen insisted, in no uncertain terms, upon maintaining the high calling of a true poet who could not be confined to the tastes of a single group.

While Cullen had no doubts that being a poet was a sacred calling, he seemed to have many doubts about what he should do to earn a living, to sort out his personal life, and to keep his muse alive. During the 1930s he wrote and published *One Way to Heaven* (1932), a novel about Harlem's social classes and religion. This double-plotted novel, dealing with the love affair of the lower-class Sam and Mattie and with the "salon" life of Constancia Brandon's New Negro set, was not an unqualified popular or critical success. The portraits of the folk characters, like the trickster Sam and the good Mattie, were judged powerful and effective, as were the scenes of their love and the ironies of the role religion played in their relationship. However, that plot did not seem to fit well with the exaggerated, satirical, ironic portraits of Constancia's set. Cullen never wrote another novel, possibly as much because he found novel writing too time consuming as because of the novel's poor reception. Poetry and a definite means of earning his living did not seem to come either. Since he was well known and associated with the best of New Negro poetry and literature, as well as well educated, Cullen was offered a position in the Department of English Literature at Dillard University in New Orleans in 1934. Although his appointment was announced in the New York newspapers, Cullen decided not to accept this offer, nor the others he apparently received, to teach in southern schools. One of the main reasons for his refusal was that he had received offers only from southern schools. Cullen wanted to stay in the North partly to be near his family, but mostly to enjoy the opportunities afforded blacks and to avoid the humiliating day-to-day contacts with a Jim Crow society, which had made his trips to the South so galling, and which had made his attitude toward life in the United States and toward white people so bitter and angry at times. Trying to earn a living and to preserve his muse, he became a junior high school French teacher and eventually taught creative writing at Frederick Douglass Junior High School, an all-black school with a primarily white staff in New York. Joining the staff in 1934, Cullen remained there until his death in 1946.

During his twelve years as a full-time schoolteacher, Cullen continued to write, to read his poetry and lecture, and to serve his community. He worked on the education committee for the 1935 commission that investigated the causes of the New York riot. In 1943 he wrote to the newspapers about the lamentable repetition of the 1935 riot's causes, which precipitated the 1943 riot in New York. While reading at Fisk University in Nashville in 1944, he was offered the Chair of Creative Literature there, but once again he turned down employment in the South to remain at his New York post.

Cullen wrote less poetry during this period. He was continually active, and on 27 September 1940 he married Ida Mae Roberson, a woman he had known since 1930, and settled happily with her. Lack of time and energy, probably resulting from the amount of work he did teaching school and from his development of high blood pressure, might have contributed to the decline in poetry writing, but his interests seemed to have changed as well. In 1935 he published *The Medea and Some Poems*, consisting primarily of his translation of Euripides' *Medea*, which had favorable reviews, although it was not as widely noticed as his previous books. In 1940 he published a book of poems for children, *The Lost Zoo*, and in 1942 a book of stories for children, *My Lives and How I Lost Them*. According to Cullen these works were written in collaboration with his feline friend Christopher Cat, who told him the stories that he recounted poetically. *The Lost Zoo* tells stories of the animals who did not get on the ark, although they had been invited, and hence passed out of the world. The animals' names, such as "The Snake-That-Walked-Upon-His Tail," "The Ha-Ha," the "Squililigee," and the humorous, ironic stories show no diminution of Cullen's imagination. Nor has his verse lost its music, as the opening lines indicate: "You've heard, no doubt, of the Dinosaur/The Dodo bird, and the African Roc;/But the Wakeupworld, shaped like a clock,/And the lazy Sleepamitemore,/The Pussybow that could mew and barks,/The lonely Squililigee,/The Treasuretit that loved the dark,/Nobody's heard of these but me." Delightful, yet full of subtle criticism of human behavior, the poetry in *The Lost Zoo* is well suited to an audience of older children but is in no way slight.

Cullen also pursued his interest in drama in the 1940s. He and Arna Bontemps collaborated on adapting Bontemps's novel *God Sends Sunday* (1931) for the stage. Their play, *St. Louis Woman*, written between 1939 and 1940, was being considered for Broadway production as a musical and for a Hollywood film version with Lena Horne in 1945. Difficulties in getting the play or the film produced arose, as did serious opposition from some members of the black community who believed the kinds of character and plot in the play were "degrading" to black people because of the "low life" of bars, racetracks, and violent love triangles depicted. As Hughes had been attacked as the "poet lowerate," pun intended, of Harlem for daring to depict black life in black idiom, Cullen the traditional versifier now faced censure not for lack of "color" in his work but for the wrong kind. As a result of these problems, the play was not produced in Cullen's lifetime.

Cullen's poetic activities in 1945 were much less controversial. Just before his death from high blood pressure and uremic poisoning in 1946 he had selected the poetry by which he wanted to be known. From *Color* to *The Lost Zoo*, he culled the poems which were the essence of his vision of poetry and of his lyrically tuned ear for traditional verse for *On These I Stand: An Anthology of the Best Poems of Countee Cullen* (1947). In this collection, published posthumously, Cullen gathered his "Heritage" (with its Christian and pagan conflict expressed in vibrant colorful images), his sonnets, his ironic epitaphs, such as "For a Lady I Know" ("She even thinks that up in heaven/Her class lies late and snores,/While poor black cherubs rise at seven/To do celestial chores"), "To Certain Critics" and the unpopular "The Black Christ," poems praising France and cats from *The Medea and Some Poems*, *The Ballad of the Brown Girl*, and poems from *The Lost Zoo*, such as "The Wake-up-world." Choosing poems written according to the method that had been at once his strength and his weakness—conservative versification coupled with exclusion of emotions he considered inappropriate for poetry—Cullen included what he believed was his best work in *On These I Stand* and clearly revealed the character of what Gwendolyn Brooks was to call his "careful talent."

His death, unlike his birth, was an event of public note, and his funeral was an occasion for public participation and mourning. While critics may have felt that the "careful talent" revealed in the whole body of his poetry was less than what had been promised in his early work, Cullen created a rich heritage of brown beauty in verse for what Gwendolyn Brooks called "every lover of lyrical richness." If the body of poems was small and, ironically, anthologized more in collections of black poetry than in volumes of American poetry, Cullen's life and art represented, as his friend Owen Dodson said, "the noblest way" of expressing the urge to lyrical song and the hope for a day when color would not limit human achievement.

Bibliography:

Margaret Perry, *A Bio-Bibliography of Countee P. Cullen* (Westport, Conn.: Greenwood Press, 1971).

Excellent source of information about Cullen's life, his works, reviews of his works, and critical articles and books about him.

References:

Houston A. Baker, Jr., *A Many-Colored Coat of Dreams: The Poetry of Countee Cullen* (Detroit: Broadside Press, 1974).
A fine, well-written reading of Cullen's poetry and its symbols by an important Afro-American critic who explores Cullen's influences and his inner splits and tensions.

Stephen H. Bronz, *Roots of Racial Consciousness: The 1920s: Three Harlem Renaissance Authors* (New York: Libra Publishers, 1964).
A study focusing on the problem of Cullen's relationship to his race consciousness in his writing.

Eugenia Collier, "I Do Not Marvel, Countee Cullen," in *Modern Black Poets*, edited by Donald B. Gibson (Englewood Cliffs, N.J.: Prentice-Hall, 1973), pp. 69-83.
An essay which examines the Cullen poem "From the Dark Tower" in detail as typical of a Negro Renaissance theme depicting being trapped in an unjust system and flowering into blackness despite the trap.

Arthur P. Davis, *From the Dark Tower. Afro-American Writers 1900-1960* (Washington, D.C.: Howard University Press, 1974), pp. 73-83.
A detailed chronology of Cullen's life, excellent bibliography of primary and secondary works, and brief interpretive essay on the themes and problems of Cullen's writing.

Blanche Ferguson, *Countee Cullen and the Negro Renaissance* (New York: Dodd, Mead, 1966).
A good source of information about Cullen's life, work, and connections with other Negro Renaissance writers and the publishing establishment.

Nathan I. Huggins, *Harlem Renaissance* (New York: Oxford University Press, 1971), pp. 206-210.
Against the backdrop of a description of the New Negro Movement, Huggins interprets Cullen's art as the result of a conflict between Cullen's ideas of what art should be and his racial consciousness.

Blyden Jackson, "Largo for Adonais," in *The Waiting Years: Essays on American Negro Literature* (Baton Rouge: Louisiana State University Press, 1976), pp. 42-62.
Originally published in the year of Cullen's death, 1946, this tribute to him explores the paradoxes of his work and life and argues that his poetry is limited.

Margaret Perry, *Silence to the Drums: A Survey of the Literature of the Harlem Renaissance* (Westport, Conn. & London: Greenwood Press, 1976), pp. 31-56.
Good source of information about reviews of Cullen's work during his lifetime and Cullen's ideas about his writing.

J. Saunders Redding, *To Make a Poet Black* (College Park, Md.: McGrath, 1968), pp. 108-112.
Evaluation of Cullen's writing by an important Afro-American critic who identifies *Color* as Cullen's best work and *The Black Christ* as his worst, giving reasons based on Cullen's style of writing and understanding of reality.

Eugene B. Redmond, *Drumvoices: The Mission of Afro-American Poetry* (Garden City, N.Y.: Anchor/Doubleday, 1976), pp. 179-185.
Brief survey of Cullen's life, themes, and various interpretations of his work with many bibliographical references.

Alan R. Shucard, *Countee Cullen* (Boston: Twayne, 1984).
A biographical and critical study of Cullen's life and writing.

Darwin Turner, *In a Minor Chord: Three Afro-American Writers and Their Search for Identity* (Carbondale: Southern Illinois Press, 1971), pp. 60-88.
Important essay by a prominent Afro-American scholar surveying Cullen's life and works, discussing various interpretations, and evaluating Cullen's achievement.

Jean Wagner, *Black Poets of the United States From Paul Laurence Dunbar to Langston Hughes*, translated by Kenneth Douglas (Urbana, Chicago & London: University of Illinois Press, 1973), pp. 283-347.

Extremely detailed scholarly study which presents the controversial thesis that Cullen had a lyrical gift and was troubled by his origins, his religion, and his racial consciousness in ways that strangled his expression.

Papers:
Cullen's papers are at the libraries of Atlanta University and the University of California, Berkeley, and in the James Weldon Johnson Collection at the Beinecke Library, Yale University.

F. Scott Fitzgerald

This entry was updated by Alan Margolies (City University of New York) from the entry by Scott Donaldson (College of William and Mary) in DLB 9, American Novelists, 1910-1945, Part 2.

Places	St. Paul, Minn. Princeton Montgomery, Ala.	Great Neck, Long Island New York City	Paris The Riviera Hollywood

Influences and Relationships	John Keats
	Joseph Conrad
	H. G. Wells
	Compton McKenzie
	H. L. Mencken
		Ring Lardner
		Maxwell Perkins
		Edmund Wilson
		Ernest Hemingway
		Zelda Sayre Fitzgerald
			Monsignor Cyril
			   Sigourney Webster
			   Fay
			Sheilah Graham

Literary Movements and Forms	Romanticism Realism	The Popular Short Story	Social History

Major Themes	The American Dream
	Idealism
	The Effect of Money
	   and Power
		College Life
		Romantic Love
		American East vs.
		   American West
			American History
			Personal Aspiration
			Disillusionment
			Success and Failure

Cultural and Artistic Influences	English Romantic Poetry	Motion Pictures	Catholicism
Social and Economic Influences	The Depression Prohibition The Jazz Age	The Expatriate Movement	Materialism World War I

See also the Fitzgerald entries in DLB 4, American Writers in Paris, 1920-1939, DLB Yearbook 1981, *and* DLB: Documentary Series 1.

BIRTH: St. Paul, Minnesota, 24 September 1896, to Edward and Mollie McQuillan Fitzgerald.

EDUCATION: Princeton University, 1913-1917.

MARRIAGE: 3 April 1920 to Zelda Sayre; child: Frances Scott.

DEATH: Hollywood, California, 21 December 1940.

BOOKS: *This Side of Paradise* (New York: Scribners, 1920; London: Collins, 1921);
Flappers and Philosophers (New York: Scribners, 1920; London: Collins, 1922);
The Beautiful and Damned (New York: Scribners, 1922; London: Collins, 1922);
Tales of the Jazz Age (New York: Scribners, 1922; London: Collins, 1923);
The Vegetable (New York: Scribners, 1923);
The Great Gatsby (New York: Scribners, 1925; London: Chatto & Windus, 1926);
All the Sad Young Men (New York: Scribners, 1926);
Tender Is the Night (New York: Scribners, 1934; London: Chatto & Windus, 1934);
Taps at Reveille (New York: Scribners, 1935);
The Last Tycoon, edited by Edmund Wilson (New York: Scribners, 1941; London: Grey Walls, 1949);
The Crack-Up, edited by Wilson (New York: New Directions, 1945; Harmondsworth, U.K.: Penguin, 1965);
The Stories of F. Scott Fitzgerald, edited by Malcolm Cowley (New York: Scribners, 1951);
Afternoon of an Author, edited by Arthur Mizener (Princeton: Princeton University Library, 1957; London: Bodley Head, 1958);
The Pat Hobby Stories, edited by Arnold Gingrich (New York: Scribners, 1962; Harmondsworth, U.K.: Penguin, 1967);
The Apprentice Fiction of F. Scott Fitzgerald, 1909-1917, edited by John Kuehl (New Brunswick, N.J.: Rutgers University Press, 1965);
F. Scott Fitzgerald In His Own Time: A Miscellany, edited by Matthew J. Bruccoli and Jackson R. Bryer (Kent, Ohio: Kent State University Press, 1971);

F. Scott Fitzgerald (collection of Matthew J. Bruccoli)

The Basil and Josephine Stories, edited by Bryer and Kuehl (New York: Scribners, 1973);
Bits of Paradise: 21 Uncollected Stories by F. Scott and Zelda Fitzgerald, edited by Scottie Fitzgerald Smith and Bruccoli (New York: Scribners, 1973);
F. Scott Fitzgerald's Ledger, edited by Bruccoli (Washington, D.C.: Bruccoli Clark/NCR Microcard Books, 1973);
The Great Gatsby: A Facsimile of the Manuscript, edited by Bruccoli (Washington, D.C.: Bruccoli Clark/NCR Microcard Books, 1973);
The Notebooks of F. Scott Fitzgerald, edited by Bruccoli (New York: Harcourt Brace Jovanovich/Bruccoli Clark, 1978);
F. Scott Fitzgerald's St. Paul Plays: 1911-1914, edited by Alan Margolies (Princeton: Princeton University Library, 1978);
The Price Was High: The Last Uncollected Stories of F. Scott Fitzgerald, edited by Bruccoli (New York: Harcourt Brace Jovanovich/Bruccoli Clark, 1979);
Poems 1911-1940, edited by Bruccoli (Bloomfield Hills, Mich. & Columbia, S.C.: Bruccoli Clark, 1981).

F. Scott Fitzgerald was a writer very much of his own time. As Malcolm Cowley once put it, he lived in a room full of clocks and calendars. The years ticked away while he noted the songs, the shows, the books, the quarterbacks. His own career followed the pattern of the nation, booming in the early 1920s and skidding into near oblivion during the depths of the Depression. Yet his fiction did more than merely report on his times, or on himself as a prototypical representative, for Fitzgerald had the gift of double vision. Like Walt Whitman or his own Nick Carraway, he was simultaneously within and without, at once immersed in his times and able to view them—and himself—with striking objectivity. This rare ability, along with his rhetorical brilliance, has established Fitzgerald as one of the major novelists and story writers of the twentieth century.

The source of Fitzgerald's talent remains a mystery. Edward Fitzgerald, his father, came from "tired, old stock" with roots in Maryland. His job with Proctor and Gamble took the family to Buffalo and Syracuse for most of his son's first decade. Then the company let Edward Fitzgerald go, and he returned to St. Paul blaming no one but himself and going daily to an office where there was not much for him to do. He drank more than he should have but had beautiful manners that he taught to his only son. Edward Fitzgerald's great-great-grandfather was the brother of Francis Scott Key's grandfather, and if Scott Fitzgerald claimed a closer relationship, it was hardly his fault. He had after all been christened Francis Scott Key Fitzgerald, and his mother, Mollie, was inordinately proud of the Key connection she had married into. Her own family could offer no pretensions to aristocracy, certainly. Philip Francis McQuillan, her father, had emigrated from Ireland in 1843 and built a substantial wholesale grocery business in St. Paul. From him may have stemmed the energy that fueled Scott Fitzgerald's production of 160 stories and four and a half novels. Equally important, probably, was Fitzgerald's sense of having come from two widely different Celtic strains. He had early developed an inferiority complex in a family where the "black Irish half . . . had the money and looked down on the Maryland side of the family who had, and really had . . . 'breeding.' " As a boy Scott used to imagine that he was born of royal blood but had turned up on the Fitzgeralds' doorstep. He loved his father, but could hardly respect him. His feelings about his mother were even more complicated.

Mollie Fitzgerald had lost two children to epidemics before her bright, handsome Scott came along. No beauty herself, she spoiled her son and loved to show him off. When company called, he was trotted out in his Little Lord Fauntleroy suit to recite or sing and accept the applause. Until he was fifteen, he later remarked, he did not know anyone else was alive. Mollie was also extremely ambitious for her son socially. Though Catholic, Irish, and the son of an unsuccessful businessman, Scott went to dancing school with children of St. Paul's elite. At an unusually early age he became interested in girls, and still more interested in the game of adolescent courtship. In his "Thoughtbook" at the age of fourteen he put down the names of his favorite girls of the moment. Marie Hersey was the prettiest, Margaret Armstrong the best talker. He wanted to be first in the affections of both and saw no need to draw the line at two. "Last year in dancing school I got 11 valentines and this year 15," he wrote. It was a game that he enjoyed playing and that he played better than most. A few years later he wrote for the benefit of his younger sister, Annabel, a closely detailed set of instructions about how to attract boys. Later, in "Bernice Bobs Her Hair" (1920), he presented some of the same advice in fictional form.

As a youth Fitzgerald revealed a flair for dramatics, first in St. Paul, where he wrote original plays for amateur production, and later at the Newman School in Hackensack, New Jersey, and at Princeton, where he composed lyrics for the university's famous Triangle Club productions. He also carried on an extensive correspondence with debutantes and subdebutantes. For Fitzgerald, boy-girl relationships amounted to a kind of contest in which there could be only one winner. There is ample evidence that he regarded man-woman relationships in much the same way, except that as he grew older the game turned into an increasingly bitter and sometimes violent conflict. During the hectic party season in St. Paul, Christmas of his sophomore year at Princeton, Fitzgerald more than met his match in the charming Ginevra King of Chicago, Lake Forest, and the great world of wealth and family background. They dated a few times and conducted a long and heated correspondence, but in the end, almost inevitably, Fitzgerald lost her. There is a legend that Ginevra's father told Scott that "poor boys shouldn't think of marrying rich girls." Whether he said it or not, Fitzgerald intuited such a message and tried to work off some of his disappointment in a number of his most power-ful stories, beginning with "The Debutante," published in the *Nassau Lit* in January 1917 and later included in *This Side of Paradise* (1920).

By the time that famous first novel appeared in 1920, Fitzgerald was engaged to marry yet another enchanting girl, Zelda Sayre of Montgomery, Alabama, the daughter of a judge and by all accounts a belle of shockingly unconventional behavior. But Rosalind Connage in *This Side of Paradise* derives from Ginevra King, and it is she who rejects Amory Blaine because he is poor and hasn't much by way of prospects. "I can't be shut away from the trees and the flowers, cooped up in a little flat, waiting for you," she tell Amory. And: "I don't want to think about pots and kitchens and brooms. I want to worry whether my legs will get slick and brown when I swim in the summer." As she tells another suitor, "Given a decent start any girl can beat a man nowadays."

It was characteristic of Fitzgerald, who was one of the most autobiographical of writers, to transform his own experience into fiction. Later he was to appropriate Zelda's life in all its tragic dimensions for use in his stories and novels. But in this first novel, which sold more than forty thousand copies in 1920, the focus was on Fitzgerald himself, thinly disguised as the protagonist Amory Blaine, and on the people he had come to know and the events that had befallen him in his young life, particularly during that part of it spent at the Newman School in Hackensack and at Princeton. At Newman Fitzgerald had encountered Father Cyril Sigourney Webster Fay, a worldly Catholic convert who delighted the boy by recognizing his potential and treating him like an adult. For a time Fitzgerald's Catholic roots threatened to emerge. At Princeton he had met John Peale Bishop, a young literary man who headed the *Nassau Lit*, Princeton's literary magazine, and became, along with Edmund Wilson, a friend for the long haul. Fay and Bishop appear in *This Side of Paradise* as Monsignor Darcy and Thomas Parke d'Invilliers, respectively, and it would be easy enough to list actual models for other characters in the novel. Always the emphasis stays on Amory, however. With people and events alike, as Andrew Turnbull observed, "Fitzgerald adhered to the Renaissance and Romantic conception of the writer as a man of action who experiences his material at first hand—not from lack of imagination, but so he can write about it more intensely."

This Side of Paradise became popular in large part because it portrayed the habits and customs of the young postwar generation. The youths do little more than kiss casually, take an occasional drink, and treat their parents rudely, but in 1920 that was enough to brand them as rebels, even if no one was sure what they were rebelling against. For his part, Amory Blaine is a remarkably tame and impeccably moral young man who flies from the arms of a seductive chorus girl as if she were an agent of the devil. He even utters some high-sounding phrases about democratic socialism. But his principal interest, and that of the novel, is in pursuing two not entirely unrelated goals. Amory seeks to win the golden girl and to achieve recognition as a leader at Princeton. His failure to win Rosalind is hardly Amory's fault, since he could not have prevented his family's loss of wealth. But his failure at Princeton is another matter.

Like Fitzgerald, Amory Blaine throws himself into the work of the Triangle Club (and, in Amory's case, the *Daily Princetonian*). He thus neglects his studies to the point where he is eventually ineligible to accept the rewards that would have been his if he had managed even a fair academic record. Like Fitzgerald, Amory spends too much time and energy analyzing the social system at Princeton as a kind of glamorous country club (this aspect of the book outraged some sons of Nassau and drew a letter of objection from Princeton's president). At the end of *This Side of Paradise*, Amory Blaine has presumably matured. "I know myself, . . . but that is all," he announces. It is doubtful.

In form *This Side of Paradise* is less a novel than the collected works, to 1920, of its twenty-three-year-old author. Fitzgerald embeds poems, play fragments, and short stories within his sprawling book. As James Miller was to observe, the result reads like what H. G. Wells called the novel of saturation. Yet for all its shortcomings of structure, theme, and character, *This Side of Paradise* still possesses one unmistakable sign of genius. It has life, and though the times and the customs have changed, the vitality remains.

Maxwell Perkins at Scribners recognized this at once and encouraged Fitzgerald through two revisions of his book, much of which he completed while serving as a second lieutenant in the United States Army. From the beginning Perkins believed in Fitzgerald's talent and was not afraid to show it. He became Fitzgerald's lifelong friend and financial benefactor. He fought for his au-

Fitzgerald with his father around the turn of the century (collection of Matthew J. Bruccoli)

stories, which drained him of time and energy that might otherwise have gone into novels. Some of the stories are brilliant, some very moving. Many of the best are included in *The Stories of F. Scott Fitzgerald* (1951), edited by Malcolm Cowley. Others are much less successful, but even in the least effective Fitzgerald almost always struck a grace note that stamped the story as indisputably his own. Thus in *Flappers and Philosophers* most of the stories are undistinguished, but two— "Bernice Bobs Her Hair" and "The Ice Palace," a well-crafted story contrasting North and South— belong with the best of his tales.

Scott and Zelda Fitzgerald were married in New York in the spring of 1920 and spent much of the next few years in and around New York, living variously in the city, in Westport, Connecticut, and Great Neck, Long Island, with sojourns in Europe for a first look at that continent and in St. Paul for the birth of their daughter, Scottie. They were never to alight anywhere long enough for it to seem like home, for Fitzgerald seems to have inherited an abiding restlessness from his parents. But during the New York years the two Fitzgeralds made themselves famous (some might say notorious) for their unconventional style of life and incessant partying. Fitzgerald earned a reputation as a symbol of the Jazz Age that he was never to rid himself of during his lifetime. But he also continued his frantic story production and widened his circle of literary acquaintants to include, for example, Ring Lardner, George Jean Nathan, and H. L. Mencken. The influence of Mencken, especially, emerged in his second novel, *The Beautiful and Damned* (1922).

This is Fitzgerald's bleakest novel, infected by a tone of cynicism. Not even Fitzgerald seems to care particularly about Anthony and Gloria Patch, his handsome young couple who decline in dignity and promise as they sue for the inheritance that will make them independently wealthy and—they anticipate—blissfully happy. When the money finally comes their way, however, Anthony has virtually lost his mind and Gloria's beauty has begun to fade and harden. Much of the book consists of talk, with Maury Noble (modeled on Nathan) delivering himself of a good many dark and clever speeches. The novel sold surprisingly well but did not advance Fitzgerald's reputation. Nor did the satirical play about American politics, *The Vegetable* (1923), which he wrote the following year in hopes of a Broadway production and financial killing. The play got as far as

thor within Scribners during times when it seemed foolish to do so, like the long dry spell between *The Great Gatsby* (1925) and *Tender Is the Night* (1934). Fitzgerald wryly imagined how it must have been for Perkins in a late self-deprecatory story called "Financing Finnegan" (1938). Perkins's efforts were worth the trouble. The house of Scribners brought out all of Fitzgerald's books during his life and continues to publish them, in hundreds of thousands of copies, to this day.

With *Flappers and Philosophers* (1920) Scribners established a policy of following up each Fitzgerald novel with a book of his stories. In book form the stories sold less well than the novels, but they brought princely sums from the magazines. At one stage the *Saturday Evening Post* was paying Fitzgerald four thousand dollars per story, but the Fitzgeralds spent money so lavishly that they were almost always in debt. Their extravagance forced Fitzgerald to write more and more an out-of-town tryout in Atlantic City, where it fizzled out because of a terrible second act. If they did nothing else, *The Vegetable* and *The Beautiful and Damned* provided convincing evidence that Fitzgerald was not cut out to be a satirist. His writing was most successful when it was most deeply felt, when some part of Fitzgerald identified with his characters.

Both the novel and play touched on themes that were to dominate Fitzgerald's work for the next fifteen years: the effects of money and power on those who have too much of them and the excruciating dilemma of the young man—not necessarily poor but not rich either—who falls in love with a golden girl, wealthy, beautiful, and often cruel. These same themes emerged in several brilliant stories Fitzgerald wrote in the first half decade of the 1920s. "May Day" (1920), a novella-length tale, provides an episodic view of New York City on May Day 1919, cutting from scenes of a society dance to a socialist newspaper office to a mob of war veterans. The protagonist of the story, Gordon Sterrett, is a weakling who commits suicide rather than face marriage with the lower-class woman who has seduced him. As in *The Beautiful and Damned*, Fitzgerald supplies no one for the reader to identify with, but in "May Day"—manifestly a slice-of-life story—it matters far less, since there are a number of sharply drawn characters to *dislike*. Least appealing of all, significantly, are a hypocritical (and rich) Yale classmate of Sterrett's and a shallow (and rich) debutante who was attracted to Sterrett when he was in less straitened circumstances. Conversely, the debutante's brother—an economics professor and socialist—emerges as the only really admirable figure in "May Day," thus providing early evidence of the leaning to the left that characterized Fitzgerald's political stance.

Two stories of 1922, "The Diamond as Big as the Ritz" and "Winter Dreams," concentrate on young men in contact with the world of wealth. "The Diamond as Big as the Ritz," a fantasy, portrays the genteel viciousness of the Braddock Washingtons, who live atop a huge diamond of a mountain, feel annoyed when they must murder houseguests to keep the secret of its location, and assume they can buy their way out of any difficulty. In the final scenes Washington attempts to bribe God to avert an aerial attack on his mountain. John Unger, the young man who had come to visit the Washingtons on holiday from school, escapes with the lovely, totally impractical, and exquisitely selfish Kismine

Washington and her sister Jasmine, as their father, his bribe having failed, blows up the mountain.

"Winter Dreams" hits closer to home. In fact, it is one of the few Fitzgerald stories obviously set in and around White Bear Lake, the summer playground of St. Paul's elite. Dexter Green first encounters Judy Jones while he is caddying at her club. He quits on the spot because he realizes that she sees him as a servant, and he quite consciously begins to make something of himself in order to earn her approval. "The little girl who had done this was eleven," Fitzgerald reveals, "beautifully ugly" now but "destined after a few years to be inexpressively lovely and bring no end of misery to a great number of men." In time Dexter does attract her attention, but she treats him cavalierly as only one in a parade of beaux. Eventually Dexter makes a success in business and then on Wall Street, where he hears that Judy has married a man from Detroit who rather mistreats her and that her beauty has faded. "Most of the women like her," he is told. Dexter can hardly believe his ears, and the news devastates him, destroying his dream of Judy: "Something had been taken from him" and "the grief he could have borne was left behind in the country of illusion, of youth, of the richness of life, where his winter dreams had flourished."

Like Dexter, most of Fitzgerald's male characters celebrate the ideal at the expense of the real. Only the world of illusion can sustain their emotional intensity; only in dreams can they shut out the sometimes terrifying everyday world. So the twelve-year-old Rudolph Miller in "Absolution" (1924), which is the discarded beginning for *The Great Gatsby*, retreats into his imaginary self, Blatchford Sarnemington, when threatened by divine punishment. Like James Gatz, Rudolph feels himself superior to his parents, and especially to his religiously stern but financially unsuccessful father.

Regarded as background for the character of Gatsby, "Absolution" is most interesting in its strongly religious orientation. Having lied, rather innocently, at confession, Rudolph is convinced that he will be struck dead when he takes communion. When he survives that trauma, however, and discovers that his priest has gone quite mad, Rudolph/Blatchford is tempted to reject conventional Catholicism and seek a more secular image to adore. In an uncannily prophetic speech, the priest warns against the costs of such materialistic worship. Go and see an amusement park at night, he advises the startled boy. "You'll see a big wheel made of lights turning in the air, and a long slide shooting boats down into the water. A band playing somewhere, and a smell of peanuts—and everything will twinkle. . . . It will all hang out there in the night like a colored balloon—like a big yellow lantern on a pole." Then the priest pauses, frowns, and adds: "But don't get up too close, for if you do you'll only feel the heat and the sweat and the life." *The Great Gatsby* tells the story of a man who got too close.

Fitzgerald wrote *The Great Gatsby* in France, where he and his wife and daughter were to spend most of the last half of the 1920s. The novel bears almost no resemblance in form to those that had come before. In Jay Gatsby, née James Gatz, Fitzgerald created far more than just another Amory Blaine seeking his fortune in the world, for in his misguided romantic way Gatsby stands for a deeper malaise in the culture—a sickness that drives young men to think that riches can obliterate the past and capture the hearts of the girls of their dreams. Gatsby's dream girl, hardly worthy of his romantic quest, is Daisy Fay Buchanan, wife to the safely (not newly) rich Tom Buchanan. She and Gatsby had met and fallen in love during the war, when Jay was a young officer with no money or position:

> eventually he took Daisy one still October night, took her because he had no real right to touch her hand.
>
> He might have despised himself, for he had certainly taken her under false pretenses. I don't mean that he had traded on his phantom millions, but he had deliberately given Daisy a sense of security; he let her believe that he was a person from much the same stratum as herself—that he was fully able to take care of her. As a matter of fact, he had no such facilities—he had no comfortable family standing behind him, and he was liable at the whim of an impersonal government to be blown anywhere about the world.
>
> But he didn't despise himself and it didn't turn out as he had imagined. He had intended, probably, to take what he could and go—but now he found that he had committed himself to the following of a grail. He knew that Daisy was extraordinary, but he didn't realize just how extraordinary a 'nice' girl could be. She vanished into her rich house, into her rich, full life, leaving Gatsby—nothing. He felt married to her, that was all.

When he went overseas, she married Buchanan. The novel tells the story of his attempt to get Daisy back some four years later. In the mean-time he has made a great deal of money, partly from bootlegging liquor; Daisy has borne a daughter; and Tom has taken as his mistress Myrtle Wilson, the wife of the owner of a garage in the ash heaps that lie along the road about halfway between West Egg and Manhattan. Told so badly, the novel sounds like material for the pulps. But the story is not told that way at all, but through the informing intelligence of Nick Carraway, an almost perfect narrator.

Clearly, Fitzgerald had been reading Joseph Conrad and discovered in his use of the character Marlow as teller of the tale a way of distancing himself from his story without sacrificing intensity. Nick Carraway functions as an ideal Marlow in *The Great Gatsby*, for he is connected by background to the Buchanans (Daisy is his cousin; he had been at Yale with Tom) and by proximity to Gatsby (he rents a small house near Gatsby's garish mansion), and he has—he tells us—cultivated the habit of withholding judgments. Nick does not particularly like Tom, even to begin with, but he knows and understands Tom and his milieu. At first, Gatsby is a mystery to Nick. He spends too ostentatiously and entertains too lavishly. Besides giving parties, Gatsby wears pink suits, drives yellow cars, and is in business with the man who fixed the World Series. Yet before the tragic end—when in a case of mistaken identity for which Tom and Daisy Buchanan are jointly responsible, Myrtle Wilson's husband kills Gatsby—Nick comes to see that the Buchanans were "careless people . . . who smashed up things and creatures and then retreated back into their money or their vast carelessness, or whatever it was that kept them together, and let other people clean up the mess," and he realizes that Gatsby, the bootlegger who followed his dream, was "worth the whole damn bunch put together." Coming from Carraway, no saint himself and a bit of a snob, a man who "disapproved" of Gatsby from beginning to end as he would disapprove of any other parvenu, that judgment takes on absolute authority.

Gatsby's greatness lies in his capacity for illusion. Had he seen Daisy for what she was, he could not have loved her with such single-minded devotion. He comes to recapture Daisy, and for a time it looks as though he will succeed. But he must inevitably fail, because of his inability to separate the ideal from the real. Everything he has done, and it is clear that much of what he has done is on the shady side of the law, Gatsby has done in order to present himself as worthy of

Fitzgerald with his wife, Zelda, and their daughter, Scottie, in Paris around 1925 (collection of Matthew J. Bruccoli)

mind to mundane reality. *The Great Gatsby* abounds in touches like these.

The Great Gatsby has inspired probably as much critical commentary as any other twentieth-century American novel, but it is so intricately patterned and tightly knit, so beautifully integrated through a series of parallels, that it hardly seems possible that criticism will exhaust the novel. If *This Side of Paradise* resembles the Wellsian novels of saturation, where everything is included, *The Great Gatsby* epitomizes the Jamesian novel of selection, where every detail fits and nothing is superfluous. It is the kind of novel—and there are not many—that gets better each time one rereads it.

The reviews for *The Great Gatsby* were the most favorable so far. Most notably Gilbert Seldes proclaimed that Fitzgerald "has mastered his talents and gone soaring in a beautiful flight, leaving behind him everything dubious and tricky in his earlier work, and leaving even further behind all the men of his own generation and most of his elders." He praises Fitzgerald's ability to report on "a tiny section of life . . . with irony and pity and a consuming passion," calling the novel "passionate . . . , with such an abundance of feeling for the characters (feeling their integral reality, not hating or loving them objectively) that the most trivial of the actors in the drama are endowed with vitality," and he also recognizes that Fitzgerald's characters "become universal also. He has now something of extreme importance to say; and it is good fortune for us that he knows how to say it."

Fresh from *The Great Gatsby*, Fitzgerald wrote "The Rich Boy" (1926), another of his very best stories. In a sense "The Rich Boy" might be regarded as a form of revenge on such careless people as the Buchanans. The mere possession of a great deal of money seems to confer on Anson Hunter, protagonist of the story, certain rights and privileges unthinkable for the penurious. He drinks to excess and feels no need to apologize; he takes advantage of women and feels no remorse; he breaks up his aunt's love affair and ignores the suicide of her lover. For all his power Anson suffers from a fatal lack of emotional capability. He cannot care about anyone other than himself. He has no illusions. He cannot love.

"The Rich Boy" appeared in *All the Sad Young Men* (1926), the volume of stories that followed *Gatsby*. Other than that collection, however, Fitzgerald published no book between 1925 and 1934. Late in his life Fitzgerald wrote his daughter that he should have said upon finishing

Daisy. By crassly materialistic ends he hopes to capture the ideal girl. Toward the end, Nick reflects, Gatsby must have realized that Daisy was not the golden girl after all, that she too had sprung from the material world and was made of all-too-human stuff, but those are Nick's thoughts, not necessarily Gatsby's. For all Fitzgerald lets us know, Gatsby dies with his dream intact, and then it is left to Nick to arrange for the service and erase the dirty word from the steps of Gatsby's house and to clean up the mess.

Though hundreds had come to Gatsby's parties, hardly anyone comes to his funeral. His father is there, a shiftless and uneducated man who even while standing in his son's mansion prefers to admire the photograph of that mansion. So is Owl Eyes, who had been startled to find that the books in Gatsby's library were real, even though their pages were uncut. Like the books, Gatsby was the real thing, but unformed, unlettered, and for all his financial cunning, ignorant. Like his father he preferred the picture in his

The Great Gatsby, "I've found my line–from now on this comes first. This is my immediate duty–without this I am nothing." In fact, he did launch immediately into a preliminary version of *Tender Is the Night* when he had completed *The Great Gatsby,* but that long, sprawling, powerful novel was to go through repeated false starts before it finally emerged. Meanwhile, the Fitzgeralds played on the Riviera and in Paris with, among others, Gerald and Sara Murphy (whose physical appearance and social gifts Fitzgerald transplanted to Dick and Nicole Diver) and Ernest Hemingway.

The story of the friendship between Fitzgerald and Hemingway makes a sad chapter in American literary history. When they met at the Dingo bar in Paris in the spring of 1925, Fitzgerald had already established himself as an important novelist while Hemingway was still a literary tyro who had yet to publish his first book in America. Nevertheless, Fitzgerald did everything he could to promote Hemingway's career, occasionally to the extent of ignoring his own. At first Hemingway responded warmly to such generosity, but it was part of his character to resent assistance from others and he eventually turned on Fitzgerald, denigrating him and his work in a series of public and private attacks.

Unlike her husband, Zelda Fitzgerald was never taken with Hemingway (nor he with her). She regarded him as "bogus," a "poseur." After a time she even accused her husband of a homosexual liaison with Hemingway, but that dubious charge came in the wake of storms that were tearing their marriage apart and driving her toward the brink of madness. In 1924 she had a brief affair with a French aviator, and her husband became steadily more dependent on liquor. Often left alone while he toured the bars and eager to find a creative outlet for herself–so, at least, runs the thesis of Nancy Milford's biography–Zelda Fitzgerald threw herself into studying ballet, taking lessons from the distinguished Madam Egorova and working harder than the other aspirants to make up for beginning so demanding a career in her late twenties instead of her early teens. In April 1930 Zelda cracked from the strain and went off to the first of the series of sanatoriums–this one in Switzerland–that were to serve as refuges for the rest of her life.

In the fall of 1931 the Fitzgeralds limped home to Montgomery. Fitzgerald suggested what the years in Europe had cost them in the autobiographical "Babylon Revisited" (1931). That story,

one of his best, tells of Charlie Wales's attempt to gain custody of his daughter Honoria. His wife had died, a victim of the reckless and expensive life they led during the boom years, and Honoria has gone to live with her Aunt Marion while Charlie recuperates from his long binge. Now he is whole, or nearly so, and returns–sober, steady, and reliable–to reclaim his little girl. Rather unluckily, some former drinking companions burst in as final arrangements are being made, and at the end it is clear that Charlie will have to wait a while longer before he recovers Honoria–and his honor. He will come back again, though, for "he wanted his child, and nothing was much good now, beside that fact. He wasn't young any more, with a lot of nice thoughts and dreams to have by himself."

Fitzgerald's own dream had begun to fade too, but he had less control over his drinking than Charlie Wales. After touching bottom in 1935 and 1936, a process vividly described in the "Crack-Up" essays, he finally began to master the demon of alcohol. Meanwhile, his stories had lost some of their appeal. In the "Basil" stories (nine in all, written in the late 1920s) Fitzgerald had effectively called up recollections of himself as a boy growing up romantic. And the five "Josephine" stories, published in 1930 and 1931, poignantly depicted the disillusionment of a young girl who, though beautiful and rich as always, had dared to dream like one of Fitzgerald's young men. The *Saturday Evening Post* printed the Basil and Josephine stories but continued to seek from Fitzgerald tales of young love triumphant, and these he would no longer produce. His attempts to write instead about what was closest to him–the amusements and trials of raising his daughter, Scottie, his own alcoholism, and encounters with nurses–had carried little appeal for the mass market that the *Saturday Evening Post* and *Collier's* and *Redbook* aimed at. So as the Depression wore on he could no longer command high prices from the magazines. On the verge of his "emotional bankruptcy," he staked a great deal on *Tender Is the Night,* a novel which failed to achieve the financial and critical success he hoped for.

Only part of the trouble was Fitzgerald's own. He had worked and reworked so much material for so long that it became difficult to stitch the parts into a whole. Yet there was little objection to the book's lack of integration. Instead a few critics condemned the subject matter, as if to write of affluent Americans in Europe–however unfavorably they might be portrayed—was to commit a politico-literary crime. Other critics felt that the downfall of Dick Diver had been insufficiently prepared for, but here they were guilty of superficial reading. Even in the opening section of the novel, when Diver is lovingly depicted through the eyes of the smitten movie actress Rosemary Hoyt, Fitzgerald plants the seeds of doubt. "Save among a few of the toughminded and perennially suspicious," the narrator says of Dick, "he had the power of arousing a fascinated and uncritical love." The trouble with Diver is that he is constantly driven to charm and coax and cajole until he succeeds in awakening that uncritical love in others, mostly women. What was a game for Amory Blaine has become for Dick Diver a way of life.

The curious thing is that he—a psychiatrist whose very profession depends upon changing others' patterns of behavior—can do nothing to escape his own obsession. He wants to be the greatest psychiatrist who ever lived, Doctor Diver admits (at Princeton Fitzgerald had confessed his ambition to become one of the greatest writers who ever lived), but he also wants to be loved, if he can fit it in. "He sometimes looked back with awe at the carnivals of affection he had given, as a general might gaze upon a massacre he had ordered to satisfy an impersonal blood lust." In the end he can fit in nothing except his attempts to generate love, which destroy him as a serious man.

The military metaphor introduced above threads through the novel, emphasizing Fitzgerald's conviction that Dick and Nicole, like many others, are engaged in a war from which only one of them will survive unscathed. Dick proposes that their eventual fate parallels that of postwar Western civilization. As he observes in his conversation with Abe North during a visit to the trenches:

> "This western-front business couldn't be done again, not for a long time. The young men think they could do it but they couldn't. They could fight the first Marne again but not this. This took religion and years and plenty and tremendous sureties and the exact relation that existed between the classes. The Russians and Italians weren't any good on this front. You had to have a whole-souled sentimental equipment going back further than you could remember. . . .

> ". . . Why, this was a love battle—there was a century of middle-class love spent here. This was the last love battle."

> "You want to hand over this battle to D. H. Lawrence," said Abe.

> "All my beautiful lovely safe world blew itself up here with a great gust of high explosive love," Dick mourned persistently.

Dick Diver declines steadily throughout *Tender Is the Night*, until he drifts off to the small towns of upstate New York, still working his charm on any female, no matter how young, who might respond. Nicole, however, regains her soundness of mind and with it the callousness of the very rich toward those who can be of service to them, for once again Fitzgerald includes an attack on their irresponsibility. In Paris Nicole goes on a monumental buying spree that bewilders Rosemary, but it is symptomatic of the Warrens of Chicago.

> Nicole bought from a great list that ran two pages, and bought the things in the windows besides. Everything she liked that she couldn't possibly use herself, she bought as a present for a friend. She bought colored beads, folding beach cushions, artificial flowers, honey, a guest bed, bags, scarfs, love birds, miniatures for a doll's house and three yards of some new cloth the color of prawns. She bought a dozen bathing suits, a rubber alligator, a traveling chess set of gold and ivory, big linen handkerchiefs for Abe, two chamois leather jackets of kingfisher blue and burning bush from Hermes—bought all these things not a bit like a high-class courtesan buying underwear and jewels, which were after all professional equipment and insurance—but with an entirely different point of view. Nicole was the product of much ingenuity and toil. For her sake trains began their run at Chicago and traversed the round belly of the continent of California; chicle factories fumed and link belts grew link by link in factories; men mixed toothpaste in vats and drew mouthwash out of copper hogsheads; girls canned tomatoes quickly in August or worked rudely at the Five-and-Tens on Christmas Eve; half-breed Indians toiled on Brazilian coffee plantations and dreamers were muscled out of patent rights in new tractors—these were some of the people who gave a tithe to Nicole, and as the whole system swayed and thundered onward it lent a feverish bloom to such processes of hers as wholesale buying, like the flush of a fireman's face holding his post before a spreading blaze. She illustrated very simple principles, containing in herself her own doom, but illus-

The Fitzgeralds at the Riviera, circa 1926 (collection of Matthew J. Bruccoli)

trated them so accurately that there was grace in the procedure. . . .

When the Warrens want something, they buy it. When Nicole wanted Dick Diver—and the family determined she needed a doctor in the house—she made herself irresistible to him. Her beauty helped, and her vulnerability, but so did her impressive wealth; and as the years wear on, Diver lets himself be more and more compromised by accepting the favors that her money can buy for them both. Fitzgerald is obviously of two minds about Nicole, as he had been about Daisy and Rosalind and the rest of the golden girls whose beauty and vitality almost redeem, for him at least, whatever defects of character lie underneath. About Baby Warren, her sister, he conveys no such ambiguity. Like Anson Hunter, Baby commands but cannot love. Something "wooden and onanistic" hovered about her person, and she is hardly to be preferred even to the homosexuals and bisexuals who inhabit the expatriate community.

Among these minor characters who represent various levels of sexual and psychological deterioration, Dick Diver can shine "with a fine glowing surface," at least at the beginning. But it is only glitter after all, and he has been "lucky Dick" too long and so is ill prepared for the rejections and rebuffs that come to him as to every man. On the whole, Diver is a likable character.

He possesses charm and ability, and he sincerely wants to be right and do good. But he is a weak man, too, unable to scourge himself of his overwhelming need to be loved and therefore susceptible to any and all cries of help, even when they come from two probable lesbians he really cares nothing about.

Amory Blaine had claimed to know himself at twenty-three, but the real knowledge came more than a decade later, with a character who truly understood himself and still could not prevent his fall. Diver is at once Fitzgerald's most complex character and the one who best represents the author's mature understanding of his own psychological makeup. When Fitzgerald describes his own shortcomings in the "Crack-Up" essays, written a year after *Tender Is the Night*, what is wrong with F. Scott Fitzgerald turns out to be almost exactly what is wrong with Dick Diver.

The reviews for *Tender Is the Night* were generally positive, but many reviewers expressed reservations, some commenting that the book was diffuse, not as well integrated as *The Great Gatsby*. Malcolm Cowley called it "a good novel that puzzles you and ends by making you a little angry because it isn't a great novel also," finding in it "a divided purpose that perhaps goes back to the author himself," and offering a persuasive definition of Fitzgerald's double vision: "Fitzgerald has always been the poet of the American upper bourgeoisie; he has been the only writer able to invest their lives with glamor. Yet he has never been sure that he owed his loyalty to the class about which he was writing. It is as if he had a double personality. Part of him is a guest at the ball given by the people in the big house; part of him has been a little boy peeping in through the window and being thrilled by the music and the beautifully dressed women–a romantic but hardheaded little boy who stops every once in a while to wonder how much it all cost and where the money came from." Cowley adds that this dual perspective works well in Fitzgerald's earlier books, but in *Tender Is the Night* the division has become emphasized: "The little boy outside the window has grown mature and cold-eyed: from an enraptured spectator he has developed into a social historian. At the same time, part of Fitzgerald remains inside, among the dancers. And now that the ball is ending in tragedy, he doesn't know how to describe it–whether as a guest, a participant, in which case he will be writing a purely psychological novel; or whether from the detached point of view of a social historian." Yet, Cowley explains that he has pointed out the shortcomings of *Tender Is the Night* because he likes the novel so much, and he calls its chief virtue "a richness of meaning and emotion–one feels that every scene is selected among many possible scenes and that every event has pressure behind it. There is nothing false or borrowed in the book: everything is observed at first hand."

Actually, as recent criticism has demonstrated, *Tender Is the Night* is a far better integrated novel than has been generally supposed. Arthur Mizener, among others, considers it Fitzgerald's most complex achievement. Yet the novel has undoubtedly suffered, to some degree, from its author's reputation for frivolity. Be careful not to use any advertising copy about "gay resorts," Fitzgerald warned Max Perkins. He wanted *Tender Is the Night* taken seriously. And so, inspired by doubts about the shape of his book, Fitzgerald tried to rearrange it to begin chronologically, with a history of Diver's past, rather than with Rosemary and others on the Riviera. In 1951 Scribners brought out a version of the novel which adopted this structure, put together by Cowley following Fitzgerald's notes. This version made it clear at once that *Tender Is the Night* was a novel about a psychiatrist (not an actress) and that the psychiatrist had certain problems that would return to haunt him. But in telling so much so soon, it sacrificed the reader's

sense of discovery. The critical consensus favors the original 1934 version, which is the one now available in bookstores.

He left his capacity to hope, Fitzgerald once wrote, on the roads that led to Zelda's sanatorium. But he also acquired something as a consequence of the misfortunes that visited his wife and himself: a conviction that life was not supposed to be happy and that it didn't matter, since the only thing that mattered, the only dignity, came from doing one's work. Deeply in debt and forced to pay hospital bills for Zelda and school bills for Scottie, Fitzgerald went to Hollywood in 1937 to recoup his credit and regain a sense of his own worth.

M-G-M, which hired him on a six-month contract at $1,000 a week, with an option at $1,250 a week for the next year, knew it was taking a chance. In two previous visits to Hollywood he had produced nothing that reached the screen. More recently, Fitzgerald had announced his "emotional bankruptcy" in the "Crack-Up" essays in *Esquire*. Furthermore, on his fortieth birthday in September 1936, a reporter from the *New York Post* had tracked down an obviously alcoholic Fitzgerald in Asheville, North Carolina, and written a devastating piece about this supposedly ruined chronicler of the Jazz Age. *Time* magazine picked up parts of the interview, and Fitzgerald, dejected, made a halfhearted attempt at suicide. Finally, readers of Fitzgerald's stories would have ascertained something of a self-portrait in Joel Coles, a screenwriter who manages to get rather drunk and make a fool of himself at a Hollywood party in "Crazy Sunday" (1932).

So Fitzgerald went to California very much under the surveillance of his employers and of himself. He rightly saw his contract there as representing a last chance to prove himself as a writer and a man. He did good work for M-G-M, particularly on *Three Comrades*, but that was to be his only screen credit, and when his contract was not renewed after eighteen months, he stayed afloat with a series of free-lance script jobs and by churning out Pat Hobby stories for $250 each. He also tried to keep a tight rein on his alcoholism during the time that was left to him, and found in Sheilah Graham a woman who cared deeply enough to help him in that battle.

In the last year of his life Fitzgerald stole time from his screen writing and stories to begin *The Last Tycoon* (1941), an unfinished novel of great promise. Its protagonist, Monroe Stahr, is the most admirable of Fitzgerald's heroes. A poor boy from New York, Stahr has become the head of a major studio, which he tries to run single-handedly by virtue of his vast energy and indisputable talent. Great men of an earlier time, perhaps, might have succeeded in such an attempt. But the world has become too complicated and materialistic and overorganized, and Stahr's ship eventually founders.

On the technical side of moviemaking, he is a genius. The most effective part of the book consists of two chapters on "The Producer's Day," as reported by Cecilia Brady, daughter of another studio executive. Here as in *The Great Gatsby* Fitzgerald strove for economy of detail, a tight structure, and a reliable outside narrator. Cecilia–half in love with Stahr–was to play the Nick Carraway role of observer. As she reconstructs his day, Stahr convinces a sniffily superior Englishman that writing for films will demand the best he can give. He consoles a dejected leading man about his temporarily flagging sexual powers. He manipulates a story conference to achieve the change in plot he is seeking. He smoothly removes a director who has let his leading lady terrorize the set. He stifles a rumor that promises to end the career of a talented cameraman. He looks for and finds Kathleen Moore, the girl he had seen on the lot during the earthquake the night before. He entertains a prince from Denmark. And he persuades investors from New York that it will do the company good to make a prestigious picture that is certain to lose money.

In time, though, as Fitzgerald's notes for his incomplete novel make clear, the money men from New York were no longer amenable to Stahr's reasoning. And in the last section of *The Last Tycoon*, written before Fitzgerald's death, Stahr is badly out of his depth when he tries to beat up a Communist union leader determined to organize his writers.

There is a love story in this novel, too, a more explicitly passionate love story than any Fitzgerald had written before. But Stahr loses his Kathleen to a greater passion, his determination to rule his studio as one man. The real romance in *The Last Tycoon* is Stahr's romance with his creative work. The tragedy is that there is no longer a place for tycoons, even in so fresh a segment of the modern world as motion pictures.

Despite his failure, there is something magnificent in Stahr's goal: "He had flown up very high to see, on strong wings, when he was young. And while he was up there he had looked on all the kingdoms, with the kind of eyes that can

Fitzgerald in Hollywood, 1940 (collection of Matthew J. Bruccoli)

stare straight into the sun. Beating his wings tenaciously–finally frantically–and keeping on beating them, he had stayed up there longer than most of us, and then, remembering all he had seen from his great height of how things were, he had settled gradually to earth."

". . . in a 'longshot' he saw a new way of measuring our jerky hopes and graceful rogueries and awkward sorrows, and that he came here from choice to be with us to the end. Like the plane coming down into the Glendale airport into the warm darkness." Fitzgerald underscores his stature by implicit comparisons with Andrew Jackson and Abraham Lincoln. Here as in all novels since *The Beautiful and Damned*, he wanted to place the contemporaneous activities of his characters into a wider historical context (he had linked Diver, significantly, with General Grant). Much of Fitzgerald's reading, which included Marx and Nietzsche and, most influential of all, Oswald Spengler, led him to anticipate the collapse of capitalism and the democratic institutions of Western nations. In his novels–and in many stories as well, even for markets where happy endings were expected–his protagonists meet eventual defeat. But this basic pessimism did not stem totally from books like Spengler's *Decline of the West*, since from the beginning, as Fitzgerald put it in "Early Success" (1937): "All the stories that came into my head had a touch of disaster in them–the lovely young creatures in my novels went to ruin, the diamond mountains of my short stories blew up, my millionaires were as doomed as Thomas Hardy's peasants."

Fitzgerald's duality of perspective enabled him to identify with Gatsby and his dreams and yet to stand back with Nick Carraway and see how ridiculous this self-styled "young rajah" was. Part of him was romantic, forever seeking the uncapturable ideal. Part was realistic, aware of the rot festering beneath the glittering surface. And linked with this double vision of himself and his times was a remarkable verbal gift which cannot be adequately described, only quoted. The closing words in *The Great Gatsby* work thematically to tie his modern tale to its historical background, but they stay in the mind not for that reason at all but because of their powerful rhetorical appeal. Nick has been reflecting on how Long Island must have struck Dutch sailors' eyes three hundred years earlier: as "a fresh, green breast of the new world. . . . For a transitory enchanted moment man must have held his breath in the presence of this continent, compelled into an aesthetic contemplation he neither understood nor desired, face to face for the last time in history with something commensurate to his capacity for wonder." Then: "And as I sat there brooding on the old, unknown world, I thought of Gatsby's wonder when he first picked out the green light at the end of Daisy's dock. He had come a long way to this blue lawn, and his dream must have seemed so close that he could hardly fail to grasp it. He did not know that it was already behind him, somewhere back in that vast obscurity beyond the city, where the dark fields of the republic rolled on under the night.

"Gatsby believed in the green light, the orgastic future that year by year recedes before us. It eluded us then, but that's no matter–tomorrow we will run faster, stretch out our arms farther. . . . And one fine morning–

"So we beat on, boats against the current, borne back ceaselessly into the past."

To an extent Fitzgerald's reputation still suffers from his image as the Jazz Age playboy who did not take his craft seriously enough. The obitu-

aries in 1940, when he suffered a heart attack, obviously reflected that image. The irascible Westbrook Pegler went so far as to accuse him of being a crybaby whose characters drank gin "in silver slabs" while they sniffled "about the sham and tinsel of it all." And few of the obituary writers took adequate cognizance of his development since his first two novels. Edmund Wilson did yeoman work to alter these misperceptions of his Princeton friend by editing *The Last Tycoon* and *The Crack-Up* (1945), a potpourri of essays, letters, notes, and critical appreciations of Fitzgerald's work from other well-established writers.

In his review of *The Last Tycoon*, Stephen Vincent Benét took to task the "self-righteousness" of those obituary writers who, instead of reviewing Fitzgerald's work, "merely reviewed the Jazz Age and said that it was closed. Because he had made a spectacular youthful success at one kind of thing, they assumed that that one kind of thing was all he could ever do. In other words, they assumed that because he died in his forties, he had shot his bolt. And they were just one hundred percent wrong, as 'The Last Tycoon' shows." He goes on to call Fitzgerald "a writer who strove against considerable odds to widen his range, to improve and sharpen his great technical gifts, and to write a kind of novel that no one else of his generation was able to write," and, comparing *The Last Tycoon* to other Hollywood novels, he concludes that Fitzgerald's novel "shows what a really first-class writer can do with material–how he gets it under his skin. . . . Had Fitzgerald been able to finish the book, I think there is no doubt that it would have added a major character and a major novel to American fiction." Even in its unfinished form, says Benét, the novel is "a great deal more than a fragment." In it he finds the "wit, observation, sure craftsmanship, the verbal felicity that Fitzgerald could always summon. . . . But with them there is a richness of texture, a maturity of point of view that shows us what we all lost in his early death."

Benét concluded his review by announcing that "the evidence is in. You can take off your hats now, gentlemen, and I think perhaps you had better. This is not a legend, this is a reputation–and, seen in perspective, it may well be one of the most secure reputations of our time." But it was not until the early 1950s, with the publication of Arthur Mizener's biography *The Far Side of Paradise* (1951) and Budd Schulberg's novel *The Disenchanted* (1950)–based in part on his friendship with Fitzgerald in

Hollywood–that the boom of public interest in Fitzgerald commenced.

Since that time almost anything written about Scott or Zelda Fitzgerald has attracted considerable attention. Most of the attention has concentrated on their lives as a romantic cautionary tale, or–in the case of Nancy Milford's *Zelda* (1970)–as a sad story of a woman thwarted by her husband's career. Andrew Turnbull's *Scott Fitzgerald* (1962) drew on his own childhood acquaintance with Fitzgerald to evoke a moving portrayal of the writer during the trying years in the mid 1930s. In *F. Scott Fitzgerald–A Critical Portrait* (1965), Henry Dan Piper combined biographical research with critical insight to produce what remains one of the most useful books on Fitzgerald.

Happily, the tendency since 1965 has been to focus on the corpus of novels and stories Fitzgerald left behind, and the best scholarship has come from those who have worked with the storehouse of Fitzgerald materials at the Princeton University Library. Matthew J. Bruccoli's *The Composition of* Tender Is the Night: *A Study of the Manuscripts* (1963) demonstrated how illuminating such textual study might be. Bruccoli was also the moving force behind the creation of both the *Fitzgerald Newsletter* and the *Fitzgerald/Hemingway Annual* as repositories for research on Fitzgerald. The invariable conclusion of all who have studied Fitzgerald's manuscripts is that he was far from frivolous in his approach to writing, even when it was aimed at popular markets like the *Saturday Evening Post*. Instead, he formed himself into an accomplished craftsman and meticulous reviser, whose best work, touched with genius, belongs with the best of his great contemporaries.

Letters:

The Letters of F. Scott Fitzgerald, edited by Andrew Turnbull (New York: Scribners, 1963; London: Bodley Head, 1964).
> The first and most important collection of letters, despite its correction of Fitzgerald's spelling and punctuation.

Dear Scott/Dear Max: The Fitzgerald-Perkins Correspondence, edited by John Kuehl and Jackson R. Bryer (New York: Scribners, 1971; London: Cassell, 1973).
> An important and fascinating collection of letters between Fitzgerald and his editor at Scribners.

As Ever, Scott Fitz–Letters Between F. Scott Fitzgerald and His Literary Agent Harold Ober, edited by Matthew J. Bruccoli and Jennifer Atkinson (New York & Philadelphia: Lippincott, 1972; London: Woburn Press, 1973).
> Interesting for its many revelations about the relationship between author and agent.

Correspondence of F. Scott Fitzgerald, edited by Bruccoli and Margaret M. Duggan with Susan Walker (New York: Random House, 1980).
> Valuable because of the many important letters here that Turnbull did not include in *The Letters of F. Scott Fitzgerald*.

Bibliographies:

Jackson R. Bryer, *The Critical Reputation of F. Scott Fitzgerald: A Bibliographical Study* (Hamden, Conn.: Archon Books, 1967; supplement, 1984).
> An annotated list of all reviews of Fitzgerald's work as well as all articles and books written about the novelist. Extremely valuable for the researcher.

Matthew J. Bruccoli, *F. Scott Fitzgerald: A Descriptive Bibliography* (Pittsburgh: University of Pittsburgh Press, 1972; supplement, 1980).
> A list of works by Fitzgerald. Lists books (with extensive bibliographical description), contributions to books, appearances in magazines and newspapers, as well as appearances elsewhere. Contains facsimiles of title pages of first editions of books. Extremely valuable for the researcher and book collector, and a model of its type.

Biographies:

Arthur Mizener, *The Far Side of Paradise* (Boston: Houghton Mifflin, 1951; revised, 1965).
> The first biography. Somewhat outdated by more recent work, but still worth reading.

Andrew Turnbull, *Scott Fitzgerald* (New York: Scribners, 1962).
> Extremely readable. Has a personal tone; Turnbull, as a young man, knew Fitzgerald.

Matthew J. Bruccoli, Scottie Fitzgerald Smith, and Joan P. Kerr, eds., *The Romantic Egoists* (New York: Scribners, 1974).
> A fascinating book of photographs and text about the lives of Zelda and Scott Fitzger-

ald. Much of this is from their scrapbooks now at Princeton University Library.

Bruccoli, *Scott and Ernest: The Authority of Failure and the Authority of Success* (New York: Random House, 1978).
The literary and personal relationship between Fitzgerald and Hemingway.

Bruccoli, *Some Sort of Epic Grandeur* (New York: Harcourt Brace Jovanovich, 1981).
Extremely important because it contains far more information than any other biography of Fitzgerald.

André Le Vot, *F. Scott Fitzgerald: A Biography* (Garden City, N.Y.: Doubleday, 1983).
A well-written life, but adds little to what is known.

James R. Mellow, *Invented Lives: F. Scott and Zelda Fitzgerald* (Boston: Houghton Mifflin, 1984).
Mellow believes that the Fitzgeralds were "masters of invention" "creating new versions of themselves, putting themselves into their stories, acting out their stories in real life."

References:

Joan M. Allen, *Candles and Carnival Lights: The Catholic Sensibility of F. Scott Fitzgerald* (New York: New York University Press, 1978).
Discusses Catholicism in Fitzgerald's life and how it affected his writing.

Matthew J. Bruccoli, *The Composition of* Tender Is the Night: *A Study of the Manuscripts* (Pittsburgh: University of Pittsburgh Press, 1963).
Excellent study of manuscripts and typescripts for his fourth novel.

Bruccoli, *"The Last of the Novelists": F. Scott Fitzgerald and "The Last Tycoon"* (Carbondale: Southern Illinois University Press, 1977).
A study of the manuscripts and typescripts for the purpose of reconstructing Fitzgerald's method of composition.

Jackson R. Bryer, *F. Scott Fitzgerald: The Critical Reception* (New York: Burt Franklin, 1978).
A valuable collection of contemporaneous reviews of Fitzgerald's work.

Bryer, ed., *The Short Stories of F. Scott Fitzgerald: New Approaches in Criticism* (Madison: University of Wisconsin Press, 1982).
Excellent collection of essays by such authors as Carlos Baker and James W. Tuttleton examining Fitzgerald's short fiction from a number of viewpoints. Includes an informative list of published criticism of the short stories.

Tony Buttitta, *After the Good Gay Times* (New York: Viking, 1974).
A memoir of Fitzgerald in Asheville, North Carolina, in 1935. Fascinating, but since it was written years later from notes and memory it is impossible to know how much actually happened this way.

Malcolm Cowley and Robert Cowley, eds., *Fitzgerald and the Jazz Age* (New York: Scribners, 1966).
Background material for a controlled research paper on Fitzgerald and the 1920s.

K. G. W. Cross, *F. Scott Fitzgerald* (Edinburgh: Oliver & Boyd, 1964).
A brief study of Fitzgerald's life and work.

Wheeler Winston Dixon, *The Cinematic Vision of F. Scott Fitzgerald* (Ann Arbor: UMI Research Press, 1986).
An overview of Fitzgerald's screen work, mainly valuable for its historical survey.

Scott Donaldson, *Fool for Love* (New York: Cogden & Weed, 1984).
A probing study of the influence of women on Fitzgerald's life and work.

Donaldson, ed., *Critical Essays on F. Scott Fitzgerald's "The Great Gatsby"* (Boston: G. K. Hall, 1984).
Reprinted essays, articles, and letters as well as five new essays.

Kenneth Eble, *F. Scott Fitzgerald*, revised edition (New York: Twayne, 1977).
A brief study of Fitzgerald's life and work. Includes some perceptive looks at some of the short stories not widely discussed elsewhere.

Eble, ed., *F. Scott Fitzgerald: A Collection of Criticism* (New York: McGraw-Hill, 1973).
Mainly a reprinting of worthwhile articles and excerpts from books.

Maxwell Geismar, *The Last of the Provincials* (Boston: Houghton Mifflin, 1943), pp. 287-352.
Discusses the "cleavage" between the "psychological" novels (*The Beautiful and Damned* and *Tender Is the Night*) and the "social" novels (*The Great Gatsby* and *The Last Tycoon*).

William Goldhurst, *F. Scott Fitzgerald and His Contemporaries* (Cleveland: World, 1963).
Discusses the relationship between Fitzgerald and Edmund Wilson, H. L. Mencken, Ring Lardner, and Ernest Hemingway.

Sheilah Graham, *College of One* (New York: Viking, 1967).
The teacher was Fitzgerald; the student was Sheilah Graham–these are the books and other materials that Fitzgerald assigned in his "college of one."

Graham and Gerold Frank, *Beloved Infidel* (New York: Holt, 1958), pp. 173-338.
Excellent personal description of Fitzgerald's last years in Hollywood.

Ernest Hemingway, *A Moveable Feast* (New York: Scribners, 1964), pp. 147-186.
Hemingway's memories of Scott and Zelda. Fascinating, but one can't be certain how much of this actually happened and how much was the result of Hemingway's penchant to fudge the truth.

John A. Higgins, *F. Scott Fitzgerald: A Study of the Stories* (Jamaica, N.Y.: Saint John's University Press, 1971).
An important study that evaluates all of Fitzgerald's short stories and relates them to the novels.

Frederick J. Hoffman, ed., *"The Great Gatsby": A Study* (New York: Scribners, 1962).
Articles, essays, and other documentation related to Fitzgerald's third novel. In his introduction Hoffman says, "It is designed to document Fitzgerald's career, but also critically and variously to assess the worth of his greatest achievement."

Alfred Kazin, ed., *F. Scott Fitzgerald: The Man and His Work* (Cleveland: World, 1951).
Compiled only some eleven years after Fitzgerald's death, this collection of tributes, reviews, and essays, a good number pub-lished during Fitzgerald's lifetime, reflects the great esteem many felt for him.

Marvin J. LaHood, ed., *"Tender Is the Night": Essays in Criticism* (Bloomington: Indiana University Press, 1969).
A good collection of previously published essays about Fitzgerald's fourth novel.

Richard D. Lehan, *F. Scott Fitzgerald and the Craft of Fiction* (Carbondale: Southern Illinois University Press, 1966).
An interesting study of Fitzgerald that "attempts to place Fitzgerald within the traditions of nineteenth- and twentieth-century literature" and shows the influence of Keats, Swinburne, Wilde, Frank Norris, and Conrad, among others.

Robert Emmet Long, *The Achieving of "The Great Gatsby": F. Scott Fitzgerald, 1920-1925* (Lewisburg, Pa.: Bucknell University Press, 1979).
A study of Fitzgerald's early writing that led to *Gatsby*. Also discusses the influence of Conrad and others; places the work in the literary milieu of its time.

Sara Mayfield, *Exiles from Paradise: Zelda and Scott Fitzgerald* (New York: Delacorte, 1971).
A personal reminiscence by a friend who knew Zelda for some forty years. Extremely opinionated at times; controversial.

Nancy Milford, *Zelda* (New York: Harper & Row, 1970).
Fascinating biography of Zelda Fitzgerald. When published contained much new material.

Arthur Mizener, ed., *F. Scott Fitzgerald–A Collection of Critical Essays* (Englewood Cliffs, N.J.: Prentice-Hall, 1963).
Another collection of previously published essays on the novelist's life and work, including articles by Lionel Trilling, Leslie Fiedler, and Arthur Mizener.

Sergio Perosa, *The Art of F. Scott Fitzgerald* (Ann Arbor: University of Michigan Press, 1965).
Analyzes each of Fitzgerald's major works and examines the relationships between them.

Henry Dan Piper, *F. Scott Fitzgerald–A Critical Portrait* (New York: Holt, Rinehart & Winston, 1965).

A good early critical biography, somewhat outdated by more recent scholarship.

Piper, ed., *Fitzgerald's "The Great Gatsby"* (New York: Scribners, 1970).

A Scribner Research anthology which includes excerpts from essays (some complete) and books for the purpose of compiling a controlled research paper.

Frances Kroll Ring, *Against the Current: As I Remember F. Scott Fitzgerald* (San Francisco: Creative Arts Books, 1985).

A brief but fascinating look at the last twenty months of Fitzgerald's life through the eyes of his then young secretary.

Charles E. Shain, *F. Scott Fitzgerald* (Minneapolis: University of Minnesota Press, 1961).

An extremely brief biographical and critical introduction to the novelist and his work.

Robert Sklar, *F. Scott Fitzgerald, The Last Laocoön* (New York: Oxford University Press, 1967).

The influence on Fitzgerald of the late-nineteenth-century genteel tradition in America. Interesting discussions of the novels and many of the short stories.

Milton R. Stern, *Critical Essays on F. Scott Fitzgerald's Tender Is the Night* (Boston: G. K. Hall, 1986).

Good collection of essays and excerpts from books written from the 1930s to the 1980s, with a bibliography of criticism of the novel.

Brian Way, *F. Scott Fitzgerald and the Art of Social Criticism* (New York: St. Martin's Press, 1980).

Fitzgerald as social novelist in the tradition of Henry Adams, Henry James, and Edith Wharton. Good discussion of *Gatsby* and *Tender Is the Night*.

James L. W. West III, *The Making of* This Side of Paradise (Philadelphia: University of Pennsylvania Press, 1983).

An interesting study of the manuscripts and how Fitzgerald wrote his first novel.

Papers:

Fitzgerald's papers are at the Princeton University Library.

Robert Frost

This entry was updated by Donald J. Greiner (University of South Carolina) from his entry in DLB 54, American Poets, 1880-1945, Third Series, Part 1.

Places	Vermont Massachusetts Bread Loaf Writers' Conference	Gloucestershire, England Amherst College Dartmouth College	New Hampshire San Francisco London
Influences and Relationships	Ralph Waldo Emerson William Wordsworth Henry David Thoreau	Ezra Pound Edward Thomas Wilfred Gibson	Edwin Arlington Robinson
Literary Movements and Forms	American Poetic Renaissance	Modernism	Romanticism
Major Themes	Nature as "Nonhuman Otherness" Religious Uncertainty Mutability Form vs. Confusion	The Contrast between Rural and Urban Points of View Humanity's Relation- ship with Nature	Breakdown of Com- munication within Families Relationship between Matter and Spirit
Cultural and Artistic Influences	The Philosophy of William James Darwin's Theory of Evolution	Henri Bergson's *Creative Evolution*	Lucretius's Theory of Atomism
Social and Economic Influences	Decline of New England Breakdown of Traditional Values	The Depression Presidency of John F. Kennedy	Presidency of Franklin D. Roosevelt

BIRTH: San Francisco, California, 26 March 1874, to William Prescott and Isabelle Moodie Frost.

EDUCATION: Dartmouth College, 1892; Harvard University, 1897-1899.

MARRIAGE: 19 December 1895 to Elinor Miriam White; children: Elliott, Lesley, Carol, Irma, Marjorie, Elinor Bettina.

AWARDS AND HONORS: Phi Beta Kappa Poet, Tufts College, 1915; Phi Beta Kappa Poet, Harvard University, 1916; elected to the National Institute of Arts and Letters, 1916; Levinson Prize (*Poetry* magazine), 1922; Pulitzer Prize for *New Hampshire*, 1924; Golden Rose Trophy (New England Poetry Club), 1928; elected to the American Academy of Arts and Letters, 1930; Pulitzer Prize for *Collected Poems*, 1931; Russell Loines Poetry Prize (National Institute of Arts and Letters), 1931; Phi Beta Kappa Poet, Columbia University, 1932; Charles Eliot Norton Professor of Poetry, Harvard University, 1936; Pulitzer Prize for *A Further Range*, 1937; Gold Medal for Poetry (National Institute of Arts and Letters), 1939; Ralph Waldo Emerson Fellow in Poetry, Harvard University, 1939; Phi Beta Kappa Poet, Tufts College, 1940; Gold Medal (Poetry Society of America), 1941; Phi Beta Kappa Poet, Harvard University, 1941; Phi Beta Kappa Poet, William and Mary University, 1941; Pulitzer Prize for *A Witness Tree*, 1943; Gold Medal (Limited Editions Club), 1949; American Academy of Poets Award, 1953; Medal of Honor (New York University), 1956; Gold Medal (Poetry Society of America), 1958; Medal for Achievement in the Arts (Harvard University), 1958; Consultant in Poetry for the Library of Congress, 1958; Emerson-Thoreau Medal (American Academy of Arts and Sciences), 1958; Huntington Hartford Foundation Award, 1958; Congressional Gold Medal, 1962; Edward MacDowell Medal, 1962; Bollingen Prize in Poetry, 1963; forty-four honorary degrees, including honorary M.A., Amherst College, 1920; honorary M.A., University of Michigan, 1922; Litt.D., Yale University, 1924; Litt.D., Harvard University, 1937; Litt.D., Kenyon College, 1945; Litt.D., Duke University, 1948; Litt.D., Oxford University, 1957; Litt.D., Cambridge University, 1957; Litt.D., National University, Ireland, 1957; L.H.D., Hebrew Union College, 1960.

DEATH: Boston, Massachusetts, 29 January 1963.

SELECTED BOOKS: *Twilight* (Lawrence, Mass.: American Printing House?, 1894; Charlottesville: Clifton Waller Barrett Library, University of Virginia, 1966);
A Boy's Will (London: David Nutt, 1913; New York: Holt, 1915);
North of Boston (London: David Nutt, 1914; New York: Holt, 1914);
Mountain Interval (New York: Holt, 1916);
Selected Poems (New York: Holt, 1923; London: Heinemann/New York: Holt, 1923);
New Hampshire (New York: Holt, 1923; London: Grant Richards, 1924);
Several Short Poems (New York: Holt, 1924);
Selected Poems (New York: Holt, 1928);
West-Running Brook (New York: Holt, 1928);
A Way Out: A One Act Play (New York: Harbor Press, 1929);
The Lovely Shall Be Choosers (New York: Random House, 1929);
The Cow's in the Corn: A One-Act Irish Play in Rhyme (Gaylordsville, Conn.: Slide Mountain Press, 1929);
Collected Poems of Robert Frost (New York: Holt, 1930; London: Longmans, Green, 1930);
The Augustan Books of Poetry: Robert Frost (London: Benn, 1932);
The Lone Striker (New York: Knopf, 1933);
Selected Poems: Third Edition (New York: Holt, 1934);
Three Poems (Hanover, N.H.: Baker Library, 1935);
The Gold Hesperidee (Cortland, N.Y.: Bibliophile Press, 1935);
From Snow to Snow (New York: Holt, 1936);
A Further Range (New York: Holt, 1936; London: Cape, 1937);
Selected Poems (London: Cape, 1936);
Collected Poems of Robert Frost (New York: Holt, 1939; London: Longmans, Green, 1939);
A Witness Tree (New York: Holt, 1942; London: Cape, 1943);
Come In and Other Poems, edited by Louis Untermeyer (New York: Holt, 1943; London: Cape, 1944); enlarged as *The Road Not Taken* (New York: Holt, 1951);
A Masque of Reason (New York: Holt, 1945);
The Pocket Book of Robert Frost's Poems, edited by Untermeyer (New York: Pocket Books, 1946);
The Poems of Robert Frost (New York: Modern Library, 1946);

Robert Frost (Jacob Lofman, Pix)

Steeple Bush (New York: Holt, 1947);

A Masque of Mercy (New York: Holt, 1947);

A Sermon (New York: Spiral Press, 1947);

A Masque of Reason: Containing A Masque of Reason, A Masque of Mercy . . . Steeple Bush and Other Poems (London: Cape, 1948);

Complete Poems of Robert Frost, 1949 (New York: Holt, 1949; London: Cape, 1951);

Hard Not To Be King (New York: House of Books, 1951);

Aforesaid (New York: Holt, 1954);

Robert Frost: Selected Poems (Harmondsworth, U.K.: Penguin, 1955);

A Remembrance Collection of New Poems (New York: Holt, 1959);

You Come Too (New York: Holt, 1959; London: Bodley Head, 1964);

Dedication/The Gift Outright/The Inaugural Address (New York: Holt, Rinehart & Winston, 1961);

In the Clearing (New York: Holt, Rinehart & Winston, 1962; London: Holt, Rinehart & Winston, 1962);

Robert Frost: His 'American Send-Off'–1915, edited by Edward Connery Lathem (Lunenburg, Vt.: Stinehour, 1963);

Selected Poems of Robert Frost (New York, Chicago, San Francisco & Toronto: Holt, Rinehart & Winston, 1963);

Robert Frost: Farm-Poultryman, edited by Lathem and Lawrance Thompson (Hanover, N.H.: Dartmouth Publications, 1963);

Robert Frost and the Lawrence, Massachusetts, 'High School Bulletin': The Beginning of a Literary Career, edited by Lathem and Thompson (New York: Grolier Club, 1966);

Selected Prose of Robert Frost, edited by Hyde Cox and Lathem (New York, Chicago & San Francisco: Holt, Rinehart & Winston, 1966);

The Poetry of Robert Frost, edited by Lathem (New York, Chicago & San Francisco: Holt, Rinehart & Winston, 1969);

Robert Frost on Writing, edited by Elaine Barry (New Brunswick: Rutgers University Press, 1972);

Robert Frost: Poetry and Prose, edited by Lathem and Thompson (New York, Chicago & San Francisco: Holt, Rinehart & Winston, 1972).

OTHER: Reginald Cook, *Robert Frost: A Living Voice,* includes speeches by Frost (Amherst: University of Massachusetts Press, 1974), pp. 36-195.

When Robert Frost died on 29 January 1963, the public mourned the loss of what it thought was the grandfatherly old bard of the nation, the most beloved poet of the century, the gentle writer of simple nature lyrics. Nothing could have been further from the truth. Though indeed loved and mourned by his public, Frost was anything but the kindly rural sage he pretended to be. Just as the accessible surface level of his poems hid deeper ambiguities and dread, so the glare of his public career masked the pain of his private life. In the years since his death, biographical revelations and critical appraisals have torn off the mask to expose a Frost the public never knew: a flawed man with more than his share of personal tragedy, a major poet with more than his share of fear.

Indeed, along with Ezra Pound, T. S. Eliot, and Wallace Stevens, Frost is now firmly regarded as one of the undisputed masters of modern American poetry. Rarely given credit during his lifetime for his ideas about poetic form and technique, he was nevertheless a primary force in the American poetic renaissance that took place after 1910. Unlike Pound and Eliot, he did not fight a public battle to define a private goal—modernism—as his two great contemporaries did through their articles and reviews; and unlike Stevens, he did not formalize his theories in scholarly lectures later published as essays. Frost publicized himself widely and well, but he used newspaper interviews and private conversations to shape his mask and to share his ideas. Most of all, he spoke his mind in hundreds of extraordinary letters and in several informal essays, only a few of which were published in his lifetime.

After his death, however, with the publication of *Selected Letters of Robert Frost* (1964), *Selected Prose of Robert Frost* (1966), *Interviews with Robert Frost* (1966), and the first volume (1966) of Lawrance Thompson's three-volume biography, readers could for the first time study the extent of Frost's contributions to the technical underpinnings of American poetry in an invigorating era. From the letters, for example, they could determine that though Frost was nearly forty years old before he found a publisher for his first book, he confidently seized the day. On 6 August 1913, a few months after the London publication of *A Boy's Will* (1913), Frost wrote to his former student John Bartlett: "I am one of the few artists writing. I am one of the few who have a theory of their own upon which all their work down to

the least accent is done. I expect to do something to the present state of literature in America."

What Frost did to American literature is now history. Writing in a period dominated by free verse, in a time, as he said in 1935, when poetry was "tried" without punctuation, without capital letters, metric frame, content, phrase, epigram, coherence, logic, consistency—"it was tried without ability"—Frost insisted that poetry have a definite form, that it be dramatic, and that it rely on voice tones to vary the "te tum" effect of the traditional iambic rhythm. Frost chose 4 July 1913 to declare his independence from the ephemeral innovation that bewitched American poets after 1910. He wrote to Bartlett: "To be perfectly frank with you I am one of the most notable craftsmen ·of my time. That will transpire presently. I am possibly the only person going who works on any but a worn out theory . . . of versification. You see the great successes in recent poetry have been made on the assumption that the music of words was a matter of harmonized vowels and consonants. Both Swinburne and Tennyson arrived largely at effects in assonation. But they were on the wrong track or at any rate on a short track. They went the length of it. Any one else who goes that way must go after them. And that's where most are going. I alone of English writers have consciously set myself to make music out of what I may call the sound of sense." One can only admire the confidence of the unknown forty-year-old poet dismissing followers of the Victorian giants while touting himself as the writer able to "do" something lasting and true.

How right he was; for though he would go on to become the finest modern American master of the sonnet form, Frost's primary contribution to poetic technique is his theory of the "sounds of sense" or "sentence sounds." Uniting the regularity of the iambic meter with the freedom of the speaking voice, Frost revolutionized blank verse. His poems often sound so much like talk that they look like vers libre, and his first readers did not know how to react. Reviewing *North of Boston* (1914), Ford Madox Hueffer (Ford Madox Ford), for example, quoted the first seven lines of "Mending Wall" and pronounced the technique a "truly bewildering achievement" (*Outlook*, 27 June 1914). Although Hueffer stopped short of urging free verse on Frost, he was not sure of what the poet had done. But Frost knew what he was doing, and it was not vers libre. In the case of "Mending Wall," it was blank verse, an untraditional blank verse, a blank verse that eschews the metronome to unify irregular speech rhythms and the regular iambic pentameter line.

Frost again wrote to Bartlett (22 February 1914) to explain his position:

> I give you a new definition of a sentence: A sentence is a sound in itself on which other sounds called words may be strung.
>
> ....
>
> The sentence sounds are very definite entities. . . .
>
> . . . They are gathered by the ear from the vernacular and brought into books. . . .
>
> A man is all a writer if *all* his words are strung on definite recognizable sentence sounds.

Clearly fascinated by the variety of the speaking voice, Frost also had philosophical matters in mind. His commitment to sentence sounds is part of his commitment to form. Frost's great subjects are confusion, fear, uncertainty–what he defines in "West-Running Brook" as "The universal cataract of death/That spends to nothingness. . . ." Confusion is the natural state of affairs, but Frost tries not to despair because he believes that confusion is a limitation humanity can react against and thereby create form. No man-made form is permanent, and thus Frost coins his famous definition of poetry as "a momentary stay against confusion" ("The Figure a Poem Makes"). He knows that humanity's greatness is its struggle to create form in the face of nothingness. Frost's insistence on stanzas, meter, and sentence sounds in poetry reflects his lifelong preoccupation with the necessity for form. As he explains in another letter (circa 21 March 1935): "The background is hugeness and confusion shading away from where we stand into black and utter chaos; and against the background any small man-made figure of order and concentration. . . . To me any little form I assert upon it is velvet, as the saying is, and to be considered for how much more it is than nothing."

Many of Frost's illuminating letters about his theory of poetry were written in England; for, like Pound and Eliot, Frost had to leave America to find an audience. The story of his struggle to become a poet is a story of courage and guilt, genius and pain; and contrary to general opinion it did not begin in New England.

Robert Lee Frost was born on 26 March 1874 in San Francisco, the first child of William Prescott Frost, Jr., of New Hampshire and Isabelle Moodie of Scotland. Although Frost's father was a Phi Beta Kappa graduate of Harvard, he was also a hard drinker who moved to Califor-

nia to earn a living in journalism and politics. When he died of tuberculosis in 1885 at the age of thirty-four, Frost's mother took Frost and his younger sister, Jeanie (born 25 June 1876), eastward across the continent, where she began a career as a schoolteacher in New Hampshire and Massachusetts.

She was also Frost's teacher. Indulging his distaste for school and his lack of discipline that occasionally manifested itself in laziness, Isabelle Frost let her son skip classes while she filled him with heroic tales of grandeur and glory. Despite the informality of his preparation, however, Frost passed the entrance requirements and matriculated in the Lawrence (Massachusetts) High School in September 1888.

His high school years were crucial. Attracted to classical languages and literature and romantic lyric poetry, Frost took his initial, tentative steps toward a career in poetry. He worked hard, remembered his mother's tales of heroism, and published his first poem, "La Noche Triste," a ballad inspired by W. H. Prescott's *History of the Conquest of Mexico* (1843), in the *Lawrence High School Bulletin* (April 1890). Later editor of the *Bulletin,* Frost contributed other schoolboy poems (for example, "A Dream of Julius Caesar") as well as editorials; and when he was graduated in June 1892, he was both class poet and covaledictorian.

The student who shared the academic honor with him was Elinor Miriam White, his future wife. The triumph of their graduation was tarnished by the threat of their separation, for in the fall of 1892 Frost was to enter Dartmouth while Elinor attended St. Lawrence. Although they were not officially married until 19 December 1895, evidence suggests that they conducted a private wedding ceremony in the summer of 1892.

Frost began classes at Dartmouth in September 1892, but the lack of discipline that characterized his earlier years reasserted itself: he did not finish the first term. Publicly explaining that his mother needed help with unruly students in the Methuen, Massachusetts, district schools, but in truth fearful that Elinor White would be attracted to other men while at St. Lawrence, Frost returned home. He divided his time between teaching and working in a mill, and he blamed Elinor for his dropping out of Dartmouth. Unwilling to work long at any regular job, he nevertheless argued that Elinor should abandon her own studies and marry him. Elinor's determination to finish college plus Frost's jealousy of her intellectual accomplishments were the first signs of a friction that would shadow their life together from before their marriage until her death on 21 March 1938. One need only read "The Subverted Flower," which Frost withheld from publication until 1942, after Elinor died, to glimpse the domestic tension of these years.

Frost's frustration was so great that it caused one of the most extraordinary adventures of his career. Hoping to become a poet, but reluctant to earn a living while learning how, Frost was understandably elated when the New York *Independent* accepted "My Butterfly" for its 8 November 1894 issue. Not only did his first professional poem bring him payment of fifteen dollars; it also persuaded him that he could support himself by writing. Still resentful of Elinor's education, and unable to accept criticism from any quarter, Frost again pressed Elinor to leave St. Lawrence. When she pointed to his lack of prospects, he privately printed "My Butterfly" and four other poems in a two-copy edition he named *Twilight* (1894), traveled to St. Lawrence to give Elinor a copy as proof of his promise as a poet, and promptly destroyed his own copy when she did not respond with the enthusiasm that he believed he deserved (the remaining copy is housed in the Clifton Waller Barrett Library of the University of Virginia). In fall 1894 he made the astonishing decision to travel to the Dismal Swamp of Virginia, where he hoped to lose himself, suffer serious injury, or die as a means of punishing Elinor for what were doubtless imaginary grievances but real pain.

Needless to say, he survived. Frost got back to Lawrence, Massachusetts, where he worked briefly as a reporter for the *Daily American* and the *Sentinel* and then as a teacher in a Salem, New Hampshire, public school (fall 1895). At the same time Elinor, having graduated from St. Lawrence the previous June, began teaching at the private school that Isabelle Frost had established in Lawrence. Following his marriage to Elinor on 19 December 1895, Frost also taught at his mother's school. He continued to write, publishing "The Birds Do Thus" in the *Independent* (20 August 1896), and the next month the Frosts celebrated the birth of their first child, Elliott (25 September 1896). Later Frost deemed most of the poems he published in the 1890s unworthy of collecting. In September 1897 he went to Harvard as a special student. His stay at Harvard was stimulating because of his study of classical languages and the philosophy of William James. Suffering from an illness suspected to be tuberculosis and knowing Elinor was about to give birth to their second child, Lesley (born 28 April 1899), Frost withdrew from Harvard after eighteen months, without taking a degree. The Frosts' marriage suffered a severe blow when their first child died on 8 July 1900, a tragedy that became one of the catalysts for "Home Burial" (*North of Boston*, 1914). Sensing the pressure caused by grief in a marriage already fraught with tension, Frost's grandfather bought a farm in Derry, New Hampshire, and allowed the couple to live on it. Frost could never bring himself to acknowledge his grandfather's financial aid, but he lived on the Derry farm from October 1900 to September 1909.

The decade in Derry was a turning point. Among the most artistically creative of his career, these years saw Frost write many of the poems that later appeared in his first three books. Yet public recognition was elusive, for he could not crack the stranglehold that conservative editors kept on the leading literary journals of the day. Suffering bouts of depression, and jolted by the deaths of his mother in 1900 and his grandfather in 1901, he had to endure both physical debilitation and the loss of the two people who had supported him through his long years of failure. The ever-generous grandfather left him the Derry farm and an annuity—which Frost was once again reluctant to acknowledge. With little regular income beyond the inheritance, and few prospects for making his name as a poet, Frost soon had a large family: Lesley, Carol (born 27 May 1902), Irma (27 June 1903), Marjorie (29 March 1905), and Elinor Bettina (18 June 1907-21 June 1907).

The irony is that the annuity provided the financial edge he needed to write. Vindictive toward those who he insisted doubted him and guilty for his refusal to elevate family over art, Frost began to live according to his famous dictum that one must create "a momentary stay against confusion." He continued to write, and in so doing he used art to order despair. In spring 1906 he accepted a part-time teaching position at Pinkerton Academy, an appointment he kept until he moved to Plymouth, New Hampshire, in 1911 to teach in the Plymouth Normal School. When he sold the Derry farm in November 1911, he closed out one of the most frustrating but productive periods of his life.

The second turning point was less than a year away. Although he managed to publish "The Tuft of Flowers," "Ghost House," "The Trial by Existence," and other poems during the Derry years, he had to place them in such journals as the obscure *Derry Enterprise, Youth's Companion,* and the conservative *Independent.* His great sonnets went unrecognized; his revolutionary blank verse went unread. Like Pound and Eliot, Frost could not find an American audience; like Pound and Eliot, he left America. On 23 August 1912, when Frost and his family sailed for England, he began the journey that would culminate in his long-sought status as a premier poet of the age.

By leaving his country, Frost both escaped a repressive atmosphere for art and discovered a receptive environment for artists. Pound was there, as were T. E. Hulme, William Butler Yeats, Ford Madox Hueffer, and Edward Thomas–all writers who helped to change the course of literature. He also spent time with the Georgian poets Wilfred Gibson and Lascelles Abercrombie and with Harold Monro, owner of the Poetry Bookshop. They gave him the audience he needed, not for the sake of his vanity–though that was important too–but for the sake of his art. Yet one should remember that the stay in England was not a line of demarcation that divided his poetry between apprentice work done in Derry and mature work completed abroad. Although Frost had written in rural obscurity before encountering the urban stimulation of London, he had nevertheless worked on such major poems as "The Death of the Hired Man," "An Old Man's Winter Night," "Hyla Brook," and "The Oven Bird" before he crossed the ocean. What he needed was a vigorous exchange of ideas, an opportunity to debate the issues that sparked modernism. He found it in England.

Success came quickly. In September 1912 Frost arrived in London; in October the firm of David Nutt accepted *A Boy's Will;* in April 1913 the book appeared; and in May 1913 Ezra Pound published in *Poetry* the first important American review of a Frost book. From today's perspective, *A Boy's Will* is Frost's weakest collection. Although he was struggling to break from the outmoded language and rhythms of the late Victorians, some of the poems–"Into My Own" and "My Butterfly" among them–illustrate the verbal inversions and "poetic" language that one does not associate with the typical Frost. In later collections he omitted three of the poems in *A Boy's Will* as

undeserving–"Asking for Roses," "Spoils of the Dead," and "In Equal Sacrifice"–as well as the prose glosses included in the table of contents for all but two of the thirty-two poems.

Yet *A Boy's Will* has its successes. One must admire the confidence that persuaded Frost to exclude the masterful poems he had already completed in order to arrange his first book to trace a boy's growth from self-centered idealism ("Into My Own") to a mature recognition of love ("A Line-Storm Song") and loss ("Reluctance"). Generally a collection of love lyrics for Elinor, *A Boy's Will* also points to the great themes of fear and uncertainty in the face of nature's nonhuman otherness that would preoccupy Frost for much of his career. "Mowing" may be the best loved of these early poems, with its colloquial language, its graceful command of the sonnet form to show manmade order confronting uncaring nature, and its unromantic insistence that the fact of work is an end in itself, that the lonely laborer need not look for a transcendental message as he lays "the swale in rows" with the same care he would use to compose a poem. "Mowing" is indeed impressive, but "Storm Fear" is the joy of the collection.

In terms of theme and technique, "Storm Fear" offers evidence in Frost's very first book that he was not a writer of gentle nature lyrics no matter what the public wanted to believe. Thematically, the concise description of the isolated man nearly overwhelmed by the beastlike storm foreshadows such later important poems as "Bereft" (*West-Running Brook,* 1928) and "The Most of It" (*A Witness Tree,* 1942). The speaker's strength–"Two and a child"–seems ironic when measured against the inexorably creeping storm. All Frost can rely on is man-made order, the poem itself, momentarily to stay the confusion. Theme merges with technique because just as the speaker's "strength" is less than adequate, so the form of the poem begins to crumble. Frost, of course, confidently controls the dissolution of the form, but he also suggests the inevitable diminishment of human order when the rhymes fall free of traditional rhyme schemes and when the iambic pentameter line breaks down. The line "How the cold creeps as the fire dies at length–," with its spondees and pentameter beat, illustrates the poet-figure's wavering effort to reassert human control; but some lines are as short as "Ah, no!," and the speaker finally wonders whether he will be able to save himself "unaided." Thus "Storm Fear" is also a poem about poetry. Creating art, man stands up to "the universal cataract of

In White

A dented spider like a snow-drop white
On a white Heal-all, holding up a moth
Like a white piece of lifeless satin cloth —
Saw ever curious eye so strange a sight? —
Portent in little, assorted death and blight
Like the ingredients of a witches broth? —
The beady spider, the flower like a froth,
And the moth carried like a paper kite.

What had that flower to do with being white,
The blue Brunella every child's delight?
What brought the Kindred spider to that height?
(Make we no thesis of the miller's plight.)
What but design of darkness and of night?
Design, design! Do I use the word aright?

RF.

A 1912 version of Frost's poem "Design," collected in A Further Range *(by permission of Alfred C. Edwards, trustee and executor for the Estate of Robert Lee Frost; courtesy of the Henry E. Huntington Library and Art Gallery)* death," but all human order is momentary and must be continually affirmed.

With its unusual technique and rejection of romantic notions of nature, "Storm Fear" looks forward to "After Apple-Picking," perhaps Frost's finest poem and a key lyric in his second book, *North of Boston*. The Georgian poets praised *A Boy's Will* because they approved of Frost's emphasis on nature, but it was Pound who brushed aside the lingering echoes of Victorian poeticisms to hear the sounds and cadences of a modern voice. Pleased with Frost's first book, Pound was enthusiastic about the second, writing a shrewd review for *Poetry* (December 1914) and claiming later that he had "hammered" Frost's "stuff" into that influential journal.

Although today *North of Boston* is considered Frost's strongest overall collection, it is the book that puzzled early readers, Ford Madox Hueffer among them. When it appeared in 1914, free verse was in the vanguard of the poetic renaissance. Readers knew that such fine poems as "Home Burial" and "A Servant to Servants" were not composed in traditional forms, but they also recognized that these poems were not as militantly experimental as Pound's. Unprepared for dramatic-dialogue poems structured around what Frost called "sentence sounds," and thus mistaking the poems for free verse, they were unable to assimilate the unusual merger of the regular pentameter line and the irregular rhythms of speech. These poems are not free verse but blank verse, and the technique is Frost's major contribution to American prosody.

Frost was very much aware of what he had accomplished. Now forty years old, the father of a family, and still all but obscure, he sent letter after letter to friends in the United States, defining his technique and urging them to publicize his achievement. He had every right to feel proud. With these poems of alienation and shattered communication, Frost confronted typical modernist concerns. Many readers remember "The Death of the Hired Man," for example, for its poignant portrait of Mary's mercy overwhelming Warren's judgment as she persuades her husband to let the hired man return home, which is memorably described as "Something you somehow haven't to deserve," but more masterful poems in *North of Boston* are "Home Burial," "After Apple-Picking," and "The Wood-Pile."

Although Frost often denied an autobiographical framework for "Home Burial," pointing to the death of his sister-in-law's child as the catalyst, one cannot ignore the more likely connection between this remarkable poem and the death of the Frosts' first son in 1900 at age four. Frost refused to read "Home Burial" in public because the emotion overwhelmed him, and his biographer Lawrance Thompson reports that Elinor could not overcome her grief following the boy's death, declaring that the world was evil. Amy in "Home Burial" makes the same sad statement.

Written in 1912 or 1913, "Home Burial" illustrates the innovative poetry that Frost had completed in time for *A Boy's Will* but withheld because the technique did not complement the lyrics of his first collection. Frost was justifiably proud of his technical virtuosity. Specifically pointing to the lines

"But the child's mound—"

                      "Don't, don't, don't, don't," she cried.

he wrote to John Cournos (27 July 1914):

> I also think well of those four "don'ts" in Home Burial. They would be good in prose and they gain something from the way they are placed in the verse. Then there is the threatening
>
>   "If—you—do!" (Last of Home Burial)
>
> It is that particular kind of imagination that I cultivate rather than the kind that merely sees things, the hearing imagination rather than the seeing imagination. . . .
>
> . . . I should say that they were sufficiently self expressive.

The lines are indeed "sufficiently self expressive," but they baffled Jessie B. Rittenhouse, secretary of the Poetry Society of America, who complained that Frost would be more successful if he exchanged the rigors of poetry for the ease of the short story.

"Home Burial" is, of course, more than dazzling technique. Its sympathetic contrast of opposing ways to grieve, its skill at jerking the reader's sympathy back and forth between husband and wife, and its unblinking understanding that the couple's sex life has also died—the graveyard is "Not so much larger than a bedroom . . ."—indicate that not only a baby but also a home has been irrevocably buried. Alienation is unrelieved in this poem.

A different sort of fear rests at the heart of "After Apple-Picking." More the fear of uncertainty than that of marital dissolution, the poem is one of several in the Frost canon in which the poet ponders what he later named as humanity's greatest terror: that mankind's best effort may not be good enough. Although the reader notes immediately that the first word of the title is "after," he cannot determine for sure what has been concluded: a day, a season, or a lifetime of work. Such ambiguity shapes the poem as Frost gracefully explores ideas of aspiration, completion, bewilderment, questioning, and possible death. Both speaker and reader are aware of the inviting association between apples and humanity's expulsion from Eden, but one of the enduring pleasures of the poem is that neither speaker nor reader is certain how far the association should be pursued. If the relationship is no more than decorative metaphor, then the speaker has successfully concluded a significant task–no matter what it literally is–and may reach for his rest in peace. But he cannot be sure; and thus if the mythological allusions to Eden carry meaning, then the speaker has finished a life's work only to be uncertain about whether finality or rebirth is at stake.

The suggestions of hazy speculation are precisely rendered ("I cannot rub the strangeness from my sight") and are nicely supported by the uncertain iambic-pentameter line that Frost first experimented with in "Storm Fear." As in the earlier poem, the lines in "After Apple-Picking" rhyme without a formal rhyme scheme, and the iambic-pentameter line breaks down as the speaker realizes the precariousness of his predicament. Always a crucial issue with Frost, man's creation of form is necessary but momentary. In the haunting "After Apple-Picking," he unifies technique and theme to illustrate how confusion confronts man despite his very best effort to contain it. *North of Boston* is full of such considerations.

Following the triumph of *North of Boston* and the outbreak of World War I, Frost and his family returned to the United States, arriving on 22 February 1915 to find the American edition of *North of Boston* already published by Henry Holt. With reviews by Pound and Amy Lowell supporting him, he soon was recognized as an acknowledged leader of the new poetry. Within four months Holt had also published *A Boy's Will*, and Frost was named Phi Beta Kappa Poet at Tufts. Within four years he had a third collection published, was elected to the National Institute of Arts and Letters, was named Phi Beta Kappa Poet at Harvard, was hired as a professor by Amherst College, and was awarded the first of his

forty-four honorary degrees, by Amherst. He must have taken special pleasure in accepting invitations and applause from the very editors and peers who had ignored him. But still jealous of recognition given other poets (he called Edgar Lee Masters, for example, "my hated rival"), and distrustful of those who disagreed with him in the slightest way, he carefully molded the mask of the gentle farmer-poet that the public would know him by for the next fifty years. Hiding the man but helping the poet, the mask enabled Frost to use art to order life.

The glare of publicity also persuaded Henry Holt to rush *Mountain Interval* (1916) into print before Frost thought the collection was ready. Always a careful arranger of the poems in his books, Frost was disappointed by the organization of *Mountain Interval*. Yet the collection includes many of his most popular poems, among them "Birches," "The Road Not Taken," and "The Oven Bird." And while the book as a whole is not as fearful as *North of Boston*, it offers the unusual "The Hill Wife" as an account of loneliness and despair. Best of all, *Mountain Interval* contains "An Old Man's Winter Night," a superior poem by any standard and one of the best Frost ever wrote.

Probably begun as early as the winter of 1906-1907, "An Old Man's Winter Night" is, Lawrance Thompson speculates, one of twelve poems in *Mountain Interval* that Frost was working on before the publication of *A Boy's Will*. The creativity of the Derry years sustained him through several collections, and Frost himself recognized the extraordinary achievement of "An Old Man's Winter Night." He wrote to Sidney Cox (circa 7 December 1916) that "An Old Man's Winter Night" is "Probably the best thing in the book . . . ," and he told Harriet Monroe, editor of *Poetry*, that " 'Old Man' is the flower of the lot, isn't it?" (circa 7 January 1917).

Reading "An Old Man's Winter Night," one is bewildered by the public's acceptance of Frost's mask. This poem is no lyric of gentle nature and benevolent tone but a sad, precise accounting of man's unfortunate fate. People age, lose the spark of the creative mind (note the light imagery in the poem), and tumble toward despair. "An Old Man's Winter Night" joins T. S. Eliot's "Gerontion" (1920) as two modern masterpieces that dismiss Robert Browning's Victorian sentiment in "Rabbi Ben Ezra" (1864): "Grow old along with me!/The best is yet to be,/The last of life, for which the first was made."

Frost's old man has no one to grow old for, and he faces only the worst. True to his understanding of nature as implacable, nonhuman otherness, Frost dramatically communicates the man's inner terror by couching it in terms of external threat: "All out-of-doors looked darkly in at him." Pitifully left to his own devices while stumbling through empty rooms, the old man mistakenly fears that the dark night menaces him personally. This poem is a forceful example of confusion overwhelming the human "stay," for nothing the old man tries has any effect whatever. Frost stresses the pervasiveness of the alienation when he suggests parallels between the man and his house: "his snow upon the roof" is his white hair and "His icicles along the wall" his tears. Even the pun on "the pane in/empty rooms" offers no smile. With memory wrecked by the grip of age, and with consciousness dimmed like a fading light, the old man has no option except sleep. Yet as Frost shows in "After Apple-Picking," sleep is not necessarily the rest of renewal. In "An Old Man's Winter Night," imagery and tone suggest that this is the final sleep of life. Frost ends this impressive poem by indirectly including all humanity on the darkening plain: "One aged man–one man–can't keep a house,/A farm, a countryside. . . ."

With this poem as proof that he was at the height of his creative power, Frost began the journeys of what he later called "barding around"– teaching and reading at universities and colleges. The first example of the modern poet in residence, Frost resigned from the Amherst faculty in January 1920 and accepted a post at the University of Michigan in September 1921. From November 1923 to June 1925, he was back at Amherst before returning to Michigan for the academic year 1925-1926. In September 1926 he again returned to Amherst, where he had various appointments to the faculty until June 1938. During these years he also lectured at the Bread Loaf Writers' Conference in Vermont, and from May 1939 to fall 1943 he was on the faculty at Harvard. Resigning at Harvard, he accepted a position at Dartmouth College that continued until 1949, but in October 1949 he went back to the college where the "barding around" all began–Amherst– and was given a life appointment as Simpson Lecturer in Literature.

Frost was rarely a full-time professor at these schools; his duties were primarily to lecture, to meet with students, and to teach a series of classes from time to time. Both college and poet gained from the association, but Frost knew that his first obligation was to write. In 1923 he published *New Hampshire* (which he impishly dedicated to Vermont and Michigan), the collection that brought him the first of his four Pulitzer Prizes. Although the long title poem testifies to his continuing commitment to sentence sounds and blank-verse narratives, it also illustrates a disturbing tendency that would characterize parts of the books that were to follow: a proclivity to use certain poems as soapboxes from which he could comment on everything from government interference to psychoanalysis. These editorial poems are often cute and occasionally clever, but from today's vantage point they seem little more than vehicles for his conservative social and political beliefs, as in the following lines from "New Hampshire": "Lately in converse with a New York alec/ About the new school of the pseudo-phallic." Frost was taking advantage of his hard-won public acclaim to broadcast his private views, but one doubts that the Pulitzer Prize was awarded for such minor efforts.

The Pulitzer committee recognized that the pleasure of *New Hampshire* was not politics but poetry. Full of such superior lyrics as the unusually rhymed "A Star in a Stoneboat," the comically diabolical "Two Witches," and the often-anthologized "Fire and Ice," *New Hampshire* also includes Frost's best-known poem, "Stopping by Woods on a Snowy Evening." The overfamiliarity of this poem does not mean that it is overpraised. Schoolchildren have memorized it and critics have debated it, but to this day "Stopping by Woods on a Snowy Evening" remains as frustratingly ambiguous as it is deceptively simple.

One of the most explicated poems in all American literature, "Stopping by Woods on a Snowy Evening" deserves its place alongside the many novels and stories that ponder the fate of those who dare to plunge beyond the safety of the clearing to the darkness of the woods. Frost knew that the lyric had immortality written all over it. On 2 May 1923 he wrote to Louis Untermeyer that "Stopping by Woods on a Snowy Evening" was his "best bid for remembrance." How right he was. He even embellished the aura surrounding the poem by claiming for years that he wrote it with "one stroke of the pen." Although Lawrance Thompson has shown that Frost's claim is false, the apparent simplicity of the poem and of its composition adds to its fame. The truth is, of course, that "Stopping by Woods on a Snowy Evening" was nearly as difficult to write as it is to interpret, and the interlocking rhyme scheme gave him the most trouble. The first draft (now in the Jones Library in Amherst, Massachusetts) reveals that the beginning of the famous final stanza originally read:

The woods are lovely dark and deep
But I have promises to keep
That bid me give the reins a shake. . . .

Clearly committing Frost to another stanza of interlocking rhymes rather than permitting him to conclude with a flourish, the draft of the last quatrain would have left the poem open-ended. But Frost wanted an ending that was definite in terms of technique yet ambiguous in terms of meaning. Twenty-eight years after writing "Stopping by Woods on a Snowy Evening," he revealed his difficulty to Charles Madison: "I might confess the trade secret that I wrote the third line of the last stanza of Stopping by Woods in such a way as to call for another stanza when I didn't want another stanza and didn't have another stanza in me, but with great presence of mind and a sense of what a good boy I was I instantly struck the line out and made my exit with a repeat line."

The repeat line–"And miles to go before I sleep,/And miles to go before I sleep."–is at the heart of the ambiguity. Those who favor the standard reading of the poem argue that the line stresses the speaker's rejection of his fascination with the dark trees in order to honor his commitment in the lighted village. Those who insist on a more radical interpretation suggest that the dark trees are as unknowable as Melville's ocean and Hawthorne's forest and that the strongest lure in the poem is not to mundane promises but to ultimate concerns–perhaps death itself. "Stopping by Woods on a Snowy Evening" supports both readings, but one might also consider that the greatness of the poem rests in part in its ambiguity and that the ambiguity derives from the speaker's hesitation. Literally, he has not moved at the end of the final stanza, and metaphorically he is frozen with indecision. Stuck in the clearing–a significant location in American literature–between the safety of the village and the invitation of the woods, the traveler is unable to choose. To select the comfort of safety is to deny the freedom of the unknown. Frost knows this truth, as do Cooper and Poe and Hawthorne and Melville and Twain, and thus he writes a poem not in praise

Frost at Pinkerton Academy, 1910 (collection of Mrs. Grace Simonds Pettengill)

of indecisiveness but about the costs of making a choice. Concerned throughout his long career with the "hearing imagination," he offers a subtle hint in the last stanza to which all interpretations should finally return: the soft sounds of the rhyme words suggest hypnotism and reverie. The speaker's end is his beginning, stopped beside the alluring woods on the very darkest evening of the year.

In 1928, five years after *New Hampshire*, Frost made a nostalgic return to England and also published *West-Running Brook*. Although the last two poems in the book, "The Bear" and "The Egg and the Machine," unfortunately look back to the social concerns of "New Hampshire" as well as forward to the politically oriented poems in *A Further Range* (1936), the collection as a whole is a rich display of Frost's considerable skill with the short lyric. No one poem stands out, though the title poem is surely important with its rumination on the "universal cataract of death" and man's obligation to resist the void via the conscious creation of form. Yet the inclusion of such lyrics as "Spring Pools," "On Going Unnoticed," "Bereft," "Tree at My Window," and "Acquainted with the Night" makes *West-Running Brook* an impressive volume indeed.

Most of these poems are darkly disturbing, uncertain of man's importance, unsure of his final strength. If nature feeds on itself, as it unfailingly does in the lovely "Spring Pools," then what chance does humanity have in the face of such force? In the perfectly formed "Spring Pools," with its two six-line stanzas, each composed of one sentence, Frost observes a natural continuity that ironically has loss at the heart of the cycle. Nature and its foliage are "dark," and all the poet can do is acknowledge but not identify the silent power that relies on destruction to create beauty which is itself ephemeral. His warning is sadly inadequate: "Let them think twice before they use their powers/To blot out and drink up and sweep away/. . . ." Not pools but man himself is overwhelmed in the little-known "On Going Unnoticed." In only sixteen lines Frost establishes three separate tones as the individual moves from quizzical contemplation of his place in nature's vastness to pleading and finally to resignation at the recognition that he is insignificant. Nonhuman otherness neither cares nor notices–a modern dilemma for humanity–and Frost knows that it is "As vain to raise a voice as a sigh" in the face of nature's strength. One is back in the world of "Storm Fear," written at about the same time as the first draft of "On Going Unnoticed" (1901-1902). Understating man's triviality, Frost metaphorically reduces the span of life from three score and ten to a single hour: "You linger your little hour and are gone,/And still the woods sweep leafily on,//. . . ." All the poignancy of the predicament is in the simple word "still."

Frost's skill at compressing the human dilemma into a few words is evident throughout the volume. In the sixteen-line "Bereft," for example, he echoes "An Old Man's Winter Night" and makes the terror of nature's storms a metaphor for the disorder of man's fear. Stressing the *un*loveliness of nature, alluding to the evil in Eden by equating the coiling leaves with a striking snake, Frost even hints that the speaker's terror is compounded because he is left with God. References to the Gospel of John, with its emphasis on the "word," suggest not religious comfort but malicious gossip, and by the end of this short, powerful, and disturbing poem the speaker's secret is revealed: he is alone. Even when Frost changes the locale from nature to city, uncertainty rests at the center of the poem. In the famous "Acquainted with the Night," for example, he writes a terzarima sonnet, again to illustrate how outer loneliness is a metaphor for inner despair. The strict form of the lyric testifies to Frost's control of his material, but the speaker has no such solace. Dropping his eyes, standing still, listening on the saddest city street, all he knows is that the interrupted cry from across the way is not to call him "back or say good-by." The surreal atmosphere of "Acquainted with the Night" is unusual in the Frost canon, and the poem is all the more fearful because neither Frost nor the speaker–nor the reader–can identify the cause of the despair. These and other dark lyrics in *West-Running Brook* spoke the lie of Frost's mask in 1928, but they also inadvertently foreshadowed the personal disasters of his most tragic decade.

Private losses undercut public gains in the 1930s. Although Frost won Pulitzer Prizes for *Collected Poems of Robert Frost* (1930) and *A Further Range* (1936), and although he won the Russell Loines Poetry Prize in 1931 and was appointed Charles Eliot Norton Professor at Harvard in 1936, he lost the heart of his family between 1934 and 1940. His daughter Marjorie, a favorite, died horribly of puerperal fever in 1934. Four years later Elinor died of cancer and a heart attack; she lingered conscious and alert for days, but she refused to admit her husband of forty-three years into her bedroom. Finally, his adult son Carol committed suicide in 1940, leaving a family that Frost generously took under his protection.

Even *A Further Range*, one of his strongest and most complex volumes, came under attack by such influential commentators as R. P. Blackmur, Newton Arvin, and Rolfe Humphries. In many ways the negative criticisms were unfair because they took issue with political preferences instead of artistic achievement. An artist has the right to be judged on his best work, and parts of *A Further Range* are proof that Frost was still at the top of his form. Blackmur and others did not see it that way, however, and Frost never again received the near-unanimous critical approval that he had enjoyed since his return from England in 1915. The problem was that he published *A Fur-*

ther Range in the midst of the Great Depression, with fascism about to invade Europe and war about to engulf the world. Stunned by these legitimate signals of disaster, the negative critics rejected what they took to be Frost's casual, conservative politics as expressed in ."A Lone Striker," "Build Soil," "To a Thinker," and the famous "Two Tramps in Mud Time."

In "A Lone Striker," they objected to the suggestion that an individual worker's personal whim is worth more than his commitment to the mill; in "Build Soil," they objected to the suggestion that individual self-reliance is more valuable than social programs; in "To a Thinker," they objected to what they perceived as an attack on President Roosevelt; and in "Two Tramps in Mud Time," they objected to the apparent insensitivity toward men in need of jobs, not realizing that the poem is more about poetry than work. The negative commentators could justifiably have criticized the artistic value of these and other poems, for the witty but often arch tone does not lend itself to writing of the first rank. The poems named are far from Frost's best, but the political climate in 1936 was such that public figures who paraded their conservatism were suspect.

The irony is that *A Further Range* contains some of Frost's finest, most enduring work. One would be hard pressed to compile a list of the essential Frost without considering "Desert Places," "A Leaf-Treader," "Neither Out Far nor In Deep," "Provide, Provide," and most of all "Design." Dark poems all, these short lyrics show Frost confronting what he called the background of "hugeness and confusion shading away . . . into black and utter chaos." Writing poetry permitted him a momentary sense of form; one has to admire his courage and determination not to be beaten down by anyone's death but his own.

Yet one does not turn to these poems for solace. If there is comfort, it is not in the message but in the technique, the art itself. In "Desert Places," for example, "A blanker whiteness of benighted snow" engulfs the universe, the countryside, and the individual himself with the frightening ambiguity that the color white suggests. In "Neither Out Far nor In Deep," which Lionel Trilling called "the most perfect poem of our time," the nursery-rhyme stanzas and rhythms expose the simpleness of humanity that thinks it looks for truth while seeing only emptiness. This desolation and despair are magnified in "Design," surely one of Frost's masterpieces.

Begun in 1912 in an early version called "In White" and originally written to defend Henri Bergson's *Creative Evolution* (1907; English translation, 1911) against the charge of atheism, the poem was revised as "Design" and first published in 1922. Questions about an all-powerful God may have inspired the poem, but no reader of American literature can study "Design" without noting affinities with Poe's *The Narrative of Arthur Gordon Pym* (1838) and Melville's *Moby-Dick* (1851), especially the chapter titled "The Whiteness of the Whale." For white–ambiguous and fearful–dominates the poem. But whereas white in Poe and Melville is associated with alluring mystery and the paradoxical combination of destruction and grandeur, white in "Design" suggests nothingness and the void. The confidence of the first words, "I found," dissolves to the final uncertainty, "If design govern in a thing so small."

The form of the poem is likewise significant, for "Design" is one of the most unusual sonnets in the language. An Italian sonnet with its organization purposely distorted by its theme, "Design" reverses the expected order of octave and sestet. Rather than pose a problem in the octave and answer it in the sestet, as an Italian sonnet traditionally does, thereby indicating the confidence of resolution, "Design" describes an event in the octave and then questions it in the sestet. There is no resolution because none is possible. Apparently insignificant when first examined, the drama of the white spider devouring the white moth on a white flower that should have been blue is finally so horrible that Frost uses only three rhymes, instead of the traditional five, as if he had to consolidate his art to contain his bafflement.

Visions of innocence ("dimpled," "snowdrop"), puns ("right," "appall"), and allusions to *Macbeth* ("witches broth") are all offered as counterweight to the relentless truth of the sonnet, and all fail. For "Design" probes the only two possibilities regarding man's relationship with a deity: either the fatal meeting of the spider and the moth is accidental, and design does not govern in such matters; or the fatal meeting is planned, and design governs all. Both prospects are fraught with terror. If design does govern, then man has no chance in the grip of such meaningless negation; if design does not obtain, then all is mindless accident. The "If" at the end of the poem is not reassuring. All Frost can do is write a tightly organized sonnet and hold on.

He had to hold on in his life, too. In the wake of the personal tragedies of these years, Frost suffered severely from guilt and depression. Some of his adult children accused him of sacrificing family to art, and he felt deeply the disparity between public acclaim and private truth. His daily life disorganized and his future bleak, he finally reasserted the resolution and courage that had seen him through the long, early years of neglect. The person who made the difference was Kathleen Morrison, wife of a Harvard professor and the woman who diplomatically helped him reorder his life. Acknowledging his debt, Frost dedicated *A Witness Tree* to Mrs. Morrison.

The fourth of his collections to win a Pulitzer Prize, *A Witness Tree* is also the last of his totally satisfying volumes. In 1942 he still had twenty years to live and great poems to write, but never again would he collect so many fine poems in one book. The table of contents reads like an honor roll of Frost's most graceful, darkly powerful lyrics: "Beech," "All Revelation," "The Most of It," "November," and "The Rabbit Hunter." The collection also includes "The Gift Outright," which Frost would read two decades later at the inauguration of President Kennedy, as well as two poems that offer contrasting views of love and marriage: the masterful "The Silken Tent" and the disturbing "The Subverted Flower."

A one-sentence sonnet carefully constructed so as not to show its seams, "The Silken Tent" is a love lyric that echoes the gentle homage of similar poems in *A Boy's Will*. It is, however, a much finer achievement than anything in the first book, and it convincingly casts the woman in the metaphor of a tent to stress her freedom within the "countless silken ties of love and thought." The metaphor is so persuasive that the reader becomes caught up in the poet's vision of the woman instead of the woman herself. Such is not the case with the little-known, surprisingly depressing "The Subverted Flower."

Unresolved to this day is the question of when it was written. Thompson reports Frost's claim that a draft of "The Subverted Flower" was completed in time to include the poem in *A Boy's Will* (1913), but no one has found the draft. Frost's memory may have been correct, but the fact remains that the technique of the poem is much closer to his later work. If Frost's claim has merit, then, significantly, he withheld publication of "The Subverted Flower" for thirty years, until after Elinor's death.

One can see why. Apparently autobiographical in nature, "The Subverted Flower" unexpectedly explores a sexual crisis that occurred during Frost's courtship of Elinor. When one recalls the poet's pressure on his future wife to marry before she was graduated from college, one understands the embarrassment this frank poem might have caused Elinor had Frost offered it to the public while she was alive. Their marriage was shaky enough. Perhaps more than any other poem, "The Subverted Flower" can startle the unprepared reader out of his misinformed interpretation of Frost as a benign composer of gentle lyrics. As disturbing as it is revealing, the poem traces the mixture of passion, frigidity, bestiality, and parental inhibition that threatens young love. In seventy-three lines of predominantly iambic trimeter, a rhythm consciously chosen to suggest the gait of running animals, Frost deliberately rhymes every line but one. That line—"If this has come to us"—is the question of the poem, for the embarrassed boy realizes that love has not come to "us." To complete the rhyme would be to complete the affair, but love is impossible when the inhibited girl mistakes the boy's gentle offering as a bestial gesture that might lead him to "pounce to end it all." She, of course, is the animal, with her frigidity and her compliance with her mother's determination to draw her "backward" behind the safe walls of an ironic Eden. Possessing a "too meager heart," the girl demoralizes the boy while denying herself. "The Subverted Flower" is the most unexpected poem in the Frost canon.

With his life apparently back in order, Frost published three more books in the 1940s: *A Masque of Reason* (1945), *A Masque of Mercy* (1947), and *Steeple Bush* (1947). The first two are blank-verse dramatic narratives that probe the question that had intrigued Frost for much of his life: whether man's best effort would be good enough in heaven's sight. More memorably examined in "After Apple-Picking," perhaps, this query provides a general frame for Frost's comic yet serious investigation of Job's suffering in *A Masque of Reason* and Jonah's rebellion in *A Masque of Mercy*. The poems take a playful attitude toward God's lofty opaqueness, and they should be read in context with *A Sermon* (1947), which Frost delivered in the Rockdale Avenue Temple in Cincinnati, Ohio, on 10 October 1946. After listening to Rabbi Victor E. Reichert's prayer based on Psalm 19, Frost took verse 14 and built both the informal sermon and the for-

Frost with Melvin B. Tolson (courtesy of the Tolson family)

mal *A Masque of Mercy* around the plea "may our service ever be acceptable unto Thee." Frost was never sure that it was. While he publicly proclaimed in "The Lesson for Today" (*A Witness Tree*), that he had a "lover's quarrel with the world," he privately knew that his quarrel was primarily with God.

Frost's concern is also evident in *Steeple Bush*. A collection that clearly exposes a marked diminishment of artistic power, *Steeple Bush* is too full of insignificant editorials that lack even the skill and perceptiveness of the politically oriented poems of *A Further Range*. Frost was, after all, seventy-three years old in 1947, and one could expect some undistinguished work. Yet *Steeple Bush* is memorable because it includes "Directive," the last great poem of his career and one of the finest he ever wrote.

Written between 1944 and 1946, "Directive" is as much about poetry as it is about religion, and it caps Frost's long pondering of the relationship between art and faith. Theodore Morrison (Kathleen's husband) reports that the germ of the poem may have been Frost's conversation with Hyde Cox, during which the poet was delighted to learn that Christ spoke in parables not

because they were clear but because the wrong listeners would not be able to understand them. True to his lifelong disparagement of his peers, Frost joked that "Directive" was his "Eliot poem" because it refers to the Holy Grail, but the religious considerations in the poem are serious: "tatters hung on barb and thorn" (Crucifixion) and "Too lofty and original to rage" (God). Frost later explained that "the key word in the whole poem is source–whatever source it is."

His comment suggests an understanding of the human dilemma, that mankind is forever uncertain of its own value. For Frost himself, the source was not faith but art. Morrison quotes the poet: "You can't be saved unless you understand poetry–or you can't be saved unless you have some poetry in you." Frost's sense of the extrareligious meaning of the word "source" is clear, but he also indirectly refers to a comment that he made years before in the essay "Education by Poetry: A Meditative Monologue" (1931) that all thinking except mathematical is metaphorical. Those not at home in metaphor will have little chance with religious parables, great poetry, or life itself.

Writing some of the most distinguished blank verse of his career, Frost begins "Directive" with a line of ten monosyllables and concludes with the word "confusion." His sense that poetry was "a momentary stay against confusion" sustained him through many decades, and it is significant that the last notable poem in his canon explores the notion in a religious context. Having different meanings for different people, the source for Frost was always poetry. And, thus, when he ends "Directive" with "Here are your waters and your watering place./Drink and be whole again beyond confusion," he is talking about himself. Art was his sacrament of communion.

The last fifteen years of his life were a succession of public honors. The Nobel Prize, the award he coveted most, eluded him, but he garnered everything else. *Complete Poems of Robert Frost, 1949* was published in May 1949, and the Limited Editions Club awarded him the Gold Medal as "that American author who is considered to have written the book most closely approaching the stature of a classic." On 24 March 1950, the United States Senate extended felicitations on his birthday. In August 1954 the State Department sent him to Brazil as a delegate to the World Congress of Writers. The state of Vermont even named a mountain after him in May 1955. In May 1957 the State Department sent him to London on a goodwill mission, and a year later he was appointed Consultant in Poetry to the Library of Congress. In September 1960 Congress authorized a Congressional Gold Medal for Frost, and President Kennedy awarded it to him in March 1962.

No other writer in American history had received such official acclaim, and it seems unlikely that any will in the future. Frost achieved the pinnacle when, on 21 January 1961, he participated in the inauguration of President Kennedy and said "The Gift Outright" from memory after his failing eyesight prevented him from reading lines composed especially for the occasion. Perhaps too confident of his relationship with the United States government and suffering the debilitation of advanced age, Frost tarnished his friendship with President Kennedy when he returned from an official mission to the Soviet Union in September 1962. Nearly eighty-nine years old, and within four months of his death, he made thoughtless remarks to reporters about America's liberalism, and he thereby unintentionally misrepresented both the president and Premier Nikita Khrushchev. The president never again spoke to him.

Just before this disappointment, Frost published *In the Clearing,* his last book, in March 1962. Taken as a collection, the book is unsuccessful. No poem is memorable, and the most important one, the long "Kitty Hawk," is significant more for its affirmative evaluation of the affinity between the spiritual and the material than for its art. "The Gift Outright" is included as part of Frost's lines for the Kennedy inauguration, but it had been published earlier in *A Witness Tree.*

When read in the context of the canon, however, *In the Clearing* is in one way a dramatic conclusion to a career. By 1962 Frost had been associated with poems about dark woods for fifty years, and his last volume is no exception. Two short lyrics, "The Draft Horse" and "In Winter in the Woods . . . ," wrap up a theme and a metaphor that had linked him to the great considerations of American literature all his artistic life. In the eerie "The Draft Horse," the speaker untypically crosses the clearing to enter the woods, appropriately described as a "pitch-dark limitless grove." Disaster "deliberately" strikes. The suggestion of what might have happened to the poet-figure in "Stopping by Woods on a Snowy Evening" is uncanny.

More important than "The Draft Horse," by virtue of its placement in the volume, is the otherwise slight "In Winter in the Woods. . . ." Reading Frost's complete poems, one should recall that the first poem in the first book is a dark-woods poem, and that it thus sets up the last poem in the last book. In "Into My Own" (*A Boy's Will*), Frost takes an amused look at the youth who plunges into the dark trees, a metaphor for investigating the self, and who then claims that the adventure merely confirms what he already knows. The speaker in "In Winter in the Woods . . ." is not so serene. A poem of old age with its four o'clock afterglow and "shadowy tracks," the lyric completes the metaphorical cycle begun in "Into My Own," but it completes it with the hallmark of the dark-woods poems: ambiguity. The final words are "another blow," and the reader is never sure whether the speaker has suffered another blow from nature or delivered one instead. Clarity is negated when one leaves the clearing for the trees. Frost always knew that. Yet he also knew that the effort had to be made, again and again and again.

When he died on 29 January 1963, just twenty-four days after winning the Bollingen

Prize for poetry, Frost's popularity had almost obscured his achievement. Adulation of the figure had clouded recognition of the art, and the public was not prepared for the shocking revelations about his life that poured out in quick succession as letters, memoirs, and biographies appeared in the 1960s. Bernard De Voto once rebuked Frost for being a "good poet but a bad man," but that judgment is also too simple. Burdened with more than his share of spite, selfishness, and fear, the poet also had more than his share of courage, tenacity, and genius. In the final analysis, of course, not the poet but the poems matter. Frost had predicted in 1913 that he would "do" something to the current sad state of American literature.

He kept his word.

Letters:

The Letters of Robert Frost to Louis Untermeyer, edited by Louis Untermeyer (New York: Holt, Rinehart & Winston, 1963; London: Cape, 1964).
Invaluable but unindexed source of information about Frost's opinions of poetry and his contemporaries.

Margaret Bartlett Anderson, *Robert Frost and John Bartlett: The Record of a Friendship* (New York: Holt, Rinehart & Winston, 1963).
Interesting account, based on letters, of Frost's long friendship with the Bartlett family to whom he expressed many of his theories of poetry.

Selected Letters of Robert Frost, edited by Lawrance Thompson (New York, Chicago & San Francisco: Holt, Rinehart & Winston, 1964).
The most valuable and comprehensive collection of Frost's letters; thoroughly indexed and annotated.

Family Letters of Robert and Elinor Frost, edited by Arnold Grade (Albany: State University of New York Press, 1972).
Significant collection that is especially important for its account of Frost's relationship with wife and children.

Robert Frost and Sidney Cox: Forty Years of Friendship, edited by William R. Evans (Hanover, N.H. & London: University Press of New England, 1981).

Collects dozens of previously unpublished letters between Frost and one of his most admiring critics.

Interviews:

Interviews with Robert Frost, edited by Edward Connery Lathem (New York, Chicago & San Francisco: Holt, Rinehart & Winston, 1966; London: Cape, 1967).
Significant source of Frost's opinions on poets, poetry, and politics.

Bibliographies:

Donald J. Greiner, "Robert Frost, The Poet as Critic: An Analysis and a Checklist," *South Carolina Review,* 7 (November 1974): 48-60.
Checklist of Frost's uncollected critical essays and remarks.

Joan St. C. Crane, *Robert Frost: A Descriptive Catalogue of Books and Manuscripts in the Clifton Waller Barrett Library University of Virginia* (Charlottesville: University Press of Virginia, 1974).
Comprehensive descriptive bibliography of the premier Frost collection.

Frank and Melissa Lentricchia, *Robert Frost: A Bibliography, 1913-1974* (Metuchen, N.J.: Scarecrow, 1976).
Lists primary and secondary materials, including reviews of Frost's work, scholarly essays, and general articles.

Biographies:

F. D. Reeve, *Robert Frost in Russia* (Boston: Little, Brown, 1964).
Short account of Frost's 1962 visit to the Soviet Union.

Lawrance Thompson, *Robert Frost: The Early Years, 1874-1915* (New York, Chicago & San Francisco: Holt, Rinehart & Winston, 1966); *Robert Frost: The Years of Triumph, 1915-1938* (New York, Chicago & San Francisco: Holt, Rinehart & Winston, 1970); Thompson and R. H. Winnick, *Robert Frost: The Later Years, 1938-1963* (New York: Holt, Rinehart & Winston, 1976); these three volumes abridged by Edward Connery Lathem, with Winnick, as *Robert Frost: A Biography* (New York: Holt, Rinehart & Winston, 1982).
Official, indispensable, but controversial biography of Frost.

Kathleen Morrison, *Robert Frost: A Pictorial Chronicle* (New York: Holt, Rinehart & Winston, 1974).
Informal account of Frost's life by his secretary during his final two decades.

William H. Pritchard, *Frost: A Literary Life Reconsidered* (New York: Oxford University Press, 1984).
Excellent study of Frost's life and work that questions many of the conclusions in Lawrance Thompson's official biography.

Stanley Burnshaw, *Robert Frost Himself* (New York: George Braziller, 1986).
Account of Burnshaw's friendship with Frost that directly challenges Lawrance Thompson's official biography.

References:
Reuben A. Brower, *The Poetry of Robert Frost: Constellations of Intention* (New York: Oxford University Press, 1963).
A thorough analysis of the Frost canon, with judicious comparisons to the work of other poets.

Reginald L. Cook, *The Dimensions of Robert Frost* (New York: Rinehart, 1958).
A discussion of Frost's poetry and poetics supported by the poet's own comments.

James M. Cox, ed., *Robert Frost: A Collection of Critical Essays* (Englewood Cliffs, N.J.: Prentice-Hall, 1962).
Excellent collection of major critical essays on the poet's work.

Philip L. Gerber, *Robert Frost* (New York: Twayne, 1966; revised, 1982).
Reliable introduction to Frost.

Gerber, ed., *Critical Essays on Robert Frost* (Boston: G. K. Hall, 1982).
Major collection of thirty-one essays that span the scope of Frost's entire career.

Donald J. Greiner, *Robert Frost: The Poet and His Critics* (Chicago: American Library Association, 1974).
Analysis of the development of and changes in Frost criticism and of how Frost's poetry has been read in different eras.

Dorothy Judd Hall, *Robert Frost: Contours of Belief* (Athens: Ohio University Press, 1984).
A study of religious themes in Frost's poetry.

John C. Kemp, *Robert Frost and New England: The Poet as Regionalist* (Princeton: Princeton University Press, 1979).
Thoughtful analysis of how Frost consciously used the myth of New England and of how his reliance on it was detrimental to his later work.

Frank Lentricchia, *Robert Frost: Modern Poetics and the Landscapes of Self* (Durham: Duke University Press, 1975).
An invigorating study that uses modern philosophy and contemporary critical theory to define Frost as a modernist.

John F. Lynen, *The Pastoral Art of Robert Frost* (New Haven: Yale University Press, 1960).
A convincing argument for the importance of the entire pastoral tradition in poetry when evaluating Frost's symbols and point of view.

George W. Nitchie, *Human Values in the Poetry of Robert Frost: A Study of a Poet's Convictions* (Durham: Duke University Press, 1960).
A serious inquiry into the limitations of Frost's art that finally deny him the stature of major poet.

Richard Poirier, *Robert Frost: The Work of Knowing* (New York: Oxford University Press, 1977).
A persuasive defense of Frost as a major poet that combines close readings of the poems and analyses of the poet's affiliations with William James, George Santayana, and Ralph Waldo Emerson.

Radcliffe Squires, *Major Themes of Robert Frost* (Ann Arbor: University of Michigan Press, 1963).
Careful readings of the poems to identify Frost's primary themes.

Jac L. Tharpe, ed., *Frost Centennial Essays*, 3 volumes (Jackson: University Press of Mississippi, 1974, 1976, 1978).
The most comprehensive collection of new essays on Frost.

Lawrance Thompson, *Fire and Ice: The Art and Thought of Robert Frost* (New York: Holt, 1942).
> Early critical study of Frost's technique by the scholar who became the poet's official biographer.

Linda W. Wagner, ed., *Robert Frost: The Critical Reception* (New York: Burt Franklin, 1977).
> Comprehensive anthology of reviews of Frost's major books.

Earl J. Wilcox, ed., *Robert Frost: The Man and the Poet* (Rock Hill, S.C.: Winthrop College, 1981).
> A collection of new essays by major Frost critics.

Papers:
Significant collections of Robert Frost's papers are in the libraries of the University of Virginia, Amherst College, and Dartmouth College; and the Huntington Library in San Marino, California.

Ernest Hemingway

This entry was updated by James Nagel (Northeastern University) from his entry in
DLB 9, American Novelists, 1910-1945, Part 2.

Places	Oak Park, Ill. Key West, Fla. Havana, Cuba	Paris Spain Italy	Africa Walloon Lake, Mich.
Influences and Relationships	Sherwood Anderson F. Scott Fitzgerald Gertrude Stein	James Joyce Ezra Pound John Dos Passos	Mark Twain Stephen Crane Ford Madox Ford
Literary Movements and Forms	Proletarian Literature Imagism Impressionism	Realism Naturalism	Modernism Minimalism
Major Themes	Stoicism and Courage War Man in Nature	Code of Conduct Sexual Love	Death Individualism
Cultural and Artistic Influences	Existentialism Modern Painting	The "Lost Generation" Sport	Bullfighting Hunting and Fishing
Social and Economic Influences	World War I World War II	Spanish Civil War The Depression	Expatriation

See also the Hemingway entries in DLB 4, American Writers in Paris, 1920-1939; DLB Yearbook 1981; DLB Yearbook 1987; *and* DLB: Documentary Series 1.

BIRTH: Oak Park, Illinois, 21 July 1899, to Clarence Edmonds and Grace Hall Hemingway.

MARRIAGES: 3 September 1921 to Hadley Richardson (divorced); child: John Hadley Nicanor. 10 May 1927 to Pauline Pfeiffer (divorced); children: Patrick, Gregory Hancock. 21 November 1940 to Martha Gellhorn (divorced). 14 March 1946 to Mary Welsh.

AWARDS: Pulitzer Prize for *The Old Man and the Sea*, 1953; American Academy of Arts and Letters Award of Merit, 1954; Nobel Prize, 1954.

DEATH: Ketchum, Idaho, 2 July 1961.

SELECTED BOOKS: *Three Stories & Ten Poems* (Paris: Contact Editions, 1923; Bloomfield Hills, Mich.: Bruccoli Clark, 1977);
in our time (Paris: Three Mountains Press, 1924; Bloomfield Hills, Mich.: Bruccoli Clark, 1977);
In Our Time (New York: Boni & Liveright, 1925; London: Cape, 1926; revised edition, New York: Scribners, 1930);
The Torrents of Spring (New York: Scribners, 1926; Paris: Crosby Continental Editions, 1932; London: Cape, 1933);
The Sun Also Rises (New York: Scribners, 1926); republished as *Fiesta* (London: Cape, 1927);
Men Without Women (New York: Scribners, 1927; London: Cape, 1928);
A Farewell to Arms (New York: Scribners, 1929; London: Cape, 1929);
Death in the Afternoon (New York & London: Scribners, 1932; London: Cape, 1932);
Winner Take Nothing (New York & London: Scribners, 1933; London: Cape, 1934);
Green Hills of Africa (New York & London: Scribners, 1935; London: Cape, 1936);
To Have and Have Not (New York: Scribners, 1937; London: Cape, 1937);
The Spanish Earth (Cleveland: J. B. Savage, 1938);
The Fifth Column and the First Forty-nine Stories (New York: Scribners, 1938; London: Cape, 1939);
For Whom the Bell Tolls (New York: Scribners, 1940; London: Cape, 1941);

Ernest Hemingway

Across the River and Into the Trees (New York: Scribners, 1950; London: Cape, 1950);
The Old Man and the Sea (New York: Scribners, 1952; London: Cape, 1952);
Hemingway: The Wild Years, edited by Gene Z. Hanrahan (New York: Dell, 1962);
A Moveable Feast (New York: Scribners, 1964; London: Cape, 1964);
By-Line: Ernest Hemingway, Selected Articles and Dispatches of Four Decades, edited by William White (New York: Scribners, 1967; London: Collins, 1968);
Islands in the Stream (New York: Scribners, 1970; London: Collins, 1970);
Ernest Hemingway, Cub Reporter: Kansas City Star Stories, edited by Matthew J. Bruccoli (Pittsburgh: University of Pittsburgh Press, 1970);
Ernest Hemingway's Apprenticeship: Oak Park, 1916-1917, edited by Bruccoli (Washington, D.C.: Bruccoli Clark/NCR Microcard Editions, 1971);
The Nick Adams Stories (New York: Scribners, 1972);

88 Poems, edited by Nicholas Gerogiannis (New York & London: Harcourt Brace Jovanovich/ Bruccoli Clark, 1979);

The Garden of Eden (New York: Scribners, 1986);

The Complete Short Stories of Ernest Hemingway (New York: Scribners, 1987).

Ernest Hemingway is one of the most celebrated and most controversial of American writers. He is seen variously as a sensitive and dedicated artist and as a hedonistic adventurer, as a literary poseur and as the stylistic genius of the century. His personal life has become so involved with his work that the two are virtually inseparable in scholarly inquiry: critics persist, with some justification, in reading characters in his works as "real" people and in assuming that events and attitudes in the fiction directly correspond with those in Hemingway's personal life. Hemingway was a strong man of definite opinion, who lived a vigorous life devoted to artistic creation and to active participation in the world. He was said to fill a room the moment he walked into it, and in those around him he inspired something close to hero worship. As Carlos Baker has said in *Ernest Hemingway: A Life Story* (1969), the standard biography, at an early age Hemingway developed the "willed determination to be a free soul, untrapped by tradition, living his life in accordance with pragmatic principles." His behavior inspired admiration in some people and astonishment and dismay in others, including his parents, but no matter what his stature as a person, his position as a writer of enormous talent and influence is well established.

Ernest Miller Hemingway was born in Oak Park, Illinois, the second child of Dr. Clarence Hemingway, a general practitioner, and Grace Hall Hemingway, who had once aspired to an operatic career. In his youth his mother cultivated his interest in the arts, particularly in music and painting, and his father developed his natural love of sport and outdoor life. His father was a stern disciplinarian who insisted that his children adhere to Christian principles and decorum, and he demanded that things be done "properly." As a boy Ernest led an active life, participating, without great distinction, in swimming, football, and boxing despite some limitations in coordination and in the sight of his left eye. While still in high school he began writing journalistic pieces and poems for the school newspaper and experimenting with stories. Although writing never came eas-

ily for him, he was apparently deeply interested in it at an early age.

After he graduated from Oak Park High School in 1917, he was given a junior position on the *Kansas City Star*, a leading newspaper of the period. The *Star* had developed a stylebook for its reporters that required the forming of direct, vigorous, declarative sentences, a practice that had a permanent influence on Hemingway's style. This period of his life ended in May 1918 when he volunteered for war duty with the Red Cross ambulance corps and left for service on the Italian front. There, on 8 July, after only a few weeks of service, he was hit by both a mortar and machine-gun fire, treated in a Milan hospital and decorated as one of the first Americans wounded in Italy, and returned home to Oak Park a celebrity in an Italian officer's cape. In the long months of convalescence with his family he turned to writing short stories based on his experiences. At other times he camped and fished in northern Michigan, where his family had a cottage and where he had spent a good portion of his youth.

Eventually, however, Hemingway was forced by his parents to seek remunerative employment. By chance he was offered a position in Toronto in 1920 as companion to a lame boy of eighteen, a situation which led to his introduction to the *Toronto Star*. Although he was not given a job as a reporter, he was allowed to write articles at space rates, and after his marriage in 1921 to Hadley Richardson he was able to arrange a correspondent post with the newspaper, filing stories from Paris and other points in Europe. Paris was a highly artistic and inspiring environment for a beginning writer, for living on the Left Bank were many of the best writers in English, among them James Joyce, Ezra Pound, Gertrude Stein, and Ford Madox Ford.

Since he was writing only occasional pieces for the *Star*, Hemingway had time to devote to his own literary development, and he filled his notebooks with poems and impressionistic vignettes, working always for concentration and sharp, evocative descriptions. Unfortunately for literary historians, most of these early efforts were lost when his valise was stolen from a train compartment, but what remains indicates clearly the development of his basic principles of narration: leaving key elements of plot out of a story but contriving to have them affect the reader nonetheless; developing a plot on two levels simultaneously, one explicit and one implicit; restricting the narrative perspective to objective descriptions and matters of fact that a sensitive reader could use to infer the psychological conflicts at the heart of the story. In these years Hemingway had difficulties in getting his fiction published, but he had early success with "My Old Man," a story heavily influenced by Sherwood Anderson's work, and with "Out of Season" and "Up in Michigan," stories more uniquely his own. These stories appeared along with a selection of his poetry in *Three Stories & Ten Poems*, published by Robert McAlmon's Contact Publishing Company in Paris in 1923, in an edition of 300 copies. In the following year William Bird's Three Mountains Press published *in our time* in Paris in a limited edition of only 170 copies. The volume is made up of eighteen brief, impressionistic prose vignettes that vividly portray dramatic episodes. In 1925 this volume was enlarged and was published in New York by Boni & Liveright as *In Our Time*, which contained not only the brief sketches of the earlier volume but fifteen of Hemingway's finest stories, including "Indian Camp," "Soldier's Home," and "Big Two-Hearted River."

In 1926 Scribners published Hemingway's *The Torrents of Spring*, a parody of Sherwood Anderson's *Dark Laughter*. There is reason to believe that he used this satirical novel to break his contract with Boni & Liveright, who also published the better-known Anderson, to clear the way for a new contractual agreement with Scribners. In any event Boni & Liveright refused the novel, and Hemingway published it with Scribners, a relationship he maintained to the end of his life.

By 1926 Hemingway had been praised by such illustrious literary figures as F. Scott Fitzgerald, Gertrude Stein, and Sherwood Anderson. He was regarded as a young author with a stirring vitality and a unique style, a promising writer from whom more would be heard. With the publication in October of that year of *The Sun Also Rises*, a novel based on his years in Paris and Spain after the war, the period of apprenticeship closed, and Hemingway emerged from it an established writer of international acclaim whose first major effort equaled or eclipsed anything written by his mentors. The publication of his short stories in *Men Without Women* (1927) added to his growing reputation. But his professional success coincided with familial turmoil; in the fall of 1926 Hemingway had left Hadley Hemingway and their son Bumby, born in 1923, for Pauline Pfeiffer, a woman he had come to know in Paris.

They decided to leave Europe, eventually settling in Key West, Florida, in the fall of 1928. Thus began a peripatetic domestic existence for Hemingway that was eventually to involve Montana, Idaho, Cuba, Africa, Spain, Italy, and various other points around the world. The year 1928 brought near-tragedy and death: in June, Pauline Hemingway, small of stature, gave birth to a son, Patrick, by a traumatic cesarean section; in December Dr. Hemingway, suffering from diabetes and related complications, committed suicide with a revolver. The incident of Patrick's birth Hemingway re-created, with a tragic conclusion, in *A Farewell to Arms* (1929), his first genuine commercial success, selling 80,000 copies within four months of publication. This novel treated the experiences of Frederic Henry on the Italian front in the First World War and his eventual desertion to Switzerland with Catherine Barkley, only to have Catherine die in childbirth. In 1931 the last of Hemingway's children was born, his third son, Gregory, again by cesarean section.

The 1930s were a decade of personal adventure, and Hemingway hunted in the American West and in Africa, fished the Gulf Stream of Cuba and Florida, and covered the Spanish civil war as a correspondent. He wrote an extended essay on bullfighting, *Death in the Afternoon* (1932), which is still considered a valuable treatment of its subject. A collection of stories, *Winner Take Nothing*, appeared in 1933. *Green Hills of Africa*, an account of adventures on safari, was published in 1935 and was followed, in 1937, by *To Have and Have Not*, one of the weakest of Hemingway's novels. But his most notable involvement during this period was his work on behalf of the Loyalist cause in Spain. Ostensibly a reporter covering the war for the North American Newspaper Alliance, in 1937-1938 Hemingway helped raise money for medical supplies and ambulances by speaking in the United States against the spread of fascism in Europe, and he helped with the production of *The Spanish Earth*, a pro-Loyalist film designed to enlist foreign aid for their cause. Out of this experience as well he wrote a play, *The Fifth Column*, which was published in 1938 along with *The First Forty-nine Stories*. But the most important work to come from his time in Spain was *For Whom the Bell Tolls* (1940), a brilliant novel about Robert Jordan, an American Spanish instructor who fights with the Loyalist forces.

The period before and during World War II brought changes to Hemingway's life. In

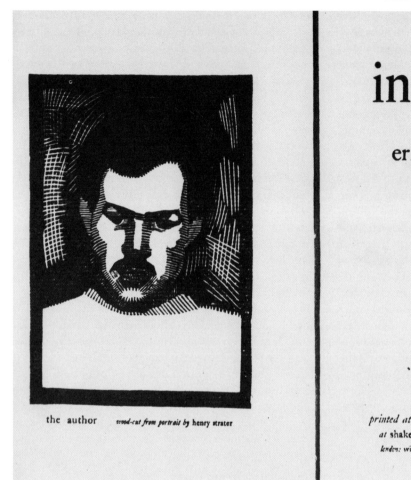

the author   *wood-cut from portrait by henry strater*

in our time

by

ernest hemingway

A GIRL IN CHICAGO: Tell us about
the French women, Hank. What are
they like?
   BILL SMITH: How old are the French
women, Hank?

LEVAVI OCVLOS
MEOS IN MONTES

paris:
printed at the three mountains press *and for sale
at* shakespeare & company, *in the rue de l'odéon;*
london: william jackson, *took's court, cursitor-street, chancery lane.*

1924

Frontispiece and title page for Hemingway's 1924 collection of eighteen prose vignettes

1940 he divorced Pauline Pfeiffer and married Martha Gellhorn, a vibrant and determined reporter with whom he had covered battles in Spain. Together they established their home in the Cuban village of San Francisco de Paula near Havana, where Hemingway was to live most of the rest of his life. With the outbreak of the war in Europe he outfitted his fishing boat *Pilar* as an anti-submarine vessel and for nearly two years searched, unsuccessfully, for German submarines in the Gulf of Mexico, events later given fictional treatment in *Islands in the Stream* (1970), a novel published after his death. In 1944 he went to England as a correspondent for *Collier's*, accompanying Martha Hemingway, who had gone the year before but had returned to be with her husband. Hemingway flew missions with the R.A.F., covered the landing in Normandy, and attached himself to Allied forces in France during the remainder of the war, sometimes serving as scout and interrogator as well as journalist, activities which

led to his decoration with the Bronze Star. This period also saw his gradual estrangement from his wife and his deepening involvement with Mary Welsh, also a journalist covering the war, and after his third divorce they were married in Havana in 1946.

Back in Cuba, Hemingway worked on a novel about a colonel named Richard Cantwell who is involved with a beautiful young woman in Venice just before his death. Entitled *Across the River and Into the Trees*, the book seemed nearly a parody of Hemingway's characteristic style and themes, and it was a disappointment to nearly everyone when it appeared in 1950. He had much better fortune with *The Old Man and the Sea* in 1952, which was not only a commercial success but won the Pulitzer Prize. This honor was followed in 1954 by the award of the Nobel Prize for Literature. Beyond these literary triumphs, Hemingway's adventurous life continued with an African safari with Mary Hemingway in 1953, during which he suffered serious head and abdominal injuries in a plane crash, and with a period in Spain covering the rivalry between two famous matadors, Antonio Ordóñez and Luis Dominguín, the account of which was published as "The Dangerous Summer." After the coming to power of Fidel Castro in Cuba, Hemingway moved his home permanently to Ketchum, Idaho, where he continued work on a series of sketches of life in Paris during the early years of his career, a volume published after his death as *A Moveable Feast* (1964). But age was difficult for him. A lifetime of dangerous physical adventure had taken its toll in numerous injuries, including several concussions, many of them severe. In addition he was suffering from hypertension, mild diabetes, and depression, for which he was given electric shock treatments. He became confused, suspicious, and aggressively suicidal; he agonized that he could not write, and he was convinced that he was being watched by government agents. After his release from the Mayo Clinic in Minnesota, he returned home to Idaho, and on 2 July 1961, in the early morning, he selected a favorite shotgun and committed suicide.

But Hemingway's death did not bring an end to interest in him and his work. Indeed, he is more widely read and taught now than he was at any point in his lifetime. Although he has been most admired for his novels, his other works have received renewed attention, especially his short stories. Hemingway wrote over one hundred short stories in two main periods: 1923-1927, during which he wrote about Nick Adams and other figures in Michigan and Italy in World War I; and 1933-1936, during which he dealt largely with more mature figures in a wider range of settings, including Africa and Florida. A few of his stories–including "The Killers," "The Snows of Kilimanjaro," "A Clean, Well-Lighted Place," and "The Short Happy Life of Francis Macomber"–are as well known as his best novels and are some of the finest stories in English.

A study of the short stories reveals a good deal about Hemingway's characteristic themes and artistic devices. They depict a harsh and disillusioning world in which traditional values have become irreconcilable with a new view of life. Casting aside social conventions, the characters find little to sustain them apart from "codes" of conduct surrounding specialized conditions (such as bullfighting, hunting, or fishing). Applied to everyday life, these codes provide dignity and meaning in an otherwise absurd and pointless world in

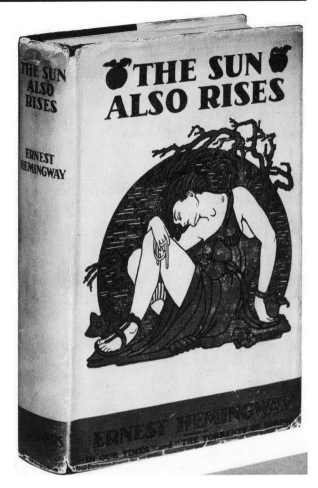

Dust jacket for Hemingway's 1926 novel

which age, war, or psychological despair ensure a tragic destiny. Crucial to conveying these ideas were Hemingway's methods, especially his sparse and economical style, which captured precisely the right tone for the portrayal of modern life. Hemingway abandoned the traditional expository mode of developing a story in favor of restricted narrative methods that allowed characters to reveal themselves through their dialogue and actions, and meanings to develop from situations without authorial comment. One of his key theories was the "iceberg" principle, according to which only a fraction of the meaning of a scene shows on the surface; the rest must be inferred from the individual details. A similar device was synecdoche, the traditional rhetorical device in which a part of something comes to signify the whole, as a few characters might come to stand for an entire generation. These devices, and the use of multiple narrators in some of the stories, help to portray a world in which there are few certainties, in which the comforts of traditional assumptions have been stripped away, and in which violence, conflict, and death are inescapable realities.

Hemingway's fiction began in a sense with the publication of a series of vignettes in *in our time* (1924), brief impressionistic episodes that capture in fiction what the imagists put into their abbreviated poems, emotional and intellectual constructs captured in instants of time. In each paragraph Hemingway presented the details and events that communicated what it was like to be part of a civilian retreat in war, to shoot German soldiers coming over a wall, or to observe the execution of political prisoners by a firing squad. In these episodes several important characters are introduced, including a "Nick," who soon becomes a continuing character known as Nick Adams. And several incidents that recur in later works are here suggested, among them a prayer by an insincere but frightened Christian, a bullfighter facing a bull readying for a charge and later being killed himself, and a man being hanged. All are rendered with acute sensory detail, understatement, brevity, and emotional detachment, an impressionistic methodology that was to form the core of Hemingway's fiction.

The Nick Adams stories illustrate these points. As Philip Young established in an excellent early study, *Ernest Hemingway* (1952), these stories are central to Hemingway's fiction in that the adventures of Nick provide a psychological history for nearly all of Hemingway's protagonists, a record of trauma and disillusionment that leaves Nick disturbed at an early age, unable to sleep at night, desperately clinging to anything that can help him retain his tenuous grasp on sanity. As a young boy, in "Indian Camp" (*In Our Time*, 1925), Nick is present while his father, Dr. Adams, performs a cesarean section on an Indian woman with a jackknife and no anesthetic. After the operation Nick sees that her husband has committed suicide by slitting his throat. Nick's feelings are never directly expressed in this story, but his emotions of shock and tragic loss are evoked by the concluding image which shows Nick trailing his hand in the water as his father rows the boat home. Life holds out many such experiences for Nick. In "The Battler" (*In Our Time*) he meets a boxer who has suffered so many concussions that he has lost his mind, and in "The Killers" (*Men Without Women*, 1927) he sees another boxer who knows he is going to be killed by gangsters but resigns himself to his fate. Wounded on the Italian front in World War I,

Nick is shocked by his war experiences, and "In Another Country" (*Men Without Women*) and "A Way You'll Never Be" (*Winner Take Nothing*, 1933) show him, disillusioned and cynical, having a difficult time retaining his sanity. In Hemingway's best Nick Adams story, "Big Two-Hearted River" (*In Our Time*), Nick is back from the war and on a fishing trip in northern Michigan trying to find something to sustain him emotionally. The details of building a proper camp, catching grasshoppers, and landing trout thus become psychological indicators of how well Nick is coping with life. "Fathers and Sons" (*Winner Take Nothing*) shows Nick years later with a son of his own still searching for ways of dealing with the trauma of his youth, especially his father's suicide. Sensitive, strong, but always vulnerable to the tragedies of life, Nick is in many ways the most important character in Hemingway's fiction in that what happens to him can be used as an indicator of the backgrounds of the other characters. In effect, the Nick Adams stories are indirect narratives in which adventure is used to portray the psychological consequences of violent and disturbing events.

Hemingway's stories involving characters other than Nick Adams develop similar themes. In one of the earliest stories, "Up in Michigan" (*Three Stories & Ten Poems*, 1923), written in Paris in 1921, the naive Liz Coates, infatuated with Jim Gilmore, a blacksmith, experiences disillusionment about sexual relations. After they make love, Jim falls asleep in a drunken stupor, showing Liz none of the affection and tenderness for which she had hoped. Written in the repetitious style of Gertrude Stein to indicate the simplicity of the characters' thoughts, the story portrays the harsh transition from youthful romanticism to a realistic view of modern life. "A Day's Wait" (*Winner Take Nothing*) reveals the resignation and shock of a young boy's erroneous belief that he is dying of fever, whereas "Soldier's Home" (*In Our Time*) is another story about the emotional effects of war. Harold Krebs returns from war having lost all of his faith in religion and in bourgeois American ideals. When his parents insist that he pray and look for a respectable job, he finds that he cannot. "Fifty Grand" (*Men Without Women*) exemplifies the continuing motif that everyone must take a beating in life. In a complex double cross, a boxer named Jack must abide a low blow without falling in order to lose a fight and win the money his family needs. A similar situation occurs in "The Undefeated" (*Men Without Women*), a

Hadley and Ernest Hemingway at Chamby, Switzerland

bullfighting story that illustrates in another setting the pain of what must be endured.

These basic ideas are further developed in a score of similar stories, three of which deserve special comment. In "The Short Happy Life of Francis Macomber" (*The Fifth Column and the First Forty-nine Stories*, 1938) a weak American husband, Macomber, is abused and dominated by his adulterous wife, Margot, who has a brief affair with the guide, Robert Wilson, during their African safari. Macomber disgraced himself by running from a wounded lion, after which his wife seized the advantage to humiliate and torture him by flaunting her affair. Led by Wilson, Macomber conquers his fear while hunting buffalo and makes it clear that he will play a more assertive role in the future. Then, in a richly ambiguous scene, he is killed by his wife as she shoots at a charging buffalo and hits her husband in the head. Here the "code hero" concept is given its most complex treatment, as Macomber is transformed from a weak man to a strong and re-

spected one. Told from the point of view of five narrators, this compelling story is one of Hemingway's finest in both theme and method. "The Snows of Kilimanjaro" (*The Fifth Column and the First Forty-nine Stories*), another excellent African story, portrays a writer dying of gangrene after a routine injury. As he passes the hours before his death, he laments having betrayed his talent to marry a rich but frivolous woman who has helped him to waste his time and energy on pointless adventures. The drama of the story is characteristically understated, having more to do with Harry's review of his life and his uneasy marriage than with physical events. When he dies there is a scene of postmortem narration as he describes being flown over the mountain in a plane. "A Clean, Well-Lighted Place" (*Winner Take Nothing*), perhaps Hemingway's finest story, is simple in plot but complex in its philosophical themes. An old man, living alone and without friends, derives satisfaction from having a drink each evening in a clean café. Two waiters attend him, a young, married waiter eager to close the bar and go home and an older waiter who is himself isolated and who sympathizes with the old man. After work the old waiter goes to a bodega where he prays "Hail nothing full of nothing," a prayer of existential emptiness and despair, of *nada*. As have so many other characters in the short stories, the old waiter has lost his faith in conventional values and now feels an unfathomable emptiness and pointlessness in his life, one expressed in his insomnia and desperate need for "A Clean, Well-Lighted Place." The stories thus trace characters from childhood to old age while developing themes of disillusionment, anguish, vulnerability, and ultimate defeat, themes that Hemingway helped forge into a central definition of "modernist" life.

But Hemingway's reputation rests primarily on his major novels, which are regarded by many scholars as among the finest in American literature. The first of these, *The Sun Also Rises*, caused a sensation when it appeared in 1926. It quickly became a celebrated statement of the views of the "lost generation," views that combined disillusionment with traditional values, brought on in part by World War I, with a new hedonistic attitude, exemplified by the female protagonist, Lady Brett Ashley. It was the first major depiction of the lives of American expatriates in Paris in the 1920s, and American adolescents responded to it immediately, imitating its dialogue and tone of hopeless love; young women cut their hair and adopted clothing inspired by Brett; young men came to think of themselves as being part of the aftermath of the war, even if they were too young to have participated in it.

The novel is narrated in a spare and idiomatic style by Jake Barnes, an American correspondent in Paris who was severely wounded in the war and has been left impotent. As he reveals later, he is in love with Brett, and she with him; because their love cannot be consummated, they find it torture to be together. But their love is the most stable relationship in the novel, and in times of trouble they inevitably come to one another for comfort. The early sections of the novel are deceptively celebrative in tone, however, concentrating on the fervor of expatriate life in Paris. Jake tells about Robert Cohn, a young Jewish writer from Princeton who is living with Frances Clyne, a possessive and insecure woman he quickly tires of. When Jake impulsively picks up a prostitute, he reveals to her that he is "sick" and she indicates that she is too; indeed, everyone is "sick." There is truth in her pronouncement, for nearly all of Jake's friends in Paris are seeking desperately for some unattainable happiness or fulfillment: Brett in romantic conquest, Cohn in romantic novels or, later, in his affair with Brett, and others of the group in their frantic celebration. Even the wealthy Greek, Count Mippipopolous, who carries arrow wounds from earlier wars, shares in this apparently joyous revel. The serious underside of this life is revealed largely through Jake's psychological turmoil, a vestige of trauma of the war, that at times nearly incapacitates him. He suffers from insomnia; when his "head starts to work" he is emotionally unstable, crying in the night and remembering how he met Brett in England when she was a nurse. Brett, too, has her troubles: her fiancé died of dysentery during the war; she made a bad marriage to acquire a title; now she plans to marry Mike Campbell, a Scottish bankrupt who cannot control his drinking and has no hopes for the future.

The second section of the novel is more dramatic and more positive. The central action covers the journey of Jake and his friends to Spain for the fiesta and bullfighting; on the way Jake and Bill Gorton stop for a few days in Basque country to fish for trout. Here, in a quiet, natural setting, Bill and Jake relax and fish and engage in humorous banter touching on all the serious themes of the novel: religion, expatriation, sex, love, and the aftermath of the war. They are joined in their fishing by a generous and sensitive Englishman named Harris who, along with Bill, is one of the few positive portraits in the novel. Leaving the Basque region, Jake and Bill go on to Pamplona for the running of the bulls and the fiesta, during which the principal drama is the courtship of Brett. Before the fiesta Brett had run off to San Sebastián with Robert Cohn for a romantic weekend. Now Cohn feels a proprietary interest in her despite her engagement to Mike Campbell and her growing attraction for Pedro Romero, a young bullfighter. Jake, an aficionado, a person who loves and truly understands bullfighting and its ritual, explains the proceedings to Brett and the others. However, he loses the respect of Montoya, another aficionado, when he violates the code by introducing Brett to Pedro. The competition for Brett finally erupts into a fight, with Robert Cohn knocking down Jake and Mike and then beating Pedro badly without being able to subdue him. Despite his injuries Pedro fights the bulls heroically the next day and then runs off with Brett. The fun and adventure of the fiesta has, by its conclusion, become grimly unromantic.

The final section of the novel is very brief and deals with the denouement of the fiesta. As the group disperses, Jake goes to San Sebastián to recover. There he gets a telegram from Brett in Madrid. She has left Pedro and needs Jake's help. He arrives after an all-night train ride to discover that Brett left Pedro out of conscience, not wanting to ruin him. The dialogue of this section is especially memorable, as when Brett says to Jake: "You know it makes one feel rather good deciding not to be a bitch." "Yes." "It's sort of what we have instead of God." Jake and Brett then drive off in a taxi dreaming about the life they might have had together: "Yes," Jake says. "Isn't it pretty to think so?"

The novel ends where it began, with Brett and Jake trapped in a hopeless love for each other. None of the major problems have been resolved, none of the characters have achieved any sort of lasting fulfillment: they are truly of the "lost generation." Hemingway prefaced his novel with two quotations: "You are all a lost generation," attributed to Gertrude Stein, and a passage from Ecclesiastes that begins, "one generation passeth away, and another generation cometh; but the earth abideth forever. . . ." Stein's remark points to the disillusionment and emptiness of the novel and to the existential notion that life is fundamentally pointless and absurd, ideas well developed by the events of the novel. The biblical passage has a much more subtle relationship to the novel in its promise of natural continuity and renewal, of a cycle of fortunes from conclusions to beginnings once again. Aside from the brief fishing trip, the vulnerable nobility of Pedro, the love between Brett and Jake, there is little optimism, but there is the suggestion that if the lives of this generation have been ruined by events beyond their control, there will nevertheless be another generation that may yet find meaning in their lives.

These themes owe their intensity to other factors in the novel, especially to Jake's understated yet effective narration. He is on the outside of the world he portrays, unable to participate fully in it, and yet he is an informed and perceptive recorder of its frenetic drama. Like Nick Adams, he knows the proper codes of behavior, and he judges harshly those, like Robert Cohn, who do not. He has been physically and psychologically wounded in the war in ways that have irrevocably changed his life, but he is still a sensitive and prescient human being who matters enormously. Much of the skill of the novel is in its portraying so sympathetically the lives of a "lost" group of people who were intelligent and sentient and yet leading hopeless lives, who were in some way the victims of historical tragedies of epic force. In this sense the characters of *The Sun Also Rises* epitomize a generation by portraying the anguish of the Western world over the European war, over the shattered illusion of peaceful order that had been irrevocably lost.

Hemingway's second major novel, *A Farewell to Arms*, is often regarded as his best artistic achievement, a nearly perfect blend of subject and method. It is a story of love and war set in Italy from 1915 to 1917 and covering the life of Frederic Henry, an American serving in the Italian army who falls in love with Catherine Barkley, an English V.A.D. in an Italian hospital. As the novel opens, Frederic, a surgeon named Rinaldi, and their unit are stationed in Gorizia near the Austrian front. They spend much of their time drinking and visiting the bawdy house for officers, much to the displeasure of the priest, who counsels them to respect traditional spiritual values and simple domestic life. This position makes the priest an easy target for the jests of the men. Rinaldi introduces Frederic to Catherine Barkley, a beautiful woman still grieving over the death of her fiancé the year before. In her desperation she imagines that he has come back to

her in the form of Frederic, who cynically cooperates in the sham in hope of sexual conquest. With this awkward beginning the early stages of their romance are tinged with an irony and deceit that mocks the norms of traditional love stories. As the fighting resumes, Henry is called to the front to evacuate the wounded only to be injured himself when his dugout is hit by a trench mortar shell, fracturing his skull and lacerating his right knee and foot. After preliminary treatment he is transported to a hospital in Milan where he is reunited with Catherine.

Frederic now discovers that he genuinely loves her, and, after major surgery on his knee, they begin an idyllic affair that lasts throughout the summer. He suggests that they marry, but Catherine is concerned that if they do so she will be sent back to England and away from him. In the early autumn Frederic is ordered to the front just as Catherine reveals that she has become pregnant. Back with his unit, he discovers that the men have become cynical and bitter about the war. The priest, on the other hand, has grown in confidence. Rinaldi complains that Frederic now acts like a married man. For his part, Frederic has grown suspicious of noble rhetoric and talk of heroism and begins to see the war as the result of political incompetence and poor leadership on both sides. As he reaches the front the Austrians attack, and, after some ineffectual skirmishing, the Italian army begins a disorganized and confused retreat from Caporetto, the central event of the novel.

The main highways are clogged with civilians and endless columns of soldiers, so Frederic leads his ambulance unit along rural roads where they find food in an abandoned farmhouse. His group is joined by two retreating soldiers and two women who are fearful for their safety. As one of the cars becomes mired in the muddy road, the soldiers flee against Frederic's orders, and he shoots the sergeant, missing the other man. After one of his ambulance drivers is shot by a sniper and another runs away, Frederic is left with only Piani as a companion on the retreat, and he comes to resent the incompetence of the Italian army and to feel that the Italians are more of a threat to him than the Germans and Austrians. This feeling is borne out as he attempts to cross a bridge over the Tagliamento River, at which point the Italian guards are shooting officers and anyone in an Italian uniform who speaks with an accent. Since he is vulnerable on both counts, Frederic dives into the river and

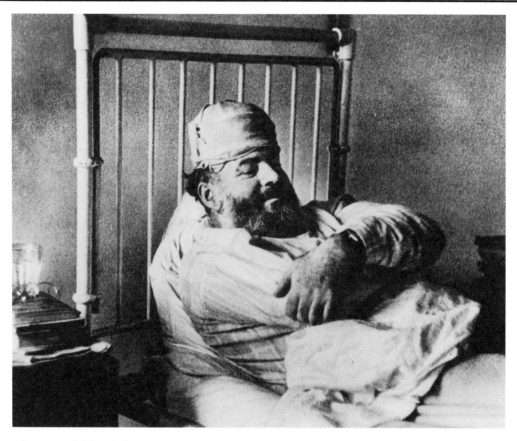

Hemingway in an English hospital recuperating from a 1940 car crash. The accident occurred in London during a blackout.

floats downstream protected by a log. Eventually he makes his way on board a freight train and back to Milan. On the way he has forsaken the war and made his "separate peace," a common theme in Hemingway's works, and now struggles only to maintain his sanity and to get back to Catherine.

In Milan Frederic learns that Catherine has been moved to Stresa, and dressed in civilian clothes, he follows her there. Catherine's closest friend, Helen Ferguson, expresses her dismay at Catherine's pregnancy, but the two lovers join in a warm reunion. Frederic has a billiard game with Count Greffi in the hotel, and then Frederic and Catherine escape into Switzerland by rowing up the lake during the night. Here they enjoy a peaceful autumn in a chalet near Montreux awaiting the birth of their child, moving to Lausanne to a better hospital as the time for delivery draws near. Catherine, who has been warned that she is dangerously narrow in the hips, has difficulties giving birth, and the surgeon delivers a stillborn child by cesarean section. Catherine begins to hemorrhage internally and quickly dies. The novel

ends with Frederic leaving the hospital and walking back to the hotel in the rain.

The first thing that must be established about these events is that they do not grow directly out of Hemingway's personal experience. There are some parallels: Hemingway served in the ambulance corps, was wounded in the knee, recovered in a hospital in Milan, and had a flirtation, probably not an affair, with a nurse. But much is different, as Michael S. Reynolds has pointed out in a remarkably fine study, *Hemingway's First War* (1976). Frederic Henry serves in the Italian army for two years (1915-1917), leaving the military after the disastrous retreat from Caporetto. Hemingway did not arrive in Italy to work for the Red Cross ambulance corps until the summer of 1918. When he wrote the novel he had never seen the Tagliamento River nor the Venetian plain where much of the action takes place, nor had he been to many of the other locations of the novel. He had researched books and newspapers to get his details right and then rendered Frederic's experiences with such impressionistic immediacy and psychological veracity that they radiate intense realism, the mark of a truly great writer.

The central artistic fact about these events is that they are told from a first-person, retrospective point of view: Frederic Henry recites this narrative some time after the final events have taken place. Catherine and their child are dead now; he has become disillusioned with war and cynical about traditional values but feels the need to review the most dramatic period of his life. He not only recaptures the bare events but imposes upon them his subsequent insights, that, for example, "The world breaks every one and afterward many are strong at the broken places." Reviewing this developing tragedy, Frederic is now able to remember early warnings of impending disaster, from Catherine's narrowness of the hips, to her seeing everyone dead in the rain, to the dead flowers he sees before her operation. In a larger sense Catherine's death and his loss are the personal manifestation of the destruction and despair pervading Europe and America during and after the war. Frederic's loss and emptiness are representative of emotions widely felt without specific justification. This emotional condition is the genesis of the lost generation: the inception of their psychological trauma, the beginning of their disillusionment and cynicism, the end of their faith in religion and convention as guides to fulfillment.

Frederic Henry finds it impossible to adhere to traditional values under wartime conditions, but he finds strength and meaning in love and personal relationships, in a secularization of the very things the ineffectual priest had advocated at the beginning. Ultimately the greatest wisdom comes from simplicity, from Catherine's confidence in their self-justifying devotion, Rinaldi's commitment to being a good surgeon, the priest's regard for his family and agrarian values. These are the things that truly matter, but even these are vulnerable and subject to ultimate defeat. Frederic shares much with Brett and Jake Barnes, who also lose everything in the war, and even more with Nick Adams, whose insomnia, separate peace, and mental instability duplicate Frederic Henry's condition.

To Have and Have Not is Hemingway's most inventive and experimental novel and, at the same time, one of his least successful. In this book Hemingway attempted more with narrative methodology than he had previously and revealed more social awareness than had any of his previous efforts. One reason that the book contains cer-

tain incongruities is that it began as two separate short stories about the central character, Harry Morgan, an ex-policeman from Miami who runs a charter boat in Florida and Cuba during the Depression. The two stories were well received, and Hemingway decided to expand the stories into a novel contrasting the "haves" and the "have nots" in Havana and Key West. He added one more incident involving Harry and a series of other episodes and sketches which establish contrasts in economic and social status, in personal integrity, and in familial contentment. The most dramatic device of the novel is its multiple narrative perspectives which give the reader indications of how various characters view the central action and emphasize how little any one perspective reveals of the full complexity of the events. The cause of Harry Morgan's death, for example, is never understood by any of the other characters in the novel, nor can any of them be certain that his friend Albert Tracy is actually dead. This ironic limitation of knowledge helps create a narrative of considerable suspense and emotional intensity.

The story of Harry Morgan is told in three episodes. The first introduces him as a tough but resourceful character struggling to eke out a living by using his boat for a fishing charter. Against a violent background of competing Cuban revolutionary factions, he becomes impoverished when a wealthy client leaves the country without paying him. Desperate for money, he agrees to a dangerous scheme to land Chinese refugees on the Florida coast. Disgusted with the treachery of the operation, Harry kills the organizer of the smuggling racket and lands the refugees back in Cuba. This episode is followed by an equally violent rum-running story in which Harry and his companion, Wesley, are both wounded, Harry eventually losing his arm. They are spotted by a government official, and Harry's boat is taken from him. The final episode has him involved in transporting Cuban revolutionaries from Florida to Cuba after they have robbed a bank. Certain they mean to kill him, Harry has a gun battle with them in which he is fatally wounded. He dies in a hospital, leaving behind his wife and three daughters. Throughout, he is portrayed as a resourceful individualist with a heroic capacity for stoic endurance, courage, and sacrifice, a portrait of the American proletarian hero who is quick with his fists, proud of his sexual abilities, and coldly calculating in moments of danger.

These qualities are forced into bold relief by contrast with the problems of other characters. Chief among these is Richard Gordon, a playboy socialite who writes undistinguished novels and who is a failure as both writer and man. At one point his wife leaves him with a bitter denunciation of his deficiencies. Other characters are also highlighted for their contrasting qualities: a homosexual couple on the verge of severing their relationship, a wealthy grain broker who cannot sleep for worry over his fraudulent income tax returns, a family aboard a yacht whose outstanding characteristic is that they are happy and love each other, and the wife of a Hollywood director who masturbates in the night out of frustration with the men in her life. These and other characters contrast thematically the fate of the doomed Harry Morgan, whose relentless individualism is no match for a hostile social and economic environment. Like many other Hemingway protagonists, including Robert Jordan of *For Whom the Bell Tolls*, Harry has fought bravely but has been defeated.

Hemingway's next novel, *For Whom the Bell Tolls* (1940), is generally regarded as his most ambitious artistic endeavor. It is a complex narrative covering the last week in the life of Robert Jordan, an American who is fighting with the Loyalist forces in the Spanish civil war, in May 1937. He has been ordered to destroy a bridge behind enemy lines to prevent rapid Fascist movement following a Loyalist attack. To assist him Jordan has the aid of a guerrilla band of peasants and gypsies led by Pablo, a formerly brave man who has lost his nerve witnessing atrocities to civilians. Others in the band include Anselmo (an uneducated but sensitive old man), Rafael (an irresponsible man who causes much trouble), and Maria (a beautiful young woman who was raped by Fascist sympathizers and whose head was subsequently shaved to indicate her collaboration with the enemy). When Jordan announces his mission, Pablo opposes it: destroying a bridge in their territory will call attention to their sanctuary and endanger his people. After a bitter dispute the other members of the band side with Jordan. Late that night he is joined in his sleeping robe by Maria, with whom he begins a brief but intensely romantic affair.

As the group prepares to blow up the bridge, a powerful woman, Pilar, tells two dramatic stories, one recounting how Pablo's band executed Fascist sympathizers by throwing them over a cliff and another remembering the struggles of Finito, a small bullfighter who was terrified in the ring. After a survey of the bridge Jordan enlists the aid of El Sordo, another guerrilla leader, who has horses and men to assist in the effort. Meanwhile the group decides to kill Pablo because he might endanger the assault on the bridge. They relent, however, when Pablo says he now favors the effort. Later, Jordan and Maria enjoy another night together. In the morning Jordan shoots an enemy cavalry officer who stumbles onto their camp and then is deeply moved as he reads through the letters the man had in his pocket. At the same time the remainder of the Fascist unit attacks the camp of El Sordo, killing everyone and beheading the leader. Anselmo subsequently discovers the bodies and then reports the equally disquieting news that the Fascists are aware of the forthcoming attack. Jordan sends a messenger, Andres, to headquarters with the information. Meanwhile, Maria tells Jordan the story of the death of her parents and of her own capture and rape.

As the time for the attack on the bridge nears, the action intensifies. Andres is delayed in reporting his information by the incompetence and bureaucracy of the officers in charge, and his message is too late to stop the offensive. Pablo steals the detonators for the dynamite in the night but returns in the morning to rejoin his band. Anselmo is killed as the bridge explodes, and Jordan discovers that Pablo has murdered his own men to get their horses. As they retreat across a road under fire, Jordan's leg is broken when his horse falls under him. Knowing he cannot go with the rest, Jordan says farewell to Maria. They leave him lying beneath a tree to delay the advance of the enemy forces, and it is certain that he will be killed.

But the bare facts of the plot do not do justice to the richness of the novel. The title, taken from a John Donne meditation that begins "No man is an *Iland*," implies a universal context for the tragedy of Robert Jordan: all civilization is diminished by his death as it is, in a larger sense, by the Fascist victory in Spain. Jordan is another of Hemingway's code heroes. He has a realistic skepticism about what the war will actually accomplish, but he dedicates himself fully to the cause nonetheless. In contrast to Frederic Henry, he makes no separate peace. Throughout there is a sense, pervasive in Hemingway's works, that existential man is morally responsible for his judgments; by the nature of his commitments he will ultimately be judged. And Jordan's loyalties are

broadly humanitarian rather than narrowly partisan, for he perceives the Spanish war as merely
the opening battle of a struggle with Fascist
forces that will ultimately lead to a larger war in
Europe. In personal terms Jordan is haunted by
a heritage of violence: he has memories of his
grandfather's distinguished Civil War record and
his father's suicide. His death at the end, rejecting suicide to face the Spanish cavalry, is a moral
victory for him.

　　In terms of technique the novel is nearly perfect. The language suggests that the dialogue
and thought occur in Spanish and are then translated into an English that conveys the idiomatic
grace of the original. There is a distinctly Iberian
style to the book that does much to underscore
the local folkways and superstitions that play an
important role. The characterizations are classic:
the profane Earth Mother in Pilar, the fearful "ruined" leader in Pablo, the courtly elegance of El
Sordo, the beautiful victim in Maria, all complement the varied personalities of the gypsies and
peasants who join them and help to create a secondary level of interest in the Spanish character, defined by both its nobility and violence. The numerous vignettes told by Pilar and Maria and the
others are among the most compelling narratives
in English. In nearly every respect, art and
theme complement each other throughout the
novel with dramatic grace, making it one of the
masterpieces of modern fiction.

　　After the enormous artistic success of *For
Whom the Bell Tolls* Hemingway entered the worst
decade of his career, one that began with World
War II and ended with the publication of an unfortunate and uneven novel, *Across the River and Into
the Trees* (1950). The failure of the novel was ironically not so much a problem of subject as of technique. Always before Hemingway's style and
craftsmanship had shaped indifferent subjects
into compelling and arresting art; in this instance
he chose a dramatic set of circumstances to portray, but his aesthetic sensibility, for the second
time in his life, failed him.

　　The basic situation could have made for an
excellent novel. An aging, fifty-one-year-old
American army colonel, Richard Cantwell, leaves
his Italian headquarters in Trieste to drive to Venice to spend the weekend with a beautiful, young
countess named Renata and to enjoy a morning
of duck shooting before returning to duty.
Cantwell has a serious heart condition that he
knows will soon end his life, and he thinks often
of death: of the deaths of his friends in Italy in

*Hemingway, March 1954, displaying hand injuries sustained
in a plane crash in Africa*

the First World War, of the many killed by Fascist
forces in the Spanish civil war, of the loss of half
of the regiment under his command in France in
World War II, of his own impending demise. As
a professional soldier, he has been much involved with war, and it has shaped his mind. He
thinks of strategic positions and lanes of retreat
even when being seated in a restaurant. At times,
in the manner of Nick Adams and Jake Barnes,
his mind starts working, torturing him with memories. An even more constant reminder of war is
his injured right hand, misshapen from an old
wound.

　　Cantwell's driver, Sergeant Jackson, is impre-
cise and obtuse, and Cantwell is curt with him, as
he is with many subordinates. But in Venice he is
united with Renata, and they enjoy a day together drinking and dining in a fashionable hotel
and making love in a gondola. He is more than
thirty years older than she is, but their love is intense and consuming, strained only by their mutual knowledge that he will soon die. Revealingly,
he calls Renata "daughter," and, indeed, he plays
a paternal role with her, lecturing her on events
in the war, sharing with her his insights into life
and death. Cantwell allows Renata, now properly
instructed, to join him and the *Gran Maestro* in

101

the mock society known as *El Ordine Militar, Nobile y Espirituoso de los Caballeros de Brusadelli*, a group which parodies the aficionado concept. The *Gran Maestro* and Cantwell share a mutual respect and affection that goes back to World War I, and they also share dangerous cardiac conditions. Suffering from severe angina, Cantwell says goodbye to Renata, taking her portrait with him, and leaves for a morning of duck shooting. He knows he will never see her again, and he arranges his affairs carefully. At the Tagliamento River Cantwell has words with a recalcitrant boatman before a period of unsatisfying shooting. Back in the car, seized with a heart attack he knows he will not survive, he climbs into the backseat to die.

The basic events, although a bit melodramatic, might have been developed into a fine novel. Some of the situations and characters are thematically enriching. Renata, whose name means "reborn," is the same age Cantwell was when he was wounded at Fossalta in the First World War; in their long discussion he frequently reviews the events of his youth, weighing and assessing his life. Her youth and innocence create an atmosphere of hope and assurance, a concentration on the present, for a dying and cynical man with no future. There is a continual development of the theme of death, from the killing of ducks, to the Germans Cantwell has killed, to his contemplation of his own death, to his cryptic comment "Love is love and fun is fun. But it is always so quiet when the gold fish die." Cantwell is also a considerable character, with a tragic past and a capacity for both violence and tenderness. His memories of the destruction of his regiment in France through the incompetence of his superior officers explain in part his cynical self-reliance and his lack of remorse in thinking of his death, as do his thoughts of his three failed marriages. These retrospective scenes also develop the most subtle theme of the novel, the perpetual reality of the past in the present. Cantwell will never be free of what has happened to him. And he is a man of a certain amount of cultural awareness, speaking and thinking often of painters and writers and historical events, such as the founding of Venice.

But much is wrong with the novel, and its weaknesses come on nearly every level. Style is usually the most artistically satisfying element in Hemingway's novels, but in *Across the River and Into the Trees*, despite a certain elegiac charm, the style is often absurd. Hemingway was betrayed by adverbial excess and by a general assumption, unfortunately common in his work and life, that the performance of routine tasks of everyday life somehow constitutes actions of remarkable intelligence. Cantwell does not merely take the champagne out of the ice bucket, he reaches for it "accurately and well." The lovers kiss "true" over and over, putting their arms around one another "gently and well." Renata does not simply eat, she chews "well and solidly on her steak"; Cantwell urges her to "sleep good and well." The *Gran Maestro* does not "feel affection" for the Countess; when he looks at her "his heart rolled over as a porpoise does in the sea." In dealing with sex Hemingway's descriptions become corny. In clitoral stimulation Cantwell's hand "searched for the island in the great river with the high steep banks"; and the lovemaking concludes with similar metaphoric gaucherie: "When the great bird had flown far out of the closed window of the gondola, and was lost and gone, neither of them said anything."

Beyond style there are other things awry. Cantwell and Renata often sound empty-headed, agreeing to "think of nothing." For a grizzled army colonel to talk this way with an Italian countess seems ridiculous. There is also a certain amount of cruelty in the thinly disguised portraits of Sinclair Lewis, as a writer with a pitted face who knows Venice only through his Baedeker, and of Martha Gellhorn, as a previous wife of limited talent and overweening ambition. If the novel is redeemed, it is done so in part by the psychological portrait of Cantwell, by Hemingway's graphic descriptions of the scenes of Venice and the surrounding area, and by his understated treatment of Cantwell's death. But these matters notwithstanding, *Across the River and Into the Trees* is generally regarded as the weakest of Hemingway's novels and a near-parody of his other work.

In the late 1940s, and at various periods thereafter, Hemingway worked on a long narrative in four parts he tentatively entitled "Sea Novel." The unifying subject was the sea, in its many forms, and human attitudes toward the sea. He never completed his work on this book, although nearly all of it was eventually published. Three of the sections, originally called "The Sea When Young," "The Sea When Absent," and "The Sea in Being," were published in 1970 as *Islands in the Stream;* the fourth section appeared earlier, in 1952, as *The Old Man and the Sea.*

Hemingway had published the basic plot of *The Old Man and the Sea* in 1936 in an essay entitled "On the Blue Water," which recounts the story of an old fisherman who hooks a giant marlin that tows him out to sea. After days of struggle he finally lands the fish only to have it attacked by sharks. He battles the sharks with all the weapons he has on board but is finally beaten and is crying in his boat, exhausted, when some fishermen find him. The plot of *The Old Man and the Sea* retains the central events of this sketch but introduces several elements that create sympathy for the fisherman, Santiago, highlight important themes in his conflict, and provide an ironic context that deepens the tragic nature of his life.

The novel begins at a point when Santiago has fished for eighty-four days without a catch. He is a thin old man with heavily scarred hands from years of fishing, and he lives alone in poverty in a small village in Cuba. He has no family, but he enjoys the affection and loyalty of Manolin, a young boy he has taught to fish and who brings him food. Together they discuss baseball, admiring the courage of Joe DiMaggio, who plays well despite a painful heel condition. When the old man sleeps, he dreams of youth, of the African beaches he visited when young, and of the lions he saw playing on them.

As he rows out of the harbor in the morning, a good deal is revealed about him, especially his love for the sea and the creatures within it, with whom he feels a kinship. Well out to sea he hooks a huge marlin that tows the boat farther out. Thus begins the first phase of his ordeal, his three-day fight to land his fish. Weak from lack of food, fighting a younger and stronger fish, Santiago recognizes his vulnerability: he could be seriously injured; he could die of exhaustion. Interspersed in the description of his long battle are memories, reflections, and dreams that reveal Santiago's simple but noble personality. He remembers catching a female marlin and discovering that her mate refused to leave her and stayed with her by the side of the boat. He reflects on the fate of a bird who lands briefly on his skiff and who faces exposure to predatory hawks as he flies back to shore. Such thoughts renew his sense of the tragic beauty in nature and heighten his feelings of respect and love for the marlin he is attempting to kill. He feels betrayed in this effort by his age and by his left hand, which sometimes develops cramps. When the marlin finally jumps for the first time, he can see that it is

longer than the skiff; it will take an enormous effort to land such a fish. In the lulls during the struggle he thinks of those things which bolster his spirit and give him strength, of the lions and the great DiMaggio, of his own arm-wrestling triumph in a match that lasted an entire day. Finally, on the third day, the marlin weakens and Santiago pulls him alongside the skiff and harpoons him.

The second phase of his ordeal begins when a Mako shark picks up the scent of the marlin and attacks him, tearing huge chunks out of his side. Santiago kills the shark with a harpoon but loses the weapon when the shark sinks to the bottom. He knows more sharks will come and that he will be unable to drive them away. His thoughts turn, during the long journey home, to notions of defeat and destruction, and he feels that he is responsible for losing his catch because he fished too far out, violating his luck. He resolves to fight the sharks to the death, but eventually every knife or club he has breaks, and the sharks eat all of the marlin. Santiago returns to shore exhausted and beaten. Manolin weeps when he sees the old man sleeping in his bed, his hands torn from the fishing lines. Meanwhile, at the harbor, tourists totally misunderstand what has happened, thinking that the old man had caught a shark. At home, with Manolin sitting at his side, the old man dreams of the lions.

It is a poignant tale, and it evokes natural and elemental themes. The youth and strength of Manolin, the marlin, DiMaggio, and the lions contrast with Santiago's age and infirmity, but his dignity and tenacity are equal to any. The care and sympathy of Manolin for the old man evoke themes of compassion, respect for age and ability, love of child for father. The imagery of the novel implies parallels between Santiago's trial and that of Christ, parallels that suggest mythic dimensions. But the power of the novel is in its simple beauty, in the style that describes Santiago's adventure and thoughts, and in his attempts to earn a humble livelihood and to live with dignity. In these concerns Hemingway captured the tragic elements of the struggle for existence of all earthly creatures.

Many of these same ideas, although with a different emphasis, are present in *Islands in the Stream*, especially the use of the sea as a platform for the human drama of life and death. The manuscript of the novel, never polished nor approved for publication by Hemingway, was cut and shaped by Charles Scribner, Jr., and Mary Hem-

ERNEST HEMINGWAY
The Garden of Eden

A NOVEL

Dust jacket for Hemingway's posthumously published novel which appeared in 1986

ingway and finally published to mixed reviews. Curiously, American reviewers were initially unsympathetic to the novel, lamenting its autobiographical overtones, its episodic plot, and its unpolished style, while British reviewers were more enthusiastic, welcoming this addition to the Hemingway canon and stressing its moving portrayal of loneliness. More extended criticism in the years that followed has generally expressed these same points of view.

As published, the novel is broken into three discontinuous units of action: "Bimini," which deals with the visit of three boys to their father, Thomas Hudson, a painter; "Cuba," which documents Hudson's life in Cuba after the death of his sons; and "At Sea," which depicts Hudson's activities as head of a unit chasing German submarines in the Caribbean in World War II. Apart from Hudson, there is little continuity of characters, nor are there major developments of theme from one section to another.

In "Bimini" the central concern is for family, for Hudson's sons by his two former marriages, and for the new family of comrades he has assembled on his island. The central event is a visit from his three sons, Tom, David, and An-

drew. Together they fish, swim, dine, and talk, the boys reviewing school and friends for their father, Tom reliving his childhood in Paris (where, as the oldest child, only he has lived) for the benefit of the other two boys. There are two especially dramatic events in this section: an intense and nerve-wrenching scene in which David, skin diving with his brothers, suddenly becomes the intended prey for a shark, and another long and agonizing scene in which David hooks a marlin and fights with him for hours, with somewhat more technologically advanced equipment than Santiago's, only to lose him at the last moment. But the emphasis throughout is on Hudson's love for his children and his first wife and his loneliness when they are away from him. Besides his children there are other members of this extended family, among them Joseph, a houseboy who cares deeply for Hudson and the children; Roger Davis, a writer; and Eddy, an alcoholic who is at his best in times of trouble. Together they form a group to replace the family Hudson has lost, one in which there is concern for domestic regularity, mutual affection, respect for culture, and promise for the future, and so it is all the more tragic when his sons David and Andrew are killed in an automobile accident along with their mother (Hudson's second wife), and Thomas Hudson loses his family, in effect, for the third time.

The emphasis in the "Cuba" section is on love—familial love, love of work, love of animals, and carnal love in a variety of expressions. The dominant underlying emotion of the section is Hudson's love for his dead sons and the nearly overpowering grief he feels when he allows himself to think of them. Although in the first section it was clearly David who was the favorite, in this part he thinks most often of Tom, the only child of his first marriage. His most immediate love, however, is for Boise, one of his many cats, with whom he shares affection with beautiful simplicity. At times his feeling for Boise is clearly inextricable from his memories of his sons: his memories of Boise as a kitten are enriched by the knowledge that his sons were alive then. His other memories often involve sensual love: his affair with a princess aboard a ship, his sexual exploits with three Chinese girls, his relationship with Honest Lil, a somewhat heavy, if accommodating, local prostitute. But the section ends with his most intense love, his love for his first wife, an actress, who stops briefly in Cuba while on tour. It is this scene of their mutual acknowledgment of the death of their son Tom and the impossibility of their ever marrying again that explains Hudson's willingness to risk danger in the final section of the novel: Hudson wishes to die to escape the pain he is forced to live with.

The tension of "At Sea" thus derives from Hudson's implicit death wish and the danger of his present circumstances: commanding a reconditioned fishing boat on its search for German submarines. Manned by a ragtag collection of enthusiastic amateurs, supplied with only light weapons, Hudson's boat is vulnerable and unlikely to survive the encounter with a submarine her commander desires. The theme of death permeates the section, giving the ending of the novel a sense of tragic inevitability.

"At Sea" is artistically stronger than the first two sections. Its narrative pace is steady, its characters more sharply drawn, its dialogue brisk and realistic. The section is basically one episode of progressively intensified action. And the prose exhibits some of Hemingway's best impressionistic style. But the central unifying idea centers on death, from the villagers killed by the Germans Hudson pursues to Hudson's own wound at the end. Along the way death appears in many forms, from the pig who swims to his death to Hudson's dreams of the deaths of his fawn and dog in his youth. Much has changed from the earlier sections: in place of the love of family and work, there is now the intensity of purpose and the certainty of death. The family group has been replaced by a disputatious military group. Sexual love has been transmogrified to bring death rather than life, for Hudson now sleeps with a pistol that he thinks of as a woman. War has converted the things of normal life into destructive and threatening forms. Hudson's dreams and memories of happier times deepen the sense of tragic loss: he thinks of Paris and young Tom, of days spent hunting, of his family, of painting, and of the satisfaction of good work. The concluding action rings with ironic tragedy. Hudson succeeds in capturing the German boat, but the remaining enemy crew ambush Hudson and critically wound him. At the end of the novel he lies dying on his boat, thinking that he will never paint again and listening to one of his crew, Willie, plead with him not to die.

As subsequent criticism has indicated, *Islands in the Stream* was a welcome addition to Hemingway's fiction, but it is not one of his major novels. It has less structural unity than his first novels, less thematic development, less technical coherence in such matters as narrative perspec-

tive. And there are some major flaws: Hudson's sons die offstage with no foreshadowing, a deus ex machina event that seems unnecessarily abrupt and contrived. Sometimes Hudson's ability to elicit love and admiration from those around him seems not to be justified by any evidence of extraordinary sensitivity or intelligence or wit on his part. And, unique among Hemingway's novels, too much is told and too little shown in some of Hemingway's best impressionistic prose, some stirring adventure, fine portraits of children and animals, and a wrenching evocation of Hudson's psychological anguish in the later sections of the novel.

One of the most biographically controversial of Hemingway's novels is *The Garden of Eden*, which appeared in 1986. A heavily edited work, selected and shaped out of a much longer incomplete manuscript, it is nevertheless a novel worthy of serious consideration. As the novel opens, David Bourne, a writer, and his wealthy wife, Catherine, are on their honeymoon in the south of France. Although they make love and cavort in the manner of newlyweds, there are indications of trouble in their relationship even in the first chapter: David is not writing and resents it; Catherine is uncertain about her sexual identity; and David ends the chapter by saying goodbye to her in his thoughts. As the novel progresses, it becomes evident that Catherine is jealous of David's devotion to his craft, which she supports with family money. There are further indications that Catherine prefers to exchange sexual roles with him.

In book two they move to the coast of northern Spain, where David resumes his writing. Almost at once Catherine begins drinking too much and is bitter about his work and press clippings. Catherine goes into town to get a man's haircut, deepening her sexual transformation, which solidifies when she tours the Prado Museum in Madrid as a boy. At this point in the novel, less than a month after the wedding, David knows the marriage is over. They decide to go back to France, where David, attempting to hang on to the marriage, agrees to have his hair cut and dyed to match Catherine's. When they later make love, Catherine calls him a girl. To further complicate their relationship, they meet a beautiful young woman named Marita, who falls in love with both of them. Soon they are each making love to Marita, who gradually begins to replace Catherine in David's mind.

Despite the disruption in his personal life, David's writing goes well; that, he thinks, is "what you have left." He begins work on a story about crossing a volcanic desert in Africa, and he takes pleasure in remembering his deceased father and making him live again in the fiction. Marita takes an interest in David's work, and as she becomes the supportive figure in his emotions, Catherine begins to fear for her sanity. David knows he has lost Catherine, and he prefers to live in his story. Catherine tears up David's story, saying that she hates it and she hates him. At this point, David, faced with pain and betrayal in his marriage, begins his most important work, one about pain and betrayal on an elephant hunt in Africa many years ago.

In the story the boy Davey and his dog track an elephant his father had been pursuing. The boy admires the animal but knows his father and their guide, Juma, want to find it and kill it. As they draw near the elephant, Davey feels he has betrayed a noble animal, an emotion deepened when they realize the elephant has stopped to visit the skeleton of another elephant. At this point Davey rejects the values of his father and begins to feel the animal is his brother. The next day Davey's father shoots the elephant, and Davey knows that things will never be the same between him and his father. His father, too, knows that he can never trust his son again. It is a poignant and dramatic moment. David has lived with the powerful emotions in this scene all these years.

Marita reads the story, is moved by it, and feels proud of David. Catherine, on the other hand, insults David's writing and subsequently burns both his reviews and his stories. The marriage has come to an end. When Catherine leaves to return to Paris, Marita and David are left together, she taking on the role of wife. With her encouragement David begins writing again, recapturing the story that Catherine had destroyed. He feels that he knows his father better than he did before, and he writes well. The novel ends on this optimistic note.

What is important about this novel is that it is Hemingway's most direct statement about the relationship between experience and the creative imagination, as David uses the feelings of the present to lead him to a fictional exploration of the past, with pain and betrayal as the links between them. The novel has many passages about how a writer lives in his work and about how his fiction and his life interrelate. On another level the theme of sexual reversal connects this novel with Hemingway's early fiction, particularly *The Sun*

Also Rises, *A Farewell to Arms*, and *For Whom the Bell Tolls*. The fact that David is involved with two women in a bisexual triangle has also occasioned a good deal of biographical speculation, none of it substantiated. The hunting story, one of Hemingway's best, reveals a depth of empathy for another living creature that is missing in much of his other work, save for Santiago's feelings for the marlin in *The Old Man and the Sea*.

Hemingway's artistic reputation rests solidly on his major short stories and on the best of his novels, *The Sun Also Rises*, *A Farewell to Arms*, *For Whom the Bell Tolls*, and *The Old Man and the Sea*. His literary productivity in other genres was much less substantial and has received proportionately less attention, but it does deserve at least brief comment. *The Torrents of Spring*, Hemingway's parody of Sherwood Anderson's *Dark Laughter*, received mixed reviews when it first appeared in 1926, with the distinguished poet Allen Tate arguing that Hemingway's parody was better than the novel satirized. Most of the other reviewers, however, felt that although it effectively pointed to weaknesses in Anderson's characteristically naive narrators and primitive characterizations, the novel failed as a work of art. The title, which Hemingway borrowed from Turgenev, alludes to sexual torrents that find expression in an absurd cast of characters that mimics the people portrayed in Winesburg, Ohio, a favorite location for Anderson's stories. Hemingway effectively mocks the innocent sentimentalism of Anderson's world but without creating a work interesting within itself, as Henry Fielding had done in *Joseph Andrews* (1742), one of his satires of Samuel Richardson's *Pamela* (1740-1742). Indeed, the chief interest in the book today derives from its role in Hemingway's highly advantageous break with Horace Liveright's publishing firm, which also published Anderson, and a new arrangement with Scribners, a move that benefited him for the rest of his life.

Death in the Afternoon (1932), Hemingway's first extended work of expository prose, was well received and is generally regarded as the finest discussion of bullfighting in English. It is a handbook of bullfighting which attempts to make intelligible for the novice the complex language, ritual, and drama of what Hemingway regarded as a tragedy rather than a sport. But it ranges beyond bullfighting to discuss at length the Spanish character and various issues in literature and modern life, including the scenes in war that he had earlier written about in fiction. The basic insight that Hemingway offers into bullfighting, as Arthur Waldhorn has observed, is that it does not involve killing for its own sake but "killing to give man respite from his own tragedy by imposing it upon the bull." Thus man, through stylized ritual that demands the risk of life itself, gains temporary victory over death.

Green Hills of Africa (1935) represents a further experiment in nonfiction prose. It is an essentially autobiographical account of an African safari Hemingway enjoyed in 1933-1934. He explained the point of it in a foreword: "The writer has attempted to write an absolutely true book to see whether the shape of a country and the pattern of a month's action can, if truly presented, compete with a work of the imagination." The demands he placed upon himself were essentially twofold: to tell the truth; to present an honest record in an artistically satisfying way. To make art out of life requires a sense of order, and Hemingway shaped the experiences depicted into four units of action, each constituting a variation on the theme of the "pursuit" of the hunter: "Pursuit and Conversation," "Pursuit Remembered," "Pursuit and Failure," and "Pursuit as Happiness." As the sections progress, Hemingway provides detailed accounts of hunting and beautiful descriptions of landscape. There is action in the chase, conflict between man and beast, competition between Hemingway and his fellow hunter, Karl, who beats him at nearly every turn, and psychological growth as the author learns to deal with the success of others. There is character interest in the contrasting portraits of various African guides, the most intriguing of whom is M'Cola, and in a variety of companions, Pop, Kandisky, and others. There is the humor of good fellows enjoying an outing together but relatively little serious thematic development. Hemingway himself becomes something of a "code hero," shooting well and dealing with wounded animals properly, yet there is the unsound assumption that the enjoyment of killing animals contains within itself a justification of the action. One point of continuing interest is the contemplation of writing and of other writers. Among the American authors Hemingway admires, he mentions Mark Twain, Stephen Crane, Henry James, and William Faulkner. He also praises James Joyce, Tolstoy and Dostoyevski, Flaubert and Stendhal. But apart from observations of isolated interest, the book as a whole does not compare favorably with Hemingway's fiction, does not captivate attention as do his best novels,

and does not give the sense of a satisfying whole. Some critics have found it boring, but most have pronounced it to be a worthy experiment in autobiography that achieves a modest success.

Hemingway's one experiment in drama was *The Fifth Column*, a play about the Spanish civil war written in the autumn of 1937 and performed in New York in the spring of 1940. Since dialogue had always been one of the best components of his fiction, there was a general feeling among critics that Hemingway had a good deal of potential as a dramatist. Unfortunately, the play was unsuccessful both critically and commercially. It features Philip Rawlings as a correspondent in Madrid who is heavily involved in the Loyalist cause. That this situation is remarkably close to Hemingway's own experience was not lost on drama critics. Indeed, Carlos Baker, a leading Hemingway scholar, has complained that the author gave Rawlings "so many of his own personal traits, desires, and illusions that the feeble dramatic structure of the play buckled under the load." But surely another weakness of the play was Hemingway's loss of artistic objectivity in his passionate advocacy of the Loyalist cause, a weakness he had skillfully avoided in *For Whom the Bell Tolls*. This advocacy is also evident in *The Spanish Earth*, a documentary film that Hemingway helped produce in conjunction with John Dos Passos, Lillian Hellman, and Archibald MacLeish. As Carlos Baker has explained, Hemingway's contribution was the writing of the sound track. The film, which recounts the experiences of a young man named Julian, depicts the need for agrarian reform in Spain, putting land back in the control of peasants to use for agricultural purposes. This film, which Hemingway showed to President Roosevelt in the White House, helped to raise money in support of the Loyalist cause.

The most successful of Hemingway's nonfiction works is *A Moveable Feast* (1964), a collection of autobiographical sketches covering his life in Paris from 1921 to 1926. Written in the late 1950s, when Hemingway's health was faltering and his career nearly over, the twenty essays deal with a period when he was struggling to establish himself as a writer, when his health was good and he was productive and optimistic, and when his marriage to Hadley Hemingway was still going well. Ironically, although he was working in part from notes taken during the 1920s, Hemingway was at this late period in his life writing the best prose of his career. His style is richly impressionistic and evocative. His eye for meaningful detail and his ear for capturing nuances in speech were never better.

For these sketches Hemingway presented dramatic individual scenes rather than summary statements of what the experience had been. He portrayed himself as a struggling writer more devoted to his craft than those around him who fritter away their time and energies on literary gossip and trivial socializing. There are brilliant descriptions of Paris, of the Place Contrescarpe in winter, the atmosphere of the Café des Amateurs, and of the other struggling writers who befriended him. He recalls going to the Musée du Luxembourg to view the Impressionist paintings, and he offers the notable comment that he was learning to write by studying the paintings of Cézanne. His representations of other writers are particularly interesting, not so much for what they reveal about other people but for what they suggest about Hemingway's attitudes toward his fellows near the end of his life. Here, in effect, Hemingway repays with vengeance his old debts for slights and insults over the years. Gertrude Stein, who had supported and encouraged him during the 1920s, is portrayed as looking like a "peasant woman." According to this account, Hemingway breaks off their friendship when he overhears her in a lesbian quarrel with her lover, Alice B. Toklas. Wyndham Lewis is described as a frog, Ford Madox Ford as a pretentious fraud, and Zelda Fitzgerald as a hawk who delighted in ruining her husband's career. Indeed, the Fitzgeralds are treated with great condescension. Scott Fitzgerald is depicted as a social child, unable to drink even moderately without becoming unconscious, a man who hires a cockney nanny for his daughter because he wants her to grow up with a fine English accent. He is portrayed as sexually insecure, a hypochondriac, a writer with talent but no discipline or commitment. On the other hand, there are loving portraits of Hadley Hemingway and their son, Bumby, and of the nobility of Ezra Pound and the kindness of Sylvia Beach. For its sharp descriptions of scene and character, for its record of literary struggle and growth, but even more for the controlled elegance of its style *A Moveable Feast* established Hemingway among the masters of expository prose.

Hemingway will never have much critical reputation as a poet despite the fact that his career began, as did that of William Faulkner, with verse. As a schoolboy he was publishing humorous poems in the newspaper *Trapeze* and the liter-

ary magazine *Tabula* at Oak Park High School. Later, in 1923, he placed six poems in Harriet Monroe's *Poetry: A Magazine of Verse* and *Three Stories & Ten Poems* with Contact Publishing Company. After that his poetic career quickly faded. Only twenty-five poems in his career, juvenilia aside, were published, and by 1929 he had written seventy-three of what were ultimately published in *88 Poems* (1979), edited by Nicholas Gerogiannis.

In general, Hemingway's poems fall into three categories of compositional form: juvenile humor, imagism, and expository love poems to Mary Welsh, who became his fourth wife. His juvenile poems are of the most ordinary sort, reflecting the common prose of athletic roughness pressed into poetic service. "Oh, I've never writ a ballad/And I'd rather eat shrimp salad" is representative of this type. Hemingway's "imagistic" poems are somewhat more interesting, especially since they are preceded by one-sentence "prose poems" that are roughly the prosaic equivalents of Ezra Pound's verse. Each of these curious pieces captures in a sentence a kinetic portrait of a streetwalker on the Boulevard Madelaine at night or a fallen horse at the races in Auteuil. Similarly, his early poems often reflect this imagistic impulse, including such "Athletic Verse" as "The Tackle" and "The Punt": "The sodden thump of a pigskin being kicked,/And the ball rises higher and higher in the air/While the grimy, muddy figures race down the field." Some of these poems reveal a clear inspiration from the verse of Stephen Crane in their pithy observations of universal injustice. Despite the fact that Hemingway's natural gifts were for linguistic precision and sharp impressionistic scenes, these poems are ultimately weak in precisely those areas in which his prose is strong. His use of rhyme and rhythm is generally obtrusive, his wit insistent, his point graphically emphasized. In addition, his predilection for barracks humor, profane phrases, and explicit sexuality offended many readers. His late poems to Mary Welsh, written during World War II, perpetuate these tendencies, but their redeeming feature is their emotive power in suggesting psychological reactions to war: bitter revulsion from death and destruction, fascination with death, admiration for courage and sacrifice. The best of these is "Poem to Mary (Second Poem)," which begins "Now sleeps he/With that old whore Death/Who, yesterday, denied her thrice." It is a powerful poem which entwines the horror of war with love and courtship, ending, after a portrayal of grim realities in battle, with the rejection of religion and an emphatic call for love and compassion in the context of human misery. This poem, and a few of the others, deserve to be examined seriously by students of American literature.

Hemingway's reputation will forever rest on an uneasy blending of the myth of his personal adventures with the artistic merit of his best fiction. But it is as artist that he deserves the attention of posterity. He was, without doubt, one of the finest prose stylists in English. He captured in stunning stories and novels the uncomfortable realities of his age and forced into public consciousness a realization of the brutalities of war and their lingering psychological effects. His stories of Nick Adams depict the adolescent agonies of a generation; his novels, especially *The Sun Also Rises, A Farewell to Arms*, and *For Whom the Bell Tolls*, record for all time the emotional turmoil of modern warfare and, in a larger sense, of modern life. And by concluding his career with *The Old Man and the Sea* he showed that even in the anguish of modern life there is nobility in human perseverance and dignity in devotion to performing a task well. Whatever failings he had as a man, and there were many, as a writer he was sometimes nearly perfect. It is the integrity of his craft, a richness beyond legend, that will forever endure.

Letters:

Ernest Hemingway: Selected Letters, 1917-1961, edited by Carlos Baker (New York: Scribners, 1981).

    The single best source of Hemingway's letters.

Bibliographies:

Philip Young and Charles W. Mann, *The Hemingway Manuscripts: An Inventory* (University Park & London: Pennsylvania State University Press, 1969).

    A description of the manuscripts now in the John F. Kennedy Library in Boston.

Audre Hanneman, *Ernest Hemingway: A Comprehensive Bibliography* (Princeton: Princeton University Press, 1967; supplement, 1975).

    These two volumes comprise the best primary bibliographies available in book form, but they do not contain all the posthumous works.

Catalog of the Ernest Hemingway Collection at the John F. Kennedy Library, 2 volumes (Boston: G. K. Hall, 1982).

    The first volume is a guide to the manuscripts and to outgoing and incoming correspondence (A-L), the second to incoming correspondence (M-Z), photographs, newspaper clippings, and other material.

Biographies:

Carlos Baker, *Ernest Hemingway: A Life Story* (New York: Scribners, 1969).

    The first, and most reliable, comprehensive biography.

Mary Welsh Hemingway, *How It Was* (New York: Knopf, 1976).

    A sensitive and often revealing account of the marriage between Mary Welsh and Hemingway.

Scott Donaldson, *By Force of Will: The Life and Art of Ernest Hemingway* (New York: Viking, 1977).

    A discussion of the central themes (such as fame, money, death, and religion) that play a central role in Hemingway's life and art.

Matthew J. Bruccoli, *Scott and Ernest: The Authority of Failure and the Authority of Success* (New York: Random House, 1978).

    An account of the personal and literary relationship between F. Scott Fitzgerald and Hemingway.

Peter Griffin, *Along With Youth: Hemingway, The Early Years* (New York: Oxford University Press, 1985).

    A biography of Hemingway's youth through his marriage to Hadley Richardson in 1921, treating fiction as unquestioned fact.

Jeffrey Meyers, *Hemingway: A Biography* (New York: Harper, 1985).

    A Freudian biographical study of Hemingway's life.

Michael Reynolds, *The Young Hemingway* (New York: Blackwell, 1986).

    An excellent study of Hemingway's life in the period from 1919 to 1921, with a fine section on Oak Park, Illinois.

Kenneth S. Lynn, *Hemingway* (New York: Simon & Schuster, 1987).
An unsympathetic psycho-biography of Hemingway that cannot be trusted for humane good judgment.

References:

Carlos Baker, *Hemingway: The Writer as Artist*, fourth edition (Princeton: Princeton University Press, 1972).
A biographical interpretation of Hemingway's fiction as works of symbolism.

Sheridan Baker, *Ernest Hemingway: An Introduction and Interpretation* (New York: Holt, Rinehart & Winston, 1967).
An excellent brief introduction to Hemingway's life and career.

Jackson J. Benson, *Hemingway: The Writer's Art of Self-Defense* (Minneapolis: University of Minnesota Press, 1969).
An exploration of the role of irony in Hemingway's major fiction.

Benson, *The Short Stories of Ernest Hemingway: Critical Essays* (Durham, N.C.: Duke University Press, 1975).
An excellent source of information, including both original and reprinted essays, about all of Hemingway's major stories.

Charles A. Fenton, *The Apprenticeship of Ernest Hemingway* (New York: Farrar, Straus & Young, 1954).
A valuable exploration of Hemingway's journalism and early fiction, especially *In Our Time*.

Fitzgerald/Hemingway Annual, 1969-1979.
An excellent collection of original articles, published once each year.

Joseph M. Flora, *Hemingway's Nick Adams* (Baton Rouge: Louisiana State University Press, 1982).
A detailed examination of the stories about Nick Adams.

Sheldon Norman Grebstein, *Hemingway's Craft* (Carbondale: Southern Illinois University Press, 1973).
The best single study of Hemingway's fiction as works of art.

Bernice Kert, *The Hemingway Women* (New York: Norton, 1983).
A comprehensive discussion of the women in Hemingway's life and work.

James Nagel, ed., *Ernest Hemingway: The Writer in Context* (Madison: University of Wisconsin Press, 1984).
Twelve original articles on the life and works of Hemingway, including essays by Patrick Hemingway, Charles Scribner, Jr., and Tom Stoppard.

Bernard Oldsey, *Hemingway's Hidden Craft: The Writing of* A Farewell to Arms (University Park: Pennsylvania State University Press, 1979).
A detailed examination of the opening and closing chapters of the novel as well as its title.

Michael S. Reynolds, *Hemingway's First War: The Making of* A Farewell to Arms (Princeton: Princeton University Press, 1976).
An excellent study of the biographical and historical background of Hemingway's novel of World War I.

Reynolds, The Sun Also Rises: *A Novel of the Twenties* (Boston: Twayne, 1988).
An excellent introduction to the novel for beginning students.

Reynolds, ed., *Critical Essays on Ernest Hemingway's* In Our Time (Boston: G. K. Hall, 1983).
Original and reprinted essays that comprise the best single source of information on Hemingway's first important book.

Earl Rovit, *Ernest Hemingway* (New York: Twayne, 1963).
An assessment of Hemingway's place in literature, particularly with regard to his use of transcendental thought.

Bertram Sarason, *Hemingway and the Sun Set* (Washington, D.C.: Bruccoli Clark/NCR Microcard Editions, 1972).
Memoirs by people who knew Hemingway in Paris in 1925, correlating events and characters in the novel with what happened that summer.

Linda Welshimer Wagner, *Ernest Hemingway: A Reference Guide* (Boston: G. K. Hall, 1977).
A useful, annotated, secondary bibliography of scholarship on Hemingway.

Wagner, *Hemingway and Faulkner: Inventors/Masters* (Metuchen: Scarecrow, 1975).
A comparative examination of the two writers in the early years of their careers, particularly with regard to their poetry and major fiction as well as the influence of imagism.

Wagner, ed., *Ernest Hemingway: Six Decades of Criticism* (East Lansing: Michigan State University Press, 1987).
An anthology of reprinted and original criticism covering the full range of Hemingway's career.

Arthur Waldhorn, *A Reader's Guide to Ernest Hemingway* (New York: Farrar, Straus & Giroux, 1972).
The best single introduction to Hemingway's life and works for the beginning student.

Emily Watts, *Ernest Hemingway and the Arts* (Urbana: University of Illinois Press, 1971).
A study of the influence of painting, architecture, and sculpture on Hemingway's fiction, especially with regard to Cézanne and the Impressionists.

Philip Young, *Ernest Hemingway: A Reconsideration* (University Park: Pennsylvania State University Press, 1966).
A psycho-critical study of Hemingway's fiction as following in the tradition of Mark Twain in its emphasis on the emotional effects of violence and trauma.

Papers:
Ernest Hemingway's papers are located at the John F. Kennedy Library in Boston, Massachusetts.

Robinson Jeffers

This entry was updated by Robert Ian Scott (University of Saskatchewan) from his entry in DLB 45, American Poets, 1880-1945, First Series.

Places	California	Ireland	
Influences and Relationships	Mark Van Doren George Sterling James Rorty	Babette Deutsche Judith Anderson William Wordsworth	Aeschylus Sophocles Euripides
Literary Movements and Forms	Romantic Poetry	Greek Tragedy	Naturalism
Major Themes	The Decline & Ultimate Extinction of the Human Race	The Futility of War The Tragedy of Hubris	The Insignificance of Humanity
Cultural and Artistic Influences	Darwin's Theory of Evolution Buddhism	Lucretius's Theory of Atomism Pantheism	The Copernican Universe Medicine
Social and Economic Influences	World War I World War II Overpopulation	Destruction of the Environment	The Threat of WW III

BIRTH: Pittsburgh, Pennsylvania, 10 January 1887, to Annie Robinson Tuttle and William Hamilton Jeffers.

EDUCATION: University of Western Pennsylvania (now University of Pittsburgh), 1902-1903; B.A., Occidental College, 1905; University of Southern California, 1905-1906, 1907-1910; University of Zurich, 1906-1907; University of Washington, 1910-1911.

MARRIAGE: 15 August 1913 to Una Call Kuster; children: Maeve, Donnan Call, and Garth Sherwood.

AWARDS AND HONORS: D.H.L., Occidental College, 1937; D.H.L., University of Southern California, 1939; Levinson Prize (*Poetry* magazine), 1940; Chancellor, American Academy of Poets (1945-1956); Eunice Tietjens Memorial Prize (*Poetry* magazine), 1951; Union League Civic and Arts Foundation Prize (*Poetry* magazine), 1952; Borestone Mountain Poetry Award, 1955; Academy of American Poets Fellowship, 1958; Shelley Memorial Award (Poetry Society of America), 1961.

DEATH: Carmel, California, 20 January 1962.

SELECTED BOOKS: *Flagons and Apples* (Los Angeles: Grafton, 1912);
Californians (New York: Macmillan, 1916);
Tamar and Other Poems (New York: Peter G. Boyle, 1924);
Roan Stallion, Tamar, and Other Poems (New York: Boni & Liveright, 1925; London: Leonard & Virginia Woolf at the Hogarth Press, 1928; enlarged edition, New York: Modern Library, 1935);
The Women at Point Sur (New York: Boni & Liveright, 1927); enlarged as *The Women at Point Sur and Other Poems* (New York: Liveright, 1977);
Poems (San Francisco: Book Club of California, 1928);
An Artist (Austin: Privately printed by John S. Mayfield, 1928);
Cawdor and Other Poems (New York: Liveright, 1929; London: Leonard & Virginia Woolf at the Hogarth Press, 1929);
Dear Judas and Other Poems (New York: Liveright, 1929; London: Hogarth Press, 1930);
Stars (Pasadena: Flame Press, 1930);

Robinson Jeffers

Descent to the Dead (New York: Random House, 1931);
Thurso's Landing and Other Poems (New York: Liveright, 1932);
Give Your Heart to the Hawks and Other Poems (New York: Random House, 1933);
Return, An Unpublished Poem (San Francisco: Gelber, Lilienthal, 1934);
Solstice and Other Poems (New York: Random House, 1935);
The Beaks of Eagles (San Francisco: Printed for Albert M. Bender, 1936);
Such Counsels You Gave to Me & Other Poems (New York: Random House, 1937);
The Selected Poetry of Robinson Jeffers (New York: Random House, 1938);
Two Consolations (San Mateo: Quercus Press, 1940);
Be Angry at the Sun (New York: Random House, 1941);
Medea: Freely Adapted From the Medea of Euripides (New York: Random House, 1946);
The Double Axe & Other Poems (New York: Random House, 1948; enlarged edition, New York: Liveright, 1977);
Poetry, Gongorism and A Thousand Years (Los Angeles: Ward Ritchie Press, 1949);

Hungerfield and Other Poems (New York: Random House, 1954);

The Loving Shepherdess (New York: Random House, 1956);

Themes in My Poems (San Francisco: Book Club of California, 1956);

The Beginning & the End and Other Poems (New York: Random House, 1963);

Selected Poems by Robinson Jeffers (New York: Random House, 1963);

Cawdor: A Long Poem, Medea, after Euripides (New York: New Directions, 1970);

The Alpine Christ & Other Poems, edited by William Everson (Monterey: Cayucos Books, 1973);

Tragedy Has Obligations (Santa Cruz: Lime Kiln Press, 1973);

Brides of the South Wind: Poems 1917-1922, edited by Everson (Monterey: Cayucos Books, 1974);

What Odd Expedients and Other Poems, edited by Robert Ian Scott (Hamden, Conn.: Shoe String Press, 1981);

Rock and Hawk: A Selection of Shorter Poems, edited by Robert Haas (New York: Random House, 1987);

The Collected Poetry of Robinson Jeffers, edited by Tim Hunt, 1 volume to date (Stanford: Stanford University Press, 1988).

PLAY PRODUCTIONS: *Medea*, New York, National Theatre, 20 October 1947;

The Tower Beyond Tragedy, New York, ANTA Playhouse, 26 November 1950.

OTHER: "Mirrors" [short story], *Smart Set*, 40 (August 1913): 117-118.

Because he thought "poets lie too much," Robinson Jeffers said in his foreword to *The Selected Poetry of Robinson Jeffers* (1938), he decided "not to pretend to believe in . . . irreversible progress; not to say anything because it was popular . . . unless I myself believed it; and not to believe easily." Such skepticism antagonizes some, but Jeffers's descriptions of human misery and unimportance in a divinely beautiful universe have won a remarkably large audience. His 1938 volume, *The Selected Poetry of Robinson Jeffers*, had eleven printings, and the 1935 Modern Library edition of *Roan Stallion, Tamar, and Other Poems* had seventeen (some forty thousand copies); his *Medea* (1946), with Judith Anderson in the title role, became a success on Broadway in 1947 and then an international success.

John Robinson Jeffers's education began early, before he was three and a half, with tutoring by his mother and then by his father, the Professor of Biblical and Ecclesiastical History and the History of Doctrine at the Western Theological Seminary, a Presbyterian institution in Pittsburgh. Jeffers then attended private schools in Pittsburgh, Germany, and Switzerland; by age twelve he had read widely in English, French, German, Latin, and Greek. In 1902, when he was fifteen, he entered the University of Western Pennsylvania (now the University of Pittsburgh) but transferred to Occidental College in 1903 when his father's health prompted a move to Los Angeles. At Occidental, Jeffers studied astronomy, geology, ethics, history, economics, rhetoric, biblical literature, and Greek, among other subjects, and edited the college's literary magazine. In 1905-1906 he took graduate courses in literature at the University of Southern California and fell in love with a student in one of his classes, Una Call Kuster, then twenty and already married; Jeffers was eighteen. After spending the 1906-1907 academic year at the University of Zurich, where he studied literature, history, and philosophy, Jeffers studied medicine for three years at the University of Southern California (including a semester when he taught physiology) not to become a doctor but to continue preparing himself as a poet.

Jeffers went to the University of Washington in Seattle in 1910, thinking that this time separation might end the affair with Una Kuster, and that as a forester he could both save trees and have time to write. But in 1912 he inherited $9,500 and had no sooner gone home to Los Angeles than he met Una Kuster again. She got an amicable divorce, which the Los Angeles newspapers considered a scandal and gave such misleading headlines as "Parents Wash Hands of It." Jeffers married Una in August of 1913; their first child, Maeve, was born 5 May 1914 and died the next day. They had planned to live in Europe, but the outbreak of World War I and the advice of a friend, poet Frederick Mortimer Clapp, led them instead to Carmel at the northern end of the Sur coast of California that September, and there they stayed, apart from vacations in Ireland and in Taos, New Mexico, and one lecture tour around America, until Una Jeffers died in Carmel in 1950, and Jeffers died in 1962.

Jeffers wrote his first poem when he was ten. A cousin who lost it remembered years later that it concerned a snake–perhaps the garden snake which the first letter in *The Selected Letters of Robinson Jeffers, 1897-1962* (1968) says he killed that year. At fourteen he read and imitated the poems of Thomas Campbell and Dante Gabriel Rossetti, and at sixteen he first had his poems published–two in the December 1903 issue of *Aurora,* Occidental College's literary magazine. One of them, the sonnet "The Measure," concludes that compared to the immensity of the universe, only space, eternity, and God are "truly great," a point he continued to make for the rest of his life. In June 1904 Jeffers first received payment for a poem, twelve dollars for "The Condor," by winning a contest sponsored by the *Youth's Companion.* It was the first of Jeffers's many poems admiring condors, vultures, eagles, hawks, pelicans, and gulls, all capable fliers (in 1899, when twelve years old, Jeffers had tried to fly with homemade wings).

When he inherited money in 1912, Jeffers paid a Los Angeles printer to publish his first book, *Flagons and Apples,* which no one reviewed; its thirty-three embarrassingly naive and stilted love poems later made Jeffers wish that he had destroyed the whole edition. His marriage and his move to the Sur coast ended such foolishness; there for the first time he saw "people living– amid magnificent unspoiled scenery–essentially as they did in Homer's Ithaca," he said, and he made those people and that coast his subject for the rest of his life, setting most of his long narratives in actual places there (see the map at the end of Robert Brophy's *Robinson Jeffers, Myth, Ritual and Symbol in His Narrative Poems* or the earlier, less complete map at the end of Lawrence Clark Powell's *Robinson Jeffers, The Man and His Work*).

Jeffers first began describing that coast and its people in his second book, *Californians,* published by Macmillan in 1916. In the introduction to his 1974 edition, William Everson argues that Jeffers could not feel free to express his view of the universe as God and of humanity as tragically foolish until his father died in December 1914. The violence, insanity, and sex in Jeffers's narratives might have shocked his father–they have certainly shocked some reviewers–but Jeffers did not begin to write these narratives until his mother had died, in 1921, and after he had discovered the universality of human suffering and conceived of the universe as the God which both creates us and saves us from such suffering. *Californians* shows little sign of either discovery; Jeffers's realization of the suffering in World War I apparently came suddenly, between the sum-

mer of 1916 and the spring of 1917, provoking his next and longest poem, the long-lost "The Alpine Christ." Ten years afterward, Jeffers called it "useless and absurd," naive in its "use of Christian mythology," and refused to permit the publication of even a part of it, but with this poem his later success began. He wrote the poem before the United States had entered the war, but after the miseries of trench warfare and the German invasion of Belgium had become widely known. Jeffers reacted with horror, pity, and disgust, a mixture of feelings which helped provoke what Jeffers later called "the accidental new birth" of his mind. As his wife explained it, "The conflict of motives on the subject of going to war or not was probably one of several factors that, about this time, made the world and his own mind much more real and intense to him. Another was building Tor House [the Jefferses' home]. As he helped the masons shift and place the wind and waterworn granite I think he realized some kinship with it and became aware of strengths in himself unknown before. Thus at the age of thirtyone there came to him a kind of awakening such as adolescents and religious converts are said to experience." Jeffers turned thirty-two on 10 January 1919 and helped build his house the following summer.

In the winter of 1971-1972 William Everson found 147 of the 227 typed pages of "The Alpine Christ" in the collection of Jeffers's papers at the Humanities Research Center of the University of Texas at Austin; Jeffers had used the blank sides of those pages for later poems. That find reveals what seems to be Jeffers's first written response to the universality of human suffering. Unlike his later poems, "The Alpine Christ" (which Everson included in *The Alpine Christ & Other Poems,* 1973) accepts Christianity as literally true. The poem begins with a conference in heaven in which Satan congratulates God for having had World War I make life on earth worse than Hell. God cannot disagree, so Christ returns to earth to save mankind from itself again, only to vanish at the end, having accomplished nothing as the war continues. Jeffers seems to have written the poem because the suffering distressed him, turned to Christianity for some help or explanation, but found in writing the poem that Christianity could not help or explain away the misery for him. The poem remains naive and much too long, but it was a fortunate failure because from it Jeffers learned to become an original poet. In just four years the deaths of his first

Tor House and Hawk Tower

child, of his father, and then of millions in World War I had led him from imitating Rossetti (while writing about himself in *Flagons and Apples*) to imitating Wordsworth (while writing about ranch families and hermits in *Californians*) to imitating "Prometheus Unbound" and *Paradise Lost* (while writing about whole countries suffering in "The Alpine Christ"). He apparently took the next step –to writing tragedies that consider the human species and the universe as a whole–because, unlike Shelley, Jeffers could not believe any revolution would end human suffering and because, unlike Milton, Jeffers did not think Christianity could justify it. As a result, Jeffers found an unchristian way in which mankind might suffer less by learning more.

Jeffers's concern with suffering began his conversion in 1916-1917, but it remained distractingly incomplete until he helped build his home in the summer of 1919. Then, as he came to admire its granite and the rest of the universe for their unhuman beauty and permanence, he gained a peaceful self-surrender and increased awareness. By so expanding his awareness beyond himself and humanity, he had made his troubles seem vanishingly small and had found the detached yet compassionate awareness which makes the poems he wrote from that summer on unlike anyone else's. He went on to write more than three hundred poems, almost all of them prais-

ing what he repeatedly called "the enormous beauty of the universe." As he explained to a reader years later, "When you are excited by something that seems beautiful or significant, you want to show it to others." He had discovered for himself the basic point of Buddhism–that selfishness blinds us, causing misery which we can and should avoid–and that he could transcend that selfishness by looking beyond himself to suffering humanity, as he did in his tragedies, and to the universe.

Jeffers said that he rejected Buddhism as well as Christianity, apparently because the misleading descriptions of Buddhism then available in the European languages made Jeffers think of Buddhism as self-centered. In "Theory of Truth," the poem with which Jeffers chose to end *The Selected Poetry of Robinson Jeffers*, he describes Buddha as "willing to annihilate Nature . . . to annul the suffering" of mankind, as if Buddha thought that he could make the universe not exist, a delusion which Jeffers understandably rejected. In "Credo," with which Jeffers ended the Modern Library edition of *Roan Stallion, Tamar, and Other Poems*, he made that contrast clearer still. His "friend from Asia . . . believes that nothing is real except as we make it," but Jeffers believed (as he also said in *Themes in My Poems*, 1956) exactly the opposite: the world makes us, and its "heartbreaking beauty will remain when there is no heart to break for it." Jeffers's misunderstanding of Buddhism was apparently caused by Western mistranslations of the Buddhist term *nirvana*, the state of mind which Buddhists want to achieve. Despite such translations, nirvana does not mean oblivion or any annihilation of the universe; it means a detached yet compassionate awareness of much more than the self, much like the cosmic perspective which Jeffers's poems advocate and display.

William Everson also recovered parts of Jeffers's next book, *Brides of the South Wind* (1974), which several New York publishers had rejected in 1921-1922. Not even Jeffers seems to have kept a copy of it, perhaps because he used much of it in later books. Apparently it contained Jeffers's earliest tragic narratives, in which unbridled selfishness brings misery to families on the Sur coast, thus demonstrating how not to behave, or so some of the fragments and Jeffers's later tragedies suggest. In both his tragedies and his short poems, Jeffers suggested that seeing the world's enormous beauty and our own unimportance should console us and keep us from the mistakes which cause so much misery. Radcliffe Squires has claimed that Jeffers's view echoes that of Arthur Schopenhauer's *The World as Will and Idea* (1819), which expresses precisely that Western misunderstanding of Buddhism which Jeffers explicitly rejects in "Credo" and "Theory of Truth," among other poems, and in his comment in *Themes in My Poems* (1956). Arthur Coffin and others have seen Jeffers as following Friedrich Nietzsche's philosophy, though apparently only the comment in *Thus Spake Zarathustra* (1883-1892)–that poets lie too much–had much effect on Jeffers. His awareness of the cycles of life, including the decline and extinction of whole cultures and species, ours included, came not from Nietzsche, but from his knowledge of archaeology, history, and evolution. Jeffers seems to have been most influenced by scientific discoveries from Copernicus on, by Greek tragedy, by the bitingly realistic early Greek lyric poet Archilochus, and by the philosophies of Lucretius and Baruch Spinoza. Like Lucretius, Spinoza, and many scientists, Jeffers described the universe as one interconnecting, infinite, and eternal system which we can and need to understand. He believed, as Stuart Hampshire has said Spinoza did, that "If we would improve human beings, we must study the natural laws of their behavior as dispassionately as we would study the behavior of trees and horses. . . ." Hampshire

adds that in the seventeenth century only Spinoza "seems somehow to have anticipated modern conceptions of the scale of the universe, and of man's relatively infinitesimal place within the vast system . . ." while other philosophers and literary people, except perhaps Pascal, "still implicitly thought in terms of a man-centered universe. . . ." Hampshire concludes that "To Spinoza it seemed that men can attain happiness and dignity only by identifying themselves . . . with the whole order of nature, and by submerging their interests in this understanding. . . . it is this aspect of Spinoza's naturalism, the surviving spirit of Lucretius against a greater background of knowledge, which most shocked and baffled his contemporaries and successors."

Such factually accurate humility still shocks and baffles many. Jeffers expressed this cosmic perspective in vividly sensed metaphors and examples, rather than in the abstractly logical language of Spinoza's philosophy, but the moral remains the same despite the difference in methods. As Bertrand Russell noted when writing about Spinoza during World War II, "it is comforting to reflect that human life, with all that it contains of evil and suffering, is an infinitesimal part of the life of the universe. Such reflections . . . may not constitute a religion, but in a painful world . . . [they] are a help toward sanity and an antidote to the paralysis of utter despair." Such reflections may not constitute a supernatural religion, but like Lucretius and Spinoza, Jeffers made them the basis for a more modestly matter-of-fact religion which notices and tries to do something to alleviate human suffering; because he mentions evil and suffering, however, some critics called Jeffers a sadist. Near the end of his life, in *Hungerfield and Other Poems* (1954), he recapitulated his view in "De Rerum Virtute," a title that emphasized its resemblance to the worldview Lucretius had expressed in *De Rerum Natura*. Both Jeffers and Lucretius believed that virtue comes from an accurate knowledge of the world, including an unflattering recognition of human mistakes, their causes and their results, and not from pious ignorance, no matter how good we may think our intentions.

Jeffers saw his poems as expressing not just a scientifically accurate knowledge of the universe (as they do), but also a mystical experience of the universe as God, appreciating its size and beauty and our unimportance–a view he felt humanity in general needs. As he said in *Themes in My Poems*, his poems "also express a protest against human narcissism. . . . If a person spends all his emotions on his own body and states of mind, he is mentally diseased. . . . It seems to me . . . that the whole human race spends too much emotion on itself. The happiest and freest man is the scientist investigating nature, or the artist admiring it; the person who is interested in things that are not human. Or, if he is interested in human beings, let him regard them objectively, as a very small part of the great music. Certainly humanity has its claims, on all of us; we can best fulfill them by keeping our emotional sanity; and this by seeing beyond and around the human race" to the universe which Jeffers thought "so beautiful that it must be loved." Jeffers used the clinical term *narcissism* accurately here, perhaps as a result of his medical training; and, according to Christopher Lasch's *The Culture of Narcissism* (1978), this emotional affliction is becoming increasingly common in our culture.

Perhaps because no publisher had accepted *Brides of the South Wind,* the book he wrote before *Tamar,* Jeffers had *Tamar and Other Poems* published at his own expense in April 1924 by the New York City printer Peter G. Boyle; Jeffers had noticed Boyle's advertisement in the *New York Times Book Review.* Six months later, enthusiastic reviews by Babette Deutsch, James Rorty, and Mark Van Doren suddenly made Jeffers famous, leading Boni and Liveright to publish a larger volume, *Roan Stallion, Tamar, and Other Poems,* in 1925. These reviewers hardly mentioned Jeffers's cosmic perspective and his protest against narcissism, but they did admire his ability to tell a story vividly. "Tamar" retells chapter thirteen of the second book of Samuel, setting the title character's story on the California coast by Point Lobos, two miles south of Jeffers's home, from December 1916 to the following August.

Jeffers's version begins when Tamar's brother drunkenly rides his horse over a cliff; she nurses and then seduces him, becomes pregnant, seduces a neighbor to force a marriage, and then, in her disgust with everyone involved, provokes a confrontation which ends when her family's farmhouse burns, killing them all. In his foreword to *The Selected Poetry of Robinson Jeffers,* the poet says the poem grew from the biblical story, from Shelley's "The Cenci," and from the "introverted and storm-twisted beauty of Point Lobos," presumably including the burned-out house which actually stood where the poem ends; the owner reputedly read the poem and said it was "a hell of a thing to write about a fel-

low's ranch!" The places and local legends of the Sur coast suggested many of Jeffers's poems. The isolation of its people made destructive emotional behavior easy, and the wilderness and weather provided metaphors and a backdrop for those emotions.

The seductions, incest, insanity, and violence of "Tamar" horrified some readers. An anonymous editorial writer for the 9 January 1926 issue of the *San Francisco Monitor* complained that "Jeffers has the power of Aeschylus, the subtlety of Sophocles," and so is "intrinsically terrible," without seeming to notice that terror may have a moral purpose and result. Not until Robert Brophy's *Robinson Jeffers, Myth, Ritual and Symbol in his Narrative Poems* appeared in 1973 did a critic show just how closely Jeffers had followed Aeschylus, Sophocles, and Euripides. Jeffers's long poems repeatedly use the five-part plot structure of Greek tragedies (introduction, complication, crisis, catastrophe, denouement) and their seasonal metaphors; both describe suffering and death as necessary for knowledge and new life. Jeffers divided "Tamar" into seven numbered sections: one and two introduce Tamar's brother's fall and recovery; three through five present the complicating seductions; six describes the crisis and catastrophe in which Tamar symbolically dies to be reborn as a willfully selfish child who bullies her family until she indirectly causes their death by fire in part seven, the denouement which completes the plot and solves their problems by ending the characters. The poem dates these stages of its plot by the moon and tides, stars and weather, to show its characters' lives as both parts and products of the world's much larger cycles, cycles Jeffers repeatedly called "the great music" we need to hear. Tamar's loves begin in spring and end in a fire in the sterile heat of August, the dead season in California's Mediterranean climate. That end seems both the epitome and the result of reckless passions in a situation so corrupt that perhaps only fire could purify it and so let new lives start. As Gilbert Murray explained in the second chapter of *The Classical Tradition in Poetry* (1927), tragedies celebrate the cycle of the seasons and sacrifice human scapegoats to ensure the continued survival of life in general, and so does "Tamar."

With this poem, Jeffers began a series of experiments with tragedy. Five years after "Tamar" appeared, Joseph Wood Krutch claimed in *The Modern Temper* (1929) that the scientific discoveries which diminish our sense of our own importance make any modern tragedy impossible; but Jeffers's tragedies repeatedly mention these discoveries: his characters' tragic mistakes result from selfishly ignoring the human unimportance these discoveries reveal, and the misery these mistakes cause shows how dangerous ignorance can prove to be.

In 1925 Jeffers's tragedy "Roan Stallion" made that unimportance more explicit, but it became notorious for another reason: some misread it as describing a sexual relationship between a horse and a woman. In fact, it does not; it describes her glimpse of the more than merely human beauty of the universe which the horse exemplifies, as she realizes when she briefly escapes the degrading circumstances of her life. When her husband tries to abuse her again, she runs to the horse for protection; the horse has become her god. It kills the husband, and then, moved by "some obscure human fidelity," she shoots the horse, only to realize too late that she has destroyed what had meant god and power, glory and freedom to her. As the poem suggests in an often noticed but generally misunderstood reference to releasing energy by splitting atoms, she has had her chance to learn and change by suffering, to grow beyond her depressingly human limitations, but like most of us, she wastes that chance, a point Jeffers went on to make again.

Also in *Roan Stallion, Tamar, and Other Poems,* in "The Tower Beyond Tragedy," Jeffers rewrote a Greek tragedy for the first time, to show how to escape tragedy. Tamar's narcissism kills her and five others; the woman in "Roan Stallion" survives, but without the liberation she might have had. In "The Tower Beyond Tragedy," his version of Aeschylus's *Oresteia,* Jeffers has his Orestes grow beyond the blind emotions which cause such tragedies. He begins with Agamemnon's triumphal return from the Trojan War, a situation Agamemnon's wife Clytemnestra complicates by killing him, causing her son Orestes to kill her, a crisis resolved by a catastrophe. Orestes then regains his sanity by realizing that his feelings do not matter. He escapes what might otherwise have become an endless and pointless cycle of tragedy after tragedy by learning from tragedy, and giving up the political power he won by killing his mother and her lover. Jeffers's Cassandra foresees not just individuals but whole cultures caught in such cyclic tragedies. If we have such a cosmic perspective, we might avoid the delusions of importance which cause tragedies, or might learn from tragedies not to repeat such mistakes,

or so Jeffers kept suggesting, a hope apparently provoked by World War I and made to seem more desperate by World War II. Jeffers had not intended "The Tower Beyond Tragedy" for the stage, but it appeared with some success on Broadway in 1950, with Judith Anderson as Clytemnestra. Apparently the granite tower Jeffers built next to his house in 1920-1924 provided the title and central metaphor of the poem, which suggested that a selfless sense of kinship with the universe, which includes granite and stars, birds, and the ocean (what Jeffers saw from his tower), can help us escape the all-too-human emotional blindnesses which cause so much misery. So Jeffers found, as he built and lived in his house and tower, and wrote about those subjects. His house and tower still stand, a national literary historical monument defying the real estate developers who have planned to demolish the house and tower and subdivide what little remains of Jeffers's property.

In 1927 Jeffers's next book, *The Women at Point Sur,* confused even his friends. This 175-page poem concerns a Reverend Dr. Barclay, whose name and delusion seem a parody of Bishop George Berkeley (whose name is pronounced "Barclay") and his philosophy that the world exists only as and because God perceives it. Jeffers's Barclay is so upset by his only son's death in World War I that he renounces his country and Christianity. Failing to notice anyone else's suffering, he comes to think of himself as the prophet of some new religion, and then as God. When an earthquake shakes him, it surprises him, but he claims that he created it and controls the world, when, in fact, he cannot control anything, himself included. When he looks at the universe of millions of galaxies which astronomers were then just beginning to photograph, Barclay sees all that immensity as only his own eye reflected, looking back at itself. Like Narcissus, he thinks the world exists only as his mirror when in fact, like an eye, he exists only as a dependent part which cannot survive alone; he dies because he will not learn that lesson. He behaves so immorally because he cannot imagine how anyone else might feel. He rapes his daughter–Jeffers repeatedly used incest as a metaphor and example of narcissism–and wanders off into the wilderness, hopelessly lost, to die of exhaustion while claiming that he is God and inexhaustible, as if his words could cause miracles. Like the logical positivists, semanticists, C. S. Peirce (but very few other poets apart from Lucretius and the Ger-

Robinson and Una Jeffers with their twin sons, Donnan Call and Garth Sherwood, at Tor House

man Christian Morgenstern), Jeffers regarded words as only words, inevitably abstract, at best approximate, and quite unmagical, a skepticism which seems a part of his humility for himself and mankind in general.

Apparently to avoid the confusion caused by *The Women at Point Sur,* Jeffers promptly made his next tragedy, "Cawdor," shorter and simpler, using the plot of Euripides' already proven *Hippolytus* (he used it again for his play "The Cretan Woman," published in 1954 in *Hungerfield and Other Poems*). In its first section, the poem "Cawdor" introduces the dangerously beautiful and resentful Fera, first seen emerging from a range fire leading her blind and dying father; they have nowhere to go and no money. Her name means "wild," and she is: she cynically marries the smugly self-confident fifty-year-old rancher Cawdor to save her father and proceeds to complicate Cawdor's life disastrously when her father dies. Cawdor's son (Jeffers's Hippolytus) will not let Fera seduce him (parts two through seven), and, in a spiteful refusal to accept such limitations or to consider anything but her own emotions, she provokes a crisis by claiming the son has raped her. In his bewildered innocence, he flees from his father's anger only to fall to his death in the dark (parts seven through ten). Fera then provokes a catastrophe by telling the truth (parts eleven through fifteen); like Oedipus,

Cawdor then blinds himself when he realizes how blind he has been (part sixteen). The poem celebrates the world's cycles by depicting fires that destroy old lives to make new life possible–as in "Tamar," a metaphor suggested perhaps by the fires California ranchers used to set, burning the old grass each fall to make more new grass grow the next spring, as at the beginning of "Cawdor"; Fera's emotions obviously resemble that fire.

The poem's fire metaphors also include two descriptions of dreams caused by death. In section seven, Fera's father's remembered failures produce a series of increasingly self-indulgent and simpleminded fantasies as his brain cells decompose, disconnecting first from the world and then from one another, a process Jeffers compares to the slow fire of decaying wood as it shines weakly in the dark; the process soon ends in a numb dark silence. In section fifteen, a caged eagle dies and dreams of soaring up as the earth dwindles beneath it–a remarkable anticipation of the view astronauts began having as their rockets took off some forty years later–until it finds its peace in the very heart of light and fire, the source of life, the sun. The bird's dream explodes outward, making it more aware of the universe beyond itself; the man's fantasies collapse inward, ignoring everything but his own self-pity and the contemptibly petty greediness which kept his life frustrating. Like many of Jeffers's other women, Fera proves fearlessly emotional, and spectacularly destructive as a result; though Jeffers deplores the misery they cause, he seems to admire such characters, as well as finding the misery they cause morally instructive.

As Jeffers told his bibliographer S. S. Alberts, the title poem of his next book, *Dear Judas and Other Poems* (1929), "was written in 1928, with the thought of presenting the only divine figure still living in the minds of people of our race, as the hero of a tragedy. The Japanese Nō plays, in which the action is performed by ghosts revisiting the scenes of their passions, no doubt influenced my conception."

In this poem, the ghosts of Judas, Jesus, and the Virgin Mary comment on what happened almost twenty centuries ago, just before and after the Crucifixion, giving the audience the benefit of their hindsight and three firsthand points of view. Their comments make Judas's behavior seem understandably human, and perhaps even admirable: Judas prudently and compassionately foresaw that any attempt at rebellion against the occupying Romans would cause widespread misery and so tried to prevent it by having its most probable leader detained. In this attempt to avoid still worse oppression, Judas succeeds disastrously well: he becomes a tragic fool as his well-meaning mistake makes possible not just the human sacrifice with which Christianity began, but also the misery which Christianity has helped cause since then, a mistake Jesus forgives because it made his glorification possible. Judas remains unconsoled, because his mistake has consequences which go on for centuries, consequences he did not want and cannot prevent. His betrayal is an impressive example of how good intentions can lead straight to Hell, when a seemingly small act has enormous and mostly unexpected consequences. Jeffers had not imagined that anyone would ever produce "Dear Judas" as a play and seemed quite unsurprised when a production of it was banned in Boston in 1947 because, the mayor said, it might stir up religious feelings.

Jeffers's success with an unchristian view of the world and humanity predictably offended some critics, most notably Yvor Winters, who wrote that because Jeffers saw the world as God, and in terms of a textbook in physics, Jeffers had "abandoned narrative logic" as well as ethics. Winters seems to have meant that nothing which did not agree with his own view could make sense. He claimed that Jeffers's poems are "defective" be-

cause they have no rational plots or structures, and so cannot be paraphrased, though Winters did paraphrase two of them, both inaccurately. Winters claimed that Jeffers's poems only repeat images, "with no rational necessity for any order . . . the order being determined wholly by the author's feeling about the graduation of importance or intensity." Such a comment may describe *The Waste Land* accurately, but not any of Jeffers's more than 440 poems except one twenty-line lyric Winters did not mention, "The Maid's Thought," which first appeared in *Tamar and Other Poems* in 1924. That poem begins with the girl saying, "listen, even the water is sobbing for something"; seventeen lines later she says what she wants, having progressed step by step from the ocean to plants to animals to herself, with each example of longing more intense and important to her than the one before. The whole series neatly recapitulates the evolution of life which she epitomizes, and which will continue if she gets what she wants, not an act without consequences despite Winters's claim that none of Jeffers's characters do anything that has any meaning or consequence. Winters said literature should be judged by the accuracy of its perceptions, a principle which may also apply to the criticism of literature. Winters claimed Jeffers used "the terminology of modern physics" but mentioned no examples, perhaps because Jeffers used so few such terms, and he seemed unable to admit how vividly and accurately Jeffers described the world, a point Horace Lyon documented in *Jeffers Country* (1970), a collection of some of Jeffers's previously published poems illustrated by Lyon's photographs. Though Winters says Jeffers does not describe the world as a botanist would, "The Maid's Thought" mentions precisely what a botanist would notice in that particular place and season: the "sulphury pollen dust" of the pines, the broom, deerweed, wild iris, globe tulips, and bronze bell in blossom, and all referred to by nontechnical names.

Though Winters managed to ignore them almost totally in his survey of the methods of organizing poetry, Jeffers used the rhetorical structures–tragic plots and other sequences, seasonal metaphors and other comparisons–which have been basic to poetry at least since Aeschylus. Winters's argument that Jeffers's poems have no moral meaning or coherence depends upon the curious assumption that because scientific discoveries reveal the causes, results, and circumstances of what we do, such knowledge leaves us unable

Pencil drawing of Jeffers by Sadie Adriani, circa 1950 (by permission of the Jeffers Collection, Occidental College Library)

to make choices or to understand anything, as if we can be free, moral, and intelligent only when ignorant. From "Tamar" on, Jeffers's poems say and show why we need to escape such self-pitying and irresponsible ignorance, and to know what misery it causes, a matter-of-fact morality Winters ignored. For instance, he called such plots as that of "The Loving Shepherdess" in *Dear Judas and Other Poems* "non-narrative" because it is "reversible," and he paraphrased that poem as about "a girl who knows herself doomed to die . . . in childbirth . . . [who] wanders over the countryside . . . turned cruelly from door to door . . . until finally the girl dies. . . ." The plot depends on two obviously irreversible changes, pregnancy and death, and shows that the girl dies as a result of her self-centered ignorance, including the delusion that her baby is the world and God, so she thinks that she contains it rather than it containing her. The result seems the opposite of the *Odyssey*. The male Odysseus returns home with great success by cheating and killing others; the shepherdess wanders from her home to her death alone, hurt-

ing no one but herself and failing at everything she tries, which makes her delusion of importance as the creator of the world and God pathetically understandable but no less dangerous as a compensation for her failures. As Aristotle said of the *Odyssey*, the rest is anecdote. In both cases, all the anecdotes describe and explain the central character's behavior and help to determine what happens next in memorably vivid ways.

Jeffers wrote little criticism, but as *The Selected Letters of Robinson Jeffers* shows, he answered questions from readers. He wrote a helpful foreword to *The Selected Poetry* (1938), as well as *Themes in My Poems* (1956) for his only lecture tour, and *Poetry, Gongorism and A Thousand Years* for the 18 January 1948 *New York Times* (republished as a book in 1949). As his poem "Self-Criticism in February" shows, he knew what critics said, and why he thought them wrong:

> *And now*
> *For the worst fault: you have never mistaken*
> *Demon nor passion nor idealism for the real God.*
> Then what is most disliked in those verses
> Remains most true. *Unfortunately. If only you could*
> *   sing*
> *That God is love, or perhaps that social*
> *Justice will soon prevail.* I can tell lies in prose.

The "more massive violence" he had predicted promptly came in World War II. While much modern poetry became notorious for its obscurity and its retreat from public subjects, Jeffers apparently thought he had something important to say to mankind about mankind and the world we inhabit, and so tried to say it clearly, offending some.

By 1929 Jeffers had written nine tragedies in seven years and thirty or more shorter poems, establishing himself as one of the most widely read and discussed American poets. He was the first to appear on the cover of *Time*, the 4 April 1932 issue, some twenty years before T. S. Eliot did. As Jeffers later said, he felt tired by 1929 and wanted to rest by "playing dead for a few months. Foreign travel is like a pleasant temporary death; it relieves you of responsibilities and familiar scenes and duties." Jeffers and his wife and twin sons went to Ireland and Britain for the second half of 1929; the result was *Descent to the Dead*, sixteen short poems about the dead of those islands, published as a separate book in 1931 and included in *Give Your Heart to the Hawks* in 1933.

Once home again in 1930 Jeffers began a series of narratives whose painful ends still demonstrate the need for an unselfish detachment from otherwise blinding emotions. Most of them are without the plot structure of Greek tragedy, as if he had decided to avoid repeating himself and to find new forms for tragedy by writing something like naturalistic novels in verse. In "Thurso's Landing," published in 1932, a stupidly jealous husband and a resentfully unfaithful wife destroy each other. His strength and courage and her passion prove worse than useless without some detached intelligence, a moral point obscured by so much misery and confusion.

In "Margrave," also in *Thurso's Landing and Other Poems*, Jeffers contrasts the useless self-pity of a condemned medical student's last hours with the outward-looking discoveries about the universe which astronomers make. The student's consciousness only makes him more miserable–he knows precisely what hanging will do to him–and more pathetic as well as despicable; he kidnapped a little girl to get money to continue his education and then killed her, a plot suggested by the then famous but now forgotten Hickman case. Considering how miserably we behave, Jeffers said, no wonder the whole universe seems to be recoiling from us as if in horror. Astronomers had then just discovered the red shift in the light from galaxies which indicates that other galaxies are moving away from us as the universe expands–a staggering metaphor, but readers may refuse to consider so depressing and despicable a character as the medical student as a representative example of humanity and may not appreciate Jeffers's disgust as a result of a long-tried compassion.

In "Give Your Heart to the Hawks" Jeffers seems less exasperated, perhaps because he has made his characters more likable. The poem presents a family on the Sur coast destroyed by their reactions to a single disastrously emotional moment, and here Jeffers at least began with a Christian organizing archetype to replace the plot structure and seasonal metaphors of Greek tragedy. The poem begins with Michael Fraser's playfully putting a harmless snake up his sister-in-law's leg as she picks apples, as if they were Adam and Eve in Eden, and Jeffers meant to invite Freudian interpretations. Their happy time soon ends: in the next scene, at a drunken party on the beach below, her husband kills a rattlesnake and then either jealously kills his brother Michael or helplessly watches him fall from the cliff (in emotional moments he cannot distinguish between his guilty fantasies and fact). Because he cannot "give his heart to the hawks" (cannot detach what he sees from his blindly human emotions), he loses his sanity and then his life while trying to escape from his fantasies. His pregnant wife survives because she can and does love unselfishly, caring for others while knowing that the world does not depend on her. Her husband had thought his guilt ruined everything, making the whole world hate him, and so he slaughtered the cattle he thought were pursuing him. His wife has only one such self-important delusion, that the child she carries "will change the world," and so the tragedy may happen again.

In 1933 Jeffers returned to Greek plots: "At the Fall of an Age," in *Give Your Heart to the Hawks and Other Poems*, shows the dead of the Trojan War come back from Hades to take Helen of Troy to the woman with whom she grew up. Blaming Helen for the war, in which the woman's husband died, that woman has Helen killed and kills herself, the last of Helen's many victims. In "Resurrection," in *Solstice and Other Poems* (1935), a soldier who died in World War I temporarily returns from death to haunt the guilty, a dramatic device Jeffers used again in "The Love and the Hate," the first half of the title poem about World War II in *The Double Axe & Other Poems* (1948). Jeffers wrote about ghosts as early as 1924, in "Tamar," and seemed to like to think of his ghost haunting his granite home for centuries to come. Despite Yvor Winters's claims, Jeffers was not altogether a determinist; he had his inconsistent and often moving moments of belief in the supernatural.

In the title poem of *Solstice and Other Poems* Jeffers also used a Greek plot, retelling Euripides' *Medea* as he would again more successfully in his *Medea* (1946). After his successes from "Tamar" to "The Loving Shepherdess" in 1924-1929, Jeffers seemed to need to find new sources and forms for tragedy, and he used the supernatural more often in his narrative poems, as if he had begun to find a strictly naturalistic worldview too bleak, or too limiting for what he wanted to say.

Solstice and Other Poems also includes "At the Birth of an Age," Jeffers's one tragedy using a Teutonic legend. It describes a stupidly petty and suicidal squabble between three brothers, leaders of a minor Germanic tribe, and their sister, who became Attila's consort because they had murdered her husband. The squabble has results they cannot even imagine: because it also kills the general who might otherwise have conquered the disintegrating Roman empire, Attila suffers his only defeat (as in fact he did, near Châlons, a hundred miles east of Paris, in the year A.D. 451), and Europe remains Christian. The victims seem dwarfed by the enormous consequences of their passionate ignorance, and at the end of the poem Jeffers makes them seem still smaller, still more pathetically limited and foolish in their pride, by contrasting them with the universe as a whole, as personified by Odin (the god of wisdom, conflict, and death in Teutonic and Norse mythology), who tortures himself in order to discover everything, which is to say, his own identity. Here Jeffers restates the traditional moral of Greek tragedies–to know who you are by knowing your limits, and so to do nothing excessively–not just in terms of another mythology, but also in terms of scientific discoveries about the universe that limits and creates us. He seems to suggest that if we discover enough we may save ourselves from the often miserable effects of ignorance. As scientists have from Newton or Galileo on, Jeffers sees the universe as one totally interconnecting network of forever-changing yet forever-balancing forces; he also sees those changes as producing not just the consciousness of his universe-as-God, but ours as well. At its most intense, consciousness becomes painful, but without it we cannot learn, so like Jeffers's Odin we must keep on balancing between opposing forces to survive.

Jeffers's view parallels the Buddhist and Taoist view of the universe as yin and yang, a perpetual balancing of mutually dependent opposites, and the Buddhist and Hindu metaphor of the universe as Indra's net (Indra is the Hindu god of the heavens). In his net, every part of the universe reflects and affects every other. Jeffers never mentions Indra and may have independently rediscovered the world-as-God-as-net metaphor which he used at least sixty times. He might also have borrowed it from Newton's law of gravitational attraction, in which every particle of the universe reflects every other, a point made clear in the astronomy textbook which Jeffers read at Occidental. As the physicist Fritjof Capra has since said in *The Tao of Physics* (1975), apparently without knowing about Jeffers, this view is basic to physics and astronomy, and to both Eastern and Western mysticism, as in William Blake's "Auguries of Innocence," which starts

To see a World in a grain of sand
And a Heaven in a wild flower,
Hold Infinity in the palm of your hand,
And Eternity in an hour.

The net metaphor and Newton's law suggest that every part of the universe is what it is, does what it does, because of all the rest, and so (as these lines may say) each part in part reflects the whole universe. These lines also seem a recipe for mystical experience; *innocence* may mean that selflessly detached compassionate awareness which Jeffers and Buddhists advocate. Jeffers saw the sheer size and beauty of the universe as both revealing our unimportance and consoling us: see the planet as a grain of sand or as an eyeball (as Jeffers did in "The Eye," 1948), and mankind becomes too small to see, and our individual troubles vanish–a liberation resented by those who prefer to cling to their self-important miseries, and misunderstood by critics who called Jeffers nihilistic, inhuman, and immoral. But if we see the universe as a net of cause-result relationships, as Jeffers did, we may choose what we do much more carefully, knowing that every act has its consequences, some of them irreversible, and so become more morally and ecologically responsible. The word *ecology* means the net of relationships between each species or individual and his environment, and, as with a net, disturbing any part inevitably affects all the rest. Thus, for Jeffers, if we see our feelings as only our feelings, and relatively unimportant, and as often misleading distractions, we may become less selfish, less harried by such misery-causing emotions as ambition and greed, and so become more compassionate and responsible because more aware of individuals and of the universe beyond ourselves.

In 1937 Jeffers continued his experiments with sources and forms for tragedy by writing one based on the old Scots border ballad "Edward," whose last line gave Jeffers his title for the poem and for the book containing it: *Such Counsels You Gave to Me* (1937). In the ballad, a man with wife and children takes his mother's counsels and kills his father but is then forced to go into exile and curses her. Jeffers makes the young man an unmarried medical student whose health and sanity break down from overwork after his father refuses to go on paying for his education. He murders his father but refuses to avoid punishment or to let his mother seduce him. Like many of Jeffers's tragic fools, he seems haunted by a ghostly counterpart of himself which tells him what he could have done, increasing his anguish without helping him succeed; he cannot see beyond that projection of himself to see anything objectively.

In 1938 Jeffers put together *The Selected Poetry of Robinson Jeffers* and then, just before flying over the Sierra Nevada to Death Valley that Easter as the passenger in an open-cockpit biplane with his younger (and only) brother, Hamilton, left his wife a note in which he anticipated his possible death on that flight. He included his will and directions for his funeral, asking "to be cremated as cheaply, quickly, and quietly as possible, no speech, no meeting nor music, no more coffin than may be necessary, no embalming, no flowers. . . . Put the ashes a few inches deep . . . near our little daughter's ashes" in the yard by the house. Meanwhile, he said that he had "no desire to die before writing another poem or two," and that he "should love to know" his wife and sons "for hundreds of years," but he neither shrank from nor welcomed death. When he did die, in 1962, his directions were followed.

In the summer of 1938, perhaps because he would not become Mabel Dodge Luhan's pet poet in Taos to replace D. H. Lawrence, Luhan encouraged a younger woman to try distracting Jeffers. Una Jeffers shot herself, perhaps by accident, and not seriously; the Jefferses avoided Luhan after that. The incident had its aftermath, as Jeffers's note later that year reveals. It begins,

> Una, *I can't write* . . . and writing–during the past 30 years–has become one of the conditions of life for me. . . .
> I believe I'll have a new birth . . . something will happen, and *life through this hell come home to me . . . ,*

as it had in 1917-1919 in "the accidental new birth" of his mind which made his original poetry possible.

Apparently Jeffers turned to Buddhism for that rebirth, because his next long narrative, "Mara" in *Be Angry at the Sun* (1941), is named for the temptress who tried unsuccessfully to distract Buddha from enlightenment. With Jeffers's tragic fool, she succeeds, and his self-pity and disgust with World War II drive him to suicide. Jeffers's Mara may owe something to Sir Edwin Arnold's best-selling biography of Buddha, *The Light of Asia,* first published in 1879. Buddha's distractions begin with

> The Sin of Self, who in the Universe
> As in a mirror her fond face shown,

And crying "I," would have the world say "I"

—the narcissistic mistake Jeffers's tragic fools, especially Barclay and the loving shepherdess, repeatedly make.

In his foreword to *Be Angry at the Sun,* Jeffers apologized for his "obsession with contemporary history" before and during World War II. It threatened his detachment and his patience and left many of his poems from 1939 on pinned to particular events and dated. In one, "The Day is a Poem (September 19, 1939)," Jeffers calls Hitler

> A man of genius: that is, of amazing
> Ability, courage, devotion, cored on a
>   sick child's soul
>   ....
>   a sick child
> Wailing in Danzig; invoking destruction and wailing
>   at it.

Hostile reviewers sometimes quoted "genius" out of context while calling Jeffers a Fascist and not adding that *genius* can mean "the evil spirit dominating a situation" or that Jeffers also described Hitler as a dangerous and contemptible psychotic. Hitler disgusted but also interested Jeffers as a spectacular example of the sort of delusion best avoided. In poem after poem, Jeffers tried to make such delusions unattractive by showing their ignoble causes and painful results.

"The Bowl of Blood," the other long poem in *Be Angry at the Sun,* shows Hitler in April 1940 consulting a fortune-teller because his invasion of Norway seems about to fail, and he does not know what to do next (it is now known that Hitler did consult an astrologer then for that reason). But as a compulsive talker, Hitler tells his own fortune only to ignore it, thus helping make it come true. He says he will not repeat Napoleon's mistake of getting trapped by invading Russia before finishing England and will shoot himself rather than surrender as Napoleon did. Hitler did shoot himself in April 1945 just as Jeffers had predicted in May or June 1941, when or just before Hitler invaded Russia. The popular impression of Jeffers as a misanthropic hermit hiding in his tower has misled many a hostile critic; in fact, few other poets in America have taken such risks to comment on current public events to predict the culture's future in order to warn and help their readers, or been so resented for trying.

Jeffers could neither ignore the war nor suppose his warnings could prevent it. He regarded it as a "tragic farce," with millions of victims but no heroes. Any tragedy he might have written about the whole war would have been bewilderingly long and complicated and, worse, might have made Hitler seem sympathetic as its central figure and victim. "The Bowl of Blood" solves both problems: it concentrates on a few minutes in which Hitler seems contemptible in his stupidity and self-pity while so many others die, and doomed because he will not learn even when he unwittingly happens to tell the truth, a poetically just fate for so compulsive and lavishly rewarded a liar.

As the poems about the war which Jeffers left out of his books show even more clearly (see the posthumous collection *What Odd Expedients*, 1981), the war left Jeffers often more disgusted and despairing than detached because mankind suffers so much, while learning so little. Many of his poems of 1933-1961 read like choruses for a tragedy never written, a tragedy he might have felt no one would want to read, because the tragic fools and victims are whole countries and cultures, the readers included. He spent the war years writing shorter poems and smaller tragedies, including the adaptation of Euripides' *Medea* Judith Anderson requested.

Medea made Jeffers wealthy enough to keep his house as Carmel's taxes kept increasing; the play opened on Broadway on 20 October 1947 with Judith Anderson as Medea, and has since been produced in Scotland, England, Denmark, Italy, France, Portugal, Australia, and on Broadway again in 1982, and translated into four languages. Jeffers had seen only five plays before he wrote it, one of them his own *The Tower Beyond Tragedy*, but he made *Medea* move quickly from the first speech, in which Medea's nurse wishes Medea had never met the Greek adventurer Jason, to Jason's utter humiliation an hour later. As in Euripides' tragedy, Jason plans to marry a princess and exile his first wife, Medea, and their two sons, although he knows she killed members of her family to save him and so cannot go home. She arranges for sanctuary elsewhere, gives the princess a golden robe which burns her and her father alive, and kills Jason's sons. In Euripides' version, the gods then carry Medea away; in Jeffers's, she walks away, leaving an utterly defeated Jason to live on in misery, forever discredited for having so violated her love and trust.

With *The Double Axe & Other Poems* (1948), Jeffers offended the patriotic by describing World War II as a slaughter best avoided, and possibly also by his "rejection of human solipsism and recognition of the transhuman magnificence" of the universe on which our lives depend. He said we need his "philosophical attitude," which he unfortunately called Inhumanism, because "It seems time that our race began to think as an adult does, rather than like an egocentric baby or insane person. This manner of thought and feeling is neither misanthropic nor pessimist, though two or three people have said so and may again. It involves no falsehoods, and is a means of maintaining sanity in slippery times. . . . It offers a reasonable detachment instead of love, hate and envy" which cause tragedies, including "The Love and the Hate," the first half of the title poem. The second half shows how to survive by having so skeptical a detachment. Like Bodhidharma (470-543), who began Zen Buddhism, Jeffers's Inhumanist lives alone in the mountains and turns away would-be disciples by challenging them with riddles to make them think and to make them see the beauty of the universe beyond themselves.

In the summer of 1948 Jeffers and Una made their third trip to Ireland, where Jeffers nearly died of pleurisy; they got back to California to find that Una had cancer. She died in his arms in September 1950, leaving Jeffers desolate. He survived to write *Hungerfield & Other Poems*, published in 1954, and the poems his son Donnan and his biographer Melba Berry Bennet collected in *The Beginning & the End and Other Poems*, published in 1963, the year after Jeffers's death. He began "Hungerfield" by hoping that somewhere, somehow, Una might still live, but he admits in a few lines that he knows she has died, so he thinks of Hungerfield, the man who temporarily defeated death. Watching his mother die of cancer, Hungerfield decides to wrestle with death and stop him, as Hungerfield thinks he did when wounded in World War I. He does, and, for a few agonizing hours no one appreciates, no one dies. Then the dam bursts: Hungerfield's wife, child, and brother die, and Hungerfield burns his house, killing himself, but his mother escapes to live two more years. The poem portrays death as a needed mercy, as Jeffers apparently needed to think then; he also thought of Una living serenely on as a part of the lovely natural world. After 1958 he suffered illness after illness and died in his sleep on 20 January 1962.

Letters:

The Selected Letters of Robinson Jeffers, 1897-1962, edited by Ann N. Ridgeway (Baltimore: Johns Hopkins Press, 1968).
Includes letters in which Jeffers explains some of his ideas and poems but does not include many of Jeffers's letters to his wife.

Bibliographies:

S. S. Alberts, *A Bibliography of the Works of Robinson Jeffers* (New York: Random House, 1933).
Contains very detailed information about Jeffers's book up to 1933, but Jeffers wrote much after that; includes some of Jeffers's earliest surviving poems, not found in his books.

Alex A. Vardamis, *The Critical Reputation of Robinson Jeffers* (Hamden, Conn.: Shoe String Press, 1972).
Useful list of almost all the books, articles, and reviews about Jeffers's work up to 1972, with very brief summaries of many, but much useful work has been done since 1972.

Biography:

Melba Berry Bennett, *The Stone Mason of Tor House: The Life and Works of Robinson Jeffers* (Los Angeles: Ward Ritchie Press, 1966).
Uncritical biography by an old friend of Jeffers, with a few mistakes; very informative about his life, and also useful because it includes much of Jeffers's *Themes in My Poems* and *Poetry, Gongerism and A Thousand Years,* not easily available elsewhere, in which Jeffers does much to explain his poetry.

References:

Joseph Warren Beach, *The Concept of Nature in Nineteenth Century Poetry* (New York: Macmillan, 1936), pp. 542-546.
Brief comment on an important aspect of Jeffers's poetry, his response to nature.

Terry Beats, "Robinson Jeffers and the Canon," *American Poetry,* 5 (Fall 1987): 4-16.
Explains why some critics and reviewers have disliked or ignored Jeffers.

Robert J. Brophy, Afterword to *Dear Judas and Other Poems* (New York: Liveright, 1977), pp. 131-153.
Explains *Dear Judas* as a passion play and the structure and meaning of *The Loving Shepherdess.*

Brophy, *Robinson Jeffers, Myth, Ritual and Symbol in His Narrative Poems* (Cleveland: The Press of Case Western Reserve University, 1973).
Explains the structure and meaning of *Tamar, Roan Stallion, The Tower Beyond Tragedy* and *At the Birth of An Age* as tragedies.

M. Webster Brown, "A Poet Who Studied Medicine," *Medicine Journal and Record,* 130 (6 November 1929): 535-539.
Shows how vividly and accurately Jeffers describes characters' symptoms (and so proves wrong Hyatt H. Waggoner's claims that Jeffers wrote abstractly.

Frederic Ives Carpenter, *Robinson Jeffers* (New York: Twayne, 1962).
Useful general introduction, less detailed but more complete than Lawrence Clark Powell's 1940 study of Jeffers.

Carpenter, "The Values of Robinson Jeffers," *American Literature,* 11 (January 1940): 353-366.
Disproves the assertions of Hyatt H. Waggoner and Yvor Winters, who claim that Jeffers was without moral standards.

Arthur B. Coffin, *Robinson Jeffers: The Poetry of Inhumanism* (Madison: University of Wisconsin Press, 1971).
Attempts to explain Jeffers's philosophy.

James Daly, "Roots Under the Rocks," review of *Tamar and Other Poems, Poetry,* 26 (August 1925): 278-285.
One of the reviews responsible for Jeffers's sudden fame.

Babette Deutsch, "Brains and Lyrics," review of *Tamar and Other Poems, New Republic,* 43 (27 May 1925): 23-24.
Another of the reviews that made Jeffers suddenly famous.

Fraser Bragg Drew, "The Gentleness of Robinson Jeffers," *Western Humanities Review,* 12 (Autumn 1958): 379-381.

Shows that despite what some say, Jeffers was kind, not cruel, and objected to violence.

William Everson (Brother Antoninus), *Robinson Jeffers: Fragments of an Older Fury* (Berkeley: Oyez, 1968).
Describes how Jeffers's poems involve the most basic religious feelings.

Horace Gregory, "Poet Without Critics: A Note on Robinson Jeffers," *New World Writing: Seventh Mentor Selection* (New York: New American Library, 1955), pp. 40-52.
A general description of Jeffers's poems from *Tamar* in 1924, but excluding those in *Hungerfield* (1954) and *The Beginning & the End* (1963).

"Harrowed Marrow," *Time,* 19 (4 April 1932): 63-64.
Proven recognition of Jeffers's fame.

Eva Hesse, "Poetry as a Means of Discovery: A Critico-Theoretical Approach to Robinson Jeffers," *American Poetry,* 5 (Fall 1987): 17-34.
Explains what Jeffers meant by saying we need to "uncenter the human mind from itself " (become less egocentric).

William Savage Johnson, "The 'Savior' in the Poetry of Robinson Jeffers," *American Literature,* 15 (May 1943): 159-168.
Examines how skeptically Jeffers regarded would-be saviours among his characters and in history.

James Karman, *Robinson Jeffers: Poet of California* (San Francisco: Chronicle Books, 1987).
Good general introduction to Jeffers and his poetry as products of their times.

William H. Nolte, *Rock and Hawk: Robinson Jeffers and the Romantic Agony* (Athens: University of Georgia Press, 1975).
Shows Arthur B. Coffin, Radcliffe Squires, and other critics to be wrong in their view of Jeffers as a misanthropist.

"Pagan Horror from Carmel-by-the-Sea," *San Francisco Monitor,* 9 January 1926, p. 8.
Hysterical but half-admiring religious reaction against Jeffers as a writer, without Christian sensibilities but with the power of, the Greek tragic poets.

Lawrence Clark Powell, *Robinson Jeffers, The Man and His Work* (Pasadena: San Pasquel Press, 1940).
The first long study of Jeffers, now incomplete but still valuable because Powell knew Jeffers, because of Jeffers's own comments in this book, and because it begins to compare Jeffers with Lucretius.

Robinson Jeffers Newsletter (1962-).
Now edited by Robert J. Brophy of California State University at Long Beach, this publication contains many articles and notes and bits of information about Jeffers's life and writing.

James Rorty, "In Major Mold," review of *Tamar and Other Poems, New York Herald and Tribune Books,* 1 March 1925, pp. 1-2.
Another of the reviews that first made Jeffers famous.

Robert Ian Scott, "The Great Net: The World as God in Robinson Jeffers' Poetry," *The Humanist,* 46 (January/February 1986): 24-29, 46.
Views Jeffers's poems as meaningful in six ways and as moral because they help make us less selfish, and less blind to what we and the world are.

Scott, "Robinson Jeffers' Tragedies as Rediscoveries of the World," *Rocky Mountain Review of Language and Literature,* 29 (Autumn 1975): 147-165.
Presents Jeffers's tragedies (his long narrative poems) as descriptions of experiments by which the way of the world may be learned.

Radcliffe Squires, *The Loyalties of Robinson Jeffers* (Ann Arbor: University of Michigan Press, 1956).
A sympathetic but mistaken attempt to describe Jeffers as a follower of Schopenhauer's philosophy.

Mark Van Doren, "First Glance," review of *Tamar and Other Poems, Nation,* 120 (11 March 1925): 268.
A review by a major critic that helped make Jeffers famous.

Hyatt H. Waggoner, *The Heel of Elohim: Science and Values in Modern American Poetry* (Norman: University of Oklahoma Press, 1959), pp. 74-180, 201-202.

Claims (but does not prove) that Jeffers's poetry is abstract, amoral nonsense, and that his science is outdated.

Yvor Winters, *In Defense of Reason* (New York: Swallow Press/William Morrow, 1947), pp. 30-74.

An unsuccessful attempt to describe Jeffers's poems as incoherent and amoral.

Robert Zaller, *The Cliffs of Solitude: A Reading of Robinson Jeffers* (New York: Cambridge University Press, 1983).

Describes Jeffers's poems and attempts to explain why he wrote them, using psychoanalytic theories.

Papers:

The bulk of the Jeffers papers are at the Humanities Research Center of the University of Texas at Austin. Occidental College in Los Angeles has some three hundred pages of unpublished poems by Jeffers, most of them written between 1917 and 1920.

James Weldon Johnson

This entry was updated by Michael D. Senecal from the entry by Keneth Kinnamon (University of Arkansas) in DLB 51, Afro-American Writers from the Harlem Renaissance to 1940.

Places	Jacksonville, Fla. Fisk University, Nashville, Tenn.	Venezuela Atlanta University	New York City Nicaragua
Influences and Relationships	Booker T. Washington W. E. B. Du Bois Walt Whitman	John Rosamond Johnson Brander Matthews	Frederick Douglass Paul Laurence Dunbar
Literary Movements and Forms	Vernacular Poetry Journalism	Autobiography	Harlem Renaissance
Major Themes	Black Influence on American Culture	Racial Identity	Miscegenation

Cultural and Artistic Influences	Tin Pan Alley
	Black American
	  History
	Slave Traditions
		Minstrel and
		  Vaudeville
		Afro-American
		  Religious Tradition
			American Popular
			  Music
			Negro Spirituals

Social and Economic Influences	NAACP Racism	Black Bourgeoisie Educational Reform	The Law

BIRTH: Jacksonville, Florida, 17 June 1871, to James and Helen Louise Dillet Johnson.

EDUCATION: A.B., Atlanta University, 1894; Columbia University, 1903-1906.

MARRIAGE: 10 February 1910 to Grace Nail.

AWARDS AND HONORS: Honorary A.M., Atlanta University, 1904; Litt.D., Talladega College, 1917; Litt.D., Howard University, 1923; Spingarn Medal, 1925; Rosenwald Grant, 1929; W. E. B. Du Bois Prize for Negro Literature, 1933; Lewis Carroll Shelf Award for "Lift Every Voice and Sing," 1971.

DEATH: Wiscasset, Maine, 26 June 1938.

SELECTED BOOKS: *The Autobiography of an Ex-Colored Man* (Boston: Sherman, French, 1912); republished as *The Autobiography of an Ex-Coloured Man* (New York & London: Knopf, 1927);
Fifty Years and Other Poems (Boston: Cornhill, 1917);
God's Trombones; Seven Negro Sermons in Verse (New York: Viking, 1927);
Black Manhattan (New York: Knopf, 1930);
Saint Peter Relates an Incident of the Resurrection Day (New York: Privately printed, 1930);
Along This Way; The Autobiography of James Weldon Johnson (New York: Viking, 1933; Harmondsworth, U.K. & New York: Penguin, 1941);
Negro Americans, What Now? (New York: Viking, 1934);
Saint Peter Relates an Incident: Selected Poems (New York: Viking, 1935).

OTHER: *The Book of American Negro Poetry*, edited by Johnson (New York: Harcourt, Brace, 1922; enlarged, 1931);
The Book of American Negro Spirituals, edited by Johnson (New York: Viking, 1925);
The Second Book of American Negro Spirituals, edited by Johnson (New York: Viking, 1926); republished with *The Book of American Negro Spirituals* in *The Books of American Negro Spirituals* (1940).

PERIODICAL PUBLICATIONS: "Self-Determining Haiti," *Nation*, 111 (August 1920): 236-238, 265-267, 295-297, 345-347;
"Lynching: America's National Disgrace," *Current History*, 19 (January 1924): 596-601;

James Weldon Johnson (courtesy of the Schomburg Center for Research in Black Culture, the New York Public Library, Astor, Lenox and Tilden Foundations)

"Making of Harlem," *Survey Graphic*, 6 (March 1925): 635-639;
"Romance and Tragedy in Harlem," *Opportunity*, 4 (October 1926): 316-317, 330;
"Race Prejudice and the Negro Artist," *Harper's*, 157 (November 1928): 769-776;
"The Dilemma of the Negro Author," *American Mercury*, 15 (December 1928): 477-481;
"Negro Authors and White Publishers," *Crisis*, 36 (July 1929): 228-229;
"Communism and the Negro," *New York Herald Tribune Magazine*, 21 July 1935, pp. 2, 25, 27.

Versatility is the most salient characteristic of the life and career of James Weldon Johnson. Equipped with restless intelligence, abundant energy, and "an abhorrence of spare time," he crowded almost a dozen occupations into a busy lifetime, excelling in most of them: teacher, school principal, journalist, lawyer, songwriter, diplomat, novelist, poet, civil rights crusader, anthologist, professor. Throughout his various activities three concerns persisted. First, he was usually involved in education in one way or another, viewing it both as a route to individual achievement and as a means of racial advancement. Second, he devoted his considerable talents mainly to the service of his race, notably during his decade and a half as a major leader of the National Association for the Advancement of Colored People (1916-1930), and in other ways at other times of his life. Third, through his belletristic writing and his anthologies he was both contributor to and preserver of the Afro-American literary tradition, linking the nineteenth century to the Harlem Renaissance.

Johnson's family background encouraged achievement and cultural pursuits. His father, James Johnson, was a self-educated man who, as a waiter in New York and a headwaiter in Nassau and then in Jacksonville, Florida, achieved economic security and adopted middle-class values. While in New York he met and courted Helen Louise Dillet, a young woman of African-French-English ancestry, a native of Nassau who had grown up in New York, received a good education, and developed her musical talent. When Dillet returned with her mother to her native island in 1861, James Johnson followed her and secured a position in a large hotel. They were married in 1864 and prospered initially, but an economic recession forced the couple and their infant daughter to move to Jacksonville, a rapidly expanding city becoming an important tourist center. Here were born James William (changed in 1913 to Weldon) Johnson and, two years later, John Rosamond Johnson.

Growing up in an increasingly secure middle-class home with books and a piano, young James was inculcated with strict notions of integrity by his father and with intellectual and artistic interests by his mother. The first black woman public schoolteacher in Florida, Helen Johnson encouraged a love of learning in her children, whom she taught at home before they attained school age and again in the classroom at Stanton School. From her they learned to read and to play the piano. A precocious child, James was quickly reading Charles Dickens, Sir Walter Scott, John Bunyan, and Jacob and Wilhelm Grimm. Formal education at Stanton School extended only through the eighth grade, from which James graduated in 1887, but travel and friends had a broadening effect. While still a small child he accompanied his family on a visit to Nassau, and in 1884 he spent a summer in New York with his grand-

mother and her sister. He took a Whitmanesque pleasure in the bustling movement and noise of the great city: "I loved the ferryboats—the rushing crowds, the stamping teams and yelling teamsters, the tooting whistles, the rattling windlasses and clanging chains when we left and entered the ship." As he further recalled in his autobiography, *Along This Way* (1933), "I was born to be a New Yorker." This cosmopolitan sense of self was reinforced by his friendships with Ricardo Rodriguez Ponce, a Cuban youth from whom he learned Spanish; Judson Douglass Wetmore (the "D—" of *Along This Way*), the near-white prototype for the protagonist of *The Autobiography of an Ex-Colored Man* (1912); and, somewhat later, a cultured and widely traveled white physician named Dr. Thomas Osmond Summers, for whom he worked as an assistant and with whom he traveled to Washington on a professional trip. Reading literary erotica and religious agnosticism in Dr. Summers's library, young Johnson expanded his interests in additional directions.

His development continued at Atlanta University, where he matriculated in the preparatory division after graduation from Stanton. In 1894 he received the A.B. degree from the collegiate division. At least as important as the rather rigorous academic curriculum, he received an education in racial issues from which he had been somewhat sheltered in Jacksonville. This other education included, he remembered forty years later, "preparation to meet the tasks and exigencies of life as a Negro, a realization of the peculiar responsibilities due to my own racial group, and a comprehension of the application of American democracy to Negro citizens." Not only was race a constant topic of discussion and debate among the undergraduates, but Johnson spent two summers teaching in a black rural school near Hampton, Georgia, an invaluable experience with a mode of black life new to him. In the summer before his senior year he traveled to Chicago to work in the great Columbian Exposition. Here on "Colored People's Day" he heard the aged Frederick Douglass speak and the young Paul Laurence Dunbar read from his poetry. With Dunbar, who was not yet famous, he quickly initiated a friendship and literary relation that would continue for many years.

Upon graduation and not yet twenty-three years of age, Johnson left Atlanta University as a member of a singing quartet touring New England to raise money for the institution. Back in Jacksonville in the fall as principal of Stanton, now perhaps the largest public school in the state, he was thoroughly prepared by education, travel, and experience to assume his self-defined role as "leader and helper to my race." In addition to improving Stanton by adding ninth- and tenth-grade courses, he attempted to educate the city's adult black community by starting a newspaper, the *Daily American,* which was published for eight months in 1895 and 1896. In his editorials Johnson promoted racial self-help while defending civil rights for the race against the resurgence of white supremacy. The financial failure of the newspaper was disappointing, but he hoped other avenues to racial leadership could be opened. Although not a single black person had ever been admitted to the Florida bar, Johnson began to read law in the office of a friendly white attorney. After a year and a half he passed a rigorous bar examination despite the obvious racial hostility of the examiners. As a lawyer, however, he found routine paperwork tedious, and his continuing duties at Stanton occupied much of his time. Johnson was growing restless in Jacksonville, too small an arena to contain either his talents or his ambitions. Furthermore, racial restrictions were tightening as the new century began.

The pattern of Johnson's career alternated between administrative and artistic roles. He had written poetry in college and even before, and the postgraduation concert tour had revived his earlier interest in music. When his brother John returned to Jacksonville in 1897, after successfully having studied at the New England Conservatory of Music and after having completed a tour with a black variety show, James was ready to resume creative activity. Together the brothers wrote "Tolosa, or The Royal Document," which was "a comic opera satirizing the new American imperialism" in a Gilbert-and-Sullivan mode. James supplied the story and lyrics while his brother composed the music. A trip to New York in the summer of 1899 did not lead to the production of the work, as the brothers had hoped, but it did introduce them to some of the key figures of the musical stage, including Oscar Hammerstein. Among the celebrated black theatrical personalities they met were the comedians Bert Williams, George Walker, and Ernest Hogan and the musicians Bob Cole, Will Marion Cook, and Harry T. Burleigh. Cook had collaborated on the operetta *Clorindy, or the Origin of the Cakewalk* (1898) with Paul Laurence Dunbar, who, now famous, renewed his friendship with Johnson. The life of

Johnson in the mid 1870s

black bohemia in New York fascinated the schoolmaster; Jacksonville certainly had nothing comparable. "I now began to grope toward a realization of the importance of the American Negro's cultural background and his creative folk art," he was to write in *Along This Way,* "and to speculate on the superstructure of conscious art that might be reared on them."

The creative side of Johnson's personality was now in the ascendancy. While still in New York, he wrote with his brother and Bob Cole the song "Louisiana Lize," selling it to a popular white singer. Returning to Jacksonville, he wrote one of his best dialect poems, the plaintive love lyric "Sence You Went Away," which was published in *Century* in 1900, the first time the author appeared in print in a national magazine. With his brother he shortly afterward wrote "Lift Every Voice and Sing," which was to become known as the "Negro National Anthem." Back in New York the following summer (and the summer thereafter), the brothers formed a songwriting partnership with Bob Cole. Almost immediately successful in bringing out hit songs, the team nevertheless worked at a disadvantage with the Johnsons in Florida most of the year. After a fire destroyed a large area of Jacksonville, including the Stanton School, and after an ugly and dangerous personal encounter with state militiamen brought in to keep order, Johnson's hometown seemed even less attractive than before. The school was rebuilt, shoddily, and he returned to work as principal. A romance with a teacher from Tampa briefly competed with the allure of Tin Pan Alley, but in the fall of 1902 he resigned from Stanton, moved to New York, and devoted himself to the team of Cole and Johnson Brothers.

The trio produced dozens of songs, including such hits as "Under the Bamboo Tree," "The Congo Love Song," "My Castle on the Nile," "I Ain't Gwinter Work No Mo'," "The Maiden with the Dreamy Eyes," "Nobody's Lookin' But de Owl and de Moon," "I've Got Troubles of My Own," "Tell Me, Dusky Maiden," "Mandy, Won't You Let Me Be Your Beau," "The Old Flag Never Touched the Ground," and "Oh, Didn't He Ramble." The income these songs brought was welcome, and the life was glamorous, on Broadway and on tours across the United States and in Europe; however, Johnson had serious reservations about such ephemeral work as genuine artistic expression. Reading Walt Whitman's *Leaves of Grass* (1855) in 1900, he became aware of the limitations of the dialect poetry he had been writing, depending as it did on white stereotypes of black life. Similarly, the vogue of coon songs on the musical stage catered to racist attitudes. To achieve their popularity, Cole and Johnson Brothers had to work in this medium and to meet its expectations. Johnson managed to avoid the worst crudities of the genre, but in so doing he universalized his subjects by appealing to the bland sentimentalities of popular taste in love songs. At any rate, he had begun formulating plans for more serious literary work. In his spare time, he began a course of graduate study at Columbia University, especially under the well-known critic Brander Matthews, who both respected his work in the popular theater and encouraged his more ambitious ventures.

Through the good offices of a political friend, Charles W. Anderson, Johnson's career now took another turn, leading far away from New York. As the most influential black Republican in the city and a close friend of Booker T. Washington, Anderson exerted the leverage needed to secure Johnson a minor diplomatic post, that traditional sinecure for literary types. At the end of May 1906 Johnson arrived in Puerto Cabello, Venezuela, on the Caribbean, as United States consul. Here he did indeed find time for his writing, producing numerous poems and making good progress on a novel. His next consular position, a slightly more desirable one in Corinto, Nicaragua, kept him busier dealing with business affairs, political unrest, and then revolution (1909-1912). But in 1910 he took a furlough to marry Grace Nail, the cultivated daughter of a prosperous New York tavern owner and real estate dealer, and he also found time to complete the novel *The Autobiography of an Ex-Colored Man* and to see it through the press. It was published anonymously by a small Boston house in 1912 while the author was still in Nicaragua.

The Autobiography of an Ex-Colored Man tells the story of a light-skinned black man who finally crosses the color line and passes as white. Born in Georgia, the son of a prominent white man and his well-kept mistress, whose "skin was almost brown," he is moved, while still a small child, with his mother to Connecticut, where they are established in a comfortable cottage. The monthly checks sent from Georgia are supplemented by the mother's work as a seamstress, making possible a genteel upbringing with a piano and books available in the home. But neither his quick mind nor his musical talent can shelter the boy from trauma when he discovers his racial identity through a humiliating episode at school. His father visits their house when the boy is twelve but decreases his contact with his illicit family afterwards, not even responding several years later when the mother appeals to him in her last illness. She dies soon after her son's graduation from high school, leaving him quite alone in the world.

The protagonist's adult life drifts rather aimlessly. Returning to Georgia to matriculate at Atlanta University, he has his savings stolen on his second day in the city. Moving on to Jacksonville, he goes to work in a cigar factory and prepares to settle down and marry a schoolteacher. Instead, he is laid off and decides to go to New York, where he falls into the sporting life, becoming adept at gambling and playing ragtime music. Catching the fancy of a wealthy white man, he accompanies him to Europe, living first in Paris, then in Amsterdam and Berlin. In the latter he finally forms a goal for his existence: he would "voice all the joys and sorrows, the hopes and ambitions, of the American Negro, in classic musical form." Returning to the States, he disembarks in Boston, and, after sampling the life of the black middle class there, he travels south to Washington, Richmond, and Nashville. With Macon as a point of departure, he moves out into the Georgia hinterlands absorbing rural life, folk culture, and its musical expression. Witnessing a lynching overwhelms him with racial shame, however, and he decides to return to the North and pass for white. Thoroughly emulating white values, he attends business college, gets a job, saves assiduously, and then speculates successfully in New York real estate. Marrying a white woman completes his transformation into "an ex-colored man," but at the end of the novel he realizes that he has "sold [his] birthright for a mess of pottage."

The Autobiography of an Ex-Colored Man is a novel, not an autobiography, but by issuing it anonymously Johnson hoped that it would be read as a true-life story, giving it greater authenticity and impact than a work perceived as a mere piece of fiction. Certainly the protagonist is not Johnson himself, who could not pass for white and would not have wanted to. Nevertheless, the sources of the novel lie largely in Johnson's own experiences and friendships. His boyhood friend Judson Douglass Wetmore eventually passed and married two white women, the second a southerner. Like the protagonist of the novel, Wetmore, too, became wealthy. On the other hand, many of the episodes parallel events in Johnson's own life. The Pilgrim's Progress and Grimms' fairy tales were read by the novelist and his fictional character at a comparable age. Like his creator, the protagonist was disappointed in the drab backwardness of Atlanta, with its unpaved streets and lack of other urban amenities. Life in the Tenderloin district of New York attracted the protagonist as it had Johnson, who records his response in Along This Way: "an alluring world, a tempting world, world of greatly lessened restraints, a world of fascinating perils; but, above all, a world of tremendous artistic potentialities." In Paris the fictional character stays with his patron at the Hotel Continental and frequents a large café, where he improves his French by speaking with attractive young women. The author with his brother and Bob Cole stayed at the same hotel and worked on his French in the same way. Author and character responded to London as well as Paris in similar ways. Returning to the United States and traveling south, the protagonist encounters revival meetings like those John-

Grace Nail Johnson

son attended as a child with his grandmother, even including an actual singing leader, "Singing Johnson," whom the writer was later to describe in his preface to The Book of American Negro Spirituals (1925). Most importantly, both Johnson and his fictional character were attracted to the riches of black folk expression and wished to make it available to a larger audience by rendering it in more artistic form.

Utilizing such biographical sources in The Autobiography of an Ex-Colored Man, Johnson presents a complex, psychological self-portrait of a weak, confused, vacillating, self-indulgent man, yet one who is capable of noble impulses and actions. Victimized by the circumstances of his birth as a "tragic mulatto," alienated from both races, he is victimized even more by the racist values which permeate American society and to which he finally yields. The first-person narration which Johnson employs allows the reader to observe closely the self-serving–often self-deceptive–habit of mind which the protagonist brings to all his experience. At the same time the point of view engages the reader's concern and even compassion, for the character surely has deep problems that admit of no easy solution. His first problem is the basic question of identity. As a child the protagonist assumes that he is white, absorbing the racism of his schoolmates. When he uses a racial epithet in a conversation with his mother, she reprimands him but does not tell him the truth. He does not learn he is black until he is required to sit down in his classroom after the principal asks the white students to stand. Humiliated, he confronts his mother. She equivocates, admitting that she is not white, but insisting that his "father is one of the greatest men in the country" and has imparted to their son "the best blood of the South." Shielded by his doting mother, herself an adorer of white values, he is ill equipped to manage the forced transition (his first "passing") from white to black. Never really gregarious, he now becomes solitary, spending most of his time with books and music. When his mother dies, his alienation is complete. Seeing large groups of black people for the first time when he travels to Atlanta to attend college, he is revolted by "the unkempt appearance, the shambling, slouching gait and loud talk and laughter of these people." He is able to enter "the freemasonry of the race" only by way of "the best class of coloured people" he later meets through music teaching and church attendance in Jacksonville. In outlining the tripartite class division of southern blacks, the protagonist identifies with the black bourgeoisie, who as "the advanced element of the coloured race . . . are the ones . . . who carry the entire weight of the race question; it worries the others very little." Fortunately, social exclusivity is a compensation for the burden, for where their numbers permit, these "advanced" members of the race have created a "society possessing discriminating tendencies which become rules as fast as actual conditions allow." But his identification with this group, as with all others, is tenuous, for he also socializes with his coworkers at the cigar factory, and he slips easily into black bohemia when he goes to New York. When he goes to Europe, rescued by the wealthy white man "who was the means by which I escaped from this lower world," he lives as a white man, for, as his friend tells him, he is one "by blood, by appearance, by education, and by tastes." Finally he decides to pass back into black life, committing himself to his music. In the South again, his response to black life more aesthetic than spontaneous, his commitment cannot survive the shock of the lynching he witnesses. Having passed from white to black, from black

back to white, and from white to black again, he decides to pass permanently into the white world. In a last gesture toward racial loyalty he reveals his race to his white fiancée, who at last overcomes the shock and accepts him in marriage, bearing a dark-haired daughter and a fair son ("a little golden-headed god") before dying young.

Obviously ambivalent about racial identity and corresponding cultural values, the protagonist also seems sexually ambiguous. Pampered by his mother, raised without a father, shy with girls, emotionally volatile, he develops a close friendship with an older dull-witted but devoted boy. Of much briefer duration is his unspoken puppy love for an older girl. Even briefer is the account of falling in love with a young woman in Jacksonville, an episode dismissed in two sentences, but the story of his close attachment to his rich, white, male friend is related at length. "A clean-cut, slender, but athletic-looking man" with a "tinge of grey about his temples," the cultured gentleman first appears at the black nightclub where the protagonist plays ragtime. Sitting "languidly puffing cigarettes," he is so pleased by the playing and the person of the narrator that he sends him five dollars. Soon he is the main source of income for the protagonist, who plays for his parties and his private pleasure, often for hours at a time. The relationship grows "familiar and warm," the narrator noting that "he had a decided personal liking for me." When a wealthy white woman with a black lover later invites the protagonist to drink champagne with her at the club, the lover appears and shoots the woman. Badly shaken by this outcome of interracial heterosexual love, the protagonist walks the streets until he is picked up by his millionaire friend, who takes him home to spend the night and then to Europe the following day. Johnson carefully refrains from making the homosexual theme explicit, but when the protagonist resolves to return to the South and its music, the point seems obvious: "I dreaded the ordeal of breaking with my millionaire. Between this peculiar man and me there had grown a very strong bond of affection," so strong, indeed, that reminiscences of their relationship "could easily fill several chapters."

Confused about his racial and sexual identities, the protagonist, like Ralph Ellison's invisible man, lacks even a name, making his grasp of who he is even more tenuous. As Robert Stepto has shown in *From Behind the Veil* (1979), the pro-

Mother Night.

Eternities before the first-born day,
Or o'er the first sun fledged his wings of flame
Calm Night, the everlasting and the same,
A brooding mother, over chaos lay.

And whirling suns shall blaze and then decay,
Shall run their fiery courses and then claim
The haven of the darkness whence they came,
Back to the Nirvanic peace shall grope their way.

So when my feeble sun of life burns out,
And sounded is the hour for my long sleep
Shall I, full weary of the feverish light,
Welcome the darkness without fear or doubt,
And, heavy-lidded, I shall softly creep
Into the quiet bosom of the Night.

u—|u—|u—|u—|u—

Pto Bello.
Dec. 1908.

Manuscript (by permission of Mrs. O. J. O'Kala and P. Richard Megali, the Estate of James Weldon Johnson) tagonist symbolically violates his heritage, even as a child in Georgia, when he digs up colored glass bottles in the flower bed of his house, an African survival intended to signify the "flash of the spirit." Much later, as a man in New York, he notes on the walls of the nightclub the photographs of Frederick Douglass and other notables but comments only that because they are autographed they are "a really valuable collection," the value imputed to them more monetary than cultural. Above all, even his music, by which he intends to embrace black culture and perpetuate it, is actually a betrayal of it. To give "classic form" to ragtime or spirituals is to impose an alien white structure inimical to the essence of the music. Even when he wishes to, the protagonist cannot divest himself of white values. As a piano player, his finest achievement is a ragtime version of Mendelsohn's "Wedding March." Then he is inspired by a German who "had taken rag-time and made it classic" to bastardize music in a similar way. He himself recognizes that his motives are mixed. His selfish desire for eminence in an unexploited musical field is as important as his sincere desire to bring black music as racial expression to a wider audience.

When in the final chapter the ex-colored man avows "white man's success"–money–as his new goal, he is only fulfilling a paternal prophecy: on his evening visits to the house in Georgia, his father had given the child shiny coins to be saved, the final one a ten-dollar gold piece drilled through the middle and tied around the boy's neck, where it stayed for most of his life. Materialism of the gilded age, not racial values or even artistic expression, wins the struggle for the ex-colored man's soul, but to his credit he does not rest easy in its triumph. In contrast to leaders of the race struggling for justice, he realizes at the end of the novel, he has only "a vanished dream, a dead ambition, a sacrificed talent." Too weak to achieve tragic stature, the ex-colored man at least deserves our pity. Cut off from the sustaining force of black culture, he is exposed to the destructive forces of white racism and materialism. Denied a coherent identity, he must inhabit a marginal psychological as well as social territory. The final irony of a novel whose mode is ironic is that his white success is his black–and human–failure.

The Autobiography of an Ex-Colored Man achieves more psychological depth and complexity of characterization than any previous Afro-American novel or autobiography, but, like that of its predecessors, its literary artistry is compromised by long expository digressions on the American racial situation for the edification of the white reader. In these passages it is often difficult to tell whether the narrative voice is that of character or author, a difficulty which blurs rather than enhances the characterization. When Johnson attempts to dramatize this exposition, as in the long, contrived smoking-car debate on racial matters in chapter 10, the effect is an impeded narrative. Despite this failure to resolve artistic and didactic aims, a perennial problem in Afro-American literature, Johnson's novel is a significant achievement for its time, giving memorable expression to an important theme and preparing the way for the mature fictional art that was to come later in the century.

The Autobiography of an Ex-Colored Man was little noticed, receiving only a handful of reviews, but "Fifty Years," an occasional poem celebrating racial progress since the Emancipation Proclamation, won much praise after its appearance in the *New York Times* on 1 January 1913. By this time Johnson had returned from Nicaragua on leave to handle his father's estate. Blocked in his efforts to secure a more desirable consular post, he resigned from the diplomatic service in September. After a year in Jacksonville, he returned to New York and began journalistic work for the *New York Age*, agreeing to provide "conservative and constructive" editorials on a variety of topics, mainly concerning the race. Actually, he was unequivocal, even somewhat militant, in pressing for equal rights and racial cooperation, if rather conservative on nonracial issues. Moreover, he resumed his political activity, attacking Woodrow Wilson and supporting Charles Evans Hughes in the presidential election campaign of 1916. All the while he was writing poetry and preparing the collection *Fifty Years and Other Poems*, which was published by the Cornhill Company of Boston late in 1917.

Of the sixty-five poems in the volume, only ten had been previously published in periodicals (*Century*, the *Scroll*, the *Independent*, the *Crisis*, and the *New York Times*). Like his friend and sometime model, Paul Laurence Dunbar, Johnson wrote both standard English verse and dialect poetry. As Dunbar had separated the dialect poems in *Majors and Minors* (1896), Johnson relegated the dialect poems in his book to a section called "Jingles and Croons," containing sixteen poems, five on love and the others on a variety of topics conventionally associated with the black rural South. In his preface to *The Book of American Negro Poetry*, published only a few years after *Fifty Years and Other Poems*, Johnson complained: "The Negro in the United States has achieved or been placed in a certain artistic niche. When he is thought of artistically, it is as a happy-go-lucky, singing, shuffling, banjo-picking being or as a more or less pathetic figure." Dialect poetry, he concluded, "is an instrument with but two full stops, humor and pathos." He could have been describing his own dialect poetry, which generally tended to confirm the stereotype, but one wonders why Johnson accepted such limitations. Were white expectations so dominant that he had to eschew the religious and protest themes of black folk songs and folk poetry? Instead of more significant themes, "Jingles and Croons" contains poems about stealing poultry ("Answer to Prayer" and "An Explanation"), eating watermelons and opossums ("The Seasons," "Possum Song," and "July in Georgy"), and playing the banjo ("A Banjo Song"). Some of the jingles are humorous enough ("The Rivals," "Tunk"), and some of the croons achieve genuine pathos ("Sence You Went Away," "De Little Pickaninny's Gone to Sleep"). Furthermore, Johnson's versification is fluent and facile. Consider these stanzas from "Sence You Went Away":

> Seems lak to me de stars don't shine so bright,
> Seems lak to me de sun done loss his light,
> Seems lak to me der's nothin' goin' right,
>   Sence you went away.
>
> Seems lak to me de sky ain't half so blue,
> Seems lak to me dat ev'ything wants you,
> Seems lak to me I don't know what to do,
>   Sence you went away.

Nevertheless, his dialect poetry does not rise to Dunbar's standard. "Ma Lady's Lips Am Like de Honey" seems a contrived, overelaborated, and sentimental version of Dunbar's "A Negro Love Song," and "A Plantation Bacchanal" and "A Banjo Song" are feeble efforts, compared to Dunbar's robust "The Party," to depict the festive side of black life.

Dunbar himself disparaged his dialect poetry ("a jingle in a broken tongue"), preferring the medium of conventional English verse. Johnson shared this preference. The first eleven poems in *Fifty Years and Other Poems* treat racial themes: racial progress, the composers of the spirituals, a black educator, black military valor, the mammy, Lincoln, lynching, slavery, interracial sex. The

original version of the title poem contained forty-one quatrains reviewing racial history in America from the introduction of the first slaves in 1619 to 1913, concentrating on the fifty years since emancipation and ending, in the last fifteen stanzas, in a despairing view of present impediments to further progress. On reconsideration, the poet decided to delete the final portion, thereby achieving coherence and the uplift required by the occasion at the expense of a more balanced view of racial history. Still, there is some dialogue between despair and hope beginning with stanza eighteen. Perhaps hope wins too easily and the poem lacks complexity, but "Fifty Years" does achieve the confident, resounding tone and the inspirational message Johnson felt to be appropriate to public poetry:

> O brothers mine, today we stand
>   Where half a century sweeps our ken,
> Since God, through Lincoln's ready hand,
>   Struck off our bonds and made us men. . . .
>
> Courage! Look out, beyond, and see
>   The Far horizon's beckoning span!
> Faith in your God-known destiny!
>   We are a part of some great plan.
>
> Because the tongues of Garrison
>   And Phillips now are cold in death,
> Think you their work can be undone?
>   Or quenched the fire lit by their breath?
>
> Think you that John Brown's spirit stops?
>   That Lovejoy was but idly slain?
> Or do you think those precious drops
>   From Lincoln's heart were shed in vain?
>
> That for which millions prayed and sighed,
>   That for which tens of thousands fought,
> For which so many freely died,
>   God cannot let it come to naught.

More impressive, though, are the sterner poems "To America," "Fragment," and "Brothers." The first two, "Fragment" especially, argue effectively that the national injustice to black people brings divine retribution. "Brothers" conveys a similar message. In lynching a brutalized black criminal, the lynchers are brutalized, making lynchers and lynched brothers through their brutalization. Among the racial poems, "The White Witch" is also noteworthy. Its admonition to black men to beware of white women develops a view of the psychosexual dimension of racism remarkably prescient for its time.

Johnson in his mature years (courtesy of the Schomburg Center for Research in Black Culture, the New York Public Library, Astor, Lenox and Tilden Foundations)

Most of the remaining poems in the collection are conventional fin de siècle verse, a bit world-weary, singing for love and idleness, rather facile, not deeply felt. Most are rhymed, but a half-dozen are not. Such a poem as "Deep in the Quiet Wood" certainly does not improve on its model, Whitman. "The Suicide" is more effective, almost achieving colloquial authenticity, and "Girl of Fifteen" is not without a certain psychological interest. All in all, however, *Fifty Years and Other Poems* represents only a modest achievement, neither comparable to nor a precursor of the brilliant *God's Trombones* (1927), published ten years later.

From about the turn of the century Johnson had known the influential ally of Booker T. Washington, Charles W. Anderson, but he had known W. E. B. Du Bois almost as long. In the summer of 1916 upon the invitation of Joel E. Spingarn and at the urging of Du Bois, Johnson attended the important Amenia Conference on racial issues. A few months later he received from Spingarn an offer to become field secretary of the National Association for the Advancement of

Colored People, which had been organized in 1910 by whites and blacks to provide a more militant vehicle for racial protest than Washington offered. Accepting the position in December, Johnson was to prove extremely effective in organizing local branches throughout the country, greatly expanding the membership of the organization. He also made an investigative trip to Haiti, exposing the abuses of American occupation of that country in a series of articles for the *Nation* in 1920. Later in the same year he became general secretary (the chief executive position) of the NAACP. Throughout the 1920s he provided effective leadership, aided by such subordinates as Walter White and William Pickens. Emphasizing legal action, publicity, and political pressure, Johnson coordinated the most effective movement against racism of its time. Even when he failed to win an immediate goal, as in the defeat of the Dyer Anti-Lynching Bill, he called the country's attention to the issue of racial injustice.

"I got immense satisfaction out of the work which was the main purpose of the National Association for the Advancement of Colored People," Johnson recalled in *Along This Way*: "at the same time, I struggled constantly not to permit that part of me which was artist to become entirely submerged." Official duties, including much travel and public speaking, occupied most of his time, but he managed to compile three important anthologies in the 1920s. The first of these, *The Book of American Negro Poetry* (1922), has pioneering importance as the first such collection ever made. In it Johnson includes thirty-one poets, all of whom lived well into the twentieth century. Earlier poets are not included, but Johnson discusses Phillis Wheatley, Jupiter Hammon, George Moses Horton, Francis Watkins Harper, James Madison Bell, and Albery A. Whitman in his long preface sketching the development of Afro-American poetry. This preface also examines some of the poems represented in the anthology, giving special praise to William Stanley Braithwaite and Claude McKay, and expounds on some of Johnson's favorite themes: the distinctive contribution of blacks to American cultural expressions (folktales, spirituals, cakewalk, ragtime), the importance of literature and art as proof of equality and the measure of a people's greatness, and the limitations of the dialect tradition (nevertheless copiously represented in the collection). *The Book of American Negro Poetry* appeared a bit too early to include the important younger poets of the Harlem Renaissance–Langston Hughes,

Countee Cullen, Arna Bontemps—but it helped to foster a favorable climate for that literary movement by earning respect for black poetry and expanding its audience. When a revised and enlarged edition of the anthology appeared in 1931, Johnson did give a generous sampling of the work of the new poets.

The other two anthologies, *The Book of American Negro Spirituals* (1925) and *The Second Book of American Negro Spirituals* (1926), likewise increased respect for black creativity. With musical arrangements by John Rosamond Johnson and Lawrence Brown, the two books offered a rich collection of 122 songs with a long preface to the first volume and a shorter one to the second. These prefaces combine a historical account with aesthetic and linguistic analyses. Johnson explains that blacks had come to take pride in the spirituals, once thought crude and backward, and that whites were increasingly recognizing them as valuable contributions to the national culture. The publication of the volumes greatly accelerated this process of appreciation. Almost all the reviews were favorable, including those by such black critics as W. E. B. Du Bois and Walter White and by white critics such as H. L. Mencken, Mark Van Doren, and Carl Van Vechten.

It is ironic that Johnson, an avowed agnostic, contributed so significantly to increased respect for the soulful richness of black Christianity. Before collecting spirituals, he had paid tribute in "O Black and Unknown Bards" to their creators. Religious themes appear elsewhere in his poetry, as in "Prayer at Sunrise" and in the untitled envoi to *Fifty Years and Other Poems*. But these are overshadowed by the superb achievement of *God's Trombones; Seven Negro Sermons in Verse*. The individual titles are "Listen, Lord—A Prayer," "The Creation," "The Prodigal Son," "Go Down Death—A Funeral Sermon," "Noah Built the Ark," "The Crucifixion," "Let My People Go," and "The Judgment Day." Two of the best of these, "The Creation" and "Go Down Death—A Funeral Sermon," had previously appeared in periodicals, the former in the *Freeman* in 1920. Johnson began work on "The Creation" after hearing a black preacher in Kansas City in 1918, but his interest in the poetic potential of the material preceded this occasion: "I had long been planning that at some time I should take the primitive stuff of the old-time Negro sermon and, through art-governed expression, make it into poetry. I felt that this primitive stuff could be used in a way similar to that in which a composer makes use of a folk theme in writing a major composition. I believed that the characteristic qualities: imagery, color, abandon, sonorous diction, syncopated rhythms, and native idioms, could be preserved and, at the same time, the composition as a whole be enlarged beyond the circumference of mere race and given universality."

This plan was fully realized in "The Creation," in particular, and in *God's Trombones*, as a whole. The analogy to the plan of the protagonist of *The Autobiography of an Ex-Colored Man* is clear, but the form and language of Johnson's poems are far more faithful to their folk sources. Eschewing regularities of meter, rhyme, or length of line, *God's Trombones* relies on speech rhythms—especially syncopation—and the biblical narratives to give structure to the poems. Instead of the often-stilted diction of his verse in formal English or the contrived cuteness of the dialect of "Jingles and Croons," the language of the collection is easy, colloquial, sinewy, yet capable of a vast range of emotion, as illustrated by the following lines from "Go Down Death—A Funeral Sermon":

Weep not, weep not,
She is not dead;
She's resting in the bosom of Jesus.
Heart-broken husband—weep no more;
Grief-stricken son—weep no more;
Left-lonesome daughter—weep no more;
She's only just gone home.

Day before yesterday morning,
God was looking down from his great, high
   heaven,
Looking down on all his children,
And his eye fell on Sister Caroline,
Tossing on her bed of pain.
And God's big heart was touched with pity,
With the everlasting pity.

And God sat back on his throne,
And he commanded that tall, bright angel stand-
   ing at his right hand:
Call me Death!
And that tall, bright angel cried in a voice
That broke like a clap of thunder:
Call Death!—Call Death!
And the echo sounded down the streets of
   heaven
Till it reached away back to that shadowy place,
Where death waits with his pale, white horses.

In this volume, rather than conventional melancholy or plantation stereotypes, Johnson expresses the dignity and depth of the racial religious experience in its own idiom, but in a way that does indeed appeal finally to the universal hunger for spiritual consolation. Ranging from cosmic grandeur of awesome proportions to fiery denunciation of sinners to the most tender solicitude for bereavement, the themes of *God's Trombones* receive expression that has the inevitability, resonance, and emotional authority of great art. Johnson's finest literary achievement, the book was favorably reviewed by such fellow luminaries of the Harlem Renaissance as Du Bois, White, Countee Cullen, and Alain Locke, as well as by white poets and critics like Joseph Auslander, Arthur Guiterman, Harriet Monroe, and Harry Alan Potamkin.

Unfortunately, Johnson wrote very little new poetry in the last eleven years of his life. *Harper's* published a love poem entitled "Futility" in 1929. *Saint Peter Relates an Incident of the Resurrection Day* was issued privately in 1930 and then included in *Saint Peter Relates an Incident: Selected Poems* (1935) together with thirty-seven poems (some in revised or retitled form) from *Fifty Years and Other Poems* and five poems previously uncollected. The title poem of the last collection is a witty and bitter satire on race prejudice evoked by a news account of a government project to send some white and black mothers of soldiers fallen in World War I to France to visit the graves of their sons. White mothers were to go on a first-class ship, followed by black mothers on a separate and less adequate vessel. The poem itself deals not with this incident, but with St. Peter's account of a future Jim Crow episode. Excavating the tomb of the unknown soldier on the great getting-up morning, superpatriotic white groups discover that he is black and wish to reinter him. Instead, he enters heaven singing "Deep River." Johnson achieves only partial success in this satire, for he does not reconcile the simple faith of the black soldier and the sophisticated skepticism of the narrative voice. Only by putting aside his own agnosticism, as he did in *God's Trombones,* could the poet successfully celebrate the resources of black religion.

During the late 1920s the strain of the hard work of the NAACP combined with his creative activity began to tell on Johnson, then in his mid fifties. When Edwin Embree of the Rosenwald Fund offered him a fellowship in 1929, he eagerly accepted it, taking leave from his organiza-

tional duties. As it turned out, Johnson did not resume his position but resigned at the end of 1930. Shortly thereafter he accepted the Adam K. Spence Chair of Creative Literature at Fisk University. This position allowed the leisure for the literary life that had always competed with activism for Johnson's allegiance.

Johnson's writing of the 1930s is more retrospective and historical than creative, however. Aside from the satirical poem, the major works of this period are *Black Manhattan* (1930), a popular historical treatment of black life in New York, and *Along This Way* (1933), a magisterial autobiography. The first of these two accounts sketches the general history of blacks in New York through the nineteenth century in the first sixty pages; the bulk of the book is devoted to black theatrical, musical, and literary developments in the city and to the rise of Harlem as "the recognized Negro capital" not only of America but the world. *Black Manhattan* emphasizes positive developments and ignores the growth of slum conditions in the 1920s. By the time the book was published the Depression was setting in, quickly making Johnson's optimism seem obsolete.

Much more durable is *Along This Way*, an autobiography that Carl Van Doren correctly called "civilized in temper, ironical, urbane, deft and reflective." Lacking the drama or intensity of other classic black autobiographies such as *Narrative of the Life of Frederick Douglass* (1845), *Black Boy* (1945), and *The Autobiography of Malcolm X* (1965), *Along This Way* complements these with its sophistication and variety of experiences related. Equally valuable for its record of the author's childhood, its account of the important events and personalities of his public life, and its statements of his literary purposes, Johnson's autobiography is less revealing of his private personality. The reserve and detachment characteristic of writers of his generation are always maintained. His wife, Grace Nail, more than fifteen years his junior, is not mentioned a single time in the last hundred pages of the work. Even when he discusses religion or politics, he tends to move toward generalization rather than to probe psychological sources. For our sense of the private man then, we have to rely on the covert hints of his fiction and some of his poetry, but as a record and commentary on his public and literary careers in the full contexts of race and history, *Along This Way* is matched only by the work of his great friend and contemporary, *The Autobiography of W. E. B. Du Bois* (1968).

Along This Way ends with speculations about the future of black people in the United States. These are adumbrated in a short book published the following year, *Negro Americans, What Now?* (1934). The four chapters of this work outline choices for resolving the racial problem, resources available to black people, techniques and policies needed, and a conclusion with a personal coda. Rejecting emigration, physical force, communism, and separatism, Johnson embraces integration as the only feasible course, naming the NAACP as the most useful organization to coordinate the considerable black power of numbers and institutions into a cohesive force. Actual implementation of integration, Johnson argues, will involve education of whites and blacks, greater involvement in the political process, increased pressure to enter the labor movement and the business community, more cultivation of interracial relations, a combination of conservatism and radicalism in racial leadership, and literary and artistic activity that will demolish old stereotypes. Nothing in this program—essentially the NAACP program—is new, but all of it is argued with the calm, commonsensical manner characteristic of Johnson. A cautious, middle-class thinker on questions of political economy, Johnson predictably gives scant attention to the wide ramifications of the country's severe economic crisis. One might complain, too, that his gradualism is too slow. Still, Johnson's own career as writer and activist offered undeniable proof that progress in racial matters was possible. He had reasons for his optimism.

Johnson's life came to an abrupt end on 26 June 1938, when he was killed in a car-train accident while traveling to his summer home in Maine. The accomplishments of his career, literary and otherwise, constitute a major and imperishable part of the history of Afro-American experience and expression in the early twentieth century.

Bibliography:

Robert E. Fleming, *James Weldon Johnson and Arna Wendell Bontemps: A Reference Guide* (Boston: G. K. Hall, 1978).
Well-researched bibliographies of criticism and reviews of the works of two Afro-American contemporaries.

Biography:

Eugene Levy, *James Weldon Johnson: Black Leader, Black Voice* (Chicago & London: University of Chicago Press, 1973).
Narrative of Johnson's life and career in all its aspects, supported by creative use of source material and historical context.

References:

Houston A. Baker, "A Forgotten Prototype: *The Autobiography of an Ex-Colored Man* and *Invisible Man*," *Virginia Quarterly Review*, 49 (Summer 1973): 433-449.
Comparison of Johnson's *The Autobiography of an Ex-Colored Man* with Ralph Ellison's 1952 novel *The Invisible Man*, focusing on their common theme of personal identity.

Robert A. Bone, *The Negro Novel in America*, revised edition (New Haven & London: Yale University Press, 1965), pp. 45-49.
Survey of black American fiction that views Johnson's *The Autobiography of an Ex-Colored Man* as an ironic commentary on the assimilationist impulse in Afro-American society.

Stephen H. Bronz, *Roots of Negro Racial Consciousness, the 1920s: Three Harlem Renaissance Authors* (New York: Libra Publishers, 1964), pp. 18-46.
Brief critical survey of the careers of Johnson, Countee Cullen, and Claude McKay in which Johnson's *The Autobiography of an Ex-Colored Man* is viewed as an essentially tragic commentary on "passing."

Richard A. Carroll, "Black Racial Spirit: An Analysis of James Weldon Johnson's Critical Perspective," *Phylon*, 32 (Winter 1971): 344-364.
Reassesses the then-prevailing view that Johnson's literary criticism was traditionalist and superficial, finding instead that Johnson's portrayal of black writing is a positivist precursor of the views of purveyors of the black aesthetic of the 1960s and 1970s.

Eugenia Collier, "The Endless Journey of an Ex-Coloured Man," *Phylon*, 32 (Winter 1971): 365-373.
Credits Johnson's *The Autobiography of an Ex-Colored Man* with being the first compassionate discussion of the dilemma of the near-white black person and an insightful

comment on the "dual heritage" of American blacks.

Collier, "James Weldon Johnson: Mirror of Change," *Phylon,* 21 (Winter 1960): 351-359.
Sees in Johnson's dialect poetry a greater ironic content than is displayed in earlier work, such as that of Paul Laurence Dunbar, because Johnson has handled some of the darker aspects of Afro-American life.

Robert E. Fleming, "Contemporary Themes in Johnson's *Autobiography of an Ex-Coloured Man,*" *Negro American Literature Forum,* 4 (Winter 1970): 120-124, 141.
Shows that Johnson's treatment of themes of identity, self-hatred, matriarchy, and race relations is paralleled in the work of later black authors such as Ralph Ellison, James Baldwin, Richard Wright, and Ann Petry.

Fleming, "Irony as a Key to Johnson's *The Autobiography of an Ex-Coloured Man,*" *American Literature,* 43 (March 1971): 83-96.
Contends that the narrator in Johnson's *The Autobiography of an Ex-Colored Man* is the source of the novel's irony.

Marvin P. Garrett, "Early Recollections and Structural Irony in *The Autobiography of an Ex-Coloured Man,*" *Critique: Studies in Modern Fiction,* 13 (December 1971): 5-14.
Details Johnson's use of the narrator's memories in *The Autobiography of an Ex-Colored Man* to indicate his feeling of guilt and his desire to justify his "white" life.

Addison Gayle, Jr., *The Way of the New World: The Black Novel in America* (Garden City, N.Y.: Doubleday, 1975), pp. 109-116.
Historical-critical survey of novels by black Americans emphasizing sociological and ideological aspects of the tradition.

Richard Kostelanetz, "The Politics of Passing: The Fiction of James Weldon Johnson," *Negro American Literature Forum,* 3 (March 1969): 22-24, 29.
Brief summary of the tragic theme of *The Autobiography of an Ex-Colored Man*: "Passing" produces not contentment, but guilty alienation.

Richard A. Long, "A Weapon of My Song: The Poetry of James Weldon Johnson," *Phylon,* 32 (Winter 1971): 374-382.
Characterizes Johnson's dialect poetry as apologetic propaganda and his serious poetry as militant, prideful propaganda.

Maurice J. O'Sullivan, Jr., "Of Souls and Pottage: James Weldon Johnson's *The Autobiography of an Ex-Coloured Man,*" *CLA Journal,* 23 (September 1979): 60-70.
Reading of *The Autobiography of an Ex-Colored Man* as a tragic demonstration of the destructive, belittling effects of race passing.

Roger Rosenblatt, *"The Autobiography of an Ex-Colored Man,"* in his *Black Fiction* (Cambridge: Harvard University Press, 1974), pp. 173-184.
Views the narrator of *The Autobiography of an Ex-Colored Man* as a kind of black hero who earns his hero status "not by fighting his destiny, but by embracing it" and then by struggling to cope with the consequences.

Stephen M. Ross, "Audience and Irony in Johnson's *The Autobiography of an Ex-Coloured Man,*" *CLA Journal,* 18 (December 1974): 198-210.
Declares that the ironic interpretation of *The Autobiography of an Ex-Colored Man* ignores Johnson's compassion for the narrator.

Joseph T. Skerrett, Jr., "Irony and Symbolic Action in James Weldon Johnson's *The Autobiography of an Ex-Coloured Man,*" *American Quarterly,* 32 (Winter 1980): 540-558.
Attempts to synthesize the tragic and ironic interpretations of Johnson's *The Autobiography of an Ex-Colored Man.*

Robert B. Stepto, *From Behind the Veil: A Study of Afro-American Narrative* (Urbana: University of Illinois Press, 1979), pp. 95-127.
Analysis of Johnson's literary career in a sophisticated survey of black American fiction as a symbol of the collective quest of black America.

Jean Wagner, *Black Poets of the United States: From Paul Laurence Dunbar to Langston Hughes,* translated by Kenneth Douglas (Urbana: University of Illinois Press, 1973), pp. 351-384. Includes a survey of Johnson's poetic career in historical context.

Wendell Phillips Whalum, "James Weldon Johnson's Theories and Performance Practices of Afro-American Folksongs," *Phylon*, 32 (Winter 1972): 383-395.

Explains the stylistic origins of Johnson's spiritual music.

Papers:

Johnson's papers are included in the James Weldon Johnson Collection of Negro Arts and Letters deposited in the Beinecke Library of Yale University.

Ring Lardner

This entry was updated by Richard Layman from the entry by Elizabeth Evans (Georgia Institute of Technology) in DLB 11, American Humorists, 1800-1950, Part 1.

Places	Great Neck, Long Island	Niles, Michigan	Chicago
Influences and Relationships	Hugh Fullerton F. Scott Fitzgerald	Maxwell Perkins H. L. Mencken	George S. Kaufman Grantland Rice
Literary Movements and Forms	Short Story Vernacular Humor	Epistolary Fiction	Journalism
Major Themes	Vulgarity of the Rising Middle Class Misogyny	The Difficulty of Communication Alcoholism	Baseball Materialism Misanthropy
Cultural and Artistic Influences	Broadway Theater	Musical Drama	Sport
Social and Economic Influences	Black Sox Scandal Prohibition	The Depression	The Jazz Age

See also the Lardner entry in DLB 25, *American Newspaper Journalists, 1901-1925.*

BIRTH: Niles, Michigan, 6 March 1885, to Henry and Lena Phillips Lardner.

EDUCATION: Armour Institute, 1902.

MARRIAGE: 28 June 1911 to Ellis Abbott; children: John Abbott, James Phillips, Ringgold Wilmer, Jr., David Ellis.

DEATH: East Hampton, New York, 25 September 1933.

BOOKS: *Bib Ballads* (Chicago: P. F. Volland, 1915);
You Know Me Al (New York: Doran, 1916);
Gullible's Travels, Etc. (Indianapolis: Bobbs-Merrill, 1917; London: Chatto & Windus, 1926);
My Four Weeks in France (Indianapolis: Bobbs-Merrill, 1918);
Treat 'Em Rough (Indianapolis: Bobbs-Merrill, 1918);
The Real Dope (Indianapolis: Bobbs-Merrill, 1919);
Own Your Own Home (Indianapolis: Bobbs-Merrill, 1919);
The Young Immigrunts (Indianapolis: Bobbs-Merrill, 1920);
Symptoms of Being 35 (Indianapolis: Bobbs-Merrill, 1921);
The Big Town (Indianapolis: Bobbs-Merrill, 1921);
Say It with Oil (New York: Doran, 1923);
How to Write Short Stories (New York: Scribners, 1924; London: Chatto & Windus, 1926);
What of It? (New York: Scribners, 1925);
The Love Nest and Other Stories (New York: Scribners, 1926; London: Allan, 1928)–augmented with works from *What of It?*
The Story of a Wonder Man (New York: Scribners, 1927);
Round Up: The Stories of Ring Lardner (New York: Scribners, 1929; London: Williams & Norgate, 1935);
June Moon, by Lardner and George S. Kaufman (New York: Scribners, 1930);
Lose with a Smile (New York: Scribners, 1933);
First and Last, edited by Gilbert Seldes (New York: Scribners, 1934);
Shut Up, He Explained, edited by Babette Rosmond and Henry Morgan (New York: Scribners, 1962);

Ring Lardner (courtesy of Ring Lardner, Jr.)

Some Champions: Sketches and Fiction by Ring Lardner, edited by Matthew J. Bruccoli and Richard Layman (New York: Scribners, 1976);
Ring Lardner's You Know Me Al: The Comic Strip Adventures of Jack Keefe (New York: Harcourt Brace Jovanovich/Bruccoli Clark, 1979).

PLAY PRODUCTION: *June Moon*, by Lardner and George S. Kaufman, New York, Broadhurst Theater, 9 October 1929.

Ring Lardner began his writing career as a newspaperman, first covering routine assignments for a local paper in South Bend, Indiana, then moving to Chicago where he was a sports reporter specializing in baseball. In many ways, his work always showed the pressure of newspaper deadlines and the lesson a successful baseball reporter learns–to be entertaining when the game gets dull. As important as his newspaper writing was (he wrote the prestigious column "In the Wake of the News" for the *Chicago Tribune,* 1913-1919, and later a "Weekly Letter," 1919-1927, for the Bell Syndicate, which had readers from Niles, Michigan, to Yokohama, Japan), his significance as an American writer began on 7 March 1914 when the *Saturday Evening Post* published the first-person narrative of a semiliterate braggart baseball pitcher named Jack Keefe. The story was "A Busher's Letters Home." A total of six busher stories appeared in the *Post* that year, and Lardner produced three books, as well as a comic strip with cartoonist Dick Dorgan, which were based on the Keefe adventures. By 1924 Lardner was an established author at Scribners, a humorist of the first order. In 1919 he moved his family from Chicago to the East, settling first in Greenwich, Connecticut, and then in Great Neck, New York, and finally in East Hampton, Long Island. The move was not motivated by a desire to escape the Midwest for eastern culture and atmosphere. Lardner moved to the New York environs because as a writer he could make more money there and because New York was the home of Broadway. Here he continued to write throughout his life, and even when he was confined to the hospital during his last illnesses, he was writing a radio column for the *New Yorker,* "Over the Waves."

All studies of American humor in the twentieth century find in Ring Lardner one of America's most successful practitioners of humor, a writer who distinguished himself amid the competition of the day, which included such fine writers as S. J. Perelman, Don Marquis, Robert Benchley, Franklin P. Adams, and Dorothy Parker. Although his admirer and friend H. L. Mencken feared that the humor which Lardner created would be lost to subsequent generations when details and names were no longer current or in vogue, such has not been the case. Whether in parody or comic verse, satiric fairy tales or brief nonsense plays, one-liners or involved stories, Lardner's writing is distinctively funny as he sardonically examines the familiar and trivial aspects of middle-class America. When Scribners brought out *What of It?* in 1925, they also published it in a uniform edition along with *You Know Me Al, Gullible's Travels, Etc., The Big Town,* and *How to Write Short Stories,* a publishing event noted on the first page of the *New York Times Book Review* for 19 April 1925. In that issue, the Scribners ad for *What of It?* aptly points out the ser-

ious and enduring qualities of Lardner's humor: "Whoever really wants to understand the American people should read Ring Lardner. Lardner shows how they live, think, and feel. He is unspeakably funny, often comic; but there is an underlying vein of deep and poignant irony in his lightest writing which puts it far beyond the realm of the merely amusing."

Ring Lardner grew up in Niles, Michigan, the youngest in a large family whose affluent circumstances afforded a large house and grounds and kept the three youngest children at home with nurses, servants, and a tutor during their early years. Until Henry Lardner suffered serious financial losses about 1901, this style of living continued. Close to his brother Rex and his sister Anna as well as to his talented and somewhat independent mother, Lardner lived in a household where reading and amateur theatricals, interesting visitors, and family excursions made a happy childhood. By 1913 he had ruled out any serious attempt at higher education, had held a series of newspaper jobs, including managing editor of the *Sporting News* and sports editor of the *Boston American,* and had distinguished himself as a sports reporter in Chicago. By the 1920s, he was living among famous eastern people who were his friends and neighbors–Grantland and Kate Rice, Zelda and Scott Fitzgerald, Gene Buck, Ed Wynn. As a man, Lardner was paradoxical. He was a humorist who detested nothing more than having to listen to a funny story, a man who was shy even with his own children, a writer who was usually taciturn unless he had been drinking. He might have been silent for most of an evening, however, and then delivered a line which made one think he had been funny all along. At the Lambs' Club once he was with composer Paul Lannin when a Shakespearean actor walked past whose wild, unruly hair prompted Lardner to ask him, "How do you look when I'm sober?"

Lardner was six feet two inches by his teens, and bartenders never questioned his age; thus his drinking began early and subsequently became a severe problem and a contributing factor to his early death. Although he frequently went on the wagon and even sought professional help, Lardner never escaped his drinking problem any more than his alcoholic character did in "Cured!" (1931). In spite of how much he drank, his speech was clear and sensible; however, his bouts were legendary. A frequently repeated episode which occurred at the Friars' Club portrays Lardner as gentlemanly and in control, but also as a

Lardner (right) with his brother Rex and sister Anna during their high school days

man on what he himself called "a real bat." Dressed in evening clothes, he went to the club after the theater where he drank as he listened to various people play the piano. With the excuse that he did not want to return home in daylight wearing evening dress, Lardner continued to sit and drink into the third day. Finally, someone approached him with the line "Have you heard the one about–?" and to escape the rest, Lardner finally left–evening clothes notwithstanding. His son, Ring Lardner, Jr., has called the drinking an insidious problem that Ring and his wife, Ellis, tried to believe did not exist.

By his early forties, Lardner was in poor health from the chronic drinking, tuberculosis, severe insomnia, and finally a heart ailment. He died at forty-eight having written some 120 short stories, 9 or so nonsense plays, numerous magazine columns, parodies and burlesques, and hundreds of newspaper columns. His friends Scott Fitzgerald (who used Lardner as the model for Abe North in *Tender Is the Night*, 1934) and Maxwell Perkins (who was his editor at Scribners) urged him to undertake a long sustained work, but he continued to turn out the short pieces that he wrote skillfully and for which he was well paid. It is difficult to know just how much Lard-

ner valued his work. On the one hand, he never kept copies of it. When Scribners was preparing to publish *How To Write Short Stories*, Maxwell Perkins had to secure library copies of the magazines in which the stories first appeared. Needing a copy of *Gullible's Travels, Etc.*, Perkins asked Lardner to supply one and got this reply: "I have virtually gone down on my knees to the Bobbs-Merrill people [his publisher for this title] for a copy of Gullible's Travels, vainly. I haven't a copy myself. Gene Buck has, and if you just want to read it, I'll try to get it away from him for a few days. It isn't that he is so fond of it, but they have got great big bookcases." In 1930, Burton Rascoe asked Lardner about his nonsense play *I Gaspiri (The Upholsterers)*; Lardner replied that he thought it was in his book *What of It?* (it was), but he had no copy–apparently of neither the play itself nor the volume that had included it. On the other hand, Lardner gave Perkins a list of people to whom he wanted the 1925 titles sent, and in letters he remarked favorably on various stories. When Mencken praised "Some Like Them Cold," Lardner quipped, "I didn't hate it myself." To another correspondent, he wrote that "I believe I like 'Golden Honeymoon' best of my immortal works, but I don't know why." In a letter to Maxwell Perkins, Lardner declared that the stories he had ready for *The Love Nest and Other Stories* (1926) were of better quality than those in *How To Write Short Stories* (1924). He was a good short-story writer, but he indulged in no pretense about his characters, the society he pictured, or the lasting value of his own work.

Although Lardner admired writers from Dostoevski to Fitzgerald, his early interest had been baseball, a sport he knew thoroughly and enjoyed until the "rabbit ball" was introduced and until the 1919 Black Sox scandal. Even after Lardner moved to New York in 1919, sports continued to be important—he still covered the World Series several times as well as important prize fights—but after the move to the East, sports were not the consuming passion they had been. Although his writing now included much fiction, Lardner's real ambition was not to be a great fiction writer; he wanted to be a great songwriter and to be associated with Broadway shows. His songwriting career began with amateur productions in Niles as early as 1903, when Lardner was eighteen, and continued quite late in his life, when he wrote and rewrote lyrics for *Smiles*, a 1930 Ziegfeld production. His one Broadway hit was the musical *June Moon* (1930), written with George S. Kaufman. Lardner continued to write short stories and magazine articles because he could not make a living as a "songsmith" and once figured that if his time devoted to composing lyrics were measured by their returns, the result would be a ten-thousand-dollar deficit. From the year of his marriage (1911) he always lived in hope of a windfall from one of his songs; but, except for *June Moon* (based on his story "Some Like Them Cold"), the profits from Broadway-show attempts and song lyrics were slim or none.

Lardner rode the financial crest of the 1920s, getting high prices for his short stories (as much as forty-five hundred dollars for a single story at times) and a substantial sum for his "Weekly Letter." He was driven to provide his family with luxuries—an elegant house, servants, a chauffeur, private preparatory schools, long winter vacations. Improvident with drink and money, he could never save except by buying life insurance, which, after his death, was all that saved his wife from economic ruin.

Frequently, Lardner used protagonists whose observations, concerns, and ideas reveal the pettiness and viciousness of an American middle class dedicated to material progress and ignorant of grace and manners, of intellectual or cul-

tural interests. Whether midwesterners or Long Islanders, these characters exhibit their rudeness and lack of polish; they are products of the 1920s, when for many all vestiges of Victorian reticence were displaced by the effects of bootleggers and bathtub gin, the flappers of the Jazz Age, and the extravagance and permissiveness that characterized the time. Narrators like Jack Keefe, Gullible, Fred Gross, and Finch speak ungrammatical English, display limited vocabularies, and testify to their low social status and cultural background with every word they say. Others of Lardner's stories are told in "straight English" and, as one critic has said, are written with dispassionate objectivity, revealing little of Lardner himself but showing that the characters are not admirable people. Especially successful for Lardner is the epistolary method which his disingenuous characters—Jack Keefe, Fred Gross, Chas. F. Lewis, and Mabelle Gillespie—use. Often he places characters in a new and usually higher social environment than they are used to, and these comic migrations reveal the shortcomings and occasionally the common sense of these characters. Critics and reviewers contemporaneous with Lardner—particularly Clifton Fadiman—charged him with disdaining and hating his characters with a Swiftian power. Indeed, Fadiman declared that the special force of Lardner's work "springs from a single fact: he just doesn't like people. Except Swift, no writer has gone farther on hatred alone." The Fadiman attack came in the *Nation* on 22 March 1933; on 24 August—just a month before Lardner died—he refuted this attack in a letter to a friend. A passage from this letter should be read as Lardner's apologia: "I don't suppose any author either hates or loves all his characters. I try to write about people as real as possible, and some of them are naturally more likeable than others. In regard to your argument, I think the decision should be awarded to you, because I cannot remember ever having felt any bitterness or hatred toward the characters I have written about. I am grateful to you for your defense of me."

Many of Lardner's characters are not likable at all; some are vicious while others are fatuous, self-serving, or dishonest. Almost none of the marriages he portrays are happy, women (whom he basically idealized) fall short of expectations, and successful careers often end in failure. Fadiman's attack may have been extreme, but Lardner's fiction is satirical, exposing characters and their unsavory actions as well as expressing little hope that they or the conditions that produced them will get much better. Lardner was sensitive to the griefs of man, to the desperate aspirations of the middle class to get ahead, to the difficulties that come with poor health, alcoholism, and unloving marriages. His characters frequently balance on the rim of despair. At the same time, he exhibits the sustaining humor that marks his life and his work. The poignancy of the situation never obliterates the humor entirely.

Lardner's letters (published as *Letters from Ring* in 1979) show this innate and unfailing ability to be funny, the humor coming in juxtapositions, in observations of peculiar behavior, in his ability to see serious events from a balanced perspective. For instance, his courtship of Ellis Abbott lasted four years, carried on in large measure through hundreds of letters, the last of which was written 21 June 1911: "I'm very tired of writing to Ellis Abbott, and I guess this is the last letter she'll ever get from me. Our correspondence has been a very pleasant diversion–really a necessity–but I don't think I can carry it on any longer, for paper and stamps cost money." He urged Ellis's brother William to give two or three days notice before he came to visit "so we can have the dishes washed," and he sometimes would inject into a letter absurdities that characterize his nonsense plays. Between two ordinary and sensible paragraphs in a letter to the Fitzgeralds, he added an exaggerated fantasy: "Ellis had two babies this summer. They are both girls, giving us two girls and four boys, an ideal combination, we think." Letter salutations are whimsical– "Fitzgeralds one and all," "Mother II" (Ellis's mother), "Sister–and Brothers–and high school-in-law"; signatures range from "R. W. L." to "Sister Stanislaus," "Mary Esselstyn," "Resy–A Michigan Boy," "Ring*–*for ice water," "Mrs. Coppell," "F. Farmer Fox."

Lardner's first important publication, *You Know Me Al* (1916), is his most successful use of baseball in fiction, and it is his best use of the epistolary technique. Jack Keefe's letters to his hometown friend Al Blanchard in Bedford, Indiana, begin in September when Jack starts his first season in the big league (with the Chicago White Sox) and end in November of the following year when the White Sox and the New York Giants leave on a world tour. Erratic spelling, misused homonyms, errors in agreement and tense and past participles, inappropriate syntax, and a limited vocabulary create the humor that establishes Jack Keefe as the typical busher who personifies ig-

norance, brashness, naivete, and incorrigible pride. The letters to Al are remarkable on a number of levels. In the introduction to the 1959 edition of *You Know Me Al*, John Lardner, Ring's oldest son, remarked that the book contains "all the essential truth about ball-playing.... Its broader values to one side, there has never been a sounder baseball book.... If you stop to pick over the accounts of ball games, you see that each detail is correct in relation to place, weather, time of year, and the hitting, pitching, or fielding idiosyncrasies of each of a hundred players." The baseball accuracy shows attention to a sense of place which establishes the world of the fictional Jack Keefe as well as that of the real players like Eddie Cicotte, Frank Schulte, and Christy Mathewson who appear on and off the field. The style of Jack's letter writing quickly reveals his inability to see mistakes, to accept criticism, or to learn by observation. The broader values, however, have obviously outlasted the baseball details, which to a great extent are dated. The silent, long-suffering recipient of Jack's letters, Al Blanchard, exemplifies the true friend. He follows the ups and downs of Jack's career and sends him newspaper clippings of his games; he loans Jack money on four occasions, apparently at some sacrifice, although Jack squanders his salary; he listens to Jack's endless plans to return to Bedford for the off-season; he remains true and loyal to a friend who is quixotic, egotistical, and insensitive. Al's loyalty remains the steady point in the book and in Jack's life. No one in Jack's own family is ever mentioned, the women in his life (including Florrie, whom he marries) are unappealing and unloving, and his behavior on and off the baseball field makes him the object of practical jokes, not of friendship with fellow players.

Jack is manipulated and exploited by the woman he marries and by the baseball system. He rarely heeds instructions about exercising, practicing, eating properly, or following the manager's orders. His spending habits show a lack of control and values. He buys clothes and furniture he does not need, but is quite slow repaying money he owes Al (and does not repay at least one hundred dollars of it), is tight-fisted with tips as well as doctors' and lawyers' fees, and lacks manners and decorum. The social scene that Lardner presents revolves around urban life–hotel rooms or rented flats, restaurants and movies, baseball games and train schedules, beer parlors and taxi rides. It is a life on the go, a life in transit, a picture of Americans without family loyalties, traditions, rituals. Jack spends money, but never saves it; he is tricked into marrying a wife he does not love and into claiming a child that is not his. Always inept and incapable of seeing his own stupidity, Jack declares he will not sign with the White Sox for less than $3,000 per annum, but then accepts $1,500. He sends word he is marrying Hazel from San Francisco and later Violet from Detroit, but marries neither. Married to Florrie instead, he separates from her irrevocably but soon announces their reunion. He has Al arrange the lease for the little yellow house in Bedford and engage a hack to meet the train but never takes his family to live in the house nor to visit his friends. He refuses to go on the world tour with the White Sox and the Giants, but then he does. A 182-word sentence, strung together with *ands* and *buts*, reveals Jack's true nature–a decision is always subject to change: "Friend Al: I guess may be you begin to think I dont never do what I am going to do and that I change my mind a hole lot because I wrote and told you that I and Florrie and little Al would be in Bedford today and here we are in Chi yet on the day that I told you we would get to Bedford and I bet Bertha and you and the rest of the boys will be disappointed but Al I don't feel like as if I should ought to leave the White Sox in a hole and that is why I am here yet and I will tell you how it come off but in the 1st place I want to tell you that it wont make a difference of more than 5 or 6 or may be 7 days at least and we will be down there and see you and Bertha and the rest of the boys just as soon as the N.Y. giants and the White Sox leaves here and starts a round the world."

Lardner had perfect pitch in music and a perfect ear for the speech of the middle-class characters like Jack Keefe and Gullible, who speak what has long been called *Ringlish*. *You Know Me Al* is an accomplishment on the level of language alone; it is also a study in the material aspirations of many Americans who spend more than they earn and a study in the myth of the hero. Jack writes Al from "Medford, Organ," about a recent game in San Francisco. "They was the biggest crowd there that I ever seen in San Francisco and I guess they must of been 4000 people there and I wisht you could of heard them yell when my name was announced to pitch." The adulation of the four thousand is not long remembered. Jack Keefe survives through Lardner, not as a hero, but as a man marked by shortcomings,

limited intelligence, rich and ungrammatical speech, and misplaced values.

Other Lardner titles reflect his continuing interest in the middle-class character on the rise and incompatible with the world of opera, New York and Florida resorts, and big-city life– Gullible and the Missus in *Gullible's Travels, Etc.* (1917), Fred Gross and his family in *Own Your Own Home* (1919), Finch and his wife and sister-in-law Kate in *The Big Town* (1921). Of the three, only *Own Your Own Home* is epistolary–Fred's letters to his brother Charley–but the other collections are narrated in the first person in language that reflects mispronunciations and includes misspellings, grammatical errors, and profuse abbreviations. The attempts of Lardner's characters to move into the various reaches of society are always unsuccessful. Gullible and the Missus do not join the "E-light" of Chicago or Palm Beach (where the Missus is mistaken for a chambermaid), the Grosses cannot enter the suburban society when they move out from Chicago, and although Tom and Ella Finch go to New York to see LIFE and to find sister Kate a husband, they also return to South Bend, Indiana, relieved to be rid of expensive New York apartments and hotels and summer resorts. New money brings them no special grace; their language (as reported through Finch) and their manners categorize them as rubes, and their inability to learn from their experiences differs only slightly from that of the Gullibles and the Grosses.

World War I furnished the background for three timely but not very successful works: *My Four Weeks in France* (1918), in which Lardner writes as a humorous war correspondent; *Treat 'Em Rough* (1918); and *The Real Dope* (1919), about Jack Keefe's army adventures at home and abroad. The move to the East prompted one of Lardner's cleverest books, *The Young Immigrunts* (1920), a parody of *The Young Visiters*, a work supposedly written by young Daisy Ashford and published with an introduction by Sir James Barrie. Narrated by Bill (Ring, Jr.), the work conveys the hazards and amusements of family travel. One of Lardner's memorable lines occurs when Bill asks his father if he has lost the way, and the answer comes back–" 'Shut Up,' he explained."

In 1919 Lardner entered an agreement with John N. Wheeler to write a weekly humorous column for his Bell Syndicate. This contract allowed Lardner to give up daily newspaper work and move to New York; moreover, it allowed him to capitalize on his reputation as a journalist and

Ring and Ellis Lardner with their children (left to right): Jim, David, Bill (Ring, Jr.), and John (courtesy of Ring Lardner, Jr.)

as a humorist. He made a substantially larger salary than he was receiving from the *Tribune* and increased his fame, since 150 newspapers from all over North America eventually subscribed to Lardner's "Weekly Letter." In September of 1922 the Bell Syndicate began circulating the comic strip "You Know Me Al," based on Lardner's busher stories. The strip ran six days a week for three years with credit to Lardner for continuity; but although the enterprise brought him thirty thousand dollars a year, it was burdensome, even loathsome to Lardner, and he quit writing copy in January of 1925.

When Lardner was thirty-five he wrote *Symptoms of Being 35* (1921), a slight book for which he earned only $293.66 in royalties by May of 1922. Besides listing nine general symptoms of reaching this age or its vicinity, Lardner also explains that a person who reaches thirty-five reassesses things like his home. When one is thirty-five, home is where you can take your shoes off, have more soup, get coffee before a meal is finished; and "Its where they know you like doughnuts and what you think about a banana."

In 1923 Nina Wilcox Putnam and Lardner wrote what he described to Hewitt Howland (then general editor at Bobbs-Merrill) as "one of

those double stunts"–Putnam's mock attack on husbands, *Say It with Bricks*, printed with Lardner's retaliation, *Say It with Oil*. Not a title of much consequence, *Say It with Oil* does contain fine one-liners: "Wives is people that thinks 2 ash trays should ought to be plenty for a 12 rm. house." Lardner confided to Howland that his expectations for the book were modest: "Between you and me, I don't think the book will set the world afire, but it may help toward the mortgage."

The titles upon which Lardner's reputation rests are his short stories of the 1920s. *How To Write Short Stories* has an introduction spoofing the do-it-yourself writing manuals and ten stories, among them four of his best: "Some Like Them Cold," "Alibi Ike," "The Golden Honeymoon," and "Champion." Somewhat to Lardner's surprise, the book received substantial critical notice and confirmed the praise that Mencken had already given. (The book sales were moderate in 1924–some thirty-five hundred copies sold by the end of June.)

Most of Lardner's critics consider this volume the turning point in his literary career, and it marks the beginning of his association with Scribners as his publisher and with Maxwell Perkins as his editor. Scott Fitzgerald had urged Perkins to read "The Golden Honeymoon" (it had appeared in the July 1922 issue of *Cosmopolitan*), which impressed Perkins so much that he wrote Lardner about the possibility of seeing enough similar material to make up a volume. Publication plans were soon under way. Lardner accepted Perkins's suggestion for the preface, and one bit of advice to his "pupils" was that they send their stories or "yarns" to prospective editors on used paper; however, they should not send them on a postcard or by way of Morse code. Lardner also followed Perkins's advice on the arrangement of the stories, which was determined by the principle of variety. Although Perkins thought that publishers exaggerated the importance of an early position in a collection, he nevertheless gave thought to the first selection in *How To Write Short Stories*. Four of the ten were baseball stories, and Perkins did not want to emphasize that theme by using one of them at the beginning. "The Golden Honeymoon," about a trying and revealing fifty-year-wedding-anniversary trip, could not open the volume, he said, because it had appeared in Edward J. O'Brien's *The Best Short Stories of 1922*. Finally, Perkins selected "The Facts," a story about a reformed alcoholic saved from a straight life by a drunken friend, because "it will please everybody, male and female, of every sort." (Edmund Wilson, however, found this story too much made for the magazine audience.) "Some Like Them Cold" (an epistolary tale about two insipid people and their would-be love affair), a masterpiece of its kind to Perkins, came next and was followed by what Perkins thought a splendid baseball story, "Alibi Ike," about an outfielder who never runs out of excuses and who is the unwitting victim of practical jokers. Perkins regretted that "Champion," a merciless story about a sadistic boxer, came so late in the order–fifth.

On 11 June 1924 Perkins jokingly warned Lardner in a letter to avoid Forty-second Street opposite Fourth Avenue since the window display at Liggetts included a huge enlargement of his photograph that would make him a recognizable figure in that area. Scribners may have assumed that Lardner's readers were primarily newspaper followers rather than literary and academic readers, but the fact remains that *How To Write Short Stories* was reviewed by prominent people in major publications. Mencken's *American Mercury* notice chided the professors of the day for not taking Lardner seriously, conceded the limitations in the writing (Lardner's works are not profound;

he does not tap the basic sources of passion and motive; his characters share the same stupidity, transparent vanity, and shallow worth), and enthusiastically praised the American vulgate that Lardner wrote so skillfully, the extraordinary realism of his characters, and his carefully constructed plots that always seem spontaneous. Mencken charged that critics ignored Lardner because they preferred a loftier and more fashionable milieu–one they could readily find in the fiction of Edith Wharton and Henry James and Scott Fitzgerald.

Edmund Wilson found most of these stories equal to those of Sherwood Anderson and Sinclair Lewis but found Lardner as a writer still shackled to newspaper and magazine tastes and demands. Wilson's challenge echoed the urgings Perkins and Fitzgerald had already been making: if Lardner had anything more to say now was the time for him to produce such work. Wilson asked, "Will Ring Lardner, then, go on to his *Huckleberry Finn* or has he already told all he knows."

In a letter to the Fitzgeralds, Lardner noted the critical reception *How To Write Short Stories* had received and called the notices "sublime." He reported that Burton Rascoe had exaggerated in saying Lardner was better than Katherine Mansfield; nevertheless, Lardner added, the notice was still enough to get the Rascoes an invitation to come out and spend Sunday with the Lardners. A 1932 royalty statement to Lardner shows that sales of *How To Write Short Stories* exceeded the other important titles he published in the 1920s: *How To Write Short Stories* sold 20,366 copies, excellent sales for a story collection. *How To Write Short Stories* was a volume Charles Scribner sent to Sir James Barrie, who admired Lardner's work, and one that Perkins sent to John Galsworthy. Its publication marked the turning point in Lardner's literary career; however, he did not go on to produce a longer and more sustained work, to write his Huckleberry Finn.

George Ade and Finley Peter Dunne, the epitome of Chicago humorists, were influences on Lardner, and Ade's skeptical reaction to callous urban knowledge and progress was "Oh, yeah?," a phrase close in spirit to Lardner's "What of it?," a reaction that appears frequently to express a character's nonplussed attitude toward men and affairs. *What of It?* is also the title of a 1925 miscellany including articles Lardner wrote about his 1924 trip to Europe, parodies of fairy tales and bedtime stories, some magazine articles, as well as some "Weekly Letters." The volume is important primarily because it reprinted *The Young Immigrunts* and *Symptoms of Being 35*, and because it included several of his nonsense plays. As a title, *What of It?* was Grantland Rice's suggestion and one that Lardner said sounded good to him. In spite of its being more or less a potpourri, *What of It?* did have a respectable sale of over eighty-five hundred copies.

In 1926 *The Love Nest and Other Stories* was published, and among these nine stories were "The Love Nest," which portrays a supposedly ideal marriage that the wife survives only by heavy drinking; "Haircut," Lardner's tale of a despicable man's cruel deeds disingenuously narrated by a barber as he works away; and "A Day with Conrad Green," Lardner's Florenz Ziegfield story, which catches a semiliterate Broadway producer in his own deceptions. The nineteen stories from *How To Write Short Stories* and *The Love Nest* and sixteen later ones were then collected in *Round Up* (1929), a volume that gave critics an opportunity to judge Lardner's collected stories. The Literary Guild selected *Round Up* for its members, thereby enhancing Lardner's reputation and boosting his sales. The Guild distributed seventy thousand copies and Scribners, also optimistic about its acceptance, printed twenty thousand trade copies of which they sold just over fifteen thousand. (This combined sale helped make Lardner's 1929 royalty earnings $11,873.21.) Reviewers, including Lewis Mumford, Dorothy Parker, John Chamberlain, and Clifton Fadiman, generally wrote positive notices; some critics made unwarranted comparisons to Proust and Chekhov; others overstated the theme of hate; and practically all, as Jonathan Yardley charges, ignored the repetition of situation and the tendency toward sentimentality in some stories.

Nevertheless, *Round Up* is a book by which to judge Lardner's skill as a short-story writer, for it contains much of his best work. The title for this collection came from Maxwell Perkins, who, in spite of its western connotation, preferred it over "Our Kind," "Some of Ours," "Such as We," "Sorts and Collections," and "Ensemble," which was Lardner's choice. Not long after *Round Up* appeared, Lardner received an invitation to speak at the summer conference at Bread Loaf, an honor he declined, declaring himself "utterly incapable of talking, even to a small audience. It is something I tried years ago and 'swore off.'" The invitation, however, was another sign of his literary reputation.

It is true that Lardner's fiction does not match the intellectual challenge of a Faulkner or the stylistic accomplishment of a Hemingway; however, his collected stories do concern a variety of themes and display skill and versatility. By his own admission, he did not enjoy writing short stories and showed no interest in writing a novel, the suggestion Scott Fitzgerald and Maxwell Perkins made repeatedly. Lardner's heart and interest remained in the theater, where he enjoyed little success. His reputation in American letters and his influence on American writers come nevertheless from his short stories. Hemingway early acknowledged his influence and as a very young writer imitated him; upon reading *The Catcher in the Rye* (1964), Flannery O'Connor declared that Salinger owed a large debt to Ring Lardner; and Philip Roth has obvious debts to Lardner in *The Great American Novel* (1973).

As Virginia Woolf observed in commenting on *You Know Me Al*, the ritual of games provided Lardner with the order British writers found in society. At least twelve stories in *Round Up* center on games: baseball, prizefighting, golf, and bridge–the games Lardner liked best. Within these stories, however, the order and ritual of the game is not always observed; some baseball players take bribes and others refuse to field the ball, prizefighters throw matches and seek revenge, bridge players ignore rules or play viciously, and golfers cheat on their scores. Although Lardner knew and admired many baseball players, his fictional ones have grave flaws. Often they are not bright, like Elmer "Hurry" Cane, who does not know when he is being kidded or exploited since he is insensitive, gullible, and dishonest. Lardner has made the words "Alibi Ike" part of the language through his character who invented excuses without ceasing. The narrator in "Harmony" is obsessed with quartet singing and will do anything to get a tenor on the team regardless of his ball-playing ability. The quartet must practice when they are not performing and should, he thinks, continue their constant association during the off-season. Buster Elliott in "My Roomy," the psychopathic baseball player who senselessly terrorizes, destroys, and attempts to murder, and the prizefighter Midge Kelly in "Champion," who can beat a crippled brother, disavow a wife, and turn a deaf ear to family cries for assistance, are Lardner's two athletes devoid of all vestiges of humanity. Their behavior is reprehensible since they lack compassion and decency. From Jack

Keffe to Speed Parker ("Horseshoes"), Lardner's fictional athletes may indeed have great ability, but they do not have the qualities of the hero. What adulation they receive comes from "bugs," those fans who have little taste and little knowledge of the game. Certainly the 1919 Black Sox scandal, when eight Chicago White Sox players took bribes to throw the World Series, and the "fix" Lardner suspected in the 1926 Gene Tunney-Jack Dempsey fight explain, in part, his disillusionment. On the other hand, he knew that athletes were men with more innate frailties than capacities for becoming heroic figures.

Six stories in *Round Up* concern show business and the theater, where writers and tunesmiths are willing to steal the work of others ("A Day with Conrad Green," "Rhythm," and "Nora") and where the producer Lou Gregg ("The Love Nest") has taken his wife from the stage and imprisoned her in a mansion that, the narrator says, could be mistaken for the Yale Bowl. "Some Like Them Cold" and "Liberty Hall" complete this group, which represents work from 1921 to 1928, the years of Lardner's greatest earning power and popularity. In them the world of songwriting and Broadway productions is filled with arrogant, selfish, unhappy, and often mediocre people who reflect Lardner's own experience. His work for Ziegfeld was not pleasant, and he had little patience with stars who acted temperamentally. When he was writing lyrics for Ziegfeld's production *Smiles*, Fred Astaire (Lardner wrote his son John) caused Lardner's best contribution to be deleted because "the number calls for the presence of some Park Avenue women in evening dress and he doesn't want anybody to appear dressed up before his own entrance." Involved in writing song lyrics off and on throughout his life, Lardner made his fictional songwriter, Harry Hart in "Rhythm," ironically appropriate familiar opera arias as his own and then smugly comment that almost no one in the audience will know the difference. That mediocre songwriter in "Some Like Them Cold," Chas. F. Lewis, expects to turn out one hit tune a year for at least "25 grand" and thus "be on Easy st. and no more hammering on the old music box in some cabaret." Ben Drake, the successful songwriter in "Liberty Hall," is spoiled and pampered by his wife and his admirers and "was credited at the Lambs' Club with that month's most interesting bender," after being the houseguest of officious hosts.

Conrad Green, illiterate except to recognize his own name in the newspapers, is unfaithful to

Ring Lardner, 1927

his wife, conducts his business in an arrogant and boorish manner, and quite willingly steals a plot until he learns it has already been used in a show that has played a whole season at the Music Box. In "Nora," Hazlett is summoned to present his new show book to a producer and collaborators who immediately rewrite the entire plot using contrived and melodramatic episodes, creating a scene to fit the "Japanese number," and adding others to accommodate irrelevant, but extravagant, displays. "We'll write a jockey number and have about eight boys and maybe twenty-four gals in jockey suits." One song is a combination of snatches from "Sole Mio" and "La Paloma," and no sense of continuity or originality has survived. Dazed by the mutilation and transformation of his work, the writer calls his bootlegger, who can send good Scotch "but I ain't so sure of the rye. In fact, I'm kind of scared of it." Hazlett orders a case–of rye. The ending is typical Lardner–pithy, clever, and at the same time reflecting not only the era of the 1920s with the Follies and bootleggers, quick fortunes and madcap living, but also his own frustrations in theater. None of Lardner's show-business characters are really successful except the obnoxious producers Conrad Green and Lou Gregg. The writers of plays and songs have various flaws or little talent and seldom do they reach the top.

Devoted to his own family, Lardner wrote letters that witness his genuine affection for his mother-in-law as well as for Ellis's sisters and brothers. His own four sons were a constant source of pride (and each of them became a writer). Such family compatibility, however, rarely emerges in his fiction; indeed, in *Round Up* poor marriages are the rule and exist in a surprising number of circumstances. For instance, Conrad Green bought pearls for his mistress, not for his wife, who by a twist of fate gets them. Lou Gregg's wife, Celia ("The Love Nest"), longs to return to the stage but is doomed to maintain the pretense of being a happy wife and mother until she drinks herself to death. In "Haircut" and "Champion," wives are brutally abused; in "Now and Then" and "Anniversary," marriages that begin happily enough end up without love or understanding. The famous songwriter husband in "Liberty Hall" dislikes company and callously ignores his wife's need for friends. Indeed, "The Golden Honeymoon" is one of the few Lardner stories of a long-term marriage, and some critics have found it a tale of raucous, petty, and even vicious characters. The Finches and the Gullibles display unsavory manners, but they at least survive their adventures and retreat to their home territory, somewhat wiser and happier. The theme of marriage appears frequently, but seldom in the short stories does Lardner portray meaningful relationships, and never does he portray the ideally happy marriage he envisioned for himself in his courtship days.

The stories collected in *Round Up* (Ring Lardner, Jr., has called the volume his father's definitive collection) also are indicative of Lardner's humor, which comes through exaggerations, erratic spelling, the juxtaposing of homely expressions and formal diction, the speech of semiliterate characters, the visual effects of abbreviations and symbols, the wry observations of narrators, and the difference between the character's and the reader's perception. "Haircut," probably Lardner's most frequently anthologized story, ends with the barber asking his customer, "Comb it wet or dry?" Throughout the story, he has snipped away at the man's hair while gossiping

about Jim Kendall, a practical joker whose mean behavior toward his family and the townspeople render him altogether despicable. The barber reports Kendall's cruel jokes without seeing their serious effects on others and mourns Kendall's death because he was "such a card." To the reader, the barber's mundane closing remark is shocking and yet, ironically, amusing.

Much of Lardner's humor comes through details of observation. What is said is funny because the reader sees the irony or the incongruity, the wit, and often the wisdom. For example, the narrative voice makes wry comments in "The Love Nest" that reveal the foolishness of much social ritual. Lou Gregg insists that his two older daughters come downstairs to meet the guest, Mr. Bartlett: " 'This is Norma and this is Grace. Girls, this is Mr. Bartlett.' The girls received the news calmly." Mildred, the shy traveler in "Travelogue," takes along a book to read–not a romance or an adventure, but a pedantic title, "Carlyle on Cromwell and Others," given to her by a pedantic-sounding clergyman, Rev. N. L. Veach. In the same story, a touch of Chekovian humor appears as two of the three characters love to talk but will not listen to each other. Chapman tries hard to tell about his visit to the dentist, eager to display the spot where the molar has been extracted. The most he gets to say is, "Three days ago in Milwaukee–" because Hazel overshadows him with her continuous travelogue. She has been to any place mentioned and repeats all of her "wonderful" reactions to every spot from northern Michigan to San Francisco. He turns from the outgoing Hazel to the quiet Mildred, who will let him tell his dental story to his heart's content. This same device appears in "Sun Cured" when two New Yorkers are chance companions on a train bound for Florida. C. L. Walters cannot finish a sentence, much less tell about his business or his life. Walters says no more than "Now you take me–" before Fretts interrupts again with a tale of his drinking bouts, his lady friends, and the Florida vacation where he did not get "sun cured" because he never saw the beach, did not unpack his new fishing or tennis or golf paraphernalia since he was too busy drinking and partying until all hours–the activities he was supposed to avoid.

Much of Lardner's humor depends on exaggeration. The narrator in "Alibi Ike" stretches things when he describes: "Doyle cracked one and Ike run back a mile and a half and caught it with one hand"; and Ike, of course, offers outlandish excuses for the outcome of every play. When Bob and Jennie Mason ("Reunion") from Niles, Michigan, visit relatives in Sands Point, Long Island, the social distance cannot be overcome because the Masons do not play bridge or golf; moreover, Jennie's dental work is unacceptable. When she smiled, "most of the visible ones were of gold, and the work had evidently been done by a dentist for whom three members of a [golf] foursome were waiting." In "Mr. and Mrs. Fix-It" the narrator declares that "a secret is just as safe with Ada as a police dog tethered with dental floss," and the photographs on the wall of musical-show producer Louie Brock ("Nora") include "a too-perfect likeness of [his] wife, whom he had evidently married in a dense fog." Slightly akin to the tale is an absurd episode in "Horseshoes." Grimes is at bat, facing the sensational pitcher Walter Johnson in the ninth inning when Johnson's pitch "hit my bat with a curve and the ball went on the ground to McBride. He booted it, but throwed me out easy—because I was so surprised at not havin' whiffed [struck out] that I forgot to run!"

Lardner may have had some of his own baseball reporting days in mind when the nameless reporter in "Horseshoes" looks up "with a little thrill" as he recognizes the new World Series star, Grimes, sitting next to him. He comments on the distance fixed between baseball stars and newspaper reporters: "I had met Grimes one day during the spring he was with the Cubs, but I knew he wouldn't remember me. A ball player never recalls a reporter's face on less than six introductions or his name on less than twenty." Lardner, of course, was quite popular with the teams he traveled with and covered for the *Chicago Tribune*. The players called him "Old owl eyes," and perhaps they always remained somewhat puzzled that he never tolerated off-color stories, which must have been common enough to hear during the long train trips. He held certain players in high esteem; others he judged for the bushers that they were. The year Lardner died, the six baseball stories about Danny Warner, *Lose with a Smile* (1933), appeared, a volume that is thin and disappointing compared to the lively *You Know Me Al.* Although Lardner uses the epistolary method in both books, Danny's letters to Jessie lack the humor and style that are so evident in Jack Keefe's letters to Al.

Three other posthumous books are of particular importance because they make much of his work more easily accessible. (Gilbert Seldes ed-

ited *First and Last,* a collection of Lardner's nonfiction, in 1934 and also prepared the Viking *Portable Ring Lardner* in 1946. Both volumes were of great use at the time but have long been out of print.) In 1962 *Shut Up, He Explained,* with introductions by Henry Morgan and Babette Rosmond, reprinted not only *The Big Town, The Young Immigrunts,* and miscellaneous parodies and articles, but also nine nonsense plays and fourteen segments of the radio column "Over the Waves." Even though Rosmond argues that the ungrammatical humor Lardner used so well did not characterize him, it is also true that his aloofness from the Chicago literati, his avowed dislike of classical music and opera, and his willingness to distort his work for Broadway's demands suggest that at times his tastes were akin to those of Gullible and Finch. Henry Morgan contends that Lardner was a writer with "the perfect ear and the see-through eye . . . nobody writes this way any more." Morgan's assessment should not be overlooked because he gets to the heart of Lardner's talent without joining the early and late critics who emphasize his supposed hatred of his characters and the general despair and despondency in the last years of his life. "And while it may be true," Morgan says, "that an Infinite Wisdom created a lot of damned fools, it was compensated for a bit by sending among us a handful of witnesses who are at once loving and wary of their fellows, who see clearly the folly of the whole population, and can be funny about it. Ring was one of the handful." His nonsense plays, some of which were occasionally performed by members of the Algonquin Round Table crowd in revues, were received with much praise and demonstrate Lardner's writing of sophisticated humor, using the process of association and employing the non sequitur to great advantage. Maxwell Geismer argues that these plays are simpler, less philosophic, more personal, and funnier than most of the surrealistic fiction of that day; he sees the nonsense humor as "just plain funny, period. Either you laugh, or you don't." These lines from "Clemo Uti–'The Water Lilies' " are funny, but will not survive much commentary or analysis:

SECOND STRANGER: Are you married?
FIRST STRANGER: I don't know. There's a woman living with me, but I can't place her.

Over half of the twenty-six pieces in *Some Champions: Sketches and Fiction by Ring Lardner* (1976), edited by Matthew J. Bruccoli and Richard Layman, were written in the early 1930s, a time in Lardner's career when he has been portrayed by many as sick, despondent, and broken—a writer whose power to produce humor was altogether gone. Four stories from the 1930s that are included—"Poodle," "Mama," "Widow," and "Cured!"—are all written in straight English without the uneducated narrator's bad grammar and spelling problems. Furthermore, they are dark stories, taking their subject matter in mental illness, alcoholism, and death; however, Lardner by no means abandons his humor. In "Widow," John Winslow dies of heart trouble and the activities surrounding his funeral are filled with clichés ("Margaret [the widow] was one of the bravest women they had ever seen, and was bearing up beautifully"). Far from the grieving widow, Margaret hopes that Dick Randall will continue his interest toward her. Conducted at the house, the funeral service shows humor that reveals Lardner at his satiric best: "A mixed quartet from the Winslows' church sang two hymns; rather, they sang 'Just As I Am' as well as a mixed quartet can sing anything when there is no piano or organ to accompany them and they fought a losing battle with 'In the Hour of Trial,' owing to the fact that Miss Wells, the soprano, pitched it three tones too high for her own good or that of Mr. Standing, the tenor. It was abruptly decided by a vote of four to nothing to put the Amen after the second verse."

Long buried in old issues of newspapers and of the *Delineator, Redbook,* and *Good Housekeeping,* many of the pieces in these two recent collections of Lardner's works had been virtually lost to the current reading public, and in fact college-age students seldom claim to remember reading even "Haircut." The reappearance of these stories may not signal a Lardner revival, but *Shut Up, He Explained, Some Champions,* as well as a collection of Lardner's comic strips, *Ring Lardner's You Know Me Al* (1979), two recent biographical studies—Ring Lardner, Jr.'s *The Lardners: My Family Remembered* (1976) and Jonathan Yardley's *Ring* (1977)—an edition of Lardner's letters, and a full descriptive bibliography suggest that he is being read more widely now and that his position in American letters is a secure one, even though it is not one of the highest acclaim. Lardner did not take on themes that engage the great social issues of the time, but he did observe with candor and always with humor the dilemma of the middle class as they struggled to get ahead and as

they attempted to avoid the pitfalls of their own inevitable foibles.

Lardner has not been raised to the status of a major American writer and probably will not be, but criticism in the past twenty years shows that he is much admired and that he is a figure essential to a thorough study of American literature in the 1920s and 1930s. As an interpreter of middle-class life and aspirations, he is unsurpassed. Linguists are impressed with his rendering of vulgate speech, and readers of all disciplines and dispositions should be entertained and delighted with his humor. After Lardner's death, Maxwell Perkins in a letter to Ernest Hemingway (28 November 1934) spoke of Lardner in terms that are still valid; he expressed praise, affection, and reservations: "If he had written more, he would have been a great writer perhaps, but whatever it was that prevented him from writing more was the thing that prevented him from being a great writer. But he was a great man, and one of immense latent talent which got itself partly expressed." His gift for humor rarely failed him and yet he remains an enigmatic person, reserved and distant, described by his sons as "laconic, uneasy in crowds, with a mask over his emotions and a deep-seated mistrust of face values, a cynic who felt that if something could be faked it probably was."

Letters:

Ring Around Max: The Correspondence of Ring Lardner and Max Perkins, edited by Clifford M. Caruthers (DeKalb: Northern Illinois Press, 1973).
Correspondence between Lardner and his editor at Scribners. Includes many details about publication of Lardner's books between 1924 and his death in 1933.

Letters from Ring, edited by Caruthers (Flint, Mich.: Walden Press, 1979).
Lardner's collected correspondence, including the many letters he wrote his wife-to-be during their long courtship.

Bibliography:

Matthew J. Bruccoli and Richard Layman, *Ring Lardner: A Descriptive Bibliography* (Pittsburgh: University of Pittsburgh Press, 1976).

Biographies:

Donald Elder, *Ring Lardner: A Biography* (Garden City, N.Y.: Doubleday, 1956).
First biography of Lardner. Valuable for its basic information about his life and career, but at times overly laudatory and sentimentalized. Written with the assistance of family members unavailable to later biographers (except for Ring Lardner, Jr.).

Ring Lardner, Jr., *The Lardners: My Family Remembered* (New York: Harper & Row, 1976).
Family memoir by Lardner's third son, who was thirteen when his father died. Drawing from family records and recollections of friends, Mr. Lardner has assembled the best account of his father's life in New York.

Jonathan Yardley, *Ring: A Biography of Ring Lardner* (New York: Random House, 1977).
Reassessment of the facts of Lardner's life and his stature as a writer. Particularly useful on his career as a sports journalist.

References:

James DeMuth, *Small Town Chicago: The Comic Perspective of Finley Peter Dunne, George Ade, and Ring Lardner* (Port Washington, N.Y.: Kennikat Press, 1980).
Discussion of the most successful vernacular humorists in the Chicago area during the first two decades of the twentieth century. Useful for perspective it gives on the recent tradition of midwestern dialect humor.

Elizabeth Evans, *Ring Lardner* (New York: Ungar, 1979).
Solid general discussion of Lardner's fiction. Good introduction to his life and works.

Clifton Fadiman, "Ring Lardner and the Triangle of Hate," *Nation*, 136 (22 March 1933): 315-317.
Influential, though misdirected early assessment of Lardner's fiction. Argues that he is driven by bitterness and a profound hatred of mankind.

Otto Friedrich, *Ring Lardner* (Minneapolis: University of Minnesota Press, 1965).
General critical study of Lardner's works.

Maxwell Geismar, *Ring Lardner and the Portrait of Folly* (New York: Crowell, 1972).
Introductory and often superficial critical biography for pre-college readers by a well-respected literary critic.

Charles S. Holmes, "Ring Lardner: Reluctant Artist," in *A Question of Quality, Popularity and Value in Modern Creative Writing*, edited by Louis Filler (Bowling Green, Ohio: Bowling Green University Press, 1976).
Well-considered critical essay arguing that Lardner was at different times in his career primarily a humorist, a satirist, and a pessimistic nihilist.

Forrest L. Ingram, "Fun at the Incinerating Plant: Lardner's Wry Waste Land," in *The Twenties*, edited by Warren French (De Land, Fla.: Everett/Edwards, 1975), pp. 111-122.
Critical essay arguing that Lardner's humor simply masks his own disillusionment and is at base a harsh indictment of human behavior.

Walton R. Patrick, *Ring Lardner* (New York: Twayne, 1963).
Introductory study of Lardner's life and works in the standard format of the Twayne United States Author Series.

Jonas Spatz, "Ring Lardner: Not an Escape, but a Reflection," in *The Twenties*, edited by French (De Land, Fla.: Everett/Edwards, 1975), pp. 101-110.
Critical essay arguing that Lardner's fiction reflects his own sense of isolation: "the inability to give or receive love."

Howard W. Webb, Jr., "The Development of a Style: The Lardner Idiom," *American Quarterly*, 12 (1960): 482-492.
Careful study of Lardner's fictional use of vernacular speech patterns. The best discussion of Lardner's style.

Webb, "The Meaning of Ring Lardner's Fiction: A Reevaluation," *American Literature*, 31 (January 1960): 434-445.
Solid rejoinder to Clifton Fadiman's charges that Lardner was a misanthrope. Argues that the central theme of Lardner's fiction is the problem of communication.

Edmund Wilson, "Ring Lardner's American Characters," in his *A Literary Chronicle: 1920-1950* (Garden City, N.Y.: Doubleday, 1956).

Brief but important essay written in 1924 by an eminent critic that describes the importance of Lardner's short fiction and declares that his true potential will only be realized if he undertakes a novel: "Will Ring Lardner, then, go on to his *Huckleberry Finn* or has he already told all he knows?"

Norris Yates, "The Isolated Man of Ring Lardner," in *The American Humorist: Conscience of the Twentieth Century* (Ames: Iowa State University Press, 1964), pp. 165-193.

Good general critical essay about the themes of Lardner's fiction, concluding that bitterness and despair are implied by the sardonic humor of his stories. Especially useful for its placement of Lardner in the tradition of American humor.

Papers:
Most of Lardner's papers are in the Newberry Library, Chicago.

Sinclair Lewis

This entry was updated by Martin Light (Purdue University) from his entry in
DLB 9, American Novelists, 1910-1945, Part 2.

Places	Sauk Centre, Minn. Yale University	New York City	Rural Midwest
Influences and Relationships	Charles Dickens H. G. Wells	H. L. Mencken Upton Sinclair	Mark Twain Henry David Thoreau
Literary Movements and Forms	Satire Vernacular Humor	Muckraking Novel	Realism
Major Themes	Revolt from the Village Pleasures of Courtship vs. Tensions of Marriage	Escape into Nature The Divided Self Religious Hypocrisy European vs. American Values	Eastern vs. Midwestern Values Aspiration and Illusion vs. Reality
Cultural and Artistic Influences	Revolt against "Literary Gentility"	Utopianism	Evangelical Religion
Social and Economic Influences	Shifting Roles of Women Urban Growth Industrialization	Communism American Materialism The Depression	Rising Power of Labor Unions The Threat of Fascism

See also the Lewis entry in DLB: Documentary Series 1.

BIRTH: Sauk Centre, Minnesota, 7 February 1885, to Dr. Edwin J. and Emma Kermott Lewis.

EDUCATION: A.B., Yale University, 1908.

MARRIAGES: 15 April 1914 to Grace Livingstone Hegger (divorced); child: Wells. 14 May 1928 to Dorothy Thompson (divorced); child: Michael.

AWARDS: Pulitzer Prize for *Arrowsmith*, 1926 (declined); Nobel Prize, 1930; elected to the National Institute of Arts and Letters, 1935; elected to the American Academy of Arts and Letters, 1938.

DEATH: Rome, Italy, 10 January 1951.

BOOKS: *Hike and the Aeroplane*, as Tom Graham (New York: Stokes, 1912);
Our Mr. Wrenn: The Romantic Adventures of a Gentle Man (New York & London: Harper, 1914; London: Cape, 1923);
The Trail of the Hawk (New York & London: Harper, 1915; London: Cape, 1923);
The Job: An American Novel (New York & London: Harper, 1917; London: Cape, 1926);
The Innocents (New York & London: Harper, 1917);
Free Air (New York: Harcourt, Brace & Howe, 1919; London: Cape, 1924);
Main Street (New York: Harcourt, Brace & Howe, 1920; London, New York & Toronto: Hodder & Stoughton, 1921);
Babbitt (New York: Harcourt, Brace, 1922; London: Cape, 1922);
Arrowsmith (New York: Harcourt, Brace, 1925); republished as *Martin Arrowsmith* (London: Cape, 1925);
Mantrap (New York: Harcourt, Brace, 1926; London: Cape, 1926);
Elmer Gantry (New York: Harcourt, Brace, 1927; London: Cape, 1927);
The Man Who Knew Coolidge (New York: Harcourt, Brace, 1928; London: Cape, 1928);
Dodsworth (New York: Harcourt, Brace, 1929; London: Cape, 1929);
Ann Vickers (Garden City, N.Y.: Doubleday, Doran, 1933; London: Cape, 1933);

Sinclair Lewis, circa 1910

Work of Art (Garden City, N.Y.: Doubleday, Doran, 1934; London: Cape, 1934);
Jayhawker: A Play in Three Acts, by Lewis and Lloyd Lewis (Garden City, N.Y.: Doubleday, Doran, 1935; London: Cape, 1935);
It Can't Happen Here (Garden City, N.Y.: Doubleday, Doran, 1935; London: Cape, 1935);
Selected Short Stories (Garden City, N.Y.: Doubleday, Doran, 1935);
It Can't Happen Here [play] (New York: Dramatists Play Service, 1938);
The Prodigal Parents (Garden City, N.Y.: Doubleday, Doran, 1938; London: Cape, 1938);
Bethel Merriday (New York: Doubleday, Doran, 1940; London: Cape, 1940);
Gideon Planish (New York: Random House, 1943; London: Cape, 1943);
Cass Timberlane (New York: Random House, 1945; London: Cape, 1946);
Kingsblood Royal (New York: Random House, 1947; London: Cape, 1948);
The God-Seeker (New York: Random House, 1949; Melbourne, London & Toronto: Heinemann, 1949);

World So Wide (New York: Random House, 1951; Melbourne, London & Toronto: Heinemann, 1951);

The Man from Main Street: Selected Essays and Other Writings, edited by Harry E. Maule and Melville H. Cane (New York: Random House, 1953; Melbourne, London & Toronto: Heinemann, 1954);

I'm a Stranger Here Myself and Other Stories, edited by Mark Schorer (New York: Dell, 1962);

Storm in the West, by Lewis and Dore Schary (New York: Stein & Day, 1963; London: Sidgwick & Jackson, 1964).

PLAY PRODUCTIONS: *Hobohemia*, New York, Greenwich Village Theatre, 8 February 1919;

Jayhawker, by Lewis and Lloyd Lewis, New York, Cort Theatre, 5 November 1934;

It Can't Happen Here, by Lewis and John C. Moffitt, New York, Adelphi Theatre, 27 October 1936;

Angela Is Twenty-Two, by Lewis and Fay Wray, Columbus, Ohio, 20 December 1938.

The career of Sinclair Lewis is impressive in its presumption, range, and achievement. He undertook to reflect in his novels the distresses felt by a generation trying to find its way in a period of change, caught between illusion and reality, puzzled by promise and necessity. As a satirist who set himself a succession of social, geographic, and occupational problems to investigate, he faced practically every concern of readers from 1910 to 1950. He was a child of the new hope raised at the turn of the century, yet he wrote of escape into nature and the past, of the revolt from the village, and of the temptations of the city. He attempted to portray the shifting roles of women; the strains upon marriage; the ruthlessness of industrial progress; the abuses of power and money; the rival claims of West and East as well as of America and Europe; and the threats of fascism, communism, and racism.

For three decades Lewis was an important public figure whose movements and statements were news. His books topped the best-seller lists. He sought, was offered, loudly refused, and then won the important prizes, snubbing the Pulitzer but seeking and happily accepting the Nobel as the first American to win that award in literature. To the Pulitzer committee he addressed a widely published and discussed letter of rejection of the prize for *Arrowsmith* (his motive was his still-

smoldering anger that the choice of *Main Street* as winner five years before had been vetoed by a senior panel). On the occasion of the Nobel ceremony, he made a memorable address explaining, defending, and touting American writers. He was in some ways an outrageous figure who, as T. K. Whipple said, bestrode his nation like a Red Indian.

Lewis created a stock company of characters who were targeted over and over in his satires: political reactionaries, fund-raisers, doctors, Rotarians, braggarts, con men, idlers, racial bigots, nagging women, professors, preachers. He portrayed heroic figures–his pioneers, workers, doers, and worthy wives. He gave us commanding examples of hypocrisy, in reproductions of doublespeak long before Orwell, in mockery of editorials, oratory, gossip, table talk, ads, religious harangues, whining, and boosterism. His protagonists itch to get moving, restlessly traveling to the Far West, the East, and Europe, to farms, villages, small cities, metropolises, and mountain retreats. He shaped a portrait of the Midwest, creating, in the process, his own state and territory, as Faulkner was later to do with "Yoknapatawpha County" in Mississippi. Obsessively, he retold again and again the fable of our divided selves, bewildered amidst aspiration and achievement. His central story narrated the experiences of the yearning and idealistic provincial, who, having stepped forth into the world with a meager preparation of reading and advice, says in wonder at what his or her observations reveal: "How they lie! How those after-dinner speakers, politicians, preachers, novelists lie!"–and then tries to find consolation and identity in education, meaningful work, friendship, faith, and love.

Lewis's career can be divided into three phases. First there was the apprenticeship, a lengthy one lasting until his first great critical and popular success, *Main Street* (1920), published when he was thirty-five years old. During the apprentice years he wrote tales and articles for Yale's literary magazines, newspaper copy, publishers' blurbs, poetry, fillers, short stories, reviews, and five uneven novels, in which he sought his subject, his territory, his characters, his style. Then came his period of highest achievement, from 1920 to 1930, during which he put his energies into five additional and notable novels (from *Main Street* to *Dodsworth*), two lesser books, skirmishes with the Pulitzer committee, quarrels in the public forum occasioned by the picture of religion in *Elmer Gantry*, and acceptance

Lewis's first wife, Grace, with their son, Wells, who was born 26 July 1917

of the Nobel Prize. During those years his themes, social settings, values, and stock company were further explored and developed. Finally, he fell into a period of decline, from 1930 until his death, when the method, the attack, the set speeches, and the stock characters were used in additional situations, but with decreasing invention, enthusiasm, and freshness.

Harry Sinclair Lewis was born on 7 February 1885 in the frontier village of Sauk Centre, Minnesota. His father was a physician; his mother died after a protracted illness and several absences to better climates, leaving her husband and three sons. Harry, the youngest, was then six. A year later Dr. Lewis married again. Harry remembered his father as dignified and stern. Other accounts described him as habit-ridden, cold, and inflexible. He valued hard work most highly of all virtues, and scolded Harry for laziness. The son, occasionally accompanying his father on medical rounds, observed the doctor's cool competence and developed an admiration for the person who works hard and pays his debts on time, traits he ascribed to a "doer." Yet already he found dullness in such an environment and in such provincial people. To seek worthy work, apply himself to it responsibly, and yet remain interesting, alert, and witty were goals throughout Lewis's life and writing. Very early

he had decided to become a writer; he was then and always a voracious reader.

Sinclair Lewis was tall and lanky, with a pock-marked face and ill-fitting clothes. He was unable to control his alcoholism and was noted for practical jokes and long monologues with which he entertained his friends by improvising the speech and reflecting the values of evangelists, scoundrels, and boosters. He was forever restless. The constant movement from place to place in his fictional plotting only mirrors his own history. He once said of himself that he was "afflicted with Wanderlust." At thirteen he tried to run away from home to the Spanish-American War. In 1902 he left Sauk Centre for a year of pre-university training at the Academy of Oberlin College. He entered Yale University in the fall of 1903, his eagerness soon clouded by his sense of being an outsider. He began writing for the *Literary Magazine* and the *Courant* as much for contacts and friendship as for expression, and by the end of the year he was working for the New Haven newspaper as well. During his first summer vacation he sailed on a cattleboat for Liverpool, where in a mere eight days on land he encountered realities that shook loose some of his illusions about literary England. During the following two years at Yale, though reading and writing intensely, he felt more alone than ever. In the summer of 1905 he visited home with some pleasure yet with a disturbing recognition that villagers could be cruelly critical.

The following summer he explored England more satisfactorily. In October of that year he abruptly left Yale. For a month he was at Upton Sinclair's socialist community at Helicon Hall; then he spent several months free-lancing in New York City and tried a brief adventure in Panama. He returned to Yale in December 1907 and graduated in June 1908. He was a newsman in Iowa for ten weeks, and after being fired was in New York during the fall. In January 1909 he arrived in California, where he lasted a little over a year. Part of the time he worked for a newspaper in San Francisco, and all the while he was there he continued to accumulate notebooks full of observations, clippings, and story ideas; in fact, he had occasional success in publishing a few short stories. In March 1910 he became a subeditor on the *Volta Review* in Washington, D.C. That September, at twenty-five years of age, he once again reached New York City. In the next five years he held positions as advertising writer and as editor, found that he could support himself by turning out short stories, and developed his craft as a novelist.

But his wandering would continue. His summary of his travels between 1915 and 1930 lists forty states of the Union, plus Canada, Mexico, fourteen countries of Europe, and three countries of South America. At one time or another throughout his life, he established residences in New York City; rural Vermont; Williamstown, Massachusetts; London; and Paris. Yet he spoke of the long arm of the small midwestern town, whose influence never left him. Of his twenty-two novels, all but six involve midwestern protagonists or midwestern locales.

In New York City in 1912 he had met Grace Livingstone Hegger; they were married two years later. Their son, Wells Lewis, born in 1917, was killed in World War II. Grace Lewis gave her account of the marriage in her novel *Half a Loaf* (1931) and in her autobiography *With Love from Gracie* (1955). They were divorced in 1928. Sinclair Lewis and the journalist Dorothy Thompson were married soon afterward. Their son, Michael, was born in 1930. The marriage ended in divorce in 1942.

Lewis lived in Duluth, Minnesota, in the mid 1940s in an attempt to return to his midwestern roots, though at the end of two years he established a home in Massachusetts. But in 1950 he was wandering again, traveling in Italy, Switzerland, and France, even though he suffered from heart trouble. He died in Rome on 10 January 1951. His grave is at Sauk Centre, between those of his father and mother.

In the era of Lewis's youth and apprenticeship (1890 to 1920), traditional religion was giving way to newer ideas of social organization, psychology, and science. Industrialism and the industrial cities became dominant, while populations shifted from rural to urban communities, emigration (especially from eastern Europe) increased, and labor strife grew. Meanwhile, the giants of nineteenth-century American literature were either recently dead or abroad or ending their careers. The principles of literary realism found practitioners in William Dean Howells, Henry James, and Mark Twain. Opposing them, professors and editors of literary magazines who espoused a cult of idealism encouraged readers to escape into sentimental medievalism, evoked in such popular books as *When Knighthood Was in Flower* (1898), by Edwin Caskoden (Charles Major), or in Tennyson, Morris, and Swinburne. Though Lewis knew the work of the new realists,

like E. W. Howe, Edward Eggleston, Mark Twain, and Hamlin Garland, and soon would also know the work of Theodore Dreiser, Sherwood Anderson, and Edgar Lee Masters, he was strangely drawn at first to escapism, which he expressed in his early poems and stories. Later, of course, he violently turned from it, and it became part of his dialogue between romance and reality.

Of all the authors Lewis read, he most admired Dickens and Wells. In Dickens he found examples of social concern, sentiment, and caricature; he would attempt to make Dickensian social comedy in America. He saw a clear link between Dickens and Wells; Wells reinforced his sense of purpose in the novel and raised the possibility of reform through the novel. He imitated Wellsian satire, tenderness, and social ideas, and he was thereby able to break through his habitual "Tennyson and water" poetry in undertaking his first novel, *Our Mr. Wrenn* (1914), with its Wellsian hero, a "little man," who ventures on the road, inspired by images of idealized women, and whose very name, "Wrenn," resembles those of Wells's Mr. Kipps and Mr. Polly.

Having settled in New York City in 1910, Lewis worked as an editor and advertising manager first at Stokes and later at the Doran publishing company. He continued to place his poetry and short stories in undistinguished magazines for very little money and turned out a potboiler for boys called *Hike and the Aeroplane* (1912) under the pseudonym Tom Graham. Then came his first crafted novel, *Our Mr. Wrenn: The Romantic Adventures of a Gentle Man*. Wrenn, a simple young fellow in a petty and tedious job, yearns for escape. With a sudden legacy of one thousand dollars, he signs onto a cattle boat for England (as Lewis himself had done, for both author and character have dreamt of adventure in far-off romantic places). In London, Wrenn falls under the influence of Istra Nash, an expatriate would-be painter, who teaches Wrenn to "play" at life. Istra is an impossible romantic, yet she is drawn with a measure of irony and skepticism. Under her guidance Wrenn sees something of art and the old culture, meets and rejects bohemian frivolity, and listens to the clichés of art and sex. But he grows enough to reject what his dreams have led him to, and returns to New York from these European sites of pretension; at home he marries down-to-earth Nellie Croubel.

In this book Lewis takes from Wells and re-creates for himself the pattern of the quixote–the

Lewis and Dorothy Thompson outside Savoy Chapel, London, 14 May 1928, just after their marriage (Dorothy Thompson Collection, Arents Research Library for Special Collections at Syracuse University)

young adventurer who sets forth from stifling reality to live by the inspiration of his or her dreams, finds the confrontation both fulfilling and disappointing, and then, chastened and initiated, settles for a realistic life, now infused by decency, sincerity, and affirmation. In Istra Nash, Lewis begins his exploration of the shallow, nagging woman, whose chief purpose is to remake men to suit her fancy and with whom he associates his concept of "play." Such a type Lewis would employ in one variation or another in later and better novels, from *Free Air* (1919), *Main Street* (1920), *Arrowsmith* (1925), and *Dodsworth* (1929) to *Cass Timberlane* (1945) and *Kingsblood Royal* (1947).

Lewis's second book was called *The Trail of the Hawk* (1915). In an article for the *American Magazine* of April 1921 (reprinted in *The Man from Main Street*, 1953) Lewis attests to the virtues of hard work: still an advertising manager, he had written *The Trail of the Hawk* on the train to his job and at the kitchen sink in odd moments after breakfast and on the weekends. Yet the book itself is a tribute to quixotic romance, a youthful, optimistic novel that pays homage to the promises of a late-nineteenth-century boyhood. Its three

sections are called "The Adventure of Youth," "The Adventure of Adventure," and "The Adventure of Love." It opens with an account of young Carl Ericson in Joralemon, Minnesota (town and boy bear some resemblance to Sauk Centre and Lewis). Carl is called a "divinely restless seeker" of romance, a pioneer, who must follow the trail to the tawny deserts, the silent forests, the "golden China dragons of San Francisco"– forever "elsewhere." In the first of a series of scenes that Lewis duplicated in later books, Carl encounters a socialist pariah of the village who is his mentor and advises him to live in life, not in books; to be wary of refinement; to dream of going beyond the commonplaces of Joralemon, Chicago, or Paris; and to guard against the probability that love and marriage will rob him of his freedom.

The second part shows Carl as a daring aviator, wandering freely across the nation. But Carl abandons that career in mourning for the death of his best friend. The final section deals with courtship and marriage. The girl is Ruth Winslow, a "playmate" (as Lewis called such idealized yet finicky women), a "princess," who, in the name of romance, seduces a man from his work. She sometimes speaks a silly medieval jargon of "thee" and "thou," "forthfaring," and "questing" to the "land of Nowhere." After Carl and Ruth finally wed, quarrel, reconcile, and face the necessity of succumbing to a prosaic and deadly office routine, they plan an escape to South America, echoing the Wellsian notion that modern industrial society stifles the spirit.

Beginning in 1915 Lewis earned a living by producing about one short story each month. He also worked on his next book, *The Job: An American Novel* (1917). In it we see a considerable advance in Lewis's understanding of women and such related issues as woman's rights, birth control, and divorce. The protagonist is Una Golden, an ambitious young woman from a dull, small town who arrives in New York City to seek significant work and someone to love. After training at a secretarial school, Una takes a series of difficult and unrewarding jobs. She meets Walter Babson, the prince of her dreams. But Walter, too, is a seeker, and, equally restless, he wanders westward, as many of Lewis's heroes must. Then in desperation Una allows herself to be persuaded that a salesman named Julius "Eddie" Schwirtz can give her the kindness and companionship for which she yearns. Eddie's vulgarities surface after the marriage, and Una divorces him. She returns to work as a real estate agent, and through a happy coincidence she meets Walter again. Soon they will marry.

In *The Job* Lewis reaches for some new material. He tries out his imitation of salesmen's talk, later to be developed in the speech of Babbitt. He introduces some Wellsian ideas about the misuse of education and the potential good in some kinds of technology. He develops a curious mixture of Veblenian criticism of business and yet praise for it and its efficiency. He counsels patience and persistence.

The Innocents (1917) concerns an elderly couple from New York, Mr. and Mrs. Seth Appleby, who, having failed at several enterprises and having found no help or consolation from their daughter and son-in-law, become hoboes. They wander to Indiana, where they are warmly received by people who understand their home-spun values. The son-in-law comes west to reclaim them, but is humiliated by seeing the acceptance they have found. One familiar with Lewis's later novel called *The Prodigal Parents* (1938) may find interest in this early treatment of the misunderstandings of parents and children, but by and large the book is of little worth.

Finally, to close out the apprentice years, Lewis published *Free Air* (1919), about a cross-country excursion to Seattle, inspired by a similar tour he and his wife had recently made. Claire Boltwood sets out from Brooklyn Heights to drive westward with her father, who is ill. She is a "princess," drawn to the pattern of Ruth Winslow of *The Trail of the Hawk*. In Minnesota she meets Milt Daggett, an adventurous fellow who abandons his car-repair shop to follow Claire and help her along the way, as a loyal knight might do. Each time she gets into trouble, Milt arrives in his little car to save her. The novel shows Claire's ill father gaining strength as they move westward, while Claire rejects her eastern suitor, Jeff Saxton, in favor of Milt, who has the western virtues of kindness, loyalty, ingenuity, and sensitivity to beauty. At one point Milt utters the idea that the best of all possible lives would be one in which a fellow could be an engineer and "still talk of beautiful things" (that is, combine the practical life with the artistic one). It was a possibility that would puzzle many of Lewis's later protagonists: Carol Kennicott, Arrowsmith, Dodsworth, and others.

Thus, as he was about to enter his great decade of accomplishment, Lewis seemed to have prepared himself by exploring settings, characters, style, themes, and narrative modes. He had re-created the environments of Midwest and East, of farms, villages, and cities. He had found archetypal characters to his liking—young pioneers, seekers, and playful women—and had tried out the satiric voices of preachers, businessmen, and professors. He had identified some sources of discontent and had raised questions of accommodation between the practical work that one must do in an industrial society and the artistic life that must be present to enrich it. He had portrayed "play" as a value that enables one to survive by imaginative escape, but had yet to perceive it as the corrupting distraction that keeps men from accomplishing the true work they are destined to do. As it turned out, he was on the verge of making a gigantic imaginative leap that would enable him to bring these perceptions together so as to embody his myth of America in a rewardingly artistic way. He was ready to create *Main Street* (1920).

In his first masterwork Lewis found new expression for the practiced themes: the dullness of the village; the lonely and stultified lives of women; the need for love. Lewis once made the claim that he had begun writing *Main Street* in the summer of 1905 under the title "The Village Virus." But Lewis's biographer Mark Schorer doubts if any of it was written then, though the phrase "village virus" appears in Lewis's diary for that year, and though there is evidence that Lewis felt the irritations of a lonely young man who had been away to college and who could well perceive that, as he later said, village neighborliness was a fake. As he worked on *Main Street* in 1919, Lewis felt confident that he was at last achieving what he had set out to do from the beginning. His letters speak of his excitement and of the long hours that he spent composing, eight hours a day, seven days of the week.

A brief word from an "alien cynic" prefaces the book and suggests to us that the story we are to read about Gopher Prairie, Minnesota, would be the same anywhere in Ohio, Kentucky, upstate New York, or the Carolinas. We first see its heroine, Carol Kennicott, as an unmarried college girl trying to find a career. She has been a great reader of romantic books and a great fantasist of images from her reading. In this, she bears some resemblance to Emma Bovary. She dreams of the pioneer West, and of southern levees, high-stacked steamers, and Dakota chiefs. While still without a goal, she happens to meet Dr. Will Kennicott, a physician in the Minnesota village of Gopher Prairie, and she imagines that by bringing reform and artistic culture to the village she can fulfill the mission of her life. She will "turn a prairie town into Georgian houses and Japanese bungalows." But after she and the doctor marry and she enters the real situation that Gopher Prairie offers, she is shocked; the "stories"–her books–have lied to her, for they had spoken of quaint and picturesque villages, and Gopher Prairie is nothing like that. In one of the most memorable passages in the novel, Carol takes her first walk through the village, observing broken yellow buildings, a cat asleep on the lettuce in the grocery window, a greasy soda fountain, and a dusty jumble of toothbrushes, combs, and nostrums in the drugstore. Her first encounter with the villagers is hardly any better; she hears nothing but gossip, trivial talk, spite, and prejudice. These storekeepers, preachers, boosters, and housewives are given their opportunity for satiric self-exposure in lengthy monologues. To each challenging question from Carol, a villager responds with foolishness and hypocrisy about religion, education, and politics. If Carol is to reform what she finds, she indeed has her work cut out for her.

Encouraged by Miles Bjornstam, a socialist outcast who becomes her mentor, Carol continues to spread ideas and suggest reforms. She launches into projects, such as remodeling a lounge for farm wives, encouraging a self-education society, and forming a theater group. Briefly she flirts with a flimsy fellow called Erik Valborg, who shares her dreams and her sensibility but is soon frightened from the scene. Throughout all this, Will Kennicott waits with some impatience. Lewis portrays the doctor as competent, yet shallow and dull. In one of many notable encounters between husband and wife, Will calls Carol neurotic and she calls him stupid. Lewis, however, suggests something more complex than that. Though prejudiced, quarrelsome, and dull, Will is also courageous, hardworking, and self-sacrificing (as Carol realizes when she, like young Lewis with his father, accompanies the doctor on his rounds and stands by during an operation). Carol, too, is not only an idealist and enthusiast, but also a person of irritating pretensions, doubts, and despair. Lewis does well in portraying the stresses of a marriage, as he would undertake to do again in *Dodsworth* and in *Cass Timberlane*.

At one point Carol sums up what she has discovered from reading about small towns. One

image of them is idealized, she says; it suggests an abode of friendship, honesty, and contentment. In another image, they are inhabited by quaint hicks. Experience tells her, however, that the town's values are expressed in cheap motorcars, ready-made clothes, motion pictures, unread sets of books, the blessings of standardization; "it is dullness made God."

With fifty pages left in the novel, Carol rebels desperately. She leaves her husband and Gopher Prairie to go to Washington, D.C. There, we are told, she talks to interesting people and attends concerts. But after a year away, she returns home. She has lost her battle with the village, but she is convinced that she has kept faith with her ideals. Her routine becomes much as it was.

Main Street was a sensation, an immediate best-seller. People argued either that it was a libel upon the village or that it was a revelation of the truths about American pettiness and hypocrisy. One way or the other, it gave America "a new image of itself," as Schorer says. The novel's strength lies in the tension it creates between a provincial narrowness that is successfully practical yet stultifying and dull, and a sensitivity which is insecure, fantastic, and escapist. Criticism that the book lacks penetration into its characters' conflicts is mistaken, though understandably provoked by its repetitiousness and stylistic heaviness. On balance, *Main Street* is a significant achievement.

With *Main Street* a critical and popular success, Lewis took his family to Europe, in triumph rather than as a collegiate pilgrim. Having accumulated his notes for his next book, he worked in Kent, then in Rome, and was able to return to New York with a completed draft. *Babbitt* (1922) is Lewis's best novel, his greatest claim to continued attention and respect. While working on it, Lewis wrote to his publisher that this time he hoped to overcome some of the limitations thought to inhere in *Main Street*–namely its superficiality–by revealing the complexities of his central figure. George F. Babbitt would give us a surprise by breaking away from the standardized life he had heretofore led. He would want passionately "to seize something more than motorcars and a house *before it's too late*." Thus Lewis was attempting once again, but now with greater thought and skill, to portray his constant subject of the lonely and sensitive outsider, longing for freedom and searching for a meaningful life. Lewis's excitement during the writing was so great that he vowed to his publisher that soon he would have everyone talking of "babbittry," and indeed one contribution of the book is that the word *Babbitt* has entered common parlance and the dictionary.

Lewis had also put into practice a method of development which he would use thereafter. He visited various appropriate locales–Cincinnati, especially; he researched the operation of a real estate business; he wrote biographies of his characters, made a summary of their actions, drew maps of his fictional city, and compiled notes on furnishings, cars, clubs, and clothes. For this novel he invented the city of Zenith, which would also be the setting for a number of scenes in *Arrowsmith, Elmer Gantry, The Man Who Knew Coolidge,* and *Dodsworth.*

The first quarter of *Babbitt* recounts one day in the life of the protagonist, who is forty-six years old in the year 1920. It opens as George awakens on his sleeping porch (he-men sleep in the open air) from dreams of a fairy-girl, and it takes us through breakfast with his wife and three children, his attentions to his car on his drive to work, negotiations at his real estate office, lunch with his best friend Paul at the Zenith Athletic Club, more work, supper, after-dinner talk and reading (his teenage son discusses enrolling in a correspondence course in how to be a detective), and finally bed, with another dream of his golden girl.

Lewis's plans had announced that Babbitt would be the typical "TBM," the tired businessman. From the start Babbitt is discontented. He is irritable in the morning; he is puzzled by what suit to wear; he is quarrelsome with his wife and contradictory to his children. He complains to his friend Paul that he has all the things he is supposed to have: a family, a car, a house, a business, virtue. He belongs to a church; he keeps trim with prudent exercise. Yet he is not satisfied; he suffers from self-contradiction. He opposes alcohol, yet drinks; he is pledged to traffic laws, yet speeds; he is dedicated to truth, yet cheats in business and advertising. He is pledged to fidelity, yet he begins an affair. Thus caught between forces, he is constantly tired.

Unsettled by the affair, Babbitt is open for a political shift from right to left when he becomes reacquainted with an old socialist friend named Seneca Doane. Throughout a lengthy and detailed section of the book, a compassionate Babbitt emerges from his doubts, confusions, and fatigue, just as Lewis intended. But the conception does not go far enough. The satiric impulse be-

Lewis, circa 1932 (Dorothy Thompson Collection, George Arents Research Library for Special Collections at Syracuse University)

hind the book cannot be overcome. Nor could Lewis face the prospect of carrying Babbitt completely out of his milieu. Thus, though the political rebellion has a substantial foundation, the rebellion through love is permitted to have no substance at all. Babbitt's lover and her friends (called the "bunch") are a mockery, and quite predictably they have no power to tap new resources in Babbitt, who might thereby change and grow. His former friends call him back; in fact, they terrorize him into returning. At the end he is in the fold again, compliant to Zenith's social norms once more.

Reviewers of *Babbitt* praised it as better than *Main Street.* H. L. Mencken said that Babbitt, "plausible and natural, . . . simply drips with human juices." Later critics have sustained the praise, though some admit to reservations. Frederick J. Hoffman sees "two Babbitts"–a booster and a doubter; he praises Lewis's skill in portraying each "Babbitt" but wonders if Lewis could expect to combine them successfully in a unified characterization. Schorer endorses Constance Rourke's insight that Lewis was less a realist than a "fabulist." Indeed, the triumph of this book is that it brought before us an enduring perception of an American type.

Babbitt is the book, moreover, in which Lewis was most skillful in his satiric representation of American speech. Examples could be drawn from the earliest pages (in which Babbitt mutters to himself in the bathroom, "By golly, here they go and use up all the towels, every doggone one of 'em, and they use 'em and get 'em all wet and sopping . . .") or from his breakfast-table lecture to his daughter (that her "uplift and flipflop and settlement-work and recreation is nothing in God's world but the entering wedge for socialism") or from his whine of fatigue ("Oh, Lord, sometimes I'd like to quit the whole game. And the office worry and detail just as bad.") or from his lengthy speech to the real estate board ("Our Ideal Citizen—I picture him first and foremost as being busier than a bird-dog . . . ," continuing in bits and pieces gleaned from editorials and advertising slogans). Lewis had been tuning his ear and practicing his technique for this mimicry all through his apprenticeship, and he achieved his greatest success with it in *Babbitt*. From *Babbitt* through *Dodsworth* it seems to come to him easily yet still effectively, but by the late books (*Gideon Planish*, 1943, for one) his use of these voices is almost a parody of itself.

Arrowsmith (1925) gives us an affirmative view of the "myth" of America, as Lewis conceived of it. He told his publisher that he intended the book to be heroic. Afterward, he would write that he had put the best of himself into it—all his respect for learning, for integrity, for human achievement, for love and friendship. In 1941 he also wrote a mock obituary of himself in which he made explicit his identification with the book's hero by calling the piece "The Death of Arrowsmith."

Once again Lewis put into practice his recently developed method of work. He found a medical adviser in Dr. Paul de Kruif, a bacteriologist and writer of popular books on science and medicine, who directed Lewis's reading and helped him (a doctor's son to begin with) to come to an understanding of physicians, medical researchers, hospitals, and research institutions. With de Kruif, Lewis visited the Caribbean is-

lands, where he would set the novel's climactic scenes involving the plague.

A substantial portion of the book occurs in and near Zenith. Now Lewis fills out his picture of his mythic territory. He reveals the state's name, Winnemac, and tells us it is bounded by Michigan, Ohio, Illinois, and Indiana. Its university is located at Mohalis, just fifteen miles from Zenith. From *Babbitt, Arrowsmith,* and *Elmer Gantry* we learn that its capital is Galop de Vache, its river is the Chaloosa, and its important cities are Monarch, Sparta, Pioneer, Catawba, and Eureka. The locales in *Arrowsmith* also include North Dakota, Chicago, New York, and Vermont, among other places real and fictional. The novel explores innumerable characters—medical students, doctors, researchers, and workers in public health; the sincere, the hardworking; the brilliant, the average, and the incompetent; frauds, charlatans, freeloaders, and opportunists.

In many ways then, the medical profession is a metaphor for much of American life. Lewis's story of America has developed into something like this: He sees as the hero of America a midwestern, naive, inventive, optimistic, enthusiastic, hardworking young man whose strength (like Hawk's) comes from his pioneer ancestry, as we see in a brief prefatory sketch of Arrowsmith's great-grandmother crossing the frontier in a wagon. In this case the hero is a medical researcher (more than a doctor-technician but rather a doer or discoverer). The hero has a mentor who gives him old-world wisdom. In this case it is an immigrant Jew named Gottlieb, who is a brilliant researcher (though thought by some to be the devil) and who is gentle and persecuted. Following Lewis's earlier patterns, the hero encounters two kinds of women; one, called an "Improver," is pretentious, nagging, and selfish; the other is modest, loyal, and loving. The hero undergoes three kinds of testing: one comes from temptresses (princesses, playmates, Improvers); another from scoundrels, con men, and opportunists; a third from humane and practical impulses which would compromise his professional integrity.

In his research Arrowsmith has done great work, discovering an antitoxin for the plague. He marches off to the Caribbean to use it on a plague-swept island. He divides the population into two groups—those who will receive the antitoxin and those who, as a control group, will not. But his good wife Leora mistakenly exposes herself to the disease and dies, a sacrifice to Arrowsmith's impulsive forgetfulness, carelessness, and human frailty. Heartbroken and feeling increased compassion for those sick with the plague, he violates his principles of scientific method and inoculates the control group too. Now his experiment will show no proof. Meanwhile Gottlieb withers and dies. Arrowsmith, back from exile, tries to start a new life. Once again a temptress approaches. Succumbing to her invitation to "play" among her socialite friends, Arrowsmith marries her, but he soon realizes his mistake. Another mentor, Terry Wickett, appears, perhaps a mirror of Arrowsmith's best self. The hero's final act is to withdraw to a makeshift laboratory set up in a shack in the Vermont woods. Arrowsmith has abandoned marriage, parental responsibility, and society–all in the name of his search for freedom, "purity" (echoing Lewis's image of the pioneer), and hard work.

For *Arrowsmith* Lewis was offered the Pulitzer Prize, but, angered at past oversights, he refused it. His resentment had begun when the Pulitzer jury (made up of Robert Morss Lovett, Stuart Pratt Sherman, and Hamlin Garland), having recommended *Main Street* for the 1921 prize, was overruled by the trustees of Columbia University; the prize went instead to Edith Wharton for *The Age of Innocence* (1920). He also felt that perhaps *Babbitt* had been neglected two years later. On 6 May 1926 the press was given his letter to the Pulitzer committee explaining his refusal. His reasons were: (1) that he disapproved of the terms of the prize, which insist that the winning work be representative of "the wholesome atmosphere of American life"; (2) that the administrators of the prize can and do reject the recommendations of their advisory critics who make the initial selection; and (3) that if the prize continues to grow in prestige (especially with "wholesomeness" as its guideline), it may become the goal for which all writers strive by producing safe, polite, and obedient work.

Arrowsmith is a long, extravagant, and worthy book. A significant part of it is devoted to Dr. Gottlieb, who suffers persecution, who puzzles out an atheist's creed, who tutors Arrowsmith in the methodology and integrity of science, who advises Arrowsmith to "work twice as hard as you can" and endlessly test your results so as piously to assault your errors, and who consoles Arrowsmith when it turns out that his great discovery has been simultaneously found by a researcher in Europe. Critics have been divided in their reactions to Gottlieb and Arrowsmith, calling them either Faustian or adolescent. While Carl Van Doren thought that

Advertisement for Lewis's 1935 speculative novel about fascism in the United States

Arrowsmith reminded him of Daniel Boone or Leatherstocking, Warren Beck found him crude and irresponsible. Though the book includes much satire, in the interests of portraying a hero Lewis withheld all humor from Arrowsmith himself. Perhaps that is the flaw in this otherwise ambitious and successful novel, for Arrowsmith is weak as well as capable, but lacking growth and self-perception.

After completing *Arrowsmith*, Lewis paused a moment to write a light novel occasioned by a fishing trip he took into Canada. *Mantrap* (1926) hardly deserves much attention. Its protagonist is a New York lawyer named Ralph Prescott who, suffering from fatigue and anxiety, retreats westward into nature to restore his damaged nerves. His companion in the forest is a Babbitt type called E. Wesson Woodbury. After little incident except the quarreling occasioned by Woodbury's empty-headed bullying, Prescott sends Woodbury away and then finds himself involved in a rather tame romance with Alverna Easter, wife of his guide Joe Easter. Though Ralph and Alverna run off, and Ralph is able to demonstrate some new-found manhood and woodlore, Joe catches up, hardly angry at all. At the end, each member of this uninteresting triangle goes his or her own way. Ralph returns to the East with the delusion that he is a better man for the experience.

Advancing then to what may have been his most outrageous undertaking, Lewis began his research for a book on the ministry. He engaged the services of the Reverend L. M. Birkhead and began gathering information in several places, principally Kansas City, where he enlisted a dozen or more ministers in a seminar on religion. His protagonist was to be a quintessential scoundrel and charlatan named Elmer Gantry. The book begins with Elmer's childhood, follows him through his education at a seminary, and then explores three important episodes of his life, each of which involves a woman and a particular kind of fraud. The first carries him through his marriage to and abandonment of Lulu, a provincial girl he meets before his ambitions soar. The second is an extended portrait of an evangelist called Sharon Falconer (based loosely on the real evangelist Aimee Semple McPherson), ending in Sharon's death in a fire at her tabernacle. The third involves Elmer as the would-be victim of an extortion trap, after he is found in a bedroom by the husband of his lover. But he recovers his poise and his following, and the book ends with the assurance that he will prevail. His only serious antagonist has been Frank Shallard, a devout minister who cannot mount an effective counterargument to Elmer. But it is Frank who has raised whatever serious questions there are in the book concerning the church and religion.

Elmer Gantry (1927) caused an even greater stir than Lewis's previous books. Angry readers threatened bodily harm to the author. Of all commentators on it, however, perhaps Schorer is the most insightful. He calls it the noisiest novel in our literature, full of animal imagery and sounds. He finds fault with its dependence on melodrama and believes that because there was no effective counterforce to Elmer there could be none of the meaningful development a novel should have. It is, he says, a work of almost pure revulsion.

Lewis then relaxed by writing several monologues presumably spoken by a soulless Babbitt from Zenith called Lowell Schmaltz, published in *The Man Who Knew Coolidge* (1928). In the title piece, an endlessly digressive ramble on filing cabinets, Prohibition, the young, home appliances,

and golf, Schmaltz tells his fellow salesmen, relaxing in a Pullman car, that he had known President Coolidge at college and had paid him a visit in Washington (in fact, he had merely talked to a presidential secretary). In another of the book's sketches, "You Know How Women Are," Schmaltz confesses to his cousin Walt, to whom he has come for a loan, that his troubles are caused by an unhappy marriage. His insights have come from a popular guide to Freudianism; his quarrels with his wife involve their cat, dog, and canary; his wife's adviser is their hypocritical minister; and Schmaltz's solace comes from a woman he is seeing in New York City. Schmaltz's monologues are amusing revelations of his prejudices, self-contradictions, and hypocrisies.

With *Dodsworth* (1929) Lewis faced and to some extent resolved what he had over and over posed as the great question in a man's life, in the life of our culture, perhaps: could a man do meaningful work (the work of a builder) and at the same time keep a humane and artistically enhanced perspective? Furthermore, Lewis again framed this question in terms of the choice between kinds of women, as he had done in many novels before; here, one suspects, he dramatized his deteriorating marriage and his courtship of his second wife, whom he met on another of his trips to Europe. Sam Dodsworth, a citizen of Zenith, is a builder–of automobiles, at first, and of homes at the end of the book. But he is deeply troubled by the values of life, art, and history. He is, we are told by Lewis, more than a Babbitt. Fran, his wife of twenty years, is a flighty, pretentious nag. At mid-life, in 1925, Sam and Fran leave their home, children, and business to embark on a tour of Europe. Along the way Fran, who says she wants to be free but in fact wants to play, finds pretentious and shallow friends and lovers. Sam becomes exasperated, and having met Edith Cortright, a calm, perceptive woman of common sense, finally seeks a divorce. He has found the values he has sought. He will, in his new occupation as a developer of housing tracts, combine up-to-date technology with artistic design.

Dodsworth is Lewis's most serious and extensive engagement with the question of Europe, the international theme so splendidly explored by Henry James and also dealt with by William Dean Howells, Mark Twain, and Ernest Hemingway. Lewis had raised the question for himself in his youth, through reading about England and medieval knighthood. Sam yearns for Europe, as young Lewis had done. Sam has fed his imagination with picture and travel books that speak magic names: Saint Moritz, Cannes, the Grand Canal. And as his ship nears Britain he feels that he has "come home" to "Mother England." Fran wishes to travel also, but instead of to literary Europe it is to the Europe of lords, counts, aristocratic manners, and jewelry. She finds Europeans who are sympathetic to her desire to play. Of course, Sam then becomes ambivalent about Europe, and the great debate, with lengthy (though not very original or instructive) arguments, begins. Varying positions are expressed by Sam, Fran, Edith, a journalist called Ross Ireland, and several expatriate and European professors. Fran praises the "European tradition" of leisure, honor, gallantry, and culture, as against "American materialism." When, midway in the book, Ross Ireland and Sam pay a short visit to America, Ireland criticizes its dirt, noise, love of speed, anti-intellectualism, and hypocrisies about alcohol. In Zenith, Sam notices that his friends do not seem to be interested in anything. Back in Europe, Sam joins the argument again. All of this is unsettling to him, however little there may be in it that is fresh or profound. But Edith helps Sam find equilibrium. She is calm, patient, quiet, and artistic. In an era of bobbed hair, she lets her hair grow long. She praises the Italian peasants who love the earth, and she counsels Sam to learn love of earth before returning to America. Together they plan that Sam will become a builder of homes, homes properly and artistically designed. He will have unified the roles of doer and artist. He will begin a second life.

Dodsworth continues the dialogue between truth and lies, between reality and illusion, first seriously undertaken in *Main Street*, though foreshadowed in *Our Mr. Wrenn* and *The Trail of the Hawk*. The international plot, by putting the pressures of two cultures onto the protagonist, has brought him to a point of reflection and change. It is of considerable significance that the book follows the period of Lewis's estrangement from Grace Lewis, his divorce, and his courtship of Dorothy Thompson in Europe, and that therefore embedded in it are motifs of departure and renewal.

In December 1930 Lewis received the first Nobel Prize for Literature given to an American. The citation at the awards ceremony praised Lewis's portrait of small-town life in *Main Street*, his undercurrents of affection in *Babbitt*, his accuracy of research for *Arrowsmith*, and the power of *Elmer Gantry*. But nonetheless there were many people who resented his getting the award, among them academic critics and humanists such as Irving Babbitt, conservatives such as Henry Van Dyke, and older writers such as Sherwood Anderson. Lewis's acceptance speech challenged the old popular picture of America as optimistic and pastoral by pointing to contradictory and depressing conditions that paradoxically made the country the most stirring in the world. He attacked spokesmen for literary gentility, and he generously cited other American writers worthy of prize (Dreiser, Masters, Cather, Lardner, James Branch Cabell, Anderson, O'Neill) and those who were the hope of the future (Hemingway, Wolfe, Thornton Wilder, Dos Passos, and Faulkner).

It was fitting that Lewis should be recognized with a prize in 1930, for indeed as one surveys his career it seems as if he had reached a place of repose in his continued dialogue and debate. Like Sam Dodsworth he was ready for a second life. He had, for example, come to an understanding of his youthfully yearning doers and builders, recognized their playfellows as wasteful and corrupting, and reached an appreciation of the expectations of women. He had created a hero in Arrowsmith, had found value in Babbitts by creating a Dodsworth, had exposed frauds and con men. In his letters he spoke of a new beginning. But it was not to be. Perhaps he had expended all his allotted energy and capacity for invention. Perhaps, at forty-six, he was unable to respond to new ideas, too much a child of the nineteenth century. Perhaps the method that had worked well through the decade of the 1920s had become stale: to choose a social section and through research find one's way to character and story. At any rate his next book seems to be a repetition of much that he had done before. The social problem would be new to him—prison reform—but the character would be another "Una Golden," a new feminist, who searches for career, self-realization, and true love.

That is not to say that *Ann Vickers* (1933) is as cautious and romantic as *The Job*. Even with the small-town background, the socialist mentor, and other motifs constant since his apprentice novels, there are signs of development here. What is new in *Ann Vickers* is Lewis's blunt depiction of violence in scenes at the women's reformatory where Ann serves as superintendent and his acknowledgment both of homosexuality and of the possibility of satisfactory sexual experience outside of marriage. His next book, *Work of Art* (1934), was somewhat more tame. It contrasts the lives of two brothers. Ora Weagle, a writer, is a fancier of medieval dreams, while Myron, a hotel manager, is a true artist, says Lewis, and a doer. Lewis's mockery of Ora may suggest that he was still haunted by memories of those neighbors in Sauk Centre who had wondered when Harry Lewis, the dreamy adolescent, was ever going to amount to anything.

In 1935 Lewis produced a book more directly involving a political purpose than any he had written until then. *It Can't Happen Here*, Lewis's vision of how fascism might come to America, looks forward to the election of 1936 and the succeeding few years. Fort Beulah, a village in Vermont, is not very different from a midwestern village like Gopher Prairie, whose heritage of independence had come from New England. The book's hero is Doremus Jessup, editor of the town paper and a "little man" like Wrenn, Milt Daggett, and Myron Weagle. Doremus is little in name (his friends call him "dormouse"), in appearance, and in community position, yet he is stubborn, courageous, and responsible. As expected, Jessup is provided with the usual complement of women. His wife Emma is dull, plain, imperceptive, but good. His friend Lorinda is intelligent, daring, and concerned. Emma is, says Lewis, bread; Lorinda is wine. A man needs both.

The plot, however, really focuses on political matters. A politician called Senator Windrip captures the nomination for the presidency as a Democrat, wins the election of 1936, and soon turns the country into a dictatorship. (An unlikely premise is that Franklin Roosevelt and other prominent politicians could easily be pushed aside.) The plausibility of this victory of fascism derives from the effects of the Depression (mortgaged farms, people on relief) and, as Jessup remarks, the strength and appeal of such figures and organizations as Huey Long, Father Coughlin, the Ku Klux Klan, Aimee Semple McPherson, and the night riders. Tyranny *could* come to America, Jessup argues, for we have tolerated exploitation of sharecroppers, imprisonment of labor leaders, wartime censorship, and lynchings. Windrip announces a program of fifteen principles leading to the Victory for the Forgotten Men, among them control of all monies by a federal bank; disenfranchisement of blacks; prohibition of blacks and Jews from holding public office or practicing as teachers, lawyers, professors, and physicians; limits on income; and return of all women to the household. Against such ideas, Doremus upholds his faith in common sense. He asserts that the rise of tyranny is the fault of lazy-minded, ordinary citizens. Like Carol Kennicott, he reads and thinks and lectures his family and friends, not very profoundly or originally but with principles that are indeed sound. He advocates government as a partnership and favors providing a good education to all. Most important is the preservation of the "free, inquiring, critical spirit."

By 1938 the country is a shambles. Many people are in concentration camps; some have fled to Canada; others have formed resistance groups. Windrip has been sent to France, his successor has been shot, and a third cohort now holds the presidency. But the last line of the book inspirationally intones the belief that a Doremus Jessup will never die; that is, "little men," middle-of-the-road believers in democratic justice, will somehow survive and ultimately win.

With the nation threatened by economic disaster and with the example of Italy and Germany clear, Lewis deserves credit for sounding an alarm. The book was popular and sensational. The Federal Theater of the Works Progress Administration in Washington asked him to collaborate on a stage version, which opened on 27 October 1936 simultaneously in eighteen cities. (His interest in the theater had been growing: he had served as adviser to Sidney Howard on an adaptation of *Dodsworth* and had collaborated with Lloyd Lewis on a play called *Jayhawker*, 1935; later he was also to act briefly the role of Jessup in *It Can't Happen Here* in summer stock.) But aesthetically the novel had faults. The lack of depth in Lewis's analysis is indicated in the names he gave his villains: "Buzz" Windrip, Adelaide Tarr Grimmitch, Hector Macgoblin, Gen. Emmanuel Coon. He undermines his criticism of fascism by writing that Windrip, who had governed a tyrannic regime, was really a "darned good sort when you came to meet him." Flaws such as this suggest that Lewis after 1930 could not sustain his skill, interest, or inventiveness.

What followed *It Can't Happen Here* is a most curious document. Having exposed fascism, Lewis now chose to examine communism. But from politics of the nation he turned to politics of the family. Already he had been playing with two new notions: one was that young people in the 1930s led self-indulgent, wasteful lives; the other was that ordinary middle-class citizens, the sort who had been his Babbitts of a dozen years

Lewis in the role of Doremus Jessup in a 1938 production of It Can't Happen Here *by the South Shore Players, Cohasset, Massachusetts*

earlier, deserved a reassessment. There was a perverse fluctuation, a dialectic of characterizations, operating in Lewis. It had appeared in his attitude toward the "playgirls" and in his remark that villains like Windrip and scoundrels like Gantry were just good fellows. It seemed an exploitation of the theme of illusion and reality: the good would be bad, the bad would be good; the weak would succeed, the strong would fail. There were potential surprises in everyone. The unscrupulous political figure could become a loving friend. The youthful dolt could turn out to be a genius. Thus, in *The Prodigal Parents* Fred Cornplow, a Babbitt, is shown to be the salt of the earth, the foundation of democracy, the source of good sense and sound values. Lewis was fascinated by contradictions. No doubt some of his faith in the unexpected grew from the pain caused by slurs against him in childhood: he had been thought a lazy and goofy kid. Now he would show them. He had made good.

The scenes at Frederick Cornplow's home in Sachem Falls, New York, are reminiscent of those in *Babbitt*: the talk at meals, smoking the first cigar, his wife in a dull wrapper. Like Babbitt, Fred wonders why he cannot take a little time off, do crazy things, ride horseback, gamble, or take the golden road to Samarkand. Lewis praises Fred as the Eternal Doer, the dependable man through all history. The chief problem for Fred, though, is that his children are foolish and feckless. They will not take proper jobs, and they flirt with communism. Fred sees the real war as not that of country against country but of parents against children. He wants an armistice. When he and his son have mental breakdowns, their healing is their reconciliation. He asks that parents stop expecting children to accept adult ideas, and he hopes for a counterattack from parents who will reaffirm the old ways. To teach his son self-mastery, Fred retreats with him to the woods, an echo of the ending of *Arrowsmith*.

At the appearance of the book, leftists who had praised *It Can't Happen Here* felt betrayed. The book's weakness had less to do with its political ideas, however, than with its thin characterizations and sentimental plot.

Lewis's next book was *Bethel Merriday* (1940), built upon four phases in the life of a stage-struck young woman. First we learn of Bethel's childhood fantasies and playacting. Then we see her as an apprentice at a summer-stock company. Afterward, she seeks work and acting opportunities in New York. And finally we follow her on a tour of the Midwest as an understudy to Juliet in a modern-dress production of *Romeo and Juliet*. Lewis drew much of the material for the book from a two-month tour of his play *Angela Is Twenty-Two* (1938), which he had directed and in which he also appeared. At the end Bethel goes on stage in place of the drunken leading lady and does rather poorly—at least the stereotype of a sudden success is avoided. Soon she succeeds to the smaller role of Lady Capulet and may now be at the start of a career. But the book closes with Bethel's unexpected and unconvincing romance with and marriage to a promising young actor. Altogether, the book is very slight.

In the summer of 1939, while completing *Bethel Merriday*, Lewis met an eighteen-year-old actress who became his companion (though intermittently as time wore on) for the next four years. Dorothy Thompson was granted a divorce in January 1942. During World War II, Lewis's *Gideon Planish* (1943), an exposé of philanthropies, was published. If the novel draws upon any predecessor, it is *Elmer Gantry*, for it is a study of a "subject" rather than of character. Planish is a man of no talent who cons his way through his education and into a professorship at a midwestern college. Soon his wife Peony, an Improver like many earlier women in Lewis's books, takes his career in hand and plots his advancement through a series of prosperous organizations. Along the way Lewis adds a bitter and unfair sketch of his second wife, Dorothy Thompson, as Winifred Homeward, the Talking Woman. Lewis needed new inspiration, and perhaps his move back to Minnesota during the oncoming years provided it.

Cass Timberlane (1945) is a different kind of book. It is the story of a judge, age forty-one, who seeks the Quiet Mind. Now divorced from an ambitious and pushy wife, he falls in love with and marries Jinny Marshland, a vigorous young

woman of twenty-four. The setting is Grand Republic, Minnesota, which resembles Duluth, where Lewis had been living. Its subtitle, *A Novel of Husbands and Wives*, suggests that the subject here is not a profession, as was usual in Lewis's work, but marriage. The novel is without doubt Lewis's most successful effort after the Nobel Prize, perhaps for the very reason that his impetus for writing is inquiry into personal relationships rather than satiric exposure of a profession or social section such as medicine, the church, prisons, hotel management, or philanthropy. Yet Jinny is in many ways one of the princesses, and the East is again the villain, for Jinny is drawn to playful adultery and to New York. Though the ending is somewhat like a wish-fulfilling soap opera, with Jinny deathly sick and repentant, the rest of the book is convincing. Particularly effective are fifteen short sketches about the marriages of Cass's neighbors, independent episodes distributed throughout the book. Edmund Wilson wrote that the judge was well portrayed in his milieu of friends and lovers, and Wilson particularly praised the fifteen interlarded sketches. Most of all, said Wilson, it seemed as if Lewis could indeed see inside his characters and appreciate their human merits.

Kingsblood Royal (1947) undertakes a "subject" again, this time racial prejudice. Also set in Grand Republic, it tells, perhaps too melodramatically, the story of Neil Kingsblood, a conventional bank assistant, who learns by accident that he has a small fraction of black ancestry. When he makes the fact public, his friends desert him, and, exploring the black community, he dispels his own racist ideas. It was a courageous book that won Lewis an award from *Ebony* magazine for promoting racial understanding.

Lewis's last books confirm the idea that he intended to supply, beneath the mass of details of life, a mythic view of America. *The God-Seeker* (1949) is a historical novel that seems to provide a justification for his vision of modern character, theme, and action. The time is 1850. The protagonist, Aaron Gadd, is indeed a pioneer, who wants to build a new home in Minnesota, to find a proper calling, and to marry a suitable wife. He finds himself surrounded by ancestors of the con men, preachers, and Eastern romantics that plague heroes in Lewis's other books. Lewis's final book, *World So Wide* (1951), written in pain in his last year while he resided in Italy, is the story of the American in Europe once more, echoing the first novel, *Wrenn*, and the median one, *Dodsworth*. It is an enervated work.

In 1952, a year after Lewis's death, *From Main Street to Stockholm: Letters of Sinclair Lewis, 1919-1930* appeared, containing the correspondence between Lewis and his publishers. The book opens with a note to Alfred Harcourt from "slewis" at the time when Harcourt was joining Donald Brace in a new publishing venture and when Lewis, with five novels and many short stories behind him, was confidently starting *Main Street*. Throughout, Lewis gives advice on advertising, suggests pursuit of the Pulitzer and Nobel prizes, comments on his travels, and reports his enthusiasm for other writers such as H. G. Wells, Arnold Bennett, and Hugh Walpole, whom he meets in England. The letters contain important statements of intention about *Main Street, Babbitt,* and *Arrowsmith.* Though they do not reveal much about his personal life, the letters do enable us to follow his movements to England, to the Continent, and throughout America during a ten-year span and do contain guarded indications of estrangement from his wife. After the Nobel Prize he becomes angry at Harcourt and Brace. He wants a special Nobel edition of his novels and in addition asks that cheap reprints be published; he accuses the editors of not pushing his books. The collection ends with his break from Harcourt and Brace, after a close and mutually rewarding ten-year collaboration. Equally interesting are Lewis's essays and reviews, published in 1953 as *The Man from Main Street.* Here one can find some of Lewis's collegiate poems and stories, his early article on how he wrote *The Trail of the Hawk* in his spare time, his eulogy to Wells, his historical and ethnographic sketch of Minnesota, and his Nobel acceptance address, along with many other pieces.

In several polls taken during his lifetime, readers nominated Lewis as among writers very likely to be remembered and read in the century ahead; sometimes he led the list. Today, with Hemingway, Fitzgerald, Eliot, Wallace Stevens, Faulkner, and others in mind, few critics would give him a ranking anywhere near the top. But it may be that when one focuses on only two or three of his novels, he deserves more attention than he now receives. Mark Schorer supplied a useful insight when he said that Lewis, by exposing the constrictions of village life and by revealing the narrow-mindedness of Babbittry, "helped us into the imagination of ourselves."

Often critics echo an early perception made of Lewis that he never transcended his material because at heart he was the same kind of provincial and victim of the same kinds of grossness as the characters he depicted. T. K. Whipple, for instance, wrote that Lewis himself was the best proof that his own charges were just. But John O'Hara, who had learned much from Lewis yet had come to a clear understanding of Lewis's flaws, wrote to Schorer that all the observations that Lewis was merely like Babbitt ignore one factor: only Lewis saw Babbitt; all other novelists were blind to Babbitt, to Zenith, to the United States until 1922. Who else, O'Hara asked, had made such "an important discovery-creation"?

Letters:

From Main Street to Stockholm: Letters of Sinclair Lewis, 1919-1930, edited by Harrison Smith (New York: Harcourt, Brace, 1952).
Letters to and from Alfred Harcourt and Donald Brace, Lewis's publishers for a decade, containing accounts of his travels, his progress on his novels, and his suggestions about publicity.

"Fragments from a Marriage: Letters of Sinclair Lewis to Grace Hegger Lewis," edited by Speer Morgan and William Holtz, *Missouri Review,* 11 (1988): 71-98.
A selection of letters to Lewis's first wife, three showing the affectionate though childishly playful tone of their courtship and early years of marriage, and others showing an "insincere" Lewis, trying "to extricate himself from one marriage" into another.

Bibliography:

Robert E. Fleming, with Esther Fleming, *Sinclair Lewis: A Reference Guide* (Boston: G. K. Hall, 1980).
A very useful annotated bibliography to 1978, then updated in an article printed in the *Modern Fiction Studies* special issue on Lewis, edited by Martin Light.

Interviews:

Frederick Manfred, "Sinclair Lewis: A Portrait," *American Scholar,* 23 (Spring 1954): 162-184.
A conversation with Lewis about writers and writing.

Betty Stevens, "A Village Radical Goes Home," *Venture,* 2 (Summer 1956): 17-26.

Records conversations with Lewis about various national problems, including politics and racial integration, while he was in Duluth, Minnesota, writing *Kingsblood Royal*.

Stevens, "A Village Radical: His Last American Home," *Venture*, 2 (Winter 1957): 35-48.
A continuation of Stevens's "A Village Radical Goes Home."

Allen Austin, "An Interview with Sinclair Lewis," *University Review*, 24 (March 1958): 199-210.
Lewis talks of a projected novel about the labor movement (never written) and of the influence of Dickens and Wells.

Biographies:
Grace H. Lewis, *With Love from Gracie: Sinclair Lewis, 1912-1925* (New York: Harcourt, Brace, 1955).
An account of the courtship and her marriage to and divorce from Lewis by his first wife.

Mark Schorer, *Sinclair Lewis: An American Life* (New York, Toronto & London: McGraw-Hill, 1961).
A large and detailed life history with commentary on each novel, plus a checklist of all of Lewis's writings.

Vincent Sheean, *Dorothy and Red* (Boston: Houghton Mifflin, 1963).
Lewis talks about his second marriage (to Dorothy Thompson, a widely published journalist), including the courtship before and the troubles afterward which led to divorce.

References:
Daniel Aaron, "Sinclair Lewis, *Main Street*," in *The American Novel*, edited by Wallace Stegner (New York: Basic Books, 1965), pp. 166-179.
Asserts that as an exposure of the prejudices, complacency, and fear of change in a typical midwestern village, the novel was "an explosive cultural event."

David D. Anderson, "Sinclair Lewis and the Nobel Prize," *MidAmerica*, 8 (1981): 9-21.
Reviews what led to Lewis's winning the Nobel Prize for Literature in 1930 and the nature of the response afterward, defend-

ing the much-disputed choice of Lewis as its first American recipient.

Helen Batchelor, "A Sinclair Lewis Portfolio of Maps: Zenith to Winnemac," *Modern Language Quarterly*, 32 (December 1971): 401-408.
Reproduces many drawings Lewis made of Babbitt's office, home, his fictitious city of Zenith, and his fictional state of Winnemac.

Martin Bucco, ed., *Critical Essays on Sinclair Lewis* (Boston: G. K. Hall, 1986).
A useful collection of thirty-nine essays and reviews on the life and works of Lewis, some of which are listed and annotated here, including those by Flanagan, Schorer, and Grebstein, as well as Robert E. Fleming's "*Kingsblood Royal* and the Black 'Passing' Novel," which suggests that to write *Kingsblood Royal* Lewis used such sources as James Weldon Johnson's *The Autobiography of an Ex-Colored Man* (1912) and other novels about black people who "pass" as white, and James Lundquist's "The Sauk Centre Sinclair Lewis Didn't Write About," which proves "the bizarre brutality of the world Lewis knew" in boyhood as evidenced in old newspapers from Sauk Centre and a history of Stearns County, which Lewis suppressed both in his fiction and his reminiscences.

Michael Connaughton, *Sinclair Lewis at 100* (St. Cloud, Minn.: St. Cloud State University, 1985).
Collects twenty-four new essays presented at the Sinclair Lewis Centennial Conference at St. Cloud, Minnesota, in February 1985, including T. J. Matheson's "Misused Language: The Narrator's Satiric Function in Slinclair Lewis's *Babbitt*," in which he argues that the heightened praise with which the narrator of *Babbitt* describes places or events indicates Lewis's ironic disapproval.

Jack L. Davis, "Mark Schorer's Sinclair Lewis," *Sinclair Lewis Newsletter*, 3 (1971): 3-9.
An important survey of Schorer's attitudes toward Lewis in his biography and in many articles, with particular attention to Schorer's biases.

D. J. Dooley, *The Art of Sinclair Lewis* (Lincoln: University of Nebraska Press, 1967).

Points to flaws in Lewis's manner, yet credits him with offering insights about America.

George H. Douglas, "*Babbitt* at Fifty–The Truth Still Hurts," *Nation*, 214 (22 May 1972): 661-662.
Claims that Babbitt's dreams and his failure to achieve them chronicle a characteristic American life story.

John T. Flanagan, "A Long Way to Gopher Prairie: Sinclair Lewis's Apprenticeship," *Southwest Review*, 32 (Autumn 1947): 403-413.
Analyzes the gradual development of Lewis's themes and characters in the five "apprentice" novels before *Main Street.*

Maxwell Geismar, "Sinclair Lewis: The Cosmic Bourjoyce," in his *The Last of the Provincials: The American Novel, 1915-1925* (Boston: Houghton Mifflin, 1947), pp. 69-150.
Comments on the novels in detail, viewing Lewis as the historian of backward small towns and corrupt cities.

Sheldon N. Grebstein, *Sinclair Lewis* (New York: Twayne, 1962).
Provides a reliable account of Lewis's life; then analyzes in detail Lewis's best work, the novels of the 1920s.

Robert J. Griffin, ed., *Twentieth Century Interpretations of "Arrowsmith"* (Englewood Cliffs, N.J.: Prentice-Hall, 1968).
A selection of early reviews, followed by various key studies of the novel.

Hugh C. Holman, "Anodyne for the Village Virus," in *The Comic Imagination in American Literature*, edited by Louis D. Rubin, Jr. (New Brunswick, N.J.: Rutgers University Press, 1973), pp. 247-258.
Contends that Lewis measures the pretenses and falsities of his characters against the pioneering spirit.

Alfred Kazin, "The New Realism: Sherwood Anderson and Sinclair Lewis," in his *On Native Grounds* (New York: Reynal & Hitchcock, 1942), pp. 217-226.
Claims that as a social critic Lewis succeeds early in his career, but after 1930 he fails

when America and its problems pass him by.

Martin Light, *The Quixotic Vision of Sinclair Lewis* (West Lafayette, Ind.: Purdue University Press, 1975).
A study of the novels based on the literary pattern of the romantic "quixote," the young wanderer who is guided by fantasies and delusions which come into conflict with reality.

Light, ed., "Special Issue: Sinclair Lewis," *Modern Fiction Studies*, 31 (Autumn 1985).
Ten new essays on Lewis, dealing with the influence of H. G. Wells and of Edith Wharton, marriage, and alcoholism, including a bibliographic supplement to Fleming's *Sinclair Lewis: A Reference Guide*, carried forward to 1985.

Glen A. Love, "New Pioneering on the Prairies: Nature, Progress and the Individual in the Novels of Sinclair Lewis," *American Quarterly*, 25 (December 1973): 558-577.
Traces the spirit of the West in Lewis's heroes, no matter where they roam, reaching its best embodiment in the character of Dodsworth.

James Lundquist, *Sinclair Lewis* (New York: Frederick Ungar, 1973).
Provides a brief biography, followed by discussions of the novels that reaffirm Lewis's place as a social critic.

Perry Miller, "The Incorruptible Sinclair Lewis," *Atlantic Monthly*, 187 (April 1951): 30-34.
A reminiscence about conversations with Lewis during an ocean crossing to Europe, when Lewis defined his satire by speaking of the love but dislike he sometimes felt for America.

Mark Schorer, *Sinclair Lewis: A Collection of Critical Essays* (Englewood Cliffs, N.J.: Prentice-Hall, 1962).
A varied collection of reviews and interpretations of the whole spectrum of Lewis's work.

Schorer, "Sinclair Lewis and the Method of Half-Truths," in *Society and Self in the Novel, English Institute Essays*, edited by Schorer (New

York: Columbia University Press, 1956), pp. 117-144.

Lewis does only half the job of a novelist in *Elmer Gantry;* he omits tensions that might have occurred had Elmer not been created as wholly a scoundrel to be hated.

Dick Wagenaar, "The Knight and the Pioneer: Europe and America in the Fiction of Sinclair Lewis," *American Literature,* 50 (May 1978): 230-249.

The evolution of Lewis's views about Europe, principally in his first, middle, and last novels: *Our Mr. Wrenn, Dodsworth,* and *World So Wide.*

Thomas K. Whipple, "Sinclair Lewis," in his *Spokesmen* (Berkeley: University of California Press, 1963), pp. 208-229.

A balanced, fair-minded assessment of Lewis's weaknesses and accomplishments, claiming nonetheless that Lewis's satiric point of view made his limitations inevitable.

Papers:

Most of Lewis's manuscripts and letters are at Yale University; an additional important collection is at the University of Texas at Austin.

H. L. Mencken

This entry was updated by William H. Nolte (University of South Carolina) from the entry by J. James McElveen (Falls Church, Virginia) in DLB 29, American Newspaper Journalists, 1926-1950.

Places	Baltimore	New York	
Influences and Relationships	Friedrich Nietzsche George Bernard Shaw James Hunecker	Mark Twain Theodore Dreiser Thomas Henry Huxley	Alfred A. Knopf George Jean Nathan
Literary Movements and Forms	Realism The Literary Renais- sance of the 1920s	Satire The Literary Hoax Literary Criticism	Cultural Criticism Journalism

Major Themes	American Politics and
	   Government
	"The Sahara of the
	   Bozart"
		The American
		   Language
		Religion and Ethics
			The Absurdity of
			   Respectability
			Misogyny

Cultural and Artistic Influences	Reaction Against Puritanism	Classical Music	Germanic Culture
Social and Economic Influences	World War I	Marxism	Prohibition

See also the Mencken entries in DLB 11, American Humorists, 1800-1950, Part 2, *and* DLB 63, Modern American Critics, 1920-1955.

BIRTH: Baltimore, Maryland, 12 September 1880, to August and Anna Abhau Mencken.

MARRIAGE: 27 August 1930 to Sara Powell Haardt.

MAJOR POSITIONS HELD: Reporter, *Baltimore Herald* (1899-1901); editor, *Baltimore Sunday Herald* (1901-1903); city editor, *Baltimore Morning Herald* (1903-1904); city editor, *Baltimore Evening Herald* (1904-1905); editor in chief, *Baltimore Herald* (1906); news editor, *Baltimore Evening News* (1906); editor, *Baltimore Sunday Sun* (1906-1910); editor, *Baltimore Evening Sun* (1910-1917); coeditor (with George Jean Nathan), *Smart Set* (1914-1923); columnist, political correspondent, *Baltimore Sunpapers* (1919-1941); editor, *American Mercury* (1924-1933).

DEATH: Baltimore, Maryland, 29 January 1956.

BOOKS: *Ventures into Verse* (Baltimore: Marshall, Beck & Gordon, 1903);
George Bernard Shaw: His Plays (Boston & London: Luce, 1905);
The Philosophy of Friedrich Nietzsche (Boston: Luce, 1908; London: Unwin, 1908);
Men versus the Man: A Correspondence between Robert Rives La Monte, Socialist, and H. L. Mencken, Individualist (New York: Holt, 1910);
A Book of Burlesques (New York: John Lane, 1916; revised edition, New York: Knopf, 1920; London: Cape, 1923);
A Little Book in C Major (New York: John Lane, 1916);
A Book of Prefaces (New York: Knopf, 1917; London: Cape, 1922);
Damn! A Book of Calumny (New York: Philip Goodwin, 1918); republished as *A Book of Calumny* (New York: Knopf, 1918);
In Defense of Women (New York: Philip Goodwin, 1918; revised edition, New York: Knopf, 1922; London: Cape, 1923);
The American Language: A Preliminary Inquiry into the Development of English in the United States (New York: Knopf, 1919; revised and enlarged, 1921; London: Cape, 1922; revised and enlarged again, 1923; corrected, enlarged, and rewritten, New York: Knopf,

H. L. Mencken (Gale International Portrait Gallery)

1936; London: Paul, 1936); *Supplement I* (New York: Knopf, 1945); *Supplement II* (New York: Knopf, 1948);
Prejudices: First Series (New York: Knopf, 1919; London: Cape, 1920);
Heliogabalus: A Buffoonery in Three Acts, by Mencken and George Jean Nathan (New York: Knopf, 1920);
Prejudices: Second Series (New York: Knopf, 1920; London: Cape, 1921);
Prejudices: Third Series (New York: Knopf, 1922; London: Cape, 1923);
Prejudices: Fourth Series (New York: Knopf, 1924; London: Cape, 1925);
Selected Prejudices (London: Cape, 1926; New York: Knopf, 1927);
Notes on Democracy (New York: Knopf, 1926; London: Cape, 1927);
Prejudices: Fifth Series (New York: Knopf, 1926; London: Cape, 1927);
Prejudices: Sixth Series (New York: Knopf, 1927; London: Cape, 1928);
James Branch Cabell (New York: McBride, 1927);
Selected Prejudices: Second Series (London: Cape, 1927);
Treatise on the Gods (New York & London: Knopf, 1930);

Making a President: A Footnote to the Saga of Democracy (New York: Knopf, 1932);

Treatise on Right and Wrong (New York: Knopf, 1934; London: Paul, 1934);

The Sunpapers of Baltimore, 1837-1937, by Mencken, Gerald W. Johnson, Frank R. Kent, and Hamilton Owens (New York: Knopf, 1937);

Happy Days, 1880-1892 (New York: Knopf, 1940; London: Paul, Trench & Trübner, 1940);

Newspaper Days, 1899-1906 (New York: Knopf, 1941; London: Paul, 1942);

Heathen Days, 1890-1936 (New York: Knopf, 1943);

Christmas Story (New York: Knopf, 1946);

A Mencken Chrestomathy (New York: Knopf, 1949);

The Vintage Mencken, edited by Alistair Cooke (New York: Vintage, 1955);

A Carnival of Buncombe, edited by Malcolm Moos (Baltimore: Johns Hopkins Press/London: Oxford University Press, 1956);

Minority Report: H. L. Mencken's Notebooks (New York: Knopf, 1956);

The Bathtub Hoax, and Other Blasts & Bravos from the Chicago Tribune, edited by Robert McHugh (New York: Knopf, 1958);

H. L. Mencken on Music, edited by Louis Cheslock (New York: Knopf, 1961);

The American Scene: A Reader, edited by Huntington Cairns (New York: Knopf, 1965);

H. L. Mencken's Smart Set Criticism, edited by William H. Nolte (Ithaca, N.Y.: Cornell University Press, 1968);

The Young Mencken: The Best of His Work, edited by Carl Bode (New York: Dial, 1973);

A Gang of Pecksniffs, and Other Comments on Newspaper Publishers, Editors and Reporters, edited by Theo Lippman, Jr. (New Rochelle, N.Y.: Arlington House, 1975);

Mencken's Last Campaign: H. L. Mencken on the 1948 Election, edited by Joseph C. Goulden (Washington, D.C.: New Republic Book Co., 1976);

A Choice of Days: Essays from Happy Days, Newspaper Days, *and* Heathen Days, edited by Edward L. Galligan (New York: Knopf, 1980).

OTHER: Henrik Ibsen, *A Doll's House*, edited, with an introduction, by Mencken (Boston & London: Luce, 1909);

Ibsen, *Little Eyolf*, edited, with an introduction, by Mencken (Boston & London: Luce, 1909);

Ibsen, *The Master Builder, Pillars of Society, Hedda Gabler*, introduction by Mencken (New York: Boni & Liveright, 1917);

Friedrich Wilhelm Nietzsche, *The Antichrist*, translated, with an introduction, by Mencken (New York: Knopf, 1920);

Americana, edited by Mencken (New York: Knopf, 1925);

Menckeniana: A Schimpflexicon, edited by Mencken (New York: Knopf, 1928);

Sara Powell Haardt, *Southern Album*, introduction by Mencken (New York: Doubleday, Doran, 1936);

A New Dictionary of Quotations on Historical Principles from Ancient and Modern Sources, edited by Mencken (New York: Knopf, 1942);

Theodore Dreiser, *An American Tragedy*, introduction by Mencken (Cleveland & New York: World, 1946);

"The American Language," in *Literary History of the United States*, volume 1, edited by Robert E. Spiller, Willard Thorp, Thomas H. Johnson, and Henry Seidel Canby (New York: Macmillan, 1948), pp. 663-675;

H. L. Mencken Speaking (Caedmon, TC 1082, 1960).

SELECTED PERIODICAL PUBLICATIONS: "Newspaper Morals," *Atlantic Monthly*, 113 (March 1914): 289-297;

"The Motive of the Critic," *New Republic*, 27 (26 October 1921): 249-251;

"Footnotes on Journalism," *Nation*, 114 (26 April 1922): 493-494;

"Three Years of Prohibition in America," *Outlook*, 131 (24 June 1922): 502-503;

"What I Believe," *Forum*, 84 (September 1930): 133-139;

"Future of English," *Harper's*, 170 (April 1935): 541-548;

"Some Opprobrious Nicknames," *American Speech*, 24 (February 1949): 25-30.

During his lifetime H. L. Mencken was called the Great Iconoclast and the Sage of Baltimore, appellations he gained because of his journalistic writing in newspapers and magazines. However, his contributions to American letters were more extensive than those ordinarily found in one who gained fame–or, as some would describe it, notoriety–as a reporter, editor, and columnist. Mencken was the author of at least thirty books and collections of essays and criticism, including his highly acclaimed philological study, *The American Language* (1919, 1945, 1948); the popular autobiographical trilogy, *Happy Days, 1880-1892* (1940), *Newspaper Days, 1899-1906* (1941), and *Heathen Days, 1890-1936* (1943); and the fascinating volumes on politics, religion, and ethics: *Notes on Democracy* (1926) *Treatise on the Gods* (1930), and *Treatise on Right and Wrong* (1934).

Henry Louis Mencken was born in Baltimore, Maryland, on 12 September 1880. When he was three years old, his parents, August and Anna Abhau Mencken, moved to 1524 Hollins Street. There Mencken lived for all of his life except the five years of his marriage. Mencken recalled his "Introduction to the Universe" in *Happy Days, 1880-1892*, as he described Baltimore's Summer Nights' Carnival of the Order of Orioles on the evening after his third birthday: "At the instant I first became aware of the cosmos we all infest I was sitting in my mother's lap and blinking at a great burst of lights, some of them red and others green, but most of them only the bright yellow of flaring gas."

The Menckens were by any standards a closely knit family, and "Harry" and his three younger siblings, Charles, Gertrude, and August, knew a childhood fraught with the usual pleasures and perplexities of living in late-nineteenth-century Baltimore. Mencken recalled the days of his nonage in the backyard of the Hollins Street row house: "Along with my brother Charlie, who followed me into this vale when I was but twenty months old, I spent most of my pre-school leisure in it, and found it a strange, wild land of endless discoveries and enchantments.... In Spring we dug worms and watched for robins, in Summer we chased butterflies and stoned sparrows, and in Autumn we made bonfires of the falling leaves. At all times from March to October we made a Dust Bowl of my mother's garden."

When he was six years old, Mencken was enrolled at Professor Friedrich Knapp's Institute, "a seminary that catered to boys and girls of the Baltimore bourgeoisie for more than sixty years." There his recitations were sufficiently impressive for him to receive his first fifty merits, entitling him to a keenly sought prize at the close of the school year in 1888: a copy of *Grimms' Fairy Tales* "for industry and good deportment." Mencken's "academic orgies," as he termed them in his memoirs, were punctuated with pleasant experiences, especially the institute's annual picnic and the yearly parade signaling the arrival of the circus.

Mencken's family home, 1524 Hollis Street, Baltimore, Maryland. He lived in this house for most of his life.

But to Mencken the "crown and consummation" of the year at Knapp's was the annual exhibition that came soon after the picnic in June. His part on the program was usually to stand at the blackboard and display his mathematical skill by multiplying or dividing several complex numbers, to the delight of his father.

Three experiences were very likely important in Mencken's choice of a career in newspaper work. On 26 November 1888, August Mencken had dispatched his bookkeeper to the Baltimore firm of J. F. W. Dorman to purchase a Baltimore No. 10 Self-Inker Printing Press and a font of No. 214 type. These basic tools of the trade were a gift for Harry. Receipts discovered years later by Mencken indicated that the press cost $7.70 and the type $1.10. Mencken said that the details of this purchase were "of a degree of concern bordering upon the supercolossal, for that press determined the whole course of my future life. If it had been a stethoscope or a copy of Dr. Ayer's almanac, I might have gone in for medicine; if it had been a Greek New Testament or a set of baptismal grappling-irons, I might have pursued divinity. As it was, I got the smell of printer's ink up my nose at the tender age of eight, and it has been swirling through my sinuses ever since." On Christmas Day Harry and his father tried out the new equipment, and the results of their efforts were far from successful. Because both possessed a minimum of mechanical dexterity, they managed to smash most of the type. A few days thereafter, however, the eight-year-old printed his first calling card, shortening his name to H. L. Mencken because he had insufficient usable type to spell out his full name.

Mencken claimed in later years that "aside from the direct and all-powerful influence of that Baltimore No. 10 Self-Inker . . . , I was probably edged toward newspapers and their glorious miseries by two circumstances, both of them trivial." One was his discovery of the printing office of the *Ellicott City Times*, the weekly newspaper of the Maryland village where the Menckens spent the summers of 1889 and 1890. He recalled watching a young man and a boy operate an ancient Washington handpress in getting out the *Times*. Their press day was Thursday, and Mencken was there to gaze at the process at every opportunity. Mencken also remembered overhearing a conversation between his father and uncle and his father's Washington agent, Mr. Cross. After discussing the transitory eminence of the congressmen, senators, justices, and military men he met in the nation's capital, Mr. Cross said that the "real princes of Washington" were the newspaper correspondents. Mencken attributed his lifelong reverence for "the gentlemen of the Washington corps" to that conversation.

The evolution of Mencken as writer, editor, and critic can also be traced to his early discovery of his father's small library, which was shelved in "an old-fashioned secretary in the sitting room" of the Hollins Street residence. Mencken devoured the collection and was drawn especially to a set of volumes by Mark Twain. Throughout his career he asserted that *Huckleberry Finn* had a "genuinely terrific" impact on him and referred to his discovery of the work as "probably the most stu-

pendous event of my whole life." After completing what he called the "Biblioteca Menckeniana," Mencken began raiding the shelves of Baltimore's Enoch Pratt Free Library, to which he had a card beginning when he was nine years old. He continued his voracious reading until he reached adolescence, inhabiting "a world that was two-thirds letterpress and only one-third trees, fields, streets and people."

Mencken credited Professor Knapp and his staff at Knapp's Institute with preparing him so well that he was advanced a full year when he entered Baltimore Polytechnic Institute in 1892. His interests at the school, chemistry and journalism, were apparent in his first attempt to get a manuscript published in 1894. He submitted an article describing a platinum toning bath for silver photographic prints to several photography magazines, but the editors rejected it. Mencken said that had he "encountered a competent teacher of chemistry at the Polytechnic, I'd have gone in that science, and today I'd be up to my ears in the vitamins, for it was synthetic chemistry that always interested me most. But the gogue told off to nurture me succeeded only in disheartening me, so I gradually edged over to letters. . . . " He recalled that although his record at the polytechnic was "pretty good," he had little interest in most of the subjects taught. Despite that attitude Mencken excelled in the school's general examination at the end of his four years. He did so well, in fact, that he finished at the head of his class and therefore spoke at the commencement exercises in June 1896. He reminisced in *Heathen Days, 1890-1936*, "That speech must have been a dreadful thing, indeed, for I was still very young in those days, and had not yet acquired my present facility for rabble-rousing." Mencken was the youngest member of his graduating class, being three months short of his sixteenth birthday.

Mencken took the first, albeit unsuccessful, step in beginning a career in journalism the Monday after his father died on Friday, 13 January 1899. August Mencken had not viewed favorably his son's oft-expressed interest in journalism, assuming that his offspring would continue the cigar-manufacturing business he and his younger brother had begun as Aug. Mencken & Bro. in 1875. But on that 16 January Mencken appeared in the newsroom of the *Baltimore Herald* to beg a reporting job from Max Ways, the city editor he later described as "a very competent man." Even though Ways was in no hurry to satisfy Mencken's wish to join the staff, he perceived the young man's eagerness and persistence. After more than a month, during which he trekked daily to the *Herald* office after his labors at the cigar factory, Mencken's chance came. On 23 February, Ways sent him to Govanstown on the outer reaches of Baltimore to seek out the news, since the regular correspondent for the *Herald* had not reported in for six days. A tremendous blizzard had just left much of the city and its environs covered with ice and snowdrifts.

Mencken's first published news story was a product of that assignment. He wrote: "A horse, buggy and several sets of harnesses, valued in all at about $250, were stolen last night from the stable of Howard Quinlan, near Kingsville. The county police are at work on the case, but so far no trace of either thieves or booty has been found." Ways also had him prepare a notice from information that had been submitted to the *Herald* about a "kinetoscope or cineograph" exhibition of war scenes. Thus, Mencken began his career in journalism much as young reporters always have, by composing an innocuous news account and rewriting a publicity release. His forays into Baltimore's remoteness did not last long, however. Shortly Ways was assigning him to the usual variety of meetings, interviews, rallies, and concerts that young reporters also glean as part of their introduction to journalism. By summer Mencken had earned a staff position on the *Herald* at seven dollars a week. Only then did he resign his job at the cigar factory. Thus began a forty-three-year experience in the newspaper field for the man who would become a premier writer, editor, and critic, known as well for his singular writing style as for his prodigious outpouring of information and ideas. Mencken admitted in his preface to *Newspaper Days, 1899-1906* that young reporters led "a gaudy life": "I believed then, and still believe today, that it was the maddest, gladdest, damndest existence ever enjoyed by mortal youth. At a time when the respectable bourgeois youngsters of my generation were college freshmen, oppressed by simian sophomores and affronted with balderdash daily and hourly by chalky pedagogues, I was at large in a wicked seaport of half a million people, with a front seat at every public show, as free of the night as of the day, and getting earfuls and eyefuls of instruction in a hundred giddy arcana, none of them taught in schools."

Mencken's career at the *Herald* spanned seven years, and his rapid rise through the ranks is a clear indication of his growth as a skilled and competent newspaperman. He covered the police and city hall beats and wrote drama criticism as well. During his first year at the *Herald* Mencken witnessed his first hanging when four felons were executed in the Baltimore jailyard. Later, when he was the waterfront reporter for the *Herald*, Mencken and two other reporters adopted a practice he called "synthesizing news" that assured that all three wrote identical stories. A *Baltimore American* reporter with the curious name of Leander J. de Bekker offered to supply from his vivid imagination any details missing from their daily report, saving them needless legwork. "The labor-saving device was used the whole time I covered South Baltimore for the *Herald*, and I never heard any complaint against it," Mencken said. Their city editors occasionally commended the creative reporters for their accuracy.

Mencken said he developed his "theory that Service is mainly only blah" when he journeyed to Jacksonville, Florida, in May 1901 to cover his first out-of-town story. Most of the city had been destroyed by fire, and Mencken was sent to file stories about the efforts by various cities throughout the United States to help the residents. The paper was especially interested in Baltimore's relief offering, since it was produced at the instigation of the *Herald*. However, he found that the train carloads of horse blankets and Maryland rye whiskey, however well-intentioned as aid for victims of the conflagration, created more mirth than satisfaction. During those years Mencken also received assignments that introduced him to legislative reporting in Washington and in the state capital at Annapolis. When he was elevated to Sunday editor in 1901, he scrapped several undesirable features, changed writers of the long-favored travel article, and, in general, enlivened the pages. His writing for Sunday editions consisted primarily of pieces about the theater.

When Mencken was twenty-three, he was made city editor of the *Herald*, the position he held during the great fire that engulfed downtown Baltimore on 7 February 1904. He devoted an entire chapter of his *Newspaper Days, 1899-1906* memoir to that harrowing experience, explaining the change it wrought him: "It was brain-fagging and back-breaking, but it was grand beyond compare–an adventure of the first chop, a razzle dazzle superb and elegant, a circus in forty rings. When I came out of it at last I was a settled and indeed almost a middle-aged man, spavined by responsibility and aching in every sinew, but I went into it a boy, and it was the hot

Mencken and Sara Powell Haardt on 27 August 1930, the day of their marriage. Mencken was "dashed and dismayed" by her death only five years later (Baltimore News American).

gas of youth that kept me going." The *Herald* building was destroyed by the flames that consumed a square mile of city, necessitating a search for a new home for the paper. During the first three days after the fire began, the staff used the facilities of the *Washington Post*, the *Baltimore World*, and the *Catholic Mirror*. Then for five weeks the *Herald* contingent worked in the plant of the *Philadelphia Evening Telegraph*, traveling as often as necessary the 100 miles between the cities. Mencken said his "opening burst of work without a stop ran to sixty-four and a half hours, and then I got only six hours of nightmare sleep, and resumed on a working schedule of from twelve to fourteen hours a day, with no days off and no time for meals until work was over."

After the fire the *Herald* experienced several upheavals in its organization and operation. Because it was difficult to get enough advertising, due to competition with the morning *Sun* and *American* and with the *Evening News*, the pub-

lisher of the *Herald* decided during the summer of 1904 to add an evening edition. After a week, the morning edition was discontinued except on Sundays. Mencken became managing editor in 1905 and, in addition to directing the newspaper's operation, often helped with the editorial page.

While he labored at the *Herald*, Mencken's writing was not devoted solely to journalistic efforts. Though he had written verse during his teenage years, he did not make his first freelance poetry sale until the fall of 1899. He had submitted the selection anonymously, claiming it was his only after it had appeared; he was paid ten dollars. Mencken said his first poem "to make high literary society . . . was a rhymed address to my hero Kipling urging him to forget politics and go back to Mandalay." His other extracurricular writing consisted of features and news stories which he submitted to other newspapers, including the *New York Telegram*, the *New York Sun*, and the *Phila-*

delphia Inquirer. Mencken also tried his hand at more mundane forms of creative writing, such as advertising copy for a cemetery and jokes for a syndicate. He sold about two dozen stories in the early 1900s to such magazines as *Munsey's*, *Youth's Companion*, and *Frank Leslie's Popular Monthly.* During this same period he completed seven chapters of a novel set in Shakespearean England, complete with a fistfight between his protagonist and the Bard himself. The manuscript was never published.

Mencken's first column writing also took place while he worked at the *Herald.* The column, "Rhymes and Reason," appeared on the editorial page of the Sunday edition beginning in 1900, and contained some of his poetry. He said later: "I had a drawer full of verse, but I was making fewer and fewer additions to it. A large part of it consisted of dreadful imitations of Kipling, who was then my god.... In the Autumn of 1900, when I was given a weekly column on the editorial page, and invited to do my damndest, I unearthed a lot of these *Jugendwerke*, and so saved the labor of writing new stuff. They were all pretty bad, but they seemed to be well received in the office, and in December I received the singular honor of being invited by the new managing editor, [Robert I.] Carter, to do a poem for the first page.... It was blowsy stuff, God knows, but Carter professed to like it, and, good or bad, there it glowed and glittered in long primer italic on page one—glory that no other American poet, however gifted, has ever achieved, at least to my knowledge." Subsequently his columns appeared under other titles— "Terse and Terrible Texts," "Knocks and Jollies," and "Untold Tales"—and contained humor and verse and later a series of what Mencken called "buffooneries," in which he featured Baltimore politicians in the guise of ancient Romans. But probably the best of his column writing at that time was in "Baltimore and the Rest of the World," which reflected not only Mencken's humor but his personal view of his hometown.

Mencken's first book, *Ventures into Verse* (1903), was published in an edition of 100 copies by two young printers and an artist who had sought out his work for one of their first efforts at advanced typography. He recalled receiving fifty of the small volumes containing mostly the verse he had used on the *Herald* editorial page. Mencken said the copies he sent to the chief critical publications drew good reviews but only three orders. "My presentation copies seem to have

been preserved in odd corners," he wrote in *Newspaper Days*, "for when American firsts began to bring fantastic prices, in 1925, a good many appeared in the market, and at one time a clean specimen brought as much as $225."

Another of Mencken's editorial interests at the *Herald* was drama criticism; he was a second-string theater critic during Carter's tenure as managing editor, beginning in late 1900. Carter reviewed the serious plays staged in Baltimore, leaving the comedies and musicals to Mencken. Thus it was that Mencken's thought was focused on plays by George Bernard Shaw, an interest that he said led him to begin his first real book in 1904. *George Bernard Shaw: His Plays* (1905) was the first critical study of the dramatist's works. Mencken remembered the day the book's proofs arrived for his perusal. He showed them to Carter's successor as managing editor, Lynn R. Meekins, on the pretense of asking about a questionable passage, whereupon Meekins insisted that the young author take the day off to read the galleys. Mencken recalled: "So I locked myself in as he commanded, and had a shining day indeed, and I can still remember its unparalleled glow after all these years." Biographer Carl Bode maintains that Mencken's true style emerged during the writing of the Shaw book: "Many different ingredients went into it but the combination was unique. There was the love of words ... seen at its earliest in the school exercise at the Polytechnic and at its fanciest in the aborted novel on Shakespeare. There was the readiness at writing which was cultivated by his reams of copy at the *Herald* and the *Sun*, copy nearly always pushed by a deadline. And there was the urge to write clearly, in part because he needed to make the mass of newspaper readers understand him but also because he early acquired an admiration for clarity for its own sake." In January 1906 Mencken was elevated to editor, but the *Herald* closed in June. Mencken moved to the *Evening News* as news editor, but his work for his former competition was short-lived. The *Baltimore Sunpapers* hired him in July as Sunday editor, beginning an association that would continue until 1941, with a brief interruption during World War I and the addition of a short period in 1948 for political convention reporting.

Mencken brought his vibrant style and exuberant spirits to the *Sun* on 30 July 1906. Within a month he had evoked a response from the subject of one of his editorial page pieces, Col. Henry Watterson, editor of the *Louisville Courier-*

Journal: "Think of it! The staid, old Baltimore *Sun* has got itself a Whangdoodle. Nor is it one of the bogus Whangdoodles which we sometimes encounter in the side-show business–merely a double-cross betwixt a Gin-Rickey and a Gyascutis–but genuine, guaranteed, imported direct from the Mountains of Hepsidam." During his first four years on the *Sun*, as he found editing the Sunday edition less demanding, Mencken began writing editorials and reviewing plays. He asked to be relieved of the theatrical critiques, however, after he had written twenty-three consecutive unfavorable reviews during the first year. He also found the editorial writing a frustrating chore because of the anonymity and uninspired subject matter inherent in such essays.

The experience of writing his Shaw book gave Mencken the impetus to start a large volume in 1907, *The Philosophy of Friedrich Nietzsche* (1908). Two years later he brought together his correspondence with Robert Rives La Monte, a Marxist and organizer for the Socialist party, in *Men versus the Man* (1910), a debate on socialism. Mencken said that after these two nonfiction efforts, he was strictly a critic of ideas.

When the *Sun* was taken over by another owner in April 1910, Mencken was elevated to associate editorship of the new *Baltimore Evening Sun*. His duties included writing two editorials every day. He also grabbed the opportunity to begin a daily column, which he signed "H.L.M." His inimitable style–direct, humorous, and iconoclastic–found a milieu and an appreciative audience. In May 1911 Mencken was asked by the *Sunpapers* management to write a by-lined column–unusual in that day–in the manner of the British columnist Horatio Bottemly, whose irreverent essays had caught the eye of a son of one of the newspaper's major stockholders. Mencken was given the mandate to be blunt, witty, and controversial. He could direct his barbs at anyone, except perhaps the church–though that institution, too, became fair game after Mencken was attacked frequently from the pulpit.

The "Free Lance" columns began appearing in the *Evening Sun* on 8 May 1911–the first day's title, "The World in Review," was dropped after that one use–and continued until 23 October 1915. Mencken's tack was to ridicule and heap abuse on every conceivable social scheme, idiotic practice, and public or private individual, whether politician, "Uplifter," or civic leader (Honorary Pallbearer, in Mencken's lexicon). He roared, hooted, and bawled; his sarcasm and derision were rarely subtle, usually bombastic in tone. William Manchester, another Mencken biographer, notes that "it was his outrageous attitude which distinguished Mencken. He opposed everything respectable, mocked everything sacred, inveighed against everything popular opinion supported." He included these two paragraphs in the "Free Lance" for 9 May 1911, the first day on which the column's title was officially used:

> After all is said and done, how many victuals are as genuinely and constantly appetizing as pigs' feet in jelly?
> Blackamoors smear the tree trunks with whitewash and elegant Neapolitans, laying aside the razor and the pushcart, practice fearful cadenzas upon the E flat clarinet. In brief, the summer parks prepare for trade. Three weeks will see them all open. A heavy miasma from singeing popcorn and hot frankfurters. Barkers barking. The sextet from *Lucia*. Young devils ogling the girls. Babies bawling. The crowded trolley. Comedians.

A Mencken device for calling attention to absurdities or to underline his opinion was the use of exclamations, interrupting other brief, usually audacious, observations on morals, habits, books, or whatever drew his sharp eye. One such paragraph appeared in the "Free Lance" of 15 March 1913: "Boil your drinking water! Cover your garbage can! Down with rum! Down with cocaine! Down with caffeine!" After a discussion of the relative merits of caffeine and alcohol Mencken concluded: "The cigarette! The cigarette! Beware, or it will get you yet! Oh, many and many a mother's pet hath perished in its awful net! On every hand its snares are set! The cigarette! The cigarette!" Because his new column was signed–not with just initials, as had been his earlier editorial-page efforts–Mencken gained a reputation for his impudent, devil-may-care pageant of mockery and satire. Bode characterizes the "Free Lance": "But allowing for comic exaggeration, Mencken meant what he said. The rebellion was real, the criticism purposeful. The point is that it was never heavy. In its largest dimension the Free Lance represented his basic attitude towards newspaper work and toward life. He treated both like his gaudy girls in the red-light district–whom he enjoyed thoroughly but disrespectfully." With the "Free Lance" Mencken had begun "stirring up the animals," his intention from the start, and as a result he gained a notoriety that led to his pronouncements being quoted throughout the United States.

During his years with the *Sunpapers* Mencken took on other writing and editing tasks, enough to tax the endurance and skill of even the most talented journalist. But his work on books and magazines was suitable and altogether appropriate for a man with such an immense fascination with ideas and the continuing carnival of humanity. In 1914 he became coeditor with George Jean Nathan of the *Smart Set*, a magazine known for its risqué content appealing primarily to the so-called society crowd. The *Smart Set* had been founded as "A Magazine of Cleverness" in 1900 by Col. William D'Alton Mann, whose lack of success with the publication forced him to sell it in 1908 to John Adams Thayer. The publication experienced a series of editors and declining circulation during the next fourteen years. Willard Huntington Wright, predecessor of Mencken and Nathan, had become editor in 1913. He had changed the magazine's slogan to "Its Prime Purpose Is to Provide Lively Entertainment for Minds That Are Not Primitive," beginning some of the changes that Mencken and Nathan would embrace. William Manchester, in his Mencken biography, says that Wright should receive full credit for having published for one year "that magazine now considered a literary milestone." Before selling the *Smart Set* to Eugene Crowe, the owner of *Field and Stream*, Thayer fired Wright, who became a columnist for the *New York Evening Mail*. Crowe appointed Eltinge F. Warner, formerly with *Field and Stream*, to be publisher of the *Smart Set*. Warner, meeting Nathan during a voyage from Europe, asked Nathan to become editor of the magazine. Nathan agreed but insisted that Mencken be coeditor. Mencken had been book editor for the magazine since November 1908, a task he approached with his usual bluster and erudition. Nathan, a former reporter who had studied languages and the theater in Europe, had become drama editor at about the same time. Under their coeditorship the *Smart Set* became a ready market for the creative efforts of young and talented writers and an important force in the literary taste of the time.

In the fifteen years he wrote for the *Smart Set*, Mencken reviewed about 2,000 books. In his final essay in December 1923 he said he had composed 182 articles during those years, or more than 900,000 words of criticism. William H. Nolte says that Mencken "was the most powerful literary critic, in his own lifetime, that this country has produced; and his judgment of individual writers and his analysis of our literary heritage were nigh unerring." The vitality, originality, and iconoclasm of the Mencken style showed through in every essay. In December 1909, for example, he wrote under the headline "A Novel Thus Begins": "*Apologies for Love*–by F. A. Myers. ' "Do you remain long in Paris, Miss Wadsworth?" Earl Nero Pensive (!!!) inquired, as he seated himself beside her. His eyes, like beaming lights out of shadowless abysm, were transfixed upon her as by magic force....' Thus the story begins. God knows how it ends!" Mencken's sure touch with ridicule is apparent in these opening sentences of a review titled "Lachrymose Love" in February 1915: "Have you tears? Do you leak easily? Are you a weeper? Then wrap yourself in a shower-bath curtain before you sit down to *Innocent*, by Marie Corelli, for the tale wrings the lachrymal ducts with exquisite and diabolical art. Sadness, indeed, stalks through the countryside; it is a sure cure for joy in every form. I myself, a mocker at all sweet and lovely things, a professional snickerer, a saucy fellow by trade, have moaned and blubbered over it like a fat woman in *La Dame aux Camelias*. My waistcoat is a sponge. My beard is white with salt. My eyes are a brilliant scarlet...."

Mencken was considered something of a patriarch in the German-American community, but biographer Edgar Kemler says that "His allegiance was, after all, to a Germany that existed in its pure state only in his mind, and it was highly distressing for him to be reminded how much the German-Americans resembled other Americans." As Mencken's columns were thought to be more and more pro-German in the early years of World War I, the *Sunpapers* management grew apprehensive that the "Free Lance" would have a volatile influence on its audience. Bode notes that Mencken, in the "Free Lance," defended the commander of the German submarine that torpedoed the *Lusitania* and predicted that Paris would be captured and London destroyed by German armies. Announcing that the war was nearing its end, Mencken proclaimed "Deutschland Über Alles!" In October 1915 the *Sun* dropped the column, and for the next year Mencken wrote on music, literature, and the arts. He was sent to Germany as a correspondent in January 1917 and for two months dispatched accounts covering aspects of life among the troops in the trenches and the generals in Berlin. He returned to Baltimore by way of Cuba, from where he smuggled out accounts of an impending revolution through his contacts in Havana. Mencken broke with the *Sun* in March 1917 and did not resume writing for it until 1919.

Meanwhile, Mencken's sardonic and entertaining views, on subjects as varied and controversial as those in the "Free Lance," appeared in the *New York Evening Mail*, with which he had a contract for three columns a week. One of the Iconoclast's *Evening Mail* columns which gained notoriety—and provoked an especially fierce uproar from one region of the country—was "The Sahara of the Bozart," which appeared on 13 November 1917. The title of the essay, a permutation of the French *beaux arts*, was evidence of Mencken's penchant for wordplay. He phrased his scorn audaciously, true to his style of overstatement: "Nearly the whole of Europe could be lost in that stupendous region of worn-out farms, shoddy cities and paralyzed cerebrums: one could throw in France, Germany, and Italy, and still have room for the British Isles. And yet, for all its size and all its wealth and all the 'progress' it babbles of, it is almost as sterile, artistically, intellectually, culturally, as the Sahara Desert. There are single acres in Europe that house more first-rate men than all the states south of the Potomac; there are probably single square miles in America. If the whole of the late Confederacy were to be engulfed by a tidal wave tomorrow, the effect upon the civilized minority of men in the world would be but little greater than that of a flood on the Yant-tse-kiang. It would be impossible in all history to match so complete a drying up of a civilization." After he included "Sahara of the Bozart" in his 1920 collection, *Prejudices: Second Series,* Mencken became the object of hostile editorials. From Atlanta to Richmond, from Charleston to Little Rock, the outpourings of furious Southerners likened him to Satan incarnate and labeled him "an insufferable excrescence on the body of American literature," "an infernal and ignorant mountebank," and "a miserable, uninformed wretch." Mencken recalled: "It produced a ferocious reaction in the South, and I was belabored for months, and even years afterward in a very extravagant manner. . . . On the heels of the violent denunciations of the elderly Southerners there soon came a favorable response from the more civilized youngsters, and there is reason to believe that my attack had something to do with that revival of Southern letters which followed in the mid-

dle 1920s." Such was the influence Mencken was beginning to wield on public opinion.

On 18 December 1917 one of Mencken's most memorable creations—for a creation is precisely what it was—appeared in the *Mail*. The famous "bathtub hoax" was a cleverly contrived column entitled "A Neglected Anniversary." Mencken later said he composed the column with its seemingly well-documented canard because in wartime "more serious writing was impossible." The bathtub history found its way into medical reference books, other news and magazine accounts, and, in later years, onto television. Mencken lamented that no matter how much he tried to explain away his foolishness, the story continued to thrive. His essay detailed the tub's construction by Adam Thompson, a cotton and grain merchant, in Cincinnati in December 1842. The huge tub was designed to hold the body of an adult and was constructed of highly polished mahogany lined with sheet lead. The magnificent container weighed 1,750 pounds. Mencken wrote gravely that the public and the medical fraternity denounced the invention as "an epicurean and obnoxious toy from England" and as "dangerous to health." He went so far as to claim that acceptance of the tub by President Millard Fillmore was responsible for bringing the device "recognition and respectability in the United States." Fillmore was said to have visited Cincinnati when he was vice-president, and after inspecting the bathtub proceeded to bathe in the Thompson original. When he became president, he ordered a similar tub for the White House. Mencken's account had all the marks of an authentic chronicle. It sounded momentous with all its dates and names, and to the gullible reader it had credibility.

Mencken's association with the *Mail* ended when the newspaper's pro-German sympathies led to its suppression in July 1918. He then directed his literary efforts to completing *Damn! A Book of Calumny* (1918) and *In Defense of Women* (1918). At the same time he began what many consider his most notable achievement, *The American Language*, a philological study that has been highly praised since the first edition was published in 1919. Mencken himself believed the work would "outlast anything else that I have ever written." He had first written about the subject in his *Sun* column and in a subsequent series for the *Smart Set*, and he carried this intense interest in language over to the massive project that consumed thirty-eight years—from 1910 to

Mencken in Cleveland, covering the 1936 Republican National Convention

1948–while he was engaged in other editorial and writing projects. Mencken produced a thorough, penetrating, and, as always, readable analysis of enormous significance to the understanding of American English idiom. His observations about and examples of American English vocabulary, spelling, pronunciation, grammar, and syntax earned praise from scholars as well as ordinary readers. Four editions of *The American Language*, along with two supplements, reveal the orderly, systematic method of a writer enthralled by the complexities of language. In each succeeding edition, Mencken incorporated suggestions from thousands of letters and information from linguistic publications and other sources devoted to language study. The fourth edition of *The American Language* appeared in 1936, and the two supplements were published in 1945 and 1948.

Mencken became general editorial adviser for the *Baltimore Sun* after rejoining the organization in 1919. His extraordinary energy and genius for editing and writing gave value to his guidance of the *Evening Sun*, particularly after

Hamilton Owens became managing editor in 1922. Mencken helped improve both the content and the appearance of the newspaper and offered counsel and instruction in both major and inconsequential matters. In editorial conferences and in conversations with the reporters and other staff personnel Mencken revealed his skill in management.

Mencken agreed also to write occasional articles when he went back to the *Sun*, and the famous "Monday Articles" were born. His weekly columns on the editorial page helped identify Mencken as a premier journalist, a newspaperman of the first order. From 1920 until 1938 he wrote of politics, literature, personalities, places–any subjects that events or encounters suggested to his fertile journalist's mind. By the end of the series of "Monday Articles" in 1938 Mencken had moved through the Depression and into Franklin D. Roosevelt's presidency. As the "Free Lance" had brought his ideas to the attention of his hometown, the "Monday Articles" imprinted his particular brand of commentary on the psyche of America. Mencken entertained and angered, engendering responses in extreme degrees among his readers. They delighted, despised, hooted, and whooped, but they always noticed.

In 1923 both Mencken and Nathan left the *Smart Set* to become coeditors of the *American Mercury*, the periodical that, more than any other, became a bible to collegians of the 1920s. Mencken reached the pinnacle of his popularity and influence during the ten years he edited the *American Mercury*. With its Paris-green cover, the magazine was simply designed by standards of later decades but was a superb typographical specimen in its day. It was not only a status symbol but a voice of critical significance during the wild, unabashed decade of prosperity and Prohibition. When Alfred A. Knopf, Mencken's publisher since 1916, was eager to begin a new magazine, he sought Mencken to be editor. Mencken insisted that Nathan also be part of the enterprise, and so his coeditor from the *Smart Set* made the transition to the *American Mercury* to provide drama criticism and comments on the foibles of humanity. The first issue, dated January 1924, indicated editorially the course Baltimore's "bad boy" intended to follow: "The editors are committed to nothing save this: to keep the common sense as fast as they can, to belabor sham as agreeably as possible, to give a civilized entertainment." The flavor of that sentence typified the *American Mercury*'s profound and audacious tone. Mencken was an imaginative editor, and his special writing style, along with his keen insight and trenchant wit, gave the *American Mercury* a lively and intellectually stimulating quality that appealed to sophisticated and perceptive readers. He used submissions from a variety of writers, the recognized talents of the day as well as virtual unknowns.

The magazine's mélange of criticism, fiction, poetry, and essays on all manner of topics—always satiric and provocative with a note of humor, occasionally sarcastic and ironical—affected the thinking and taste of a mass of readers in the 1920s. Largely as a result of the magazine's impact, Walter Lippmann remarked in 1926 that Mencken was "the most powerful personal influence on the whole generation of educated people." Each issue of the *American Mercury* contained the "Americana" column, which consisted of brief notes taken from news clippings, wire reports, church bulletins, publicity releases—as assortment of sources from throughout the United States. The passages reflected the idiocies, imbecilities, and prejudices of the populace and appeared under state name headings with sardonic introductory sentences. The first issue's "Americana" included:

ALABAMA

Final triumph of Calvinism in Alabama, October 6, 1923:

Birmingham's exclusive clubs–and all other kinds–will be as blue hereafter as city and State laws can make them. Commissioner of Safety W. C. Bloe issued an order today that Sunday golf, billiards, and *dominoes* be stopped, beginning tomorrow.

VIRGINIA

Examples of neo-Confederate English from examination papers submitted by Virginia schoolmarms attending the Summer School at the University of Virginia:

He run down the street, but it was too late to cought him . . .

I like James Witcomb Riley, because he is not dead, and writes poems in the paper that one can see all right . . .

The flames shot into the sky a few foot above the house . . .

WASHINGTON

Hurrying on the Kingdom in the Chinook State, as reported by the *Editor and Publisher*:

Newspaper advertising was the best invest-(sic) made in 1923 by the Garden Street Methodist Episcopal Church, Bellingham, Wash., according to the pastor, the Rev. Dr. J. C. Harrison, who added that $100 worth of advertising had brought in more than $1,700 in silver plate collections.

Readers were amused by "Americana," and they found other regular features–Nathan's column on "The Theatre," Mencken's "The Library," and their collaboration on "Clinical Notes"–similarly entertaining and informative. The *American Mercury* contents had appeal that few other periodicals of that time could claim. The first issue was indicative of what was to come in the next 120 issues, all of which contained 128 pages. In addition to Mencken's and Nathan's efforts, the twenty-two selections ranged from essays on "The Lincoln Legend" by Isaac R. Pennypacker and "Stephen Crane" by Carl Van Doren to four poems by Theodore Dreiser and "Four Generations," a story by Ruth Suckow.

Mencken's own writing was direct, and his turns of phrase and superb use of language rendered his subjects memorable. On 8 December 1924, he described chiropractors in his *Baltimore Sun* column: "That pathology is grounded upon the doctrine that all human ills are caused by the pressure of misplaced vertebrae upon the nerves which come out of the spinal cord–in other words, that every disease is the result of a pinch. This, plainly enough, is buncombe. The chiropractic therapeutics rest upon the doctrine that the way to get rid of such pinches is to climb upon a table and submit to a heroic pummeling by a retired piano-mover. This, obviously, is buncombe doubly damned." Mencken summed up his feelings about religionists, particularly the more zealous, in his definition of Puritanism as "The haunting fear that someone, somewhere, may be happy." The succinct observation embodied his reaction to many of the pious causes célèbres of his time, but the furor raised by the Scopes trial in Dayton, Tennessee, in 1925 was one of Mencken's great moments, both as reporter and as social critic. The so-called monkey trial grew out of the indictment of John Thomas Scopes, a high school biology teacher who disobeyed the Tennessee law against teaching evolution. In *Heathen Days, 1890-1936*, Mencken recalled going to Dayton to cover the trial. He wrote that after the event stories about his being run out of town were pervasive, but "nothing of the sort ever happened. It is a fact that my dispatches from the courtroom were somewhat displeasing to the local susceptibilities, and that my attempts to describe the town and its people were even more so, and it is also a fact that there was talk among certain bolder spirits of asking me to retire from the scene, but beyond that it did not go." Indeed, Mencken's dispatches to the *Evening Sun* caught the flavor of the place and the event. One of them began: "It was hot weather when they tried the infidel Scopes at Dayton, Tenn., but I went down there very willingly, for I was eager to see something of evangelical Christianity as a going concern. In the big cities of the Republic, despite the endless efforts of consecrated men, it is laid up with a wasting disease. The very Sunday-school superintendents, taking jazz from the stealthy radio, shake their fire-proof legs; their pupils, moving into adolescence, no longer respond to the proliferating hormones by enlisting for missionary service in Africa, but resort to necking instead. Even in Dayton, I found, though the mob was up to do execution upon Scopes, there was

a strong smell of antinomianism. The nine churches of the village were all half empty on Sunday, and weeds choked their yards. Only two or three of the resident pastors managed to sustain themselves by their ghostly science; the rest had to take orders for mail order pantaloons or work in the adjacent strawberry fields; one, I heard, was a barber."

A prime target of Mencken's acerb pen was William Jennings Bryan, the prosecutor in the Scopes trial. Mencken attacked Bryan, hero of the fundamentalists, in a notable piece for the *Evening Sun* of 27 July 1925 that began: "Has it been duly marked by historians that William Jennings Bryan's last secular act on this globe of sin was to catch flies? A curious detail, and not without its sardonic overtones. He was the most sedulous fly-catcher in American history, and in many ways the most successful." Bryan had died the day before.

Among the hundreds of targets of his observations, caustic criticism, and ironic comments, Mencken also counted members of the press as particularly appropriate objects of scorn. Although he was a member of their breed, he had no difficulty in focusing on their shortcomings. In 1927 he wrote: "It is this vast and militant ignorance, this widespread and fathomless prejudice against intelligence that makes American journalism so pathetically feeble and vulgar, and so generally disreputable. A man with so little intellectual enterprise that, dealing with news daily, he can go through life without taking in any news that is worth knowing–such a man, you may be sure, is lacking in professional dignity quite as much as he is lacking in curiosity."

The controversy surrounding publication of "Hatrack" in the April 1926 *American Mercury* brought Mencken increased notoriety. Herbert Asbury's relatively innocuous story of a small-town prostitute stirred the Boston censors. Mencken subsequently confronted the Reverend J. Franklin Chase, secretary of the Watch and Ward Society of Boston, selling him a copy of the offending issue of the *American Mercury* on Boston Common. Mencken openly sought arrest so that he could test the obscenity charge in court. He won an injunction against Chase and a similar action against the New York postmaster, who, at Chase's urging, had sought a Post Office ban on the *American Mercury*.

Mencken commented on comedians in his *Sun* column for 18 November 1929: "Relatively few reflective persons seem to get any pleasure out of acting. They often, to be sure, delight in comedians–but a comedian is not an actor. His work bears the same relation to acting properly so called as that of a hangman, a midwife or a divorce lawyer bears to poetry, or that of bishop to religion."

The surprise announcement that H. L. Mencken would marry Sara Powell Haardt of Montgomery, Alabama, in September 1930 produced much hilarity among the acquaintances of Baltimore's premier curmudgeon. The press treated the impending nuptials with high good humor and, in some cases, scorn, as headlines trumpeted the Great Iconoclast's fall from professional bachelorhood. Editorials quoted Mencken's *In Defense of Women*, which had been considered proof of his aversion to the matrimonial state. The wedding took place in Baltimore on 27 August, a week earlier than the announced date of 3 September, to avoid the confusion the event could possibly have created.

Mencken had met Sara Haardt in 1923 when she was teaching English at Goucher College. A writer of fiction and articles in her own right, she had won over the great debunker with her wit, charm, and Victorian manner. Her frail health, although not a totally debilitating influence, always hovered over their courtship and marriage.

Before the end of its fifth year in 1928 the *American Mercury* had numerous imitators, especially among college publications, but the magazine's popularity was beginning to wane. Its circulation, more than 77,000 in 1927, was down to almost 74,000. By the close of the 1920s and the onset of the Depression, Mencken's influence, and consequently that of the *American Mercury*, had declined severely: circulation dropped to 67,000 in 1929. Criticism of Mencken from many quarters pointed to his failure to adjust to the times. His columns did not have their usual vitality, and much of the writing by contributors reflected a Menckenian formula. Nathan had departed the *American Mercury* in 1925, though he continued to write his theater column and to contribute to "Clinical Notes" until early 1930.

Mencken's bite was not totally gone, however. His suggestion for choosing legislators was published in the *Sun* on 13 April 1931: "So I propose that our Legislatures be chosen as our juries are now chosen–that the names of all the men eligible in each assembly district be put into a hat (or if no hat can be found that is large enough, into a bathtub), and that a blind moron, prefera-

Mencken returning from the hospital with his nurse, Lois Gentry, in 1951

bly of tender years, be delegated to draw out one. Let the constituted catchpolls then proceed swiftly to this man's house, and take him before he can get away. Let him be brought into court forthwith, and put under bond to serve as elected, and if he cannot furnish the bond, let him be kept until the appointed day in the nearest jail."

Mencken left the *American Mercury* in December 1933. After five years of marriage–the only period of Mencken's life that he lived away from Hollins Street–Sara died of tubercular meningitis on 31 May 1935. Mencken wrote that he was "dashed and dismayed" by her death. Their life together, he said, had been "a beautiful adventure."

In addition to his work on the *Evening Sun* and the *American Mercury*, Mencken also wrote essays for the *Chicago Tribune* from November 1924 to January 1928 and for the *New York American* from July 1934 to May 1935.

Mencken's favorite continuing news story was the political campaign. From the first two conventions he covered in 1904 for the *Herald* until his final campaign in 1948, he gloried in the hoopla and circuslike atmosphere of the quadrennial orgies. Beginning in 1920 he covered every political campaign until 1940. Although he left the *Sun* in 1941–an echo of the experience of a quarter of a century before, as he realized his feelings about the war in Europe were at odds with those of the newspaper–Mencken agreed to revel just once more in the orators, crowds, and steaming auditoriums in 1948. He ground out his usual perceptive and colorful copy on the Democratic, Republican, and Progressive conventions that year. A dispatch in June 1948 from the Republican gathering in Philadelphia revealed the old Mencken touch, as he viewed the arrival of a new technology:

> Television will take its first real bite at the statesmen of America tomorrow, and this afternoon there was a sort of experimental gumming or rehearsal in Convention Hall.
>
> It passed off well enough, all things considered, and no one was actually fried to death.
>
> But I doubt if any politician, however leathery his hide, survives that unprecedented glare of light without a considerable singeing. I was sitting quietly in the almost empty press-stand when the first 10,000-watt lamp was turned on.

Mencken's campaign coverage continued into November and the election of Democrat Harry S. Truman to the presidency.

On 23 November 1948 Baltimore's Sage had a severe stroke which left him unable to read or comprehend well what he saw or heard. His speech was also impaired. For the next eight years Mencken suffered the ultimate disability for one whose life had been built on a rare ability to communicate, a skill for choosing the right word and formulating the most colorful, the most potent statement. He died in his sleep on 29 January 1956, leaving among his millions of words a brief epitaph: "If, after I depart this vale, you ever remember me and have thought to please my ghost, forgive some sinner and wink your eye at some homely girl."

It would be possible to assign H. L. Mencken to some esoteric category that would encompass what he contributed to American letters: journalist-editor-critic-author-satirist-philologist. It would be simple enough, as many authors have found, to expound his "meaning" by quoting at length from his voluminous correspondence or his extraordinary outpouring of columns, articles, and books. Both approaches merely prove that Mencken cannot be compart-

mentalized; his works cannot be described in simple terms or limited to preconceived notions. The constant stream of commentary about Mencken, dissecting his ideas on everything from religion to ethics to politics and reviewing his life in detail, never really captures the man himself.

A great part of Mencken was his inimitable style. His words and, as a result, the works that those words produced, pulsate with pungent and potent good humor and common sense. Mencken remarked on his style in his notebooks, which have been collected in *Minority Report* (1956): "The imbeciles who have printed acres of comment on my books have seldom noticed the chief character of my style. It is that I write with almost scientific precision–that my meaning is never obscure. The ignorant have often complained that my vocabulary is beyond them, but that is simply because my ideas cover a wider range than theirs do. Once they have consulted the dictionary they always know exactly what I intend to say. . . ."

Mencken's ideas may not always have been original; his conservative-libertarian philosophy sometimes seemed contradictory. But he could grab the public's attention by stating an issue in terms that pointed up the inanity and the foolishness of man. His iconoclasm knew no limits; everything he encountered–person, object, or idea–was fair game for his particular brand of debunking. All elements of the persona of H. L. Mencken–his boisterous humor, his incisive wit, his healthy skepticism, his seemingly limitless gusto, and his innate rebelliousness–were inseparable from his thinking, his way of seeing the universe.

Mencken's dissent–his way of demolishing society's hypocrisy, of smashing the idols of human folly–set him apart from other writers of his day. His thought embraced the whole range of issues and problems that beset the first half of the twentieth century; and his writings have not aged, because mankind is subject to the same shortcomings and foibles that prevailed in his day.

Mencken's life as a journalist doubtless made him conscious of the peculiar position of those in the writing profession. In his notebooks he commented about the "unhappy man of the pen": "His feelings torture him far more than any other man is tortured, but soon or late he is able to work them off. They escape by way of his writings. Into those writings, if he lives long enough, he gradually empties all his fears and hatreds and prejudices–all his vain regrets and broken hopes–all his sufferings as a man, and all the special sufferings that go with his trade. The world, to such a man, never grows downright unbearable. There is always a sheet of paper. There is always a pen. There is always a way out." As long as there are those who long for a well-turned phrase that probes subjects that really matter, that breaks that mold of the commonplace, then there will be an audience for H. L. Mencken.

Letters:

Letters of H. L. Mencken, edited by Guy J. Forgue (New York: Knopf, 1961).

The New Mencken Letters, edited by Carl Bode (New York: Dial, 1977).

Mencken and Sara: A Life in Letters, edited by Marion Elizabeth Rodgers (New York: McGraw-Hill, 1986).

Bibliography:

Betty Adler and Jane Wilhelm, *H. L. M.: The Mencken Bibliography* (Baltimore: Johns Hopkins University Press, 1961); *Ten-Year Supplement, 1962-1971* (Baltimore: Enoch Pratt Free Library, 1971).

Biographies:

Isaac Goldberg, *The Man Mencken: A Biographical and Critical Survey* (New York: Simon & Schuster, 1925).
Early account of Mencken's life and work, written around the midpoint of his career and for that reason incomplete.

Edgar Kemler, *The Irreverent Mr. Mencken* (Boston: Little, Brown, 1950).
Biography of Mencken published two years after his disabling stroke and six years before his death.

William Manchester, *Disturber of the Peace: The Life of H. L. Mencken* (New York: Harper, 1950).
Reliable biography by one of Mencken's associates on the *Baltimore Sun*.

Sara Mayfield, *The Constant Circle: H. L. Mencken and His Friends* (New York: Delacorte, 1968).
Anecdotal memoir of Mencken and his various friends and associates, written by a school chum of Sara Haardt.

Carl Bode, *Mencken* (Carbondale: Southern Illinois University Press, 1969).
Most comprehensive biography of Mencken to date.

Douglas C. Stenerson, *H. L. Mencken: Iconoclast from Baltimore* (Chicago: University of Chicago Press, 1971).
Discusses Mencken's role as social satirist.

References:

Ernest Boyd, *H. L. Mencken* (New York: McBride, 1925).
Early study of Mencken's ideas.

Carl R. Dolmetsch, *The Smart Set, a History and an Anthology* (New York: Dial, 1966).
Reviews the history of *Smart Set*, with which Mencken was associated from 1908 to 1923, and reprints selected materials from the magazine.

John Dorsey, ed., *On Mencken* (New York: Knopf, 1980).
Collects essays by various hands.

Charles A. Fecher, *Mencken: A Study of His Thought* (New York: Knopf, 1978).
Argues that Mencken's ideas were a major force in shaping American attitudes, not only in his own time, but in later years as well.

Fred C. Hobson, Jr., *Serpent in Eden: H. L. Mencken and the South* (Chapel Hill: University of North Carolina Press, 1974).
Discusses Mencken's criticism of the American South and his negative critical reception there.

William H. Nolte, *H. L. Mencken, Literary Critic* (Middleton, Conn.: Wesleyan University Press, 1966).
Discusses Mencken as "the most powerful literary critic, in his own lifetime, that this country has produced."

Charles Scruggs, *The Sage in Harlem: H. L. Mencken and the Black Writers of the 1920s* (Baltimore: Johns Hopkins University Press, 1984).
Argues that Mencken's influence on black writers during the Harlem Renaissance has been overlooked and that, despite his some-

times seemingly racist comments, he was one of the first editors to publish the work of black authors in publications for mainstream America.

M. K. Singleton, *H. L. Mencken and the American Mercury Adventure* (Durham, N.C.: Duke University Press, 1962).
Chronicles Mencken's role in the founding and operation of the *American Mercury.*

W. H. A. Williams, *H. L. Mencken* (Boston: Twayne, 1977).

Useful, brief overview of Mencken and his work.

Papers:
The Enoch Pratt Free Library, Baltimore, has H. L. Mencken's personal library, including manuscripts, typescripts, and scrapbooks; and his correspondence, except that with twentieth-century authors and non-Marylanders, which he gave to the New York Public Library. Thirty-four other institutions and libraries are listed in Betty Adler, *A Descriptive List of H. L. Mencken Collections in the U.S.* (Baltimore: Enoch Pratt Free Library, 1967) as holding first editions of Mencken's books, original issues of magazines, or manuscripts.

Edna St. Vincent Millay

This entry was updated by Paula L. Hart (University of British Columbia) from her entry in DLB 45, American Poets, 1880-1945, First Series.

Places	Camden, Maine Greenwich Village	Steepletop Farm, Austerlitz, New York	Vassar College
Influences and Relationships	Arthur Davison Ficke Witter Bynner Edmund Wilson	Elinor Wylie William Shakespeare Andrew Marvell	Robert Browning A. E. Housman John Donne
Literary Movements and Forms	The Sonnet	Dramatic Monologue	Fairy Tales
Major Themes	The Renewing Power of Nature The Inevitability of Death	Celebration of Sexual Love Search for Beauty	Female Equality Emotional Bonds between Women
Cultural and Artistic Influences	Bohemianism	Elizabethan Drama	Opera
Social and Economic Influences	Execution of Sacco and Vanzetti Genteel Poverty	Feminism Post World War I Pacifism	World War II Propaganda

BIRTH: Rockland, Maine, 22 February 1892, to Henry Tolman and Cora Buzzelle Millay.

EDUCATION: A.B., Vassar, 1917.

MARRIAGE: 18 July 1923 to Eugen Boissevain.

AWARDS AND HONORS: *Poetry* prize for "The Bean-Stalk," 1920; Pulitzer Prize for Poetry, 1923; honorary Litt.D., Tufts University, 1925; elected to the National Institute of Arts and Letters, 1929; Levinson Prize (*Poetry* magazine), 1931; Laureate of General Federation of Women's Clubs, 1933; Litt.D., University of Wisconsin, 1933; Litt.D., Russell Sage College, 1933; honorary L.H.D., New York University, 1937; honorary Litt.D., Colby College, 1937; elected to the American Academy of Arts and Letters, 1940; Gold Medal of the Poetry Society of America, 1943.

DEATH: Austerlitz, New York, 19 October 1950.

SELECTED BOOKS: *Renascence and Other Poems* (New York: Kennerley, 1917);
A Few Figs from Thistles (New York: Shay, 1920);
Aria da Capo, Chapbook (London), no. 14 (August 1920); (New York: Kennerley, 1921);
Second April (New York: Kennerley, 1921);
The Lamp and the Bell (New York: Shay, 1921);
Two Slatterns and a King (Cincinnati: Kidd, 1921);
The Ballad of the Harp-Weaver (New York: Shay, 1922);
The Harp-Weaver and Other Poems (New York & London: Harper, 1923; London: Secker, 1924);
Poems (London: Secker, 1923);
Renascence (New York: Anderson Galleries, 1924);
Distressing Dialogues, as Nancy Boyd (New York & London: Harper, 1924);
Three Plays (New York & London: Harper, 1926; London: Cape, 1927);
The King's Henchman [score], libretto by Millay and music by Deems Taylor (New York & Birmingham, U.K.: Fischer, 1926);
The King's Henchman: A Play in Three Acts (New York & London: Harper, 1927; London: Cape, 1927);
Edna St. Vincent Millay, edited by Hughes Mearns (New York: Simon & Schuster, 1927);
Fear (New York: Sacco-Vanzetti National League, 1927);
The Buck in the Snow and Other Poems (New York & London: Harper, 1928);

Edna St. Vincent Millay around the age of thirty (courtesy of Vassar College Library)

Edna St. Vincent Millay's Poems Selected for Young People (New York & London: Harper, 1929);
Fatal Interview, Sonnets (New York & London: Harper, 1931; London: Hamilton, 1931);
The Princess Marries the Page: A Play in One Act (New York & London: Harper, 1932; London: Hamilton, 1932);
Wine from These Grapes (New York & London: Harper, 1934; London: Hamilton, 1934);
Vacation Song (Hanover, N.H.: Baker Library Press, 1936);
Conversation at Midnight (New York & London: Harper, 1937; London: Hamilton, 1937);
Huntsman, What Quarry? (New York & London: Harper, 1939; London: Hamilton, 1939);
"There Are No Islands Any More" (New York & London: Harper, 1940);
Make Bright the Arrows: 1940 Notebook (New York & London: Harper, 1940; London: Hamilton, 1941);
Collected Sonnets (New York & London: Harper, 1941);
The Murder of Lidice (New York & London: Harper, 1942);

Collected Lyrics (New York & London: Harper, 1943);

Second April and The Buck in the Snow (New York: Harper, 1950);

Mine the Harvest, edited by Norma Millay (New York: Harper, 1954; London: Hamilton, 1954);

Collected Poems, edited by Norma Millay (New York: Harper, 1956; London: Hamilton, 1957).

OTHER: "Renascence," in *The Lyric Year,* edited by Ferdinand Earle (New York: Kennerley, 1912);

Charles Baudelaire, *Flowers of Evil,* translated by Millay and George Dillon, with an introduction and a biography by Millay (New York & London: Harper, 1936; London: Hamilton, 1936).

Despite a publishing career that spanned three decades and a canon that ranges from lyrics to verse plays and political commentary, Edna St. Vincent Millay is probably best known for her early works, particularly "Renascence" (1912), *A Few Figs from Thistles* (1920), and *Second April* (1921). The first, a 214-line poem revealing a mystical view of the universe, God, and death, caused a sensation as the work of a girl just turned twenty. The second, a celebration of feminism and free love, caught the mood of Greenwich Village life in the racy postwar period of the 1920s. *Second April* showed a more honest approach to the already favorite Millay themes of death, love, and nature. Millay's admirers also commend *Aria da Capo* (1920), a verse play on the foolishness of war, and certain of her sonnets, especially "Euclid alone has looked on Beauty bare" (1923) and the sequences, "Sonnets from an Ungrafted Tree" (1923) and "Epitaph for the Race of Man" (1934).

Edna St. Vincent Millay, the first of the three daughters of Cora Buzzelle Millay and Henry Tolman Millay, was born in Rockland, Maine, on 22 February 1892. In 1900 Cora Millay divorced her husband, an educator with a fondness for poker playing, and settled with her girls in Camden, Maine, providing for the family by nursing. It is little wonder that the poet retained a lifelong devotion to the woman who encouraged in all her daughters self-reliance and a love for music and books. The musical talent of Vincent (as she was known in the family) was so obvious that a local teacher gave her piano lessons,

hoping to prepare her for a musical career. After a few years the plan was abandoned, but music remained a source of pleasure, a subject for poetry, and undoubtedly the basis for her unfailing sense of poetic rhythm.

It was Millay's early interest in literature that became dominant and soon, augmented by her responsiveness to nature, found expression in original compositions. At the age of fourteen she had a poem, "Forest Trees," published in *St. Nicholas* magazine, a popular children's periodical that printed a number of her juvenile works. At Camden High School she wrote for and eventually became editor of the school magazine. At her graduation in 1909 she recited an original poem, showing a third side of her early interest in the arts: dramatic performance.

In 1912, at her mother's urging, Millay submitted a long poem, which she entitled "Renaissance," in a contest designed to select pieces for an anthology called *The Lyric Year.* Ferdinand Earle, one of the judges, was delighted with the entry from E. Vincent Millay (as she then called herself), persuaded her to change the title to "Renascence," and fully expected the poem to win first prize. Other judges were not in agreement, and the poem ranked only fourth in the final tally. Nevertheless, when *The Lyric Year* was published in November 1912, "Renascence" received immediate critical acclaim. Two of the earliest to write their congratulations, poets Witter Bynner and Arthur Davison Ficke, became Millay's close friends.

The poem, in traditional tetrameter couplets, chronicles the poet's spiritual and emotional development. The enclosed childlike perspective of the opening, "All I could see from where I stood/Was three long mountains and a wood," soon gives way to the persistence of the inquiring mind, "And reaching up my hand to try,/ I screamed to feel it touch the sky." Extending this penetration, the young narrator feels the pressures of a sympathetic response to all humanity, driving her to death underground. A youthful will to live and the reviving power of nature in the image of rain, however, recall the transformed individual, who can now cry, "God, I can push the grass apart/And lay my finger on thy heart!" The heightened spiritual awareness gained by the imaginative experience is shown in the final stanza, which is starkly contrasting in perspective to the first: "The soul can split the sky in two,/And let the face of God shine through."

Many critics were impressed by the poem's youthful freshness, by its strong emotional impact, and by what Harriet Monroe called its "sense of infinity." Caroline B. Dow of the National Training School of the YWCA heard Millay read "Renascence" in Camden and helped her secure a scholarship to Vassar.

Millay, already in her twenties when she entered Vassar in 1914, after a semester's additional preparation at Barnard College, was very much involved in campus life as well as her studies. She published poems and plays in the Vassar *Miscellany;* acted regularly in school dramas, playing the lead in her own *The Princess Marries the Page* (published in 1932); and composed lyrics for a 1915 Founder's Day marching song. Her studies were concentrated on literature, drama, and both classic and modern languages. Critical biographer Norman Brittin notes, "Her education reinforced the influence of the classics upon her and insured that she would be a learned poet, one more like a Milton, Shelley, or Tennyson than a Whitman or Vachel Lindsay." Indeed, though her poetry would always be termed "American" in flavor, her images and allusions were often based on the classics, while her rhythms and sentiments were forever inviting comparison to established poets from John Donne to A. E. Housman.

The Vassar years, with their feminine collegiality, also had an effect on Millay's outlook, either stimulating or solidifying a healthy regard for the friendship of women and the active feminist principles that were evident in her later poetry. A spirited female independence, to be labeled "flippant" in *A Few Figs from Thistles,* displayed itself also, particularly in Millay's bridling at rigid dormitory rules. This is hardly shocking, coming from a woman in her mid twenties.

In 1917, not long after her graduation, Millay's first volume of poetry, *Renascence and Other Poems,* was published by Mitchell Kennerley. In addition to the title poem, twenty-two others, many published earlier in periodicals, were included. Critics again responded warmly to "Renascence." The other long poem, "Interim," a blank-verse monologue delivered by a young narrator who has just lost his love, fails to convey the emotional honesty of "Renascence." The dramatic framework, whether it was a device suggested by her reading of Robert Browning and other poets or her own background in theater, was used more effectively by Millay in other works. Her fresh-eyed view of nature, always a Mil-

lay strength, is captured in the childlike experience of "Afternoon on a Hill," but it is regrettably clichéd in the often-quoted line, "O world, I cannot hold thee close enough!," of the sentimental "God's World." Its "gaunt crag" and "black bluff" epitomize the artificial poetic diction of which her detractors were often to accuse her.

The last six poems in *Renascence and Other Poems* are sonnets. Though they are not remarkable, they do show indications of the uniquely feminine perspective that was to elicit praise for the best. Sonnet five, in the Shakespearean mode, projects the possible reaction of a young woman if she were to learn of her lover's death while she was in a public place. The realistic detail of the closing lines, which should give a sharp sense of the mundane trivia preventing a genuine expression of grief, instead made some readers infer indifference:

> I should but watch the station lights rush by
> > With a more careful interest on my face,
> Or raise my eyes and read with greater care
> > Where to store furs and how to treat the hair.

The final sonnet, "Bluebeard," is of interest because she quite suitably transposes the image of Bluebeard's room to that of a feminine bastion, a place of privacy which must be abandoned when profaned by male intrusion. It shows also the prominence of fairy tales as a source of her literary inspiration.

The appearance of this first volume made Millay a presence in the literary world, but it brought her no financial rewards. Millay returned to New York City, hoping to make a living through acting. She and her sister Norma moved to Greenwich Village, home of the Provincetown Players.

In the Village spirits were high and free. It was a new kind of intellectual awakening for Millay, quite different from the formalized education of Vassar. Woman's rights and free love were an accepted part of the living code, and the determination to experience life to the full was heightened by the reality of World War I, with its daily records of young lives lost. Millay had long ago shown an independence of spirit which suited her admirably to Village life. The fact that she was an attractive, slender redhead was certainly an added advantage, and the young woman who was so recently surrounded by loving female friendships soon had a line of male suitors vying for her attention. Floyd Dell was the first of the

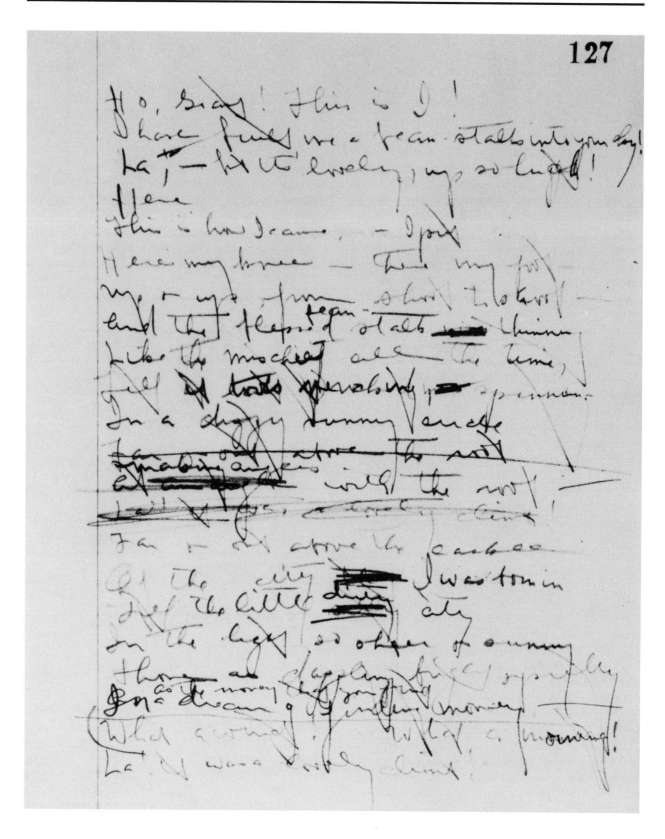

Page from the first draft for "The Bean-Stalk," published in Second April *(courtesy of the Manuscript Division, Library of Congress)*

lovers Millay was to have in the Village.

In 1918 Millay finally met Arthur Davison Ficke, with whom she had corresponded since his first congratulations on the publication of "Renascence." Ficke, an accomplished sonneteer, had obviously influenced Millay's experimentation with the form. Through their correspondence, she had come to think of the married man as her spiritual mentor. While he was in New York on his way to a military posting in France, however, they had an intense three-day affair. The emotional experience found direct expression in love letters and sonnets written to Ficke (such as "Into the golden vessel of great song") and indirectly in much of her other work. Though they were to remain lifelong friends, the ardor cooled.

The romances and all-night parties made a gay life, but the Village years were ones of poverty for Millay. She made no money from her acting and had to work hard to sell a few poems. One of her chief sources of revenue at this time was *Ainslee's*, a magazine with no literary pretensions. Since she was paid by the line, poetry did not bring a very great return, so she began turning out prose, along with some light poetry, under the pseudonym of Nancy Boyd. These pieces were later collected in *Distressing Dialogues* by "Nancy Boyd," with a coy preface by Edna St. Vincent Millay, in 1924.

In 1920 Millay met Edmund Wilson, who was later, unsuccessfully, to propose marriage to the poet. He was an editor at *Vanity Fair,* a magazine appealing to much more sophisticated tastes than *Ainslee's*. With his influence, Millay began to have most of her work published in that periodical. This brought much-needed capital to the young woman, still involved in the exciting, nonpaying world of theater: acting, writing, and directing. The *Vanity Fair* exposure also gave rise to the popularity the poet was to maintain for many years.

Her second volume of poetry, *A Few Figs from Thistles,* was published by Frank Shay in 1920. The arch tone of this collection did not please reviewers. It did, however, clearly reflect the impression the fast life and fleeting loves had made on the young woman always receptive to emotional experiences. The feelings may have been shallow, as seen in these lines from "To the Not Impossible Him"–

The fabric of my faithful love
    No power shall dim or ravel

Whilst I stay here,–but oh, my dear,
    If I should ever travel!

–but the kick at convention seen in this poem and others, such as the "First Fig" with its memorable "My candle burns at both ends," appealed to the postwar generation. Here, too, was the voice of feminism: women as well as men could be casual in their treatment of sexual love, go on with life when it was over, and look forward to the next affair. Writing much later in his *Lives of the Poets* (1961), Louis Untermeyer most clearly identified the reason for the popularity of Millay's poetry during this period: "Plain and rhetorical, traditional in form and unorthodox in spirit, it satisfied the reader's dual desire for familiarity and surprise."

Millay finished *Aria da Capo* (1920), a one-act verse play, for the 1919-1920 Provincetown Players season. It proved to be the outstanding success of the year for them. Starkly dramatic in its concept and construction, the play begins with the stock Harlequin characters Columbine and Pierrot exchanging inanities and satirizing current trends:

PIERROT.   Don't stand so near me!
    I am become a socialist. I love
    Humanity; but I hate people. Columbine,
    Put on your mittens, child; your hands are cold.

The light mood abruptly ends when Cothurnus, the masque of Tragedy, chases the Harlequins from the stage and forces the shepherds Thyrsis and Corydon to play their scene. The two friends play a game, building a wall between them with the stage props constructed of colored crepe paper, apparently cutting Corydon off from a stream. They begin to take the game seriously, their jealousy over possession deepening when Corydon finds a bowl of jewels (confetti) on his side. Before long the two have murdered each other with their carefully guarded possessions: Thyrsis poisons Corydon with tainted water from the stream, and Corydon strangles Thyrsis with a string of the precious stones. Cothurnus gives a command to cut the scene, hastily putting a table over the bodies of the slain shepherds and kicking the protruding limbs beneath it. When the Harlequins protest that they cannot continue their scene with bodies under the table, Cothurnus advises them just to pull down the table cover so that the shepherds are out of sight. They do so and resume their chatter. This harsh climax delivers a powerful statement about the folly of war and the callous disregard for human life.

The year of especially hard work brought the additional reward of a $100 prize from *Poetry* magazine for "The Bean-Stalk," which was to appear in her next published collection, *Second April* (1921). Overwork and an active life also brought illness and nervous exhaustion. At the beginning of 1921, however, she was able to sail for Europe, thanks to *Vanity Fair* editor Frank Crowninshield, who paid her a regular wage for pieces she would send from there. In the two years she spent abroad, Nancy Boyd articles comprised her chief bread-and-butter writing.

Second April, which came out in 1921, includes much of the same kind of poetry seen in earlier collections. There is the juvenile piece "Journey" with its youthful celebration of nature: "The world is mine: blue hill, still silver lake." The clear, childlike spirit that was such a true voice for Millay is also joyfully exercised in the prizewinning "The Bean-Stalk":

Ho, Giant! This is I!
I have built me a bean-stalk into your sky!
La,–but it's lovely, up so high!

In the same collection, the striking if simplistic image of "The Blue-Flag in the Bog" gives voice again to Millay's love of nature and elevates it as the only thing that makes heaven bearable to a child destroyed by a holocaust.

Even in the familiar themes, there is a pervading sense of disenchantment in the volume. "Spring" asks, "To what purpose, April, do you return again?/Beauty is not enough." "Lament" gives a poignant sense of a family's loss of the dead father through skillful use of concrete objects:

There'll be in his pockets
Things he used to put there
Keys and pennies
Covered with tobacco.

Many readers were reminded of Housman's *A Shropshire Lad*. A more personal record of loss, the moving sequence "Memorial to D.C.," for Vassar friend Dorothy Coleman, culminates in a precise image: "Once the ivory box is broken,/Beats the golden bird no more."

Norman Brittin suggests that Millay's disenchantment with New York City is evident in the collection, especially in "Ode to Silence," a technically accomplished poem on the search for peace, containing the classical allusions and poetic diction which some readers praised and others deplored. Padraic Colum called it "nothing more than a literary exercise." Undoubtedly it reflected the mental state of the poet just before leaving for Europe.

Perhaps the most highly praised qualities of the collection are the maturing outlook of the poet who cries out for continued life through his work in "The Poet and His Book" and the deft musicality of such lines as "Suns that shine by night,/Mountains made from valleys" from this poem and "There will be rose and rhododendron/When you are dead and under ground" from "Elegy Before Death."

Early in 1921, at the beginning of her stay in Europe, Millay finished the five-act verse play *The Lamp and the Bell*, commissioned for the fiftieth anniversary of Vassar's Alumnae Association. It was published by Shay in the same year. The germ of its story is the Grimm brothers' tale "Snow White and Rose Red," but the play is fleshed out as an Elizabethan drama. At a medieval Italian court the two main characters, Bianca (Snow White) and the robust Beatrice (Rose Red), become sisters when their parents marry. Like the fairy-tale characters, the sisters are devoted to each other and remain so after Bianca's ambitious mother, Octavia, contrives to have Bianca's warm vulnerability draw King Mario away from Beatrice, with whom he is falling in love. The noble Beatrice never reveals her feelings for Mario to Bianca, and when her father, King Lorenzo, dies, she ably manages his kingdom. After a period of five years, in which Bianca has given birth to two children, Beatrice is attacked by brigands while out hunting. Mario, also hunting in the area, rushes to help but is killed by Beatrice, who mistakes him for one of her attackers. Injured herself, she is taken to her castle to recuperate and is soon visited by Bianca, who wonders why she has not come to comfort her. Beatrice confesses she accidentally killed Mario, and Bianca leaves, now doubly stricken.

In a dramatically charged, if contrived, final act, Bianca is dying and Beatrice has been imprisoned by the arch villain Guido, who has been responsible for much of the duplicity. He agrees to let her go to Bianca, who has sent for her, only after she agrees to surrender herself to him. The sisters are reunited just seconds before Bianca dies. Continuity of their attachment is assured when Beatrice takes Bianca's two daughters (echoes of themselves as children). In the final scene

Beatrice's wise fool Fidelio seeks out the mourning queen to tell her that Guido has been murdered by Francesca, the woman he had scorned.

This summary gives no suggestion of the multitude of characters–ladies and lords of the court, servants, pantomime players–that provided a suitable number of parts for the alumnae extravaganza. Probably only for such an occasion could the poet feel free enough to play with the themes of female platonic love as well as feminism so freely. Though the poet herself did not take the work seriously, the drama shows how she could take an essential human truth (the firm friendship of young girls) and make it her own. Unlike the Grimms' heroines, whose adventures in the story are symbolic introductions to sexual love, after which they take their destined places as wives, Millay's protagonists insist that platonic devotion is a genuine feminine trait that does not end when one reaches marriageable age.

Though more-recent commentators, such as Brittin, have deplored the stereotypes and contrivances, and though Millay herself thought the play would surely suffer in obvious comparison to Elizabethan works, Mark Van Doren, writing in 1921, found the drama delightful, predicting it would be "best remembered as a delicate riot of gay asides and impeccable metaphors, Elizabethan to the bottom yet not in the least derivative; it bubbles pure poetry."

In contrast to *The Lamp and the Bell,* the other verse play that was published in the same year, *Two Slatterns and a King* (1921), is an easily dismissed farce in regular four-foot couplets that Millay had both written and produced at Vassar. Borrowing again from fairy tales, she used the theme of the king seeking a suitable bride. He desires the tidiest woman in the kingdom, but because of an odd series of accidents, he mistakenly chooses Slut instead of Tidy.

Millay's European travels took her to France, England, Albania, Italy, Austria, and Hungary. These were years of adventure and discovery, undoubtedly, but they were also lonely ones for the poet. Both of her younger sisters married, and Arthur Davison Ficke, whose marriage was breaking up, had already formed a close relationship with Gladys Brown. It is not surprising that Millay accepted a long-distance marriage proposal from poet Witter Bynner, Ficke's closest friend. There is some question about the seriousness of the initial proposal. In any case, after a short period of time, both agreed that the match would not work. By the spring of 1922 Millay was able to bring her mother to Europe, boosting the spirits of both women.

Despite her ill health and concentration on the Nancy Boyd pieces in 1922, Millay did publish some poetry in that year, including a pamphlet of her poem *The Ballad of the Harp-Weaver.* Her efforts were crowned with a Pulitzer Prize for poetry in 1923.

Back in New York at a party in the spring of 1923, Millay was paired with Eugen Boissevain, a man she had met at previous Village gatherings, as lovers in a game of charades. Boissevain was a forty-three-year-old businessman and widower. Though the two had shown no interest in each other before, a strong attraction developed on that single night, and the two were married on 18 July 1923. If her public was surprised that the free spirit had succumbed to marriage, it could have no quarrel with the whirlwind way she went about it. Immediately after the wedding, Boissevain took his wife to the hospital for intestinal surgery. His fatherly solicitude was to be a trademark of their marriage, as Boissevain relieved Millay from the burden of everyday details. He was also an ardent feminist and had a high regard for the significance of Millay's writing.

The Harp-Weaver and Other Poems was prepared during her convalescence and was published in 1923 by Harper and Brothers, with whom Millay was to form a lasting business association. If readers were looking for a marked maturity or some fresh insights as a result of her European travel, they must have been disappointed, for most of the poems in the collection explored themes already closely associated with the writer. John Gould Fletcher summarily dismissed the title poem as "the unforgettable rhythm of Mother Goose, the verbal utterance of a primer–all used to deal out an idea which is wishy-washy to the point of intellectual feebleness...." The poem is the sentimental story of a little boy's mother, who dies one Christmas Eve, but not before weaving on "the harp with a woman's head" an appropriate legacy:

> And piled up beside her
>   And toppling to the skies,
> Were the clothes of a king's son
>   Just my size.

The poem has been seen as an allegory of the rich cultural gifts Cora Millay had given her children, even when necessities were difficult to ob-

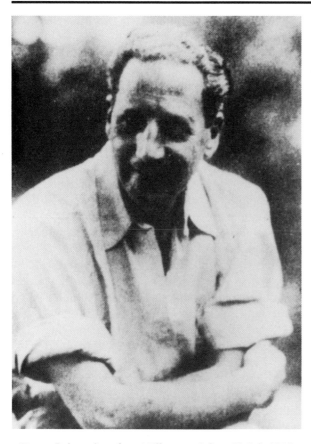

Eugen Boissevain, whom Millay married on 18 July 1923

tain. That may be the case, but the poem can also be seen as one of the more successful of the instances in which Millay used the child's voice. The simple quatrains, reminiscent of nursery rhymes, convey the child's sense of wonder, alerting the reader to the imminence of magic, and delivering the essential emotional truths possible only through the folk medium. In the third of the thirty stanzas, Millay introduces the unusual harp, and any child who knows "Jack and the Beanstalk" is aware that special magic is going to be worked. Likewise, while the conclusion may seem maudlin, it has the charm of the concluding image of Hans Christian Andersen's "The Little Match Girl."

The volume also shows the poet's continuing willingness to experiment with form while pursuing favorite themes, as in "Never May the Fruit Be Plucked," a statement about the inevitable staleness of love, delivered in free verse, with a characteristic image in its conclusion: "The winter of love is a cellar of empty bins,/In an orchard soft with rot." Those who found a mature, more-informed tone to the poems on the loss of love and the unwillingness to accept death were sur-

prised to find poems such as "The Betrothal," in which a woman coldly agrees to marry a man she does not love: "I might as well be easing you/As lie alone in bed." This tone is more appropriate to *A Few Figs from Thistles.*

Also in this collection are some of Millay's best-known sonnets. The seventeen-part series, "Sonnets from an Ungrafted Tree," gives a revealing picture of a woman returning to her estranged husband only to ease his death. Not only are the woman's memories and actions sharply focused, but the poems are filled with detailed pictures of homely New England farm life.

By far Millay's best-known sonnet is that which begins "Euclid alone has looked on Beauty bare." Millay had already received praise for her search for beauty in nature and in human beings, but here she transcends the simply personal, elevating beauty through the mathematical conceit. Mere mortals must forego the sight of beauty and hope at most for the sound of the feminized ideal: "Fortunate they/Who, though once only and then but far away,/Have heard her massive sandal set on stone." The Petrarchan octave gains auditory power from enjambment, as in "let geese/Gabble and hiss. . . ." The sestet with its startling representation of Euclid's vision as "light anatomized" is executed with a *cddccd* rhyme pattern, with the final "stone" throwing emphasis back on "Euclid alone" at the end of the eleventh line. Oscar Cargill testified to its continuing power when he wrote in 1941 that this was a poem one could return to and find something fresh.

The years that followed were busy ones, even though no major new work was published. Millay did a midwestern reading tour in 1924, finding to her disappointment that audiences knew only the poems from *A Few Figs from Thistles.* In the same year, showing an increasing public involvement in social issues, she read her poem "The Pioneer" at a National Women's Party celebration in Washington, D.C., to mark the anniversary of the Seneca Falls Equal Rights meeting. Shortly after, Millay and her husband set out on a lengthy tour which took them to the Orient, India, and France. Upon returning, they purchased a rambling old farm, which they named Steepletop, in Austerlitz, New York. It was a retreat from the city and home for the rest of their lives. Yet another peak in this eventful period was the first academic recognition of her poetry when Tufts University granted her an honorary Litt.D. degree in 1925.

In 1926 Millay was able to combine her three major talents and chief interests–poetry, drama, and music–in the libretto for *The King's Henchman*, an opera by Deems Taylor. The story recounts the tragic undoing of a tenth-century liegeman who betrays his lord's trust by marrying the woman he was sent to bring to the king, were she found acceptable. The libretto presented Millay with the kind of challenges she liked best: creating an authentic archaic flavor in the language while charging it with a genuine music and the freshness of wit, and conveying the heroic ideal of male friendship while delivering a sharp portrayal of a spirited female chafing at the confines of a male-dominated society. She succeeded, and the opera, performed by the Metropolitan Opera, was well received.

Ever sensitive to the problems of the human condition, Millay's demand for justice and equality increasingly took the form of social protest. She wrote to withdraw her name from the League of American Penwomen in 1927 because they had expelled poet Elinor Wylie, who had broken the rules of convention by living with a married man. She marched with protestors in Boston in defense of Sacco and Vanzetti and was arrested. She had an interview on their behalf with the governor of Massachusetts, but it was to no avail.

"Justice Denied in Massachusetts," the poem Millay wrote to raise public feeling against the execution of Sacco and Vanzetti, was included in her 1928 collection, *The Buck in the Snow and Other Poems*. It and the title poem employ nature images to cry against death, and both contain a bitter, poignant note in their suggestion that mankind itself is an accomplice to this waste, the first by suggesting we are willing to sit and wait for death, allowing the good earth to go to waste around us, and the second by the unstated presence of the hunter who has brought the buck to the ground. Some reviewers, such as Babette Deutsch and Louis Untermeyer, saw the collection as more of the same railing against death, but others, including Max Eastman, found more resonance in the lyrics. Though deploring the somber tone, Untermeyer was pleased by the experimentation with line, as can be seen in the final stanza of "The Anguish":

> The anguish of the world is on my tongue;
> My bowl is filled to the brim with it; there is more
>   than I can eat.
> Happy are the toothless old and the toothless

> young,
> That cannot rend this meat.

The poet insists that death, especially senseless death, must be fought against, and comfort and sense must be found in life. She found them, characteristically, in nature, the bobolink "Chuckling under the rain," and in the sublime order of music, as in the admirable Shakespearean sonnet "On Hearing a Symphony of Beethoven." In addition to her customary deft handling of form, the poet charged the poem with the intensity of the enraptured listener–"Sweet sounds, oh, beautiful music, do not cease!"–and was able to convey as well the dramatic moment of the concert itself, as other transfixed listeners for the moment bear no trace of their everyday pettiness.

Edd Winfield Parks, writing in the January-March 1930 issue of *Sewanee Review*, noted the emerging of a philosophy and considered the work a benchmark, predicting that she could not keep up the lyric intensity with the passing years.

Millay's next collection, published in 1931, was a bold undertaking. *Fatal Interview*, taking its title from a Donne line, is a sequence of fifty-two sonnets telling the story of a love affair. Recent evidence has indicated that an affair Millay had at this time with George Dillon, the much younger man with whom she was to translate Baudelaire's *Flowers of Evil*, was the inspiration for this tale of love won and lost. The first sonnet contains an allusion to Selene and Endymion, though they are not named until the final one. Love is elevated by these classical references, but the poet blends them with the voice of the modern woman, who offers love openly and with the freshness of a child. Love runs its inevitable course, echoed by the cyclical pattern of nature.

The sustained theme and its blending of classicism and sensibility gave a more reflective and universal quality to the work than in other Millay love poems, but this quality did not please all contemporary readers. Many missed the strong, purely personal note; others believed, with Allen Tate, that she had failed to probe the symbols she used as frame. But whether they saw the collection as a rejuvenation of the sonnet form or as a clever exercise in its manipulation, reviewers praised her technical performance. Sharp images and musical language abound, and both can be found in the single opening line of sonnet eleven: "Not in a silver casket cool with pearls." The same poem, an artfully constructed single sentence, displays also the poet's dramatic sureness

Millay in 1942 (courtesy of Vassar College Library)

of voice, as the guileless narrator offers love: "I bring you, calling out as children do:/'Look what I have!–And these are all for you.' "

The final sonnet of *Fatal Interview,* which Tate in his review judged her best poem to that time, is richly evocative, bringing together the picture of endlessly sleeping Endymion and a love-distracted Selene, devastatingly portrayed through fragmented images of the moon seen through clouds and reflected on the sea.

By the time *Wine from These Grapes* appeared in 1934, Millay had suffered the death of her mother and was experiencing increasing anxiety over the fate of mankind itself as global tensions escalated. These two events–one personal and one universal–dominated the contents of the volume. In light of their coincidence, it is not surprising to find a more objective viewpoint in her treatment of death. Not only was the poet mature in years, but she had traveled extensively and had obviously responded to the life she had viewed. The prevailing tone seems to be one of anger rather than the bitterness some contemporary readers sensed. In the controlled, predominantly Petrarchan sonnet sequence "Epitaph for the

Race of Man," she achieved a sharp picture of the history of living things, the best in man's nature, and the inexplainable certainty of his self-destruction. The style is rhetorical and contains some highly elaborated conceits, such as her comparison of man to a split diamond "set in brass on the swart thumb of Doom." Sonnet two, dealing with the dinosaur, is an equally astonishing but more effective picture that conveys the idea of the transiency of dominant life forms:

> His consort held aside her heavy tail,
> And took the seed; and heard the seed confined
> Roar in her womb; and made a nest to hold
> A hatched-out conqueror . . . but to no avail:
> The veined and fertile eggs are long since cold.

Reviewers such as Percy Hutchison and Harold Lewis Cook praised the sequence, many considering it one of her best. Association with "Epitaph for the Race of Man" enriches the collection's more personal poems alluding to the death of her mother. In "Childhood Is the Kingdom Where Nobody Dies" Millay, always attuned to the child's perspective, successfully captures the child's voice in free verse. The use of cataloging and extended line conveys the impatience of children who have to deal with adults who pay no attention to the important things: "To be grown up is to sit at the table with people who have died,/who neither listen nor speak." In the 1930s the whole world was filled with adults who would not listen but relentlessly prepared for war.

Millay spent 1935 working, both in New York with George Dillon and in Paris, on the translation of Baudelaire's *Flowers of Evil,* which was published in 1936. The chief feature of the translation was the retaining of Baudelaire's hexameter line. While the exercise must have appealed to the technician in Millay, the translation seemed to Allen Tate and Mary Colum a flabby English rendering that did not do credit to Baudelaire.

A more interesting project was under way in 1936, however: the controversial *Conversation at Midnight* (1937), the most experimental of Millay's works. The first copy of the work was destroyed in a hotel fire while the poet was vacationing in Florida, so it had to be completely redone. More than a hundred pages long, the work is the script of the after-dinner conversation of several acquaintances at the New York home of the independently wealthy Ricardo. The host is a liberal agnostic, and his guests include a stockbroker, a painter, a writer of short stories, a poet who is also a communist, a Roman Catholic priest, and a young advertiser. The opinions of these guests vary as much as their ages and professions. Although talk begins innocuously enough with hunting, it wanders inevitably to women and eventually to contemporary social issues, eliciting verbal attacks which very nearly lead to blows after the priest has left. At the end Ricardo pours them all a final drink, and they leave.

Though written in play form, the work has no dramatic structure and remains an exchange of diverging ideas, albeit one in which there is increasing tension. Millay used a variety of poetic forms in the delivery. At times the characters speak in sonnets, and in the humorous discussion of women their accents are those of Ogden Nash.

Peter Monro Jack and Basil Davenport applauded this distinctive break from her usual style, hailing the work as a faithful portrayal of the troubled period. Yet John Gilland Brunini, William Plomer, and John Peale Bishop were dismayed by the odd mix of line and rhythms and disappointed by the inconclusiveness of the argument.

In 1936 Millay suffered a back injury in an automobile accident. Added to her already frail health, it was to hamper her work for years. Her next collection of poetry, *Huntsman, What Quarry?,* did not appear until 1939. Its poems, composed over several years, included the same range of themes and styles that characterized the earlier volumes. There are pieces about lost love with the old sass, such as "Pretty Love, I Must Outlive You," and those with a more tolerant understanding of brief love, as "Song for Young Lovers in a City." There are also death poems, notably the sequence "To Elinor Wylie," who had died in 1928, and, of course, nature poems. The title poem, about a dramatic encounter between a young maid and the huntsman she attempts to dissuade from the chase with the offer of a warm bed, has philosophical implications in contrasting the feminine and the masculine approaches to life.

Robert Francis, recommending the collection as representative of the essential Millay, pointed to the dramatic quality of the poems—"the poet appearing in one part after another, effective in each"—as the key to success with readers. He missed, however, a consistent poetic vision. His comments surely were relevant for this volume and, indeed, provide a useful lens for viewing the entire body of Millay's work.

In the 1940s Millay could not maintain her former pacifism. The atrocities of Hitler's Germany forced her to take a different position, and she literally threw her talent into the war effort. She rightly subtitled *Make Bright the Arrows: 1940 Notebook,* but this did not excuse the prostitution of her talent or make the contents any more palatable. It must have taken every bit of Millay's considerable reading skill to make "If I address thee in archaic style–/Words obsolete, words obsolescent" approximate anything like poetry when she read it at Carnegie Hall in 1941. The intense personal voice had been a most successful idiom for Millay in the past, but lovers of poetry had to agree with Babette Deutsch, whose review claimed, "when she turns to political themes, the gay impudence of her girlhood, the sensitive curiosity of her more mature work, are lost in the shriek of a helplessly angry woman."

The Murder of Lidice, a propaganda piece written for the Writers' War Board in 1942, is an overly sentimental ballad recounting the German destruction of the Czech village through the story of two village lovers planning to marry on that very day.

The strain of these years resulted in a nervous breakdown in 1944, and recovery was slow. Several friends died in the 1940s, most notably Arthur Davison Ficke in 1945. Eugen Boissevain, her mainstay, died in August 1949. Though Millay never recovered emotionally or physically, she continued to write, planning another collection. Still at work, she died of a heart attack at Steepletop on 19 October 1950.

Mine the Harvest, published in 1954, seems a suitable concluding volume. The poet's voice often has the refreshing colloquial style that makes her letters so delightful to read, as in the untitled "I woke in the night and heard the wind, and it blowing half a gale./'Blizzard, by gum!' I said to myself out loud, 'What an/elegant/Hissing and howling, what a roar!' "

There is much close observation of nature in this volume, and, if there are hints of the wonder seen already in "God's World," the observer is seasoned by experience of many years, surprised that the now-dead snake had shared her garden all summer, and wondering if the seed of love can thrive in her stony heart as the acorn has grown into a mighty oak in "Here in a Rocky Cup."

This reflective cast, of the individual looking for an affirmation of life and the strength to endure one's declining years, is evident in such diverse poems in the collection as the untitled one beginning "The courage that my mother had" and "Tristan," with the dying lover propped against the thriving oak.

Millay's old spirit does break into the collection. "How innocent we lie among/The righteous! . . ." shows her feisty approval of taking love where it can be found. Her poetic philosophy is delightfully put forth in the sonnet "I will put Chaos into fourteen lines."

Contemporary reviewers thought *Mine the Harvest* too intellectualized for the woman who had been their poet of sensibility, but it seems a most fitting conclusion to the work of a sensitive individual who had always used her pen to let people know just where she stood with life.

By the 1950s Millay's voice was no longer reflective of the spirit of the times, and John Ciardi, in an article written shortly after her death, suggested, "It was not as a craftsman nor as an influence, but as the creator of her own legend that she was most alive for us. Her success was as a figure of passionate living." Yet in the same article he admits to being awakened in his youth to a "sudden sense of life" in her saucy lyr-ics and concludes by wondering if her place in literature will be as the reflector of youthful discoveries to be outgrown with maturity.

Ciardi was probably right in identifying youth as the audience with which Millay would always have the greatest impact. The ecstasy of first love and initial sexual experience, accompanied by the bravado necessary to survive its ending, and the stubborn insistence on life seem vital to every new generation, and her poetry continues to attract young readers able to find their feelings matched in her words.

Millay, however, should also be recognized for breaking through the boundaries of conventional subject matter for women writers, while showing the range and the depth of the feminine character. She achieved success in dramatic, operatic, and lyric composition, and her best sonnets demonstrate a masterful handling of form.

Brittin, in his revised *Edna St. Vincent Millay,* blames modernist editors of anthologies for much of the neglect of the poet in the 1950s and 1960s. Judith Nierman's 1977 bibliography of criticism and Brittin's 1982 revision, along with other recent works, give testimony to an increased interest in Millay's work, which may lead to the much-needed consideration of her mature work.

With the prominence of women's studies in the 1980s, Millay's work has received some of the serious critical study called for by Brittin. The love sonnets and sequences (especially *Fatal Interview*) have provided a field for study of the female perspective in this traditionally male form. The most provocative study of Millay's sonnets is a 1986 article by Debra Fried, "Andromeda Unbound: Gender and Genre in Millay's Sonnets." Though Fried found no evidence to elevate Millay's work to a higher place in twentieth-century letters, she presents a convincing picture of a successful revisionist coming to terms not only with the historical traditions of the sonnet but also its gender assumptions. These new critics reaffirm the quality of Millay's craftsmanship while providing new insights into basic poetic forms.

Bibliographies:

Karl Yost, *A Bibliography of the Works of Edna St. Vincent Millay* (New York: Harper, 1937).

A detailed description of Millay's publications from *The Lyric Year* (1912) to *Flowers of Evil,* also listing of appearances and music, magazine writing, magazine portraits, criticism through 1936, and an appreciative essay by Harold Lewis Cook.

Judith Nierman, *Edna St. Vincent Millay: A Reference Guide* (Boston: G. K. Hall, 1977).
A useful annotated listing of critical works from 1918 to 1973, with a concise introduction highlighting issues.

Biographies:

Norman A. Brittin, *Edna St. Vincent Millay* (New York: Twayne, 1967; revised, 1982).
A competent survey of Millay's life, major poetic and dramatic works as well as critical response to Millay's work. The 1982 revision includes an abbreviated biographical section

and new chapters on Millay's prose works and her involvement with feminist issues.

Anne Cheney, *Millay in Greenwich Village* (University: University of Alabama Press, 1975).
Concentrating on the men in Millay's life, Cheney gives a sometimes tenuous psychological profile, blending Millay's writings with real events.

Papers:

The Library of Congress, the Berg Collection at the New York Public Library, and the Beinecke Library at Yale University have the largest collections of Millay's papers. In 1986 Frank Krome donated a private collection of about two hundred Millay works to Skidmore College.

Ezra Pound

This entry was updated by Carroll F. Terrell (University of Maine) from the entry by Wendy Stallard Flory (University of Pennsylvania) in DLB 45, American Poets, 1880-1945, First Series.

Places	Paris
	London
	University of
	  Pennsylvania
		Italy
		Disciplinary Training
		  Center (Pisa, Italy)
			Spain
			St. Elizabeth's Hospital,
			  Washington, D.C.

Influences and Relationships	William Butler Yeats Henri Gaudier-Brzeska Wyndham Lewis Harriet Monroe T. S. Eliot Robert Frost	Hilda Doolittle Amy Lowell Olga Rudge James Joyce Dante Confucius	Ford Madox Ford William Carlos Williams Benito Mussolini Ernest Hemingway

Literary Movements and Forms	Imagism
	Oriental Verse
	  and Drama
		European Literary
		  Tradition
		Literary Criticism
			Vorticism
			Modernism

Major Themes	The Past
	Tragedy of War
	Intellectual Perfection
	  vs. Reality
		Political & Artistic
		  Corruption
		Civic Responsibility
			The Dual Nature of
			  Passion as Inspi-
			  ration & Destruction

Cultural and Artistic Influences	Troubadour Tradition Spanish Culture European Military History	Neoplatonism Opera Music Composition	Romance Languages Medieval Gnosticism The Bible
Social and Economic Influences	Expatriation Anti-Semitism World War II	Economic Theories (Usury) Italian Fascism	World War I Monetary Policy

See also the Pound entries in DLB 4, American Writers in Paris, 1920-1939 *and* DLB 63, Modern American Critics, 1920-1955.

BIRTH: Hailey, Idaho, 30 October 1885, to Homer Loomis and Isabel Weston Pound.

EDUCATION: University of Pennsylvania, 1901-1903; Ph.B., Hamilton College, 1905; M.A., University of Pennsylvania, 1906; further study, 1907-1908.

MARRIAGE: 20 April 1914 to Dorothy Shakespear; children: Omar Shakespear, Mary (by Olga Rudge).

AWARDS AND HONORS: *Poetry* prize, 1914; *Dial* award, 1928; Honorary doctorate, Hamilton College, 1939; Bollingen Prize in Poetry for *The Pisan Cantos,* 1949; Harriet Monroe Award, 1962; Academy of American Poets Fellowship, 1963.

DEATH: Venice, Italy, 1 November 1972.

BOOKS: *A Lume Spento* (Venice: Printed for the author by A. Antonini, 1908);
A Quinzaine for this Yule (London: Pollock, 1908);
Personae (London: Elkin Mathews, 1909);
Exultations (London: Elkin Mathews, 1909);
The Spirit of Romance (London: Dent, 1910; London: Dent/New York: Dutton, 1910);
Provença (Boston: Small, Maynard, 1910);
Canzoni (London: Elkin Mathews, 1911);
Ripostes (London: Swift, 1912; Boston: Small, Maynard, 1913);
Gaudier-Brzeska: A Memoir Including the Published Writings of the Sculptor and a Selection from his Letters (London: John Lane, Bodley Head/ New York: John Lane, 1916);
Lustra (London: Elkin Mathews, 1916; enlarged edition, New York: Knopf, 1917);
Pavannes and Divisions (New York: Knopf, 1918);
The Fourth Canto (London: Ovid Press, 1919);
Quia Pauper Amavi (London: Egoist Press, 1919);
Instigations of Ezra Pound, Together with an Essay on the Chinese Written Character by Ernest Fenollosa (New York: Boni & Liveright, 1920);
Hugh Selwyn Mauberley (London: Ovid Press, 1920);
Umbra (London: Elkin Mathews, 1920);
Poems 1918-21 (New York: Boni & Liveright, 1921);

Ezra Pound (Sylvia Beach Collection, Princeton University Library)

Indiscretions (Paris: Three Mountains Press, 1923);
Antheil and the Treatise on Harmony (Paris: Three Mountains Press, 1924; Chicago: Covici, 1927);
A Draft of XVI. Cantos (Paris: Three Mountains Press, 1925);
Personae: The Collected Poems (New York: Boni & Liveright, 1926; London: Faber & Faber, 1952);
A Draft of the Cantos 17-27 (London: John Rodker, 1928);
Selected Poems, edited by T. S. Eliot (London: Faber & Gwyer, 1928);
A Draft of XXX Cantos (Paris: Hours Press, 1930; New York: Farrar & Rinehart, 1933; London: Faber & Faber, 1933);
Imaginary Letters (Paris: Black Sun Press, 1930);
How To Read (London: Harmsworth, 1931);
ABC of Economics (London: Faber & Faber, 1933; Norfolk, Conn.: New Directions, 1940);
ABC of Reading (London: Routledge, 1934; New Haven: Yale University Press, 1934);
Make It New (London: Faber & Faber, 1934; New Haven: Yale University Press, 1935);

Eleven New Cantos: XXXI-XLI (New York: Farrar & Rinehart, 1934; London: Faber & Faber, 1935);

Homage to Sextus Propertius (London: Faber & Faber, 1934);

Alfred Venison's Poems: Social Credit Themes, as The Poet of Titchfield Street (London: Nott, 1935);

Social Credit: An Impact (London: Nott, 1935);

Jefferson And/Or Mussolini (London: Nott, 1935; New York: Liveright/Nott, 1936); rewritten in Italian and republished as *Jefferson e Mussolini* (Venice: Edizioni Popolari, 1944);

Polite Essays (London: Faber & Faber, 1937; Norfolk, Conn.: New Directions, 1940);

The Fifth Decad of Cantos (London: Faber & Faber, 1937; New York & Toronto: Farrar & Rinehart, 1937);

Confucius: Digest of the Analects (Milan: Giovanni Scheiwiller, 1937);

Guide to Kulchur (London: Faber & Faber, 1938; Norfolk, Conn.: New Directions, 1938);

What Is Money For (London: Greater Britain Publications, 1939);

Cantos LII-LXXI (London: Faber & Faber, 1940; Norfolk, Conn.: New Directions, 1940);

A Selection of Poems (London: Faber & Faber, 1940);

Carta da Visita (Rome: Edizioni di Lettere d'Oggi, 1942); republished as *A Visiting Card,* translated by John Drummond (London: Russell, 1952);

L'America, Roosevelt e le Cause della Guerra Presente (Venice: Edizioni Popolari, 1944); republished as *America, Roosevelt and the Causes of the Present War,* translated by Drummond (London: Russell, 1951);

Oro e Lavoro (Rapallo: Tip. Moderna [Canessa], 1944); republished as *Gold and Work,* translated by Drummond (London: Russell, 1952);

Introduzione alla Natura Economica degli S.U.A. (Venice: Edizioni Popolari, 1944); republished as *An Introduction to the Economic Nature of the United States,* translated by Carmine Amore (London: Russell, 1950);

Orientamenti (Venezia: Edizioni Popolari, 1944);

"If This Be Treason . . . " (Siena: Printed for Olga Rudge by Tip. Nuova, 1948);

The Pisan Cantos (New York: New Directions, 1948; London: Faber & Faber, 1949);

The Cantos (New York: New Directions, 1948; London: Faber & Faber, 1950);

Selected Poems (New York: New Directions, 1949);

Patria Mia (Chicago: Seymour, 1950);

Literary Essays, edited, with an introduction, by Eliot (London: Faber & Faber, 1954; Norfolk, Conn.: New Directions, 1954);

Lavoro ed Usura (Milan: All 'Insegna del Pesce d'Oro, 1954);

Section: Rock-Drill 85-95 de los cantares (Milan: All 'Insegna del Pesce d'Oro, 1955; New York: New Directions, 1956; London: Faber & Faber, 1957);

Gaudier-Brzeska (Milan: All 'Insegna del Pesce d'Oro, 1957);

Pavannes and Divagations (Norfolk, Conn.: New Directions, 1958; London: Owen, 1960);

Versi Prosaici (Rome: Biblioteca Minima, 1959);

Thrones 96-109 de los cantares (Milan: All 'Insegna del Pesce d'Oro, 1959; New York: New Directions, 1959; London: Faber & Faber, 1960);

Impact: Essays on Ignorance and the Decline of American Civilization (Chicago: Regnery, 1960);

Patria Mia and The Treatise on Harmony (London: Owen, 1962);

Nuova Economia Editoriale (Milan: Vanni Scheiwiller, 1962);

A Lume Spento and Other Early Poems (New York: New Directions, 1965; London: Faber & Faber, 1966);

Être Citoyen Romain, edited by Pierre Aelberts (Liège: Editions Dynamo, 1965);

Canto CX (Cambridge, Mass.: Sextant Press, 1965);

Selected Cantos (London: Faber & Faber, 1967; enlarged edition, New York: New Directions, 1970);

Redondillas (New York: New Directions, 1968);

Drafts and Fragments of Cantos CX-CXVII (New York: New Directions, 1969; London: Faber & Faber, 1970);

Selected Prose 1909-1965, edited by William Cookson (London: Faber & Faber, 1973; New York: New Directions, 1973);

Selected Poems 1908-1959 (London: Faber & Faber, 1975);

Collected Early Poems, edited by Michael John King (New York: New Directions, 1976; London: Faber & Faber, 1977);

Ezra Pound and Music: The Complete Criticism, edited by R. Murray Schafer (New York: New Directions, 1977; London: Faber & Faber, 1978);

"Ezra Pound Speaking": Radio Speeches of World War II, edited by Leonard W. Doob (Westport, Conn. & London: Greenwood Press, 1978);

Ezra Pound and the Visual Arts, edited by Harriet Zinnes (New York: New Directions, 1980);

From Syria: The Worksheets, Proofs, and Text, edited by Robin Skelton (Port Townsend, Wash.: Copper Canyon Press, 1981).

OTHER: *Des Imagistes: An Anthology,* edited, with contributions, by Pound (New York: A. & C. Boni, 1914; London: Poetry Bookshop/New York: A. & C. Boni, 1914);

Catholic Anthology 1914-1915, edited, with contributions, by Pound (London: Elkin Mathews, 1915);

'Noh' or Accomplishment, by Pound and Ernest Fenollosa (London: Macmillan, 1916; New York: Knopf, 1917)–edited, with an introduction and translations, by Pound;

Guido Cavalcanti, Rime, Italian text, edited, with notes and some translations, by Pound (Genoa: Marsano, 1932);

Active Anthology, edited, with contributions, by Pound (London: Faber & Faber, 1933);

Confucius to Cummings: An Anthology of Poetry, edited by Pound and Marcella Spann (New York: New Directions, 1964).

TRANSLATIONS: *The Sonnets and Ballate of Guido Cavalcanti* (Boston: Small, Maynard, 1912: London: Swift, 1912);

Cathay: Translations by Ezra Pound for the Most Part from the Chinese of Rihaku, From the Notes of the Late Ernest Fenollosa, and the Decipherings of the Professors Mori and Ariga (London: Elkin Mathews, 1915);

Rémy de Gourmont, *The Natural Philosophy of Love,* translated, with a postscript, by Pound (New York: Boni & Liveright, 1922; London: Casanova Society, 1926);

Odon Por, *Italy's Policy of Social Economics, 1930-1940* (Bergamo, Milan & Rome: Istituto Italiano D'Arti Grafiche, 1941);

Confucius: The Unwobbling Pivot & the Great Digest, translated, with commentary, by Pound, *Pharos,* no. 4 (Winter 1947);

The Translations of Ezra Pound, edited by Hugh Kenner (London: Faber & Faber, 1953; New York: New Directions, 1953);

The Classic Anthology Defined by Confucius (Cambridge: Harvard University Press, 1954; London: Faber & Faber, 1955);

Sophocles, *Women of Trachis* (London: Spearman, 1956; New York: New Directions, 1957);

Love Poems of Ancient Egypt, translated by Pound and Noel Stock (Norfolk, Conn.: New Directions, 1962).

Ezra Pound's influence on the development of poetry in the twentieth century has unquestionably been greater than that of any other poet. No other writer has written as much poetry and criticism or devoted as much energy to the advancement of the arts in general. Nor has any writer been the focus of such heated controversy. More widely recognized than any other writer by his poet-contemporaries for his influence on their work, he has at the same time been the most widely and bitterly condemned by critics. Opinions about Pound run the gamut from uncritical adulation to vituperative hatred.

Pound's energy was prodigious, and he applied it to his self-appointed mission of revitalizing poetry and the arts in general with an almost obsessive single-mindedness. As the artist and novelist Wyndham Lewis said of him in *Blasting and Bombardiering* (1937), "there was nothing social for him that did not have a bearing upon the business of writing. . . . He breathed Letters, ate Letters, dreamt Letters." T. S. Eliot, Ernest Hemingway, and many others have written on Pound's unselfish dedication to his making new of the arts, to the way in which, if he thought artists had promise, he would go to any lengths to help them, with complete disregard for his own convenience and with no suggestion that they were in his debt as a result. In his introduction to Pound's *Literary Essays* (1954) Eliot explained that, for Pound, "to discover a new writer of genius is as satisfying an experience as it is for a lesser man to believe that he has written a great work of genius himself. He has cared deeply that his contemporaries and juniors should write well; he has cared less for his personal achievement than for the life of letters and art." Pound had an almost infallible sense for talent and genius and a remarkable facility for making contact with major artists, often identifying them before anyone else. He was both friend and literary adviser for many of the greatest writers in English of his time: T. S. Eliot, William Carlos Williams, James Joyce, William Butler Yeats, Marianne Moore, Hilda Doolittle (H. D.), Robert Frost, and Ernest Hemingway. In addition, he helped many other writers by getting their work published, by reviewing it enthusiastically, by introducing them to one another, and even by lending or giving them money.

Knowing that Pound spent much of his life in Europe, insisted that serious American poets should be thoroughly familiar with the great works of the European literary tradition, and denounced the actions of the American government during World War II, many people have thought him "un-American"—an adoptive European. But Pound always considered himself completely American, and, when he was in Europe, he exaggerated his American accent. He wanted American writers to know the heights of European literary achievement, not to be overawed by these, but to surpass them, reasoning that "when an American in any art or *métier* has learned what is best, he will never after be content with the second-rate."

Pound saw in himself the combination of two strong and contrasting American traditions. On his mother's side was the colonial family with its "respect for tradition," in particular his grandmother Mary Parker Wadsworth Weston who, through her mother, was a member of the same Wadsworth family that had produced Joseph Wadsworth (who saved the Connecticut Charter by hiding it in the "Charter Oak") and Henry Wadsworth Longfellow. On his father's side was the pioneer family with "the most rugged kind of idealism," in particular his grandfather Thaddeus Coleman Pound.

Thaddeus Pound's colorful career held a considerable fascination for Pound who, as a child, heard a good deal about how his grandfather had built three railroad lines, owned the second store ever opened in Chippewa Falls, Wisconsin, owned a lumber company and a bottled spring water company, was one of the founders of a bank, was lieutenant governor and then acting governor of Wisconsin in 1870 and 1871, a United States congressman from 1876 to 1882, and a strong contender for the post of secretary of the interior under Garfield in 1880. After 1928 Pound viewed Thaddeus Pound as the type of selfless public servant and as an idealist upon whom he could model himself.

In the true pioneer tradition, Pound himself was born on the frontier, in Hailey, Idaho, on 30 October 1885. His father, Homer Pound, ran the land office there, but the rough-and-ready atmosphere of the town seems to have been uncongenial to Pound's rather self-consciously genteel mother, Isabel Weston Pound. She claimed that she could not stand the high altitude any longer, and the family moved to New York in the late spring of 1887 during the Great Blizzard, behind

the first rotary snowplow. The family stayed first in New York, with "Aunt Frank" (Frances A. Weston) at 24 East Forty-seventh Street, and then, when Pound was three, at Thaddeus Pound's farm in Wisconsin. In June 1889 the family moved to Philadelphia, where Homer Pound was to spend the rest of his working life as assistant assayer at the United States Mint. They lived first at 208 South Forty-third Street, West Philadelphia, then at 417 Walnut Street, Jenkintown. In 1891, they moved to 166 Fernbrook Avenue, Wyncote. In addition to local schools, Pound at seven attended the Chelten Hills School, run by the Heacock family and founded by Annie Heacock, a suffragette, and at twelve the Cheltenham Military Academy, going from there to the Cheltenham Township High School.

In September 1901, shortly before his sixteenth birthday, he entered the University of Pennsylvania, where his major professor in English was Felix Schelling. At about this time he met William Brooke Smith, a painter and the first of a series of artists in whom Pound would take a keen interest. Smith died of tuberculosis in 1908, and that same year Pound dedicated his first published book of poetry, *A Lume Spento*, to the memory of this "first friend": "mihi caritate primus William Brooke Smith. Painter, Dreamer of dreams," as one who loved "this same/beauty that I love, somewhat/after mine own fashion."

In the summer of 1898 Pound had traveled in Europe for three months with Aunt Frank, visiting England, France, Belgium, Germany, Switzerland, Italy, and Morocco. In the summer of 1902 he made a second trip to Europe, this time with his parents. Back at the university he met William Carlos Williams, beginning a firm friendship which was destined to continue, despite a variety of standoffs, largely on Williams's part, until Williams's death in 1963.

Pound transferred to Hamilton College in 1903 and completed his degree there, receiving a Ph.B. in 1905. His study of Anglo-Saxon under the Reverend Joseph Ibbotson and the instruction he received from William Shepard in French, Spanish, Italian—and, by special arrangement, in Provençal—helped to turn his literary enthusiasms in a direction that would have a decisive influence on his poetry, criticism, and translations. He claimed that the idea of writing the long poem that would eventually be *The Cantos* came to him in the course of a talk with Ibbotson, and, when he finally decided how to begin this poem, he chose to present the subject of Odysseus's descent into the underworld in a verse form that would imitate Anglo-Saxon prosody.

During this period, Pound was still very much under the influence of his religious upbringing. His parents were very actively involved in the affairs of the Calvary Presbyterian Church of Wyncote, and Pound was to recall many years later, for one of the psychiatrists who interviewed him at St. Elizabeths Hospital, that he "read the Bible regularly up to the age of sixteen years" and was, between the ages of twelve and sixteen, an "earnest Christian." In 1909 he dedicated *Exultations* to the minister of Calvary Church—the Reverend Carlos Tracy Chester—and from the letters that Pound wrote to his parents from Hamilton College it is apparent that he paid close attention to the sermons delivered by the president, Dr. Stryker, and other faculty members. In 1903 Homer and Isabel Pound began missionary work among Italian immigrants in the Philadelphia slums, and by 1905 Homer Pound was superintendent of the First Italian Presbyterian Church of Philadelphia. Pound appreciated the value of his parents' "practical Christianity" and helped them with the children's activities.

Having graduated from Hamilton in 1905, he returned to the University of Pennsylvania to take a master's degree in Romance languages. He studied English again under Felix Schelling and Latin under Walton McDaniel, working on Catullus and Ovid and, on his own initiative, investigating the works of the Italian renaissance Latinists (who appear prominently at the end of Canto 5). Yet when he applied for a fellowship to do research abroad it was to work on Spanish literature—in particular the plays of Lope de Vega—which he had been studying with Hugo Rennert and which he intended to make the subject of his doctoral thesis.

During his fellowship year, 1906-1907, he did research in the British Museum and the National Library in Madrid. He was particularly impressed by Velázquez's paintings in the Prado, and he visited Burgos, where he allowed his imagination to take him back (as in Canto 3) to the days of El Cid. He also spent some time in Paris, where he discovered Joséphin Péladan's writings, which develop the theory that the troubadours were the guardians of a "mystic extra-church philosophy or religion" which dated back to the Eleusinian mysteries.

In 1907, after one more year of graduate study, he took a teaching post in Romance lan-

Ezra Pound, circa 1903 (courtesy of the Beinecke Rare Book and Manuscript Library, Yale University)

guages at Wabash College in Crawfordsville, Indiana. That summer he had become romantically involved with Mary S. Moore, and wrote to her from Crawfordsville that "you are going abroad with me next summer . . . we need spend no futile time in disputing the matter"; it came as quite a shock to discover that she did not share his assumption that they would marry. By then he had lost his position at Wabash—partly because of the scandal resulting from his having allowed a stranded traveling actress to spend the night in his rooms—and had definitely decided to go to Europe.

Shortly after this time he began his serious courting of Hilda Doolittle, whom he had first met in 1901. Beginning in 1905, when she entered Bryn Mawr, they had spent a good deal of time together, and, after Mary Moore made it clear that she did not intend to marry him, he became engaged to H. D. Although in *End To Torment,* her memoir of Pound, H. D. claims that he was responsible for the breaking off of the engagement, in *Hermione,* a lightly veiled autobiographical account of this period in her life, it is quite clear that her overwrought state of mind and her strong attraction to a female friend, Frances Gregg, were the real causes of the increasing distance between her and Pound. He had made and hand bound for her a small book of twenty-four poems, written between 1905 and 1907, which he entitled *Hilda's Book,* and after their engagement was broken she gave it to Frances Gregg to keep for her. Although the Hilda poems are mannered and archaicized—in the worst he descends to a strained "Miltonism" and describes the perfume of a "flower mortescent" as "Marescent, fading on the dolorous brink/That border is to that marasmic sea"—he was also capable in others of a lyric gracefulness and interesting variations of cadence. He later included four of these poems in *A Lume Spento,* and of these "The Tree" has earned a place among the best known of Pound's short poems, its allusion to the myth of Baucis and Philemon looking forward to the opening of Canto 90, the central canto of the Rock-Drill sequence of *The Cantos.*

Pound left Wabash College in January 1908, and on 8 February sailed from New York to Gibraltar (several of his experiences there are recorded in Canto 22). He then spent three months in Venice. Though he was very short of money, the city was a source of romantic inspiration for his poetry, and he collected forty-four of his poems and published them in Venice under the title *A Lume Spento* in June 1908. A strong undercurrent of studied medievalism of allusion and diction runs through the poems, which—when they are not ballads—are often in the manner of Robert Browning, Algernon Swinburne, François Villon, and William Butler Yeats. Several of them, such as "Plotinus," describe poetic rapture and show his fascination with a Neoplatonic state of visionary transcendence. "Scriptor Ignotus" is dedicated to K. R. H. (Katherine Ruth Heyman), a concert pianist whom Pound had met in 1904. She was on tour in Venice, and at this point was the muse who inspired Pound—in the persona of an eighteenth-century "Dante scholar and mystic"—to conceive a "great forty-year epic." Pound took *A Lume Spento* to London in September. It was reviewed favorably in the *Evening Standard* and in America by Ella Wheeler Wilcox.

In early December Pollock and Company published a twenty-eight-page pamphlet of Pound's poems, *A Quinzaine for this Yule.* In little more than a week the hundred copies of that print-

ing sold out, and Elkin Mathews brought out a second printing of one hundred. Between 21 January and 25 February 1909 he gave a series of six lectures at the Regent Street Polytechnic on "The Development of Literature in Southern Europe," paying particular attention to the troubadours and the renaissance Latinists. At the salon of the wife of Albert Fowler (who is the "Hamish" of Canto 18) Pound met Olivia Shakespear—a novelist, a first cousin of the poet Lionel Johnson, and an intimate friend of Yeats. He was invited to tea at the Shakespear home in Brunswick Gardens, Kensington, where he met Olivia Shakespear's daughter Dorothy, whom he would later marry. He was rapidly coming to know many of the literary personages of Olivia Shakespear's generation. In the spring of 1909 he met Laurence Binyon, Maurice Hewlett, Selwyn Image, Ernest Rhys, May Sinclair, Sturge Moore, George Bernard Shaw, and Hilaire Belloc. In April 1909 Elkin Mathews published Pound's third book of poems, *Personae,* with a dedication to "Mary Moore of Trenton, if she wants it."

While his association with these writers gave him the sense of having made contact with a part of the literary establishment, the contacts that would prove to have a direct and significant influence on his own writing were those he made with the younger group of poets which had gathered around the philosopher-poet T. E. Hulme—F. S. Flint, Edward Storer, Florence Farr, Joseph Campbell, Francis Tancred, and, on occasion Padraic Colum and Ernest Rhys. Hulme, who would be killed in World War I at the age of thirty-four, was the first to expound the aesthetic principles behind imagism and to put them into practice in his poetry. Hulme's ideas about the remaking of poetry in English were much influenced by his reading of French poetry and the philosophical writings of Henri Bergson, and Pound was impressed by the lectures on Bergson's aesthetics which Hulme gave in December 1911 and February 1912. As a consequence of his relationship with Wyndham Lewis, Pound later misrepresented the nature and extent of his debt to Hulme. Lewis felt a strong sense of rivalry with Hulme, begrudged him his "discovery" of the French neoclassicists, and suspected him of championing sculptor Jacob Epstein over Lewis himself. As Pound came increasingly to admire the vitality and revolutionary nature of Lewis's painting and writing, he started to side with him against Hulme. In "This Hulme Business" (*Townsman,* January 1939) he echoed Lewis's low opinion of Bergson, contending "the critical LIGHT during the years immediately pre-war in London shone not from Hulme but from Ford (Madox etc.) in so far as it fell on writing at all."

Although this is not a fair appraisal in any objective sense of the relative aesthetic influence of Hulme and Ford, it does convey Pound's consciousness of what the development of his writing owed to these two men. His association with Ford Madox Hueffer (later Ford Madox Ford) was an introduction into a literary circle of real distinction. Hueffer's *English Review* published the work of Thomas Hardy, Henry James, William Butler Yeats, Walter de la Mare, John Galsworthy, W. H. Hudson, Norman Douglas, H. G. Wells, Joseph Conrad, Hilaire Belloc, and Wyndham Lewis, and, in June 1909 it ran Pound's "Sestina: Altaforte" and in October "Ballad of the Goodly Fere." In May 1909 he finally met Yeats, becoming a regular guest at the elder poet's "Monday evenings" and spending his Sundays with Victor Plarr discussing the "old days" of Ernest Dowson, Lionel Johnson, and the Rhymers' Club. The "Siena Mi Fe'" section of *Hugh Selwyn Mauberley* (1920), in which Plarr appears as "M. Verog," gives the reader a good idea of Plarr's topics of conversation.

By July 1909 Pound had made arrangements to give a second series of twenty-one lectures at the Polytechnic on medieval literature. (This material was published in 1910 as *The Spirit of Romance*.) The lectures began on 11 October, and both Olivia and Dorothy Shakespear had signed up for them. On 25 October *Exultations* was published. The volume contains fourteen new poems along with thirteen from his earlier books, and it received largely favorable reviews although the praise was not as unqualified as it had been for *Personae*. Altogether, the speed with which Pound had attracted the attention of the London literary establishment was quite remarkable, and he was even noticed by *Punch,* which gave notice that "Mr. Welkin Mark [Elkin Matthews] begs to announce that he has secured for the English market the palpitating works of the new Montana (U.S.A.) Poet, Mr. Ezekiel Ton, who is the most remarkable thing in poetry since Robert Browning."

In early March 1910 William Carlos Williams was in London for a week, and, before he left for Paris, Pound took pains to make his stay as interesting as possible. On 23 March Pound himself left for Paris, where he stayed for two days with the pianist Walter Morse Rummel before

going on to Italy. From Verona he traveled to Sirmione on Lake Garda, where–as apparent in such poems as "Blandula, Tenulla, Vagula," and the first of the "Three Cantos" (which appeared in *Poetry* in June 1917)–he felt strongly attracted to the "genius of the place." He felt himself inspired both by the beauty of the landscape and by his strong sense of the past: he found himself thinking not only of the Sirmio of Catullus's day but sensing also those energies which the ancients had pictured to themselves as "Etruscan gods" and as "Panisks/And oak-girls and the Maenads." Pound, like Emerson, had "transcendental" intimations and found the Neoplatonic way of conceptualizing "the radiant world . . . of moving energies" to be helpful in conveying something of the quality of transcendent experience, which he presents graphically and dramatically by describing the apparitions of pagan divinities. "A god is an eternal state of mind," he said, who becomes manifest "when the states of mind take form."

Pound valued the Provençal and Tuscan poets highly, partly because of what he believed to be their Neoplatonic sensibilities: they were the exponents of an "unofficial mysticism"–an "ecstatic religion" that could be traced back to the Eleusinian mysteries and was reserved for an elite of highly developed intellect and sensibility. Where Christianity called for the suppression of the senses as the road to spiritual enlightenment, Pound felt that in the Eleusinian tradition, approach to the divine was *through* the senses–by refining the emotions. In the Tuscan poets and particularly in Cavalcanti Pound found a similar sensibility accompanied by a rigorous intellectualism–a sophisticated "conception of the body as perfect instrument of the increasing intelligence." Although his admiration for Dante remained unwavering, he was fascinated by the "intellectual hunger" of the less orthodox Cavalcanti and his ideal of a strenuous intellectual progress toward "The Truth." At Sirmione he set for himself the goal of translating all of Cavalcanti's poetry.

In April he escorted Olivia and Dorothy Shakespear from Sirmione to Venice and then returned, setting out again in the middle of May for Verona, Vicenza, and Venice, where he stayed for a week before returning, via Paris, to London. On 10 June 1910 he sailed for America and spent the summer and fall in Swarthmore, where his parents were staying, devoting most of his energies to his translations of Cavalcanti. By November he had written the introduction for *The Sonnets and Ballate of Guido Cavalcanti* (1912). In the late fall and winter he stayed in New York and spent time with Yeats's father, artist John Butler Yeats, and with the lawyer John Quinn, who would later be a valuable patron for Lewis, Gaudier-Brzeska, Eliot, and Pound.

On 22 November *Provença,* the first American edition of his poetry, was published, and on 22 February 1911 he sailed, via England, for Paris, where he spent a good deal of time with Walter Morse Rummel, discussing the music of the troubadours and Debussy. By June he was back at Sirmione and wrote in July of his plans for a study of philosophy from Richard of St. Victor to Pico della Mirandola. He made a brief architectural tour of Northern Italy with Williams's brother, Edward, and then returned to London, stopping at Milan and Freiburg-im-Breisgau to research troubadour poetry, and at Giessen to give Hueffer a copy of *Canzoni* (published on 11 July). Hueffer literally rolled on the floor at some of the stilted language, a response which, Pound later said, "saved me at least two years, perhaps more. It sent me back toward using the living tongue."

Pound reached London in August and the next month met G. R. S. Mead, a man of many talents and wide education. Musical and a brilliant mathematician, Mead was a lover of Greek literature and a student of Eastern religions. As head of the Quest Society–a group devoted to the study of gnosticism and theosophy–he invited Pound to give a lecture on the connection between medieval gnosticism and the troubadours. In 1901 Mead had published a study of the life of the neo-Pythagorean Apollonius of Tyana, and Pound would later devote Canto 94 to this "philosopher-hero."

In October 1911 Pound was seeing a good deal of Walter Morse Rummel and of Hilda Doolittle, who were both now in London, and he had his first meeting with A. R. Orage, editor of the *New Age,* who was to have a decisive influence on the course of his career. On the practical level Orage made it possible for Pound to continue writing poetry by regularly publishing his articles–and paying for them. Pound called him, in his 1934 obituary notice, "the man whose weekly guinea fed me when no one else was ready to do so, and that for at least two years running." Yet, most important, through his association with Orage, Pound was introduced into a circle of intellectual and artistic discussion which was more rig-

orous and pragmatic and hardheadedly practical than any he had been exposed to before.

Orage was originally a Guild Socialist, and the *New Age* lived up to its claim of being "An Independent Socialist Review of Politics, Literature and Art." A. J. Penty called it "a centre of free intellectual discussion which in our time has led to nothing less than a revolution in thought on social questions," and its contributors over the next several years were George Bernard Shaw, G. K. Chesterton, H. G. Wells, Arnold Bennett, Hilda Doolittle, Katherine Mansfield, G. D. H. Cole, T. E. Hulme, Wyndham Lewis, T. S. Eliot, and, of course, Pound. With his remarkable breadth of knowledge and vision and his judicious turn of mind, Orage provided a center of gravity for this wide range of intellectual activity. His own deep interests in social reform and religious mysticism, tempered by common pragmatic sense, by what Edwin Muir called his "incorruptible adherence to reason," had a profound effect on Pound.

The vista of new talents and interests that opened up for Pound as he became acquainted with the writers of the *New Age* circle was exciting and energizing. Pound had an extraordinary affinity for people of artistic talent or genius, and his almost unerring sense of genius in others was balanced by his lack of competitiveness. No talent, however formidable, seemed to overawe him; he felt no jealousy toward other writers whom he considered talented or any need to advance his work at the expense of theirs. He had an instinctive and unself-conscious conviction of his own poetic genius and never felt threatened by the genius of others. Pound's own creativity was quickened when he was in close proximity to other sources of creative energy, and he consistently took pains to be wherever this energy was most intense.

But for his later fascination for economics, Pound's wide range of interests was already established while he was still in America; yet in England and Europe he managed to find increasingly talented exponents of the arts that he admired. In the fine arts he had begun by admiring the paintings of his friends Frank Whiteside of Philadelphia and Fred Vance of Crawfordsville, Indiana, but in Europe he turned to the futurists and vorticists, to the paintings of Wyndham Lewis and Picabia and the sculpture of Henri Gaudier-Brzeska, Epstein, and Brancusi. After his friendship with Katherine Heyman, he became acquainted with Rummel, Olga Rudge, George Antheil, Tibor Serly, and Gerhart

Münch. From his early reading of the Neoplatonists, he graduated to the esoteric investigations of Yeats, Mead, and Allen Upward, another *New Age* writer whose work *The Divine Mystery* (1913) impressed Pound deeply.

Pound's first series for Orage was "I Gather the Limbs of Osiris" (30 November 1911-22 February 1912), and, interestingly, the first of its twelve parts was a translation of the Anglo-Saxon poem "The Seafarer," which his biographer Noel Stock calls "the first clear sign of major ability." The "Osiris" articles and "Credo" (December 1911) set out Pound's new poetic program. In "Credo" he wrote of his belief in an "absolute rhythm" in poetry which "corresponds exactly to the . . . shade of emotion to be expressed"; that "the proper and perfect symbol is the natural object"; that "technique is the test of a man's sincerity," which means "the trampling down of every convention that impedes or obscures . . . the precise rendering of the impulse." He predicted a new poetry that would be "harder and saner . . . 'nearer the bone'. . . . austere, direct, free from emotional slither." These formulations show Pound becoming increasingly clear about the possibilities, suggested by Hulme's aesthetic theories, for innovation in his own poetry. In fact, it was in his note to accompany Hulme's *Complete Poetical Works* (published at the end of *Ripostes*, 1912) that Pound first used the label *Les Imagistes,* whom he identified as "the descendants of the forgotten school of 1909." Before he wrote this note, in about April 1912, Pound, Doolittle, and Richard Aldington had agreed upon three "imagist" principles: direct treatment of the subject, no superfluous words, and poetic rhythm based on the musical phrase and not on "strictness of the metronome." After a walking tour of "troubadour country," Pound was in London in August refining his ideas about poetry in light of Flint's long "Contemporary French Poetry" in that month's *Poetry Review.* Harriet Monroe's invitation to Pound to work on her projected Chicago magazine, *Poetry,* no doubt spurred Pound on. In the following months he sent her poems by Doolittle (which he signed "H. D. Imagiste," thus giving her her pen name) and by Yeats, and prose publicizing the *Imagistes:* a long letter ("Status rerum," published in the January 1913 issue), a self-interview attributed to F. S. Flint, and his celebrated "A Few Don'ts by an Imagiste" (both in the March issue). At this time, he met Robert Frost (through Flint) and reviewed Frost's first book, *A Boy's Will,* enthusiastically in *Poetry* (May

1913). He also got verse by Williams published in the *Poetry Review* (October 1912), *Poetry* (June 1913), the *Egoist* (March, August, and December 1914), and elsewhere.

Meanwhile, *Ripostes* had been published in October 1912 by Swift and Company, but the firm failed the next month, and Elkin Mathews took over the bound copies and sheets of the book, bringing out *Canzoni & Ripostes of Ezra Pound* in May 1913 and *Ripostes* alone in April 1915. Hueffer's "roll on the floor" had impressed upon Pound the need to wean himself from his mannered style, and he worked hard in the years between 1911 and 1920 until he had found his own, distinctive voice. The main weakness of the earlier verse had been its inclination to looseness and lack of inevitability. Its presentation tended to the expository and the movement of the verse to a simple forward flow. For presentation he would come to the view that "the natural object is always the *adequate* symbol" (*Poetry,* March 1913), and in the matter of verse flow he would learn how to energize his poems through the use of tension. The act of translating "The Seafarer" from Anglo-Saxon helped by requiring him to work both with the very rigid prosody of the original (with its pattern of three strongly stressed alliterating words in each line and breaks both in the middle and at the end of each line), and also with the tension between the original Anglo-Saxon vocabulary and his own modern (although archaized) English, which sometimes echoed the words of the original and sometimes could not. His close analysis, also in 1911, of Arnaut Daniel's Provençal verse with its short lines, complex rhyme schemes, and its frequently brisk, staccato, and sometimes even clashing sound patterns provided additional training in tightening up his own verbal looseness. Also, by becoming aware of the extent and persistence of the evocative power of the broken form of Greek poems that have survived only on parchment scraps and fragments, he learned that "less could be more," that he could write a more powerful poem by suggesting rather than stating, by leaving gaps and requiring his readers to exercise their imaginations in making connections and visualizing for themselves.

Already, in *Ripostes,* "The Return" shows the effectiveness of combining openness and incompletedness of form and of presentation with various kinds of tension between opposites—in this instance between how the subjects of the poem were and how they are, between the differ-

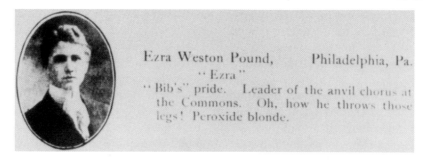

Ezra Weston Pound,   Philadelphia, Pa.
" Ezra "
" Bib's" pride. Leader of the anvil chorus at
the Commons. Oh, how he throws those
legs! Peroxide blonde.

Pound in his college yearbook, the Hamiltonian. *He graduated from Hamilton College in 1905.*

ent kinds of meter associated with these two states and between our expectations of forward movement in the verse and the counterforce of hesitation and partial reversal. His efforts in this volume to pare away his esoteric and archaic vocabulary and simplify his verse to greater concision and directness, seeking the "luminous detail," find their first full achievement in "Contemporania" (*Poetry,* April 1913), a group of poems including the much-anthologized "In a Station of the Metro." Attributing this technical breakthrough to the extreme brevity of the Japanese haiku (in an essay significantly titled "How I Began"), Pound pointed to a new area of interest and technical resource: Chinese and Japanese writing. His interest in current French writing was unabated, however; witness his decision in April 1913 to meet in person the group of writers surrounding Charles Vildrac and Jules Romains. He later wrote a seven-part series on this group for the *New Age* ("The Approach to Paris," 4 September-16 October 1913) and reviewed *Odes et Prières,* by Romains, for *Poetry* (August 1913). He learned from them a sense of indebtedness to Rémy de Gourmont. He also met John Gould Fletcher and Skipwith Cannell in Paris before he left for Sirmione and Venice, where he spent some time with Doolittle, her parents, and Aldington. From here he returned to London via Munich.

Back in London, Pound's association with Frost came to an abrupt end when Pound sent out "The Death of the Hired Man" to the *Smart Set* without bothering to consult Frost first. Characteristically, Frost's annoyance in no way lessened Pound's resolve to promote the older poet's work, and he wrote a favorable review of *A Boy's Will* for the *New Freewoman* (later the *Egoist*), for which he became literary editor in August. The *New Freewoman* published "The Serious Artist" (15 October-15 November 1913), an important statement of Pound's growing economic and politi-

cal concerns. Concurrently, despite his distaste for D. H. Lawrence personally and for what seemed to him an excessively confessional impulse in *Love Poems and Others* (1913), Pound publicized Lawrence's work by reviewing it in *Poetry* (July) and sending poems by Lawrence to both *Poetry* and the *Smart Set.* He told Harriet Weaver that "If I were an editor I should probably accept his work without reading it. As a prose writer I grant him first place among the younger men."

Pound even persuaded Yeats to consider his call for greater directness and simplicity in poetry, and Yeats was prepared to rethink his own poetic practice to some extent in the light of Pound's ideas. On 3 January 1913 he had written to Lady Gregory that Pound "helps me to get back to the definite and concrete away from modern abstractions. To talk over a poem with him is like getting you to put a sentence into dialect. All becomes clear and natural"; and, Yeats added, he was "writing with new confidence having got Milton off my back." In November of that year, Yeats invited Pound to stay with him for three months at Stone Cottage, Coleman's Hatch, in Sussex, where, in addition to working on their own poetry, they spent a good deal of time following up Yeats's interest in a comparison of Irish folklore and mythology with those of other countries. It was here that Pound first heard of James Joyce, and when Yeats found him a copy of Joyce's poem "I Hear An Army Charging" Pound immediately got permission from Joyce to include it in his anthology *Des Imagistes* which appeared in February 1914 as a number of the *Glebe* and was published as a book in March in the United States and in April in London. It was Pound who persuaded Harriet Weaver to run Joyce's *A Portrait of the Artist as a Young Man* serially in the *Egoist.*

At Stone Cottage, Pound was also busy making his own rendering of the Japanese Nō play *Nishikigi* from a verbatim translation made by

Ernest Fenollosa, an American who had taught rhetoric in Japan and was finally made Imperial Commissioner of Art in Tokyo. He had died in 1908, and, after his widow came to know Pound in 1913, she chose him as her husband's literary executor and entrusted to him sixteen notebooks of research on and translations of Chinese and Japanese works, as well as an essay, "The Chinese Written Character as a Medium for Poetry." Pound's version of *Nishikigi* appeared in *Poetry* for May 1914.

Pound had, meanwhile, been courting Dorothy Shakespear since 1911; it was not until 23 March 1914 that, overcoming her parents' objections, they announced their engagement. They were married on 20 April. On 18 January 1914 Pound, together with Yeats, Sturge Moore, Fred Manning, Plarr, Flint, and Aldington, had gone as a delegation to honor Wilfred Scawen Blunt for his services to poetry and as a champion of individual freedom. They had given Blunt a marble "reliquary" carved by the young sculptor, Henri Gaudier-Brzeska. Pound had met Gaudier in 1913 at an art show at the Albert Hall, and the friendship which developed between them would profoundly influence Pound's thinking about the arts and his attitude toward social issues. Gaudier was, as Pound saw, a sculptor of great promise; the body of work that he left—both sculpture and drawings—is an impressive achievement indeed. His death in action in 1915 at the age of twenty-three was a severe blow to Pound, not simply as a personal loss but as a symbolic instance of how those forces in a culture that lead to war simultaneously work to destroy the arts and culture itself. After Gaudier's death Pound dedicated himself with relentless determination to do whatever was in his power as a man of letters to prevent another world war. That he was bound to fail is only too clear now, but it was a defeat that he refused to concede until long after the cause was lost.

He particularly admired the fact that Gaudier's sculpture required the greatest precision and expertise because he cut directly in stone. When Yeats suggested that Harriet Monroe award £40 of Yeats's £50 *Poetry* award to Pound, this prize money went to buy two small Gaudier statues, as well as a new typewriter. When Pound sat for his bust—the "hieratic head"—he considered this one of the most memorable moments of his life: "Some of my best days, the happiest and the most interesting, were spent in his uncomfortable mud-floored studio.... I knew that if I

lived in the Quattrocento I should have had no finer moment, and no better craftsman to fill it. And it is not a common thing to know that one is drinking the cream of the ages."

Pound was to write many articles on art, the first of which was "The New Sculpture," a piece on Gaudier and Epstein, published in the *Egoist* for 16 February 1914. His continuing association with the *New Age* made him increasingly familiar with and informed about the works and views of the artists whose paintings were reproduced in its pages—Edward Wadsworth, David Bomberg, William Roberts, C. R. W. Nevinson, Walter Sickert, and most important, Wyndham Lewis. Lewis, a confirmed misanthrope, had made Pound an unusual concession in taking seriously his aesthetic judgments and in sharing his own views on art with Pound. Lewis, after a falling out with Roger Fry, had left Fry's Omega Workshops and set up his own Rebel Art Center, paying Pound the signal honor of allowing him alone to see his latest paintings, which were kept locked in a back room. Pound's admiration for Lewis's creative energy and expertise is clear from a letter that he wrote in March 1916 to John Quinn: "Lewis has just sent in the first dozen drawings ... and the thing is stupendous. The vitality, the fulness of the man.... Nobody has *any* conception of the volume and energy and the variety.... It is not merely knowledge of technique, or skill, it is intelligence and knowledge of life ... every kind of whirlwind of force and emotion. Vortex. That is the right word, if I did find it myself."

Vorticism, this new movement that Pound had named and Lewis had galvanized and focused, seemed to Pound an important step forward from imagism, which was likely to generate poems of fairly limited scope. Vorticism, rooted essentially in painting and sculpture, was concerned with a wider field of composition, with "lines of force," "planes in relation," and currents of energies which would be moving, yet in a patterned and efficient way, gravitating toward a point of maximum concentration of energy—a vortex. This new theory did not represent any departure from Pound's faith in the poetic power of the image itself, but now, when he tried to identify this power, he found that the idea of the vortex provided a useful analogy. The image was "a radiant node or cluster ... a VORTEX, from which, through which, and into which, ideas are constantly rushing."

No important poetry came out of his vorticist period, but Pound credited his association with these painters and sculptors with providing him with an entirely new sense of form. It is clear that his thinking at this time had a decisive influence in expanding his conception of the scope of his future poetry. The vorticists' emphasis on energetic and strenuous action and their attacks on whatever seemed stultifying in the society around them encouraged Pound to abandon the pose of the indolent aesthete which he had affected and to show his moral earnestness much more openly. The major vorticist assault on establishment complacency was Pound and Lewis's magazine, *Blast: A Review of the Great English Vortex,* with its eye-catching pink cover, "declamatory" typefaces, and its ridicule of whatever it judged to be inane and inert. It was very much in the vorticist spirit of cultivated outrageousness that Pound responded to Lascelles Abercrombie's call for poets to "return to Wordsworth" by challenging him to a duel. Abercrombie responded to the challenge in the spirit in which it was intended and, since it was his privilege to choose the weapons, averted the duel by deciding that they should pelt each other with unsold copies of their own books.

In the meantime, Amy Lowell was busy maneuvering herself into the position of "leader of the Imagists." Having read about imagism in *Poetry,* she had come to London in 1913 with a letter of introduction from Harriet Monroe to Pound. He found her "pleasingly intelligent," introduced her to Yeats, and asked for permission to include "In a Garden" in the *New Freewoman* and later in *Des Imagistes.* Their friendship cooled considerably when Pound became impatient because she declined to put up a large sum of money to finance a magazine which he could run for her. In July 1914 she was back in London with a plan of action. Two days after attending a vorticists dinner given 15 July at the Dieudonné restaurant in celebration of the publication of *Blast,* she gave her own imagist dinner at the same restaurant. Her plan was for a second and much larger "imagist" anthology for which contributors would choose their own poems. Pound, seeing that the result would not be imagist in any precise or authentic way, had no wish to have his work included and suggested that it would be more appropriate to call the book vers libre. She proceeded with her plan, and in 1915 Houghton Mifflin published the first of three anthologies titled *Some Imagist Poets,* with poems by Aldington, H. D., Flint, John Gould Fletcher, Lawrence, and Lowell. Pound dismissed this new pseudomovement as

"Amygisme," and his annoyance at Lowell's attempt to pass herself off as the mother of his "brainchild" seems understandable enough: her publisher was billing her as "The foremost member of the 'Imagists'–a group of poets that includes William Butler Yeats, Ezra Pound, Ford Madox Hueffer."

In September 1914 Pound met Eliot, and, as soon as he saw "The Love Song of J. Alfred Prufrock," he reported excitedly to Harriet Monroe that he had been sent "the best poem I have yet had or seen from an American" and that Eliot had "trained himself *and* modernized himself *on his own.*" He sent her "The Love Song of J. Alfred Prufrock" in October but was disgusted when she objected to it. It was not until the following June that, by a process of alternating anger and patient justification, he could persuade her, reluctantly, to include it in *Poetry.*

By that time he was working enthusiastically on the Fenollosa notebooks and in October 1914 published his translations of the Nō plays *Kinuta* and *Hagoromo* in the *Quarterly Review.* His poetic resources were challenged even more demandingly by the task of turning Fenollosa's rough translations of Chinese poems into polished verse, a task which he accomplished with impressive skill in the poems of *Cathay,* published on 6 April 1915.

As an imagist, Pound had discovered how to use for his own poetic ends the power of the carefully chosen image to attract to itself and focus and radiate from itself a complex of associations which would provoke a deeply felt and specific emotional response in the reader. As he worked with these Chinese poems, he saw how they also had been constructed around images in a way that showed their authors to have been fully aware of this principle of composition which imagism had identified and, in effect, rediscovered. Pound realized that the imagists had "sought the force of Chinese ideographs *without knowing it.*" Often in the poems of *Cathay* the focal point is an image of leaves, grasses, plants, or flowers described in a way that identifies a season of the year and in turn, at one further remove, highlights the mood of the poem's speaker. In "Song of the Bowmen of Shu" the passage of time and the falling away of hope is focused by the change from "soft fern shoots" to "old fern-stalks." In "The River Song" the coming of spring is made graphic by "the willow-tips . . . half-blue and bluer" whose "cords tangle in mist, against the brocade-like palace," and in "The River-

Merchant's Wife" the speaker's sorrow at the five-month absence of her husband radiates out from the lines "By the gate now, the moss is grown, the different mosses,/Too deep to clear them away!"

At Coleman's Hatch with Yeats again in the winter of 1914-1915–this time accompanied by his wife–Pound pressed forward with his researches into Chinese culture. He began to study Confucius in earnest, and in the three-part series "The Renaissance" (*Poetry*, February, March, and May 1915), as well as in the seven-part "Affirmations" (*New Age*, 7 January-25 February 1915), suggested that artists bent on a revival of contemporary culture could learn a good deal from the study of Chinese writings.

At the same time Pound was trying to give Joyce all the help he could. He arranged for Joyce to receive a grant of £75 from the Royal Literary Fund in September 1915, and in February 1916 he published a long article praising Joyce's play *Exiles* in the Chicago magazine *Drama*. He took every opportunity to insist on the greatness of *A Portrait of the Artist as a Young Man*, calling Joyce "by far the most significant writer of our decade." In June 1916 he got two more grants for Joyce, one of £26 and another of £100 from the Civil List.

Pound had been increasingly outraged by the spectacle of the war as he came to know more about it from the firsthand accounts of Gaudier. One of the effects of Gaudier's death in June 1915 was a hardening of Pound's attitude into a new grimness and urgency. He volunteered for service himself, and even after he was rejected by the British authorities, he later tried, again unsuccessfully, to use John Quinn's influence to arrange for him to serve with the American forces in France. A more important result of this sense of urgency was the new resolve with which he turned to the idea which he had held for several years of writing "a cryselephantine poem of immeasurable length which will occupy me for the next four decades." The following month he was working his way through William Roscoe's *The Life and Pontificate of Leo X*, which would provide much of the material for Canto 5, which he was already working on in mid December, having written early drafts of Cantos 1 through 3.

Finally, after a great deal of effort, he was able to find publishers for Joyce's *A Portrait of the Artist as a Young Man*. Harriet Weaver agreed to publish the English edition, and Pound per-

suaded John Marshall to bring out the American edition in place of a collection of Pound's own prose articles which Marshall had already accepted.

On 14 April 1916 John Lane published *Gaudier-Brzeska: A Memoir*. Pound's original Cantos 1-3 appeared in the June, July, and August numbers of *Poetry* under the general title "Three Cantos," but Pound continued to revise them, realizing that he had not yet arrived at the degree of formal precision that would be necessary if they were to provide a strong opening for his projected "cryselephantine" poem. When they appeared in the enlarged private and trade editions of *Lustra*, published in America shortly afterward, these cantos had already been revised and pared down. In March, with the financial backing of John Quinn, Pound was made a London editor of the *Little Review*, an important outlet both for his writing and for that of Eliot and Wyndham Lewis (now with the army in France). Pound and Eliot worked quite closely together between 1917 and 1921: Pound made the financial arrangements for the printing of *Prufrock and Other Observations* under Harriet Weaver's *Egoist* imprint, and their shared interests in Théophile Gautier and in Jules Laforgue led both to turn for a while to writing in more metrically regular forms. *Hugh Selwyn Mauberley* (1920) and Eliot's Sweeney poems were partly conceived as a "countercurrent" to "the dilutation of *vers libre*, Amygism, Lee Mastersism [and] general floppiness."

Pound was actively following up on his interest in music and, as William Atheling, was writing music reviews for the *New Age* (as well as art criticism under the pseudonym B. H. Dias). He was particularly concerned with reviewing troubadour music and with exploring the art of harmonizing lyric poetry with musical settings–an art which he felt had virtually died out since the time of Henry Lawes, Thomas Campion, and Edmund Waller. In Raymonde Collignon, he felt that he had found a singer who could do justice to the kind of marriage of poetry and music which he was working toward, and, when she gave a concert of Rummel-Pound troubadour songs, "William Atheling" covered this event for the *New Age* in May 1918. Collignon appears to be the woman "that sang me once that song of Lawes" to whom the "Envoi" of part one of *Hugh Selwyn Mauberley* is addressed.

Starting in December 1917 Pound began to receive chapters of Joyce's *Ulysses,* which he was arranging to have serialized in the *Little Review.* The first installment appeared in March 1918. On 29 June 1918 Knopf published *Pavannes and Divisions,* a collection of Pound's prose. In August Pound edited a "Henry James Number" of the *Little Review,* and between August 1918 and April 1919 the *Egoist* ran several of his articles on translators of Homer and of Aeschylus, one of which included his "Seafarer" rendering of Andreas Divus's *Odyssey* (which would later become the body of Canto 1). Harriet Weaver planned to publish these collected articles as a booklet, but Pound suggested that a more valuable project would be a first book of poems by Marianne Moore that had been brought to London without Moore's knowledge by H. D., Robert McAlmon, and Bryher (Winifred Ellerman), and it was duly published by The Egoist Ltd. in 1921.

After the February 1919 issue of *Poetry,* Pound was no longer its foreign correspondent; the most immediate reason for his removal after more than six years in the position was the correspondence over "Homage to Sextus Propertius," part of which appeared in the March 1919 issue of *Poetry.* Although his references in the poem to Wordsworth and to "a frigidaire patent" should be conclusive indications that Pound intended no verbatim translation or even fidelity to the original, he was attacked in *Poetry* (April) and the *Chicago Tribune* as being "incredibly ignorant of Latin." When Pound wrote to protest this criticism, in a letter to Harriet Monroe beginning "Cat-piss and porcupines," and then stopped writing to her, she took this action as a tacit resignation from his position with the magazine, and in November wrote to him to formalize it. Pound had several reasons for his highly idiosyncratic rendering of this Latin poet. His statement that he intended to "bring a dead man to life, to present a living figure" suggests a tribute, both to this particular poet and to the power of successful poetry which allows it to be revived many centuries after it was written. To some extent Pound was also using Propertius as a persona by means of which he could present his own feelings in the present—"certain emotions as vital to me in 1917, faced with the infinite and ineffable imbecility of the British Empire, as they were to Propertius some centuries earlier, when faced with the infinite and ineffable imbecility of the Roman Empire." Of course, Propertius is not Pound. Propertius's contentment with writing poetry in a minor key does not at all correspond to Pound's ambitious notion of the poetry that he himself was planning

to write. Pound was much less concerned with Propertius's point of view than he was with capturing his shrewd and easygoing tone of voice.

In writing the poem, Pound radically transformed his sense of history: where earlier he tended to adopt the stance of the poet drawn back to the past, even yearning toward its pastness, now he began to draw the past into the present. Instead of explicitly displaying his own emotions, he began to keep himself and his feelings well "behind the scenes," choosing to impress the reader with his discrimination through his artistry and with his self-confidence through his proprietorial attitude toward the great art of the past. Wordsworth and the Frigidaire in "Homage to Sextus Propertius" serve as rather extreme instances of this attitude, showing Pound flaunting the advantage which he automatically had by being alive and writing at a time when Propertius was dead. Pound was discovering how to draw on his love of the past for poetic capital without being nostalgic or sentimental and without fleeing from the present. "Homage to Sextus Propertius" is a major step forward in the process of establishing the assured poetic voice that was a prerequisite for a rethinking of *The Cantos.*

In May 1919 Pound and his wife traveled to Paris and then spent most of the summer in the "troubadour country" of the south of France, staying in Toulouse and visiting Nîmes, Arles, Avignon, and the ruins of Montségur in the Pyrenees, the site of the massacre of the Albigensians, where now there was "wind space and rain space/ no more an altar to Mithras." (Pound recalled this summer's touring in Cantos 48 and 76.) In September, when they returned to London, the *Little Review* began its serialization of Fenollosa's "The Chinese Written Character as a Medium for Poetry," and in October John Rodker's Ovid Press published *The Fourth Canto* in a limited edition of forty copies. That same month the Egoist press published *Quia Pauper Amavi,* which included both the early Cantos 1-3 and "Homage to Sextus Propertius." Although Eliot and Ford reviewed this book favorably, bad reviews in the *Observer* of 11 January and the *Spectator* of 7 February 1920 annoyed Pound.

Pound was writing drama and ballet reviews for the *Athenaeum.* Also, in March 1920, his review of Maj. C. H. Douglas's *Economic Democracy* appeared in the *Little Review.* He had met Douglas in 1918 and had come increasingly to share Orage's conviction of the extreme importance of Douglas's Social Credit theories. Also in

Victor Plarr, T. Sturge Moore, William Butler Yeats, Wilfrid Scawen Blunt, Ezra Pound, Richard Aldington, and F. S. Flint at Newbuildings, 18 January 1914 (courtesy of the Fitzwilliam Museum)

March he was made correspondent for the American *Dial,* and in April Boni and Liveright in New York published his *Instigations,* a collection of critical essays and the complete text of "The Chinese Written Character." By 3 May Pound and his wife were in Venice, where he began *Indiscretions,* an account of his childhood and family history which, although it renamed the people involved and affected to deal with their exploits in an "off-hand" or arch manner, was both factually reliable and revealing about the genuine interest he felt in his ancestors. Starting in May 1920, the *New Age* published *Indiscretions* in twelve installments (it was published as a book in 1923). Before *Indiscretions* began to appear in the *New Age,* Dorothy Pound's health dictated a move to Sirmione, and Pound prevailed upon Joyce to visit him there (accompanied by his son) on 8-9 June, during which time Pound persuaded him to make Paris his base, rather than Trieste.

In June Elkin Mathews published *Umbra,* a selection of Pound's early poems, and John Rodker published 200 copies of *Hugh Selwyn Mauberley.* The writing of the Mauberley se-

quence was a decisive stage in the evolution of Pound's thinking about his role as a poet. The sequence makes clear how the shock of World War I (and of Gaudier's death in particular) and the increasing insight into larger social issues, which he owed to his association with Orage and Douglas, had made his earlier exclusive preoccupation with purely aesthetic concerns seem now to be irresponsible. In the first poem of the sequence he writes of this earlier "aesthete-self," whom he calls E. P., and then disowns him, "killing him off" by calling this poem a funerary ode. In the remaining twelve poems of the sequence, he deplores the "tawdry cheapness" of standards of public taste in the arts; the way in which a writer such as Arnold Bennett, who caters to these standards, is successful while such a committed stylist as Ford is neglected; the hardships of the poets of "the Nineties"; and the death of any Dionysiac vitality or reverence for the mysteries. In particular he deplores the tragedy of the war and the disillusion that followed it, when those who did survive came "home to many deceits,/home to old lies and new infamy;/

usury age-old and age-thick/and liars in public places." Poem five leaves no doubt about the relative importance in his eyes of the lives of young men and the cultural monuments of the past:

> There died a myriad,
> And of the best, among them,
> For an old bitch gone in the teeth,
> For a botched civilization,
>
> Charm, smiling at the good mouth,
> Quick eyes gone under earth's lid,
> For two gross of broken statues,
> For a few thousand battered books.

In part two of the sequence he presents and decisively disowns Mauberley, the ineffectual, self-absorbed hedonist whom Pound intends to be the exaggerated projection of the kind of writer E. P. might have become had he kept to his purely aesthetic concerns. By creating this caricature, Pound was justifying his belief that a failure to make his poetry more socially conscious would be poetically self-destructive. Mauberley's energies ebb away until he is capable of "Nothing, in brief, but maudlin confession,/Irresponse to human aggression."

Pound's feeling of disgust with the disillusioned mood of postwar London and its hidebound literary establishment had already made him consider living elsewhere, and Paris seemed the most likely alternative. He was back in Paris from Italy in June 1920 and in July helped the Joyce family to settle there, but he still thought of London as his base and moved back there that autumn. One of the reasons for his return was the money he could make as drama critic for the *Athenaeum,* and so, when he was fired from this position shortly after arriving from Paris, he was angry at not having been told earlier. His *Dial* letters were increasingly full of praise for the artistic vitality of Paris; he was enthusiastic about his discovery of the poetry of Jean Cocteau, and in January 1921 he left England for France. Until April he stayed at St. Raphael on the Côte d'Azur and then settled in Paris at 70 bis, rue Notre Dame des Champs.

Pound's three years in Paris were transitional ones for his career—a time for reorienting his thinking about his future role as a socially committed writer and also for making some important decisions about *The Cantos.* After the stuffiness of London, Paris seemed to be a more energetic place, where it was easier to put ideas into action. In the United States the Society for the Prevention of Vice had managed to bring a halt to the serialization of *Ulysses* in the *Little Review,* and Huebsch as well as Boni and Liveright had decided not to publish it as a book; but in Paris, Sylvia Beach of the Shakespeare and Company bookstore undertook to publish it herself, and Pound took it upon himself to collect subscriptions. It was in Paris at this time that, with considerable help from Pound, Eliot's *The Waste Land* (1922) found its final form. *The Waste Land* manuscripts, published in 1971, show exactly the extent of Pound's contribution, why Eliot would tell Gilbert Seldes of the *Dial* that Pound is "the most important living poet in the English Language," and why Eliot dedicated the poem "For Ezra Pound/*il miglior fabbro.*" When Eliot was presented with the 1922 *Dial* award of $2,000, he wrote to John Quinn that his only regret was that the award had come to him before having been given to Pound.

In his Paris years Pound established his own assured poetic stance, developing the voice and control that would give unity and integrity to his individual opening Cantos and build up the momentum that would give an inevitability to the ordering of their sequence. We can see how radical a development was involved when we compare Cantos 1-3 as they appeared in *Poetry* to Cantos 1 and 3 of the poem as it now stands. In the early version, the poet's preoccupation with the difficulty of finding an appropriate voice is to a large extent the subject of the poetry. The original Cantos 1 and 2 in particular tend to be rambling, verbose, and, when he discusses his anxiety, prosaic, while his recurring indecisiveness deprives them of any forward impetus. The revised version uses the self-contained second half of the original Canto 3 for revised Canto 1 and cuts most of the original Cantos 1 and 2. The revised Canto 3 contains some greatly abbreviated sections from the original Canto 1 and preserves the passage on El Cid from the original Canto 2; the rest is very heavily cut indeed. (The sources of these, and of all the cantos, are recorded in Carroll F. Terrell's *A Companion to the Cantos of Ezra Pound,* 1980, 1984.)

Barbara Eastman has traced the complex history of the text; it is sufficient to note here that Cantos 4-7 first appeared in *Poems 1918-21* (December 1921) and the "Malatesta Cantos" (now numbered 8-11) in Eliot's *Criterion* (July 1923). They were later revised. These cantos focus on other kinds of difficulty: the dual nature of passion as inspiration and destruction (Canto 4), the apparent incompatability of any vision of intellectual perfection with actual reality (Canto 5). Pound clearly identifies with the dilemmas of people who struggle to get things done against great odds, perhaps with the hope of only limited success. In a climate of post-world-war disillusion, the achievements of Sigismundo Malatesta, a Renaissance patron of the arts whose life is the subject of Cantos 8-11, are a salutary example of what one man can do "outside the then system, and pretty much against the power that was, and in any case without great material resources."

Though Pound was living in Paris at this time, he was regularly visiting Italy, and in these cantos he is drawing on his Italian research. These years in Paris are more a source of Pound's musical than of his poetic inspiration: his friendship with the young American violinist Olga Rudge spurred his musical ambitions, and he turned to her (as well as to Agnes Bedford, concert pianist and lifelong friend of Wyndham Lewis) for help in composing an opera using the poetry of Villon as libretto. Unable to play the piano, Pound bought a bassoon, whereupon Lewis, suspecting Bedford's complicity in this purchase, asked her: "do you think it is an act justified by the facts of existence, as you understand them?" Pound also got help from George Antheil, whom he met in June 1923 and whose musical theories became the subject of Pound's *Antheil and the Treatise on Harmony* (1924). Once Pound finished his opera, he turned to composing music for the violin. An abbreviated concert version of *Le Testament* was performed in Paris on 29 June 1926; the whole work was broadcast by the BBC on 26 October 1931.

Pound's "On Criticism in General" was published in Eliot's *Criterion* in January 1923 and in 1929, revised as *How to Read*, was serialized in the *New York Herald Tribune Books* (it was published as a book in 1931). Here he distinguished three "kinds of Poetry"—*melopoeia*, "wherein the words are charged, over and above their plain meaning, with some musical property which directs the bearing or trend of that meaning"; *phanopoeia*, "a casting of images upon the visual imagination"; *logopoeia*, " 'the dance of the intellect among words.' "

There was much about the ambience of the expatriate life-style in Paris that Pound was bound to find uncongenial. The anomie, the directionlessness, and the hard drinking of the "Lost Generation" were antithetical to Pound's energy, earnestness, and optimism—he had no enthu-

siasm for or even interest in "decadence." He was, however, a strong advocate of sensuousness, and his 1922 translation of Rémy de Gourmont's *Physique de l'Amour; essai sur l'instinct sexual,* with an earnest and rather embarrassingly silly postscript, suggests that he felt the need to establish his willingness to enter into the Parisian spirit, and to demonstrate that he was, although no decadent, certainly no "Puritan."

In October 1924 the Pounds left Paris for Rapallo, where, after a while, they settled into a top-floor apartment at Via Marsala 12, on the seafront. In mid December they went to Sicily for several months, and in late January 1925 in Paris William Bird's Three Mountains Press published *A Draft of XVI. Cantos* in a limited edition with capitals designed by Henry Strater. Where the "Malatesta Cantos" celebrated Sigismundo Malatesta as patron and as survivor in a hostile time, Canto 12 provides twentieth-century contrasts and comparisons with a tribute to John Quinn which in tone foreshadows the "Hell Cantos" (14-15). Canto 13's serene introduction of Confucius sharply contrasts with the "Hell Cantos," in which Pound invents his own counterpart to a circle of Dante's *Inferno,* describing in repulsive detail the fates of corrupt politicians, war profiteers, financiers, agents provocateurs, slum owners, usurers, vice crusaders, newspaper owners, imperialists, and monopolists, as well as "betrayers of language," the pusillanimous, bigots, liars, the envious, the pompous, the litigious, bores, and—sounding like a holdover from *Blast*— "lady golfers." The serious offenders belong in either or both of the major categories—"obstructors of knowledge,/obstructors of distribution." With Plotinus taking the place of Dante's Virgil as his guide, the poet comes up out of this hell into the sunlight, and in Canto 16 finds himself at "Hell-Mouth."

Schooled by the Social Credit theory of Major Douglas, Pound had become increasingly certain that, were it not for the machinations of the "obstructors of knowledge" and "obstructors of distribution," the common sense of an informed public would have been alert to prevent a tragedy like World War I. Having expressed his outrage so stridently and graphically in the Hell Cantos, Pound settles in Canto 16 for a calm rehearsal of fact. Even the death of Gaudier, which had distressed him so much, is reduced to the matter-of-fact comment "And Henri Gaudier went to it,/and they killed him,/And killed a good deal of sculpture" and to the elegiac vignette of "an arm upward, clutching a fragment of marble," being sucked down into "the lake of bodies."

As the opening canto of a new section of the poem, Canto 17 (set in Venice) is almost a poetic counterpart to the new beginning which Pound had made by choosing Italy as his new permanent home. Although he had made Rapallo his home base, Venice would always be the most important "magnetic center" for him in Italy, personally as well as culturally. From the 1930s on, he spent his summers there with Olga Rudge; he would finally settle there after his return to Italy following World War II and his incarceration in St. Elizabeths and would eventually be buried there. Pound's relationship with Venice was not simple: although its inimitable architecture, painting, and sculpture was a great source of inspiration so that he found "in Venice more affirmations/ of individual men/ . . . than any elsewhere," the very excellence of its art challenged him in a somewhat forbidding way; for the very "completedness" of Venice seemed to exclude him and to send him off to another, less overwhelming setting in which he could create his own art. Two levels of reality alternate in Canto 17: the city itself is never seen in full daylight and so seems strangely artificial and insubstantial. The sunlit landscapes are settings for the apparition of the gods–of Diana, Dionysus, Hermes, and Persephone. For example, in Canto 21, while the city of the present is seen only in the half-light of sunset, the goddesses appear in a moonlight which blurs clear distinctions and the gods themselves have become "discontinuous."

The main event of Canto 26 is the arrival in Venice in 1438 of the Byzantine emperor and the patriarch of Constantinople who are on their way to the Council of Ferrara-Florence to ask the pope for military aid to defend Constantinople against the Turks. Politically a failure, their mission was culturally important for leading to the meeting of Gemisthus Plethon and Cosimo de'Medici and to the founding of the Platonic Academy in Florence. The canto is a focal point for this section of the poem (17-27), since in it appear many of Pound's important Renaissance characters who happen to be in Venice on this occasion.

Canto 20–Pound's warning to himself to resist the siren song of an escapist aestheticism–is an organizing center for the autobiographical material, and Niccolò d'Este, who made Ferrara a center for arts and letters during the fifteenth cen-

tury, is important in both, tying these focal points together. Cantos 18, 19, 22, and 27 deal with the problematical present, with 18 and 19 concentrating on crooked financial deals, monopolies, racketeering, and war profiteering. Canto 22 identifies financial success with crooked practice and castigates economist John Maynard Keynes ("Mr. Bukos") who, at a time when two million men were out of work, said that the reason for the high cost of living was "Lack of Labour." Canto 27 suggests that Europe, with no responsible political leadership, is drifting out of civilization.

Cantos 17-19 were published in the Autumn/ Winter 1925/1926 issue of the Paris little magazine *This Quarter*. On 9 July 1925 Mary, Pound's daughter by Olga Rudge, was born in Bressanone in the Italian Tyrol, and for the rest of this year and the next Pound did very little writing, concentrating mainly on music–on concerts by Rudge and Antheil and on the performance of *Le Testament*. On 10 September 1926 Dorothy Pound had a son, Omar, born in the American Hospital in Paris. On 22 December 1926, Boni and Liveright published *Personae*, Pound's choice of the poems that he wished to remain in print. In spring 1927 he started his own magazine, the *Exile*, which lasted for four issues until fall 1928. At this time, encouraged by Ford, he was considering a lecture tour of the United States–although nothing was to come of this plan–and corresponding with H. L. Mencken, refusing to acknowledge the fact that Mencken's unregenerate cynicism was the antithesis to his own earnest optimism.

In the fall of 1927 he turned, as he so often did, to Cavalcanti and to Confucius for reassurance that harmony and order were still possible despite all evidence to the contrary. He was working on a translation of Cavalcanti's *canzone* "Donna mi prega," and on 17 October 1927 he finished a translation of Confucius's *Ta Hio*. He had begun reading Confucius seriously in 1915, in connection with his work on Fenollosa, and he came increasingly to rely on the wisdom of the *Four Books* as a source of order and a stabilizing influence in a life that was to become progressively frenetic and chaotic. Originally he was particularly interested in the *Ta Hio* (*The Great Learning*) and the *Analects*. Confucius had studied the histories of China to learn about the operation of moral laws in the state, and Pound came to see the Confucian concern with civic order as far preferable to "the maritime adventure morals of Odysseus" and to the values of "the Homeric world . . . of ir-

Ford Madox Ford, James Joyce, Ezra Pound, and John Quinn at 70 bis, rue Notre Dame des Champs, 1923

responsible gods, a very high society without recognizable morals, the individual responsible to himself."

In February 1928 Yeats and his wife took an apartment in Rapallo. Pound, busy preparing an Italian edition of Cavalcanti's complete works, excerpted a part of his commentary for publication in the March 1928 *Dial* as "Medievalism and Medievalism (Guido Cavalcanti)" and sent a translation of "Donna mi prega" for the July number. *A Draft of the Cantos 17-27* was published by John Rodker in September. The final issue of Pound's *Exile* carried forty pages of Williams's writing, and the November *Dial* included Pound's article "Dr. Williams' Position." Williams wrote to thank him for his "great interest and discriminating defence of my position" and insisted "nothing will ever be said of better understanding regarding my work than your article in *The Dial*."

In early 1929 Pound was studying the works of the German anthropologist Leo Frobenius, who in Pound's view had revolutionized anthropological study by "reading" surviving artifacts to discern the general state of the culture that produced them. Pound was attracted to his notion

that the "reader" could become sensitized to the "Paideuma" of a period, which Pound defined as "the complex of ideas which is in a given time germinal, reaching into the next epoch, but conditioning actively all the thought and action of its own time." It was this "active element" that Pound was particularly concerned to identify and do all he could to strengthen, and his increasing conviction that postwar Europe was drifting toward another war made him turn to Mussolini as the only Western leader who, in his eyes, showed any sign of taking any active and constructive measures against it.

From 1930 on, Pound lived during the summers in Olga Rudge's house in Venice while Dorothy Pound spent time in England. He now began to devote much energy to an ongoing letter-writing campaign to impress upon any American politician or public figure who would listen to him the need for economic reform. In August 1930 Nancy Cunard's Hours Press published *A Draft of XXX Cantos* (with initials designed by Dorothy Pound), and when Cantos 31-33 appeared in *Pagany* for July 1931 his change of emphasis was clear. He had chosen to make the personal take second place to the issues of civic

233

responsibility and the need for economic reform. *Eleven New Cantos: XXXI-XLI* (1934) moves from the good sense of Jefferson and Adams to Jackson and Van Buren's fight against the Second United States Bank, and ends with a celebration of Mussolini's efforts to curtail the power of the "usurers."

In Cantos 31-33 Pound turned again to the technique he had used in the Malatesta Cantos, building cantos out of extracts from the writings of the characters he is presenting. Now he used *The Writings of Thomas Jefferson*, which Eliot had given him ten years earlier, and *The Works of John Adams*. Pound saw the letters between the two men from 1813 to 1826 as "a Shrine and a Monument" and used these and other documents to comment on human irrationality and the rarity of leaders with good sense. Quoting Adams on the "arbitrary, bloody and . . . diabolical" nature of absolute power, these cantos remind the reader that the evils of the problematical present, attacked in *The Cantos,* had been diagnosed long ago by the greatest of America's founders and point to Senator Brookhart of Iowa's attack on the Federal Reserve Board's practices as a contemporary instance of political integrity.

Canto 34, constructed from excerpts from *The Diary of John Quincy Adams,* and Canto 37, on Van Buren's role in preventing the recharter of the privately owned Bank of the United States, appeared in *Poetry* for April 1933 and March 1934 respectively. In January 1932 Edizioni Marsano of Genoa published *Rime,* Pound's long-projected edition of Cavalcanti. This project had engaged Pound's attention since 1928. Originally planned as a bilingual edition (which was abandoned when the Aquila Press failed), it finally appeared as a critical edition of the Italian texts (with a few translations by Pound). He sent a copy of this work to the University of Pennsylvania, but it was not, as he hoped, accepted in lieu of a doctoral dissertation. In the summer of 1932 he drafted a second opera, *Cavalcanti,* which was not performed until 1983.

In 1932 Pound had also been busy writing articles and newspaper items; between 1932 and 1940 he contributed more than 60 to the Rapallo newspaper *Il Mare* and more than 180 to the *New English Weekly,* which Orage began to publish in 1932 after his return to London–and to "full-time Social Credit"–from his stay in America. In the summer of 1932 Pound met the futurist Fillippo Marinetti in Rome and was impressed with his energy and enthusiasm. At this time

Ford visited Pound in Rapallo, and Olga Rudge made a transcription of their conversation. She translated it into Italian, publishing it, in an interview format, in the 20 August issue of *Il Mare* (her English retranslation appeared in the August 1947 issue of *Western Review*). Ford arranged for Farrar and Rinehart's publication of *The Cantos of Ezra Pound* (1933), a pamphlet of tributes to Pound by fifteen of his fellow writers, including, in addition to Ford, Hemingway, Eliot, Joyce, Hugh Walpole, and Archibald MacLeish. This pamphlet was to be advance publicity for the Farrar and Rinehart edition of *A Draft of XXX Cantos,* which appeared on 15 March 1933. Louis Zukofsky, who at Pound's suggestion had edited the "objectivist" number of *Poetry* (February 1931), traveled to Rapallo for a visit in 1933.

In 1932 Pound worked with F. Ferruccio Cerio on a film scenario about the history of Italian Fascism which was printed but not published that December (the film was never made), and on 30 January 1933, Pound was granted an official audience with Mussolini. The Duce, looking over a copy of *A Draft of XXX Cantos,* pronounced it *"divertente,"* which Pound chose to see as an incisive perception that his purpose in the poem was to "delight" as well as to instruct. Pound was similarly impressed when in response to Pound's comment that he wanted to put his ideas in order, Mussolini asked "Why?" Yet at least as important as showing Mussolini his poem was the opportunity this interview gave Pound to present the Duce with a list of suggested fiscal and economic reforms. Pound's interest in the Fascist regime extended only to its social and economic policies. Early in his regime Mussolini had made significant social and economic innovations, which understandably led Pound to see the Duce as the humane and responsible ruler for which he had been searching; yet he was clearly not justified in closing his mind, as he did, to the mounting evidence during the late 1930s of Mussolini's mental and moral deterioration.

Many of Mussolini's reforms of the 1920s were in accord with Pound's theories. Under the Fascists a country that was in many ways essentially feudal was modernized and industrialized according to a coherent, long-range program that had been largely worked out as early as 1921 and 1922. A deficit of four hundred million lire was replaced, by 1925, with a balanced budget, and by 1929 Italy's industrial output had doubled so that its rate of industrial productivity was higher than that of France, Germany, or England. After 1926

Mussolini created an "insulated economy" to protect domestic prosperity against foreign exploitation, and he centralized and increased state control of banking. His social welfare legislation was thoroughgoing and highly successful, and he also involved the government in support of culture and the arts. Pound saw the histrionic face of fascism—the parades, military drills, and rousing speeches—as unimportant window dressing, reflecting an Italian love of public display and having nothing to do with the commitment to social and fiscal reform which, to him, was fascism proper. He was annoyed that the British and American press dwelt only on the histrionic and easily mocked.

Right after his interview with the Duce, Pound began *Jefferson And/Or Mussolini* (1935), the purpose of which was to assure his reader that Mussolini, like Jefferson, was the "OPPORTUNIST who is RIGHT," that, because he faced such impediments to effective political action, he had to act unilaterally to accomplish any substantial reform, and that his good faith guaranteed that he would not abuse his power. Pound was completely sincere in these statements, but he did acknowledge that "any thorough judgement of MUSSOLINI will be in a measure an act of faith, it will depend on what you *believe* the man means, what you believe that he wants to accomplish." Although the book was written by February 1933, it was not published until April 1935, after having been rejected, Pound claimed, by forty publishers.

On 16 April 1933 Faber and Faber published Pound's short book *ABC of Economics,* the most lucid and helpful digest of his economic views. In 1934 he was busy working on *The Cantos* and writing more than one hundred articles on economic and political reform. On 8 October *Eleven New Cantos: XXXI-XLI* was published in New York. Canto 41, the last of this sequence, begins with a tribute to Mussolini for having provided grain, a safe water supply, and decent housing for large numbers of Italians and for his stand against usury, graft, and corruption. Although increasingly Pound's impulse was to put economic reform before purely literary matters, 1934 also saw the publication of *ABC of Reading* in May and of *Make It New*—a selection of his earlier writings on literature—in September. Also in 1934 James Laughlin came to stay in Rapallo as a student-disciple of Pound's. He took on the editorship of the literary section of *New Democracy,* the magazine of the American Social Credit party,

and called it "New Directions," the title he would later use when, also at Pound's suggestion, he began his own publishing company.

In 1935 Pound maintained his steady flow of articles on economics and wrote letters to anyone, particularly in America, who would give his fiscal theories a hearing. He had made contact with Henry A. Wallace, secretary of agriculture; with the historian and member of Roosevelt's "Brain Trust" W. E. Woodward; and with the Republican congressman George Tinckham, whom he thought would make a good president. But 1935 was to prove a crisis year for Pound. Mussolini's invasion of Abyssinia on 3 October revealed a new side of the Duce which would alienate the considerable sympathy for his regime that had existed up to that time in Britain and America. The invasion confronted Pound with a dilemma. It had been an article of faith with him that Mussolini was interested only in domestic reforms and was strongly opposed to war. The Abyssinian invasion showed that this belief was unfounded, but Pound had staked so much on his original notion of Mussolini that he could not bear to abandon it. From this point on he began to lie to himself about Mussolini's good faith, trapping himself in a mind-set which would require him to rationalize or to try to explain away increasingly blatant evidence that he had been mistaken. This was the beginning of an inexorable process of self-delusion that would lead Pound farther and farther away from contact with the reality of the political situation in Italy. The propaganda of the regime told him what he wanted to hear about the benevolent and peace-loving Duce, and he accepted it at face value. After Abyssinia he carried photographs of alleged Abyssinian "atrocities," which he eagerly presented to people as explanation of Mussolini's change of policy.

Hemingway had already made his dislike of Mussolini clear to Pound back in 1933, but the *New Democracy* for 15 October 1935 carried a very favorable review of *Jefferson And/Or Mussolini* by Williams, who was himself strongly committed to Social Credit. The main voice of warning about the Duce and the one that stood the best chance of getting Pound's attention was that of Orage, but to Pound's great shock, Orage died suddenly on 6 November 1935, shortly after having made a BBC broadcast on Social Credit, which Pound had been able to pick up on his radio in Rapallo. It seems as though, at the time when Pound most needed the counsel of common sense and restraint, the voice that could

Ezra and Dorothy Pound (courtesy of Omar Pound)

poleon, which, Pound claimed, had harmful consequences for all Europe by strengthening England and Austria, who gave the usurers free reign. Drawing up his case against the usurers in Canto 46, Pound adopted a new, grimmer mind-set, and the undertone of the whole sequence is elegiac: the celebration of sexuality in Canto 47 and of precise definition and the value of expertise in Canto 48 are muted by a sense of the transitoriness of human life and human achievements. In the meditative "Seven Lakes Canto" (49) the poet enters the "dimension of stillness," but through a rather claustrophic isolation, and in his "Lament Against Usura" in Canto 45–the most intense and heartfelt of this sequence–there is not rage against the usurers, as in the "Hell Cantos," but a concern for those who suffer from Usura's stranglehold over all the forces of vitality.

But Pound was not given to despair or inertia, and 31 July 1938 saw the publication of *Guide to Kulchur*. The book is not so much a reliable guide in any objective way to the cultural phenomena Pound considers as it is a revelation of Pound's state of mind: both of the way he thought and of what he thought. It shows clearly the split between the two very different states of mind into which he fell, depending on whether he was dealing with the arts or with economics and politics. This split persisted and widened over the following years: what he said in one state of mind gives at best a partial indication of how he thought in the other. What he said of the arts is generally reasonable, well considered, and consistent with his earlier views, and this is also generally true of his views about economic theory; but when he tried to account for the current economic and political situation, instead of reasoning carefully he rationalized and relied increasingly on a conspiracy theory about the causes of war and poverty: "We know that there is one enemy, ever-busy obscuring our terms; ever muddling and muddying terminologies, ever trotting out minor issues to obscure the main and the basic, ever prattling of short range causation for the sake of, or with the result of, obscuring the vital truth." More and more, Pound would come to see a deliberate and conscious conspiracy. Altogether, *Guide to Kulchur* provides a highly reliable insight into Pound's state of mind and his most pressing interests in the late 1930s. The similarity of his economic views to those of Odon Por, whose book *Italy's Policy of Social Economics, 1930-1940* Pound would translate in 1941, encouraged Pound to feel that there was a good chance

offer him this counsel most persuasively and with most chance of being heard was suddenly silenced. For Pound, Orage was irreplaceable.

Since the summer of 1933, Pound had been actively involved in organizing concerts in Rapallo with Olga Rudge and the pianist Gerhart Münch as "musicians in residence" joined by visiting musicians whenever possible. Pound and Olga Rudge were responsible for a revival of interest in the works of Vivaldi. In addition to presenting these works in concert, Olga Rudge traveled to Turin to catalogue the Vivaldi material in the National Library, and both she and Pound lectured and wrote articles on the composer.

In February 1936 Pound's best-known canto, the "Usura Canto" (45), was included with Canto 46 in the London magazine *Prosperity*, and on 3 June 1937, the complete *Fifth Decad of Cantos* (Cantos 42-51) was published.

Canto 50 follows the history of Tuscany from the time of the Medici until the defeat of Nafor Social Credit policies to be implemented by Mussolini, as did the ease with which he was able to get his articles on economics published in the Italian press.

In October 1938 Olivia Shakespear died, and Pound traveled to London to help settle her estate. He saw many old friends, including Eliot and Lewis, who painted an oil portrait of the poet and sold him some of his drawings. Shortly after his return to Italy, Pound decided to travel to America the following year, and in April 1939 he sailed from Genoa to New York, where he spent time with Cummings and with Gorham Munson of the American Social Credit Movement, whose *Aladdin's Lamp* (1945) is still the best book on Social Credit. In late April he went to Washington and met the senators and congressmen with whom he had been in correspondence. Williams, who met Pound in Washington by chance, wrote to Allen Tate that he found Pound "very mild, depressed and fearful." Since Pound's purpose in coming to America was to convey his insights into economics and the "real" nature of the political situation in Italy to politicians willing and able to act on them, he was clearly despondent at his lack of success. Back in New York in early May, he saw Ford, Katherine Heyman, Zukofsky, Marianne Moore, and Mencken. He visited Fordham University and Harvard, where he stayed with Theodore Spencer and was recorded reading some of his own poetry. In Cambridge he also met Archibald MacLeish, and he traveled to New Haven and to Rutherford, New Jersey, where he spent a night with Williams. At Hamilton College, on 12 June, he received an honorary degree, as did the journalist H. V. Kaltenborn, and Pound disrupted Kaltenborn's luncheon speech to protest what he saw as a misrepresentation of Mussolini. On 29 June 1939 Ford died in France at Deauville, and Pound wrote an obituary article, "Ford Madox (Hueffer) Ford; Obit," which was published in the August issue of *Nineteenth Century and After*.

Although the burden of all Pound's Social Credit theorizing was that under the present economic system periodic wars were inevitable, the prospect of war in Europe was one that Pound found unbearable. This belief may explain his refusal to "take sides" on the Spanish civil war, as Nancy Cunard's June 1937 questionnaire asked him to. By calling it a "sham conflict" he was trying to pretend to himself that it was not a "real war" and therefore that the cause of preventing war in Europe was not yet lost. By September 1939 this pretense was no longer possible. As soon as war started he wrote to anyone in America whom he thought could be instrumental in keeping the country out of the war, but he found little grounds for hope. In September both Tinckham and Mencken wrote to Pound that Roosevelt was determined to involve America. So desperate was Pound that he considered returning to the United States early in 1940 despite his failure to influence policy on his previous visit.

The Vivaldi "revival" continued, and Olga Rudge arranged a Vivaldi week (16-21 December 1939), sponsored by the Accademia Musicale Chigiana of Venice, in Siena. Some of the works performed were from scores in the Library of Congress and in the Sächsische Landesbibliothek in Dresden–the Dresden library destined to be destroyed in the firebombing–scores which Pound had arranged to have microfilmed. Olga Rudge also compiled a Vivaldi catalogue.

By September 1939 Pound had sent off *Cantos LII-LXXI* to Faber, who published them on 28 January 1940. We can see from the beginning of Canto 52, and from his publisher's cancellation of some of Pound's anti-usury lines, that his decision to concentrate in this sequence on Chinese history and on John Adams was, at least in part, a way of counteracting his growing tendency to fall into rantings against the usurers. This decision enabled him to consider present problems from the vantage point of the past and to adopt a more contemplative perspective on the discouraging prospect of the impediments to social justice. Although the straightforward chronological survey that the "Chinese History Cantos" supply makes them the most accessible sequence in the poem, they are only of a secondary level of intensity. In writing this sequence Pound, following Confucius's advice, surveyed the whole of Chinese history up to 1780. Inevitably, his commentary is rather cursory; by the middle of Canto 54, the prosaic style and the increasing use of slang and abbreviation suggest that he was moving hurriedly, superficially, and mechanically through material of no compelling interest. But the section on Confucius is of particular interest.

Instead of eulogizing Confucius, Pound presents the events of his life in an understated way which is consonant with the fact that in his lifetime there was great corruption and suffering and that he was denied the opportunity to put his ideas into action. Although he was able during his life to make so little impact upon social conditions, after his death his ideas went into action with enormous force, and Pound observes that "every durable dynasty since his time has risen on a Confucian design."

Distressed by the lack of impact that his own ideas were having, Pound felt an affinity with Confucius and, in the next sequence, with John Adams, who continued to reaffirm his disinterested principles throughout his political career even after it was clear, from bitter experience, how rarely political ideals could be enacted without being adulterated by considerations of greed, personal ambition, and "the spirit of party." Earlier, Pound had praised Jefferson as the man of action, the "OPPORTUNIST who is RIGHT . . . who has certain convictions . . . and batters and forms circumstance with them," but now that "circumstance" seemed increasingly intractable, Pound was more inclined to value the deliberateness, steadiness, and tenacity of Adams, whom he calls in Canto 62 "the clearest head in the congress/1774 and thereafter" and "the man who at certain points/ . . . /saved us by fairness, honesty and straight moving."

In these cantos Pound kept to the order of the pieces in *The Works of John Adams*. Cantos 62-65 show Adams in action; Cantos 66 and 67, taken from his political essays, show how he used his mastery of the law to demonstrate the legality of his countrymen's demands for guarantees of their basic rights and freedoms. Cantos 68 and 69 cover his diplomatic missions to France, Britain, and the Netherlands, and Cantos 70 and 71, taken from his letters, show him reflecting on the destructive effects of factionalism and on religion and human nature in general. Later, Pound would describe the "Brothers Adam" as "our norm of spirit" and as an "unwobbling pivot"–a particularly apt metaphor for the role of the "Adams Cantos" as a central fixed point for the whole poem. They look backward to Cantos 31-34 and Canto 37, and forward not only to the Thomas Hart Benton and Andrew Jackson Cantos (88 and 89) but to all the many passages in the later cantos that deal with the theme of law.

After Cantos 52-71 were finished, Pound had planned to change the emphasis of the poem from economics to matters of belief and philosophy–to write a "paradiso." He hoped that the American philosopher George Santayana, who was then living in Rome, would be able to answer some of his questions about philosophy, and he did meet Santayana in January and again in December of 1939. Pound invited Santayana to collaborate with him and Eliot in writing a book on

"The Ideal University, or The Proper Curriculum," but the philosopher declined, saying that while they were "reformers, full of prophetic zeal and faith in the Advent of the Lord" he was not, and so such an undertaking would be "impossible morally" for him.

Mussolini declared war on Britain and France on 10 June 1940, and in late 1940 Pound began to broadcast speeches over Rome Radio. He was still insisting that Mussolini was "for peace" which, by now, required him to rationalize away such overwhelming evidence to the contrary that his view of the international political situation seemed clearly psychotic. He had convinced himself that because Mussolini's main goal was economic justice, he must be antiwar also. For Pound, to oppose Mussolini was to oppose economic justice and peace, so Roosevelt and Churchill were usurers' puppets and warmongers, who had forced their countries into a war they knew they could not win. Mussolini's choice of Hitler as ally "proved" to Pound that the Führer was not a warmonger, so Pound convinced himself that the real villains were a conspiracy of international–predominantly Jewish–bankers. As his paranoia increased, what had been denunciations of bankers became anti-Semitic allegations about a Jewish plot to undermine gentile culture.

By this time he was so obviously speaking out of a personal, psychological compulsion that his views should not be called Fascist propaganda. If Allied listeners had been able to recognize the premises that lay behind Pound's cryptic, staccato commentary, they would have automatically dismissed his allegations as insane, but the abrupt turns of thought and changes of subject made it almost impossible to get any sense of a coherent argument at all. A friend of H. D.'s, who monitored these broadcasts for the British government, said they were "baffling, confused, confusing," and their "message, whatever it was" was not "doing any harm or any good to anybody." His intentions do not seem to have been treasonous, and there is no evidence that the speeches had any effect on the Allied war effort. Pound wrote to the U.S. attorney general: "I have not spoken to the troops, and have not suggested that the troops mutiny or revolt," and he was sincere in believing that the views he broadcast were not "incompatible with his duties as a citizen of the United States of America."

In 1939 and 1940 Pound had explored the possibility of getting back to America, and in the fall of 1940 he made preparations to leave Italy.

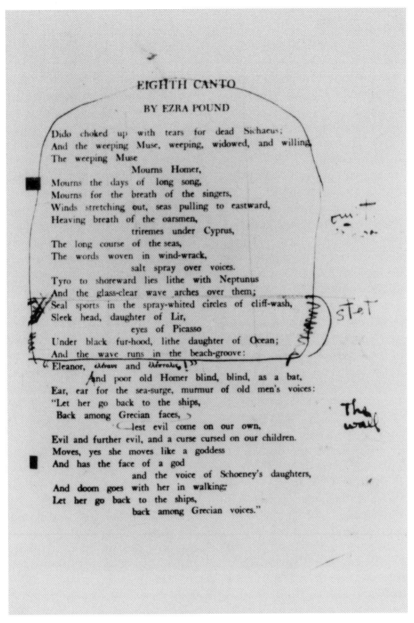

Page from the proofs of the original Canto 8 as it appeared in the May 1922 issue of the Dial, *revised by Pound as part of Canto 2 in* A Draft of XVI. Cantos *(1925) (used by permission of the Ezra Pound Literary Property Trust)*

In October he tried to get on a clipper ship at Genoa, since the only alternative route was through occupied France to Spain and Lisbon, but no American ships were sailing from Mediterranean ports, and after Pearl Harbor one impediment to his return was the fact that he would have to leave behind his parents, both in their eighties, his father with a broken hip that would not mend. When Italy's surrender to the Allies was announced on 8 September 1943, Pound, who had previously heard on the BBC of his indictment in July for treason, was already on his way by foot from Rome to Gais, in the Italian Tyrol, where his daughter was living with the peasant family by which she had been raised. It was a journey of 450 miles, and, although he was able to take a train from Bologna to Verona, he made much of the journey on foot, sleeping wherever he could and arriving with feet swollen and blistered from the ill-fitting walking shoes he had borrowed from the Degli Ubertis. They had also lent him a large-scale map, and it was only when he got to Verona that he realized that it was a military map and that, had he been caught with it, he might have been taken for a spy. His main reason for making the journey was finally to tell Mary what had been kept from her until that time—the fact that her mother was not his wife.

He stayed at Gais for several weeks and then traveled to Rapallo via Milan. He seems to have stopped on the way at Salò, where Mussolini had set up his "New Republic" that September, and during the next sixteen months he contributed thirty-five articles to *Il Popolo d'Alessandria,* one of the papers of the Salò Republic. In November at a big Fascist congress in Verona, Mussolini had presented a new economic program. Its emphases were exactly in keeping with Pound's own views, and it seemed further evidence to him that the Duce was the economic reformer he had taken him for.

Back in Rapallo he clung to the forlorn hope that the cause of economic reform under Italy's leadership was still not lost. Writing in Italian, he issued several manifestos, had posters printed bearing Confucian maxims and Social Credit slogans, and published six books and pamphlets with the Venetian publishing house, Edizioni Popolari. Of these, *Orientamenti* (1944), a collection of his economic and political articles; *Jefferson e Mussolini* (1944), a rewriting of *Jefferson And/Or Mussolini*; and a translation into Italian of Confucius's *The Unwobbling Pivot* were burned after the liberation, the title of this last—*Ciung Iung. L'Asse* [Pivot/Axis] *che non vacilla* (1945)—making it almost inevitable that it be mis-indentified as Fascist propaganda.

By the end of 1944 he had written, also in Italian, Cantos 72 and 73, in which the poet is visited by a series of ghosts. First the ghost of Marinetti admits that he wanted war while Pound wanted peace but that they were both blind, Marinetti lacking in self-knowledge and Pound blind to the times. Then the ghost of Manlio Dazzi appears. Dazzi links the two cantos together, having translated Mussato's *Ecerinis* (a place about Ezzelino de Romano, whose ghost speaks later in this canto) and having helped Pound to edit his Italian edition of the *Rime* of Cavalcanti, whose ghost is the main voice in Canto 73. Ezzelino, included among the tyrants in the *Inferno,* here rises up in rage to denounce the betrayers of Mussolini's Italy, while in Canto 73 Cavalcanti celebrates the courage of a peasant girl from Rimini, who, having been raped by a Canadian soldier, deliberately led a party of his fellow soldiers across a mine field, killing twenty of them as well as herself.

In the spring of 1944 the Pounds had had to leave their seafront apartment as it was requisitioned by the Germans, and they had no choice but to move in with Olga Rudge in Sant' Ambrogio on the hill above the bay. Here Pound was working on a translation of Mencius when, on 2 May 1945, two armed partisans ordered him to follow them to their headquarters at Chiavari. No one was interested in him there, but he was determined to turn himself over to the American authorities and asked to be driven to Lavagna. From there he was taken by MP's to Genoa, where he was interrogated by the FBI. On 24 May he was taken to the Disciplinary Training Center, north of Pisa, an internment camp for some 4,000 American soldiers, and confined in an additionally reinforced "segregation cell" with cement floor and heavy-gauge wire-mesh sides. The heat and dust during the day and the bright light trained specifically on his cell during the night, together with his anxiety about his eventual fate, were an increasing mental and physical strain. At his most depressed it seemed as though the sharp spikes of the cut ends of the steel mesh were a tacit invitation to suicide. He was, after a while, allowed a cot and a pup tent, but he was overcome by claustrophobia, panic, and fear and on 18 June was moved to a tent in the part of the medical compound reserved for those prisoners who were officers. He was allowed writing materials and given use of the dispensary typewriter once the dispensary was closed for the night, on the theory that "letting him write would be good therapy and good preventative medicine." The result was some of his finest poetry.

He had few books—the Bible, the Confucian *Four Books,* a Roman Catholic chaplain's field book, and M. E. Speare's *Pocket Book of Verse,* found in the latrine. He found other material in the details of his surroundings—men entering and leaving through the main gate nearby; soldiers on sick call, identifiable by their names stenciled in white on their green fatigues; the orchards, fields, and mountains surrounding the camp; the moon and stars, the sun and clouds, the morning mists, the birds on the stockade fencing, the grasses, wasps, and crickets. But most of all he could call on what remained "in the mind indestructible"—his memories of the past. The dominant mood of this sequence is meditative, nostalgic, and reverential. Prevented from acting, he was now freed from his irresistible compulsion to carry on his war against Usura—freed to rediscover his compassion, humility, and contrition and belatedly to begin the painful process of introspection and self-analysis. The climactic moment of the sequence is the poet's vision, in Canto 81, of the eyes of the women he has loved which, with their reassurance of forgiveness–"nor any pair showed anger"–lead him to his great affirmation: "What thou lovest well remains/the rest is dross/What thou lov'st well shall not be reft from thee/What thou lov'st well is thy true heritage."

At the same time his response to Confucius's writings became more personal and more profound. He became attentive to Confucius's insistence on the need for self-examination and self-criticism and to his advice on attaining self-sufficiency and serenity in adversity. He became interested in the *Chung Yung* (*The Unwobbling Pivot*), the most metaphysical of the *Four Books,* and he translated it into English in a way that "neoplatonized" it, making his description of the "process"–the "perfect way" of the *tao*–echo the radiation of the light of the Neoplatonic One.

It was more than four months before Pound's family was able to see him again. Dorothy Pound was allowed to visit him on 3 October and 3 November, and Olga and Mary Rudge came on 17 October. On the night of 16 November 1945, Pound was taken by jeep to Rome to be flown to Washington. Omar Pound, serving with the American army, arrived at the camp the next day to find Pound gone and carried the news to Rapallo. Pound was indicted a second time on 26 November on nineteen counts of treason, a motion for bail was denied, and on 13 February 1946 a jury found him mentally incompetent to stand trial. He was placed in St. Elizabeths Hospital for the insane. In July, Dorothy Pound came to Washington and moved into a basement apartment in a rundown neighborhood near to St. Elizabeths. She stayed there, attending to his correspondence in the mornings and visiting him every afternoon, for the rest of the nearly twelve years that he was there. On 11 February Pound's lawyer Julian Cornell filed a petition for a writ of habeas corpus for Pound to be released into the care of his wife. Although the District Court refused, Cornell was optimistic that an appeal to the Supreme Court would succeed, but on 13 March Dorothy Pound asked him to withdraw the appeal.

On 20 February 1949 the Fellows of American Letters of the Library of Congress awarded the annual Bollingen Prize to *The Pisan Cantos,* which had been published as a book on 30 July 1948. Before this time, reviews of the volume had been generally favorable, with no mention of anti-Semitism. In fact, the only anti-Semitic lines in the sequence, written before Pound had any knowledge of the concentration camps, are a reiteration of the ancient stereotype of the financially naive gentile outsmarted by the sharp practice of the Jew: "the yidd is a stimulant, and the goyim are cattle/in gt/proportion and go to saleable slaughter/with the maximum of docility" (Canto 74). After he was given the Bollingen Prize, however, the *Saturday Review of Literature* mounted an anti-Pound and anti-T. S. Eliot campaign, which soon turned into a broad-based and acrimonious controversy. Robert Hillyer's *Saturday Review* articles drew strong protest, and John Berryman circulated a petition protesting them. Eighty-four critics and writers signed this petition, and after the *Saturday Review* refused to publish it, it appeared in the *Nation* for 17 December.

In the meantime, Pound seemed reconciled to his imprisonment and quietly complied with the hospital routine. For thirteen months he had been in Howard Hall, the maximum security building for the criminally insane. His mental condition deteriorated under the strain of life in the "hell-hole," and he became claustrophobic and afraid of a complete mental collapse. A second application for bail was denied, but, as a compromise, he was moved on 4 February 1947 to Chestnut Ward, where the inmates were not dangerously insane. Now Dorothy Pound, who had previously been allowed to see him for only fifteen minutes a day, could spend the afternoons with him. Many admirers visited him over the years, mainly writers and critics, including Eliot, Williams, Cummings, Marianne Moore, Tate, Charles Olson, Robert Lowell, Elizabeth Bishop, Conrad Aiken, Langston Hughes, Mencken, MacLeish, Zukofsky, and Juan Ramón Jiménez. Not all who wanted to visit were allowed to come. Requests to visit had to be made in writing and cleared with Pound, and he absolutely forbade any interviews and was able to exercise a good deal of control over the topics of conversation.

During his years in St. Elizabeths, Pound was psychologically in limbo. His wartime views and state of mind remained virtually unchanged. Neither psychiatrists nor friends could diagnose his problem accurately enough to be able to help him to understand and overcome it, and, in the absence of any completely reliable source of psychological support, he was careful to avoid introspection and self-analysis as far as possible. While it might seem logical to assume that the circumstances of his confinement were a painful ordeal which threatened his mental stability, in one sense the fact of his imprisonment offered him considerable protection against the mental anguish that would have accompanied self-confrontation. Certain in his own mind that it had never been his intention to betray America, and, realizing that he was only in prison now because he had been accused of treason, he could see his present condition as punishment for a crime he had not committed. Since his imprisonment must have seemed punitive rather than therapeutic, self-accusation must have seemed redundant, perhaps dangerously masochistic.

Depending on the subject at issue, he chose evasiveness, self-protection, or affirmation, and these responses determine the three main levels of intensity of the cantos in *Rock-Drill* (1955) and *Thrones* (1959). The weakest passages are those born of evasion. Because he had not yet confronted his "usurers' conspiracy" theory of war, he automatically retreated to it under the pressure of anxiety or frustration or–as happened in St. Elizabeths–when someone like the self-avowed white racist John Kasper encouraged him, passing himself off as a serious economic reformer. By 1972 he would come to see that the main cause of economic injustice was human weakness: "re USURY: I was out of focus, taking a symptom for a cause. The cause is AVARICE." But he did not see this fact while he was incarcerated and, because he was still involved in rationalizing his conspiracy theory, he often settled in the cantos he was writing for commentary which is cryptic and fragmentary, reiterating in a rather pro forma fashion points he had made frequently before.

The passages written more from a self-protective than from an evasive impulse are more successful, for they follow closely written sources whose own integrity disciplines and tightens the writing, and in those he affirms those values which are the root of civic morality–benevolence, mutuality, filiality, and prudence. But the most successful passages–as fine as anything in *The Pisan Cantos*–are the more personal, reflective, and lyric sections, which affirm without question his faith in a divine force that is the source of all creative power and of all natural order. Borrowing from Neoplatonism, Christianity, and other religions, he visualized this force as

a feminine principle, calling it "Lux in diafana./Creatrix," but he could only apprehend it fleetingly, trapped as he was for so much of the time at "the dulled edge beyond pain" (Canto 90). In these passages the poet's struggle to raise himself above despondency long enough to capture a visionary moment of revelation is followed by the inevitable falling back to the drabness of life in the hospital, "under the rubble heap." The paradisal state of mind is authentic but "jagged,/For a flash,/for an hour./Then agony,/then an hour,/then agony" (Canto 92).

Pound called this force, as it operates in human affairs, Amor, choosing as an epigraph for Canto 90 a quotation from Richard of St. Victor which translates: "The human soul is not love, but love flows from it, and therefore it does not delight in itself, but in the love which comes from it."

In these cantos the power of Amor emanates from the eyes of a beloved woman, inspiring the intellect to philosophical insight, the moral sense to virtuous action and the imagination to artistic creation such as Beatrice inspired in Dante, Giovanna in Cavalcanti, and Eleanor of Aquitaine in Bernart de Ventadour. Reproaching himself for having shown insufficient compassion in the past, Pound now describes himself, in the words of Confucius, as "counting his manhood and the love of his relatives the true treasure." In both *Rock-Drill* and *Thrones* he celebrates the power of benevolence and also the inspirational influence of two young visitors to St. Elizabeths–Sherri Martinelli ("Flora Castalia") and Marcella Spann, in whose presence the hospital grounds become metamorphosed into a temple precinct and the trees into marble columns.

The dominant mood at the conclusion of *Thrones* is one of calm resignation at the realization that there is no triumphant conclusion either to the poet's quest for the earthly paradise or to the poem itself. To keep alive the intellectual light is to be committed to an unremitting struggle against obscurantism. "Oak boughs alone over Selloi," from the *Trachiniae* recalls the revelation of the dying Hercules–"what/SPLENDOUR,/IT ALL COHERES," but this moment of resolution is followed by three references to new journeys to be made. John Bunyan's Christian, beginning his journey to the Celestial City, is directed by Evangelist to make for the light shining "over wicket gate." Odysseus, helped after his shipwreck by Leucothea, must resume his voyage home. Dante, calling back to the reader "in the dinghy ... astern there," is about to embark upon the writing of his *Paradiso.*

In addition to his cantos Pound also worked in St. Elizabeths on his translations. His *Great Digest and the Unwobbling Pivot* was republished in 1951, and a collection of his translations was published in 1953. Of the three thousand classic Chinese odes, Confucius had selected the three hundred which he considered indispensable, and Pound undertook to translate them all, filling thirty spiral notebooks between 1946 and 1950 with notes and characters, and publishing his translations as *The Classic Anthology Defined by Confucius* (1954). That same year his *Literary Essays* were published. In addition, his translation of Sophocles' *Women of Trachis* was broadcast on the BBC (25 November 1954) before appearing in book form in November 1956. In 1952 Olga Rudge visited him, and the following year his now-married daughter spent three months in Washington.

By January 1957 Archibald MacLeish was working actively to obtain Pound's release and to this end had drafted a letter to the attorney general signed by Eliot, Hemingway, and Frost. On 18 April 1958, the indictment was dismissed and Pound was free to leave St. Elizabeths. Because of passport problems, he remained in the country for two months, during which time he made visits to Wyncote and to Williams in Rutherford. He sailed for Genoa on 30 June 1958, with his wife and Marcella Spann en route to Brunnenburg, his daughter's castle in the Tirol where, for the first time, he met his grandchildren, Walter and Patrizia de Rachewiltz. At first he was in excellent spirits, working on the manuscripts for *Thrones* and sorting papers and letters, but before long his unresolved anxieties became increasingly oppressive. In January 1959 he went to stay in Rapallo with his wife and Marcella Spann, and, after touring through Italy in the spring, they settled in an apartment in Rapallo for the summer. By October Spann had returned to America, and Pound had written to Mary that he wanted to return to Brunnenburg "to die." His sense that his life's work was a failure was only temporarily alleviated by a birthday telegram from Eliot assuring him that his position as a great poet was secure. The self-punishing effects of his remorse took a heavy toll mentally and physically. He resisted eating and was afflicted with slowness of speech and movement, sometimes remaining completely still for hours at a time. He subjected himself to relentless self-accusation and was obsessed with un-

Pound late in his life (photograph by Jonathan Williams)

founded anxieties about his health. His physical condition deteriorated because of his resistence to eating, and by the summer of 1960 he had to be treated at a clinic at Martinsbrun, returning there in June 1961 after spending some time at a clinic in Rome the previous month for treatment of a urinary infection. In 1962 and 1963 he underwent prostrate surgery.

By 1962 he was speaking less and less, but his delay and slowness in responding were at the level of communication rather than at the level of thought. This fact is clear from his replies to Donald Hall's questions in the long interview published in the *Paris Review* (Summer/Fall 1962). Neither his memory nor his sense of orientation were impaired, and when he did talk his comments were precise and correct. His holding back from speech seemed of a piece with the problem he had from 1965 on in initiating physical movements and in carrying one through once it was begun. From 11 March to 16 April 1966 he was at the Clinic for Nervous and Mental Illnesses of the University of Genoa, where his condition was carefully studied. His psychiatrist's findings were very much of a piece with those of Dr. Overholser at St. Elizabeths–that, while he was rational and in touch with reality at almost all points, in one area–the assigning of blame–his thinking appeared psychotic. Where in St. Elizabeths he had believed in the culpability of an international conspiracy of usurers, now he castigated himself. He was not suffering merely from "senile depression," and his psychiatrist noted that he was not depressive except in the one area of self-accusation. He also noted that during trips Pound was sometimes capable of essentially normal activity, and this continued to be the case up until the time of his death. On 4 February 1965 he had attended the T. S. Eliot memorial service in Westminster Abbey and then had traveled to Dublin to see Yeats's widow. In the summer of 1965 he attended the Spoleto Festival, and in October, after his eightieth birthday, he visited Greece. In July 1966 he traveled to Paris and in June 1969 spent two weeks in America as the guest of James Laughlin, visiting Hamilton College on the occasion of the presentation of an honorary doctorate to Laughlin and spending time with Valerie Eliot, Hemingway, Lowell, and Marianne Moore.

In 1969 he published *Drafts and Fragments of Cantos CX-CXVII*. On those rare occasions when he could be persuaded to talk, he sometimes dismissed his *Cantos* as a complete failure, saying that they were "a botch" and that his writing was "stupidity and ignorance all the way through"; yet *Drafts and Fragments of Cantos CX-CXVII* contains a more balanced assessment. Having chosen all his life to dwell more on how things might ideally become than on how they were, he had finally to acknowledge that he could neither see a solution to the social problems he deplored nor bring his poem to the "paradisal" conclusion he had projected–that it "nor began nor ends anything" (Canto 114). He confronted this realization steadily, and the prevailing undertone of these cantos is a calm resignation which at times slips into the poignantly elegiac and at other times rises to affirmation. He celebrated the healing power of music and of all forms of beauty and in particular his realization that "the truth is in kindness" (Canto 114)–that "Justification is from kindness of heart/and from her hands floweth mercy" (Canto 113).

He persisted in his self-accusation and now saw clearly "That I lost my center/fighting the world" (Canto 117) but, rather than escaping into rationalization, fatalism, or self-pity, he chose the painful course of contrition without self-exculpation, "the mind as Ixion, unstill, ever turning" (Canto 113). Although he was oppressed by the fact that "my errors and wrecks lie about me./And I am not a demigod,/I cannot make it cohere," he had not lost the faith that "it coheres all right/even if my notes do not cohere" (Canto 116). Feeling that he was "A blown husk that is finished," he was still aware that "the light sings

eternal/a pale flare over marshes" (Canto 115) and that, even if the light is glimpsed only fitfully, even "A little light, like a rushlight [can] lead back to splendour." Here, in this most poignant and moving sequence of the *Cantos*, he managed "To confess wrong without losing rightness" (Canto 116).

Stoic in his silence, he remained active until the end. He could make the long walk from Olga Rudge's house via the Accademia Bridge to the Piazza San Marco, and he was photographed shortly before his death, very thin, but standing dignified and erect, looking at the roses in the garden of friends in Venice. He died in his sleep on 1 November 1972, and his funeral service was performed on 3 November in the Benedictine Abbey on the Island San Giorgio Maggiore. He was buried on the Venetian cemetery island of San Michele.

A summary of Pound's poetic achievement invites the frequent use of superlatives. He saw earliest and most clearly and formulated most thoroughly and emphatically the new principles by which twentieth-century poetry would operate. He realized and illustrated in his own work the importance of precision of diction and of vividness and specificity of presentation. He was most bold in experimenting with different kinds of openness of form. He may well have had the most perfect ear of all the poets of his age, and, while urging poets to respect the natural cadences of the speaking voice and to resist nineteenth-century distortions of word order, he produced the most beautiful and musical verse cadences. In *The Cantos* he wrote the most difficult poem of the period with the most numerous and far-ranging allusions, but also the most moving lyrical passages–a poem that is probably the most unread and so offers the most to be discovered.

Letters:

The Letters of Ezra Pound 1907-1941, edited by D. D. Paige (New York: Harcourt, Brace, 1950; London: Faber & Faber, 1951);

Pound/Joyce: The Letters of Ezra Pound to James Joyce, edited by Forrest Read (New York: New Directions, 1967; London: Faber & Faber, 1969);

Letters to Ibbotson, 1935-1952, edited by Vittoria I. Mondolfo and Margaret Hurley (Orono, Maine: National Poetry Foundation, University of Maine, 1979);

Letters to John Theobald, edited by Donald Pearce and Herbert Schneidau (Redding Ridge, Conn.: Black Swan, 1981);

Pound/Ford: The Story of a Literary Friendship, edited by Brita Lindberg-Seyersted (New York: New Directions, 1982);

Ezra Pound and Dorothy Shakespear: Their Letters 1909-1914, edited by Omar Pound and A. Walton Litz (New York: New Directions, 1984);

The Letters of Ezra Pound and Wyndham Lewis, edited by Timothy Materer (New York: New Directions, 1985);

Selected Letters of Ezra Pound and Louis Zukofsky, edited by Barry Athearn (New York: New Directions 1987).

A revealing picture of both poets in a private dialogue about the art of poetry and how ideas should take form. Out of this correspondence the objectivist movement was born.

Bibliography:

Donald Gallup, *Ezra Pound: A Bibliography* (Charlottesville: University Press of Virginia, 1983).

Biographies:

Charles Norman, *Ezra Pound,* revised edition (New York: Minerva, 1969);

Noel Stock, *The Life of Ezra Pound* (New York: Pantheon, 1970);

Mary de Rachewiltz, *Discretions* (Boston: Little, Brown, 1971);

C. David Heyman, *Ezra Pound: The Last Rower* (New York: Viking, 1976);

James H. Wilhelm, *The American Roots of Ezra Pound* (New York: Garland, 1985).

References:

Michael Alexander, *The Poetic Achievement of Ezra Pound* (Berkeley: University of California Press, 1979).

Impressive and knowledgable account based on a superior command of both classical and medieval sources.

David Anderson, *Pound's Cavalcanti: An Edition of the Translations, Notes and Essays* (Princeton: Princeton University Press, 1982).

The final word for our time about Pound's lifelong work on Tuscan poet Guido Cavalcanti.

Massimo Bacigalupo, *The Forméd Trace: The Later Poetry of Ezra Pound* (New York: Columbia University Press, 1980).

A necessary resource for the study of Pound's later work; because of Bacigalupo's Italian connections, his book contains a wealth of information not found elsewhere.

Walter Baumann, *The Rose in the Steel Dust: An Examination of the Cantos of Ezra Pound* (Coral Gables: University of Miami Press, 1967).

A valuable introductory account dealing with *The Cantos.*

Ian F. A. Bell, *Critic as Scientist: The Modernist Poetics of Ezra Pound* (London & New York: Methuen, 1981).

A scholarly examinations for those interested in linguistic criticism.

Jo B. Berryman, *Circe's Craft: Ezra Pound's "Hugh Selwyn Mauberley"* (Ann Arbor: UMI Research Press, 1983).

Argues that the poem reflects two distinct points of view, that of Pound himself and that of the fictional poet Mauberley.

Christine Brooke-Rose, *A ZBC of Ezra Pound* (Berkeley: University of California Press, 1971).

A seminal work which helped to refocus the whole critical tradition of *The Cantos.*

Ronald Bush, *The Genesis of Ezra Pound's Cantos* (Princeton: Princeton University Press, 1976).

Opened up new territory about the growth of Pound's own changing ideas about the form as well as the content of his long poem.

William M. Chace, *The Political Identities of Ezra Pound and T. S. Eliot* (Stanford: Stanford University Press, 1973).

Analyzes the political leanings of Pound and his friend and fellow poet; well written and presented but now dated.

Donald Davie, *Ezra Pound* (New York: Viking, 1976).

Brief but stunning account of the poet.

Davie, *Ezra Pound: Poet as Sculptor* (New York: Oxford University Press, 1964).

Views Pound's eclecticism as the moving force behind his work and as a key for understanding his poetry.

Earle Davis, *Vision Fugitive: Ezra Pound's Economics* (Lawrence: University of Kansas Press, 1968).
A first inquiry into Pound's economic theories, but now dated. Contains a summary of what Pound called "red herrings." Davis, like most other writers on this subject, is not aware that Pound's concern was with monetary policy and not economics per se.

L. S. Dembo, *The Confucian Odes of Ezra Pound* (Berkeley: University of California Press, 1963).
Good introduction to Pound's Oriental verse.

Mary de Rachewiltz, *Discretions* (Boston: Little, Brown, 1971); republished as *Ezra Pound, Father and Teacher* (New York: New Directions, 1975).
This account by Pound's illegitimate daughter is the first and still the best book to show Pound as a human being struggling to find himself and his identity in a dozen significant ways.

T. S. Eliot, *Ezra Pound: His Metric and Poetry* (New York: Knopf, 1917).
Excellent work on Pound's poetry by his contemporary, T. S. Eliot; should be read and re-read.

Wendy S. Flory, *Ezra Pound and The Cantos: A Record of Struggle* (New Haven: Yale University Press, 1980).
Successfully redefines the focus of criticism of Pound's *Cantos*.

Christine Froula, *A Guide to Ezra Pound's Selected Poems* (New York: New Directions, 1983).
A delightful book; essential for introducing Pound in any classroom.

Froula, *To Write Paradise: Style and Error in Pound's Cantos* (New Haven: Yale University Press, 1984).
This 205-page book explores the massive amount of materials and the dozens of versions Pound wrote to get the final Canto IV.

Based on several years of work at the Yale archives.

Hugh Kenner, *The Poetry of Ezra Pound* (New York: New Directions, 1951).
All criticism of Pound dates from this book.

Kenner, *The Pound Era* (Berkeley: University of California Press, 1971).
Indispensable survey which separates the valuable from the dross in the growing mass of works about Pound; contains a stunning wealth of new data.

James Longenbach, *Stone Cottage: Pound, Yeats, and Modernism*: (New York: Oxford, 1988).
A detailed and fascinating look at the critical years (1913-1916) during which Pound took a number of new directions. Corrects the record and brings new light to the formation of the controversial Pound.

Peter Makin, *Pound's Cantos* (London & Boston: Allen & Unwin, 1985).
The best recent book on *The Cantos* and the first one to explore Pound's special attitude toward the mystic tradition. It shows how the Eleusinian rites related to the arcanum as the major unifying theme of the poem.

Makin, *Provence and Pound* (Berkeley: University of California Press, 1979).
By far the best book on Pound's study of the Provençal poets, by an authority on the subject.

Jean-Michael Rabate, *Language, Sexuality and Ideology in Ezra Pound's Cantos* (Albany: State University of New York Press, 1986).
An informed European presents the results of twenty-five years of thinking about the Pound canon in this refreshing analysis of *The Cantos*.

M. L. Rosenthal, *Sailing into the Unknown: Yeats, Pound and Eliot* (New York: Oxford University Press, 1978).
The most complete exploration of the interrelationships of these three giants.

Leon Surette, *A Light From Eleusis: A Study of Ezra Pound's Cantos* (Oxford: Clarendon Press, 1980).

The first book to explore the rites of Eleusis in detail; essential to the study of *The Cantos*.

James J. Wilhelm, *The American Roots of Ezra Pound* (New York: Garland, 1985).

The first book in a trilogy planned to correct a mass of errors in all previous biographies concerning Pound's ancestry. Wilhelm traveled widely and examined every document.

Papers:

The majority of the Pound papers are in the Ezra Pound Archive of the Beinecke Library, Yale University. Other papers are in the Berg Collection of the New York Public Library, the Houghton Library of Harvard University, the Newberry Library in Chicago, and the libraries of Hamilton College, Cornell University, and the University of Pennsylvania. The Lilly Library of Indiana University has about 12,000 letters to Ezra and Dorothy Pound, dating from 1945-1953.

Gertrude Stein

This entry was updated by William B. Adams from the entry by Meredith Yearsley in DLB 54, American Poets, 1880-1945, Third Series, Part 2.

Places	Oakland, Cal. Harvard University	Baltimore, Md. (Johns Hopkins University)	Paris
Influences and Relationships	Pablo Picasso William James Alice B. Toklas Ernest Hemingway	Virgil Thompson Gustave Flaubert Paul Cézanne Mabel Dodge	Sherwood Anderson Alfred North Whitehead
Literary Movements and Forms	The Oral Tradition in Poetry	Experimental Fiction Prose Portrait	Hermeticism
Major Themes	Lesbianism Rejection of the Patriarch	The Nature of Language	The Inner Lives of Women
Cultural and Artistic Influences	Linguistics Post Impressionist Painting & Cubism Dada	Henri Bergson's Theory of Time German Language Psychology	Conceptual Art Opera Neoromantic Painting
Social and Economic Influences	The "Lost Generation" Expatriate Movement	World War I	World War II

248

See also the Stein entries in DLB 4, American Writers in Paris, 1920-1939 *and* DLB 78, American Short-Story Writers, 1880-1910.

BIRTH: Allegheny, Pennsylvania, 3 February 1874, to Daniel and Amelia Keyser Stein.

EDUCATION: A.B., Harvard University, 1898; Johns Hopkins Medical School, 1897-1901.

AWARD: Médaille de la Réconnaissance Française, 1922.

DEATH: Neuilly-sur-Seine, 27 July 1946.

BOOKS: *Three Lives: Stories of The Good Anna, Melanctha and The Gentle Lena* (New York: Grafton Press, 1909; London: John Lane, Bodley Head/New York: John Lane, 1915);

Portrait of Mabel Dodge at the Villa Curonia (Florence, Italy: Privately printed, 1912);

Tender Buttons: Objects, Food, Rooms (New York: Claire Marie, 1914);

Have They Attacked Mary, He Giggled. (West Chester, Pa.: Printed by Horace F. Temple, 1917);

Geography and Plays (Boston: Four Seas, 1922);

The Making of Americans, Being A History of A Family's Progress (Paris: Contact Editions, 1925; New York: A. & C. Boni, 1926; London: Owen, 1968); abridged as *The Making of Americans, The Hersland Family* (New York: Harcourt, Brace, 1934);

Descriptions of Literature (Englewood, N.J.: George Platt Lynes & Adlai Harbeck, 1926);

Composition as Explanation (London: Leonard & Virginia Woolf at the Hogarth Press, 1926);

A Book Concluding with As a Wife Has a Cow, A Love Story (Paris: Editions de la Galerie Simon, 1926; Barton, Millerton & Berlin: Something Else Press, 1973);

An Elucidation (Paris: transition, 1927);

A Village Are You Ready Yet Not Yet A Play in Four Acts (Paris: Editions de la Galerie Simon, 1928);

Useful Knowledge (New York: Payson & Clarke, 1928; London: John Lane, Bodley Head, 1929);

An Acquaintance with Description (London: Seizin Press, 1929);

Lucy Church Amiably (Paris: Plain Edition, 1930; New York: Something Else Press, 1969);

Dix Portraits, English text with French translations

Gertrude Stein, circa 1895 (courtesy of the Beinecke Rare Book and Manuscript Library, Yale University)

by Georges Hugnet and Virgil Thomson (Paris: Libraire Gallimard, 1930);

Before the Flowers of Friendship Faded Friendship Faded, Written on a Poem by Georges Hugnet (Paris: Plain Edition, 1931);

How to Write (Paris: Plain Edition, 1931; Barton: Something Else Press, 1973);

Operas and Plays (Paris: Plain Edition, 1932);

Matisse Picasso and Gertrude Stein with Two Shorter Stories (Paris: Plain Edition, 1933; Barton, Berlin & Millerton: Something Else Press, 1972);

The Autobiography of Alice B. Toklas (New York: Harcourt, Brace, 1933; London: John Lane, Bodley Head, 1933);

Four Saints in Three Acts, An Opera To Be Sung (New York: Random House, 1934);

Portraits and Prayers (New York: Random House, 1934);

Lectures in America (New York: Random House, 1935);

Narration: Four Lectures (Chicago: University of Chicago Press, 1935);

The Geographical History of America or The Relation of Human Nature to the Human Mind (New York: Random House, 1936);

Is Dead (N.p.: Joyous Guard Press, 1937);

Everybody's Autobiography (New York: Random House, 1937; London & Toronto: Heinemann, 1938);

A Wedding Bouquet, Ballet Music by Lord Berners, Words By Gertrude Stein (London: J. & W. Chester, 1938);

Picasso [in French] (Paris: Libraire Floury, 1938); translated into English by Alice B. Toklas (London: Batsford, 1938; New York: Scribners/London: Batsford, 1939);

The World is Round (New York: William R. Scott, 1939; London: Batsford, 1939);

Paris France (London: Batsford, 1940; New York: Scribners/London: Batsford, 1940);

What Are Masterpieces (California: Conference Press, 1940; expanded edition, New York, Toronto, London & Tel Aviv: Pitman, 1970);

ida A Novel (New York: Random House, 1941);

Petits Poèmes Pour un Livre de Lecture, French translation by Madame la Baronne d'Aiguy (Charlot, France: Collection Fontaine, 1944); republished in English as *The First Reader & Three Plays* (Dublin & London: Maurice Fridberg, 1946; Boston: Houghton Mifflin, 1948);

Wars I Have Seen (New York: Random House, 1945; enlarged edition, London: Batsford, 1945);

Brewsie and Willie (New York: Random House, 1946);

Selected Writings, edited by Carl Van Vechten (New York: Random House, 1946);

In Savoy, or Yes Is for a Very Young Man (A Play of the Resistance in France) (London: Pushkin, 1946);

Four in America (New Haven: Yale University Press, 1947);

The Mother of Us All, by Stein and Virgil Thomson (New York: Music Press, 1947);

Blood on the Dining Room Floor (Pawlet, Vt.: Banyan Press, 1948);

Two (Hitherto Unpublished) Poems (New York: Gotham Book Mart, 1948);

Last Operas and Plays, edited by Van Vechten (New York & Toronto: Rinehart, 1949);

Things As They Are, A Novel in Three Parts by Gertrude Stein, Written in 1903 but Now Published for the First Time (Pawlet, Vt.: Banyan Press, 1950);

Two: Gertrude Stein and Her Brother and Other Early Portraits [1908-12], volume 1 of *Unpublished Works of Gertrude Stein* (New Haven: Yale University Press/London: Cumberlege, Oxford University Press, 1951);

In a Garden, An Opera in One Act, libretto by Stein, music by Meyer Kupferman (New York: Mercury Music, 1951);

Mrs. Reynolds and Five Earlier Novelettes, volume 2 of *Unpublished Works of Gertrude Stein* (New Haven: Yale University Press/London: Cumberlege, Oxford University Press, 1952);

Bee Time Vine and Other Pieces 1913-1927, volume 3 of *Unpublished Works of Gertrude Stein* (New Haven: Yale University Press/London: Cumberlege, Oxford University Press, 1953);

As Fine As Melanctha (1914-1930), volume 4 of *Unpublished Works of Gertrude Stein* (New Haven: Yale University Press/London: Cumberlege, Oxford University Press, 1954);

Absolutely Bob Brown, Or Bobbed Brown (Pawlet, Vt.: Addison M. Metcalf Collection, 1955);

Painted Lace and Other Pieces 1914-1937, volume 5 of *Unpublished Works of Gertrude Stein* (New Haven: Yale University Press/London: Cumberlege, Oxford University Press, 1955);

Stanzas in Meditation and Other Poems [1929-1933], volume 6 of *Unpublished Works of Gertrude Stein* (New Haven: Yale University Press/ London: Cumberlege, Oxford University Press, 1956);

Alphabets & Birthdays, volume 7 of *Unpublished Works of Gertrude Stein* (New Haven: Yale University Press/London: Oxford University Press, 1957);

A Novel of Thank You, volume 8 of *Unpublished Works of Gertrude Stein* (New Haven: Yale University Press, 1958; London: Oxford University Press, 1959);

Gertrude Stein's America, edited by Gilbert A. Harrison (Washington, D.C.: Robert B. Luce, 1965);

Writings and Lectures 1911-1945, edited by Patricia Meyerowitz (London: Owen, 1967); republished as *Look at Me Now and Here I Am: Writing and Lectures, 1909-1945* (Harmondsworth & Baltimore: Penguin, 1971);

Lucretia Borgia, A Play (New York: Albondocani Press, 1968);

Motor Automatism, by Stein and Leon M. Solomons (New York: Phoenix Book Shop, 1969);

Selected Operas and Plays, edited by John Malcolm Brinnin (Pittsburgh: University of Pittsburgh Press, 1970);

Gertrude Stein on Picasso, edited by Edward Burns (New York: Liveright, 1970);

I Am Rose (New York: Mini-Books, 1971);

Fernhurst, Q.E.D., and Other Early Writings (New York: Liveright, 1971; London: Owen, 1971);

A Primer for the Gradual Understanding of Gertrude Stein, edited by Robert Bartlett Haas (Los Angeles: Black Sparrow Press, 1971);

Reflections on the Atomic Bomb, volume 1 of *The Previously Uncollected Writings of Gertrude Stein,* edited by Haas (Los Angeles: Black Sparrow Press, 1973);

Money (Los Angeles: Black Sparrow Press, 1973);

How Writing is Written, volume 2 of *The Previously Uncollected Writings of Gertrude Stein,* edited by Haas (Los Angeles: Black Sparrow Press, 1974);

The Yale Gertrude Stein: Selections (New Haven & London: Yale University Press, 1980).

PERIODICAL PUBLICATIONS: "Normal Motor Automatism," by Stein and Leon M. Solomons, *Psychological Review,* 3 (September 1896): 492-512;

"Cultivated Motor Automatism," *Psychological Review,* 5 (May 1898): 295-306;

"Henri Matisse" and "Pablo Picasso," *Camera Work,* special number (August 1912): 23-25, 29-30;

"From a Play by Gertrude Stein," *New York Sun,* 18 January 1914, VI: 2;

"Aux Galeries Lafayette," *Rogue,* 1 (March 1915): 13-14;

"A League," *Life,* 74 (18 September 1919): 496;

"Two Cubist Poems. The Peace Conference, I and II," *Oxford Magazine,* 38 (7 May 1920): 309;

Review of *Three Stories & Ten Poems* by Ernest Hemingway, *Chicago Tribune,* European edition, 27 November 1923, p. 2;

The Making of Americans, transatlantic review, 1 (April 1924): 127-142; 1 (May 1924): 297-309; 1 (June 1924): 392-405; 2 (July 1924): 27-38; 2 (August 1924): 188-202; 2 (September 1924): 284-294; 2 (October 1924): 405-414; 2 (November 1924): 527-536; 2 (December 1924): 662-670;

"The Life of Juan Gris The Life and Death of Juan Gris," *transition,* no. 4 (July 1927): 160-162;

"Bibliography," *transition,* no. 15 (February 1929): 47-55;

"Genuine Creative Ability," *Creative Art,* 6 (February 1930), supplement: 41;

"Scenery and George Washington," *Hound & Horn,* 5 (July/September 1932): 606-611;

"Basket," *Lion and Crown,* 1 (January 1933): 23-25;

Review of *Roosevelt and His America* by Bernard Faÿ, *Kansas City Star,* 20 January 1934;

"Why Willows," *Literary America,* 1 (July 1934): 19-20;

"Plays and Landscapes," *Saturday Review of Literature,* 11 (10 November 1934): 269-270;

"Completely Gertrude Stein: A Painting Is Painted as a Painting," *Design,* 36 (January 1935): 25, 28;

Review of *Puzzled America* by Sherwood Anderson, *Chicago Daily Tribune,* 4 May 1935, p. 14;

"English and American Language in Literature," *Life and Letters Today,* 13 (September 1935): 19-27;

"A Portrait of the Abdys," *Janus* (May 1936): 15;

Dialogue with Nunez Martinez, *Ken,* 1 (2 June 1938): 103-104;

"The Situation in American Writing" [symposium], *Partisan Review,* 6 (Summer 1939): 40-41;

"Ballade," *Confluences,* 11/12 (July 1942): 11-12;

"Liberation, Glory Be!," *Collier's,* 114 (16 December 1944): 14-15, 61-63; 114 (23 December 1944): 51, 74-76;

"Now We Are Back in Paris," *Compass* (December 1945): 56-60;

"Capital, Capitals," by Stein, with music by Virgil Thomson, *New Music,* 20 (April 1947): 3-34;

"I Like American and American," *'47,* 1 (October 1947): 16-21;

"Jean Atlan: Abstract Painting," *Yale French Studies,* no. 31 (May 1964): 118.

Just as the postimpressionists and cubists made us see paint and then made us see painting, Gertrude Stein made us see words and then made us see writing. Immensely various and wide-ranging, her work amounts to a systematic investigation of the formal elements of language (parts of speech, syntax, phonetics, morphemics, etymology, and punctuation) and of literature (narrative, poetry, prose, drama, and genre itself). In the course of these investigations, as Marianne DeKoven has pointed out, Stein reinvented literary signification (in "the most substantial and successful body of experimental writing in English"), creating a language that both disrupts conventional modes of signification and provides alternatives to them: "The modes Stein disrupts are linear, orderly, closed, hierarchical, sensible, coherent, referential, and heavily focused on the signified. The modes she substitutes are incoherent, open-ended, anarchic, irreducibly multiple, often focused on what Roland Barthes calls the 'magic of the signifier.' "

America, Gertrude Stein believed, was the first nation to enter the twentieth century. Although she lived in France for most of her writing life, she was most emphatically an American, and, as she wrote in her 1938 book on her friend Pablo Picasso, she felt completely in tune with "the century where nothing is in agreement, neither the round with the cube, neither the landscape with the houses, neither the large quantity with the small quantity." Again and again, stimulated by her undergraduate training in philosophy and psychology (notably with William James), she asked and investigated deceptively simple questions that reflected key issues of the century: questions to do with being, time, entity, identity, mind, language, and human nature—questions addressed by Alfred North Whitehead (a close friend of Stein's), Bertrand Russell, Martin Heidegger, and Ludwig Wittgenstein. What is knowledge? What is mind? What is human nature? What is poetry? What is prose? What is literature? What is composition? What do these *do*? She knew that, even in asking these questions, she was suggesting a new vocabulary of thought. Like Wittgenstein, she realized that she must invent a way of showing what could not be written *about*. Writing *about* things, explaining, was a nineteenth-century way of seeing: in the twentieth century there had to be ways of seeing what seeing itself was. In her work, as in Wittgenstein's thinking, the subject disappears as the telling, the seeing, and the language system itself are placed in the foreground. She investigated in literature what would later be documented by theorists such as Roland Barthes, Marshall McLuhan, and Jacques Derrida.

Stein's writing may be roughly divided into three groups: relatively straightforward narratives—*Three Lives: Stories of The Good Anna,*

Melanctha and The Gentle Lena (1909) and the best-selling memoirs *The Autobiography of Alice B. Toklas* (1933), *Everybody's Autobiography* (1937), and *Wars I Have Seen* (1945); critical and exegetical work—*Composition as Explanation* (1926), *Lectures in America* (1935), *Narration* (1935), and *What Are Masterpieces* (1940); and works which demolish conventional notions of poetry, prose, and genre—her still lifes, portraits, geographies, plays, novels, librettos, series, and philosophical discourses. Most of her writing falls into this third group, and in an important sense she discovered writing qua writing—a poetry of thinking, seeing, and hearing grounded in the activity of language. "Language as a real thing is not imitation either of sounds or colors or emotions it is an intellectual recreation," she wrote in one of her American lectures. "And so for me the problem of poetry was and it began with *Tender Buttons* to constantly realize the thing anything so that I could recreate that thing." She was and is a poet's poet, whose work is a technician's paradise of innovations.

During Stein's lifetime, however, her innovative writing, often the butt of reviewers' parodies, received little recognition or understanding. Her achievement was mostly overshadowed by her celebrated role as American eccentric in Paris and hostess of the popular salons she and her brother Leo Stein held in their Paris studio/apartment at 27, rue de Fleurus, which became a mecca for tourists, writers, and artists. Championing the modern movement, Leo and Gertrude Stein, with their older brother and sister-in-law, Michael and Sarah Stein (who lived nearby on the rue Madame), amassed a major collection of postimpressionist and modernist art—works by Paul Cézanne, Paul Gauguin, Henri de Toulouse-Lautrec, Edouard Manet, Henri Matisse, Pablo Picasso, Pierre Bonnard, Juan Gris, and others. Not only did Gertrude Stein form close relationships with Picasso, Matisse, Georges Braque, Robert Delaunay, and Marie Laurencin, she also became acquainted with such avant-garde writers as Max Jacob and Guillaume Apollinaire, the flamboyant promoter of the cubists. Leo Stein, who at the time of his sister's arrival in Paris in 1903 had decided to devote himself to painting and art criticism, was at first the dominant force in the salons. But when Gertrude Stein wholeheartedly embraced cubism—which Leo Stein could not—it was she who became the driving force, with the able support of her lifelong friend and lover Alice B. Toklas. After Gertrude and Leo had separated in 1913 or 1914 and some of Gertrude

Stein with Alice B. Toklas in Venice, circa 1908 (courtesy of the Beinecke Rare Book and Manuscript Library, Yale University)

Stein's early work (which Leo Stein thought nonsense) had been published, 27, rue de Fleurus became a literary mecca (rivaling Pound's and Joyce's), where Gertrude met and coached such writers as Ernest Hemingway and Sherwood Anderson and began a series of literary friendships that was to include, among others, Bravig Imbs, Edith Sitwell and her brothers, Ford Madox Ford, Robert McAlmon, Scott Fitzgerald, and Natalie Clifford Barney. Visitors also included writers as various as Hilda Doolittle (H.D.), William Carlos Williams, John Dos Passos, Mina Loy, and Djuna Barnes and, significantly, composers—Erik Satie, George Antheil, Aaron Copland, and Virgil Thomson (who appreciated the rhythmical elements of Stein's work, collaborated with her on operas, and set many of her pieces to music).

Stein's influence is readily discernible in the writing of such major poets as Louis Zukofsky, in, for example, his work with prepositions, in his playful epigrammatic pieces, and in the dense multivalent composition of longer works such as

"A" (which he began writing in 1927 and completed in 1974) and *80 Flowers* (1978). Robert Duncan's work, *Writing Writing* (1964), *From the Laboratory Notebooks* (1969), and *A Book of Resemblances* (1966; which includes his Stein imitations), also reflects her influence as does the work of such Canadian poets as Steve McCaffery, George Bowering, and B. P. Nichol and the "concrete" and "sound" poets of the 1960s. Perhaps the most wide-reaching offshoot of Stein's work, however, has occurred in the writing of the so-called L=A=N=G=U=A=G=E poets (Lyn Hejinian, Bruce Andrews, Charles Bernstein, Diane Ward, Bob Perelman, and others) whose work (which appears in little magazines such as L=A=N=G=U=A=G=E, *Roof,* and *This*) emerged in the 1970s and 1980s. These writers share with Stein an interest in the surfaces, opacity, and polysemy of language, and, like Stein, they approach writing as universally poetic.

"Why in fact have we not heard more generally from American scholars upon the writings of Miss Stein?," asked William Carlos Williams in an article for the Winter 1930 issue of *Pagany* (which he wrote with the silent collaboration of Zukofsky) —they connected her work with that of Laurence Sterne. Forty years after her death, with the emergence of theories about texts from Roland Barthes and Jacques Derrida, the academic establishment is only beginning to understand her achievement.

On 3 February 1874 Gertrude Stein was born to Amelia Keyser and Daniel Stein in Allegheny, Pennsylvania. She was the youngest of a planned family of five children and was deeply impressed by the fact that she would not have been born at all if two other children had not died in infancy. It was a fact that strengthened her bond with the second youngest of the family, her brother Leo. Being the youngest was a role that suited her, however: "It is better if you are the youngest girl in a family to have a brother two years older," she wrote in *Everybody's Autobiography,* "because that makes everything a pleasure to you, you go everywhere and do everything while he does it all for you and with you which is a pleasant way to have everything happen to you." This pleasant way was to continue for Gertrude for nearly forty years: throughout her childhood, university training, and early career she remained very close to Leo. For the rest of her life, "Baby Woojums"—as she became known to Alice B. Toklas ("Mama Woojums") and close friends—

expected and received care and protection from others, even as a Jew in Nazi-occupied France.

In the spring of 1875 the family moved to Vienna, followed by another move to Passy, France, in 1878, as Daniel Stein pursued various business interests. In Europe the family lived a comfortable, prosperous life, full of treats, dancing lessons, and excursions for the children, who in Vienna had a Hungarian governess and a Czech tutor. This early exposure to a mélange of languages (Stein spoke German and French before she spoke English) apparently fascinated Stein even at the time: "Our little Gertie is a little Schnatterer," wrote her Aunt Rachel, who lived with the family in Vienna. "She talks all day long and so plainly.... [and] toddles around the whole day & repeats everything that is said and done." Here perhaps were the beginnings of Stein's lasting interest in the habits and forms of language. It was not until 1879 when the family returned to America to live with the Keyser grandparents in Baltimore that Gertrude had her first experience of "proper" English. Even then, most of the English she heard was that of an immigrant family, none of whom spoke the language very well.

In 1880, when Gertrude Stein was six, the family moved to California, where Daniel Stein had invested in the San Francisco street railway. Here they spent a happy first year at Tubb's Hotel in Oakland: "I do love Tubb's hotel very well with Eucalyptus and palms," Stein wrote forty-one years later in "A Sonatina Followed by Another"–eucalyptus and palms would always mean for her Tubb's Hotel. The following year (1881) the Steins rented a ten-acre farm, the rambling "Old Stratton House," on the eastern outskirts of Oakland. Stein described it in her 1,000-page novel *The Making of Americans:*

There was, just around the house, a pleasant garden, in front were green lawns not very carefully attended and with large trees in the center whose roots always sucked up for themselves almost all the moisture, water in this dry western country could not be used just to keep things green and pretty and so, often, the grass was very dry in the summer, but it was very pleasant then lying there watching the birds, black in the bright sunlight and sailing, and the firm white summer clouds breaking away from the horizon and slowly moving. It was very wonderful there in the summer with the dry heat, and the sun burning, and the hot earth for sleeping; and then in the winter with the rain, and the north

wind blowing that would bend the trees and often break them, and the owls in the wall scaring you with their tumbling.

....

In the summer it was good for generous sweating to help the men make the hay into bales for its preserving and it was well for ones growing to eat radishes pulled with the black earth sticking to them and to chew the mustard and find roots with all kinds of funny flavors in them, and to fill ones hat with fruit and sit on the dry ploughed ground and eat and think and sleep and read and dream and never hear them when they would all be calling; and then when the quail came it was fun to go shooting, and then when the wind and the rain and the ground were ready to help seeds in their growing, it was good fun to help plant them, and the wind would be so strong it would blow the leaves and branches of the trees down around them and you could shout and work and get wet and be all soaking and run out full into the strong wind and let it dry you, in between the gusts of rain that left you soaking. It was fun all the things that happened all the year there then.

She led a carefree life, roaming the countryside with Leo, being educated erratically, sometimes with governesses, sometimes at schools (there is no record of her graduation from Oakland High School), developing the habit of doing what she wanted, not what teachers had in mind for her. Holding themselves apart from the rest of the family, Leo and Gertrude reveled in each other's company, reading together Jules Verne, Mark Twain, George Eliot, and all of Shakespeare, as well as science handbooks, encyclopedias, and history books. Already they were regularly attending art galleries, theater, and opera.

Family life was easygoing and undisciplined. With Daniel Stein increasingly involved in his job as vice-president of the Omnibus Cable Company, the children were left in the hands of their indulgent mother, whom Gertrude described in *The Making of Americans* as "very loving in her feeling to all of her children, but they had been always ... after they stopped being very little children, too big for her ever to control them. She could not lead them nor could she know what they needed inside them." In 1885 Amelia Stein became too weak with illness to manage the large house, and the family moved to a smaller one in Oakland, where the children helped to care for her. She died of cancer in 1888. But the children apparently took her death in stride: "we had all already had the habit of doing without her," Gertrude Stein wrote in *Everybody's Autobiography*.

Three years later (1891) Daniel Stein died, releasing the children from the tyranny of his erratic and domineering ways. Leo and Gertrude Stein, who thought him aggressive and illiterate, had never liked him. For Gertrude Stein, fathers and fathering would remain synonymous with arbitrary authority: "There is too much fathering going on just now and there is no doubt about it fathers are depressing," she later wrote, commenting on the dictatorships and the political atmosphere of the 1930s.

When Michael Stein, the eldest child (then twenty-six), took over the guardianship of the younger children–Simon (twenty-three), Bertha (twenty), Leo (nineteen), and Gertrude (seventeen)–he found his father's finances had deteriorated. "I was most awfully shocked when Mike brought home my father's business books and Leo and I went through them with him," Gertrude wrote later; "There were so many debts it was frightening." But Michael Stein soon became branch manager of the Central Pacific Railway, to whom he sold his father's relatively worthless cable-company holdings, and the five children were provided with enough income to free them from having to earn a living. As Gertrude Stein put it, "Mike's own statement was that he knew if it was not done he had us all on his hands because none of us could earn anything . . . to live on and something had to be done." In 1892 the family dispersed, Gertrude and Bertha Stein moving to Baltimore to live with their mother's sister and Leo Stein transferring from the University of California at Berkeley to Harvard. "I left the more or less internal and solitary and concentrated life I led in California and came to Baltimore," Gertrude Stein recalled, "and lived with a lot of my relations and principally with a whole group of very lively little aunts. . . . they did have to say and hear said whatever was said. . . . That inevitably made everything said often. I began then to consciously listen to what anybody was saying and what they did say while they were saying what they were saying." The next year (1893) Gertrude Stein followed Leo Stein to Harvard, entering Harvard Annex (which was renamed Radcliffe College in 1894).

Like Leo Stein, she studied psychology with William James, who deeply impressed her: "Prof. James . . . is truly a man among men," she wrote in a theme for her English composition teacher,

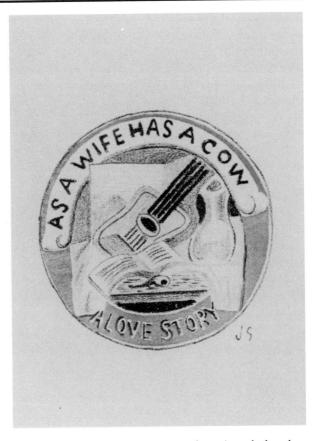

Front cover for Stein's experiment to determine whether there was any real difference between poetry and prose (Sotheby Parke Bernet, Sale #3966)

poet William Vaughn Moody–"a scientist of force and originality embodying all that is strongest and worthiest in scientific spirit; a metaphysician skilled in abstract thought, clear and vigorous and yet too great to worship logic as his God, and narrow himself to a belief merely in the reason of man." From James she learned methods of scientific investigation and the value of an open mind ("If you reject anything that is the beginning of the end as an intellectual," she was to recall his saying), both of which informed her appreciation of visual art and her own writings for the rest of her life. Under James's supervision she conducted experiments with automatic writing designed to reveal the character of the subconscious mind in normal subjects. The poetic quality and the repetitiveness of the subjects' writings were immediately recognized by Stein and her coresearcher Leon Solomons (with Solomons she published an article, "Normal Motor Automatism," in 1896, and she published another independently in 1898). James's theories of the human being (people think themselves as thinkers), knowledge (they know things by acquaintance or by knowledge about them), consciousness (they think in a continuously present stream), and identity (they sense identity by recognizing sameness along the continuum of their thoughts and perceptions) are reflected in much of Stein's writing. Particularly in her early creative work–including *Three Lives* (1909), *The Making of Americans* (1925), and "A Long Gay Book" and "Many Many Women" (both in *Matisse Picasso and Gertrude Stein with Two Shorter Stories*, 1933)–she continued exploring things she had studied under James, such as the identity of her characters as it is revealed in unconscious habits and rhythms of speech, the classification of all possible character types, and the problem of laying out as a continuous present knowledge that had accumulated over a period of time. Her investigations of identity led her eventually to a new concept: entity–the memory-free mode of consciousness that occurs in the act of doing anything, when the individual cannot be conscious of his identity.

Although she did not receive her Harvard A.B. until 1898, Gertrude Stein began to study medicine at Johns Hopkins University in the fall of 1897 in preparation for a career in psychology. But after losing interest, she abandoned her medical studies in 1901, except for doing some brain research in 1902. During this time she spent her summers in San Francisco with the Michael Steins and in Europe with Leo Stein (whose trip around the world in 1895 and permanent move away from Baltimore in 1900 very likely made it difficult for Gertrude Stein to stay there). Like Leo Stein, she was more and more attracted to Europe. With him she traveled to Tangier, Granada, and Paris in 1901 and then to Italy and England in 1902 (spending much of her time in London reading English literature in the British Museum).

In the winter of 1903 she began early drafts of *The Making of Americans* while living in New York with Mabel Weeks and several other women. It was here that she wrote "Q.E.D." (published posthumously as *Things As They Are*, 1950, and later in *Fernhurst, Q.E.D., and Other Early Writings*, 1971), the story of her painful and traumatic love affair with May Bookstaver during her last years at Johns Hopkins, an affair complicated by Bookstaver's involvement with another woman, Mabel Haynes. During 1904-1905 she reexamined the three-cornered affair in another story, "Fernhurst," based on a scandal at Bryn Mawr. Parts of this story became melded into *The Making of Americans*. Both stories are convoluted and obscure (somewhat in the style of Henry James), a style that disappeared in her next works, *The Making of Americans* and *Three Lives*.

In the fall of 1903 Gertrude Stein left behind her in America the disappointments of her medical studies and her friendships and found herself plunged into the "atmosphere of propaganda," as Leo called the barrage of talk among artists and literati who gathered every Saturday evening at 27, rue de Fleurus in Paris. By the age of thirty, the following year, Gertrude Stein had made up her mind to settle down with Leo Stein in Paris and to devote herself to writing. She wrote of this time in *The Making of Americans*: "It happens often in the twenty-ninth year of a life that all the forces that have been engaged through the years of childhood, adolescence and youth in confused and ferocious combat range themselves in ordered ranks. . . . the straight and narrow gate-way of maturity and life which was all uproar and confusion narrows down to form and purpose and we exchange a great dim possibility for a small hard reality."

Gertrude Stein's exposure to painters and the concepts of interest to visual artists had a profound effect on her writing. During the summer of 1904 with Leo Stein in Fiesole, she saw the Charles Losier collection of Cézannes in Florence and began purchasing paintings. "Everything I have done has been influenced by Flaubert and Cézanne," Stein said in an interview with Robert Haas in 1946 (she translated some Flaubert stories in 1909); "this gave me a new feeling about composition. Up to that time composition had consisted of a central idea, to which everything else was an accompaniment and separate but was not an end in itself, and Cézanne conceived the idea that in composition one thing was as important as another thing. Each part is as important as the whole, and that impressed me enormously, . . . so much that I began to write *Three Lives* under this influence." Stein considered the highly acclaimed "Melanctha" (the second part of *Three Lives*), which recounts the story of a Negro woman, the "quintessence" of "this idea of composition." It was an idea that also helped to shape Stein's other early prose works–*The Making of Americans*, "A Long Gay Book," and "Many Many Women"– works where the reader is often forced away from any sense of larger movement or central idea by detailed and minute repetitions and variations in phrasing.

The Steins' purchase of Matisse's controversial *La Femme au Chapeau* in 1905 led to friendship with the painter and an introduction to Picasso, who soon became a regular at the rue de Fleurus gatherings, bringing with him Max Jacob, Guillaume Apollinaire, Marie Laurencin, and a crowd of other artists, patrons, and critics. Almost immediately, Gertrude and Picasso became friends. Sharing a roughness of manner and childlike enthusiasm, isolated in the world of their creative imaginations by an unfamiliar language, each had begun to sense his own genius. In 1906, although he had not worked from a model for eight years, Picasso asked to paint her portrait. During the ninety sittings their friendship deepened as they talked about theories of composition: "I began to play with words then," Stein told Haas in 1946. "I was a little obsessed by words of equal value. Picasso was painting my portrait at that time, and he and I used to talk this thing over endlessly. At this time he had just begun on cubism. And I felt the thing I got from Cézanne was not the last in composition. . . . I felt . . . I had to recapture the value of the individual word, find out what it meant and act within it." Not long after, she began thinking of this problem in terms of literary portraiture: "I began then to want to make a more complete picture of each word, and that is when the portrait business started." Her investigations and reinvention of portraiture continued alongside other literary interests off and on for the rest of her life. Wendy Steiner suggests this evolved through three phases: the portraits of 1908-1911 are concerned with character types (for example, "Two. Gertrude Stein and Her Brother," "Five or Six Men," "Italians," and "A Kind of Woman"); the portraits of the second phase (1913-1925) are concerned with visual elements and then with "melody" (for example, "Portrait of Mabel Dodge at the Villa Curonia," "Guillaume Apollinaire," and "Susie Asado"); and the portraits of 1926-1946 are concerned with entity, or what Stein called "self-contained movement" (for example, "Jean Cocteau," "Georges Hugnet," and "Bernard Fay"). In "Portraits and Repetitions" (one of the lectures she gave in America during 1934-1935) Gertrude Stein described the evolution of her investigations, explaining that while she was writing *The Making of Americans,* "by listening and talking I conceived at every moment the existence of some one" (stressing the immediacy, continuous present, and nature of seeing and things seen). She went on,

it was like a cinema picture made up of succession and each moment having its own emphasis. . . .

Then as I said I had the feeling that something should be included and that something was looking and so concentrating on looking I did the Tender Buttons because it was easier to do objects than people if you were just looking. Then I began to do plays to make the looking have in it an element of moving and during this time I also did portraits that did the same thing. In doing these things I found that I created a melody of words that filled me with a melody that gradually made me do portraits easily by feeling the melody of any one. And this then began to bother me because perhaps I was getting drunk with melody and I do not like to be drunk. . . .

I began again not to let the looking be predominating not to have the listening and talking be predominating but to once more denude all this of anything in order to get back to the essence of the thing contained within itself . . . some portraits . . . I . . . think did do what I was then hoping would be done.

. . . perhaps two that did it the most completely . . . were portraits of Georges Hugnet and Bernard Faÿ.

Like a painter whose works reflect the sequence of discoveries he makes in techniques that will capture perception, techniques that are perceptions in themselves, Stein was embarked on an exploratory reinvention of literary possibility–a "dynamic program of theory, experimentation, discovery and new theory" as Steiner calls it–that was to continue through all her writings. But, like the painters who stimulated her, she found almost no one in the first decades of the century who understood what she was doing.

Born into the bohemian middle class in San Francisco, Alice B. Toklas had become acquainted with the Michael Steins during their various trips there to check on their real estate and business holdings. When she arrived in Paris in the fall of 1907 with her friend Harriet Levy, she immediately contacted the Steins, and, as she noted in *What Is Remembered* (1963), went to meet them—an event she was never to forget: "In the room were Mr. and Mrs. Stein and Gertrude Stein. It was Gertrude Stein who held my complete attention. . . . She was a golden brown presence, burned by the Tuscan sun and with a golden glint in her warm brown hair. She was dressed in a warm brown corduroy suit. She wore a large round coral brooch and when she talked, very little, or laughed, a good deal, I

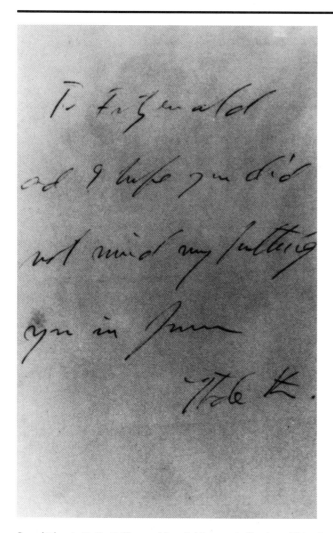

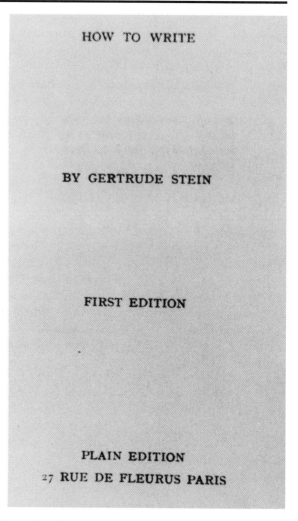

HOW TO WRITE

BY GERTRUDE STEIN

FIRST EDITION

PLAIN EDITION
27 RUE DE FLEURUS PARIS

Inscription to F. Scott Fitzgerald and title page (collection of Matthew J. Bruccoli). The inscription refers to the line "That is the cruelest thing I ever heard is the favorite phrase of Gilbert."

thought her voice came from this brooch. It was unlike anyone else's voice–deep, full velvety like a great contralto's, like two voices. She was large and heavy with delicate small hands and a beautifully modelled and unique head." Later she would recall when they met Alfred North Whitehead, "He was my third genius for whom the bell rang. The first two had been Gertrude Stein and Picasso."

Toklas herself, Mabel Dodge recalled, "was slight and dark, with beautiful gray eyes hung with black lashes–and she had a drooping, Jewish nose, and her eyelids drooped, and the corners of her red mouth and the lobes of her ears drooped under the black folded Hebraic hair, weighted down, as they were, with long heavy Oriental earrings.... Alice wore straight dresses made of Javanese prints.... She looked like Leah, out of the Old Testament, in her half-

Oriental get-up–her blues and browns and oyster whites–her black hair–her barbaric chains and jewels–and her melancholy nose. Artistic."

With Gertrude Stein, Alice Toklas was immediately caught up in the world of art and artists. She took French lessons from Picasso's mistress Fernande Olivier. At her first salon, she recalled, "The room commenced to be crowded. There were not only French but Russians, a few Americans, Hungarians and Germans. The discussions were lively but not entirely friendly. A very small Russian girl was holding forth explaining her picture, a nude holding aloft a severed leg. It was the beginning of the Russian horrors." Even more lively was the famous Banquet Rousseau in honor of painter Théodore Rousseau which she attended with Gertrude Stein at Picasso's studio in late summer or autumn 1908. Some thirty guests, including Apollinaire, Braque, Jacques Vaillant,

Jacob, and Laurencin, drank more and more wine while the ordered dinner did not arrive. Stein and Toklas, who later found that a pet donkey from a neighboring café had eaten the flowers off her hat, were asked but declined to sing American Indian songs. Rousseau was made to play his violin. Apollinaire sang songs and recited poems.

During the summer of 1908 Toklas and Harriet Levy took a villa near the Steins in Fiesole. Back in Paris, Toklas learned to type and began transcribing *The Making of Americans*, taking over as Gertrude Stein's handmaiden from Etta Cone, who had typed *Three Lives* (completed in 1906 but not published until 1909). Already Gertrude and Leo Stein had disagreed about Gertrude Stein's writing and their views on art, and it was clear to Gertrude Stein that she must look elsewhere for sustained emotional support. Sometime late in 1908, she chose a life, as husband and wife, with Alice Toklas, who moved to 27, rue de Fleurus early in 1909. Henceforth Toklas not only looked after the household and typed Stein's manuscripts, she responded to them and encouraged Stein, she read proofs (beginning with those for *Three Lives*), she sought out publishers and saw that manuscripts were safely stored, and she protected Stein from unwanted intrusions. "Fernande was the first wife of a genius I was to sit with," Stein has Toklas recall in *The Autobiography of Alice B. Toklas* (1933), "The geniuses came and talked to Gertrude Stein and the wives sat with me."

Toklas would also figure prominently in Stein's writings, sometimes under her own name, sometimes under pet names, such as "Pussy" or "Ada" (as in the portrait "Ada"), sometimes as the addressee of valentines or love poems, and sometimes as a counterpoint voice in dialogues (for example, in the long poem "Lifting Belly") or in snatches of conversation from daily life.

During the years before World War I, while cubism was reaching its zenith, Stein's inventions in her search for "the value of the individual word" strayed further and further from conventional semantic relations. The referentiality in the 1909 portraits of Matisse and Picasso ("One whom some were certainly following was one who was completely charming") gave way to the opacity and obscurity of the 1912 *Portrait of Mabel Dodge at the Villa Curonia*–"The only reason there is not that pressure is that there is a suggestion. There are many going. A delight is not bent. There had been that little wagon."–and finally exploded into what DeKoven calls the "fecund incoherence," rich in sound, image, and suggestion and dense with open-ended connections, of *Tender Buttons* (1914). Stein also wrote during this time some astonishingly lyrical portraits, notably 'Susie Asado' and 'Preciosilla,' both inspired by flamenco dancing she had seen during her sojourn in Spain in 1912. "The strict discipline that I had given myself," Stein wrote of this work, "the absolute refusal of never using a word that was not an exact word all through the *Tender Buttons* and what I may call the early Spanish and *Geography and Plays* period finally resulted in things like 'Susie Asado' and 'Preciosilla' etc. in an extraordinary melody of words and a melody of excitement in knowing that I had done this thing."

It was while staying with Mabel Dodge at her villa in Florence in the fall of 1912 that Stein had composed her portrait of Dodge, who immediately had 300 copies printed and bound them in Florentine wallpaper. Dodge's distribution of these pamphlets among the literati in New York, along with the appearance of the Matisse and Picasso portraits in the August 1912 issue of Alfred Stieglitz's magazine *Camera Work*, had a marked effect on Stein's reputation as a herald of international modernism. Dodge herself wrote an article on Stein for *Arts and Decorations* magazine. After a trip to London in 1913 in search of publishers and the appearance of *Tender Buttons* (published by the poet Donald Evans at his Claire Marie press) in 1914, Stein was regularly courted as an important member of the modernist movement. More and more visitors–including Roger Fry, Wyndham Lewis, Henry Lamb, Augustus John, Jacob Epstein, Nancy Cunard, Lady Ottoline Morrell, Marcel Duchamp, and Francis Picabia–came to the rue de Fleurus Saturday evenings to see Gertrude Stein and the Picassos rather than Leo Stein, who had come to loathe cubism. By the spring of 1914 Gertrude and Leo had divided up the treasures they had collected since their life together in Baltimore in 1897 and parted for good, Leo Stein moving to Florence and Gertrude staying on at 27, rue de Fleurus.

"Poetry," Stein wrote in *Lectures in America,* "is essentially a vocabulary just as prose is essentially not.... a vocabulary entirely based on the noun.... concerned with using with abusing, with losing with wanting, with denying with avoiding with adoring with replacing the noun." The "vocabulary" was not a lexicon of terms but a repertoire of activities. In *Tender Buttons* there began to evolve some of the most revolutionary ideas about poetry yet to emerge in English: "in *Tender Buttons* I was making poetry . . . but in prose I no longer needed the help of nouns and in poetry did I need the help of nouns. Was there not a way of naming things that would not invent names, but mean names without naming them."

Divided into three sections ("Objects," "Food," and "Rooms"), the work presents a series of still lifes with titles such as "A Chair," "A Frightful Release," "Water Raining," "Roastbeef," "Lunch," "End of Summer," and "Way Lay Vegetable." The subsections, varying from one line to several pages in length, are characterized throughout by great energy and ebullience as unexpected phrases jar and collide, often counterpointing a simple sentence structure that suggests the discourse of reasoned exposition. The pieces are not intended to be imagist, nor are they intended to be translated into one final right meaning. They are instead, as Marjorie Perloff has noted, "constructing a way of happening rather than an account of what has happened, a way of looking rather than a description of how things look." The words enact, are equivalent to, the energy of the thing seen. Thus in "A Box" foursidedness is reflected in the number of phrases beginning "out of," just as enclosedness is reflected in the grammatical structure of the last clause, which forces the reader back into the sentence to sort out the syntax:

> Out of kindness comes redness and out of rudeness comes rapid same question, out of an eye comes research, out of selection comes painful cattle. So then the order is that a white way of being round is something suggesting a pin and is it disappointing, it is not, it is so rudimentary to be analysed and see a fine substance strangely, it is so earnest to have a green point not to red but to point again.

Other examples of this method include "A Sound"–"Elephant beaten with candy and little pops and chews all bolts and reckless reckless rats, this is this."–"Sugar," which begins, "A violent luck and a whole sample and even then quiet. Water is squeezing, water is almost squeezing on lard. . . ." and "Celery":

> Celery tastes tastes where in curled lashes and little bits and mostly in remains.

> A green acre is so selfish and so pure and so enlivened.

Pieces such as these and the rhythmic and evocative "Susie Asado" (in *Geography and Plays,* 1922), Marjorie Perloff has pointed out, must be read as multiple interlocking and open-ended systems in which each element and system is as important as any other. In "Susie Asado" such systems include the sound patterns of flamenco-dance rhythms, the system of erotic suggestions in phrases such as "the wets," the pun on "sweet tea" or "slips slips hers," and the system of effects suggesting something like a Japanese tea ceremony in a garden–"told tray," "sash," "rare bit of trees," and the Japanese sound of the name Susie Asado:

> Sweet sweet sweet sweet sweet tea.
>> Susie Asado.
> Sweet sweet sweet sweet sweet tea.
>> Susie Asado.
> Susie Asado which is a told tray sure.
> A lean on the shoe this means slips slips hers.
>> When the ancient light grey is clean it is yellow, it is a silver seller.
>> This is a please this is a please there are the saids to jelly. These are the wets these say the sets to leave a crown to Incy.
>> Incy is short for incubus.
>> A pot. A pot is a beginning of a rare bit of trees. Trees tremble, the old vats are in bobbles, bobbles which shade and shove and render clean, render clean must.
>>> Drink pups.
>> Drink pups drink pups lease a sash hold, see it shine and a bobolink has pins. It shows a nail.
>>> What is a nail. A nail is unison.
>>> Sweet sweet sweet sweet sweet tea.

When war broke out in August 1914, Stein and Toklas were visiting the Whiteheads at their home, Lockridge, in Wiltshire, Stein having just signed a contract with John Lane for the English edition of *Three Lives*. Other guests included Bertrand Russell, George Moore, and Lytton Strachey. What had begun as a weekend visit turned into a six-week sojourn before they went back to Paris in October. Portraits of the guests and snatches of their conversation are captured in Stein's poem "Lockridge" (in *Bee Time Vine,* 1953).

"I very well remember at the beginning of the war being with Picasso on the boulevard Raspail when the first camouflaged truck passed," Stein recalled in *Picasso:*

It was at night, we had heard of camouflage but we had not yet seen it and Picasso amazed looked at it and then cried out, yes it is we who made it, that is cubism.

Really the composition of this war, 1914-1918, was not the composition of all previous wars, the composition was not a composition in which there was one man in the centre surrounded by a lot of other men but a composition that had neither a beginning nor an end, a composition of which one corner was as important as another corner, in fact the composition of cubism.

At first, frightened by the zeppelin raids in 1915, Stein and Toklas fled to Barcelona and then to Palma de Majorca, where they stayed over the winter. But in 1916, encouraged by the outcome of the Battle of Verdun, they returned to Paris and volunteered their services to the American Fund for the French Wounded. Their assignment was to distribute medical supplies, and for this purpose Gertrude purchased and drove "Aunt Pauline" (or "Auntie"), the first of a series of Ford cars that she owned. After the war she bought "Godiva," so named because her dashboard was bare of all accessories. Fords had special significance for Stein because they were repetitions, all modeled on a prototype and manufactured in series, a form which she regarded as particularly modern and which she tried in her own work in pieces such as "Descriptions of Literature," "Lifting Belly," and "Patriarchal Poetry," where a word or phrase ("a book," "lifting belly," and "patriarchal poetry," in these cases) is repeated in a series of forty to a hundred or more varying sentences.

To some extent Stein and Toklas resumed their old life when they returned to Paris in 1916. Picasso was there bringing with him Erik Satie and Jean Cocteau, both of whom became friends of Stein's. But cubism, as an avant-garde art form, was dead (one of its original publicists, Apollinaire, would never recover from war wounds, dying in 1918)–a new art movement, Dada, was on the horizon. Stein's work after 1914 never returned to the cryptic word kaleidoscope of *Tender Buttons*. Full of the joyfulness of phrases such as "a little lounge a clean piece of murder girder," the short poems of 1913 (collected in *Bee Time Vine*) are similar in their effects to *Tender Buttons*. But many of them reveal new explorations, such as the incorporation into the carefully chosen words of a dramatic format where Stein plays on both the character names and their dialogue, as in these lines from "In":

(I no)

> He is says.
> He is says he is. says.
> He is says
> He is says

(B)

> Nine Tea
> Nine tea times.
> Nine tea times four tea.
> Nine tea four tea.

By 1914, in pieces such as the long poems "Oval" and "Emp Lace," both in *Bee Time Vine*, Stein was choosing words not so much for their individual dynamism as for their rhythmical effects in repetitions, as, for example, these lines from "Oval":

> Wipe.
> Wipe it.
> Wipe with it.
> With it.
> Wipe.
> Wipe lay it.
> Wipe loan lying.
> Wipe.
> Wipe with.
> Wipe with stretches.

Whereas the *Tender Buttons* poems had been justified at both margins, Stein now began to work in lists, which allowed her to incorporate the dynamic of dramatic dialogue, as, for example, in the long poem "Lifting Belly" (written during 1915, 1916, and 1917 in Majorca, Paris, and in Perignan and Nimes, where she was assigned by the American Fund):

> I do not mention roses.
> Exactly.
> Actually.
> Question and butter.
> I find the butter very good.
> Lifting belly is so kind.
> Lifting belly fattily.

Lists of short sentences were often varied by very long highly rhythmical sentences, as in this sentence from "Emp Lace":

> Cow come out cow come out cow come out come out cow cow come out come out cow cow come out cow come out cow come out come out cow cow come out come out cow cow come out cow come out cow come out cow come out cow cow come out cow come out.

The sheer diversity of play in Stein's work during this period (and with much of her work from this point on in her career) defies categorization. DeKoven has labeled this period "Voices and Plays" while Haas has pointed out Stein's interest in both the audible world in general and the movement and relations of things and people in space. But her explorations included the reinvention of genre concepts (for example, by labeling writings "geography" or by making "Sonnets that Please" which seem to be like sonnets but do not look like them) and the challenging of any assumptions about structure that capture her attention (for example, a forty-one-part play, "Counting Her Dresses," in *Geography and Plays*, where each part is divided into two to seven one-line "acts," or a play, "The King or Something," also in *Geography and Plays*, divided into ninety-seven "Pages"). Stein changed forever the meaning of terms such as "poem" and "play."

Always sensitive to rhythms in the sounds she heard every day, Stein recreated in the poems, plays, and portraits of this period everything from snatches of conversation, war news, the sound of her car, or machinery in the street to nursery rhymes, aphorisms, and the act of sex. The long poem "A Sonatina Followed By Another" (in *Bee Time Vine*), for example, doodles its way through the rhythms of nursery rhymes: "Come along and sit to me sit with me sit by me, come along and sit with me all the next day too." (echoing "London Bridge is Falling Down"); "I wish I was a fish with a great big tail, a polly wolly doodle a lobster or a whale." (echoing "Patticake"). The title of this poem refers to Stein (who was not a musician) improvising on the piano, and the piece proceeds very much as though someone is trying this or that melody or rhythm and then meandering on to another.

Rather than particular things singled out and intensely seen (as in the still lifes of *Tender Buttons*), the objects, people, and activities in the work of this period come primarily from Stein's daily life. "Lifting Belly," for instance, with its erotic undercurrent ("Kiss my lips. She did./Kiss my lips again she did."), begins with references to burning olive wood in Majorca, is full of references to Alice Toklas, "Baby" (Gertrude), and objects from their daily life (apricots and decorated candles), and ends with references to Aunt Pauline (her first Ford) and to Miss Cheatham, someone she knew in Nimes. The phrase "lifting belly," repeated again and again, is not so much defined (it ceases to have any reference at all

after the twentieth repetition, a discovery about language we all make as children) as used to pace the flirtatious rhythm in the piece.

Stein was delighted to see the American troops ("doughboys") when they arrived in 1917, having not seen so many Americans together since her last trip to the United States in 1904. Pieces like "Work Again," "Decorations," and "Won" are among the war poems (collected in *Geography and Plays* and *Bee Time Vine*) that refer to them. Another war poem, "Accents in Alsace" (in *Geography and Plays*), begins,

Act I. The Schemils.

Brother brother go away and stay.
Sister mother believe me I say.
They will never get me as I run away.

....

The Schemmels.
Sing so la douse so la dim.
Un deux trois
Can you tell me wha
Is it indeed.

It ends with the lyrical,

Sweeter than water or cream or ice. Sweeter than bells of roses. Sweeter than winter or summer or spring. Sweeter than pretty posies. Sweeter than anything is my queen and loving is her nature.

Stein and Toklas were sent to Alsace in 1918 to help provide relief for civilians. So dedicated to the volunteer effort were they that they sold their last Matisse, the once controversial *La Femme au Chapeau*, in order to take the assignment. At the end of the war the French recognized their services with the Médaille de la Réconnaissance Française.

"If you write not long but practically every day you do get a great deal written," Stein remarked. By 1921 an enormous number of manuscripts had accumulated; only a small portion of them could be included in the collection entitled *Geography and Plays* brought out by the Four Seas Company of Boston in 1922. Many would not be published until after Stein's death, when they appeared in the Yale edition of the unpublished writings, which includes *Bee Time Vine and Other Pieces 1913-1927* (1953), *Painted Lace and Other Pieces 1914-1937* (1955), and *As Fine As Melanctha (1914-1930)* (1954) with five other volumes.

"For me the work of Gertrude Stein consists in a rebuilding, and entire new recasting of life,

Stein in 1937, standing in front of Pablo Picasso's 1906 portrait of her (courtesy of Edward M. Burns)

in the city of words," wrote Sherwood Anderson in his introduction to *Geography and Plays*. "Here is one artist who has been able to accept ridicule, who has even foregone the privilege of . . . wearing the bays of the great poets, to go live among the little housekeeping words, the swaggering bullying street-corner words, the honest working, money-saving words, and all the other forgotten and neglected citizens of the sacred and half forgotten city." Although the book firmly established Stein's reputation in literary circles, its reviews were seldom flattering. Typically she received acclaim and appreciation from writers, such as Mina Loy, while critics and journalists, such as H. L. Mencken, denounced the book as "dreadful stuff, indeed."

The book did not bring the "gloire" Stein had long sought. But this lack was offset somewhat by her being sought out as teacher in the early 1920s by writers such as Sherwood Anderson and Ernest Hemingway, whose work she affected. She read all of Hemingway's manuscripts,

consoled him in 1922 when his wife left the only manuscripts for all but two of the stories he had written on a train, and encouraged him to have enough confidence in his writing to take a year off from journalism. Eventually Hemingway was able to give her something in return: first he arranged for the serialization of *The Making of Americans* in Ford Madox Ford's *transatlantic review,* and then when the magazine folded before the entire work could be published, he persuaded Robert McAlmon's Contact Editions to publish it in book form in 1925. Akin to Joyce's *Ulysses* (1922) and Proust's *Remembrance of Things Past* (1913-1927) in its encyclopedic nature, this massive work narrates the history of America, of life's passage from birth to death, and of Stein and her family; explores habits of attention and quirks in the movement of thought; and evolves a grammar of continuous present–its publication was something she had long awaited.

In 1922, tired after the preparation of *Geography and Plays*, Toklas and Stein had retired for several months to Saint-Rémy in Provence. "It was during this winter," Stein wrote in *The Autobiography of Alice B. Toklas,* "that Gertrude Stein meditated on the use of grammar, poetical forms and what might be termed landscape plays." The following year (1923) they took their first annual summer in the country around Belley and thus began the Saint-Rémy or romantic/bucolic period in Stein's writing, full of cows, oxen, sheep, birds, streams, brooks, hills, valleys, and meadows. The writing itself sometimes went on outdoors, much in the manner of a painter with his easel, as Virgil Thomson recalled: "The scene took place in a field, its enactors being Gertrude, Alice, and a cow. Alice, by means of a stick, would drive the cow around the field. Then at a sign from Gertrude, the cow would be stopped; and Gertrude would write in her copybook. After a bit she would pick up her folding stool and progress to another spot, whereupon Alice would again start the cow moving around the field till Gertrude signaled she was ready to write again." The shift in her work was reflected by a shift in her interests in art during the 1920s to the nonabstract neoromantic painters: Christian Bérard, Pavel Chelishev, Leonid Berman, and Francis Rose.

Stein's works of this period include the landscape plays (such as "A Saint in Seven," written in 1922 and published in *Composition as Explanation,* 1926), the long poem "Patriarchal Poetry" (written in 1927 and published in *Bee Time Vine and Other Pieces 1913-1927,* 1953), *A Novel of Thank You* (written in 1925-1926 and published in 1958), *An Acquaintance with Description* (written in 1926 and published in 1929), "As a Wife Has a Cow" (written and published in 1926), and *Lucy Church Amiably* (written in 1927 and published in 1930)–named after a church in the town of Lucey, near Belley–and *Four Saints in Three Acts* (written in 1927 and published in *Operas and Plays,* 1932). There were also shorter pieces about the Saint-Rémy area: "A Comedy Like That," "The Four Regions," and "Capital Capitals" (a conversation among the four capitals, Aix, Arles, Avignon, and Les Beaux, which was set to music by Virgil Thomson and performed in New York in 1929). Stein's "landscape plays" are balanced compositions that have the stasis of a landscape painting but at the same time the activity of things in relation to one another (as in a play). Saints, because they are magical simply by existing, are also landscapes. "In *Four Saints,*" Stein said, "I made the Saints the landscape. All

the saints that I made and I made a number of them because after all a great many pieces of things are in a landscape all these saints together made my landscape." By calling her compositions "saints" or "landscapes," Stein invented new ways to think about literature and avoided the worn-out expectations conjured up by words such as "poem" or "novel."

One problem Stein was investigating in this work was whether there was any real difference between poetry and prose. Many of these pieces, though they purported to be novels or prose, are extremely lyrical, as in this sentence from "As a Wife Has a Cow: A Love Story":

> Happening and have it as happening and having it happen as happening and having to have it happen as happening, and my wife has a cow as now, my wife having a cow as now, my wife having a cow as now and having a cow as now and having a cow and having a cow now, my wife has a cow and now. My wife has a cow.

Another example of the lyricism of Stein's work during this period is this passage from "A Saint in Seven":

> In pleading sadness length of sadness in pleading length of sadness and no sorrow. No sorrow and no sadness length of sadness.
> A girl addresses a bountiful supply of seed to feed a chicken. Address a bountiful supply of trees to shade them. Address a bountiful supply to them.

Lucy Church Amiably, which Stein called "A Novel of romantic beauty and nature and which Looks Like an Engraving," also exhibits this poetic quality:

> Very little daisies and very little bluettes and an artificial bird and a very whited anemone which is allowed and then after it is very well placed by an unexpected invitation to carry a basket by an unexpected invitation to carry a basket back and forth back and forth and a river there is this difference between a river here and a river there.

As in the poetry of *Tender Buttons,* Stein was still concerned with meaning (re-creating) things without naming them: "I found in longer things like Operas and Plays and Portraits and Lucy Church Amiably . . . that I could come nearer to avoiding names in recreating something. . . . And here was the question if in poetry one could lose the noun as I had really and truly lost it in prose would there be any difference between poetry and prose.... I decided and Lucy Church Amiably had been an attempt to do it, I decided that if one definitely completely replaced the noun by the thing in itself, it was eventually to be poetry and not prose which would have to deal with everything that was not movement in space." She was beginning to discover that all writing that was not newspaper writing was poetry. She was also investigating the simple but profound question: how to write–investigations that culminated in the book by that title published in 1931.

Concurrently she was investigating grammar, trying to create paragraphs or long sentences that had both the "unemotional" balance of a sentence (where unity is based on static syntactic relationships) and the "emotional" movement of a paragraph (based on a series of sentences). Poems of this period, such as "As Eighty" in *Bee Time Vine*, reflect this interest in grammar.

Much of Stein's writing, as DeKoven has pointed out, has been devoted to demolishing and replacing the worn-out conventions and hierarchical orders of discourse invented by patriarchal society. But the long poem "Patriarchal Poetry" is not "about" this concern; rather it places the term "patriarchal poetry" into the multiple suggestive incoherent mode of discourse it is opposed to, where it stands out like a rock, meaning nothing and heard only as a drum beat. " 'Patriarchal Poetry' is not cubistic at all," wrote Virgil Thomson, who knew Stein while she was composing it, "not angular or explosive or in any way visual. It is rounded, romantic, visceral, auditory, vastly structured, developed like a symphony." Beautifully musical, the piece modulates through highly rhythmical interweavings of word motifs often reminiscent of the repeated squeakings and jerkings of a piece of machinery: "Is it best to support Allan Allan will Allan Allan is it best to support Allan Allan will Allan best to support Allan will patriarchal poetry Allan will patriarchal poetry Allan will patriarchal poetry is it best to support Allan...." Its final lines resound with the long drawn-out cadence of the symphonic finale:

Patriarchal poetry has to be which is best for them at three which is best and will be be and why why patriarchal poetry is not to try try twice.
  Patriarchal Poetry having patriarchal poetry. Having patriarchal poetry having patriarchal poetry. Having patriarchal poetry. Having patriarchal poetry and twice, patriarchal poetry.

He might have met.
  Patriarchal poetry and twice patriarchal poetry.

In 1925 Edith Sitwell, after an unsuccessful attempt to have Hogarth Press publish *The Making of Americans,* realized that Gertrude Stein needed more publicity, and she therefore arranged for Stein's first lectures, which were given in 1926 at Oxford and Cambridge. For the occasion Stein, by then fifty-two, wrote *Composition as Explanation* (1926), in which she outlined with deceptive simplicity the crucial entanglement of the time at which artistic composition occurs, the composition itself and the composition (that is, make-up) of the artist's generation or historical period. The lectures were a great success and shortly afterward resulted in, among other things, the publication of another collection of pieces: *Useful Knowledge* (1928). Stein was by now regularly published in such magazines as the *Little Review, Vanity Fair,* and *transition.* Her work had appeared through the 1920s in such avant-garde publications as *Broom, This Quarter, Black & Blue Jay, Blues,* and *Pagany.* But her work simply was not getting published quickly enough, and in 1930 Toklas published *Lucy Church Amiably,* the first of the five Plain Editions, printed in monotype on cheap paper and bound with simple covers. Toklas did the distribution herself.

Stein and Toklas were living at this time a pleasantly domestic life of gardening, preserving, and baking cakes (Toklas's specialty) in their summer residence at Bilignin. Basket, the white poodle they had acquired in 1928 (so named because Toklas thought he should "carry a basket of flowers in his mouth"), had made a dog lover of Stein. "I am I because my little dog knows me," she would write in 1935: ones's identity was the self that others knew. The story of how they acquired their summer retreat provides a typical example of Gertrude Stein's childlike egotism and dependence on others to work things out for her. As Toklas recalled later, "one day from the valley below we saw the house at Bilignin and Gertrude said, I will drive you up there and you can go and tell them that we will take their house. I said, But it may not be for rent. She said, The curtains are floating out the windows. Well, I said, I think that proves someone is living there." When they discovered that the lieutenant who lived there had no intention of moving, Stein arranged for him to be promoted so he would be posted elsewhere and have to move.

They signed the lease papers in spring 1929, having only seen this seventeenth-century villa from the outside. "Inside," Janet Hobhouse says, "was the furniture of the descendants of Brillat-Savarin himself. Outside was a lovely semi-formal garden, with gravel walks and flower beds. There were little balconies and shutters and a spectacular view of the countryside. It was a perfect home for a woman of letters."

At the end of her second decade in the twentieth century Stein made an important discovery about poetry: "there was something completely contained within itself and being contained within itself ... moving, not moving in relation to anything not moving in relation to itself but just moving.... Well it was an important thing.... because it made me realize what poetry really is." The portrait of Bernard Faÿ written in 1929, she felt, was one of the pieces where she achieved this self-contained movement:

> Patience is amiable and amiably.
> What is amiable and amiably.
> Patience is amiable and amiably.
> What is impatience.
> Impatience is amiable and amiably.

The movement here is delightful and quite comic. The first three lines swing along in a care-free forward lilt which is suddenly halted by the opposition in the fourth line. But, like a happy-go-lucky person, who is not long depressed by the perplexities of life, the fifth line picks up the lilt again, swinging the opposition along with it. Perhaps Bernard Faÿ was such a person, but it really does not matter.

The following year, Stein recalled, she began again to worry about the difference between poetry and prose: "As this thing came once more to be a doubt inside me I began to work very hard at poetry.... At that time I wrote Before the Flowers of Friendship Faded Friendship Faded and there I went back again to a more or less regular form to see whether inside that regular form I could do what I was sure needed to be done and also to find out if eventually prose and poetry were one or not one."

Before the Flowers of Friendship Faded Friendship Faded (the second Plain Edition, 1931) began as a free translation of Georges Hugnet's poem *Enfances* but quickly became a Steinian étude in which she experimented with conventional poetic rhythms:

> They will be white with which they know they
> see, that darker makes it be a color white for me,
> white is not shown when I am dark indeed with
> red despair who comes who has to care that they
> will let me a little lie like not I like to lie I like to
> live I like to die I like to lie. ...
>
> ....
>
> A little lake makes fountains
> And fountains have no flow,
> And a dove has need of flying
> And water can be low[.]

Just as Noam Chomsky would later use nonsense combinations of words to reveal purely syntactic relations in language, Stein used incoherent sentence combinations to reveal the movement of thought and rhythm that occurs in conventional poetry.

Publication plans originally were to print the two poems side by side, presenting the book as a collaboration. But when it came time to go to press Hugnet insisted on treating Stein's work merely as a translation. The two poems were never published together in book form, although they appeared on facing pages in *Pagany* (Winter 1931). Instead Toklas brought out Stein's poem as a Plain Edition, with a clear message to Hugnet in the title.

Early in the 1930s Stein came to the conclusion that "There could no longer be form to decide anything, narrative that is not newspaper narrative but real narrative must of necessity be told by any one having come to the realization that the noun must be replaced not by inner balance [such as the syntactic balance of sentences] but by the thing in itself and that will eventually lead to everything"–a universal form: writing. "Winning His Way: A Narrative Poem of Poetry," a fifty-six-page poem written in 1931 (published in *Stanzas in Meditation and Other Poems [1929-1933]*, 1956), reflects this concern with the melding of poetry and prose. "The 'story,' as a structure of consecutive happenings to be followed, has been pretty thoroughly destroyed by its explosion or transubstantiation into lyricism," notes Donald Sutherland, "and the 'narrative' is now almost entirely in the verbal and lyrical events of the poem itself, which moves at an astonishing pace."

> They could. See. Seem. In proportion.
> This. Was. As if. A shock. Of. Then.
> Who. Are hours. With. That. It. Was oftener.
> Thinking. In their heart. Sublime.
> Nicely. Known. Should they. Better. Belie.
> If they ask. Of it. To be better. Soon.

Stein singing "On the Trail of the Lonesome Pine," her favorite song, at Bilignin, summer 1937 (photograph by W. G. Rogers; courtesy of the Beinecke Rare Book and Manuscript Library, Yale University)

If "Winning His Way" transubstantiates narrative into lyricism, "Stanzas in Meditation" (150 pages long), written in 1932, transubstantiates ideas: "it came to Gertrude Stein," Sutherland points out, that "after all grammar and rhetoric are in themselves actualizations of ideas and the beginning, perhaps, of a conversion of ideas into poetry, since they are in their way shapes or schemes, aesthetic configurations. . . ." In "Stanzas in Meditation," he adds, "Stein solved the problem of keeping ideas in their primary life, that is of making them events in a subjective continuum of writing. . . . about ideas about writing." Stanza XII is a meditation on the thought configuration suggested by the word "which":

She was disappointed not alone or only
Not by what they wish but even by not which

Or should they silence in convincing
Made more than they stand for them with which.

Sutherland, who places the poem with Pound's *Cantos* and T. S. Eliot's *Four Quartets* in the "tradition of the long, rambling, discursive poem whose interest and energy are primarily in the movement of the poet's mind writing," likens the "tense and elegant behavior of the syntax" to the vibrant line in the drawings of Gabrielle Picabia (a close friend of Stein's) and describes its musicality as "a rhetorical accent rather than a properly temporal element. . . . an intensive, as against a progressive, metric . . . [where] both the temporality and the spatiality . . . are 'ideal'–functions of the sense, of the articulate 'thoughts' succeeding each other in a meditation."

Stein was discovering here what she would later call "entity"–"the moment you are you without the memory of yourself." The writing in "Stanzas in Meditation" not only occurs at such moments but forces the reader into that mode of consciousness. In "Stanzas in Meditation," as Sutherland points out, "The nowness and thisness of a thought, not its connections with past or future thoughts or with an objective context of thoughts, are the conditions of its life, and of thought generally at its most vibrant." In the same way, Stein would argue in "What are Masterpieces," it is entity–the memory-free mode of consciousness–that is crucial to the creative work of the genius or the masterpiece, not "identity"– the self-conscious or audience-oriented mode, structured as it is by the memory of past experiences. In the same vein, Wendy Steiner points out that Stein's late portraits sought "to present the individual as an entity, as a degree, a mode, of movement"–not in relation or comparison to anything else.

Diagramming entity involves diagramming the reader's thought as it is bombarded with juxtapositions of sentences of various rhetorical movements or forces, and the interweaving of phrases that sometimes do and sometimes do not objectivize themselves or particular words. This process is apparent in these selections from "A French Rooster. A History," one of the shorter poems of this period, which was written in 1930 and published in *Stanzas in Meditation:*

II

Pottery needs the damp
It needs noise hardly at all
It is less different from porcelain
It is less well known.

....

XII

Our by relief
In mentioning either
They will generously lead
In patience weather
They will make it be
Relieve their holding
It is in August
That they will be there.

These lines from another 1930 poem, "Abel" (published in *Stanzas in Meditation*), are also an example of Stein's diagramming:

Blame means does it
Halve means like it

Shoulder means hours now
Women mean like it
Who makes their care
To please running with ease[.]

In "Narrative" (also written in 1930 and collected in *Stanzas in Meditation*), as in many other works, Stein asks, What is the entity of the form itself ?:

A narrative now I know what a narrative is, it is not continuous it must contain that they wish and are and have been and it is that they lean in and together.

This is what a narrative is it does not need to be in remain it is that they include in conclude in into remain.

Two events in Stein's life during the 1930s helped to highlight for her the issue of identity versus entity. The first was the great success of *The Autobiography of Alice B. Toklas* (1933), which brought her her first income from writing and made her come to terms with for the first time the way an audience changes the writing: "When you are writing before there is an audience anything written is as important as any other thing and you cherish anything and everything that you have written. After audience begins, naturally they create something that is they create you, and so ... something is more important than another thing, which was not true when you were you that is when you were not you as your little dog knows you." That is to say, the audience tends to make one write out of one's identity rather than one's entity, which results in inferior work.

Stein, who was not really interested in conventional biographical prose writing, had wanted Toklas to write her autobiography for some time. But when Toklas did not get around to it, Stein took the task on herself, perhaps, as Sutherland suggests, as a relief from the intense concentration of writing "Stanzas in Meditation." Since it was written entirely from Toklas's point of view, reproducing very well her clipped, laconic speech, Stein had ample license to build exactly the legend of herself that she chose, only at the end revealing herself as the true author. Some old friends and acquaintances of Stein's, who thought they had been misrepresented, banded together and complained bitterly in "Testimony Against Gertrude Stein," which was published in the February 1935 issue of *transition*. But the public loved the book, in both America and Paris. It was reprinted as a Literary Guild selection in August 1933. "La Gloire," for which she had waited so long, had arrived.

Her agent soon began to pressure her to take advantage of it with a lecture tour, the second event that would bring identity/entity to the fore: as she lectured she heard more and more what the audience heard and was confronted again and again by her identity for them. For some time she resisted the trip, until one of the "doughboys" she had known during World War I, William Rogers (whom she called "Kiddie"), who had since become a reporter, came to Bilignin and persuaded her. A whole boatload of reporters came out to the S.S. *Champlain* to meet her when she arrived in New York on 24 October 1934. "Why don't you write the way you talk?," one asked. "Why don't you read the way I write?," Stein answered. She had a tremendous ability to communicate her intelligence and wit both in lectures and question periods.

While she was lecturing in the East, she took her first airplane trip to Chicago to see *Four Saints in Three Acts*. The production, with music by Virgil Thomson, choreography by Frederick Ashton, and an all black cast, had been extremely popular since its Broadway run, which opened in February. Crisscrossing back and forth to university, college, and cultural group audiences, her five-month tour included Philadelphia, Boston, Chicago (her favorite city, where Robert Hutchins and Mortimer Adler arranged for her to give seminars for the Great Books program at the University of Chicago; her lectures were later published as *Narration*), Baltimore, Charlottesville, New Orleans, Dallas, Austin, Houston, Pasadena, and San Francisco. By the time she returned to Paris on 12 May 1935, she had become a seasoned air traveler (who saw the lines of Picasso and Braque in the landscape below) and had visited almost every corner of the country. She had had tea at the White House and been entertained royally everywhere she went. And she had acquired a new publisher, Bennett Cerf of Random House, who agreed to publish one book by her each year.

In 1936 she lectured again at Oxford and Cambridge, presenting *What Are Masterpieces,* which examined the relationship of identity/entity to masterpieces and genius. During the trip to America, she had begun contributing pieces to various journals on such subjects as "American Food and American Houses." This "identity" writing for audiences continued through her last years and included among other things a series of articles on money in 1936, *Everybody's Autobiography* (1937), *Paris France* (1940), "The Winner Loses, A Picture of Occupied France" (*Atlantic Monthly*, November 1940), and *Wars I Have Seen* (1945), for which she kept a journal through World War II.

The "entity" writing in Stein's final years, however, resulted in some of her most philosophical work, including *Four in America* (1947), *The Geographical History of America or The Relation of Human Nature to the Human Mind* (1936), *ida a Novel* (1941), *Brewsie and Willie* (1946), "Dr Faustus Lights the Lights" (in *Last Operas and Plays,* 1949), and *The Mother of Us All* (1947). In *Four in America* she examined the relationship between identity (public role) and entity (independent quality of genius) by placing four "geniuses," Henry James, George Washington, Ulysses S. Grant, and Wilbur Wright, into roles they did not have. In *The Geographical History of America*, she tried to distinguish human mind (entity) from human nature (publicly defined identity). She spent the summer after her American tour at Bilignin mulling over these problems in the company of Thornton Wilder. Artistic endeavor, Stein believed, was a process of discovering what one knows regardless of the interests of any audience. "All the thousands of occasions in the daily life go into our head to form our ideas about these things," she said to Wilder. "Now if we write . . . these things we know flow down our arm and come out on the page. The moment before we wrote them we did not really know we knew them; if they are in our head in the shape of words then that is all wrong and they will come out dead; but if we did not know we knew them until the moment of writing, then they come to us with a shock of surprise. . . . Now of course there is no audience at that moment. . . . At that moment you are totally alone at this recognition of what you know." Characteristically work of this period proceeds as a series of propositions, queries, conclusions, and meditative games somewhat in the manner of Wittgenstein's *Philosophical Investigations* (1953).

All through the rumblings of war in the late 1930s, Gertrude Stein had firmly believed it would not happen, regarding it mainly as an intrusion upon her work. But, as she had seen change was a principle of art, she came also to accept it as a principle of life. When the landlord terminated the lease for 27, rue de Fleurus in 1938, Stein and Toklas moved happily to 5, rue Christine: "We were tired of the present which also was the past because no servant would stand the kitchen, there was no air in the house, the garage they had built next door had made it uncomfortable." When Basket, who had been painted and photographed almost as much as his mistress, died later that year, Stein and Toklas acquired another white poodle, Basket II. And when war was declared in September 1939, they quickly packed away their belongings in Paris and returned to Bilignin for the winter, where they coped with shortages in a spirit of adventure, chopping wood, making jam, and going on long walks in search of firewood. When they ran out of money, they "ate Cézanne." *Mrs. Reynolds* (1952), a novel Stein began in 1940, is largely an account of the experiences of a woman like herself in occupied France. Eventually they were forced to give up even Bilignin, when the lease expired in 1943. They moved to Le Colombier in nearby Culoz, where in August German officers were billeted, followed by Italian troops in September. Stein and Toklas did not live without anxiety. More than once they set out to leave. But the villagers, who knew exactly who they were and who could easily have denounced them as Jews, loved them, protected them, and encouraged them to stay. The mayor of Culoz, in fact, kept their names off the official records required by the Germans.

Just as Stein had reveled in the company of the "doughboys" in 1917, so also she welcomed the American troops in France in 1944. For her their arrival marked the end of the war. Toklas baked her victory cake; in December they moved back to Paris; and from then until Stein's death in 1946, she surrounded herself with GIs, talking to them, entertaining them wherever she went, and catching the rhythms of their voices in one of her last works, *Brewsie and Willie.*

On 19 July 1946 Gertrude Stein collapsed on her way to stay at a country house lent to her by Bernard Faÿ. She was immediately rushed to the American Hospital at Neuilly, where against medical discretion she ordered that the doctors operate. On 23 July she made her will, providing for Toklas out of the estate, making Toklas and Allan Stein executors, bequeathing her Picasso portrait to the Metropolitan Museum in New York and her unpublished manuscripts to the Yale University Library, and providing Carl Van Vechten, her lifelong friend and supporter, with the funds to publish all of her unpublished work. Then she settled in to wait, heavily sedated and in considerable pain, for the operation on 27 July. She died of inoperable cancer while still under anesthesia. "What is the answer?," she had asked Toklas just before her death. Toklas remained silent. "In that case what is the question?," Stein added.

How do we read this writing, that, along with the work of Alain Robbe-Grillet, Samuel Beckett, John Barth, Donald Barthelme, and William S. Burroughs, questions our defining notions of poetry, narrative, language, writing, literature, and finally the world? Stein might well ask of her critics some forty years after her death: "Why don't you read the way I write?" Very few have dealt with her work as twentieth-century art that, as Marianne DeKoven notes, "*must* reflect the . . . fragmented twentieth century reality, with its subjectivist epistemology, its emphasis on nonrational areas of the mind, its notion of consciousness as a chaotic flow of private associations, its vision of events as acausal, of time as nonlinear, of truth and reality as plural and undetermined. . . . [where] art is no longer seen as primarily representative or mimetic."

Posing a direct challenge to the assumptions of academic literary criticism in general, Stein's work has not lent itself to the hermeneutic and thematic textual explications that have dominated critical approaches in the twentieth century. Commentary has abounded with marginalizing terms such as "hermetic," "difficult," "experimental," and "inaccessible," which do nothing to come to terms with the very real and rich patterns, designs, and demands of Stein's writing. Following Richard Bridgman, a number of critics have focused on erotic readings of Stein's work, applying the label "erotic" to phrases which are simply affectionate and completely ignoring the dense collage of other effects and activities in the writing. Stein's work is full of references to people, places, and objects from her daily life, but biographical approaches, which attempt to attach some extrinsic or objective meaning to it, are a distraction from the aesthetic object of the texts and a denial of their essential multiplicity. Stein herself firmly believed that writing as art had nothing to do with the facts of daily living (identity): though it might contain those facts, its wellspring was located in the part of our beings that is unconscious of daily worries and pleasures (entity). The writing neither invites interpretive criticism, nor does it need it. Almost completely interlocking in its vocabulary, likely at any moment to involve anything from punning transliteration of foreign languages to challenges of the whole gamut of formal assumptions, her work is virtually impossible to generalize about and, as Stein intended, cannot be known or understood through explanation. Rather the writing exemplifies her thought and is emblematic, in its pluridimensionality, of the twentieth century.

The best introduction to Stein's work is her own exegetical and critical writing (*Composition as Explanation, Lectures in America, Narration, What Are Masterpieces,* and *How Writing is Written*) and her interview with Robert Bartlett Haas. The introductions to the Yale editions of unpublished writings, particularly the one to *Stanzas in Meditation* by Donald Sutherland, are valuable—as are the introductions to *The Geographical History of America* and *Four in America* by Thornton Wilder and the introduction to *How to Write* by Patricia Meyerowitz. Haas's *A Primer for the Gradual Understanding of Gertrude Stein* provides the most useful general approach to Stein's writing, since it presents the work in Stein's own terminology and in its chronological sequence as an evolution of investigations.

The emergence of semiotics and critical techniques from the work of Barthes, Derrida, and Kristeva, among others, has resulted in the late 1970s and the 1980s in criticism, notably from Marjorie Perloff and Marianne DeKoven, that begins to come to terms with the great diversity, play, resonance, and perception in Stein's work. But those who characterize her writing as a series of styles do it an injustice, for this approach suggests both the inappropriate distinction between style and content and the inaccurate notion that the work proceeded in a neat orderly progression. Nor is the word "experiment" accurate: "Artists do not experiment," Stein said, "Experiment is what scientists do; they initiate an operation of unknown factors in order to be instructed by its results. An artist puts down what he knows and at every moment it is what he knows at that moment." We have still to learn to read as Stein wrote.

Always a writer's writer, Stein's influence is still growing. The persistent activity of her artistic vision makes her a major writer of this century, comparable in the magnitude of her perception and achievement to her contemporaries Ezra Pound and James Joyce.

Interview:

Robert Bartlett Haas, "Gertrude Stein Talking: A Transatlantic Interview," *Uclan Review,* 8 (Summer 1962): 3-11; 9 (Spring 1963): 40-48; 9 (Winter 1964): 44-48.

Letters:

Sherwood Anderson/Gertrude Stein Correspondence and Personal Essays, edited by Ray Lewis White (Chapel Hill: University of North Carolina Press, 1972).
White's editing highlights and clarifies without intruding; the letters provide candid insight and document one of the few continuously cordial relationships Stein was to have with another author.

Dear Sammy Letters from Gertrude Stein & Alice B. Toklas, edited by Samuel M. Steward (Boston: Houghton Mifflin, 1977).
Although the memoirs included here contain little useful information about Stein, the letters and photographs more than compensate for this lack.

The Letters of Gertrude Stein and Carl Van Vechten 1913-1946, 2 volumes (New York: Columbia University Press, 1986).
Music critic Van Vechten was a tireless promoter and publicist of Stein. This collection illustrates an enduring friendship and the struggle to place Stein's work before a public.

Bibliographies:

Robert Bartlett Haas and Donald Clifford Gallup, *A Catalogue of the Published and Unpublished Writings of Gertrude Stein* (New Haven: Yale University Library, 1941).
Details the Yale exhibition of 1941 but is superceded by more recent bibliographies.

Robert A. Wilson, *Gertrude Stein: A Bibliography* (New York: Phoenix Bookshop, 1974).
A comprehensive primary reference source, dealing with published works of Toklas as well.

Ray Lewis White, *Gertrude Stein and Alice B. Toklas: A Reference Guide* (Boston: G. K. Hall, 1984).
Chronological listing of primary and secondary sources, especially useful for locating periodical reviews and commentary; most entries contain brief quotes from the work to indicate content.

Biographies:

W. G. Rogers, *When this you see remember me: Gertrude Stein in person* (New York & Toronto: Rinehart, 1948).
An interesting memoir, especially helpful to those studying Stein's lecture tour of America.

Elizabeth Sprigge, *Gertrude Stein: Her Life and Work* (New York: Harper, 1957).
The first biography of Stein, factual and dry; surpassed in organization and depth by later works.

John Malcolm Brinnin, *The Third Rose: Gertrude Stein and Her World* (Boston: Little, Brown, 1959).
Fairly complete and well written, but due to inaccuracies more recent sources should be consulted.

James R. Mellow, *Charmed Circle: Gertrude Stein & Company* (New York & Washington: Praeger, 1974).
The best biography of Stein available to date– detailed and well researched; contains interesting, lively accounts of Stein's artistic and personal relationships.

Janet Hobhouse, *Everybody Who Was Anybody: A Biography of Gertrude Stein* (New York: Putnam's, 1975).
Dissects Stein's homosexuality based on Leon Katz's analysis of the Stein notebooks but presents a sketchy view of other aspects of Stein's life; excellent photographs.

References:

Richard Bridgman, *Gertrude Stein in Pieces* (New York: Oxford University Press, 1970).
One of the more comprehensive critical texts; examines almost all the material available at the time and explains many vague areas but falls short of providing an overall portrait of Stein's development in only 340 pages.

Marianne DeKoven, *A Different Language: Gertrude Stein's Experimental Writing* (Madison: University of Wisconsin Press, 1983).
Documents and analyzes Stein's varied concepts and her effects on the avant-garde in literature.

Irene Gordon, ed., *Four Americans in Paris* (New York: Museum of Modern Art, 1970).
Includes six critical essays, Stein's portraits of Matisse and Picasso, a catalogue of the Stein family's art collection, and Leo Stein's *More Adventures*, as well as numerous photographs.

Robert Bartlett Haas, Introduction to *A Primer for the Gradual Understanding of Gertrude Stein,* edited by Haas (Los Angeles: Black Sparrow Press, 1971).
A cross section of Stein's writings with helpful explanations; useful to the Stein novice as a starting point.

Shirley Neuman and Ira B. Nadel, eds., *Gertrude Stein and the Making of Literature* (Boston: Northeastern University Press, 1988).
An anthology of critical essays varying from technical studies to an examination of Stein's lecture style; contains the first complete publication of Stein's "Realism in Novels."

Wendy Steiner, *Exact Resemblance to Exact Resemblance: The Literary Portraiture of Gertrude Stein* (New Haven: Yale University Press, 1978).
An in-depth consideration of Stein's development of the portrait as a literary form and its relation to cubism; also provides a comprehensive listing of Stein's portraits.

Donald Sutherland, *Gertrude Stein: A Biography of Her Work* (New Haven: Yale University Press, 1951).
Strongly biased toward Stein, this first published overview of her works should be used as a foundation in conjunction with later, more objective examinations of her works.

William Carlos Williams, "The Work of Gertrude Stein," *Pagany,* 1 (Winter 1930): 41-46; collected in *Selected Essays of William Carlos Williams* (New York: Random House, 1954), pp. 113-120.
An aid to an initial understanding of Stein's purposes and goals, despite some rather bizarre analogies.

Papers:

The major repository for Stein materials is the Beinecke Library at Yale University, which has most of Stein's manuscripts, correspondence, and un-published notebooks. There are also significant collections at the Bancroft Library, University of California at Berkeley, and the University of Texas at Austin.

Jean Toomer

This entry was updated by Rudolph P. Byrd (Carleton College) from the entry by Nellie McKay (University of Wisconsin-Madison) in DLB 51, Afro-American Writers from the Harlem Renaissance to 1940.

Places	New York City Washington, D.C.	Sparta, Ga. Chicago	Doylestown, Pa.
Influences and Relationships	P. B. S. Pinchback Waldo Frank George I. Gurdjieff	Sherwood Anderson Gorham Munson Georgia O'Keeffe	Hart Crane Walt Whitman
Literary Movements and Forms	Harlem Renaissance American Modernism	Imagism	Surrealism
Major Themes	Alienation Growing Dependence upon Technology Dissolution of Traditional Values	Southern Black Rural Experience The Relevance of the Past "Passing" for White	Psychological and Spiritual Development vs. Materialism and Conventional Values
Cultural and Artistic Influences	Institute For the Harmonious Development of Man (Gurdjieffian Philosophy)	Quakerism Buddhism The Bible	
Social and Economic Influences	Rise of Industrialism	Materialism	Miscegenation

See also the Toomer entry in DLB 45, *American Poets, 1880-1945, First Series.*

BIRTH: Washington, D.C., 26 December 1894, to Nathan and Nina Pinchback Toomer.

EDUCATION: University of Wisconsin-Madison, 1914; Massachusetts College of Agriculture, Amherst, 1915; American College of Physical Training, Chicago, 1916; University of Chicago, 1916; New York University, 1917; City College of New York, 1917.

MARRIAGES: 20 October 1931 to Margery Latimer (deceased); child: Margery. 1 September 1934 to Marjorie Content.

DEATH: Doylestown, Pennsylvania, 30 March 1967.

SELECTED BOOKS: *Cane* (New York: Boni & Liveright, 1923);
Essentials (Chicago: Lakeside Press, 1931);
An Interpretation of Friends Worship (Philadelphia: Committee on Religious Education of Friends General Conference, 1947);
The Flavor of Man (Philadelphia: Young Friends Movement of the Philadelphia Yearly Meetings, 1949);
The Wayward and the Seeking: A Collection of Writings by Jean Toomer, edited by Darwin Turner (Washington, D.C.: Howard University Press, 1980);
The Collected Poems of Jean Toomer, edited by Robert B. Jones and Margery T. Latimer (Chapel Hill: University of North Carolina Press, 1988).

OTHER: *Balo: A One Act Sketch of Negro Life,* in *Plays of Negro Life,* edited by Alain Locke and Montgomery Gregory (New York & London: Harper, 1927), pp. 269-286;
"Race Problems and Modern Society," in *Problems of Civilization,* edited by Baker Brownell (New York: Van Nostrand, 1929);
"York Beach," in *The New American Caravan,* edited by Alfred Kreymborg, Lewis Mumford, and Paul Rosenfeld (New York: Macaulay, 1929), pp. 12-83;
"Blue Meridian," in *The New Caravan,* edited by Kreymborg, Mumford, and Rosenfeld (New York: Norton, 1936), pp. 633-654;

Jean Toomer (courtesy of the Prints and Photographs Collection, Moorland-Spingarn Research Center, Howard University)

"Five Vignettes," in *Black American Literature: Poetry,* edited by Darwin Turner (Columbus, Ohio: Merrill, 1969).

PERIODICAL PUBLICATIONS: "Banking Coal," *Crisis,* 24 (June 1922): 65;
"Oxen Cart and Warfare," *Little Review* (Autumn/Winter 1924-1925): 44-48;
"Easter," *Little Review,* 11 (Spring 1925): 3-7;
"Reflections," *Dial,* 86 (1929): 314;
"White Arrow," *Dial,* 86 (July 1929): 596;
"As the Eagle Soars," *Crisis,* 41 (April 1932): 116;
"Brown River, Smile," *Pagany,* 3 (Winter 1932): 29-33;
"Of a Certain November," *Dubuque Dialogue,* 1 November 1935;
"See The Heart," *Friend's Intelligencer,* 104 (9 August 1947): 423;
"Chapters from *Earth-Being,*" *Black Scholar,* 2 (January 1971): 3-14.

　　When the writers of the early Harlem Renaissance read *Cane* in 1923, in the words of Arna Bontemps, they "went quietly mad." No prior literary description of the Afro-American experience had reached its level of artistic achievement. Jean

Toomer, the author of *Cane,* had been mostly associated with progressive white writers of the late 1910s and early 1920s, such as Hart Crane and Sherwood Anderson, but the black avant-garde writers claimed him as their own. *Cane* was called the herald of a new day in Afro-American letters, and Toomer was perceived as the most promising Negro writer. It was an auspicious beginning for a new author. Although Toomer continued writing for his whole life, the promise of his masterpiece was not matched again in his published work. By the end of the 1920s Toomer and *Cane* seemed to have disappeared from the world of letters; they remained largely unknown to the reading public for nearly forty years. Then in 1951, *Cane* was republished, and by 1969 it had made a dramatic comeback from obscurity. A new generation of thinkers confirmed earlier appraisals of Toomer's book, hailing *Cane* for its critical achievement as well as for its intrinsic worth as the first major book to affirm cultural assumptions of the Harlem Renaissance of the 1920s.

Nathan Eugene Toomer, the son of Nina Pinchback and Georgia planter Nathan Toomer, was born in Washington, D.C., on 26 December 1894. Although known by the surname Pinchback for most of his early life, he used his father's last name as an adult, and when he began to write, he changed Eugene to Jean. He spent his early years in Washington in the home of his maternal grandparents to which his mother had returned after her husband deserted her in 1895. Toomer's grandfather Pinckney Benton Stewart Pinchback had been a powerful politician associated with the Louisiana governor's office in the era of Reconstruction. The Pinchbacks were a racially mixed family. In the autobiographical essay "On Being An American," Toomer described his background as "Scotch, Welsh, German, English, French, Dutch, Spanish, with some dark blood." Although the Pinchbacks were sufficiently fair-skinned to have been considered white, P. B. S. claimed *he* was a Negro and built his career on that claim. Toomer himself could not readily be identified as black. Until 1906 he lived in his grandparents' home on Bacon Street, in a wealthy white neighborhood which he recalled as being unblighted by prejudice. An assertive child, Toomer found the main source of conflict in his life to be his domineering grandfather. After a devastating illness in 1905 and an eight-month-long convalescence in 1906, Toomer moved to white neighborhoods first in Brooklyn and then to New Rochelle, New York, with Nina

Pinchback and her white second husband. He returned to Washington after his mother's unexpected death in 1909.

By 1910, the Pinchbacks had suffered severe financial losses. They had moved into a less affluent, black section of the city. Toomer attended the M Street High School, Washington's secondary school for Negroes. Later Toomer often said that he had an advantage over most other people in knowing the truth about race, for he had lived in both the white and black worlds as a member of each group. In 1914, after having given the matter of his racial identity some thought, he reasoned that he would consider himself an American, neither white nor black. He was convinced that almost all Americans were descended from a number of bloodlines, but that they were just not yet aware of it. He pondered his national identity in his early "The First American." His decision to adopt an American identity had a major impact on his literary career as well as on all other significant events in his subsequent life.

Although he worried about whether his having graduated from a black high school would affect his reception at college, in 1914 he enrolled at the University of Wisconsin-Madison, intending to study agriculture. However, by the end of the year he changed his mind, and he left school shortly after the Christmas vacation. In the four years that followed, Toomer attended as many colleges, and he changed his academic interests just as frequently. In 1915 he entered the Massachusetts College of Agriculture; in 1916 he enrolled at both the American College of Physical Training in Chicago and the University of Chicago; in the 1917 summer session, he entered the City College of New York. He remained at no institution long enough to earn a degree. Each time he began with high hopes, but each time some difficulty arose that he could not overcome, and he left. In 1919 he decided to become a writer.

Jean Toomer's interest in literature began in early childhood, he relates in "Chapters From *Earth-Being:* An Unpublished Autobiography" (*Black Scholar*, 1971), when his Uncle Bismarck introduced him to the world of books and imagination. Every night Bis would retire after dinner "in bed with a book, cigarettes, and a saucer of sliced peaches prepared . . . in a special way, and read far into the night. Sometimes he would write, trying his hand at fiction." He began to include Toomer in his nightly ritual, introducing him to new ideas and having discussions about

Toomer's mother, Nina Pinchback, circa 1890 (courtesy of Marjorie Content Toomer)

them with the boy. When Toomer went to New Rochelle, initially he had difficulty making friends, but he discovered the public library and began to read intensively stories of knights and chivalry: books about King Arthur and the Knights of the Round Table, Sir Galahad and Sir Lancelot, and the Quest for the Holy Grail. As a child, he loved the outdoors, and was fond of bicycling, baseball, swimming, and tennis. He also learned to sail in New Rochelle and was given a small boat of his own in which he spent much of his time exploring the waters of the Long Island Sound. His first attempts at writing included materials he recalled from these early outdoors experiences. In high school, where his love of reading continued, Shakespeare and Dickens were his favorite writers.

Although Toomer became aware of the possibilities of a literary life while he was in Wisconsin, he did not give the idea serious consideration until later. At City College in 1917, he began to read George Bernard Shaw and Henrik Ibsen, whose works made him aware of the relationship between literature and society. Soon after, he discovered Walt Whitman's writings. Romain Rolland's *Jean Christophe* and Goethe's Wilheim Meister novels helped him see how the creative imagination and psychology could be made to serve each other.

Living in New York in 1919, he met many of the up-and-coming young American writers of the day. Among these were Edwin Arlington Robinson, Witter Bynner, Van Wyck Brooks, and Waldo Frank. Frank and Toomer became close friends and were part of Greenwich Village's artistic society. The scope of his reading expanded significantly after he decided to pursue a career in writing. He recalled later that during that time he read the works of Fyodor Dostoyevski, Leo Tolstoy, Gustave Flaubert, Charles Baudelaire, Sinclair Lewis, Theodore Dreiser, Sigmund Freud, Robert Frost, and Sherwood Anderson, with whom he was to have an extended correspondence. He also read books on Buddhist philosophy, Eastern teachings, occultism and theosophy, and the Christian Bible as literature, and magazines, including the *Dial,* the *Liberator,* the *Nation* and the *New Republic.* During this difficult period of apprenticeship, he wrote essays, articles, poems, short stories, and reviews, but nothing he wrote satisfied him, and he linked his ineptness to internal disharmony. He was sure he would not find his literary voice until he solved the problem of his internal disorganization, and he saw no immediate escape from the dilemma this presented to him.

Toomer's life and writings were deeply affected by his search for internal harmony, which was tangentially related to the issue of racial identity. His search for spiritual concord later became synonymous with his search for higher consciousness. He entered into his early adulthood determined to find a system through which he could bring the physical, emotional, and intellectual parts of himself into harmony. His quest for such a system compelled much of his attention through the remainder of his life and, ultimately, was the defining criterion of his happiness, success, shortcomings, and disappointments.

In the summer of 1921 Toomer was living in Washington again, taking care of his ill, aging grandparents, and trying to write, but having no success in this latter endeavor. He met the principal of a small, rural, black school near Sparta, Georgia, who needed someone to take over the management of his institution for a short time. Toomer was invited to take the temporary position, and he welcomed the opportunity as a respite from the drudgery of housekeeping and the frustrations of his unrealized literary efforts. He was also curious about the South and its folk culture. In September he went to Sparta.

Struck by the beauty and power of the people and the land, in spite of racial segregation, poverty, and the unpolished state of the culture, Toomer lived among the rural people with whom he worked. He had a "shack" off by himself, where, he noted, the mud came up through the floorboards when it rained, but which gave him the opportunity to observe the folk while they went about their daily affairs. For the first time he heard the women singing at sunset while they prepared supper, and he heard spirituals sung by musically untrained people. He realized the special quality in their emotional responses to these songs. He saw firsthand the brutality, hardships, and social and economic oppression experienced by southern black people, as well as the internal strength and dignity of the black folk culture.

Toomer responded emotionally to this new environment, feeling for the first time in his life a sense of inner balance that enabled him to begin to write in a way that satisfied him. He immersed himself in the spirituality of the experience, and he found his voice. Before he left Georgia in November, he sent a poem to a New York journal, and on the train back to Washington he began to compose the narratives which became the first section of *Cane*. By the end of the year this part of the book was completed; by early spring 1923 the entire book was done.

When Toomer had first begun writing, he had not conceived of a book. He wanted only to set down in prose and poetry his vision of the southern black rural experience. While he was in the South he had been in close correspondence with Waldo Frank, and by the time he had returned to New York early in 1922, Frank advised him to combine his pieces into a book and promised to recommend it to his own publisher, Boni and Liveright.

Taking advantage of the climate of experimentation in language and form that was being fostered by many of the white writers he then knew, Toomer combined prose narratives, poetry, prose poems, and drama to delineate his total experience. The book, an artistic, balanced exploration of the black experience in white America,

revolves around the central analogy between the hard and grinding work that takes place before the syrup can come from the cane, and the fortitude of a people resisting physical and psychological oppression.

Toomer arranged his pieces in a format intended to unify the rural southern and urban northern black experiences. *Cane*'s focus is circular, moving from black Georgia folk culture to northern city culture, and back to the South, where both experiences merge, if not collide. Even his narrative perspective reinforces the circular thematic structure of the work. The first two sections of the book feature a narrator who is most often a detached observer of the action. It is clear that he is less familiar with Georgia than he is with the cities, for in the first section, he makes several attempts to develop close relationships with the women, but he is unable to do so. They elude him physically, intellectually, and spiritually. He has more success with women in the second section, except in the case of a woman who shares qualities with her country sisters. In the last section of the book, the narrator and central character, Ralph Kabnis, blend into one, rarely becoming distinguishable from each other. Kabnis has both a northern and a southern identity. He moves painfully from resistance to his "other" self, to acknowledgement of the whole history of the self, to expectation of acceptance of his divided self.

The first section, set in Georgia, is made up of twelve poems and six vignettes of the lives of women. Against the background of the grinding and boiling of cane and the stirring of the sweet syrup, black men from the community gather in the night to tell stories around the hot, fragrant, copper cauldron. Toomer's imagery in these sketches is taken mainly from nature, making this section the most lyrical, vivid, mystical, and sensuous part of the book. The initial effect of the imagery can be deceptive, however, for Toomer also weaves dissonance, sarcasm, irony, and harsh realism into the fabric of these vignettes. The lyrical beauty of dusk on the horizon at the beginning of the section metamorphoses into the evil eye of a "blood burning moon" at the finale. The narratives and poems between these two points focus on the conflicts, insecurities, and pressures that beset southern life.

The six women, five black and one white, are symbols of the history of women in the South. The black women are identified with nature, and to varying degrees, they are beautiful, in-

Toomer with his Uncle Bismarck, who encouraged Toomer's early interest in literature (courtesy of Marjorie Content Toomer)

nocent, sensuous, sometimes strong, but always vulnerable, misunderstood, and unpossessable. As nature has always been helpless against the onslaughts of industrialization and the technological advances of the modern age, so, too, are the women desecrated by racial and sexual oppression. The women experience alienation, madness, and death, emblemizing the embattled state of black people and black folk culture. Jean Toomer's women are of the earth because they are sensuous and fecund, but they are not earth mothers. They do not nurture; they, like the land, are ravaged.

The single white woman in the group is as poor and as oppressed by the rigid system of racial segregation as the black women. Toomer understood clearly that black and white people in the South were interdependent in significant ways and that it was impossible to separate the groups' experiences in any comprehensive survey of southern life. Through this character Toomer demonstrates that rigid codes of racial oppres-

sion, partly justified by their perpetrators as means of protecting southern white women, can oppress society as well.

The first section of the book ends in a confrontation: a black man is lynched for daring to date the same woman that a white man dates, and the white community has its satisfaction in the knowledge that the status quo remains intact. The black woman who is left behind is the final victim. Surrounded by chaos and brutality, she sinks into madness.

Cane's second section comprises a kaleidoscope of impressions of the more sophisticated, but narrowing, urban styles of life in Washington, D.C., and Chicago.

Throughout the seven prose pieces and five poems, Toomer's tone and language evoke sensations associated with the vibrations of city life, and the imagery reflects the effects of industrialization and mechanization on human beings in the urban environment. There are only rare images of nature here, no dusky sunsets or golden colors illuminate the landscape, and there is no lyricism. The black people of this section, descendants and survivors of the black southern folk culture, are seeking new homes in the urban North, where man has subdued nature. The migration of people from the South was motivated by hopes of finding a larger life, one outside of southern racism, but the refugees discover only new and different restrictions in the place they had hoped would be the promised land. Yet, there is a crude energy in this section, and it comes from the tension in the people's will to resist and survive the arbitrary restraints of this world.

Toomer's main focus is on the effects on the black spirit of the physical and psychological oppression of northern social and economic institutions. He fastens on the ultimate failure of black people, as a group, to achieve emotional and spiritual wholeness in America. In addition to external restrictions in the North, the newcomers are also in danger of self-imposed psychological restraints. Several of the selections address this issue and show how new value systems replace old ones in the psyche of the recently transplanted urbanites, before they can fully comprehend the meanings of the new. Thus, Toomer suggests that a positive black identity can be attained through an understanding of the past. The burdens of an oppressive history can be used as lessons to shape the future.

Toomer takes the reader back to Georgia, in the third part of the book, where Ralph Kabnis, a black northerner, experiences a nightmare in the canebrake. The earlier focus on mysticism, sensuality, nature, and the elusiveness of women is replaced by a focus on the fear and ambivalence that result from a milieu in which racial oppression is a way of life. In this self-contained drama, Kabnis comes as a schoolteacher; he is also a poet who dreams that he will become the voice of the South. But Kabnis is the victim of impotency and uncertainty as he searches for his identity in the land of his ancestors. His journey toward that goal incorporates the alienation, ambivalence, and sense of oppressive control that are all part of the black heritage.

Kabnis is aware of the beauty and worth of the waning folk culture, and he wishes to catch its parting song in order to rekindle its spirit to the world. He will do this by bringing together the forces of anger, exploitation, evil, and the will to survive, which have always been elements in black American folk culture. But before he can realize his goal, he must first acknowledge and assimilate the humiliation and pain of the past; he must be disabused of his northern separateness from it.

During his Georgia stay Kabnis learns many things about southern history and the nature of southern white oppression of black people. By the end of the drama he is no longer just Kabnis the northerner whose ancestors came from the South, or an enlightened black man offering gifts of education and art to his backward southern relatives; he is a black man who is beginning to understand the meaning of himself as a northerner and as a southerner, to understand what it is to be a black American.

In a choice between education, politics, and art as ways of comprehending and fusing the various elements of the black American experience into a dignified whole, Toomer chooses art. The northern black political activist, who is present in the drama for a while, leaves before the job is done, and Kabnis gives up teaching just as quickly. It is Kabnis, the poet, who remains to catch the "birthsong" of the new day and to create *Cane*.

In this book, race and sex, city and country, erudition and illiteracy, and beauty and pain are examined as parts of the experience that come together and determine black identity. The folk culture is passing, but its influence is vital among black people. The present is in flux and is itself the search for future direction. Kabnis is the black Everyman on a journey in time, to discover a concrete meaning of the American black identity.

The most enduring aspect of *Cane* is that it reveals the intrinsic strength and beauty of black American culture. In 1923 the book represented the distance between the slave heritage and the New Negro of the Harlem Renaissance. The sun and the new day at the end of the book symbolize the triumph of the strength of the folk culture. Without self-glorification or apologies for enduring oppression, *Cane* leaves the reader with a sense of positive individual and group identity.

Between the fall of 1921 and the beginning of 1923 Toomer also worked on other pieces that addressed important Afro-American themes. A short story, "Withered Skins of Berries," and two plays, *Balo* and *Natalie Mann*, are his major extant works of the period. *Balo,* a one-act folk drama, was produced by the Howard University Players during its 1923-1924 season, and was anthologized in *Plays of Negro Life* (1927), edited by Alain Locke and Montgomery Gregory. *Natalie*

Mann is an expressionist play that has never been staged. Both "Withered Skins of Berries" and *Natalie Mann* were not printed until 1980, when they appeared in *The Wayward and the Seeking*, an anthology of Toomer's previously unpublished writings edited by Darwin Turner.

All of these works have artistic merits. "Withered Skins of Berries" treats the theme of the mulatto passing for convenience. It is set in Washington, D.C., and examines the complexities of the black individual's struggle to rise above race in America. In her economic interests, the mulatto protagonist "passes" and works in an office among whites who are hostile to blacks. The language is as lyrical as the first section of *Cane*, but beyond that, it sheds light on the motivations that propel blacks to move across the color line. *Balo* is a realistic play and is noteworthy because Toomer attempts to experiment with southern black dialect. He presents a positive attitude toward the strength of the black family and community at a time when such an attitude was in decline. Following in the tradition of writers like Tolstoy and Ivan Turgenev, Toomer uses the lives of common folk as the subject of art, and he foreshadows black writers like Zora Neale Hurston, Langston Hughes and Sterling Brown, who also use the folk culture as a source of rich artistic inspiration.

Natalie Mann is important in the Toomer canon both for its experimental expressionistic style and its content. Had he been successful in having this play staged, he would have been a pioneer in the field at that time, for when it was written in 1922 only Eugene O'Neill among American dramatists had written and produced works which used similar techniques. Toomer was not only interested in imitating European stage writers who were already using expressionism, but he wanted to demonstrate that language was sufficiently flexible to "objectify mankind's spiritual struggle," and to ridicule those moral and social values which he considered destructive to the human spirit. Through this play Toomer satirizes American business, social, and materialistic ideals. The dialogue is stilted and mechanical, and the actions and expressions of the characters are exaggerated and full of distortions. Stage directions are explicit and detailed, and the players are caricatures rather than realistic characters.

Natalie Mann is the lyrical dramatization of materialism, hypocrisy, and antihumanistic values versus intellectualism, spirituality, and creativity. It examines negative aspects of black middle-class

Jean Toomer (photograph by Marjorie Content Toomer, from the Marjorie Toomer Collection)

life in Washington and focuses on one black woman's search for liberation from many of the values of this social group. In their search for social and economic upward mobility, the members of the black middle class imitate the white bourgeoisie, especially its sterile values, at great emotional and spiritual cost to themselves. Above all, they sacrifice inner well-being to a preoccupation with social status. The result is personal alienation and fragmentation in the community.

The protagonist, Natalie Mann, represents "creative revolution" in her search for honest friendships and the chance to love freely and be loved in return. Around her, the community is weak because of social pressures to conform to repressive conventions and to aspire to material gains. There is no intensity of joy or sorrow, of spontaneity and creativity in this environment. The other characters portray conscious denial of all that is natural to the human spirit. Natalie Mann repudiates this denial of life, and ultimately she completely rejects the oppressive conventions of her black middle-class upbringing.

One important aspect of this play is the prominence given to the middle-class black woman. This concern for her dilemma was echoed in other black writers of the later 1920s, especially the women, who found it difficult to escape others' expectations that they would fill traditional roles in spite of their artistic potentials. The novels of Jessie Fauset and Nella Larsen are enlightening for their insights into the conditions which Toomer, preceding them, raises in his play. Toomer was aware that women were particularly victimized in often being denied the opportunity to aspire to careers outside of their roles as wives and mothers. His own mother had been so limited. He saw also that the social attitudes that permitted this kind of oppression were destructive to the entire culture. In restricting women's options to fulfill themselves, men were restricting themselves as well, for the freedom of all depends on the freedom of the individual.

In a larger sphere, Toomer's concern in this and his other works of the early 1920s is that the spiritual heritage of mankind is in jeopardy of strangulation by the antilife forces of the modern world. This perception was central to the thinking of Waldo Frank, Gorham Munson, and the other critical thinkers who were closest to Toomer in that decade. With this group, Toomer wanted to raise American consciousness of the dangers within civilization. Radical in their time, wanting to strip away pretense and emptiness from living and to provide spirituality and deep human feelings, the writers Toomer knew experimented with new forms in language and techniques in efforts to expand literature to accommodate and convey the subjectivism of their views. It was unfortunate for Toomer that *Natalie Mann* was not allowed to reach the public at the time it was written, for it falls in so well with the progressive ideas of his peers.

In spite of his being critically acclaimed as a new leader in black letters, Toomer wanted to be no more than an American writer, and he wanted his work on the black experience to be viewed only as a part of the American experience. Upset and outraged that the book led everyone to see and think of him as a "Negro" writer, he argued publicly that there was no proof of African heritage in his family, and that he was not a Negro. With a good deal of pique, almost immediately after the publication of his book, he turned away from the friends and colleagues who had inspired and encouraged his efforts from 1919 to 1923. He set out, intellectually, to find a new source to restore the internal unity he had enjoyed during the time in which he had been writing the book. Except for his rather brief recon-

struction of Afro-American life and history in the opening sections of "The Blue Meridian," Toomer never again wrote of the Afro-American experience in the imaginative mode.

Early in 1924 he encountered the teachings and philosophy of George Ivanovitch Gurdjieff, a Greek and Armenian guru who had traveled extensively in the Orient studying theology and philosophy. Gurdjieff, viewed by his followers as prophet, priest, and teacher, arrived in the West after the Russian Revolution and World War I precluded the possibility of his opening an institute in Russia. Offering a way to obtain balance between mind, body, and soul, and to achieve full human potential through higher consciousness, he attracted a great deal of attention in the early 1920s. People from diverse backgrounds flocked to the Institute For the Harmonious Development of Man located in Fontainebleau, outside of Paris. The time was right for him, and many Western, middle-class intellectuals, disillusioned with the state of the world and searching for meaning out of the chaos of modern civilization, were willing to adopt his complicated system of psychology, philosophy, and dance in the hope of transcending ordinary human capability.

When Jean Toomer saw a demonstration of the exercises and dances and heard a lecture on the system in 1924, he thought he had found an answer to his quest. He not only joined the movement, but that summer he went to Fontainebleau, and in the fall he became a teacher of the system. By then he had cut almost all his ties with the literary world.

From 1924 to 1932 Toomer worked as a teacher of the Gurdjieff philosophy. Beginning in New York, he tried to establish a group of followers in Harlem. Those who initially turned up to listen to Toomer expound on the attributes of higher consciousness were more interested in him as the author of *Cane* than as the carrier of a new gospel of salvation. The failure of his effort is described in detail in *The Big Sea* (1940), an autobiography by Langston Hughes. Toomer went next to Chicago, where, for several years, he was successful in forming groups among the intellectuals of that city.

Although Toomer rejected the literary world in 1923, he continued to write. In the spring of 1925 a short story, "Easter," appeared in the *Little Review*. "Mr. Costyve Duditch" and "Winter on Earth," two short stories, were published in the *Dial* in 1928, and "York Beach," a novella, in the *New Caravan* in 1929. His final publication, the long poem "The Blue Meridian," appeared in the *New Caravan* in 1936. None of these works linked him publicly to his earlier literary success.

"Easter" is a work that shows Toomer in transition from the ideas that led from *Cane* to his later writings. While the book embraces a small world, the story has a universal vision. Where *Cane* is lyrical and combines symbolism and realism, "Easter" is surrealistic, and its images are absurd and grotesque. The story largely discredits the Judeo-Christian tradition as the force for the salvation of Western man.

"Mr. Costyve Duditch" was written by a Toomer secure in his mission as a Gurdjieff teacher, for Duditch represents modern man reflected in the light of that philosophy. He is a mechanical man whose life is defined by sterility, the lack of genuine feelings and emotions, and a superficial attitude toward his internal development. Duditch is independently wealthy, and he travels extensively. In his rootlessness and meaningless behavior he is unaware of his potential. Toomer sees this blindness as the universal condition of modern man, and history shows his strong beliefs in the need for a new way to reverse this state of affairs.

"Easter" and "Mr. Costyve Duditch," from a literary point of view, are Toomer's best works between *Cane* and the end of the 1920s. "Winter on Earth" is mostly philosophical discourse on the need for human beings to strive toward greater individual and collective union with the universe, and "York Beach" is similar. The goal of human life, Toomer is saying, is to develop one's highest potential to achieve higher consciousness. He incorporates ideas on the negative effects of materialism and alienation in the modern world and stresses the need for more intensive spiritual development. In most of these works, as is also the case in many of the stories in his unpublished manuscripts, the central character is a thinly disguised Jean Toomer, no longer showing the ambivalence of Ralph Kabnis, but exuding confidence in the knowledge that he has found the way to achieve full self-realization.

"The Blue Meridian," his final publication, had its genesis in "The First American," which Toomer composed at the time he pondered his racial identity before he went to college in 1924. The influences of Walt Whitman and Hart Crane are evident in the finished work, and so are those of the Gurdjieff philosophy. Toomer sings his own America, in a poem that pays tribute to all Americans of all races, religions, or creeds. Through the eyes of a Gurdjieffian utopian visionary, "The Blue Meridian" creates a myth of the evolution of a new America. In the poet's new culture, barriers dissolve, and black, white, and red men join to become the blue man, in a synthesis that potentiates spiritual energy.

Much of the language of the poem comes from Gurdjieffian thought. Man, in his ordinary state of being, is asleep, and needs to be awakened. When the union of man and the universe is effected there is awakening. This climax, in Toomer's estimation, is the triumph of man over "not-man," of birth over antibeing. From a past of blindness, mistakes, hate, and greed, men emerge to lose their prejudices and other enslaving attitudes; America can then celebrate as a whole nation.

The symbols of "The Blue Meridian" are drawn from Western and Eastern culture. The symbol of spiritual force in the poem is the Mississippi, whose images frame the work. At the beginning, this powerful river is the "sister" of the Ganges, itself as sacred as the other. At the end of the poem it is called the "main artery of the Western world," and Toomer tells us that it represents the spirit of all our people. The American eagle and the achievement of Charles Lindberg are as important as the address to the "Radiant Incorporeal," the Absolute of the universe. This combination of elements from ancient and modern worlds, technology and the natural environment, underscore Toomer's holistic philosophy through which he could finally see himself as fully integrated into the stream of all human life.

In 1932 Toomer married Margery Latimer, a novelist with New England roots, who had joined a Gurdjieff group he led in Portage, Wisconsin, that summer. Less than a year later she died giving birth to their daughter. In 1934 he married Marjorie Content, a New York woman from an upper-class financial and artistic background. They set up their home on a farm in Doylestown, Pennsylvania, where Toomer lived until his death in 1967.

Toomer's active involvement with the Gurdjieff movement lasted until the time of his first marriage, although he continued to follow many of the tenets of the philosophy for the rest of his life. In 1934 he wrote Gurdjieff and noted that while he still believed in his methods, his responsibilities as a father and husband demanded most of his time and energy, and he could no longer be active in that work. Many of Toomer's later friends believed that he had had ambitions to set up an institute of his own at Doylestown, a replica of the one at Fontainebleau. However, he was never able to secure the funds to carry out such a project.

Toomer did not find the internal harmony he felt so crucial to his happiness and achievement of full potential in the Gurdjieff movement, although that system appears to have given him the greatest encouragement toward that end. By the middle of the 1930s he was once again searching for a new system. In 1939 he took his family to India, on a trip that lasted nine months. There he conferred with gurus and sages, trying to garner the secrets of inner peace. The trip, however, was only another failure in his search, and two unfinished plays, "Columbo Madras Mail" and "Pilgrims, Did You Say?" are the records of his disappointment over the results of that pilgrimage. He returned to America depressed by the poverty and disease he saw in India, and he noted that such marginal living as he observed there made people greedy for the material things they lacked. It drained their spiritual resources.

Still in search of the internal harmony that ultimately evaded him in his work as a lecturer in the Gurdjieff movement and during his pilgrimage to India, Toomer joined the Society of Friends in 1949. Toomer found Quakerism appealing because of its emphasis upon man's direct experience with God. Because of his literary background, engaging lecture style, and courtly manner, Toomer quickly assumed important responsibilities among the Quakers in Pennsylvania. Toomer distinguished himself at the quarterly and yearly meetings of the Friends by serving on several important committees including those created to improve race relations, and also by acting as the adult adviser to the Young Friends of Philadelphia. Toomer's greatest strength as a leader in the Society of Friends was that he had a way of making others feel needed and capable.

In 1949 Toomer delivered the William Penn Lecture: his last and most important address to the Society of Friends. This address was published shortly afterward as *The Flavor of Man* and it is the distillation of Toomer's understanding of the human condition.

Although Toomer had severed connections with the writers who had been his friends and colleagues from 1919 to 1923, he had privately continued to write until the middle of the 1940s. He had made many unsuccessful attempts to have

his writings published before he finally gave up in discouragement. Among his unpublished manuscripts are several novels, plays, short stories, poems, and autobiographical fragments.

Publishers had rejected Toomer's post-*Cane* works mainly because the style and content of his writing changed drastically after he became an adherent of the Gurdjieff philosophy, and he had given up the aims of art in literature in exchange for the goals of a proselytizer. One of his lifelong friends, Gorham Munson, in an interview given in New York City in 1969, said Toomer gave up the beautiful writing he had done in that "wonderful" book, *Cane*, for something that was not beautiful in writing. His later works were largely didactic, tedious, and dull. Furthermore, many intellectuals thought Gurdjieff was a charlatan and an opportunist, and Toomer did not help his own cause by openly championing such a controversial figure.

The Wayward and the Seeking includes autobiographical works that are among the most interesting of Toomer's papers. Apart from factual data, Toomer's autobiographies, many in various stages of incompleteness, are also valuable for the insights they provide into Toomer's psyche. "Earth Being," "A New Identity," "On Being American," "Outline of an Autobiography," and "Why I Joined the Gurdjieff Work," all written between 1928 and the early 1940s, offer Toomer's perceptions of his family and his life between 1894 and the late 1920s. As early as 1929 he submitted one draft for publication, and submissions and rejections of various versions are scattered throughout the history of his career.

In selecting the aspects of his life he wished to explore and reveal through these works, Toomer aimed for a portrait that showed his Gurdjieff involvement as the outcome of his evolution from "waking-sleep" to "self-consciousness." When he looked at his early life, he tended to be indulgent and romantic. His descriptions of the various members of his family and of his childhood in Washington are idealistic. At the same time, his voice is authoritative and independent, even in his portrayals of his father whom he never saw and whose name had been banned from mention in his grandfather's house. His most interesting portraits are of his grandfather, and it is clear that Toomer both admired and rebelled against the domineering, charismatic P. B. S. Pinchback.

Toomer's use of women as central characters in his imaginative works becomes understandable through his recollections of the two women who figured most prominently in his early life, his mother and grandmother. His insights into the perceptions of women in works like *Cane* and *Natalie Mann* reflect the sympathy he felt for his own mother whose life was full of unhappiness and disappointments at the hands of her father and her two husbands. She was raised to be a lady and was never allowed to step outside of that role. Toomer identified with her helplessness and unhappiness, and he often successfully expresses the frustrations of living within such limits through the women in his writings. He also perceived quiet strength in his grandmother, noting that the gentleness of her face was deceptive. While her domain was the management of an orderly and well-organized home for her political husband, her strength was a source of support for him throughout his life.

From Toomer's autobiographies we derive the image of a man who perceived a seriousness in human existence that could not be readily understood through the normal process of everyday living. All things in the universe were connected, he knew, and he wanted to understand and ultimately control that matrix of experiences. His autobiographies are engaging and embody a serious attempt on his part to examine and "name" his experiences.

Toomer's unpublished fiction of the period of the later 1920s until the very early 1940s includes four full-length novels—"Transatlantic" (written in 1929) revised as "Eight Day World" (1933 or 1934), "Caromb" (written in 1932), "The Gallonwerps" (first written as a play in 1927 and revised as a novel in 1933), and "The Angel Begoria" in 1943.

"Eight Day World," a 436-page work, was Toomer's longest manuscript. It is the fictionalized account of his shipboard experiences on his first trip to Fontainebleau in 1924. For a long time he was convinced that it was his best work, but no one agreed to publish it. The somber "Caromb," made up of letters from Carmel, California, has its genesis in an unpleasant racial incident that Toomer and his first wife experienced during their honeymoon there in 1932. He interweaves the physical beauty of the place with the ugliness and dark underside of attitudes toward race in America. "The Gallonwerps" or "Diked" was a work for teaching with Gurdjieff groups. The theme is the power of human suggestibility, showing that Toomer was not against human manipulation in the right circumstances. The central

theme in "The Angel Begoria" is the value of religion as a unifying force between man and God. Written during World War II, he saw that America had an opportunity to lead the world in that direction.

Finally, the Toomer manuscript collections at Fisk and Yale Universities contain, among other items, thirteen poems written between 1936 and 1939 which appear to reconcile his beliefs in the spirit of mankind with the spirit of the universe. All are deeply religious. They are invocations through which the poet seeks ways to come closer to the spirit of the universe which is able to cleanse, enlighten, mend, and blend human beings into his being. As supplicator, he wishes to integrate the inner and outer man to achieve a level of consciousness that will link him to cosmic consciousness.

Toomer's distress over his inability to publish his writings or to find internal harmony was further aggravated by failing health as early as the 1930s. First, he had feelings of general weakness and a lack of energy. He blamed this condition on his lack of internal harmony. For a man who had exhibited a good deal of athletic prowess in his youth and early manhood, this physical failure was particularly difficult for him to bear. What followed was worse. He had a bout with kidney problems, for which he underwent surgery in the 1940s, and he also had trouble with his eyes. During the final years of his life he was often in a nursing home undergoing intensive treatment for these ailments. These were extremely sad times for him. He was a man who was doubly disappointed in his life, and his mental state hastened his physical deterioration. He died on 30 March 1967; the cause was listed as arteriosclerosis.

Toomer's racial ambivalence and his involvement with the Gurdjieff movement must bear most of the burden of his failure to achieve what might well have been a brilliant literary career. Nevertheless *Cane* is a solid achievement. Those who have been aware of his conscious rejection of his role as a leading black writer believe that in so doing he turned away from the promise of fame. But he rejected the boundaries of blackness because he wanted nothing less than universal identity.

Biography:
Cynthia E. Kerman and Richard Eldridge, *The Lives of Jean Toomer: A Hunger for Wholeness*

(Baton Rouge: Louisiana State University Press, 1987).
An outstanding biography; Kerman and Eldridge examine Toomer's lives as a writer, as a philosopher, and as a person of deep but waivering faith.

References:

Houston Baker, "Journey Toward Black Art: Jean Toomer's *Cane*," in *Singers at Daybreak: Studies in Black American Literature* (Washington, D.C.: Howard University Press, 1975), pp. 53-80.
An excellent examination of the major themes and recurring imagery in *Cane*.

Brian Joseph Benson and Mabel Mayle Dillard, *Jean Toomer* (Boston: Twayne, 1980).
Largely focused upon Toomer's literary career before and up to the point of *Cane*'s publication, this first book-length study of Toomer is distinguished by a perceptive reading of *Cane* and an extensive secondary bibliography.

Robert Bone, "Jean Toomer," in his *The Negro Novel in America* (New Haven: Yale University Press, 1958).
Although Bone mistakenly assumes that *Cane* is a novel, he correctly emphasizes the extent to which Toomer subverts the pastoral tradition in American and Afro-American literature.

Arna Bontemps, *The Harlem Renaissance Remembered* (New York: Dodd, Mead, 1972).
A useful but uneven collection of critical essays on Toomer and other writers of the New Negro Movement.

Bontemps, "The Negro Renaissance: Jean Toomer and the Harlem Writers of the 1920's," in *Anger and Beyond: The Negro Writer in the United States,* edited by Herbert Hill (New York: Harper & Row, 1966), pp. 20-36.
As one of the writers of the New Negro Movement, Bontemps unfairly criticizes Toomer for his decision not to limit himself to the category of Afro-American writer.

Rudolph P. Byrd, "Jean Toomer and the Writers of the New Negro Movement: Was He There With Them?," in *Harlem Renaissance:*

A Revaluation, edited by Stanley Brodwin, Amritjit Singh, and William Shiver (New York: Garland Press, 1988), pp. 35-49.
An essay that refutes the charge made by Arna Bontemps and Alice Walker that Toomer passed for white; the author also exposes Alain Locke's exploitation of Toomer's growing prestige as the author of *Cane*.

John F. Callahan, " 'By de Singin' uh de Song': the Search for Reciprocal Voice in *Cane*," in *In The African-American Grain: The Pursuit of Voice in Twentieth Century Black Fiction* (Urbana: University of Illinois Press, 1987).
A superb examination of the stories and poems in *Cane*, as well as Toomer's use of African and Afro-American oral traditions.

Frank Durham, *Studies in Cane* (Columbus, Ohio: Merrill, 1971).
Provides an excellent history of the stages in the publication of *Cane* as well as responses to the book by black and white writers of Toomer's generation.

Nellie McKay, *Jean Toomer: Artist* (Chapel Hill: University of North Carolina Press, 1984).
A superb scholarly study not only of Toomer's boyhood in Washington, D.C., but also of the major prose and verse masterpieces in Toomer's rather uneven canon.

Gorham Munson, "The Significance of Jean Toomer," *Opportunity*, 3 (1925): 262-263.
As a friend and fellow writer, Munson praises Toomer for his celebration of spiritual values.

Darwin T. Turner, "Jean Toomer: Exile," in his *In A Minor Chord: Three Afro-American Writers and Their Search for Identity* (Carbondale: Southern Illinois University Press, 1971), pp. 1-59.
Turner examines the social, cultural, and racial influences upon Toomer's development as a writer.

Jean Wagner, "Jean Toomer," in his *Black Poets of the United States,* translated by Kenneth Douglas (Urbana: University of Illinois Press, 1973).

Wagner identifies the themes that distinguish Toomer from other poets of the New Negro Movement.

Alice Walker, "The Divided Life of Jean Toomer," in *In Search of Our Mothers' Gardens, Womanist Prose* (New York: Harcourt Brace Jovanovich, 1984), pp. 60-71.
Although she identifies Toomer as a writer who influenced her personal and professional development, Walker complains, often unfairly, of Toomer's refusal to define himself as an Afro-American writer.

Papers:
Toomer's manuscript collection, at the Fisk University Archives and the Beinecke Rare Book and Manuscript Library at Yale University, includes several novels, plays, a large number of poems and short stories, and a half dozen versions and fragments of autobiographical writings.

William Carlos Williams

*This entry was updated by John Xiros Cooper (Mount Royal College) from his entry in
DLB 54, American Poets, 1880-1945, Third Series, Part 2.*

Places	Paterson, N.J. New York City	Paris	Puerto Rico
Influences and Relationships	Walt Whitman John Keats Ezra Pound Hilda Doolittle	Alfred Kreymborg Louis Zukofsky Mina Loy	D. H. Lawrence James Joyce Charles Demuth
Literary Movements and Forms	Modernism Imagism	Objectivism	Realism
Major Themes	The City as Metaphor for the Psyche Dance and Music as Metaphors for Creation Spiritual Redemption through Art	The Feminine Principle as Fecundity and Danger Primacy of the Mate- rial Object over Abstraction	Sensuous Experience as the Basis of a Poetics Nobility of the Ordinary
Cultural and Artistic Influences	Post World War I American Cultural Nationalism	Postimpressionistic Painting	Medicine Photography
Social and Economic Influences	The Depression World War II	American Political Radicalism	McCarthyism

BIRTH: Rutherford, New Jersey, 17 September 1883, to William George and Raquel Hélène Rose Hoheb Williams.

EDUCATION: M.D., University of Pennsylvania, 1906; University of Leipzig, 1909-1910.

MARRIAGE: 12 December 1912 to Florence Herman; children: William Eric, Paul Herman.

AWARDS AND HONORS: *Dial* Award, 1926; LL.D., University of Buffalo, 1946; Russell Loines Award (National Institute of Arts and Letters), 1948; National Book Award for *Selected Poems* and *Paterson (Book Three)*, 1950; fellow, Library of Congress, 1950; D.Litt., Rutgers University, 1950; D.Litt., Bard College, 1950; appointed Consultant in Poetry, Library of Congress, 1952 (did not serve); Bollingen Prize in Poetry, 1952; Levinson Prize (*Poetry* magazine), 1954; Oscar Blumenthal Prize (*Poetry* magazine), 1955; American Academy of Poets Fellowship, 1956; Brandeis University Creative Arts Medal, 1958; Pulitzer Prize for *Pictures from Brueghel and other poems*, 1963; National Institute and American Academy of Arts and Letters Gold Medal, 1963.

DEATH: Rutherford, New Jersey, 4 March 1963.

BOOKS: *Poems* (Rutherford, N.J.: Privately printed, 1909);
The Tempers (London: Elkin Mathews, 1913);
Al Que Quiere! (Boston: Four Seas, 1917);
Kora in Hell: Improvisations (Boston: Four Seas, 1920);
Sour Grapes (Boston: Four Seas, 1921);
The Great American Novel (Paris: Three Mountains Press, 1923);
Spring and All (Paris: Contact Editions, 1923);
GO GO (New York: Monroe Wheeler, 1923);
In the American Grain (New York: A. & C. Boni, 1925; London: MacGibbon & Kee, 1967);
A Voyage to Pagany (New York: Macaulay, 1928);
A Novelette and Other Prose (1921-1931) (Toulon, France: TO Publishers, 1932);
The Knife of the Times and Other Stories (Ithaca, N.Y.: Dragon Press, 1932);
The Cod Head (San Francisco: Harvest Press, 1932);
Collected Poems 1921-1931 (New York: Objectivist Press, 1934);
An Early Martyr and Other Poems (New York: Alcestis Press, 1935);

William Carlos Williams, 1938 (photograph by Charles Sheeler)

Adam & Eve & The City (Peru, Vt.: Alcestis Press, 1936);
White Mule (Norfolk, Conn.: New Directions, 1937; London: MacGibbon & Kee, 1965);
Life along the Passaic River (Norfolk, Conn.: New Directions, 1938);
The Complete Collected Poems (Norfolk, Conn.: New Directions, 1938);
In the Money: White Mule–Part II (Norfolk, Conn.: New Directions, 1940; London: MacGibbon & Kee, 1965);
The Broken Span (Norfolk, Conn.: New Directions, 1941);
The Wedge (Cummington, Mass.: Cummington Press, 1944);
Paterson (Book One) (Norfolk, Conn.: New Directions, 1946);
Paterson (Book Two) (Norfolk, Conn.: New Directions, 1948);
The Clouds, Aigeltinger, Russia, & (Aurora, N.Y.: Wells College Press/Cummington, Mass.: Cummington Press, 1948);
A Dream of Love: A Play in Three Acts and Eight Scenes (Norfolk, Conn.: New Directions, 1948);
Selected Poems (Norfolk, Conn.: New Directions, 1949; enlarged, 1968);

The Pink Church (Columbus, Ohio: Golden Goose Press, 1949);

Paterson (Book Three) (Norfolk, Conn.: New Directions, 1949);

The Collected Later Poems (Norfolk, Conn.: New Directions, 1950; revised, 1963; London: MacGibbon & Kee, 1965);

Make Light of It: Collected Stories (New York: Random House, 1950);

A Beginning on the Short Story [Notes] (Yonkers, N.Y.: Alicat Bookshop Press, 1950);

Paterson (Book Four) (Norfolk, Conn.: New Directions, 1951);

The Autobiography (New York: Random House, 1951; London: MacGibbon & Kee, 1968);

The Collected Earlier Poems (Norfolk, Conn.: New Directions, 1951; London: MacGibbon & Kee, 1967);

The Build-Up: A Novel (New York: Random House, 1952; London: MacGibbon & Kee, 1969);

The Desert Music and Other Poems (New York: Random House, 1954);

Selected Essays (New York: Random House, 1954);

Journey to Love (New York: Random House, 1955);

I Wanted to Write a Poem, reported and edited by Edith Heal (Boston: Beacon Press, 1958; London: Cape, 1967);

Paterson (Book Five) (Norfolk, Conn.: New Directions, 1958);

Yes, Mrs. Williams: A Personal Record of My Mother (New York: McDowell, Obolensky, 1959);

The Farmers' Daughters: The Collected Stories (Norfolk, Conn.: New Directions, 1961);

Many Loves and Other Plays: The Collected Plays (Norfolk, Conn.: New Directions, 1961);

Pictures from Brueghel and other poems (Norfolk, Conn.: New Directions, 1962; London: MacGibbon & Kee, 1963);

Paterson, books 1-5 and notes for book 6 (New York: New Directions, 1963; London: MacGibbon & Kee, 1964);

The William Carlos Williams Reader, edited by M. L. Rosenthal (New York: New Directions, 1966; London: MacGibbon & Kee, 1967);

Imaginations, edited by Webster Schott (New York: New Directions, 1970; London: MacGibbon & Kee, 1970);

The Embodiment of Knowledge, edited by Ron Loewinsohn (New York: New Directions, 1974);

A Recognizable Image: William Carlos Williams on Art and Artists, edited by Bram Dijkstra (New York: New Directions, 1978).

OTHER: "Rome," edited by Steven Ross Loevy, *Iowa Review,* 9 (Spring 1978): 1-65.

TRANSLATIONS: Philippe Soupault, *Last Nights in Paris* (New York: Macaulay, 1929);

Yvan Goll, *Jean sans Terre: Landless John,* translated by Williams, Lionel Abel, Clark Mills, and John Gould Fletcher (San Francisco: Grabhorn Press, 1944);

Pedro Espinosa (Don Francisco de Quevedo), *The Dog & the Fever,* translated by Williams and Raquel Hélène Williams (Hamden, Conn.: Shoestring Press, 1954).

One should perhaps always resist the temptation to sum up a writer's life and work, his "essence," by way of a single revealing anecdote. In the case of William Carlos Williams, however, a story Kenneth Burke has told captures something of that special quality of temper and feeling that pervades Williams's life and work. Some years after Williams had retired from his medical practice he, Burke, and a neighbor's dog were walking slowly along a beach in Florida. The dog was limping. Burke, hoping to help the dog, leaned down clumsily to grasp the injured paw, and the dog, suddenly frightened, nearly bit him. Williams took the paw in his left hand and started to feel around for the problem. "It was a gesture," Burke writes, "at once expert and imaginative, something in which to have perfect confidence, as both the cur and I saw in a flash." Probing the dog's padded paw "lightly, quickly, and above all *surely,*" Williams found a small burr and removed it without hurting the animal.

This "touch" for handling the body, acquired over many decades as a physician, provides, paradoxically, the best introduction to his writing, for Williams's poetics are uniquely physical. For him reality, perception, and language are materially based, and the knowledge derived from the contact of mind and earth, language and the real, leads to the same sort of awareness that comes from touching and handling, from caressing and probing and cupping the intimately known and loved. One may never be able to "place" the world's body explicitly and smoothly in some supramundane cosmology, either philosophical or religious, but one "knows" it in the same way a mountain climber knows a mountain, not by looking at a map merely, but in his fingers and arms, his feet, his knees, and the twists of his torso, knowing the mountain as a subtly variable network of textures, physical pressures, tolerances, and tastes. The physician cannot avoid this knowledge of each unique human body he touches. Dr. Williams did not, of course, entirely reject conceptual or theoretical knowledge; he merely wanted to acknowledge that the schematizing intelligence was only a small part of a writer's equipment. For him the primary function of the mind was not to classify, analyze, and transcend the world, but to lay it bare and penetrate it. Needing to get one's hands on things, to get one's hands "dirty," distinguished, he felt, the American mind from the European. If there be such a thing as "transcendence," it was achieved through the acceptance and penetration of things, not by their renunciation.

The philosophical consequences of such an orientation lead in the direction of that quintessential American idea: pragmatism. Had Williams bent his intelligence to philosophy he would no doubt have contributed a superb chapter to pragmatist theory and logic, begun in the last years of the nineteenth century by C. S. Pierce, William James, and John Dewey. His contribution would have surely emphasized the physical dimension of knowing, knowing in the body, not simply in the head. "A thing known passes out of the mind into the muscles . . ." is the perception of a poet, rather than a philosopher. Such a notion of the physicality of knowledge, its material "embodiment," to use one of Williams's favorite words, would have allowed him, Ron Loewinsohn rightly suggests, to appreciate Norman Mailer's perception that Muhammad Ali's combinations of rights and lefts in the boxing ring demonstrate as much intelligence, poise, and humor as anything to be found in the poetry of Alexander Pope or the witty verbal duels of Oscar Wilde's comedies. Although never extensively developed in the abstract, these ideas lie at the heart of Williams's aesthetics and penetrate not only his poetry but also his thinking about the cultural development of the United States as a whole.

In his thinking about American culture Williams's notion of the concrete particular led him to champion the concrete *and* the particular, to recognize and acknowledge "place" and locality as the "field" in which significant art happens. He early turned a deaf ear to the classical conception of art he heard T. S. Eliot voice in the early years of modernism, an art that upheld the universal over the particular, the abstract over the concrete, the international over the regional, the cosmopolis over "our town."

Yet Williams's position was never a mere unthinking Babbittry; it was not a position minted from fear and ignorance. It was much more positive than that. In his experience of the greatest literature and art, he was struck by the undeniable sense of place and occasion that the great works always seemed to manifest. The best art does not breathe, he believed, an ethereal atmosphere of pure thought and unbodied feeling divorced from necessary contact with the real life of a real place: "every individual, every place, every opportunity of thought is both favored and limited by its emplacement in time and place. Chinese 8th cent., Italian 12th, English 15th, French 18th, African, etc. All sorts of complicated conditions and circumstances of land, climate, blood, surround every deed that is done." In this respect Williams should be grouped with the modernist writers of very similar orientation, poets such as the Scottish modernist Hugh MacDiarmid, or the Nobel laureate from Chile, Pablo Neruda, rather than with cosmopolitan modernists such as T. S. Eliot and Ezra Pound, who were part of the modernism that flourished in the European capitals during the first three decades of the twentieth century. Of course, Williams possessed a cosmopolitan side of his own, derived from his family background, from his English father, from his mother, a woman in whom several distinct cultures joined, from travel, and from his contact with the leading modernist cosmopolites of his time. But when he finally sat down to work out his ideas and beliefs in the 1920s and after, his primary allegiances became visible; they pointed to the place he called home–the New Jersey of his birth. There, in the intense observation of his place, he made a verbal art as profound and moving as any in modern literature. And beyond his own considerable achievement he would help to make it possible for American writers to feel finally, and finely, at home in their own land, by showing them that the great humane values, the most sophisticated approaches to art, are just as accessible in the vicinity of the Passaic as they are on the Left Bank of the Seine.

He was born on 17 September 1883 in Rutherford, New Jersey, the city in which he would marry, bring up his sons, live, practice his profession, write, and eventually die. Rutherford was still a rural town of about three thousand inhabitants in the 1880s and 1890s. Williams in later years would remember that rural landscape, with its flowering trees, its meadows, and the duck hunters skirting the clumps of trees on crisp fall days. The cold copper mines that had provided the economic backbone of the region in the earlier part of the nineteenth century were already long closed, replaced by small manufacturing concerns and other commercial enterprises.

His father, William George, came from pure British stock, a fact he was never to forget even though he had been taken from England at the age of five. He was to remain a British citizen all his days. He was known as a quiet man whose business, the manufacture and distribution of eau de cologne, often took him from his family for varying lengths of time, including one trip to Latin America that lasted for an entire year. He was in every respect a late-Victorian gentleman, whose regular way of life did not change all through his working years. Perhaps under the influence of George Bernard Shaw's music journalism, he had developed a taste for the music drama of Richard Wagner. His acknowledged favorite among writers was Rudyard Kipling, the apologist and bard of the British imperial presence in what is now called the Third World. William George reflected exactly the culture and temper of liberal progressives in the North Atlantic world of the late nineteenth century. He thought of himself as a socialist, probably having come under the influence of Shaw's Fabianism. Characteristically, he was one of the founders of the liberal Unitarian Society of Rutherford, at whose services his sons sang in the choir. He understood and promoted the value of the best possible education and insisted that his sons, William Carlos and Edgar, be well-read in the classics and informed about the leading ideas of their time. He was an unbending, dignified man whose ruling passion seemed to be devotion to duty and to the Englishness he never abandoned. He was a man, William Carlos wrote in "Adam" eighteen years after his death, who tasted "the death that duty brings" and who could only be imagined with "a British passport/always in his pocket–."

His mother's family was scattered over a number of Caribbean islands, principally in Martinique and Puerto Rico. Raquel Hélène Rose Hoheb Williams (called Elena at home) was partly French, Dutch, Spanish, and Jewish. She studied art in Paris at l'Ecole des Arts Industrielles from 1876 to 1879. She remembered this happy sojourn in Paris, the "capital of the nineteenth century" as Walter Benjamin

called it, her whole life, longing to return there from her exile, first in Puerto Rico, to which she returned at the end of the 1870s, and later in Rutherford. She savored every opportunity to revisit the city of her youthful memories. She was in the charge of her physician brother, Carlos Hoheb, when she met William George Williams. On 29 November 1882 the two young people were married in Brooklyn and went to live in Rutherford, across the Hudson River from New York City.

Elena was an exotic presence in the Williams household. She did not take to the English language very well, preferring to speak her native Spanish at home, and to practice French, the language she most loved, whenever there was anyone about who knew it. She did not mix easily with the citizens of Rutherford and the Williams home received a continual procession of visitors, Elena's relatives and friends from the Caribbean and from Paris, who would arrive for long spells. It was through this contact that she was able to forget the Protestant provincialism of life along the Passaic. She was a profound influence on her eldest son, an influence William Carlos explored explicitly in *Yes, Mrs. Williams: A Personal Record of My Mother* (1959). She provided him with one dimension of the feminine presence that haunts his poetry, and she was a mirror in which he saw reflected something of himself. As he wrote in "Eve,"

> I sometimes detect in your face
> a puzzled pity for me
> your son—
> I have never been close to you
> —mostly your own fault;
> in that I am like you.

She seems to have had what is sometimes thought of as the temperament of an artist (that is, she was moody) and a hankering after gentility, insisting all her life that her family respect the canons of good taste and good manners. She longed for the elegance and refinement of Paris, yet she was also something of a puritan, expressing disappointment at the earthiness of some of her son's poetic language. She shared with her husband a love of the opera and would be heard singing arias from *La Traviata* through the house in Rutherford. "Take her to the opera" was William George's suggestion to William Carlos when he left Elena in his son's care for a year.

This exotic, passionate, yet fragile and distant woman was not the only feminine influence on Williams. His grandmother, Emily Dickinson Wellcome, who, living in the Williams home, was primarily responsible for raising him through his early years, played an even more important role. Grandma Wellcome, William George's mother (the name Wellcome came from a second marriage), took little "Willie" under her wing when he was born in 1883. At fifty she was still full of vigor and independence; she had an earthy toughness that contrasted sharply with the delicacy of her vaguely aristocratic daughter-in-law. She taught Williams the English language after it became clear that his mother was not going to make much of an effort to learn the language herself. The two women did not like each other, and occasionally Elena Williams was forced to assert her authority in the Williams household against the encroachments of her mother-in-law. Williams felt closer to his grandmother in many respects than he did to his mother. Certainly the older woman figures more centrally in his work. She became, as Paul Mariani has suggested, "the central mythic presence in Williams' young life." Fierce old Emily Wellcome is remembered in Williams's "Dedication for a Plot of Ground," "Last Words of My English Grandmother," and "The Wanderer," where, Reed Whittemore has argued, she becomes "a strange combination of muse and antimuse." Williams said in *I Wanted to Write a Poem* (1958), that "The Wanderer" "is a story of growing up. The old woman in it is my grandmother, raised to heroic proportions. I endowed her with magic qualities. She had seized me from my mother as her special possession, adopted me, and her purpose in life was to make me her own. But my mother ended all that with a slap in the puss." The tension between Elena Williams and Emily Wellcome ended in 1920 with the older woman's death. Williams romanticized his memory of her; and the feminine principle or spirit she embodied, attaining mythic proportions, was transmuted again and again in many poems and prose pieces. For Williams finally she represented two things, a kind of stubborn independence in the face of constant travail and a great, consuming fecundity, a fruitfulness made richer and more splendid by its contrast with the sterilities of a commercial and conformist America that Williams saw emerging all his life. Later, Florence Herman, Williams's wife, would provide a third dimension in the feminine ideal the poet created over his long artistic life.

It is useful for an understanding of Williams's work to emphasize his immediate environment, because, along with the work of most other modernist and postmodernist poets, his art is fundamentally autobiographical. This fact is one of the consequences of an aesthetic based on the local, the concrete, and the particular. One's own life offers itself as the immediate "stuff" of one's art. Immediacy, indeed, came to be one of the great rallying cries of modernism. Any intensive study of Williams's literary output needs to have a firm grasp of the immediate environment, both geographical and domestic, in which he lived, worked, and wrote. Yet one should, of course, avoid narrowly biographical interpretation of works of art. The biographical approach that is most productive for criticism notes the transmutation of immediate materials into the new life of those materials in the poem itself. One should not scrutinize the poem for references to particular people and events, but for what the poet has done with them, what imperative in the poem's idea these materials serve.

With his younger brother Edgar, Williams attended the public schools in his hometown through the early and mid 1890s, was taken to the Unitarian church of which his father was a founder, and indulged in all those pastimes and pleasures which, in semirural Rutherford, he was to remember fondly in *The Autobiography* (1951). In 1897, with her husband off in Argentina on business for a year, Elena Williams took her sons to Europe in order to indulge her longing to revivify the memories of her art-student days in Paris, and to look to the refinement of the boys' education. Williams was fourteen. In Europe the family set up house in Geneva, Switzerland, and the boys attended a private school with an international student body, the Chateau de Lancy. Elena Williams's aim was to have the boys acquire fluency in French, but this goal proved almost impossible because the majority of the boys in the school were British and many of the masters spoke English most of the time. By the time the family moved on to Paris for the last few months of their stay in Europe and the two brothers were enrolled in a French school, the Lycée Condorcet, their French was only slightly better than it had been when they first arrived in Geneva. Unable to function in the language of instruction at the Lycée, they were soon floundering in their work and were withdrawn from the school.

Upon the family's return to the United States in 1899, Williams and his brother were sent to private school in New York City, Horace Mann High School, near Columbia University at

Williams in 1908, during his internship at Child's Hospital in New York (courtesy of William Eric Williams)

Morningside Heights. Things went much better for them at Horace Mann, at that time one of the best, and best-known, schools on the eastern seaboard. The two boys commuted from New Jersey to Manhattan's upper West Side every school day for three years. There Williams was introduced for the first time to the systematic study of poetry under the tutelage of William Abbott, who taught Williams something of the English tradition in poetry from Geoffrey Chaucer to Alfred Tennyson. With Abbott, Williams studied the tradition, but especially John Milton, and the great romantics, William Wordsworth, Samuel Taylor Coleridge, and John Keats. Keats was particularly important, as it was his influence that pervaded Williams's earliest verses. Williams came to love Abbott—"Uncle Billy" as he was affectionately called by his pupils—and dedicated his *Selected Essays* (1954) to his memory, writing that he was "the first English teacher who ever gave me

an A." At Horace Mann, however, the *A*'s were few and far between. Williams finished three years at the school with an overall *C* average. It was in this period that he began to write his first imaginative work, keeping a series of copybooks in which he set down free-ranging, Whitmanesque ruminations. Of all the poets he had read, there may have been poets, such as Keats, who exerted specifically literary influences early on, but it was Walt Whitman in whose loose, freewheeling, passionate idiom Williams filled up his notebooks. For his formal poeticizing, however, the young Williams turned to the lessons of the great English tradition, to the works of Edmund Spenser, Keats, and Tennyson. His early poems are stanzaic and rhymed, with laboriously metered lines in which the massed iambs and trochees are "poetically" phrased. The growing influence of Keats and Tennyson dominated Williams's writing all through his college years. He did not lay aside the Keatsian burden until after the appearance of his first book, *Poems*, which he published privately in 1909.

At Horace Mann, Williams resolved to dedicate his life to writing, having tasted early the intense satisfaction which art can give the practitioner. However, his parents took for granted that an education in a suitable profession lay ahead for him, and their elder son acquiesced in that demand. His artistic ambitions remained his own secret commitment with himself.

From Horace Mann, Williams went on to the school of dentistry at the University of Pennsylvania, in Philadelphia, in 1902. Within a year he had transferred to the medical school, where he bent his energies to the rigors of training in medicine. Meanwhile he kept up with his interest in poetry. During his first semester he met Ezra Pound, who introduced him in the spring of 1905 to another young poet, Hilda Doolittle (H. D.), whose father was a professor at Penn. The connection with Pound is especially important. Although their friendship had its rocky periods, primarily caused by sometimes violent disagreements over Pound's later socioeconomic and political passions, it lasted for the rest of Williams's life. Pound was a precocious seventeen-year-old sophomore when Williams arrived at Penn as a somewhat shy nineteen-year-old freshman. The younger man, studying languages and humanities, had already developed what often passed in those days as a poet's personality. Given to flamboyance of language, gesture, and dress, Pound was living out the American afterglow of the English fin de siècle, the Yellow Nineties. However, his posturing masked, as Williams could see, a talented young man, whose passionate devotion to poetry was total. He took the young Pound's commitment to writing to heart, and it gave him an immediate contemporary model, more public and showy, that paralleled his own quieter vow.

In his high school and college years Williams was fastidiously working within the formal and thematic bounds of the English poetic tradition, a tradition codified by Francis Turner Palgrave in his widely read anthology, *The Golden Treasury of the Best Songs and Lyrical Poems in the English Language* (1861; revised and enlarged, 1891). But under the influence of Pound, he soon began to grow away from these adolescent attractions and toward something more recognizably modern. Pound's opinions, always forcefully and directly expressed, made Williams aware that the kind of Keatsian and Whitmanesque lyrics he was writing were like those of countless other versifiers, of varying degrees of competence, on both sides of the Atlantic. Pound's importance as an influence on the early Williams was precisely on this point: Pound simply made Williams aware of all the poetic work that did not need doing. Indeed the service Pound rendered Williams in this respect can be seen no more clearly than in a 1909 letter Pound wrote Williams from London responding to the New Jersey poet's first slim volume of Keatsian imitations: "I hope to God you have no feelings. If you have, burn this *before* reading." Lesser writers might have been crushed by the rest of Pound's letter. It is a tribute to Williams's sense of his own vocation that this response firmly closed the door on Palgrave forever and freed Williams to develop his own poetic practice, his own idiom, his own subject matter. Pound's placing comment comes near the end of his letter, when he says that Williams is "out of touch" with the kind of work being produced at the center of the literary world. Stacked up against poems by even writers of the second rank, *Poems* does not measure up. As Pound wrote, "Individual, original it is not. Great art it is not. Poetic it is, but there are innumerable poetic volumes poured out here in Gomorrah [London]. . . . Your book would not attract even passing attention here. There are fine lines in it, but nowhere I think do you add anything to the poets you have used as models."

Putting Williams in touch with what was thought and felt at the heart of the literary world, as London was in the years before World War I, was Pound's greatest service. Pound made Williams aware of the impossibility of pursuing the dead rituals of a moribund poetic tradition, deriving mainly from the decay of English and American romanticism. That past was perceived by the younger generation in 1909 as having made poetry unhealthily sentimental and false to the sources of its original inspiration. It accused the poetry of the nineteenth century of using a poem to ornament a feeling or, worse, to fake it, rather than making the poem the radiant vehicle for the presentation, as directly and cleanly as possible, of that which, in the world, provokes and stimulates feeling. The younger generation, of course, overstated their condemnations, but there was enough validity to their claims that, when the polemical smoke cleared, the modernist fire could be seen burning with a hard, gemlike flame. If modernism begins anywhere, it begins in this opposition to a tradition clotted with an obsessive dependence on stanzaic regularity, an unnecessarily archaic diction, and intellectual and emotional fuzziness, a kind of bloated profligacy in the spending of the devalued, inflated currencies of the past. What Pound helped Williams learn was the avoidance of "literature," in this degenerated sense of the word, how to avoid it, paradoxically, for the better health of the art. Only one hundred copies of *Poems* were printed, and of that one hundred only the whereabouts of ten are known (nine are in major research libraries). Williams, after he turned from the early sources of his art, did everything he could to discourage readers from looking into this early work. None of the poems has ever been republished in any of the collections and selections of his work over which Williams had any authority.

The first major modernist attempt to put into practice a positive poetics minted from the aggressive critique of the past was the movement known in London as *imagisme*. Although its principles had begun to be formulated as early as 1908 by T. E. Hulme, an English disciple of the French philosophers Henri Bergson and Georges Sorel, Pound quickly put himself at the center of the group, which flourished in bohemian London from 1911 to 1916. The writers involved preferred to use the French spelling of the name of their movement because the poetry of nineteenth-century France provided one of the literary sources of *imagisme*. The French writer venerated by *les imagistes* as a predecessor was Théophile Gautier, whose *Émaux et Camées* (1852) offered a model of the finely chiselled lyric, built around lucidly presented images, cleanly phrased, and exquisitely musical, a model on which an English poetic practice might be founded, a model, indeed, that not only contrasted with the concurrent Tennysonian norm, but was savored as a superior rebuke to that banal "ideal."

Hulme provided a philosophical justification for *imagisme*, but it was left to Pound to propound a set of operating procedures in an article signed by F. S. Flint, but attributed to Pound (*Poetry*, March 1913):

1. Direct treatment of the "thing" whether subjective or objective.
2. To use absolutely no word that does not contribute to the presentation.
3. As regarding rhythm: to compose in the sequence of the musical phrase, not in the sequence of a metronome.

Many scholars and critics have found it impossible to say exactly what these rules mean within the compass of the larger questions of aesthetics and the history of poetry. However, *les imagistes* knew what they meant, and the poetry produced was recognizably different from the postromantic gush against which *imagiste* restraint stood firm. Although never a charter member of the movement, Williams was receptive to its doctrines, and his poetry was profoundly influenced by it. His verse in this new style was included in the several anthologies that *les imagistes* collected and published in London. In the main, the movement helped reform Williams's rather conventional sense of poetic diction and his heavily rhetorical approach to the poem. He turned away from the early poetic practice exemplified in "On a Proposed Trip South," which he had included in his first book:

E'er have I known December in a weave
Of blanched crystal, when, thrice one short night
Packed full with magic, and oh blissful sight!
N'er so warmly doth for April grieve[.]

His new poetic is apparent in "To Mark Antony in Heaven," which appeared in Pound's anthology *Des Imagistes* (1914):

This quiet morning light
reflected, how many times
from grass and trees and clouds
enters my north room
touching the walls with
grass and clouds and trees.

The important change here is not simply the obvious renovations of diction and form; more striking is the change in "voice." In the second excerpt an individual and concretely placeable voice is speaking. It is a voice that, conceivably, might be used in everyday intercourse, under the stress or sway of certain moods or particular circumstances of feeling. The voice of the first excerpt is conventionally "poetic," a voice produced by screwing up one's inwardness into an awkwardly carried conventional poetic posture. This nineteenth-century voice, furthermore, suggests no *particular* speaker, speaking from some concrete context of situation. Instead, we hear a tradition speaking; the young man who has written these lines is merely a field of receptivities in which a poem, entirely impersonal and abstract, is happening. The slightly older man responsible for "To Mark Antony in Heaven" has shifted his ground, and the voice he has created is not simply being produced by the manipulation of certain acceptable literary conventions. It is the voice, the particular, concrete voice, of an experience, finding in the resources of words, word clusters, line breaks, an expressive language which more lucidly embodies the dynamics of things seen, things thought, things felt.

At the University of Pennsylvania Williams undertook that necessary exploration of the tradition, finding in it much to value, much to imitate, but finding finally that a great deal of it needed to be set aside, indeed rejected outright, in order to permit his talent to flower. But Ezra Pound and Hilda Doolittle were not the only influences in those years. While at Penn he met Charles Demuth, an art student, at the boardinghouse where he took his meals. This connection would prove to be as fruitful as the connection with Pound. Demuth did not have Pound's irascible and aggressive personality. A bit easier to get along with, he was also tilling a different artistic field, painting, which had the benefit of having been recognized as adjacent to poetry as early as the *Ars Poetica* of Horace in Augustan Rome. Williams and Demuth were fast friends until Demuth's death in 1934. Although his life was short, Demuth exerted an important influence on native American painting in the 1920s. The ten years before World War I, when Williams and Demuth were first getting acquainted, was a very good time to know such a painter. The same renovatory winds which had begun to blow through poetry in movements such as *imagisme* had in fact been reaching hurricane force in painting for a considerable time. Again the impetus and focus of change in the tradition of representational art had occurred under French leadership. With the impressionists as artistic forefathers, the Post-impressionists in the 1890s, Cézanne and Van Gogh principally, had pushed painting to the brink of the breakdown of the representational picture plane toward a more painterly abstractionism. The "materials" of the painter—structure, volume, texture, and, above all, color—instead of doing service in the making of oil replicas of the "real" world, became themselves the overt signs of a new way of seeing.

For Williams contact with Demuth in those years gave him access, through a knowledgeable friend, to the excitement and renovatory energy animating the avant-garde art of that time. Decades later Williams would pinpoint painting as an early and profound influence: "As I look back, I think it was the French painters rather than the writers who influenced us, and their influence was very great. They created an atmosphere of release, color release, release from stereotyped forms, trite subjects." Through his contact with Demuth, Williams learned that the painter's medium is paint, not "stereotyped forms, trite subjects." In the same way the poet's medium is language, words, not the conventional postures, dictions, and rhetorical effects of a thoroughly routine romanticism. Words became material objects that filled the mouth, pushed the mouth in odd shapes and movements, and, moreover, words were of particular places and times, and they had color and tone and accent. When words were embraced by the traditional stanzaic frameworks of nineteenth-century poetry, the prosodic conventions of measure, rhyme, and beat tended to obscure the word's uniqueness, the word's natural rhythms and accents, carried into the poem from everyday life. These rhythms and accents in an American voice were muted by the prosodic and lexical traditions of British practice. By 1913, the date of Williams's second book of poems, *The Tempers*, he had formulated the poetics to which he would devote his art for the rest of his life. He was discovering in that period the grain of the American voice, neither domesticated to the parlor sweetness of the English Georgians nor crushed by Tennyson's more formal grandeur. Instead he was writing poems such as "Della Primavera Transportata Al Morale":

a green truck
dragging a concrete mixer

passes
in the street—
the clatter and true sound
of verse—

He was establishing the primary phonic pigments of a new kind of poetic speech; it would become his signature.

Of course, it would be incorrect to suggest that Williams learned to write by looking at avant-garde pictures. Painting was an important influence that pointed him in a productive direction, but the work of finding his own approach or style was an entirely verbal one. The influence of the new painting on Williams crystallized in the famous Armory Show in 1913, an exhibition that largely introduced American audiences to Post-impressionistic European painting. The general public was outraged and rather obtuse about the new directions. The public taste was very much shaped by the conventions of three-dimensional space and what was thought to be realistic coloring. Although public reaction to the show was rather negative, the response of the younger generation of artists, writers, architects, and photographers was delight and celebration, a feeling that the massive exhibition that opened on 25th Street in New York represented a profound dilation of visual, plastic, and affective experience, an experience from which American painting and sculpture would never look back. The opening which this exhibition made in 1913 was affirmed and consolidated four years later, in the spring of 1917, in the Society of American Artists show, an event Williams attended and at which he read his futurist poem "Overture to a Dance of Locomotives":

Porters in red hats run on narrow platforms.
This way ma'am!
    —important not to take
the wrong train!

As far as the development of his own art and the new ideas about writing which Williams began to advance in his prose, he certainly did not take the wrong train. Indeed these developments would transform completely the practice of poetry in America in the twentieth century.

After finishing his medical studies in Philadelphia in 1906, he moved to New York City to intern at the French hospital for two years. From there he went to the small pediatrics unit at Child's Hospital. After six months at this second institution, where he was very unhappy with the administration, he resigned and decided to open a private practice in Rutherford. But before that he wanted to study pediatrics a little more and resolved to spend the better part of the winter of 1909-1910 in Germany in that pursuit. He left for Europe in July for a spot of touring on the Continent before proceeding to Leipzig, where he was to take up a rather lonely residence until March 1910. After taking in as much as he could at the medical college in the German city, he began the long journey back to Rutherford with a visit to his old friend Ezra Pound in London, where he caught up with some of the recent developments in poetics and where he met the important literati in that hub, or so Pound thought it, of the literary world. Through Pound he spent an evening with the great Anglo-Irish poet William Butler Yeats, who was in those years on the threshold of that change of direction that would eventually lead to a Nobel Prize and a seat in the Senate of the Irish Republic.

Back in the United States Williams returned to Rutherford to begin his medical practice, which he did in September 1910. He was promptly appointed physician for the Rutherford public schools as well. Three years before this resettlement in his hometown he had met the daughters of a prosperous German-American Rutherford family by the name of Herman. After an initial interest in the eldest of the Herman girls, Charlotte, Williams had turned his attention to the younger sister, Florence, just before his trip to Europe. Indeed only a few weeks before he left on his trip he had proposed to her and been accepted. On his return their relationship was reestablished and on 12 December 1912, after he put his practice on a sound footing, they were married. In the following year, with the help of Florence's father, they bought the house at 9 Ridge Road in Rutherford where they would live for the rest of their lives. Their two sons were born there in quick succession, William Eric on 7 January 1914 and Paul Herman on 13 September 1916. Williams settled down to a long and fruitful career both as a doctor and as a poet.

In the same year that Williams and his wife moved to 9 Ridge Road an established publisher agreed to publish a Williams manuscript. His first book in 1909 had been printed privately by a local Rutherford printer. *The Tempers* (1913) was accepted, on Pound's recommendation and urging, by Pound's own publisher in London, the small firm run by Elkin Mathews. In 1913 also Williams had four poems accepted by Harriet

The house at 9 Ridge Road in Rutherford, New Jersey, where Williams lived from 1913 until his death

Monroe's *Poetry*, a small Chicago literary magazine that found itself, occasionally to Monroe's chagrin, sponsoring the new directions poetry was taking. Williams, in a letter thanking her for accepting his work, reminded her of the important role she was playing in bringing into print the work of the American avant-garde–Sandburg, Lindsay, Pound, and himself. He called what was happening a profound revolution. He was referring, of course, to the revolution in technique, but he meant, too, an even greater revolution in perception and taste. His work also appeared in London periodicals–the *Egoist*, with which Pound was associated, and the *Poetry Review*. Finally his work was also selected for Pound's *Des Imagistes* (1914). In these venues Williams groped toward that sense of form, idiom, and content which would characterize his poetry thereafter. The poetry of *The Tempers* and his periodical verse represent a positive way of making poetry that is entirely his own. During this time he came out from under the early British influences and also from under Pound's shadow, by which his work in the 1912-1914 period had been obscured.

Having settled in Rutherford and launched his practice and having accepted the rigors and joys of raising a family, Williams, as his work was occasionally being published in London and Chicago, soon came in close contact with the writers and artists living and working in New York and its environs. The focus of this new set of contacts was the small poetry magazine *Others,* founded and edited by Alfred Kreymborg, a friend of Pound's and a New York man of letters, who in 1915 went to live in Grantwood, on the New Jersey Palisades. His small summer retreat became the rendezvous of a large group of writers and artists that included Williams, who first met Kreymborg that year. At Grantwood Williams was introduced to leading poets, artists, and critics of his day: Orrick Johns, Alanson Hartpence, Man Ray, Malcolm Cowley, Walter Arensberg, Mina Loy, Marcel Duchamp, Robert Sanborn, Wallace Stevens, and Maxwell Bodenheim.

In the developing cultural environment of early-twentieth-century America *Others* represented an extension of literary modernism from its original Chicago base at Harriet Monroe's *Poetry.* Founded in 1912, that periodical had sponsored the new poetry, at Pound's transatlantic prodding, virtually alone until the establishment of *Others* in 1915. This growth in avant-garde letters was an inevitable development, although *Others* also represented a rebuke to the Chicago group, and specifically to Harriet Monroe herself, whose commitment to modernism was marked by something less than total enthusiasm. Indeed for Williams she had not lived up to the revolutionary role he felt she was obliged to play in the fostering and promotion of the new American writing–and he told her so.

Others from the beginning saw itself in that role, and it was in its pages that Williams was first featured in his native land. The curious fact is that like a number of other American writers at that time, Pound and H. D. for example, Williams was better known to the London literary scene than to any American equivalent. However, this situation began to change in December 1916, when sixteen of his poems were included in a special number of *Others,* which also featured work by Kreymborg and Bodenheim. In that group of sixteen poems by Williams the technique, approach, orientation, and voice that would characterize his work for a lifetime can be seen fully formed. Most of the poems were quite successful and none more so than "The Young Housewife," an excellent example of the vigorous style which he had developed and a good example also of the quotidian content, his concentration, beyond the margins of the conventionally "poetical" and "literary," on the forms and substances of the everyday, to which he had turned for good, and that would in fact provide him with the material for his magnum opus, *Paterson* (1946).

At ten A.M. the young housewife
moves about in negligee behind
the wooden walls of her husband's house.
I pass solitary in my car.

Then again she comes to the curb
to call the ice-man, fish-man, and stands
shy, uncorseted, tucking in
stray ends of hair, and I compare her
to a fallen leaf.

The noiseless wheels of my car
rush with a crackling sound over
dried leaves as I bow and pass smiling.

Here Williams has turned his back on establishing a poem's measure by counting beats or syllables. The verse line has become a rhythmic unit of speech under the control of some affective disposition which the poem generates from line to line. In the old prosody, the verse line was a rhythmic unit whose sound-shape was bent to the requirements of a particular metrical scheme. Of course, within the metrical scheme considerable variation was possible. Williams's ideas about the prosodic requirements of the revolutionary poetry he and his colleagues were writing would develop from the verse practice that began for Williams in the years of World War I. Later in an essay he called "Against the Weather," published in the Spring-Summer 1939 issue of Dorothy Norman's *Twice a Year,* and in a public lecture delivered at the University of Washington in 1948, "The Poem as a Field of Action"–both collected in *Selected Essays*–he would amplify and attempt to make explicit his own prosodic practice.

With the eschewing of a metrically based prosody Williams also had to turn away from the traditional stanzaic forms and, more important, to develop a different approach to the problem of poetic structure. In metrically disciplined verse the development of the subject of the poem, the dynamics of feeling and thought which make up its internal coherence, are always played rhythmically against the requirements of recurrence in stanza and metrical pulse. Thus structure in such verse arises as a product of the variations in the chosen metrical scheme. Through varying the wavelike monotony of absolute regularity the poet is able to suggest a speaking voice and to isolate thematically important words, word clusters, line breaks, and stanza boundaries. Only through these variations and substitutions (such as the common substitution of a trochaic or spondaic foot at the beginning of

as a potential dance which the dancer makes visible or embodies in the dance proper. This consciousness more and more informs Williams's perception of the natural and gestural movements of the world around him, and more and more he begins to accentuate and bring out the beauty that lies hidden in the simplest and most natural gestures of person and thing. Such a consciousness of life itself, as gesture aspiring to the condition of dance, provides the extraordinary beauty and poignancy of a small poem such as "Arrival" in the *Sour Grapes* collection. The simple movements that accompany the preparations for love–"loosening the hooks of/her dress"–are caught in the moment when they become pure dance:

> The tawdry veined body emerges
> twisted upon itself
> like a winter wind . . . !

In the year of *The Great American Novel* (1923), Williams published a small volume of poems that represents a new plateau in his work and establishes him for the first time as a major American poet. *Spring and All* was not as formally and thematically audacious as *Kora in Hell*, and, indeed, it was neither very widely read in its time nor much appreciated whenever a rare copy of the book fell into a reviewer's line of fire. In November 1923 Marion Stroebel, an old friend and assistant to Harriet Monroe at *Poetry*, directed a rather harsh attack on the book that edged on the personally insulting. To challenge this blast, Marjorie Allan Seiffert, another poet and friend of Williams's from his *Others* days, reviewed *Spring and All* again in the April 1924 number of *Poetry*. Her review, although a pointed defense of Williams, did manage to look at the volume coolly enough to recognize its obvious strengths and the maturity of technique and vision which it represented in Williams's development as a poet. The poems, she said, were marked by an extraordinary clarity of image and a lively mobility of language. More important she pointed to Williams's own definition of art in the volume (the first edition of *Spring and All* appeared with a prose commentary, as had *Kora in Hell: Improvisations*) as an objective reality enjoying its own "separate existence," written out of a "condition of imaginative suspense." Although she did not fully understand the implications of what Williams was asserting, she had put her finger on a crucial point. Williams wrote: "Imagination is not to avoid reality, nor is it description nor an evocation of objects or situations, it is to say that poetry does not tamper with the world but moves it–It affirms reality most powerfully and therefore, since reality needs no personal support but exists free from human action, as proven by science in the indestructibility of matter and of force, it creates a new object, a play, a dance which is not a mirror up to nature. . . ."

René Magritte, the French surrealist painter, has painted a rather large picture of a rather large brown pipe on a cream-colored background. Under the pipe appear the words "Ceci n'est pas un pipe"–This is not a pipe. And of course it is not a pipe; it is a picture. Williams's best-known poem, "The Red Wheelbarrow," was untitled in the first edition of *Spring and All* and that is perhaps how it should have remained. If a title was thought necessary perhaps something along the lines of Magritte's comment on his picture might have helped generations of readers since 1923 to understand this enigmatic little poem–this is not a red wheelbarrow. "The Red Wheelbarrow" is a poem. Williams's prose comment on the nature of imagination is particularly appropriate. Imagination does not imitate or plagiarize or describe the world, nor does it evoke or put one in the mood to appreciate and gather delight from a nice barnyard scene, or a shimmering sunset outside one's window. Reality exists in its own right, is free and independent of human agency. If every human were to disappear suddenly from the earth, reality would remain intact, indestructible. Imagination is not the Xerox machine of the psyche. Imagination creates new objects; in Williams's case it creates poems. In reading "The Red Wheelbarrow" one is not being asked to look through the words at some scene which can be located in space and time. First one is dealing with an object made from words, set down in patterns; the words–because they have the capacity to stipulate objects, processes, and events–present an image, not an image *of* the world, but an image *in* the world. The verbal imagination makes separately existing things out of its verbal materials. And not just words in abstract, as one might find them in a dictionary, trailing, kitelike, a long tail of bland denotations, but words as they are shaped by mouths, and as they are cupped and held in one's ears. And not just what the words mean as abstractions, but all their connotations, their latent images and metaphors, their accents, and music. And above all in *Spring and All* one notices how words, like the sails of a yacht, can catch the wind of feeling, fill out, and drive the vessel forward.

"The Pot of Flowers" is not a moment of pure observation; its aesthetic substance is not visual. Certainly the poem presents a visual image, but its beauty lies in its words, rather than in the fidelity with which it depicts some real pot of flowers. Like an object in the world, an object with its own shape, volume, texture, and moving energy, a poem is a unique, unified, and universal object in its own right, instinct with rhythm: "flowers and flowers reversed/take and spill the shaded flame"; sound texture: "red where in whorls/ petal lays its glow . . ."; and its own organic form:

> the leaves
> reaching up their modest green
> from the pot's rim
>
> and there, . . .

form, here, suspensively construed, the word "rim" coinciding with a strophic boundary, a formal "rim."

On a literary sensibility steeped in metaphor and all the subspecies of rhetorical figuration from the poetic tradition, Williams's procedures and effects were almost entirely lost. But such splendors as are to be found in *Spring and All*, although largely indiscernible to the older generation of "versifiers," trope-mongers, and trope-consumers, whose sense of poetic rhythm was limited to the sound palette of the metrical tradition, were heard and recognized by the younger generation in the mid 1920s, young poets such as Louis Zukofsky, Charles Reznikoff, and later George Oppen and Lorine Niedecker, among many others. *Spring and All* was a turning point for Williams and for American poetic modernism. At the age of forty, Williams consolidated the accomplishments of fifteen years of experience. He showed in that volume that modernism was not a youthful mania to be abandoned with the passing of life's spring. Unlike T. S. Eliot, for whom "tradition" and conservatism were the final destination for "individual talent," Williams insisted on the efficaciousness of the revolution in art he had helped shape and extend. He was not going to turn his back on it just as it was beginning to produce a rich harvest of poetry. Someone once wrote that middle age is the moment in life when everything seems to hang on the point of being lost. In *Spring and All* nothing is lost, and the promise of a life's spring is fulfilled.

A work in the same mold as *Spring and All*— poetry, prose, fact, aesthetics, social criticism— followed in 1928. *The Descent of Winter*, which appeared in the Autumn 1928 issue of Pound's little magazine the *Exile*, contributes several astonishingly beautiful poems to Williams's oeuvre— "My bed is narrow," "that brilliant field," "To freight cars in the air," "Dahlias." It represents also spring's antagonist, the coming of winter and the darker, more deathly forces of thought, feeling, and history with which one associates the dead time of the year. The book is more clearly than *Spring and All* in journal form, beginning "9/27"–and concluding on 18 December. It explores this chill "descent" in images of pain and death–"In the dead weeds a rubbish heap/in flames"–and of pollution, physical and ethical: "That river will be clean/before ever you will be." The aesthetic point of view so forcefully articulated in the 1923 volume stands undiminished and unchanged in this new work, but there appears, in addition to aesthetics, a much wider and more intense concern with social and political matters:

> and men at the bar
>   talking of the strike
>   and cash.

"A Morning Imagination of Russia," an encomiastic ode of considerable interest, is placed at the heart of the volume, and halts, for a moment, the descent. It staunches also the hemorrhage of death imagery, beginning with the stirring of dawn–and social hope–and ending with the possibility of convalescence after sickness and decay. Social transformation is seen not in terms of political action and power, but, characteristically for Williams, in terms of closer, more immediate and tactile contact with reality:

> We have little now but
> we have that. We are convalescents. Very
> feeble. Our hands shake. We need a
> transfusion. No one will give it to us,
> they are afraid of infection. I do not
> blame them. We have paid heavily. But we
> have gotten–touch. The eyes and the ears
> down on it. Close.

Except in the eye-ear pun in the last word– "Close" as nearby, and "Close" as end of the poem–this is not an entirely successful poem qua poem; it strays into the symbolic a little too far, losing touch for a moment with Williams's usual aes-

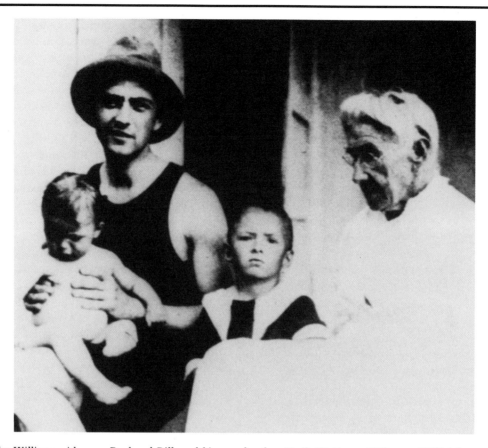

William Carlos Williams with sons, Paul and Bill, and his grandmother, Emily Dickinson Wellcome, 1917 (photograph by Irving B. Wellcome; courtesy of William Eric Williams)

thetic. Here the images take on an editorializing function, and although no one can impugn the genuineness of the feeling, the sharpness of his concern, still his usual clarity and intensity in word and rhythm has ebbed. In this regard *The Descent of Winter* is a lesser work than *Spring and All*.

However, what Williams attempts in "A Morning Imagination of Russia" is not a technical and aesthetic dead end. Nor is it new to his work. Williams's first important poem, one he placed at the head of his *The Collected Earlier Poems* (1951), is written to a similar mode and theme. "The Wanderer" (written in 1913) also uses the longer, more prosaic (which is to say, perhaps, more conversational) line as rhythmic base, wanders into symbolic utterance, and engages in social comment. This line of development, after "The Wanderer," continues, in technique at least, with his experiments in dramatic monologue, that is, assimilates Robert Browning's influence through Ezra Pound's example, in such poems as "The Death of Franco of Cologne: His Prophecy of Beethoven" and "Con Brio" (both written by 1913), extends through "History" (written in

1916) and "Tract" (written in 1917), and culminates in the earlier period in the first "Paterson" (written in 1926). This important three-page poem anticipates the *Paterson* to come in the 1940s. In the earlier "Paterson" the idea of seeing a city as a man is first used: "I see myself/in the regularly ordered plateglass of/his thoughts, glimmering. . . ." And the influential notion of poetic objectivity first articulated at length in *Spring and All* is trenchantly formulated in a phrase with which Williams will always be associated: "Say it! No ideas but in things."

The poetic problem which *The Descent of Winter* tackles, but does not adequately solve (the solution would not emerge fully until *Paterson*), is: how does one alloy the vivid intensity and clarity of a lyricism steeled on strict attendance to the image–a technique refined in the school of verbal conciseness, directness of treatment, and musicality–with the need–growing more urgent all through the 1920s–to engage the larger social and historical realities of one's time and place? How could a writer express in the medium of poetry his or her social and political concerns at the center of social life and not turn a poem into a sermon or political harangue or prose tract? If the primary notional vocabulary of poetry was the sensory image as it embodied immediate experience, how could this vocabulary be alloyed to the conceptual thinking the study of society, politics, and economics seemed to necessitate? How could the vivid rhythms of specific perception and concrete contact with things and processes be preserved in a discourse swamped by the general and the abstract?

Ezra Pound's solution in *The Cantos* involved the treatment of concepts as if they were notional images–conceptual ideograms–abstractions rooted in the concrete and real and emerging through time as the accumulated conceptual wisdom of a real people, living a concrete history, in a particular landscape. Turning his back on the theoretical knowledge generated by the experientially alienated analytical logic of Cartesian rationalism, Pound proposed and formulated in his opus an anthropological poetics, which entered a culture at the level of its characterizing concrete experiences where it recovered the knowledge that that culture had derived from meditating on those experiences. Such a knowledge was not systematic in the philosophical sense, but was wholly efficacious nonetheless as concrete knowledge, or what a philosopher might call "recipe" knowledge. Because roots of this knowledge were sunk deep in the actual lived experiences of a people, such knowledge embodied the concrete in a way a philosophical abstraction could not. Thus these conceptual ideograms offered a new way of incarnating the known and, as a result, could be handled as one handled sensory images in a poem. The poetic logic that controlled the unfolding sequence of images in a poem was the logic that made sense of the conceptual ideograms. These two kinds of images mutually vivified and supported each other–the sensory embodying actual experience, and the conceptual embodying the wisdom derived from experience. Clearly here the emphasis is on the concrete, the made, the particular–thus one can know a society better by examining the workmanship of a simple clay bowl than by reading the inflated abstractions on which a national anthem might rest; or one might find the sincerity and beauty of an actual religious ceremony more telling of a culture's values than some abstract conception of deity toward which every member of that society pays a required pro forma respect. This for Pound was the lesson to be learned from four thousand years of Chinese

civilization. It was the lesson learned by Williams contemplating the very different life of a people along the banks of the Passaic. For Williams this new orientation would culminate in *Paterson*. Before he thought through to the essentials, in form and content, of that great summative epic, he would immerse himself in a rigorous program of social observation, a program of close attention to the sound and feel of quotidian reality, a celebration, in short, of the ordinary. But he would do this in the medium of prose fiction, both short and long.

There is no time in Williams's life when he did not write poetry, but there is a period from about the mid 1920s to about 1950 when he seemed to devote a tremendous amount of his creative power to prose, starting with *The Great American Novel* in 1923. Williams, in 1925, published *In the American Grain*, a series of essays and studies of "American" heroes from Red Eric of Greenland, Columbus, Cortés, and Montezuma, on to Abraham Lincoln. This book, unrecognized in its own time, has finally achieved the status of a classic in the development of a distinctively American prose. Its early impact, light as it was, got Williams labeled an American "primitive" who had finally renounced the deracinated cosmopolitanism of cubist poetics, or so Gorham Munson, writing in the 1920s, thought. Williams's exploration of the "primitive" in America's early history was also praised by D. H. Lawrence. Like Lawrence, Williams celebrates the "beauty of lavish, primitive embrace..." glimpsed in certain exemplary lives: Samuel de Champlain, Cotton Mather, Pere Sebastian Rasles, Daniel Boone, George Washington, Aaron Burr, just to mention the subjects of six of the more interesting essays. The label "primitive" was very soon translated as a call for the restoration of "primitivism" in contemporary life. The book, of course, argues for no such thing. It locates and embodies in these superbly crafted prose essays, sketches, and "characters" the pure essence of American locality. The definitive assessment of this volume's prose style remains to be undertaken. There can be no doubt that when that assessment is done, *In the American Grain* will take its place as one of the decisive moments in the evolution of American prose.

From that work in prose Williams then moved to a novel. *A Voyage to Pagany* (1928), his first in the traditional mode, was based on the five-month trip he and Flossie Williams had taken in 1924 to Europe, where he met, especially in

Paris, a great number of the generation of writers and artists whose modernism Williams more or less shared. This novel was not well received in its own time and is not much read today. Its principal interest now lies in the light it throws on that voyage to Europe, where Williams caught up with old friends from his university days (Pound, H. D.) and the New York of the period of World War I (Robert McAlmon) or made the acquaintance of other moving spirits of the new art: James Joyce, Philippe Soupault (whose *Last Nights in Paris* Williams translated into English in 1929), and Constantin Brancusi. His meeting with McAlmon was particularly important because it instituted again for a few months a fruitful friendship that the two men had shared in New York just after World War I, a period in which they had edited the influential little magazine devoted to modernism, *Contact* (1920-1923). Although the two men would never reestablish the close professional intimacy they had shared in New York, a consequence, largely, of McAlmon's rather dissipated life in the Paris of the "lost generation," Williams would come to McAlmon's aid in subsequent years after the younger writer's return to America a broken and defeated man.

In the 1930s Williams's writings in prose continued in a veritable flood of stories, plays, and novels, including the first part of a trilogy of novels: *White Mule* (1937), which was followed by *In the Money* in 1940, and by *The Build-Up* in 1952. These three novels deal with the spiritual and social growth of a family called Stecher in the early years of the century, as they seek to assimilate themselves to the dominant values of the New World they have chosen for their field of action. Although the trilogy ends "tragically," Williams always saw this long prose work as working out of a tradition of social comedy, a comedy of manners, in which the writer was not the ethical interpreter of a family's rise and fall but someone who simply revealed what he saw without comment. There is here a wish to annihilate the self as the expressive framework of art. This effacement of the "I," one of the major narrative innovations of *White Mule,* was explored and refined in the prose works, where the issue of narrative point of view is of utmost importance in the depiction of the represented world of fiction. *The Great American Novel* of 1923 had begun in the fullness of a personal and electrically expressive ego. The *White Mule* trilogy, however, does not begin with the self as first cause; it begins with society.

This attention to the particulars of life along the Passaic, its lived density, helped orient Williams to the thematic materials of *Paterson.*

Williams began publishing collections of short stories in the early 1930s, although his short fiction had been appearing for years in the literary periodicals of his day. *A Novelette and Other Prose (1921-1931)* and *The Knife of the Times and Other Stories* were both published in 1932. *Life along the Passaic River* followed in 1938. These stories again and again capture with an unerring eye for the representative, typifying detail the feel of life in twentieth-century America. Williams was particularly adept at embodying the social and psychological tensions that emerge among his characters. As in his poetry, the sharpness with which these conflicts and struggles are depicted is achieved through the telling juxtaposition of episodes and events, and, more important, through the painstaking care for le mot juste in the phrasing. The remarkable prose stylist of *In the American Grain* writes at full stretch in the stories and novels. Concision and directness are the two obvious virtues of his style; an ear attuned to the lift and weight of the voices of real people, a speaking which energizes and focuses the style. Style is obviously the product of discipline and a poet's native inwardness with the entire expressive instrument of language. But a great and good prose style is not merely a technical accomplishment; it is also an ethical one. As Williams explained in "White Mule versus Poetry," an essay published in the August 1937 issue of the *Writer:* "The writing of the language is what interests me. So in writing . . . my greatest concern was to write with attention to marshalling the words into an order which would be free from 'lies.' "

In addition to prose, Williams was interested in the drama, both as an actor and as a playwright. As an actor he engaged in theatricals of all kinds, amateur and professional, at home and on the public stage. At home the Williamses, with their friends and acquaintances, would often sing, dance, and perform skits, sketches, and other light plays by Williams. Williams's interest in the theater, however, extended beyond his own living room. His early association with Alfred Kreymborg led to one memorable engagement as an actor in New York's Greenwich Village in 1916, his stage debut. The play, *Lima Beans,* by Kreymborg, was a dada piece in which Williams played a typical middle-class husband opposite Mina Loy's typical American housewife.

Light stuff, compounded of satiric comment on what have come to be known as middle American *mores*, slapstick, and farce, it was enjoyed by the generally bohemian audiences attracted to this sort of avant-garde entertainment. More important than the play was Williams's contact with Mina Loy, a talented, physically attractive, and modish young modernist poet who had already begun to make a reputation for herself in the small magazines—such as *Others, Poetry,* and the *Dial*—in which Williams's own work was also prominent.

From those early experiences with the theater Williams never lost his love for the stage. He went on to write a number of plays, plays generally well received in their day but now rarely performed or read. His major achievement in dramatic literature is still thought to be *Many Loves,* which was first published in the 1942 volume of *New Directions in Prose and Poetry* and collected in *Many Loves and Other Plays* (1961). *Many Loves* incorporates three one-act plays he had written for a local Rutherford drama group in 1939 and fuses them with a Pirandello-like framework written in verse. The play explores the failure of communication between the sexes and is distinguished by his sympathetic portrayal of his female characters, asserting a forward-looking sensitivity to the position of women in a society dominated by male notions of sexuality and intimacy. A second major drama, *A Dream of Love,* premiered Off-Broadway in 1949 to a warm review in the *New York Times* by playwright William Saroyan. Published in the 1948 *New Directions* annual and collected in *Many Loves and Other Plays,* this play also scrutinizes relationships between the sexes, but this time in the context of a modern marriage, focusing particularly on the problem of fidelity. His third important drama is the nightmarish *Tituba's Children* (written in 1950), a powerful cry of dissent in the midst of the anti-Communist witch-hunts that seized American political culture in the late 1940s and 1950s. Also in *Many Loves and Other Plays,* this play represents Williams's final attempt to make overt political and social statements in his art, attempts that characterized much of his work in prose, poetry, and the essay through the 1930s.

His activities in this respect during that decade and after did not entirely displace purely aesthetic and literary concerns. In the early 1930s, in the depths of the Depression, Williams's work was still to be found in the little poetry magazines that managed to hang on to patrons and readers in the socioeconomic maelstrom created by the hard times. Richard Johns's *Pagany* (Boston); Charles Henri Ford and Parker Tyler's *Blues*; *Hound and Horn,* edited by the neoclassicist critic and poet R. P. Blackmur; the *Miscellany;* Norman MacLeod's *Morada;* and others kept alive the notion of an independent, avant-garde literary culture even in an era when American society and culture were in turmoil.

Important as his contacts with these small magazines and periodicals were, none was more decisive for the middle-aged poet than his contact with Louis Zukofsky and the "objectivism" which Zukofsky began to noise in the early 1930s. The younger Brooklyn poet, a man of great skill and erudition, had already begun work on his vast masterwork, *A,* a twenty-four-part poem that Zukofsky would not finish until the 1970s. Objectivism took the *imagisme* of the first generation of modernists as its point of departure. From that base, Zukofsky developed objectivism as a way of making clearer than *imagisme* ever did the notion of the poem as embodying a radical objectivity. He extended to poetry an optical analogy, namely that a lens brings the rays of an object to a focus. The poem then embodies a mode of ontological being as an object in and for itself. In every word, Zukofsky asserted in his important prose statement "An Objective" (written in 1930), there is a potential for radical objectification based on the axiom that words are "absolute symbols for objects, states, acts, interrelations, thoughts about them." He did not want to call any verbal event "verse" that "did not convey the totality of perfect rest." This emphasis on the materiality and thing-likeness of a poem, a poem, in short, as a verbal artifact in a new and radical sense, was understood as well by *les imagistes.* However, Zukofsky attempted to articulate a more explicit and detailed poetics than the rules-of-thumb that had characterized most *imagiste* theorizing.

In this new development Zukofsky saw Williams as playing a central role. For Williams was one of the old masters of objectivism, a writer who had begun life as an *imagiste* but had worked his way well beyond that starting point and, whether he knew it or not, had intuited objectivism in practice. Trusting to his superb poetic judgment and trusting especially to his eye and ear, he had almost single-handedly devised an aesthetic worthy of capturing America itself in all its diverse, dissonant, shifting reality.

Paterson, Book V : The River of Heaven

Of asphodel, that greeny flower,

    that is a simple flower

            like a buttercup upon its

branching stem, save

    that it's green and wooden -

            We've had a long life

and many things have happened in it.

    There are flowers also

            in hell. So today I've come

to talk to you about them - of flowers

    that we both love

            even of this poor

colorless thing that no one living

    prizes

            but the dead see

and ask among themselves,

    What do we remember that was shaped

            as this thing

is shaped ? Their eyes fill

with tears.

            Of love, abiding love

it should be

    But too weak a wash of crimson

            colors it.

Page from a draft for a section that Williams dropped from Paterson (Book Five) *but later revised as "Asphodel, That Greeny Flower" (William Carlos Williams,* Pictures from Breughel. *Copyright © 1955 by William Carlos Williams. Reprinted by permission of New Directions Publishing Corporation, Agents for the Estate of William Carlos Williams. Courtesy of the Beinecke Rare Book and Manuscript Library, Yale University)*

This assessment of Williams was high praise indeed, and Williams was no doubt flattered by the younger poet's attention. Soon after Williams read Zukofsky's assessment of his position in American letters, the two men began a friendship that lasted the rest of Williams's life, a friendship and collaboration still in need of much study. Zukofsky was not, however, the only self-confessed objectivist. There were others, and Zukofsky's To Press helped put these new ideas into circulation. George Oppen, Carl Rakosi, Basil Bunting, Charles Reznikoff constituted this school of poetry revolving first around the To Press and, later, around Rakosi's Objectivist Press. It was this second small press, financed by the contributions from the poets themselves, that first published Williams's *Collected Poems 1921-1931* in January 1934.

It is arguable that contact with this group of writers during the 1930s helped Williams catch his second poetic "breath" after his annus mirabilis of 1922. Their poetry did not transform Williams's own poetic practices. Rather, it was Williams's probable realization that as a practitioner of a certain kind—one who valued sensory alertness, perceptual opportunism, clarity, sharpness of outline in image and tonality—he was now no longer the only poet of talent who adhered to an objectivist poetics, a poetics which this younger generation had named and developed. This perhaps should be emphasized: Zukofsky's adherence to a poetics of objectivism derived from a poetic practice he found in Williams's earlier work. For Williams this theoretical step was not particularly necessary; after all the practitioner qua practitioner does not need to have a theory to explain what he's been doing all along. What this development did do for Williams, however, was to make him acutely aware that the efforts of the 1920s to establish a poetics and a sensibility, divested of its old world costumes, had not been in vain. In the 1930s the objectivists were all the evidence he needed that the moment of clarity at the Armory Show in 1913 had, in fact, given birth to a new sensibility, one that had "taken" on American soil, and found its fittest expression in the energies of the American tongue. Later *Paterson* would establish the poetic efficacy of the native idiom once and for all, bringing to fruition a half-century of American modernism and, beyond that, culminating Walt Whitman's great and daring revolution in technique and theme in mid-nineteenth-century poetry.

As he readied himself and accumulated the thematic and technical materials for his own *Song of Myself* in the 1940s, Williams continued with his busy life at Rutherford, practicing medicine, writing, and keeping up contacts with friends and colleagues all over the North Atlantic world. He took a public part in many of the social and political controversies which dominated the public sphere in the 1930s. Such involvements in the next two decades would come to disappoint Williams and, in the case of the politically motivated withdrawal of his appointment as Poetry Consultant to the Library of Congress in 1952, would hurt him deeply. His medical practice flourished, and he was much loved by his patients, most of them the everyday folk of a thoroughly typical industrial town in what was then the heart of the American economy.

By the late 1930s his children, Bill and Paul, were both heading out into the world. Bill, after an undergraduate career at Williams College, proceeded to the Cornell Medical School and a distinguished career in medicine. Paul, the younger son, returned to his father's alma mater, the University of Pennsylvania, and from there went on to the Harvard Business School, marriage, and the beginnings of a career with Republic Steel in Canton, Ohio. With the bombing of Pearl Harbor both young men were swept up in the maelstrom of war. Bill, Jr., served as a medical officer in the U.S. Navy and shipped off in spring 1942 to the Pacific with an outfit of Seabees. Paul later also shipped out with the U.S. Navy, but drew escort duties on a destroyer, riding shotgun on the Allied shipping lanes across the North Atlantic. Like millions of parents across the country, Williams and his wife had to endure the agony of separation from their sons and to enter that state of anxious hope that became the psychological norm for those back home in a nation at war.

In the late 1930s Pound had put Williams in touch with a wealthy young man from Harvard, James Laughlin, who was interested in modern literature and willing to translate that appreciation into a publishing enterprise that would provide concrete and continuous support for the moderns. Laughlin's New Directions Press, with the publication of *White Mule* in 1937, for all intents and purposes became Williams's permanent publisher, although his relationship with Laughlin and the press was occasionally troubled by the poet's suspicion that Laughlin was a bit too much of a dilettante. Laughlin himself tells the story of how *White Mule* was accidentally allowed to go out of print in 1937 while he was away on a skiing vacation. Williams always knew and acknowledged that Laughlin's heart was in the right place as far as the modernist movement in literature was concerned. Indeed, even with the coming of success in the 1950s and 1960s, Laughlin never diluted the focus of his publishing program by going after potboilers and bestsellers. However, his obvious editorial daring, acumen, and taste in literature were not always complemented by an aggressive program for promotion and distribution of the works he published.

In any case, Laughlin's new press, founded in a rather casual fashion, has been persistently the most important publisher of modernist and avant-garde literature from the late 1930s to the present day. And the press served the important function of keeping in circulation the works of Williams and Pound. After years of seeing their work published by small, poorly financed presses, quickly going out of print, the two senior modernists in American letters could now depend on respectable publishing runs and a much wider circulation than they ever enjoyed before. In 1938, for example, New Directions published a new volume of Williams's collected poems that was twice as big as the Objectivist Press production of 1934 and published it in an edition of 1,500 copies rather than the much smaller number of the earlier edition.

Williams's association with New Directions could not have come at a more opportune time for he had, by 1937, already made his first substantial commitment toward the composition of *Paterson*. During the 1940s and 1950s he was gratified to watch New Directions bring out each section of the long poem as it was finished, in handsomely designed editions, on good quality paper, and with a typographical aptness to the content rarely lavished on books by the major commercial publishing houses. In 1963 New Directions would collect all five parts of *Paterson*, as well as the notes for the uncompleted part six, into one volume, which the press has kept continuously in print to the present day. In all, Laughlin would keep fourteen Williams titles on his publishing list after the poet's death in 1963.

In composing *Paterson* Williams realized the epic poem anticipated in his earlier work. "The Wanderer" (written in 1913) provided a poetic initiation into the things of the world, of which the river–"the filthy Passaic"–provided an enduring symbol. This initiatory process is presided over by the feminine principle, variously embodied as muse, fertility goddess, and the young poet's grandmother. This figure would also endure mutatis mutandis in *Paterson*.

Other anticipations were the small imagist poems such as "Proletarian Portrait," which had catalyzed Williams's earlier reputation as a poet of pure vision:

A big young bareheaded woman
in an apron

Her hair slicked back standing
on the street

One stockinged foot toeing
the sidewalk

Her shoe in her hand. Looking
intently into it

She pulls out the paper insole
to find the nail

That has been hurting her[.]

In *Paterson* these pure "lyrics" were made to serve somewhat different poetic ends. He used the image, with a new and deepening authority, as the lexical hoard for a new kind of extended poetic discourse; the image complex provided the essential building block of meaning. A poem like "Proletarian Portrait," capturing an ordinary moment in time, transforming that moment into pure spectacle, when placed in the extended continuities of *Paterson*, accumulated and released a plenitude of resonance and meaning which the naked lyric, gleaming in its denotative skin, has sloughed away. This procedure, the linking together of radiant particulars, permitted the image in its developing contexts to denote more than the thing itself, without abandoning concrete materiality for the general and the abstract:

That is the poet's business. Not to talk in vague categories but to write particularly, as a physician works, upon a patient, upon the thing before him, in the particular to discover the universal. John Dewey had said (I discovered it quite by chance), "The local is the only universal, upon that all art builds."

This, then, was to be the path to that "Rigor of beauty" which Williams had made his life's quest and which would culminate in *Paterson*.

The clearest anticipation of *Paterson,* however, was written in 1926 in a poem of the same name. "Paterson" won the *Dial* award for poetry in that year and was published in the February 1927 issue. In this poem Williams presents the central image of the later poem, the image of the city as a man, a man lying on his side by the river and peopling the place with his thoughts. But the place is not just a manifestation of his thoughts; the thoughts are also manifestations of the place, hence the poem's key phrase—"Say it! No ideas but in things."—repeated several times:

> Say it! No ideas but in things. Mr.
> Paterson has gone away
> to rest and write. Inside the bus one sees
> his thoughts sitting and standing. His thoughts
> alight and scatter—
>
> Who are these people? (how complex
> this mathematic) among whom I see myself
> in the regularly ordered plateglass of
> his thoughts, glimmering before shoes and
>   bicycles—?

This whole passage with one minor change was repeated in the opening pages of book one. It was a good place to start indicating the summative character of the books to follow. A whole life of perception, feeling, and thought cascades through the long poem like the water pouring over Passaic Falls, water that "crashes from the edge of the gorge/in a recoil of spray and rainbow mists." From this perspective, *Paterson* can be profitably compared to those summative epics of Williams's contemporary modernists, Pound's *The Pisan Cantos* (1948), Hugh MacDiarmid's *In Memoriam James Joyce,* and T. S. Eliot's *Four Quartets* (1936-1942). Indeed Hugh Kenner has recently argued that *Paterson* represents, partly at least, a response to Eliot's *Four Quartets,* Williams's last word in a feud between the two men that went back to before 1920. The verbal echo to Eliot's *East Coker* (1940) in the preface to book one is unmistakable:

> For the beginning is assuredly
> the end—since we know nothing, pure
> and simple, beyond
> our own complexities.

This statement was not intended as homage to Eliot, one giant of modern literature saluting another, but as a rebuke. While Eliot's sequence strove to transcend the local and particular, quick-

ening the deeper the poem entered its sacred, otherworldly silences, *Paterson* would be discovered, Williams wrote in his introductory remarks, in "its own idiom," rising "to flutter into life awhile.... as itself, locally, and so like every other place in the world." *Paterson* would not begin in philosophical abstractions (*Burnt Norton*) and end in silence, stillness, and annihilation (*Little Gidding*); it would hear and explore the "roar" of the falls "as it crashed upon the rocks at its base"; because, Williams explained, "In the imagination this roar is a speech or a voice, a speech in particular; it is the poem itself that is the answer."

The specifically poetic voice Williams had in the back of his mind in writing *Paterson* was not the voice of one of his immediate contemporaries, but the voice of Walt Whitman, and it is to this precursor that he pays homage at the close of his introductory remarks to the poem. Williams sees his own poem as the extension, some would say culmination, of the poetic revolution Whitman announced in the mid-nineteenth century. Whitman, wrote Williams, "always said that his poems, which had broken the dominance of the iambic pentameter in English prosody, had only begun his theme. I agree. It is up to us, in the new dialect, to continue it by a new construction upon the syllables."

Constructing "the new dialect . . . upon the syllables" carried several immediate consequences. First, the final rejection of a specifically poetic diction, the sort of specialized poeticizing language against which the early romantics, Wordsworth especially, had rebelled in the latter part of the eighteenth century. It meant also the forging of a new prosody based on the phrasal patterns of natural speech rhythms rather than the more or less fixed, repetitive pulses of traditional meters, especially the dominant iambic. To this latter task Williams was particularly devoted, going so far as to theorize about prosody and crediting himself with the discovery of a new prosodic sound-shape for American verse based on the notion of the "variable foot." This innovation he felt was not all that new; it was known and practiced by the ancient Greeks in the form of what classicists call their "lame" or "limping" iambics. In a note appended to book one of *Paterson,* he quoted John Addington Symonds on Hipponax: "In order apparently to bring the meter still more within the sphere of prose and common speech, Hipponax ended his iambics with a spondee or a trochee instead of an iambus, doing thus the utmost violence to the rhythmical structure." The quotation accords with Williams's rejection of traditional metrics in favor of a new measure–worked out in practice in the third section of book two–which he called the "relativistic or variable foot," a notion perfectly at home in the Einsteinian universe. Like the earlier *imagistes'* attention to the "musical phrase," the variable foot represents a unit of rhythmical expression determined by the rhythm and density of the poet's own perception, the nature of the subject at hand, and poet and reader's shared knowledge of the common language in which the particular perception, subject, or experience is normatively expressed. The fixed, metronomic foot of traditional metrics apes solidities and certainties that have vanished in our time. Throughout *Paterson,* the search for appropriate form involved the establishment of a new measure, a new "musical pace." Whitman's was the first heave against audition habituated to the drive and beat of the iambus; *Paterson,* Williams seems to be suggesting, would have been impossible without that bit of daring. Free verse is not free, it seems, but variable.

It has been said that writing in general, the placing of graphic symbols on the blank white page, is not simply making visible prior thought processes. Writing itself is a form of thought, and to use writing simply as a recording or reflecting medium ends by denaturing it, by robbing writing of its greatest potential. The development of Williams's poetry can be plotted as a movement toward the apprehension of writing as a uniquely material form of intellection.

The modernist rejection of traditional metrics unveiled this function of writing as thinking more clearly than ever before. The poem's lines were no longer repeatable rhythmical units in need of suitably and tautly impacted fill. Instead each line was conceived as a unique rhythmical event: fragments of necessary syntax, line length, medial pauses, juxtaposed elements, line breaks, the wide variety of possible sound effects, organic stanzaic boundaries make the thought process itself concrete. As Williams wrote in section two of book one,

> There is no direction. Whither? I
> cannot say. I cannot say
> more than how. The how (the howl) only
> is at my disposal (proposal) : watching–
> colder than stone
>
> a bud forever green,

tight-curled, upon the pavement, perfect
in juice and substance but divorced, divorced
from its fellows, fallen low–

> Divorce is
> the sign of knowledge in our time,
> divorce! divorce!

In the first line the comment about "direction" mutates into a probe of self, "Whither? I." In the second line, simple repetition–"cannot say. I cannot say"–becomes for the speaker a kind of desperate advice to himself: in other words, being unable "to say" is impermissible; he must say. The assonantal repetition in the third line–"more than how. The how (the howl) only"–makes audible, which is to say musical, the mind's agony before obstacles to saying. In these movements, some halting, some "tight-curled," words and sounds jostling against each other, the poetry is as fully alive to its own material processes as it is to its topical subjects. He returns to the subject of words in book two, section three:

> She was married with empty words:
> > better to
> > stumble at
> > the edge
> > to fall
> > fall
> > and be
> >
> > –divorced
>
> from the insistence of place–
> > from knowledge,
> from learning–the terms
> foreign, conveying no immediacy, pouring down.

This poetry approaches as closely as writing is able to unity of mind and body, to a reassociation of sensibility whereby a thought is grasped not only in the abstract spaces of the mind, but grasped also by the senses. The poet, Williams once suggested to a correspondent, possesses "knowledge in the flesh as opposed to a body of abstract knowledge called science and philosophy." *Paterson* is the embodiment of that principle.

The central topic of *Paterson* is the idea of a city. That such a topic should have suggested itself for his most ambitious work is not surprising, for the city as symbol has had as long and varied a history as has the city as dwelling. The chronicle of Western civilization can, to a large extent, be read as the history of the rise and decline of great cities: Athens, Rome, Jerusalem, Constantinople, Venice. These cities have been the key arenas in the development of Western civilization. To the physical location of these great cities, and to cities in general, a level of symbolic meaning has accumulated over the centuries. Who in Judeo-Christian civilization cannot feel the symbolic pull of the name Jerusalem or Rome? Indeed the most important symbol of paradise in Christianity is the New Jerusalem. For a thousand years the empire centered by Rome was not only a military and administrative center but a focus for all aspects of physical, intellectual, and artistic life. Its secular authority was transformed after the decline of its military power, and it became the spiritual center of Christendom until the Reformation. Even to this day Rome, for Catholics, represents the center of their spiritual world. The Anglo-Welsh poet David Jones has explored the concrete place and mystical-spiritual function of Rome in our civilization in a long poem called *The Anathemata* (1952), which curiously enough he was composing at the same time Williams was working on the central city–Paterson–of his own particular cosmos.

However, mystical insight and sacerdotal celebration of a city whose myth is more powerful than its reality have no part in the idea which Williams embodies in *Paterson*. Indeed the mystical and the otherworldly, in the traditional terms in which such matters are treated in Western culture, have been deliberately avoided; the whole tenor of his work has been toward a grasp of human beings as they are here and now. Interest in the human is paramount in his idea of the city, for *Paterson* is about man; man identified with and personifying the city. In the introductory note Williams briefly sums up this insight: "*Paterson* is a long poem in four parts [later expanded to five]–that a man in himself is a city, beginning, seeking, achieving and concluding his life in ways which the various aspects of a city may embody–if imaginatively conceived–any city, all the details of which may be made to voice his most intimate convictions." This conception encompasses both the poet's vision of reality, the real world, and his idea of man, for it is "an interpenetration both ways." Mr. Paterson is Everyman (but presented in the only way one can directly know him, as an individual–living in time, rooted in history), the sum total of his experi-

ences; he is also the city Paterson, which is the cosmos in miniature, located in specified place.

In book one (1946), "The Delineaments of the Giants," the physical location and topography of Paterson, the city, give rise to its personification as a giant lying on his right side in a bend of the Passaic River, his head near the thunder of the Passiac Falls, his back easily arched with the curve of the river.

> Eternally asleep
> his dreams walk about the city where he persists
> incognito. Butterflies settle on his stone ear.
> Immortal he neither moves nor rouses and is sel-
> dom
> seen, though he breathes and the subtleties of his
> machinations
> drawing their substance from the noise of the pour-
> ing
> river
> animate a thousand automatons. Who because they
> neither know their sources nor the sills of their
> disappointments walk outside their bodies aimlessly
> for the most part,
> locked and forgot in their desires–unroused.

Here are stated some of Williams's most intimate convictions which the city embodies: its aspect as industrial center "locked and forgot" in the permanent depression of economic decline, the closeness of nature and the determining influence of the natural phenomena which form and surround it, the alienation of those who "walk outside their bodies," isolated from their own desires and from the sources of their social and personal beings. From this opening and for the whole of book one, Williams explores what he calls "the elemental character of the place," through reiterated images, through episodic devices, and through the extended and subtle analogical framework of the connection between man and city.

Book two (1948), "Sunday in the Park," comprises what Williams called "the modern replicas" of the elements in book one. Loosely speaking, book two is an interior monologue, and one cannot help but sense James Joyce's Molly Bloom in the background here. A man spends Sunday in the park. He thinks and looks about him; his mind contemplates, describes, comments, associates, stops, stutters, and shifts, bound only by its environment. The mind belongs to a man who is by turns the poet, Mr. Paterson, the American, the masculine principle, Everyman. His monologue is interrupted by blocks of prose: para-

Passaic Falls in Paterson, New Jersey. Williams's personified Paterson "lies in the valley under the Passaic Falls/its spent waters form-
ing the outline of his back. He/lies on his right side, head near the thunder/of the waters filling his dreams! . . ."

graphs from old newspapers, textbooks, and letters, a device Williams uses throughout *Paterson.*
The park, on the other hand, is the feminine
principle, America, the women of Paterson,
Everywoman. In the reiterative symbolism of the
whole poem, the water roaring down the falls
from the park to Paterson becomes the principle
of life, and the feminine and masculine, into
which terms everything is translated, strain toward union, a state of "marriage." It never comes
off, except in imagination, and there only in tran-
sient forms.

Book three (1949), "The Library," Williams
notes, seeks "a language to make them [the modern replicas] vocal." The most philosophical of
the five books, exploring the relationship between language and reality, this book offers one
of the great defenses of language as being most
purely itself when used imaginatively. It is also
one of the great defenses of the poetics of the languages of everyday life. The great enemies in
book three are the technical abstractions of scholars and other academics. Abstraction and generalization are heard as "offense[s] to love, the mind's

worm eating/out the core, unappeased."

Book four (1951), "The Run to the Sea," Williams felt, would be "reminiscent of episodes–all
that any one man may achieve in a lifetime." The
three subjects which this part of the poem introduces in succession are, first, love–of various
kinds, each with its own frustrations–in the figure of a triangle involving a New York poet (a homosexual woman), a young nurse (the female Paterson), and the male poet as Paterson; second,
science, through the episode of a lecture on
atomic fission to which the male Paterson takes
his son (as an introduction to his heritage of the
disruptive knowledge of his time); and third,
money, greed as the cause of the concentration
of capital in a few hands and a subsequent social
corruption. These three topics all relate to the
theme of alienation (divorce, the "sign of knowledge in our time"), first introduced in book one;
and they are also intimately related to the problem of language. The question at the start of the
third part of book four keeps this overarching
theme in the whole poem firmly in sight:
"Haven't you forgot your virgin purpose,/the language?"

With the completion of book four in the early 1950s, Williams felt that *Paterson* was finished. However, as the decade passed he began thinking about the ending of book four again; as the aging poet-protagonist of the poem sensed the shifting of attitudes and moods, the closure of 1951 did not fit the situation of 1958. In *I Wanted to Write a Poem* Williams recalled this shift: "*Paterson* IV ends with the protagonist breaking through the bushes, identifying himself with the land, with America. He finally will die but it can't be categorically stated that death ends *anything*. When you're through with sex, with ambition, what can an old man create? Art, of course, a piece of art that will go beyond him into the lives of young people, the people who haven't had time to create. The old man meets the young people and lives on."

Book five appeared in 1958 without a title and dedicated

> To the Memory
> of
> Henri Toulouse Lautrec,
> *Painter*[.]

This lineation emphasized the topic of Memory as the theme of the book. The poet still calls himself Paterson, and there are significant continuities of image, idea, and metrical form carrying over from the earlier books, but Mr. Paterson is less bound by his locality and his immediate present. Here the formative idea of place is expanded to encompass time, as is only fitting in a poem written under the sign of memory. Book five is, in essence, Williams's answer to Ezra Pound's meditation on *memoria* in *The Pisan Cantos*. The book opens with a complex image of freedom, playing on the transitivity of the verb phrase "casts off ":

> In old age
>   the mind
>
>   casts off
>   rebelliously
>   an eagle
> from its crag[.]

The reader soon finds that the mind has cast itself off into memory

>   —remember
>
> confidently

only a moment, only for a fleeting moment—
        with a smile of recognition . .

With time, the poet-protagonist seems to be saying, the cognitive gives way "rebelliously" and "confidently" to the *recognitive*. The great connection that Williams makes is in the linking of recognitive and imaginative processes:

> The flower dies down
> and rots away   .
> But there is a hole
> in the bottom of the bag.
>
> It is the imagination
> which cannot be fathomed.
> It is through this hole
> we escape   .   .

When one remembers Williams's earliest "poeticizing," his imitations of John Keats, one realizes that he has come full circle in his old age. This celebration of the imagination rediscovers the inner meaning of Keats's "Ode to a Nightingale." Of course, from that early allegiance he has shucked the romantic poetic diction and the elaborate rhetorical surface. Underneath, at the core,

>   through art alone, male and female, a field of
>   flowers, a tapestry, spring flowers unequaled
> in loveliness.

In old age comes the marvelous lucidity of vivid remembrance, the pinnacle of an achieved simplicity:

> There is a woman in our town
> walks rapidly, flat bellied
> in worn slacks upon the street
> where I saw her.
>   neither short
> nor tall, nor old nor young
> her
>   face would attract no
> adolescent. Grey eyes looked
> straight before her.
>   Her
>   hair
> was gathered simply behind the
> ears under a shapeless hat.

In 1946, the year of the publication of *Paterson (Book One)*, Williams was sixty-three years old. From then until his death in 1963 recognition and public honors began to flow his way. Invitations to speak and read at a variety of venues, literary prizes, even honorary degrees began to accumulate, and Williams lived to experience a sense of satisfaction in seeing the poetry and ideas which he had begun championing before World War I taking root in the American psyche. Indeed several schools of younger poets regarded the Rutherford physician as mentor and one of the first genuine American literary classics. His home at 9 Ridge Road in those latter years of his life was visited by many friends and acquaintances, but, more important for continuity, it was also visited by the young. He also had the satisfaction of seeing his two sons return from the war intact and resume their careers in business and medicine in New York City.

Aging, however, was not all a matter of basking in his newfound celebrity. Growing old also brought death and sickness. His mother, Elena, died in 1949 at what was thought to be the age of 101; her real age (110) was not discovered until 1956 when her baptismal records were consulted. Williams was much amused by his mother's audacity in hiding her age. Problems with his own health also began to multiply, beginning with two hernia operations in 1946. In February 1948 he was struck by a heart attack, which, though slowing him down for a while, did not incapacitate him. In March 1951 he suffered the first of a series of strokes, the effects of which he struggled to overcome to continue writing. The story of this struggle is the stuff of heroism; even as he suffered, his creative impulses never flagged. A very serious stroke threatened his life in August of 1952, and this event was compounded by his difficulties in occupying the Consultancy in Poetry at the Library of Congress. His past involvement in radical politics in the 1930s and during World War II and the publication of *The Pink Church* in 1949, with its unfortunate adjective which by that time had acquired menacing overtones in the vocabulary of American political life, finally blocked his accession to this recognition of his accomplishments and importance in American letters. In early 1953 he was forced, in one of the more dishonorable episodes of American political and cultural history, to relinquish the Library of Congress appointment. From February to April of that year Williams was hospitalized for severe depression. He recovered though and continued to write and publish, harvesting the final and brilliant crop of work which completes his achievement. His third stroke hit in October 1958, shortly after *Paterson (Book Five)* was published. A sixth book was also in the works in the early 1960s but never progressed beyond the note stage. A series of strokes in 1961 finally forced Williams to give up trying to write altogether. His death on 4 March 1963 was commemorated by the posthumous award of a Pulitzer Prize and the Gold Medal for Poetry in that year.

In the last decade or so of his life Williams began to have autobiographical urgings, especially as the physical weakness of his heart became manifest after 1948. His major autobiographical statements in prose were all published in the 1950s. *The Autobiography* (1951) was directly provoked by his heart attack and his sudden awareness of the nearness of mortality. Writing an autobiography might seem an incongruous act in a poet as autobiographical as Williams. Indeed in some ways *The Autobiography* is a bit distant and casual in relating the narrative of his life. It was always in his art that Williams moved in closer to his own life, communicated with intensity and candor the held intimacies. His courtship of his wife is more vividly and intimately enacted in his novel *The Build-Up* (1952) than in *The Autobiography* of 1951. A second important autobiographical document is his reminiscence of the composition of some of his major works. *I Wanted to Write a Poem* (1958) was recorded and edited by Edith Heal in a series of conversations and interviews with the Williamses at the poet's home in Rutherford. His tribute to his mother, *Yes, Mrs. Williams: A Personal Record of My Mother* (1959), is a little-known and little-read gem of a book chronicling the life of a fascinating woman. Although the book is focused on Williams's mother, the reader learns much about Williams in an oblique way. The image of the feminine is a constant in all his work, and in this portrait of Elena Williams the reader is given a detailed look at one of the sources of this theme.

Important as these autobiographical writings are for an understanding of Williams's life and work, the last decade of his life should, more aptly for a poet, be remembered for its poetic fertility. Williams continued to progress and to explore new aesthetic territories in his late work, collected in *Pictures from Brueghel and other poems* (1962). Most of the poems in this volume extend and complicate the triadic stanza and variable-foot measure which Williams developed in *Paterson (Book Two)* and which in this period he came to call *versos sueltos*, or "loose verses," to distinguish his technique from the vers libre or "free verse" he practiced as an *imagiste* in the 1920s, but from which he eventually turned. In 1953 he told the critic John C. Thirlwall, "The iamb is not the normal measure of American speech. The foot has to be expanded or contracted in terms of actual speech. The key to modern poetry is *measure*, which must reflect the flux of modern life. You should find a variable measure for the fixed measure; for man and the poet must keep pace with this world." Many believe he comes closest to realizing this ideal in his later work. Fellow poet Kenneth Rexroth nearly asserted just such a proposition when he wrote of Williams as the first American "classic," especially in his later work: "his poetic line is organically welded to American speech like muscle to bone, as the choruses of Euripides were welded to the speech of the Athenians in the market place."

Of the many excellencies in *Pictures from Brueghel and other poems* two longer poems stand out. The first, "The Desert Music," originally published in 1954, was first read as the Phi Beta Kappa poem at Harvard University in June 1951. A poem about writing poetry, it celebrates the rediscovery of creative inspiration after a short period in Williams's life when he found himself unable to write. In this rediscovery Williams, near the beginning of the poem, seems to propose that the primary spur to creativity is having something necessary to say: "How shall we get said what must be said?//Only the poem." To embody this theme the poem develops the figure of "the dance":

> A music
> supersedes his composure, hallooing to us
> across a great distance   . .
>   wakens the dance
> who blows upon his benumbed fingers!

In 1984 this most finely wrought of Williams's later poems was set to music by the young New York composer Steven Reich.

The second notable work in *Pictures from Brueghel and other poems* is "Asphodel, That Greeny Flower," a love poem addressed to the poet's wife. It surveys their years together and recalls in vivid, clear, and distinct images those heightened states of thought and feeling which mark both the progress of their marriage and the poet's artistic development. Both these continuities intertwine in the poet's mind like the spiralling tendrils of climbing clematis. "Asphodel, That Greeny Flower" has always been associated with the end of Williams's life as a poetic statement that does double duty as a personal credo ("What power has love but forgiveness?") and an artistic manifesto ("Only the imagination is real").

In the poem's "Coda" art and life melt finally into each other and the result is as fitting an epitaph as any poet can hope to earn:

> But love and the imagination
>   are of a piece,
>   swift as the light
> to avoid destruction.

Letters:

The Selected Letters of William Carlos Williams, edited by John C. Thirlwall (New York: McDowell, Obolensky, 1957).
    A good selection of letters that reveals the poet and craftsman rather than the man.

Interviews:

Interviews with William Carlos Williams: "Speaking Straight Ahead," edited by Linda Welshimer Wagner (New York: New Directions, 1976).
    Interviews clarifying the poet's fundamental ideas about poetry.

Bibliographies:

Emily Wallace, *A Bibliography of William Carlos Williams* (Middletown, Conn.: Wesleyan University Press, 1968); with addenda included in various issues of the *William Carlos Williams Newsletter* and the *William Carlos Williams Review*.
    Good source of secondary materials on early critical reception, but needs to be updated.

Neil Baldwin and Steven L. Myers, *The Manuscripts and Letters of William Carlos Williams in the Poetry Collection of Lockwood Memorial Library, State University of New York at Buffalo: A Descriptive Catalogue* (Boston: G. K. Hall, 1978).
    Essentially an illustrated list of manuscript holdings at the State University of New York, Buffalo.

Biographies:

Mike Weaver, *William Carlos Williams: the American Background* (Cambridge: Cambridge University Press, 1971).
    Not strictly speaking a biography of the poet, but a reading of the work in biographical and cultural contexts, with lots of biographical information.

Reed Whittemore, *William Carlos Williams: Poet from Jersey* (Boston: Houghton Mifflin, 1975).

A poet's biography of a fellow poet that uses the biographical occasion to make a statement, not only about Williams, but about poetry as well.

Paul Mariani, *William Carlos Williams: A New World Naked* (New York: McGraw-Hill, 1981).

The authoritative, scholarly biography that lays bare the innumerable details of a broad, rich life.

References:

Harold Bloom, ed., *William Carlos Williams: Modern Critical Views* (New York: Chelsea House, 1986).

An excellent compilation of mainly older, and some new, short critical studies that makes available in a convenient form the established tradition of Williams scholarship.

James E. Breslin, *William Carlos Williams: an American Artist* (New York: Oxford University Press, 1970).

Solid conventional approach to the works emphasizing the traditional formal and generic issues the works raise.

Joel Osborne Conarroe, *William Carlos Williams' 'Paterson': Language and Landscape* (Philadelphia: University of Pennsylvania Press, 1970).

An important and thorough thematic study of *Paterson* with some emphasis on the problem of poetic language in the poem.

Bram Dijkstra, *The Hieroglyphics of a New Speech: Cubism, Stieglitz, and the Early Poetry of William Carlos Williams* (Princeton: Princeton University Press, 1969).

A groundbreaking study placing the work in the relevant cultural contexts, emphasizing the visual sources–in painting and photography–of the poet's imagination.

Charles Doyle, ed., *William Carlos Williams: The Critical Heritage* (London: Routledge & Kegan Paul, 1980).

Valuable reference source reprinting contemporary reviews of and articles about all the poet's important publications from 1909 to 1967.

Bernard Duffey, *A Poetry of Presence: The Writing of William Carlos Williams* (Madison: The University of Wisconsin Press, 1986).

A recent survey of Williams's writing, important for both what the author has to say about the poet and for the premises (mainly derived from Kenneth Burke's *A Grammar of Motives*) on which his theory is based.

Hugh Kenner, *A Homemade World: the American Modernist Writers* (New York: Knopf, 1975).

A general study of the genius of the American imagination with a superb chapter on Williams.

Paul Mariani, *William Carlos Williams: the Poet and his Critics* (Chicago: American Library Association, 1975).

A very useful reference summarizing the evolution of the critical response to the work over the decades of the poet's activity.

J. Hillis Miller, ed., *William Carlos Williams: a Collection of Critical Essays* (Englewood Cliffs, N.J.: Prentice-Hall, 1966).

A solid and accessible collection of essays covering all the important aspects of the poet's works.

Alan Ostrom, *The Poetic World of William Carlos Williams* (Carbondale: Southern Illinois University Press, 1966).

An interesting reading of the poet as being in essence a poet of the human, thus implicitly placing Williams's poetic world in a humanist context.

Sherman Paul, *The Music of Survival: a Biography of a Poem by William Carlos Williams* (Urbana: University of Illinois Press, 1968).

A subtle stylistic analysis of the poet's verbal world, sensitively explored in considerable linguistic detail.

Carl Rapp, *William Carlos Williams and Romantic Idealism* (Hanover, N.H.: The University Press of New England for Brown University, 1984).

Interesting but forced attempt to read the poet within the tradition of romantic idealism and to advance the novel notion of

Emerson as an important precursor to Williams's poetics.

Benjamin Sankey, *A Companion to William Carlos Williams's 'Paterson'* (Berkeley: University of California Press, 1971).
A conventional interpretation of *Paterson,* but still an excellent source of useful information about the poem.

Stephen Tapscott, *American Beauty: William Carlos Williams and the Modernist Whitman* (New York: Columbia University Press, 1984).
Explores the origins of Williams's poetics in Whitman and traces the evolution of a specifically American aesthetic sensibility in the production of a new kind of American verbal art.

Carroll F. Terrell, *William Carlos Williams: Man and Poet* (Orono: University of Maine, 1983).
An important collection of critical and biographical essays by poets and scholars covering all aspects of Williams's work.

Charles Tomlinson, ed., *William Carlos Williams: A Critical Anthology* (Harmondsworth, U.K.: Penguin, 1972).
Very useful reference, compiled by a British poet and admirer of Williams, that reprints important critical and scholarly responses to his work.

Linda Welshimer Wagner, *The Poems of William Carlos Williams: a Critical Study* (Middletown, Conn.: Wesleyan University Press, 1964).
A critical study emphasizing the poet's techniques, craftsmanship, and critical acuity by a preeminent Williams scholar.

Wagner, *The Prose of William Carlos Williams: A Critical Study* (Middletown, Conn.: Wesleyan University Press, 1970).
A companion to this scholar's study of the poems, focusing on the unity of Williams's writing both in poetry and prose.

Thomas R. Whitaker, *William Carlos Williams* (New York: Twayne, 1968).
The standard Twayne treatment: solid, reliable, thorough.

Papers:
The bulk of Williams's manuscripts and letters is housed in three libraries: the Lockwood Memorial Library, State University of New York, Buffalo; the Beinecke Rare Book and Manuscript Library, Yale University; and the Humanities Research Center, University of Texas, Austin. There are also smaller but important collections of papers at the Alderman Library, University of Virginia; the University of Delaware library; and the Lilly Library, Indiana University.

Contributors

William B. Adams ....Columbia, South Carolina

J. M. Brook ....Columbia, South Carolina

Rudolph P. Byrd...Carleton College

John Xiros Cooper ....Mount Royal College

Scott Donaldson...College of William and Mary

Elizabeth Evans...Georgia Institute of Technology

Wendy Stallard Flory ....University of Pennsylvania

Donald J. Greiner...University of South Carolina

Paula L. Hart ....University of British Columbia

Keneth Kinnamon...University of Arkansas

Richard Layman ....Columbia, South Carolina

Martin Light...Purdue University

Shirley Lumpkin...Marshall University

Alan Margolies...City University of New York

J. James McElveen ....Falls Church, Virginia

Nellie McKay...University of Wisconsin-Madison

Joseph Miller ....Vancouver, British Columbia

James Nagel..Northeastern University

William H. Nolte...University of South Carolina

Walter B. Rideout ....University of Wisconsin-Madison

Robert Ian Scott ....University of Saskatchewan

Michael D. Senecal ....Columbia, South Carolina

Carroll F. Terrell..University of Maine

Meredith Yearsley ....Vancouver, British Columbia

321

HOW TO USE A DICTIONARY
PICTURE BOOK FOR CHILDREN

How to Use a Dictionary
PICTURE BOOK FOR CHILDREN

Based on the Works of
L. RON HUBBARD

PUBLICATIONS, INC.

To the Parent or Teacher

Important information about the usage of this book is written on pages 281–283. Familiarity with and application of the data in that section can help your child get more out of the book.

Published by
Bridge Publications, Inc.
4751 Fountain Avenue
Los Angeles, California 90029

ISBN 0-88404-747-4

Printed in the United States of America

How to Study This Book

It is best to study this book with another person. This person is called your twin. A *twin* is a person's partner in study. When you have a twin you work together and make sure that you each really understand what you are studying. It makes it easier and more fun.

All through the book there are drills to do. A drill is something that a person does to practice something so that he learns it better. People always need to practice and drill things they want to get really good at.

Do all of the drills with your twin.

If you are reading this book by yourself and do not have a twin, then write down the answers to the drills on a piece of paper or find a person who can listen to you do them out loud. If there is a drill that says to take turns with your twin and you don't have a twin, just do the whole drill yourself.

Drilling will help you a lot!

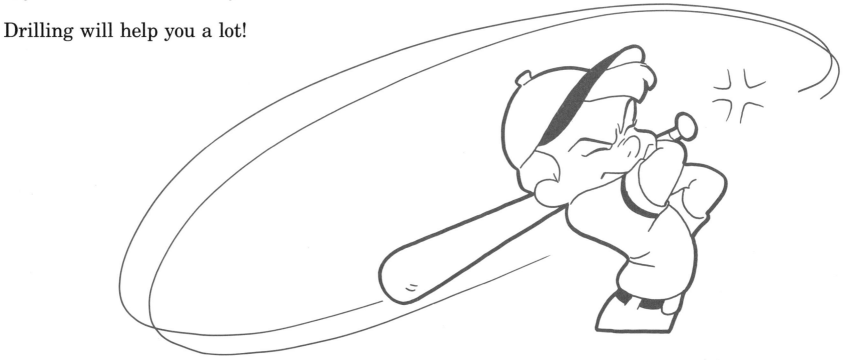

Contents

CHAPTER ONE:

WHAT IS A DICTIONARY?

Words

RUNNING
word

TALL
word

4

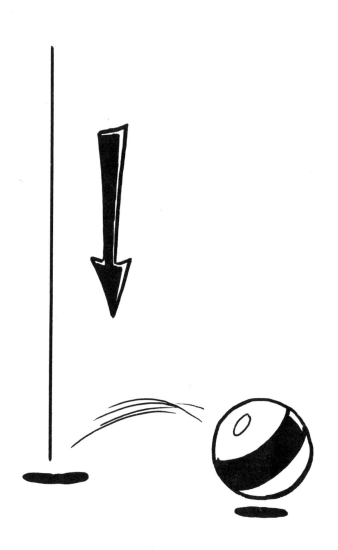

DOWN
word

APPLE
word

GIRL
word

BIRD
word

Words have meanings.

Words often have more than one meaning.

It is important to understand the meanings of words.

Joe does not understand the words.

Bob does understand the words.

A dictionary can help you understand words.

This book will show you how to use a dictionary.

What Is a Dictionary?

A dictionary is a word book.

A dictionary tells you the meanings of words and other things about words.

You can use a dictionary to find out what a word means,

how to say a word,

how to spell a word,

how to use a word and many other things about words.

Dictionaries can be very helpful.

When you know how to use a dictionary you will be able to use it easily and it will be very helpful to you.

He *does not* know how to use a dictionary.

He *does* know how to use a dictionary.

CHAPTER TWO:

DICTIONARIES

Dictionaries

This book tells you what you need to know
to use a dictionary easily.

There are many kinds of dictionaries.

Some dictionaries are very big.

There is a dictionary which has so many words that it needs many, many books to hold them all.

Dictionaries are different and they may give you the meanings of words differently.

Most dictionaries are similar though and when you learn to use one dictionary you will be able to use other dictionaries too.

CHAPTER THREE:

HOW TO FIND WORDS IN A DICTIONARY

How to Find Words in a Dictionary

letter

letter

letter

letter

letter

letter

All the letters together
are called an *alphabet*.

a
b
c
d
e
f
g
h
i
j
k
l
m
n
o
p
q
r
s
t
u
v
w
x
y
z

The alphabet can be written
in capital letters. THESE
ARE CAPITAL LETTERS.

A
B
C
D
E
F
G
H
I
J
K
L
M
N
O
P
Q
R
S
T
U
V
W
X
Y
Z

The alphabet can also be
written in small letters.
These are small letters.

a
b
c
d
e
f
g
h
i
j
k
l
m
n
o
p
q
r
s
t
u
v
w
x
y
z

To use a dictionary well you will have to know the alphabet very well and know where all the letters are very easily.

If you don't, you will spend a long time trying to look up words as you will not be able to find them easily.

Drill

Learn the alphabet forwards so you can say it to your twin all in one breath without any errors.

A B C D E F G H I J K L M N O P Q R S T U V W X Y Z

Drill

Learn the alphabet backwards so you can say it to your twin all in one breath without any errors.

Drill

Have your twin pick a letter of the alphabet and ask you what letter comes after that letter. This drill is done until you can correctly answer the question every time without needing to think about the answer.

39

Drill

Have your twin pick a letter of the alphabet and ask you what letter comes before that letter. This drill is done until you can correctly answer the question every time without needing to think about the answer.

WHAT LETTER COMES BEFORE U?

T

How Words Are Put in Order in Dictionaries

A dictionary has a section for each letter of the alphabet.

This means all the words beginning with the letter **A** are in the **A** section,

all the words beginning with the letter **B** are
in the **B** section,

all the words beginning with the letter **C** are in the **C** section and so on, in the same order as the alphabet.

Words are put in alphabetical order by their first letters, then their second letters, then their third letters and so on.

(*Floor* comes between *flat* and *foot*.)

These words are in alphabetical order.

far

fast

feed

five

flat

floor

foot

In a dictionary, these words would look like this:

Drill

Use a sheet of paper and put the following words in alphabetical order. When you are done give your paper to your twin. Your twin will check your work. The answers are at the bottom of the page.

apple　　　　box

bird　　　　shirt

flower　　　　table

zoo　　　　zebra

Entry Words

Entry words are the words being *defined* in a dictionary. To define means to tell what something means.

In dictionaries the entry words are in alphabetical order. They are usually given in dark letters.

Guide Words

At the top of each page of the dictionary, there are words written in darker letters. They are called *guide words*. Guide words show the first and last words entered on that page.

GUIDE WORDS

You can find the page of the dictionary you want by looking at the guide words on each page. Guide words help you find the words you are looking for faster.

If you know the alphabet and use the guide words you can quickly and easily find words in a dictionary.

CHAPTER FOUR:

PRONUNCIATION

Pronunciation

Pronunciation is the way something is said. Many dictionaries tell you how to pronounce a word.

If you know how to pronounce a word, you will be able to say it the right way.

A word's pronunciation is given in the dictionary following the word itself.

Dictionaries use certain marks and letters to show a word's pronunciation.

Syllable

A syllable is a single spoken sound that is a word or a part of a word.

One of the ways dictionaries show a word's pronunciation is with syllables.

Dictionaries show how words are divided into syllables.

elephant

el e phant

Many dictionaries use a dot between syllables.

el • e • phant

dot dot

Drills

1. Have your twin tell you what a syllable is. Have him or her show you a syllable in the word *eating*.

eat • ing

2. Tell your twin what a syllable is. Show him or her a syllable in the word *chicken*.

chick • en

3. Have your twin tell you how many syllables are in the following words.

can • dle

to • geth • er

dress

yes • ter • day

4. Tell your twin how many syllables are in the following words.

Jan • u • ar • y

some • thing

stu • dent

hour

Accent Mark

This is an accent mark **ʹ**

When a word has two or more syllables, one of the syllables is said with more emphasis.

el**ʹ** • e • phant

Emphasis means to say a word or syllable with more force of voice.

This emphasis is called accent.

An accent mark is a mark used to show which syllable is said with more emphasis.

elephant	**el • e • phant**	**el′ e phant**
ball	**ball**	**ball**
(This word has only one syllable so it does not have an accent mark.)		
woman	**wom • an**	**wom′ an**
father	**fa • ther**	**fa′ ther**

In some dictionaries the accent is shown with darker letters instead of an accent mark.

don key	**wom** an	**fa** ther

If someone does not put the emphasis on the correct syllable of a word, it sounds wrong. It might not be understood.

sugar　　　　Su′ gar sounds right.

Su gar′ sounds wrong.

Syllables and accent marks can help you pronounce a word correctly.

But even when you have the syllables and accent mark, you still have to know how the parts of the words should sound.

Drills

1. Tell your twin what an accent mark is. Say the following words to your twin, using the accent marks given below.

un til′

o′ ver

lid

her self′

2. Have your twin tell you what an accent mark is. Have him or her say the following words, using the accent marks given below.

but′ ter

can′ dle

moth′ er

fa′ ther

The Sounds of Letters

Most letters of the alphabet have one sound, but there are some letters that can have more than one sound.

cat

city

The **c** in *cat* has a different sound from the **c** in *city*.

If a person did not know how to say the word *city* he could think the **c** in *city* had the sound of the **c** in *cat*.

WHAT IS THIS KITY?

bed

he

The **e** in *bed* has a different sound than the **e** in *he*.

If someone said the **e** in *bed* like the **e** in *he*, people would not understand what he was talking about.

A dictionary shows you how the letters in a word sound.

Dictionaries use letters and certain marks to show how the letters in a word sound. These letters and marks are put inside parentheses.

These are parentheses ( )

A pronunciation key is an explanation of the letters and marks used to show the correct pronunciation of words.

The marks in parentheses are explained in the pronunciation key of the dictionary, which tells exactly what sounds the letters and marks stand for.

Here is an example of how dictionaries use letters to show how a word sounds.

fix (fiks)

To say *fix* correctly, you would say *fiks*.

Here is an example of how dictionaries use marks to show how a word sounds.

five (fīv)

The little line above the **i** in *fiv* is explained in the pronunciaind in the pronunciation key by showing what sound **i** stands for.

ī   ice

This means you say the **i** in *five* like you say the **i** in *ice*.

You look at the pronunciation of the word given in parentheses with the marks and symbols, and then look at the pronunciation key to get the word's pronunciation.

The marks above the letters in the pronunciation key do not have any specific meaning. They only show how the letters sound.

Here is a pronunciation key.

SYMBOL	SOUND	SYMBOL	SOUND
a	cat, act	b	bat, bag
ā	ate, say	ch	child, choice
â(r)	air, Mary	d	did, darker
ä	father, part	f	full, if
		g	go, bag
e	ten, pen	h	he, hit
ē	even, be	hw	which, where
ēr	ear, here	j	jar, just
		k	king, make
i	hit, big	l	let, all
ī	ice, denial	m	me, him
		n	no, on
o	not, box	ng	bring, king
ō	open, over	p	pay, stop
ô	all, gone	r	ran, near
oi	choice, joined	s	see, past
o͝o	book, tourists	sh	she, shoe
o͞o	too, cool	t	tell, bit
ou	out, loud	th	thing, truth
		t͟h	that, mother
u	butter, sun	v	very, live
û(r)	fur, her	w	well, away
		y	yes, you
		z	zoo, those
		zh	measure, pleasure

To use a pronunciation key to see how to say the word *city* correctly, you find the word *city* in the dictionary.

After *city* there are parentheses.

Inside the parentheses are the letters and marks which show how to pronounce *city*.

City has two syllables. The first syllable has an accent mark so it is said with more emphasis than the second syllable.

To find out what the letters in each syllable sound like look at the pronunciation key.

The first letter inside the parentheses is **s**.

Find **s** in the pronunciation key.

p	**p**ay, sto**p**
r	**r**an, nea**r**
s	**s**ee, pa**s**t
sh	**sh**e, **sh**oe
t	**t**ell, bi**t**
th	**th**ing, tru**th**

The words *see* and *past* are given.

Say *see* or *past* and listen to how the **s** sounds.

The second letter inside the parentheses is **i.**

Find **i** in the pronunciation key.

i   h**i**t, b**i**g
ī   **i**ce, den**i**al

The words *hit* and *big* are given.

Say *hit* or *big* and listen to how the **i** sounds.

The third letter inside the parentheses is **t**.

Find **t** in the pronunciation key.

s   see, pa**s**t
sh   **sh**e, **sh**oe
t   **t**ell, bi**t**
th   **th**ing, tru**th**
th   **th**at, mo**th**er

The words *tell* and *bit* are given.

Say *tell* or *bit* and listen to how the **t** sounds.

Say all the sounds together.

That is the first syllable.

The second syllable is ē.

Find ē in the pronunciation key.

e   t**e**n, p**e**n
ē   **e**ven, b**e**
er   **ear**, h**ere**

The words *even* and *be* are given.

Say *even* or *be* and listen to how the **e** sounds.

That is how the **e** sounds.

Now put the two syllables together.

sit ē

Put a little more emphasis on the first syllable because it has an accent mark.

sit′ ē

city

That is how to use a pronunciation key.

Drills

1. Using the letters and marks given on page 64, look at how the following words are pronounced and say them correctly to your twin.

2. Now have your twin use the letters and marks given on page 64 and look at how the following words are pronounced and then say them correctly to you.

first	(fûrst)		**walk**	(wôk)
born	(bôrn)		**seem**	(sēm)
scale	(skāl)		**describe**	(di skrīb′)
until	(un til′)		**happy**	(hap′ ē)
anywhere	(en′ ē hwâr)		**John**	(jon)
front	(frunt)		**thin**	(thin)
jar	(jär)		**busy**	(biz′ ē)
story	(stôr′ ē)		**waist**	(wāst)

Additional Marks Used in Pronunciation Keys

There is another mark used in pronunciation keys which is different from the other marks.

It looks like this ə.

It is called a *schwa*.

A schwa is used to show you that **a, e, i, o** or **u** are said without emphasis.

You will see this mark in the pronunciation key like this:

ə represents
a in **a**bout
e in tak**e**n
i in penc**i**l
o in lem**o**n
u in circ**u**s

The **a** in *hat* is said with emphasis. (h**a**t)

The **a** in ***about*** is not said with emphasis.
(ə bout′)

The **o** in *home* is said with emphasis. (hōm)

The **o** in *lemon* is not said with emphasis.
(lem′ən)

LEMON

Let's look at how you would use the pronunciation key to learn how to pronounce *elephant*.

To say elephant take the first syllable, **el.**

Look at the first letter. It is **e**.

Then look at the pronunciation key and find **e**.

SYMBOL	SOUND	SYMBOL	SOUND
a	cat, act	b	bat, bag
ā	ate, say	ch	child, choice
â(r)	air, Mary	d	did, darker
ä	father, part	f	full, if
		g	go, bag
e	ten, pen	h	he, hit
ē	even, be	hw	which, where
ēr	ear, here	j	jar, just
		k	king, make
i	hit, big	l	let, all
ī	ice, denial	m	me, him
		n	no, on
o	not, box	ng	bring, king
ō	open, over	p	pay, stop
ô	all, gone	r	ran, near
oi	choice, joined	s	see, past
o͝o	book, tourists	sh	she, shoe
o͞o	too, cool	t	tell, bit
ou	out, loud	th	thing, truth
		t̲h	that, mother
u	butter, sun	v	very, live
û(r)	fur, her	w	well, away
		y	yes, you
		z	zoo, those
		zh	measure, pleasure

ə represents
a in about
e in mother
i in pencil
o in carrots
u in helpful

The words *ten* and *pen* are given.

Say *ten* or *pen* and listen to how **e** sounds.

Look at the next letter.

It is **l.**

Look at the pronunciation key and find **l.**

j	**j**ar, **j**ust
k	**k**ing, ma**k**e
l	**l**et, a**ll**
m	**m**e, hi**m**
n	**n**o, o**n**

The words *let* and *all* are given.

Say *let* or *all* and listen to how the **l** sounds.

Now put **e** and **l** together using those sounds.

That is how *el* sounds.

Now look at the second syllable, **ə**.

The first **ə** in the pronunciation refers to the second **e** in elephant.

Under **ə** in the pronunciation key find **e**.

The word *mother* is given.

ə represents
a in **a**bout
e in moth**e**r
i in penc**i**l
o in carr**o**ts
u in helpf**u**l

Say *mother* and listen to how the **e** sounds.
That is how **ə** sounds.

Look at the third syllable, *fənt*.

Look at the first letter in this syllable.

It is **f**.

Look at the pronunciation key and find **f**.

d   **d**id, **d**arker
f   **f**ull, i**f**
g   **g**o, ba**g**

The words *full* and *if* are given.

Say *full* or *if* and listen to how the **f** sounds.

Look at the next letter.

It is ə.

This ə refers to the **a** in elephant.

Under ə in the pronunciation key find **a**.

ə represents
a in **a**bout
e in moth**e**r
i in penc**i**l
o in carr**o**ts
u in helpf**u**l

The word *about* is given.

Say *about* and listen to how the **a** sounds.

Look at the next letter.

It is **n.**

Look at the pronunciation key and find **n**.

l   let, a**ll**
m **m**e, hi**m**
n **n**o, o**n**

The words *no* and *on* are given.

Say *no* or *on* and listen to how the **n** sounds.

Look at the next letter.

It is **t.**

Look at the pronunciation key and find **t**.

s   **s**ee, pa**s**t
sh **sh**e, **sh**oe
t   **t**ell, bi**t**
th **th**ing, tru**th**

The words *tell* and *bit* are given.

Say *tell* or *bit* and listen to how the **t** sounds.

Put the **f**, **ə**, **n**, and **t** together using these sounds.

That is how *fənt* sounds.

Now put the syllables together using these sounds to say elephant and you will be pronouncing it the right way.

Pronunciation keys change a bit from dictionary to dictionary. But they all tell you the sounds of letters.

They are actually easy to use.

Pronunciation keys are given at the beginning of a dictionary most of the time.

A shorter pronunciation key is also given on the bottom of every page or every other page of the dictionary.

PRONUNCIATION KEY

Drills

1. Have your twin use the pronunciation key on page 80 of this book and tell you how to pronounce the following words.

accident   (ak′ si dənt)

everyone   (ev′ rē wun′)

pleasure   (plezh′ ər)

2. Using the pronunciation key on page 80 of this book, tell your twin how to pronounce the following words.

paper   (pā′ per)

butterflies   (but′ ər flīz)

running   (run′ ing)

CHAPTER FIVE:

DIFFERENT WAYS THAT WORDS ARE USED

Different Ways That Words Are Used

When speaking and writing, words are used in different ways, so that a person can say what he means. Some words are used to name things, some words are used to show action, some words describe things. Describe means to tell how things look, feel or act.

Understanding how a word is being used can help you understand what that word means exactly.

In dictionaries there are names given for the different ways a word is being used. It is important that you know what these names mean so that you understand what you read in a dictionary.

Noun
(a word that names a person, place or thing)

MAN

noun

SALLY

noun

TEACHER

noun

STUDENTS

noun

ISLAND

noun

LOVE

noun

HAMMER

noun

CITY

noun

THOUGHT

noun

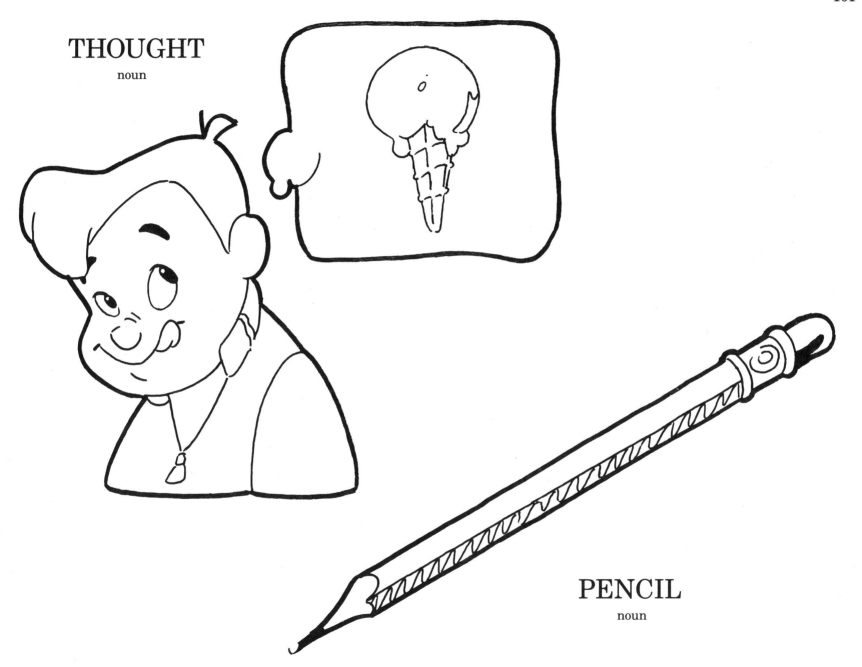

PENCIL

noun

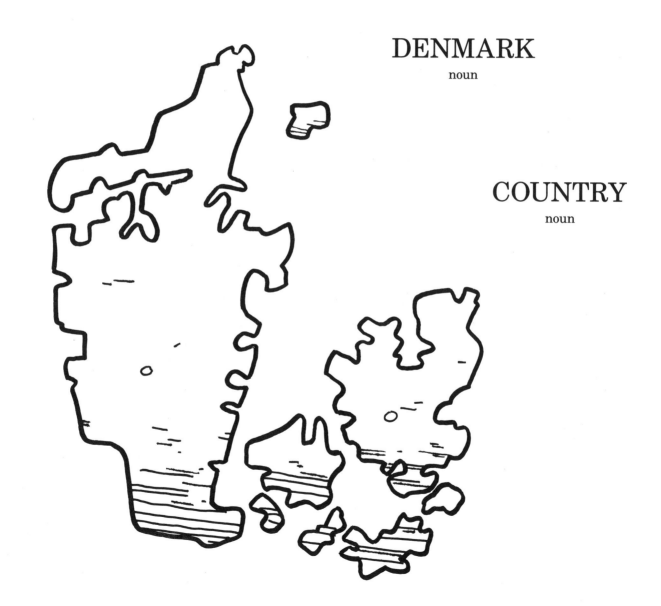

DENMARK

noun

COUNTRY

noun

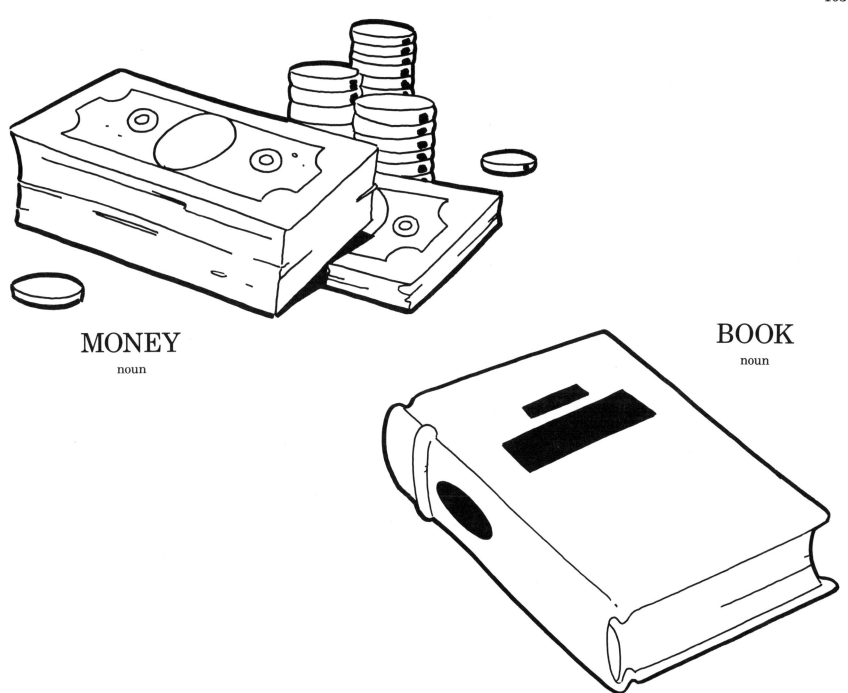

MONEY

noun

BOOK

noun

Drills

1. Give your twin ten examples of nouns.

2. Have your twin give you ten examples of nouns.

Pronoun
(any word used in the place of a noun)

IT
pronoun

HE
pronoun

THEIRS
pronoun

HERS

pronoun

HIS

pronoun

SHE

pronoun

YOU

pronoun

THESE

pronoun

THOSE

pronoun

THIS

pronoun

THAT

pronoun

WHAT

pronoun

WHO

pronoun

Drills

1. Have your twin give you ten examples of pronouns.

2. Give your twin ten examples of pronouns.

Adjective
(a name dictionaries use for a word that
describes a noun or pronoun)

TALL GIRL

adjective   noun

LITTLE GIRL

adjective   noun

GIRL

noun

BASKET
noun

FULL BASKET
adjective   noun

EMPTY BASKET
adjective   noun

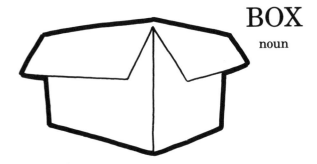

BOX

noun

SMALL BOX

adjective   noun

LARGE BOX

adjective   noun

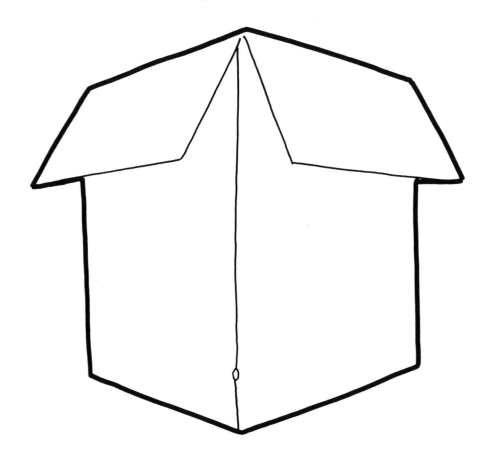

SHIRT

noun

DIRTY SHIRT

adjective   noun

TORN SHIRT

adjective   noun

BOY
noun

TWO BOYS
adjective   noun

MANY BOYS

adjective   noun

Drills

1. Give your twin ten examples of adjectives.

2. Have your twin give you ten examples of adjectives.

Verb

(a word or words that show action
or state of being)

(*State of being* means the way that something is or exists.)

Here are some examples of verbs that
show action.

JOHN **HIT** BALL

noun   verb   noun

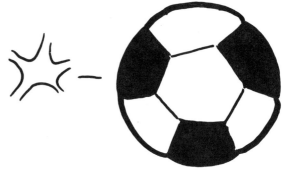

JOHN **KICKED** BALL

noun   verb   noun

JOHN **THREW** BALL

noun   verb   noun

JAN **DREW** PICTURES
noun   verb   noun

SUE **RIDES** BIKE
noun   verb   noun

SARAH **WATERS** FLOWERS
noun   verb   noun

SARAH **LIKES** SUE
noun   verb   noun

TOM PAINTS FENCE
noun   verb   noun

I EAT DINNER
pronoun verb   noun

SAM **CUTS** ROSES

noun   verb   noun

SAM **TAKES** ROSES

noun   verb   noun

TREE **FELL**

noun   verb

Here are some examples of verbs that show state of being.

TREE IS TALL
noun   verb   adjective

In this example *is* shows the state of being of the tree.

SHE **IS** ANGRY

pronoun   verb   adjective

IT **IS** PRETTY

pronoun verb   adjective

BILL **IS** TALL

noun   verb   adjective

THEY **ARE** FRIENDS

pronoun   verb   noun

A verb is not always a single word.

A verb can be made up of two or more words.

For example, the verb *is* can be used with another verb to show continuing action.

TOM **IS PETTING** DOG

noun   verb   noun

FISH **<u>IS SWIMMING</u>**

noun   verb

SHE **IS SITTING**
pronoun   verb

JOE **IS READING** BOOK
noun   verb   noun

Drills

1. Have your twin give you ten examples of verbs.

2. Give your twin ten examples of verbs.

Transitive Verb
(shows action going across to something)

Transitive means going over or across.

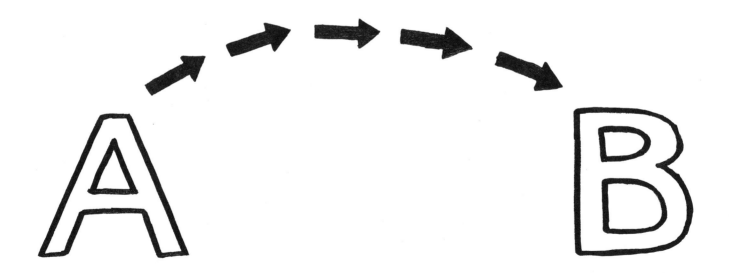

SHE **ATE** APPLE

pronoun   verb   noun

THEY **ARE PLAYING** CHECKERS

pronoun   verb   noun

TOM WON RIBBON
noun   verb   noun

SARA IS WAVING FLAG
noun   verb   noun

Drills

1. Give your twin ten examples of a transitive verb.

2. Have your twin give you ten examples of a transitive verb.

Intransitive Verb
(shows action not going across to something)

Intransitive means not transitive.

THEY **ARE PLAYING**
pronoun   verb

JOE **WON**
noun   verb

THEY <u>ARE TALKING</u>

pronoun   verb

BABY <u>IS WAVING</u>

noun   verb

Drills

1. Have your twin give you ten examples of an intransitive verb.

2. Give your twin ten examples of an intransitive verb.

Adverb

(a name dictionaries use for a word that describes a verb,
adjective or another adverb)

An adverb can describe a verb.

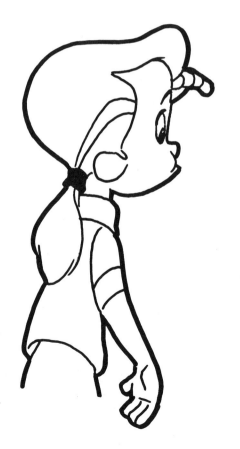

SHE <u>IS LOOKING</u>
pronoun   verb

SHE IS LOOKING **UP**

pronoun   verb   adverb

SHE IS LOOKING **DOWN**

pronoun   verb   adverb

DOG RAN **FAST**

noun   verb   adverb

DOG RAN

noun   verb

An adverb is also a word that describes an adjective.

IT IS BIG

pronoun   verb   adjective

IT IS **VERY** BIG

pronoun   verb   adverb   adjective

An adverb is also a word that describes another adverb.

RADIO IS PLAYING **LOUDLY**
noun verb adverb

RADIO IS PLAYING **TOO** LOUDLY
noun verb adverb adverb

Drills

1. Have your twin give you ten examples of adverbs.

2. Give your twin ten examples of adverbs.

Article

(a word which helps to show what
something is)

I NEED **THE** SMALL BOX

pronoun   verb   article   adjective   noun

I NEED **A** BOX

pronoun   verb   article   noun

I WANT **AN** APPLE

pronoun   verb   article   noun

THAT IS **THE** APPLE I WANT

pronoun   verb   article   noun   pronoun   verb

Drills

1. Give your twin ten examples using articles.

2. Have your twin give you ten examples using articles.

Preposition

(a word which shows the relationship between a
person, place or thing and some other word)

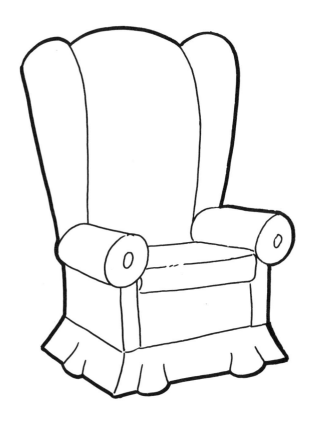

THE CHAIR

article   noun

ON THE CHAIR

preposition   article   noun

UNDER THE CHAIR

preposition article noun

BEHIND THE CHAIR

preposition article noun

BY THE CHAIR

preposition   article   noun

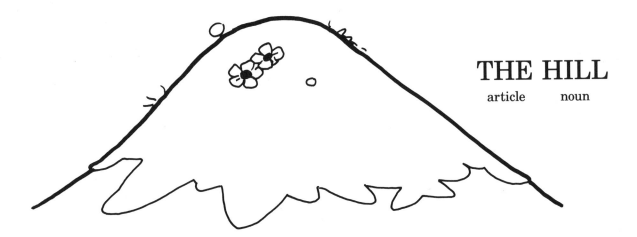

THE HILL
article   noun

NEAR THE HILL
preposition   article   noun

UP THE HILL

preposition   article   noun

DOWN THE HILL

preposition   article   noun

Drills

1. Have your twin give you ten examples of prepositions.

2. Give your twin ten examples of prepositions.

Conjunction
(a word which joins words or groups of words)

BILL **AND** TOM HAVE A BOX

noun   conjunction   noun   verb   article   noun

JOHN SEES A BOOT **AND**

noun   verb   article   noun   conjunction

A TABLE **AND** A CUP

article   noun   conjunction article   noun

WE CAN PLAY BALL **OR** SWIM

pronoun   verb   noun   conjunction   verb

BILL IS OLDER **BUT** BOB

noun   verb   adjective   conjunction   noun

IS HEAVIER

verb   adjective

Drills

1. Give your twin ten examples of conjunctions.

2. Have your twin give you ten examples of conjunctions.

Interjection

(a word or group of words that show strong feeling)

WOW THAT IS GREAT

interjection   pronoun   verb   adjective

HELP   I AM FALLING

interjection   pronoun   verb

Drills

1. Have your twin give you ten examples of an interjection.

2. Give your twin ten examples of an interjection.

You can see that words can be used in different ways to mean different things.

Some words name things. *He has an apple.*

Some words show action. *Joe can run.*

Apple is a word which names a thing. It is a *noun*.

Run is a word which shows action. It is a *verb*.

Some words show state of being. *She is happy.*

The different things words do are called the *parts of speech.* Knowing what part of speech a word is can help you understand its definition better.

Is is a word which shows state of being. It is a *verb.*

Dictionaries tell you what parts of speech words are.

Joe has a new bat.

In this example, *bat* is a noun. It names a thing.

Sam will bat.

In this example, *bat* is a verb. It shows an action.

They live in the big house.

In this example, the word *house* is a noun. It names a thing.

They house the dog there.

In this example, the word *house* is a verb. It shows they give the dog a place to live. That is an action.

CHAPTER SIX:

MARKS AND SYMBOLS

Marks and Symbols

Dictionaries use different marks and symbols.

Some of the most common marks and symbols that dictionaries use in definitions are given here so that you will know what they mean if you see them in a dictionary.

Period ●

A period shows that what has been said is completed.

JOE IS SLEEPING **.**

period

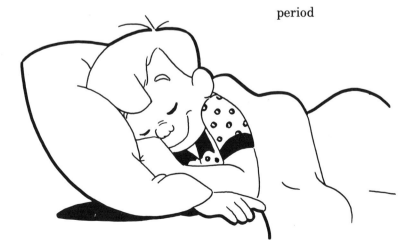

MARY HAS A BROOM **.**

period

A period shows that a word has been abbreviated.

Abbreviated means made shorter.

APARTMENT APT .

period

172

MONDAY

MON .

period

UNITED STATES OF AMERICA

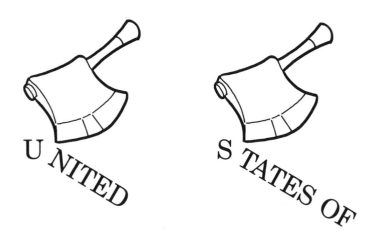

U .   S .   A .

period   period   period

A period is used after numbers or letters to separate them from what is stated following the numbers or letters.

BEFORE YOU LEAVE

1. CLOSE THE WINDOW

period

2. SWITCH OFF THE LIGHT

period

3. LOCK THE DOOR

period

Drill

1. Use a sheet of paper and write out for your twin ten examples of the correct use of a period.

Comma ,

A comma is used to separate words or groups of words from each other.

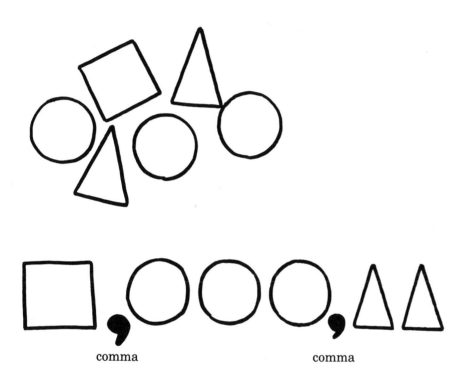

comma   comma

JOE HAS PENS, PAPER,

comma   comma

PENCILS AND BOOKS.

period

A comma is used to separate the parts of a date.

TODAY IS MONDAY,

comma

JANUARY 15.

period

A comma is used to separate large numbers.

1,000,000

comma   comma

Drill

1. Use a sheet of paper and write out for your twin ten examples of the correct use of a comma.

178

Semicolon ;

A semicolon is used to separate parts of a sentence or definition that are different, but are related (have to do with one another).

IN THE WINTER HE GOES SKIING; IN THE SUMMER HE GOES SWIMMING.

semicolon   period

behold to look at ; see
SEMICOLON

Drill

1. Use a sheet of paper and write out for your twin ten examples of the correct use of a semicolon.

Colon :

A colon is used before a list of things.

A colon is used in some dictionaries to show that the words which follow the colon are an example of the definition being given.

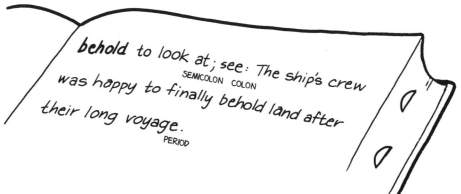

A colon is used between hours and minutes when writing the time.

3:35

colon

8:05

colon

Drill

1. Use a sheet of paper and write out for your twin ten examples of the correct use of a colon.

Apostrophe '

An apostrophe is used to show that something is owned.

apostrophe

BILL'S BICYCLE

apostrophe

THE CAR'S TIRE

apostrophe

JANE'S BABY

apostrophe

GIRL'S KITTEN

apostrophe

CHILDREN'S BALL

An apostrophe is also used to show that a
letter or letters have been left out of a word.

HE CANNOT LIFT IT.

period

apostrophe

HE CAN'T LIFT IT.

period

SHE IS NOT STANDING UP.

period

apostrophe

SHE ISN'T STANDING UP.

period

Drill

1. Use a sheet of paper and write out for your twin ten examples of the correct use of an apostrophe.

Question Mark ?

A question mark is used after a question.

WHO ARE YOU?
question mark

WHERE IS MY DOG?
question mark

190

WHAT**?**

question mark

apostrophe

IT LOOKS GOOD DOESN**'**T IT**?**

question mark

Drill

1. Use a sheet of paper and write out for your twin ten examples of the correct use of a question mark.

Exclamation Point !

An exclamation point is used to express surprise, strong feeling or to add emphasis.

HE FELL DOWN.

period

HE FELL DOWN!

exclamation point

WOW.

period

WOW!

exclamation point

Drill

1. Use a sheet of paper and write out for your twin ten examples of the correct use of an exclamation point.

Parentheses ( )

Parentheses are used to put additional information into a statement, a question or a definition.

THE FLOWERS (ROSES)
parenthesis   parenthesis

LOOK GOOD.
period

THE FRUIT (4 PEARS
parenthesis

AND 3 ORANGES)
parenthesis

IS ON THE TABLE.
period

A single parenthesis may be used after numbers or letters to separate them from what is stated following the numbers or letters.

ON THE TABLE**,** THEY SAW**:**

comma   colon

1) BOOKS

parenthesis

2) PLATES

parenthesis

3) CUPS

parenthesis

Drill

1. Use a sheet of paper and write out for your twin ten examples of the correct use of parentheses.

Quotation Marks " "

Quotation marks are used to show exactly
what someone said.

I LOVE ROSES.

period

quotation
marks

quotation
marks

SHE SAID, "I LOVE ROSES."

comma

period

Quotation marks can be used to show that a word is being referred to as a word.

quotation quotation
marks marks

SHE IS LOOKING UP "TO."

period

Drill

1. Use a sheet of paper and write out for your twin ten examples of the correct use of quotation marks.

Italics

Italics are letters that slant to the right.

ITALICS look like this.

Italics are used to set off or emphasize a word or words.

Italics are used to show the names of books, magazines and movies.

TOM *WILL NOT* EAT.

        italics   period

SHE HAS
ALICE IN WONDERLAND.

        italics   period

Italics are used to show the names of air-planes, trains, ships and so on.

THEY LEFT ON THE
SILVER ARROW.

italics   period

Italics are used to show that a word is being referred to as a word.

SHE IS LOOKING UP *TO.*

italics period

Italics are also used in dictionaries to show that the words in italics are an example of the definition being given.

house 1. a building in which people live. They are in their house.
ITALICS

In some dictionaries only the word which is being defined is in italics in the example given.

house 1. a building in which people live. They are in *their house*.
ITALICS

Drill

1. Give your twin four examples of where italics would be used.

CHAPTER SEVEN:

FORMS OF WORDS

Forms of Words

A form of a word is one of the different ways a word can be spoken or written.

SINGULAR

Singular means one.

BIRD

PLURAL

Plural means more than one.

BIRDS

BOX

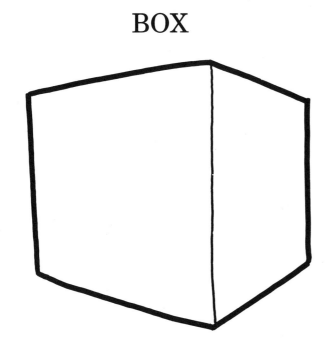

BOXES

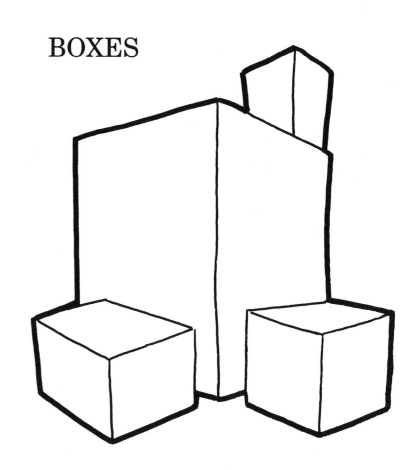

There are some words which are plural but do not have an **s** at the end.

mouse is singular

mice is plural

man is singular

men is plural

child is singular

children is plural

Other Forms of Words

EAT

Ate is a form of eat.

Eaten is a form of eat.

Eating is a form of eat.

Some dictionaries give the different forms of words. For example if you find the word *eat* in the dictionary it may also give the forms of *eat*.

Not all dictionaries give you the forms of words like this, but some do. The definition of the word being defined can be used to help understand the different forms of the word.

He *ate* the cake.

He has *eaten* the cake.

He is *eating* the cake.

This is a dash —

Some dictionaries use a dash in front of the forms of a word, to separate the forms of the word from the rest of the information given.

This is a hyphen ▬

Sometimes a hyphen is used when only the word endings are shown, not the whole word.

Some dictionaries show only the endings for the forms of a word.

CHAPTER EIGHT:

HOW WORDS ARE
DEFINED IN DICTIONARIES

How Words Are Defined in Dictionaries

The information about parts of speech, singular and plural, and the different forms of a word are usually given before the word itself is defined.

Dictionaries do this in different ways.

Here are some examples of how dictionaries give this information.

house	(hous)	*noun*
house,	hous,	*noun*
house	(hous)	noun plural houses (hou′ ziz)

A dictionary tells you the different ways in which a word can be used (the different parts of speech).

If a word has a meaning as a noun and also has a meaning as a verb then the definitions of that word as a noun are given together and the definitions of that word as a verb are given together and so on for each part of speech.

In the example below, the definitions of *house* as a noun are given first, then the definitions of *house* as a verb.

Dictionaries use different kinds of marks in the definitions of a word.

Here are some examples of how dictionaries define words. You can see that they do this in different ways.

house	(hous)	*noun* 1. a building for people to live in.

This definition begins with a number. It ends with a period. There is no example.

house	(hous)	*noun* a building for living in;

This definition does not begin with a number. A semicolon shows that is the end of the definition. (A semicolon is used in some dictionaries between the definitions.) There is no example.

If a word has more than one definition, the definitions are given one after the other. Numbers and semicolons are often used to separate definitions and parts of definitions.

---

house (hous) *noun* 1. a building for living in, especially one used as the home of a person or family. 2. a family.

Dictionaries often use abbreviations.

For example, the abbreviation for *plural* is *pl*. If you looked up *house* and saw *pl. houses*, that means that the plural of *house* is *houses*.

Most dictionaries have a section which tells you what all the abbreviations mean.

If you see an abbreviation in a dictionary and you do not know what it stands for you can usually find out in the abbreviations section of the dictionary.

The abbreviation *n.* in a dictionary means *noun.*

The abbreviations section usually comes at the beginning of the dictionary.

Words Formed from Different Parts

Sometimes in a dictionary you will see a long list of words that do not have any definitions given for them.

It is easy to find out what these words mean though.

Words are often made up of different parts. An example of this is the word:

nonhuman

This word is made of *non,* which means *not* and *human* which means *having to do with people.*

Nonhuman means *not a person or persons.*

You can see that letters were added to the beginning of *human* to make a new word: *nonhuman*.

nonhuman

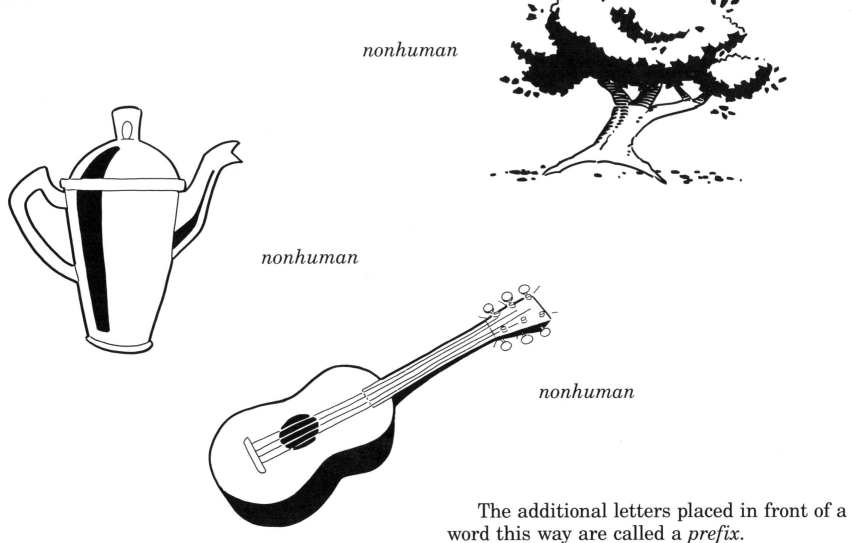

nonhuman

nonhuman

The additional letters placed in front of a word this way are called a *prefix*.

A prefix is a letter or letters added to the front of a word to make a new word.

In a dictionary, prefixes are entered as entry words and their definitions are given.

A hyphen is used with a prefix to show that the prefix is to be joined with other letters to make a complete word or to make a different word.

non-

In the dictionary, the entry would look like this:

non- (non) *prefix* not

To understand what *nonhuman* means, you look at the definition of *human.*

non, not

and

human, having to do with people.

Dictionaries do not always define all of the words that are made with prefixes. There are many, many words that can be made with the prefix *non-* and you can understand what each of these words mean by looking at the definitions of the prefixes and the definition of the word which is attached to the prefix.

Here are some more examples.

nonbreakable

nonfiction

nonliving

If a word that you are looking up is entered in the dictionary this way, then you only have to look up the prefix and the word which is attached to the prefix and then put the two meanings together and you will understand the whole word.

Letters can also be added to the end of a word to make a new word.

An example of this is the word *friendless*.

Friend is a person (or animal) one knows and likes.

In the word *friendless*, *-less* means *without*.

Friendless means *without friends*.

The additional letters placed at the end of a word this way are called a *suffix*.

A suffix is a letter or letters added to the end of a word to make a new word.

Sometimes you will find a word in the dictionary that was made with a suffix, but is not defined in the dictionary.

friend (frend) *noun* 1. a person (or animal) one knows and likes. 2. a helpful thing or quality, *the night was our friend*. 3. a person who helps or does things in support of someone or something, *a friend of the poor*. **friend' ship** *noun* **friend' less** *adjective*.

To find out what *friendless* means you would look up the definition of *friend* and then look up the suffix *-less*. If you put these two together you would have the meaning of *friendless*.

Dictionaries use hyphens with suffixes to show that the suffix is a suffix and that the rest of the word comes before the suffix.

-less

In the dictionary the entry would look like this:

-less (les) *suffix* without

Knowing how dictionaries use prefixes and suffixes is important when you are using a dictionary.

Idioms

An idiom is a group of words that has a meaning which is different from what you would have if you put the usual meanings of the words together.

Idioms are usually given in a dictionary after the other definitions have been given.

house:
1. ——
2. ——
bring the house down: to receive very loud applause.

You should always clear up any idioms which are given for a word that you are looking up in a dictionary.

CHAPTER NINE:

USING A DICTIONARY TO UNDERSTAND WORDS

Important

Definitions in dictionaries are not always complete and sometimes they are not fully correct.

Remember that dictionaries are written by people who themselves could have words they don't understand.

So do not think that they are books which have no errors and which must always be believed.

They are usually right but they are just tools.

Using a Dictionary to Understand Words

It is very important when you are trying to study or read about anything that you use a dictionary to learn the words that you don't understand.

The biggest block to learning anything is going past words that you don't understand.

That's why it is important to know how to use a dictionary!

Never go past a word you do not fully understand.

When a person reads past a word he doesn't understand then he can become confused. He can think that he is not able to learn what he is trying to learn. But this is not true. It is only that he doesn't understand all the words.

This is also the *only* reason why a person gives up on studying something and quits.

Have you ever come to the end of a page and realized you didn't know what you had just read? Well, somewhere earlier on that page you went past a word that you didn't know the meaning of.

Here's an example. "It was found that when the crepuscule arrived the children were quieter and when it was not present they were much more noisy."

You see what happens. You think you don't understand the whole idea, but the confusion comes only from one word you didn't know, *crepuscule,* which means the time from sunset to dark.

So you see, the sentence at first looked confusing, but it really only means that the children were quieter at night than they were when the sun was up.

To successfully study and learn you must look up *any* word that you don't understand or are not sure of.

Look up means to find the word in a dictionary and see what it means.

If something you are reading becomes confusing or you can't seem to understand it, there will be a word just earlier that you have not understood. Don't go any further, but go back to *before* you got into trouble, find the word you did not understand and look it up.

There is a right way to learn the meanings of a word you don't understand.

It is called *clearing* a word.

When a word is fully understood it is said to be *cleared*.

This is how you clear a word using a dictionary:

If you come across a word you don't understand in what you are reading, find the word in a dictionary.

Read the definitions and find the one that fits in the sentence you were reading.

Read that definition and then make up sentences using the word that way until you really understand that meaning. This might take many sentences, up to ten or more. That's okay. The important thing is that you understand the word.

THE PIZZA HOUSE IS MY FAVORITE PLACE TO EAT.

THEY WENT TO THE TOOL HOUSE FOR A HAMMER.

house:
1. ▭
2. a building used for any purpose.

When you understand that definition fully then do the same for each of the other definitions. Each word is cleared in this way.

When you are clearing a word, you may find a word in the definition itself that you don't understand. Look that word up too, and clear all of its definitions. Then go back to the word you were clearing.

There are many idioms in English. These are usually given in a dictionary after the definitions of the word itself. Clear any idioms that are given for the word you are looking up.

You may see other abbreviations in dictionaries.

If you see something that you do not understand, look in the front of the dictionary and find out what it means.

While using a dictionary it is very important not to go past any words, symbols or marks that you do not understand.

Most dictionaries have a section which explains what all the marks and symbols mean.

If you find something you do not understand in a dictionary, clear it.

When you understand all the words in what you are reading you can understand the whole thing.

Knowing how to use a dictionary can help you do that.

And that can make you pretty smart!

CHAPTER TEN:

DRILLS

Drills

248

HE DID NOT DRILL !

pronoun   verb   adverb   verb   exclamation
                                       point

Parts of Speech Drills

1. **noun**   Tell your twin ten nouns.

2. **noun**   Have your twin tell you ten nouns.

3. **pronoun**   Have your twin tell you ten pronouns.

4. **pronoun**   Tell your twin ten pronouns.

5. **adjective**   Tell your twin five different examples of adjectives.

6. **adjective**   Have your twin tell you five different examples of adjectives.

7. **verb**   Have your twin tell you ten verbs.

8. **verb**   Tell your twin ten examples of verbs.

9. **adverb**   Tell your twin five different examples of adverbs.

10. **adverb**   Have your twin tell you five different examples of adverbs.

11. **article**
   a. Have your twin give you five different examples using **a**.
   b. Have your twin give you five different examples using **an**.
   c. Have your twin give you five different examples using **the**.

12. **article**
   a. Give your twin five different examples using **a**.
   b. Give your twin five different examples using **an**.
   c. Give your twin five different examples using **the**.

13. **preposition** Give your twin five different examples using prepositions.

14. **preposition** Have your twin give you five different examples using prepositions.

15. **conjunction** Have your twin give you five different examples using conjunctions.

16. **conjunction** Give your twin five different examples using conjunctions.

17. **interjection** Give your twin five different examples using interjections.

18. **interjection** Have your twin give you five different examples using interjections.

19. You and your twin are to correctly say what part of speech each word in the following sentences is. You do the first one, your twin does the second one, and so on.

Sam ate ice cream.

A bird sat on the fence.

She jumped high.

I ran home.

They sang the song.

Tom and Sue helped Bob.

That is a tall tree.

Mike put his shoes in the closet.

I saw a little puppy.

I love good books.

Amy sat on the chair.

She needs a brush and some paints.

His dad is a tall man.

Lizzy has a horse.

Wow! The mountain is tall.

Her small dog ate all the food.

Punctuation Drills

1. On a piece of paper, write ten examples that show how to use a period correctly. Show them to your twin.

2. Have your twin write ten examples of how to use a period correctly and show them to you.

3. Have your twin write five examples of how to use a comma correctly and show them to you.

4. On a piece of paper, write five examples that show how to use a comma correctly. Show them to your twin.

5. On a piece of paper, write five examples that show how to use a semicolon correctly. Show them to your twin.

6. Have your twin write five examples of how to use a semicolon correctly and show them to you.

7. Have your twin write five examples of how to use a colon correctly and show them to you.

8. On a piece of paper, write five examples that show how to use a colon correctly. Show them to your twin.

9. On a piece of paper, write five examples that show how to use an apostrophe correctly. Show them to your twin.

10. Have your twin write five examples of how to use an apostrophe correctly and show them to you.

11. Have your twin write five examples of how to use a question mark correctly and show them to you.

12. On a piece of paper, write five examples that show how to use a question mark correctly. Show them to your twin.

13. On a piece of paper, write five examples that show how to use an exclamation point correctly. Show them to your twin.

14. Have your twin write five examples of how to use an exclamation point correctly and show them to you.

15. Have your twin write five examples of how to use parentheses correctly and show them to you.

16. On a piece of paper, write five examples that show how to use parentheses correctly. Show them to your twin.

17. On a piece of paper, write five examples that show how to use a single parenthesis correctly. Show them to your twin.

18. Have your twin write five examples of how to use a single parenthesis correctly and show them to you.

19. Have your twin write five examples of how to use quotation marks correctly and show them to you.

20. On a piece of paper, write five examples that show how to use quotation marks correctly. Show them to your twin.

21. On a piece of paper, write five examples that show how to use italics correctly. Show them to your twin.

22. Have your twin write five examples of how to use italics correctly and show these to you.

Dictionary Drills

You will now be doing drills on using a dictionary. You will be using a dictionary to do these drills.

While doing these drills, if you see a word, a part of speech, an abbreviation or a symbol that you do not understand, use this book to clear it up. If it is not in this book then clear it in a dictionary.

1. Without looking at the definition in this book, tell your twin, in your own words, what a dictionary is.

2. Now have your twin tell you what a dictionary is.

3. Using a dictionary, have your twin find the **R** section (the section of the dictionary which contains all the words beginning with the letter **R**). Have him show it to you.

4. Using a dictionary, find the **C** section. Show this to your twin.

5. Find the **O** section in a dictionary and show it to your twin.

6. Have your twin find the **H** section in a dictionary and show it to you.

7. Have your twin show you an entry word in a dictionary.

8. In a dictionary show your twin an entry word.

9. Open your dictionary to any page. Show your twin the guide words on that page. Open the dictionary to another page. Show your twin the guide words on that page. Do this until you can easily find the guide words on any page of the dictionary.

10. Have your twin open his or her dictionary to any page. Have your twin show you the guide words on that page. Have your twin open the dictionary to another page and show you the guide words on that page.

Have your twin do this until he or she can easily find the guide words on any page of the dictionary.

11. Have your twin use the guide words to find the following words in the dictionary and show them to you. Have your twin do this as quickly as he or she can.

 pen   acorn

 cook   winter

 start   door

 animal woman

This drill is done until you can easily and quickly find words in the dictionary. Your twin can give you more words to find in the dictionary until you can find them quickly and without any trouble.

12. Using the guide words, find the following words in the dictionary and

show them to your twin. Do this as quickly as you can.

 absent feather

 snow   rain

 owl   better

 tomorrow midnight

13. Look up the following words in the dictionary and tell your twin how many syllables they have.

 dictionary happiness

 mountain feather

 happy   action

 connect express

14. Have your twin look up the following words in the dictionary and tell you how many syllables they have.

 position location

pronunciation	contest
act	deeper
prettier	following

15. Have your twin find the pronunciation key in the beginning of the dictionary and show it to you. Have your twin find the pronunciation key at the bottom of a page of the dictionary and show it to you.

16. Find the pronunciation key in the beginning of the dictionary and show it to your twin. Find the pronunciation key at the bottom of a page of the dictionary and show it to your twin.

17. Find the following words in the dictionary and using the pronunciation key, pronounce each word correctly for your twin.

| baby | meaning |

| paper | monkey |
| cottage | yesterday |

18. Have your twin find the following words in the dictionary and using the pronunciation key, pronounce each word correctly.

loud	yellow
morning	open
together	leaf

19. Have your twin find the following words in the dictionary and show you the plural form of each of them.

| ox | man | moose |

20. Find the following words in the dictionary and find out what the plural form is for each of the words. Show them to your twin.

| woman | child | mouse |

21. Find the word *eat* in the dictionary. Show your twin the different forms that are given for *eat*.

22. Have your twin find the word *run* in the dictionary. Have your twin show you the different forms that are given for *run*.

23. Have your twin look up the following words in the dictionary and find out what part of speech each one is. Have your twin show you what he or she finds.

    Spain   ear   too

24. Look up the following words in the dictionary and find out what part of speech each word is. Show your twin what you find out.

    quite   typewriter   you

25. Look up the following words. Each of them can be used as more than one part of speech. Find each one in the dictionary and tell your twin what different parts of speech each word is.

    gold   hope   delay

26. Have your twin look up the following words. Each of them can be used as more than one part of speech. Have your twin find each one in the dictionary and tell you what different parts of speech each word is.

    skirt   give   place

27. Find a definition in the dictionary that has an example given for that definition. Show it to your twin.

28. Have your twin find a definition in the dictionary that has an example given for that definition and show it to you.

CONGRATULATIONS!

Congratulations on completing the *How to Use a Dictionary Picture Book for Children.*

You should use the data you have learned in this book every day to help you understand things better. This is an important part of being successful in life.

It makes life a lot easier and a lot more fun!

Glossary

A *glossary* is a collection of definitions or explanations that have to do with a particular subject.

On the following pages is a glossary of words and marks that are used in this book and in dictionaries. It does not contain *all* the words and marks contained in dictionaries but it has a lot of them.

At the end of the glossary there is a list of marks and symbols used in this book.

a.

abbreviation for *adjective*.

abbr.

abbreviation for *abbreviation*.

abbrev.

abbreviation for *abbreviation*.

abbreviated

shortened.

*January has been **abbreviated***.

abbreviation

abbr.

abbrev.

a shortened form of a word which stands for the whole word.

United States of America

U. S. A.

accent

when a word has two or more syllables, one or more of the syllables is said with more emphasis. This emphasis is called *accent*. (See *accent mark*.)

accent mark

a mark used to show which syllable of a word is said with more emphasis.

wom'an

adj.

abbreviation for *adjective*.

adjective

a.

adj.

one of the parts of speech given in dictionaries. It is a word that modifies or describes a noun or pronoun.

girl

small girl

tall girl

adv.

abbreviation for *adverb*.

adverb

adv.

one of the parts of speech given in dictionaries. It is a word that modifies or describes a verb, an adjective or another adverb.

She is looking.

*She is looking **down**.*

*She is looking **up**.*

ant.

abbreviation for *antonym*.

antonym

ant.

a word which has an opposite meaning to another word: *Good* is an **antonym** of *bad*.

apostrophe

This is an apostrophe '

1. a mark used to show something is owned: *Joe's bicycle.*

2. a mark used to show that a letter or letters have been left out of a word.

He cannot lift it.

He can't lift it.

3. a mark used in some pronunciation keys before the sounds of *l*, *m* and *n* in a syllable which is said without emphasis. It is used to show that when saying the word there is almost no vowel sound made in that syllable.

able (**ā b'l**)

arch.

abbreviation for *archaic*.

archaic

arch.

(of definitions) old and no longer used very often. *Thou* is an archaic word. It is an older form of the word *you*. It is sometimes used, but not very often. It would usually be given in a dictionary as *archaic*.

art.

abbreviation for *article*.

article

art.

one of the parts of speech. It is a word which helps identify something.

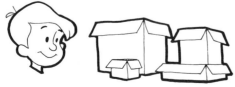

a
box

the
box

asterisk

This is an asterisk *

a mark used in some dictionaries to show that a word originated in or is mainly used in the United States (or a country other than England which speaks English, such as Canada or Australia). An example of such a word is *belittle*, a word that was brought into the English language in the United States about 200 years ago. It means, *to make seem little, less important, etc., or to speak badly of.*

---

* belittle to make seem little, less important, etc., or to speak badly of.

---

base

the part of a word used to make other words.

friendless

brackets

These are brackets **[ ]**

1. brackets are used in dictionaries to enclose additional information or directions, etc.: *She said "I wuv [love] you."*

2. brackets are sometimes used to enclose examples given in the dictionary.

> **house** 1. a building in which people live *[They are in their house.]*

Brit.

abbreviation for *British*.

British

Brit.

of or having to do with Great Britain.

cf. or Cf.

an abbreviation for the Latin word *confer*, which means *compare*. In a dictionary this means you should compare the word which you are looking up with the word following the *cf.* for additional information.

colon

This is a colon **:**

1. a mark used before a list of things.

Animals**:** dogs, cats, tigers, etc.

2. a mark used in some dictionaries to show that the words which follow the colon are an example of the definition being given.

> **house** 1. a building in which people live**:** *They are in their house.*

3. used between hours and minutes when writing the time.

5**:**00

comma

This is a comma **,**

1. a mark used to separate words or groups of words from each other: *Joe has pens, paper, pencils and books.*

2. a mark used to separate the parts of a date.

Thursday**,** January 15.

3. a mark used to separate large numbers.

$$1,000,000$$

conj.

abbreviation for *conjunction*.

conjunction

conj.

one of the parts of speech. It is a word which joins words or groups of words.

contraction

a word or words which have been shortened by using an apostrophe in place of a letter or letters that have been left out.

cannot **can't**

it is **it's**

dash

This is a dash —

a mark used in dictionaries to show a separation between groups of letters or words.

house —verb 1. to provide with a place to live.

dictionary

a word book. A dictionary contains the meanings of words and other information about them. A dictionary can be used to find out what a word means, how to say a word, how to spell a word, how to use a word and many other things about words.

dot

a mark used in some dictionaries between syllables, to show the syllables of a word.

el • e • phant

ending

the last part of something.

walk**ing**

exclamation point

This is an exclamation point **!**

a mark used to express surprise, strong feeling or to add emphasis.

Hello**!**

future tense

a verb form which shows that something will exist or will happen in the future: *You* **will go** *soon*.

glossary

a collection of definitions or explanations that have to do with a particular subject.

guide words

the words written in darker letters at the top of each page of a dictionary which show the first and last words entered on that page.

hyphen

This is a hyphen **-**

1. a mark used in dictionaries to show the forms of a word when only the word endings are given, not the whole word.

2. used in dictionaries with prefixes and suffixes to show that the prefix or suffix is joined to another word to make a complete word or to make a different word.

non- (non) *prefix* not

index

an alphabetical list of all the information given in this book, which tells which pages of the book the information is on. If you wanted to find where something is in this book then you would look in the index.

informal

the usual way that people speak and write, especially with friends, etc.; when a word is used a certain way in normal conversation or writing and is not used that way at other times it is called *informal* or *colloquial*.

Capital is used in an **informal** or colloquial way to mean, *very good*.

informally

in an informal way: *She spoke to him **informally***.

interj.

abbreviation for *interjection*.

interjection

interj.

one of the parts of speech. It is a word or group of words that show strong feeling.

***Wow!** I want one too.*

intr.

abbreviation for *verb intransitive*.

intransitive

not transitive (see *verb intransitive*).

intransitive verb

same as *verb intransitive*. (See *verb intransitive*.)

italics

letters that slant to the right. *These are **italics***.

1. italics are used in dictionaries to set off or emphasize a word or words: He is *very* tall.

2. italics are used when writing the names of books, magazines, movies, etc.: The name of the book is *Alice in Wonderland*.

3. italics are used when writing the names of airplanes, trains, ships and so on: They are traveling on the *Silver Arrow*.

4. italics are used when a word is being referred to as a word: She is looking up the word *to*.

5. italics are used in dictionaries when an example of a definition is being given.

---

house 1. a building in which people live: *They are in their house.*

---

house 1. a building in which people live: They are in their *house.*

---

key

something that explains or gives information that is necessary to understand something else: *A pronunciation **key** gives the information needed to understand the pronunciations given in dictionaries.*

-less

a suffix meaning *without.*

n.

abbreviation for *noun.*

non-

a prefix meaning *not.*

noun

n.

one of the parts of speech. It is a word used to name a person, place or thing.

girl   thought

money

obs. or Obs.

abbreviation for *obsolete.*

obsolete

obs.

Obs.

no longer in use. In dictionaries the word *obsolete* is used to point out definitions of a word which were used in the past but are not used now. An example is an obsolete definition of the word *contain.* Almost 400 years ago, the word *contain* also meant, *to view in a certain way*. An example of this would be: *The people contain even their enemy as friends*. This meaning of the word is not used anymore.

ordinary letters

normal or usual letters.

These are darker letters.
These are ordinary letters.

parentheses

These are parentheses ( )

parentheses are used to put additional information into a statement, a question or a definition: *She has the flowers (roses).*

parenthesis

see *single parenthesis.*

part of speech

one of the parts of speech (see *parts of speech*).

parts of speech

the different things words do (name a person, place or thing, show action or state of being, modify or describe another word, etc.).

past tense

pa. t.

pt.

a verb form which shows that something happened or existed in the past: *They **ate**.*

pa. t.

abbreviation for *past tense.*

period

This is a period •

1. a mark used to show that a statement is completed: *Joe is sleeping.•*

2. a mark used to show that a word has been abbreviated.

U. S. A.

3. a mark used after numbers or letters to separate them from what is stated following the numbers or letters.

house 1.• a building in which people live.

pl.

abbreviation for *plural*.

plural

pl.

a form of a word which indicates more than one person, place or thing is being talked about.

MEN
plural

prefix

a letter or letters added to the front of a word to make a new word.

nonhuman

prep.

abbreviation for *preposition*.

preposition

prep.

one of the parts of speech. It is a word which shows the relationship between a person, place or thing and some other word.

The cat is **on** *the chair.*

The cat is **under** *the chair.*

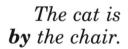

The cat is **by** *the chair.*

present tense

a verb form that is used to show a few different things:

a) present tense shows that something exists or is happening at the present moment: *The cat is in the tree.*

b) present tense is used to tell that something is true at all times: *People need food to live.*

c) present tense is used to tell about an action that is a habit or usual action: *He swims every day.*

pron.

abbreviation for *pronoun*.

pronoun

pron.

one of the parts of speech. A *pronoun* is a word which takes the place of a noun.

boy
he

cake
it

boys
them

pronounce

make the sound of a letter or word.

*He cannot **pronounce** an L sound.*

pronounced

1. made the sound of a letter or word.

*He **pronounced** the word incorrectly.*

2. said correctly: *How is this word **pronounced**?*

pronouncing

making the sound of a letter or word.

*He is **pronouncing** the word correctly.*

pronun.

abbreviation for *pronunciation*.

pronunciation

pronun.

a way of making the sound of a letter or word; the way something is said.

*His **pronunciation** of LOVE is wrong.*

pronunciation key

an explanation of the symbols used in a dictionary to show the correct pronunciation of words. (A pronunciation key is given on page 64 of this book.)

pronunciations

more than one pronunciation (see *pronunciation*).

pt.

abbreviation for *past tense*.

question mark

This is a question mark **?**

a mark used after a question: *Who are you?*

quotation marks

These are quotation marks " "

1. marks used in dictionaries to show exactly what someone said: *She said, "Hello."*

2. used to show that a word is being referred to as a word: *She is looking up the word "house."*

schwa

a mark used in pronunciation keys which looks like this ə. A *schwa* is used to show the sound of a vowel when it is said without emphasis.

semicolon

This is a semicolon **;**

a mark used to separate parts of a statement or definition that are different but which are related; sometimes used in dictionaries to separate the definitions: *In the winter he goes skiing; in the summer he goes swimming.*

sing.

abbreviation for *singular*.

single parenthesis

This is a single parenthesis)

a single parenthesis is used to separate things or to list things.

---

house 1. a) a building which can be used as a place to live for one or several families.

---

singular

sing.

a form of a word which indicates one person, place or thing is being talked about.

BIRD
singular

slang

a word or group of words that are used in a very informal way: *Chow* is **slang** for *food*.

small capital letters

SMALL CAPITAL LETTERS.

Small capital letters are used in dictionaries to show that the word in small capital letters is under its own entry in the dictionary and to find more information about the definition you are looking up you should look up the word in small capital letters.

specialized definition

a definition for a word that applies only to a certain subject, like mathematics, sports or ships.

spell

write or say the letters of a word in a particular order.

*He can **spell** CAT.*

spelled

(of the letters which make up a word) written or spoken in a particular order to make a word.

The word is **spelled** *C A T.*

spelling

the order in which letters are written or spoken to make a word.

She gave the correct **spelling** *of the word.*

star

This is a star ☆

a mark used in some dictionaries to show that a word originated in or is mainly used in the United States. An example of such a word is *belittle*, a word that was brought into the English language in the United States about 200 years ago. It means *to make seem little, less important, etc., or to speak badly of.*

☆ **belittle** to make seem little, less important, etc., or to speak badly of.

---

suffix

a letter or letters added to the end of a word to make a new word.

friend**less**

syllable

a syllable is a single spoken sound that is a word or part of a word.

woman   **wom an**

syn.

abbreviation for *synonym.*

synon.

abbreviation for *synonym*.

synonym

syn.

synon.

a word in the same language that has a similar meaning to another word in that language: *Big* and *large* are **synonyms**.

tense

comes from the Latin word *tempus* which meant *time*. Verbs express time by changing their form (sound or spelling). This is called *tense*. See *present tense*, *past tense* and *future tense*.

tr or tr.

abbreviation for *verb transitive*.

transitive

going across (see *verb transitive*).

transitive verb

same as *verb transitive*. (See *verb transitive*.)

tr. v.

abbreviation for *verb transitive*.

usage

the way or ways in which something is done or is used. Dictionaries sometimes give information on the usage of a word.

v.

abbreviation for *verb*.

vb.

abbreviation for *verb*.

verb

v.

vb.

one of the parts of speech. It is a word or words that show action or state of being: *John **hit** the ball. John **is running**. Bill **is** tall.*

verb intransitive

intr.

vi.

v.i.

a verb that shows action not going across to something: *The fish **is swimming**. She **is sitting**.*

verb transitive

tr

tr.

tr. v.

v.t.

a verb that shows action going across to something.

He **sees** the *tree*.

vi. or v.i.

abbreviation for *verb intransitive*.

v.t.

abbreviation for *verb transitive*.

Marks And Symbols

The marks and symbols below are used in this book and in dictionaries, and are explained in the glossary of this book. These are not all of the marks and symbols that are used in dictionaries, though. If you find a mark or symbol in a dictionary that is not defined in this book, you will be able to clear it using the dictionary.

' APOSTROPHE

* ASTERISK

[ ] BRACKETS

: COLON

, COMMA

— DASH

• DOT

! EXCLAMATION POINT

- HYPHEN

( ) PARENTHESES

. PERIOD

? QUESTION MARK

" " QUOTATION MARKS

ə SCHWA

; SEMICOLON

) SINGLE PARENTHESIS

☆ STAR

Important Information for Parents and Teachers

Dictionaries play an important role in any child's quest to learn.

An amazing thing about using a dictionary is that it contains many, many words, symbols and marks and often a person doesn't have a clue what all of these things mean. This can make a dictionary very hard to use.

Children are always seeking to obtain a larger and larger vocabulary. They love to learn new words and use new words. Many children like to browse through dictionaries just to see what new words they can learn! Knowing *how* to use a dictionary is a vital part of a child's learning skills.

This book starts off by giving the child an explanation of what a *word* is and explaining what a dictionary is and what it is used for. It then covers the most common terms, punctuation marks and symbols that appear in dictionaries that children most commonly use. The book fully explains how a dictionary is laid out and how to use one.

The material in this book was developed by L. Ron Hubbard in order to provide an easy way to learn what one needs to know in order to use a dictionary without running into confusions and problems. Knowing the importance of learning and study to all people, not just children, L. Ron Hubbard developed an entire technology on how to study which has helped many, many people to overcome seemingly insurmountable barriers to learning. Being able to use a dictionary is an obvious important part of being able to study any subject.

Getting the Most out of the Book

This book has been published to give children an interesting and fun way to learn how to use a dictionary.

The information is given one step at a time, without giving the reader a lot of things to learn all at once that are too hard to learn.

In working with a child to help him learn how to use a dictionary it will help if you first read the book yourself and get familiar with its contents.

In giving this book to your child and in working with him to get through the book, there is one very important datum about study which a parent or teacher must know:

THE ONLY REASON A PERSON GIVES UP A STUDY OR BECOMES CONFUSED OR UNABLE TO LEARN IS BECAUSE HE HAS GONE PAST A WORD THAT WAS NOT UNDERSTOOD.

The confusion or inability to grasp or learn comes AFTER a word that the person did not have defined and understood.

Here's an example. "It was found that when the crepuscule arrived the children were quieter and when it was not present they were much noisier." You see what happens. You think you don't understand the whole idea, but the confusion comes only from one word you didn't know, *crepuscule,* which means the time from sunset to dark.

The datum about not going by a word that one does not understand is the most important datum in the whole subject of study. Every subject a person has taken up and then abandoned or done poorly with had its words which the person failed to get defined. It is the most important barrier to study and a parent or teacher should be familiar with this data.

Handling Trouble

If the child starts to have trouble getting the data, gets confused, feels like throwing the book down or giving up on it, it is because of a word he went by that he did not know the meaning of. If this should occur then help the child by getting him to go back to where he was last doing well with the material and right at that point, or just before that, will be a word he didn't get. It needs to be found and then looked up and properly defined. There could be more than one.

"Twins"

The book is best studied with another person (called a "twin"). A twin is a study partner. Two twins would go through this whole book together, reading the text and doing all the drills together. Doing the drills is very, very important—remember it is the ability to *apply* the data that is important in study, not just learning a lot of data that you cannot then do anything with.

If it is not possible for the child or student to study the book with a twin, then he can study the book himself and write down all the answers to the drills. Sometimes the drills call for another person and so minimally he would need a parent or teacher or friend to help him with these drills.

Use in School Curricula

Numerous schools across the United States and throughout Europe now use Mr. Hubbard's educational materials to promote faster learning with increased comprehension.

Further Information

If you or your child or student encounter any difficulties in reading this book there are addresses of schools and institutions listed at the back of this book which will provide any assistance needed. They will be happy to answer any questions or give you further information about L. Ron Hubbard's technology of study and the courses and other materials offered on the subject.

———

The whole idea of this book is to give a child a basic understanding of dictionaries and the ability to *use* a dictionary so that he can and will use it when studying or learning any subject. It is next to impossible to learn a subject when you don't know the words which are used to describe that subject.

For a child it can be an important first step to a very successful life.

About the Author

L. Ron Hubbard was no stranger to education. Although his main profession was that of a professional writer, in a long, event-filled and productive life he spent thousands of hours researching in the education field, lecturing and teaching.

He was born in Tilden, Nebraska on 13 March 1911, and his early years were spent on his grandfather's ranch in the wilds of Montana. As the son of a US Navy commander, he was well on the way to becoming a seasoned traveler by the age of eight, and by the time he was nineteen he had logged over a quarter of a million miles.

He enrolled in George Washington University in 1930, taking classes in mathematics and engineering. But his was not a quiet academic life. He took up flying in the pioneer days of aviation, learning to pilot first glider planes and then powered aircraft. He worked as a freelance reporter and photographer. He directed expeditions to the Caribbean and Puerto Rico, and later, to Alaska. The world was his classroom and he studied voraciously, gathering experience which provided the background for his later writings, research and discoveries.

Some of his first published articles were nonfiction, based upon his aviation experience. Soon he began to draw from his travels to produce a wide variety of fiction stories and novels: adventure, mystery, westerns, fantasy and science fiction.

The proceeds from his fiction writing funded his main line of research and exploration—how to improve the human condition. His nonfiction works cover such diverse subjects as drug rehabilitation, marriage and family, success at work, statistical analysis, public relations, art, marketing and much, much more. But he did more than write books—he also delivered over 6,000 lectures and conducted courses to impart his own discoveries to others.

However, in order to learn, one must be able to read and understand. Therefore, L. Ron Hubbard tackled the problem of teaching others how to study. His research uncovered the basic reason for the failure of a student to grasp any subject. He discovered the barriers to full comprehension of what one is studying, and developed methods by which anyone can improve his ability to learn and to *apply* the data that he is being taught. He wrote a considerable body of work on this subject, which he termed *study technology.*

L. Ron Hubbard's advanced technology of study is now used by an estimated two million students and thousands of teachers in universities and school systems internationally. His educational materials have been translated into twelve languages to meet this worldwide demand for the first truly *workable* technology of how to study. Organizations delivering L. Ron Hubbard's study technology have been established in the United States, Australia, South Africa, Canada, Austria, Great Britain, Pakistan, Mexico, Germany, Denmark, France, Italy, Venezuela and China.

L. Ron Hubbard departed his body on 24 January 1986. His contributions to the world of education have meant new hope, better understanding and increased ability for millions of students and educators the world over.

Index

Additional Books for Students by L. Ron Hubbard

Learning How to Learn • For children, knowing how to read and being able to understand and *apply* what they read is the real key to success in their lives. With the simple steps taught in this book, written for young students, learning can become an exciting and rewarding experience.

Study Skills for Life • Written for preteens and young teenagers, this book teaches students how to *use* what they are studying so they can attain the goals they set for themselves. Using these skills, they can break the barriers to learning.

Grammar and Communication • The ability to communicate is vital to happiness and self-confidence. But getting one's communication across is dependent upon being able to speak and write correctly. The unique approach to grammar taught in this book can open the world of words to a child—granting him the strong sense of self-esteem which results from the ability to read well, write clearly and communicate effectively.

When children can learn and think for themselves, the world is an open book.

For more information on educational books and materials by L. Ron Hubbard, contact your nearest distributor:

Association for Better Living
and Education International
6331 Hollywood Blvd., Suite 700
Los Angeles, California 90028

Association for Better Living
and Education Canada
696 Yonge Street
Toronto, Ontario
Canada M4Y 2A7

Association for Better Living
and Education Eastern
United States
349 W. 48th Street
New York, NY 10036

Association for Better Living
and Education Western
United States
1307 N. New Hampshire
Los Angeles, California 90027

Association for Better Living
and Education Europe
Sankt Nikolajvej 4–6
Frederiksberg C
1953 Copenhagen, Denmark

Instituto de Tecnologia para la
Educacion A.C.
Tetla #6 Colonia Ruiz Cortines
Delegación Coyoacán
C.P. 64630, Mexico D.F.

Association for Better Living
and Education United Kingdom
Saint Hill Manor
East Grinstead, West Sussex
England RH19 4JY

Association for Better Living
and Education Russia
48 Vavilova Street
Building 4, Suite 169
Moscow 117333, Russia

Association for Better Living
and Education Australia and
New Zealand
201 Castlereagh Street
Sydney, New South Wales 2000
Australia

Association for Better Living
and Education Africa
Security Building, 4th Floor
95 Commissioner Street
Johannesburg 2001
South Africa

Association for Better Living
and Education Italy
Via Nerino, 8
20213 Milan
Italy

You can also contact any of the groups and organizations on the following pages which use L. Ron Hubbard's study technology.

Applied Scholastics Groups and Organizations

Applied Scholastics International
7060 Hollywood Blvd., Suite 200
Los Angeles, California 90028

United States of America

Arizona

Phoenix Renaissance Academy, Inc.
4330 N. 62nd St., #128
Phoenix, Arizona 85251

Scott Tutoring
4203 N. 9th Avenue
Phoenix, Arizona 85013

California

Ability Academy
PO Box 601091
San Diego, California 92160

Ability Plus School—La Canada
4490 Cornishon Ave.
La Canada, California 91011

Ability Plus School—Orange
County
333 S. Prospect
Orange, California 92669

Ability Plus School—Woodland
Hills
Dept. 503, PO Box 4172
Woodland Hills, California 91365

Academy for Smart Kids
4632 Russell Ave.
Los Angeles, California 90027

Applied Scholastics Compton
11174 Atlantic
Lynwood, California 90262

Applied Scholastics—Crescenta
Valley
7944 Day Street
Sunland, California 91040

Applied Scholastics—Los Angeles
503 Central Ave.
Glendale, California 91203

Applied Scholastics Orange County
701 W. 17th Street
Santa Ana, California 92706

Applied Scholastics—San Francisco
39355 California St. #107
Fremont, California 94538

California Ranch School
17305 Santa Rosa Mine Road
Gavilan Hills, California 92370

Carroll-Rees Academy
4474 De Longpre
Los Angeles, California 90027

Delphi Academy—Los Angeles
4490 Cornishon Ave.
La Canada, California 91011

Delphi Academy—Sacramento
5325 Engle Rd. #600
Carmichael, California 95608

Delphi Academy—San Francisco
445 E. Charleston Rd. #7
Palo Alto, California 94306

Expansion Consultants, Inc.
550 N. Brand Street 700
Glendale, California 91203

Golden Gate Apple School
379 Colusa Ave.
Kensington, California 94707

Karen Aranas Tutoring Center
933 Edward Ave. #24
Santa Rosa, California 95401

Kids Academy
1839 N. Kenmore Avenue
Los Angeles, California 90027

Kids' World School
1220 N. Berendo Ave.
Los Angeles, California 90029

The Learning Bridge
593 4th Ave.
San Francisco, California 94118

Legacy Learning Group
2789 Cornelius Drive
San Pablo, California 94806

Lewis Carroll Academy of the Arts
5425 Cahuenga Blvd.
N. Hollywood, California 91601

Los Gatos Academy
220 Belgatos Road
Los Gatos, California 95032

Mojave Desert School
44579 Temescal
Newberry Springs, California 92365

Pinewood Academy
4490 Cornishon Ave.
La Canada, California 91011

Real School
50 El Camino
Corte Madera, California 94925

Smart Apple Tutoring Service
1310 Chuckwagon Dr.
Sacramento, California 95834

VenturePlan
3300 Foothill Blvd.
Box 12570
La Crescenta, California 91224

Colorado

Applied Scholastics—Colorado
3 Paonia
Littleton, Colorado 80127

Connecticut

Ability Plus Connecticut
256 Brainard Hill Road
Higganum, Connecticut 06441

Standard Education
3 David Drive
Simsbury, Connecticut 06070

Florida

Applied Scholastics—Miami
2557 SW 31st Ave.
Miami, Florida 33133

A To Be School, Inc.
531 Franklin Street
Clearwater, Florida 34616

Jefferson Academy, Inc.
1301 N. Highland Ave.
Clearwater, Florida 34615

Studema International
PO Box 10559
Clearwater, Florida 34617

TRUE School, Inc.
1831 Drew Street
Clearwater, Florida 34625

Georgia

Lafayette Academy
2417 Canton Road
Marietta, Georgia 30066

Illinois

The Learning School, Inc.
864 E. Northwest Hwy.
Mount Prospect, Illinois 60056

Massachusetts

Applied Scholastics—New England
1500 Main Street, Suite 4
Weymouth, Massachusetts 02190

Delphi Academy—Boston
564 Blue Hill Ave.
Milton, Massachusetts 02186

Michigan

Cedars Center
1602 W. 3rd Ave.
Flint, Michigan 48504

Recording Institute of Detroit, Inc.
14611 E. Nine Mile Road
East Detroit, Michigan 48021

Minnesota

Beacon Heights Academy
12325 Highway 55
Plymouth, Minnesota 55441

Missouri
Ability School—St. Louis
14298 Olive St. Road
St. Louis, Missouri 63017

New Hampshire
Bear Hill School, Inc.
PO Box 417
Pittsfield, New Hampshire 03263

New Jersey
Ability School—New Jersey
192 W. Demarest Ave.
Englewood, New Jersey 07631

New York
Maryann's School
#2 Hillcrest
Niagara Falls, New York 14303

Ohio
Applied Scholastics—Ohio
101 W. Dunedin Rd.
Columbus, Ohio 43214

Oregon
Columbia Academy, Inc.
1808 SE Belmont
Portland, Oregon 97214

The Delphian School—Oregon
20950 SW Rock Creek Road
Sheridan, Oregon 97378

Eagle Oak School
PO Box 12
Bridal Veil, Oregon 97010

Pennsylvania
Applied Scholastics Pennsylvania
PO Box 662
Reading, Pennsylvania 19603

Texas
Austin Academy of Higher
  Learning
12002 N. Lamar
Austin, Texas 78753

Perfect Schooling, Inc.
402 Town and Country Village
Houston, Texas 77024

Utah
Ability School—Utah
913 E. Syrena Circle
Sandy, Utah 89094

Virginia
Chesapeake Ability School
5533 Industrial Dr.
Springfield, Virginia 22151

Wyoming
Great American Ski School
PO Box 427
Jackson, Wyoming 83001

Canada
Académie Phénix
9222 Chateaubriand
Montreal, Québec 42M 1X8
Canada

Applied Scholastics
  (National Office)
840 Pape Ave., Suite 209
Toronto, Ontario M4K 3T6
Canada

Berube Educational Services
114 Bourassa
St. Luc, Québec J0J 2A0
Canada

Education Alive—Halifax
2130 Armcrescent West
Halifax, Nova Scotia B3L 3E3
Canada

Education Alive—Kentville
27 James Street
Kentville, Nova Scotia B4N 2A1
Canada

Education Alive—Toronto
840 Pape Ave., Suite 201
Toronto, Ontario M4K 3T6
Canada

Effective Education School
8610 Ash Street
Vancouver, British Columbia
  V6P 3M2
Canada

Progressive Academy
12245 131st Street
Edmonton, Alberta T5L 1M8
Canada

Toronto Ability School
85 41st Street
Etobicoke, Ontario M8W 3P1
Canada

Wise Owl Tutoring
342 Blackthorn Ave.
Toronto, Ontario M6N 3J3
Canada

United Kingdom
Effective Education Association
  East Grinstead
31A High Street
East Grinstead, W. Sussex
  RH19 3AF
England

Effective Education Association
  London
2C Falkland Rd.
Kentish Town, London
England

Effective Education Association
  Scotland
31 St. Katharine's Brae
Liberton, Edinburgh EH16 6PY
Scotland

Effective Education Association
  Sunderland
9 Catherine Tce.
Newkyo, Stanley, Co. Durham
  DH9 7TP
England

Greenfields School
Priory Road—Forest Row
E. Sussex RH18 53D
England

The London Study Center
313 Finchley Road
London NW3 6EH
England

Austria
Kreativ College
Rienosslgasse 12
1040 Wien, Austria

Belgium
Brussels Ability School
Rue Auguste Lambiotte 23
1030 Bruxelles
Belgium

Study Tech Center
Clos des Palombes
1410 Waterloo
Belgium

Denmark
Amager International School
5th Floor, Graekenlandsvej 51-53
2300 Copenhagen S, Denmark

Applied Scholastics (European
  Office)
F. F. Ulriksgade 13
2100 Copenhagen O, Denmark

Applied Scholastics—Denmark
F. F. Ulriksgade 13
2100 Copenhagen O, Denmark

Foreningen for Effektiv
  Grunduddannelse Aarhus
Hammervaenget 22
8310 Tranbjerg, Denmark

Foreningen for Effektiv
  Grunduddannelse Amager
Graekenlandsvej 53
2300 Copenhagen S, Denmark

Foreningen for Effektiv
  Grunduddannelse Birkerod
Kongevejen 110 B
3460 Birkerod, Denmark

Foreningen for Effektiv
  Grunduddannelse Brondby
  Strand
Hyttebovej 20
2660 Brondby Strand, Denmark

Foreningen for Effektiv
Grunduddannelse Bronshoj
Klintevej 40
2700 Bronshoj, Denmark

Foreningen for Effektiv
Grunduddannelse Dania
Daniavej 60 Assens
9550 Mariager, Denmark

Foreningen for Effektiv
Grunduddannelse Dania
Erhvervscenter
Daniavej 60 Assens
9550 Mariager, Denmark

Foreningen for Effektiv
Grunduddannelse Glostrup
Falkevej 20
2600 Glostrup, Denmark

Foreningen for Effektiv
Grunduddannelse Grinsted
Gronlandsvej 2
7290 Grinsted, Denmark

Foreningen for Effektiv
Grunduddannelse Hvidovre
Hvidovre Alle 17
2650 Hvidovre, Denmark

Foreningen for Effektiv
Grunduddannelse Kalundborg
Dalsvinget 5
4400 Kalundborg, Denmark

Foreningen for Effektiv
Grunduddannelse Koge
Straedet 6
Stroby Egede
4600 Koge, Denmark

Foreningen for Effektiv
Grunduddannelse Naestved
H. C. Lumbyesvej 102
4700 Naestved, Denmark

Foreningen for Effektiv
Grunduddannelse Norrebro
Ravnsborggade 6, 5
2200 Copenhagen N, Denmark

Foreningen for Effektiv
Grunduddannelse Norre Sundby
Jorgenbertelsvej 17 A, 1tv
9400 Norre Sundby, Denmark

Foreningen for Effektiv
Grunduddannelse Olstykke
Sajisnej 21
3650 Olstykke, Denmark

Foreningen for Effektiv
Grunduddannelse Osterbro
F. F. Ulriksgade 13
2100 Copenhagen O, Denmark

Foreningen for Effektiv
Grunduddannelse Risskov
Flintebakken 60
8240 Risskov, Denmark

Foreningen for Effektiv
Grunduddannelse Silkeborg
Chr. D. 8. vej 12.1
8600 Silkeborg, Denmark

Foreningen for Effektiv
Grunduddannelse Slagelse
Sct. Mikkelsgade 23
4200 Slagelse, Denmark

Foreningen for Effektiv
Grunduddannelse Tastrup
Kogevej 11
2630 Tastrup, Denmark

Foreningen for Effektiv
Grunduddannelse Vadum
Ulrik Burihovej 69
9330 Vadum, Denmark

Foreningen for Effektiv
Grunduddannelse Vojens
Vestergade 58
6100 Haderslev, Denmark

Kildeskolen
Roskildevej 158
2500 Valby, Denmark

France
Applied Scholastics France
49 rue Général de Gaulle
22400 Lamballe
France

Aptitudes
11 rue Palluat de Besset
42000 St. Etienne, France

Ecole de l'éveil
11 passage Courtois
75011 Paris, France

Institute d'Aide a l'Etude
12 impasse Bonnave
42000 St. Etienne, France

Irene Chartry Tutoring Service
27 rue Andre Cayron
92600 Asnieres, France

Le Cours pour apprendre
16 rue du Bac
75007 Paris, France

Management Distribution
43 rue Volney
49000 Angers, France

Germany
Applied Scholastics—Germany
Unter Buschweg 118
5000 Köln, Germany

Applied Scholastics Aidlingen
Blumenstrasse 14
7042 Aidlingen
Germany

Applied Scholastics Augsburg
Stettenstrasse 36
8900 Augsburg
Germany

Applied Scholastics Cologne
Unter Buschweg 118
5000 Köln, Germany

Applied Scholastics Düsseldorf
Kruppstrasse 45
4000 Düsseldorf 1
Germany

Applied Scholastics Eisingen
Waldpark 2
7531 Eisingen
Germany

Applied Scholastics Euskirchen
Ringelstrasse 14
5350 Euskirchen-Billig
Germany

Applied Scholastics Hamburg
Swartenhorst 50
2000 Hamburg 71
Germany

Applied Scholastics Hünfelden
Obergasse 1
6257 Hünfelden-Ohren
Germany

Applied Scholastics Velbert
Am Neuhanskothen 51
5620 Velbert 11
Germany

Holland
Lafayette School
Vascode Ganver Straat 19
1057 CH Amsterdam
Holland

Italy
Associazione Studio Moderno
Piazza Cittadella, 13
41100 Modena, Italy

Sweden
Applied Scholastics—Sweden
Terrängvägen 39
126 61 Hägersten, Sweden

Daghemmet U-Care
Grusåsgränd 88
122 49 Enskede, Sweden

Fritidshemmet Robin Hood
Terrängvägen 39
126 61 Hägersten, Sweden

Måsens daghem
Nedre Bergsvägen 4
126 34 Hägersten, Sweden

Solrosen
Örtugsgatan 13
414 79 Göteborg
Sweden

Studema-Skolan
Terrängvägen 39
126 61 Hägersten, Sweden

Switzerland
Verein ZIEL
Postfach 5114
6002 Luzern, Switzerland

Australia
Ability Plus
32 Ryan St.
Northcote Victoria 3070
Australia

Applied Scholastics ANZO
319 Canterbury Road
Ringwood, Victoria 3134
Australia

Applied Scholastics—Canberra
36 Ebden St.
GPO Box 1910
Ainslie, Canberra, ACT 2602
Australia

Applied Scholastics—Sydney
Suite 3, Level 3
647 George St.
Sydney NSW 2000
Australia

Applied Scholastics Training Centre
#404, 3 Smail St.
Broadway NSW 2007
Australia

I Can Enhancements
1/23 Glebe Point Rd.
Glebe NSW 2037
Australia

Jenny Gellie Tutoring Services
21 Railway Parade
Hazelbrook NSW 2779
Australia

Yarralinda School
319 Canterbury Road
Ringwood, Victoria 3134
Australia

Japan
Applied Scholastics Japan
3-13-36E 1001
Kusunoki-cho, Nishi-Ku
Hiroshima
Japan 733

Malaysia
Applied Scholastics Institute
No. 42-2A, Jalan Tun Sambanthan
50470 Kuala Lumpur
Malaysia

Pakistan
Effective Education Association—
  Karachi
348 CP Berar Society, Block 7/8
Dhoraji Colony
Karachi-5, Pakistan

Africa
A+ School
28 Church Street
Halfway House
Pretoria 1685, South Africa

Affluence Management
PO Box 59779
Kengray 2100, South Africa

Education Alive—Cape Town
51 Station Road
Observatory
Cape Town 7925, South Africa

Education Alive—Johannesburg
3rd Floor CDH House
217 Jeppe Street
Johannesburg 2001, South Africa

Education Alive (National Office)
3rd Floor CDH House
217 Jeppe Street
Johannesburg 2001, South Africa

Greenfields Education Complex
PO Box 35
Akroso-Akim
Ghana, Africa

Latin America

Colombia
Instituto de Ayuda Escolar
Cra 28 No. 91-39
Sante Fe de Bogotá
Colombia

Mexico
Educacion Del Mañana
Cordobanes 47
Col. San Jose Insurgentes
03900 México D.F.

Grupo Iniciativa
Calzada de Tlalpan #934
Col. Nativitas
03500 México D.F.

ITE de México (National Office)
Tetla #6 Col. Ruiz Cortines
Coyocan
04630 México D.F.

ITE de Guadalajara
Jazmin 376 S.R.
Guadalajara, Jalisco
México

ITE de Jalapa
Corregidora #24-A
Col. Centro
Jalapa, Veracruz
México